Midwest Studies in Philosophy
Volume XIX

EDITED BY PETER A. FRENCH, THEODORE E. UEHLING, JR.,
HOWARD K. WETTSTEIN

Many papers in MIDWEST STUDIES IN PHILOSOPHY are invited and all are previously unpublished. The editors will consider unsolicited manuscripts that are received by January of the year preceding the appearance of a volume. All manuscripts must be pertinent to the topic area of the volume for which they are submitted. Address manuscripts to MIDWEST STUDIES IN PHILOSOPHY, Department of Philosophy, University of California, Riverside, CA 92521.

The articles in MIDWEST STUDIES IN PHILOSOPHY are indexed in THE PHILOSOPHER'S INDEX.

Forthcoming

Volume XX   1995 Moral Concepts

Available Previously Published Volumes

Midwest Studies in Philosophy Volume XIX

Philosophical Naturalism

Editors

Peter A. French
Trinity University

Theodore E. Uehling, Jr.
University of Minnesota, Morris

Howard K. Wettstein
University of California, Riverside

University of Notre Dame Press • Notre Dame, Indiana

Published by the University of Notre Dame Press
Notre Dame, IN 46556
Printed in the United States of America

Library of Congress Cataloging-in-Publication Data

Naturalism / editors, Peter A. French, Theodore E. Uehling, Jr.,
Howard K. Wettstein.
     p.   cm. — (Midwest studies in philosophy : v. 19)
   ISBN 0-268-01406-X
   1. Science—Philosophy.   I. French, Peter A.
II. Uehling, Theodore Edward   III. Wettstein, Howard K.
IV. Series.
Q175.P5125
501—dc20   93-8496
                                            CIP

Midwest Studies in Philosophy
Volume XIX
Philosophical Naturalism

Midwest Studies in Philosophy
Volume XIX

Direct Realism without Materialism

PANAYOT BUTCHVAROV

I

The direct realism I shall propose represents, though in a somewhat regimented way, our natural, commonsense, and phenomenologically firmly grounded view of sense perception, namely, that at least seeing and tactual feeling are simply cases of our being mentally confronted with ("aware," "conscious," of) material objects. But the direct realist need not hold (as the "naive realist" is defined by H. H. Price as holding[1]) that we cannot also perceive material objects that are not real. (This is the regimentation.) Indeed, despite his sense-datum theory, Price allowed, probably under the influence of continental phenomenology, that we can have *perceptual consciousness* of unreal objects. Price admitted that common sense is happy, "though not without vacillation," with the use of the word "perception" as a synonym of his "perceptual consciousness" but decided against so using it because it would be against the practice of "several philosophers, including Professor G. E. Moore."[2] And in *The Foundations of Empirical Knowledge,* A. J. Ayer wrote: "I am using ['perceive'] here in such a way that to say of an object that it is perceived does not entail saying that it exists in any sense at all. And this is a perfectly correct and familiar usage of the word."[3] I shall try to show that it is essential to direct *realism* even with respect to veridical perception that it allow for the possibility of direct perception of unreal objects, and thus to include what may be called "direct *irrealism.*"

The reason this is so has to do with a second, no less familiar formulation of direct realism, namely, that perception, whether veridical or not, involves no intermediaries such as sense data, sensations, ways of being appeared to, sense experiences, mental representations, ideas, images, looks, seemings, appearances, or occurrent beliefs or "acceptings" of any sort.[4] The point is not merely

1

that perceptual judgments are not inferred from, or justified by, judgments about such intermediaries. The point is that the alleged intermediaries are philosophical inventions, whether they are supposed to be particular objects, such as sense data, or properties, such as ways of being appeared to.

Clearly, these two points would be accepted by a materialist who says what she means, i.e., the uncompromising eliminative materialist. We shall see that her disagreement with direct realism would occur on a much deeper level. We may also call such a materialist a physicalist, and I shall do so in order to save words. If materialism is the view that all that exists is material, then since it is ultimately up to physics to tell us what it is for something to be material, it would be also up to physics to tell us what exists. This is all that would matter metaphysically. Whether the other natural sciences, e.g., biology, are "reducible" conceptually or semantically to physics (a most unlikely possibility) I shall not discuss. Nor shall I discuss what has been called "supervenience physicalism," beyond avowing that I find it perversely obscurantist.

That direct realism as I have stated it (it should not be confused with any other so-called direct realism) is at least *prima facie* true should be evident from the fact that what I have called intermediaries are invariably described with technical terms or grossly abused ordinary terms. I will consider here just some of these.

We do not speak of having visual sensations when seeing something unless we mean pains or tickles or itches in the eyes; nor do we say that we experience, or have a sense experience of, a person just because we see the person.[5] Indeed, it need not be true that in such a case we have any experiences at all, in the proper sense of the word, e.g., emotions, pains, tickles, itches. This point is, of course, familiar to readers of Gilbert Ryle's works. What may be less familiar is that G. E. Moore, in "A Defense of Common Sense," expressed doubt that "there is a certain intrinsic property . . . which might be called that of 'being an experience'," and that whenever one is conscious there is an event that has that property (p. 48).[6] If Ryle's grounds were linguistic, Moore's, I believe, were strictly phenomenological. The difference need not be as great as it seems. It would be surprising if ordinary language failed to reflect the phenomenological facts. It is true that in the case of tactual perception we often use the verb "to feel" ("I feel a rough surface"), but to infer from this that such tactual feelings are sensations or experiences would be to ignore the obvious ambiguity of the English word "feel." (Feeling pain, which can be quite properly described as a sensation as well as an experience, is categorically different from feeling a rough surface.)

As to beliefs, surely they are not occurrences, for if they were it should make sense to say such things as "I am believing now that p," which it does not. They may be behavioral dispositions, but then they would hardly be logically involved in perceiving, which is a kind of occurrence. The acquisition of a disposition may be an occurrence, as David Armstrong and George Pitcher have pointed out,[7] but they admit that there are perceivings that involve no such acquisitions and so feel compelled to appeal to acquisitions of such things as inclinations to believe, potential beliefs, even suppressed inclinations to believe. But while we have a very clear idea of what it is to perceive something, we have only the vaguest idea of what, if any, dispositional beliefs, to say nothing of inclinations to such beliefs, suppressed such inclinations, or potential beliefs, we acquire then. The robustness of perception can hardly be captured with gaseous notions such as these.

Of course, for perception to occur certain *causal* conditions must be satisfied. For example, in vision, light must be reflected or emitted by the object seen, it must stimulate the retina, and the optic nerve and the brain must be functioning properly. But this, I suggest, is a topic for science, not for philosophy. Indeed, according to one *philosophical* account of perception, the so-called causal theory of perception, perception *logically* involves the causal efficacy of the object perceived (thus the theory does not allow us to speak, even though we regularly do so, of perceiving, e.g., seeing, objects that are not real, as in hallucinations and dreams). And the theory ordinarily holds that the relevant causal effect of the object is precisely one of the intermediaries I have mentioned. This is so even if the effect is described just as the experience of the object (a good example of why we should avoid this technical use of "experience"). Indeed this is the view of P. F. Strawson, who claims to combine direct realism with the causal theory. But he does this by denying that causation need be a relation between distinct existences.[8]

The so-called "intuition" behind the causal theory is that the object perceived is somehow necessary for the occurrence of the perceiving. But direct realism acknowledges this: the object, even if not real, is a *logically* necessary element of the perceiving.

In fact, as H. P. Grice admitted in his classic defense of the causal theory of perception, the intuition in question seems rather to preclude a causal theory.[9] He wrote: "There is no natural use for such a sentence as 'The presence of a cat caused it to look to X as if there were a cat before him.'" To meet the objection, Grice suggests that we should not restrict the causal theory to using the verb "to cause" and allow it to use such expressions as "accounts for," "explains," "is part of the explanation of," "is partly responsible for." But all these expressions also have a natural *logical* sense, and therefore so stated the "causal theory" is no longer a causal theory but a family of theories, of which the original theory is at best only one member, direct realism being another. Of course, Grice is right that in cases where appropriate causal connections are missing (as in his example of the clock on the shelf, which is not seen even though one's "visual impression" is just as if it were, because the impression is caused by posthypnotic suggestion or direct manipulation of one's brain) we withhold the judgment that the object the perceiver claims to perceive is really perceived. But a sufficient explanation of this is that ordinarily we take for granted that perception is veridical and that in veridical perception a suitable causal connection does in fact obtain, and on discovering in a particular situation the extraordinary circumstance that it does not, we hesitate to say that perception of the object obtains, or perhaps are even left speechless.

Indeed, it may be said that the presence of an appropriate causal connection is pragmatically implied, but not entailed, by a perceptual statement, somewhat as one's making a statement implies, but does not entail, that one believes it. This is a good example of how wary we should be of relying on linguistic "intuitions." But I shall not appeal to this explanation, since the direct realist has a much simpler explanation of such hallucinations as that of Grice's clock. The perceiver sees not the real clock on the shelf but rather an unreal clock that is otherwise just like it.

It is an illusion to suppose, as some defenders of the adverbial theory of sensing do, that if the relevant causal effect is a way of being appeared to, then the causally efficacious object is directly perceived.[10] What one is really aware of, according to this theory, is the way one is appeared to, which according to the leading defender of the theory, Roderick M. Chisholm, is a self-presenting property of one, one's having that property being self-evident to one. (Chisholm offers a purely epistemic definition of "self-presenting," but I believe he would also use it in its usual phenomenological sense). In the latest (1989) edition of his *Theory of Knowledge,* he writes: "In the case of being appeared to, there is something, one's being appeared to in a certain way, that one interprets as being a *sign* of some external fact" (Chisholm's italics).[11] And: "if, for example, you look outside and see a dog, then you see it by means of visual sensations that are called up as a result of the way the dog is related to your eyes and nervous system. In seeing the dog, you are also aware of the visual sensations (but it would be a mistake to say that you *see* them). Whether sensations ever *do* present us with such things as dogs is a difficult question . . ." (Chisholm's italics).[12] Another adverbialist, Alvin Plantinga, writes: "My perceptual beliefs are not ordinarily formed on the basis of *propositions about* my experience; nonetheless they are formed on the basis of my experience . . . you form the belief . . . *on the basis of* this phenomenal imagery, this way of being appeared to" (Plantinga's italics).[13]

Such theories can (and usually do) stipulate that the object causing the way one is appeared to is perceived, but this violates the ordinary sense of "perception," according to which perception is a mode of awareness. On the other hand, if they allow that one is directly aware of the object, the states of being appeared to being logically independent from that awareness and it from them,[14] then we have at best a rather uneconomical version of direct realism, moreover one encumbered with all of the difficulties of the adverbial theory.[15]

Of course, we can say that the object appears to the perceiver, but so far we have just a strained way of saying that the perceiver perceives the object, not a theory of perception. And the standard locutions of the forms "appears *F*," or "seems *F*," or "looks *F*" are in most cases used as cautious substitutes for "is perceived to be *F*" or "is perceived as *F*." But it is best to avoid these locutions in the philosophy of perception because they encourage us to start speaking of "appearances" and "ways of being appeared to." How can we do this? Simply by speaking of perceiving qualities *in* (or on) the material objects we perceive even if the objects do not really have those qualities, i.e., even if the qualities perceived are not qualities *of* the objects. If an object is blue and "appears" blue to us, we may say that we perceive blue in the object and that the object is blue. If the object is white but "appears" blue to us, then we may say that we still perceive blue in the object but the object is not blue. All this would be especially clear if we followed G. F. Stout and D. C. Williams and regarded individual things as bundles of *particular* qualities. I shall return to this point.

A similar remark can be made regarding theories that appeal to the occurrence of "perceptual experiences." If by "perceptual experience" they mean simply perceiving, then they merely introduce needless terminological confusion. If they mean something caused by the object perceived, then a perceptual experience is likely to be what I have called an intermediary, and the theory would be incompatible with direct realism as I have defined it.

The direct realist view is that all that is *logically* involved in perceiving is the perceiver, the awareness or consciousness properly called perceiving in ordinary discourse (that there is this element is evident from the fact that being unconscious entails not perceiving anything), and the object perceived. But the object need not exist. It is chiefly in this respect that direct realism differs from the so-called disjunctive view recently defended by Hinton, Snowdon, and McDowell.[16] Roughly, this view (at least as presented by Hinton) accepts direct realism with respect to veridical perception and avoids commitment to objects or events such as sense data or experiences by denying that veridical and nonveridical perception have a common sort of element. The proposal is that a disjunction such as "It is either a perception or an illusion" is the best description of what seems to be a case of perception.

Why not accept this view? One reason is that it tells us nothing philosophically informative about the second disjunct by merely labeling it "illusion" (or "appearance"). But the main reason is that it does not do justice to the undeniable phenomenological fact the sense-datum theorists relied upon, namely, that there is no intrinsic difference between (veridical) perception and illusion. Our direct realism, however, does do justice to it in the most obvious and quite natural way: by regarding both as perception and identifying the difference between them as one between their objects, namely, respectively, real and unreal objects. (Hinton[17] quotes Gilbert Ryle's well-known admission that "There is something in common between having an afterimage and seeing a misprint. Both are visual affairs."[18] Ryle recognizes that this fact constitutes a problem for his denial that there are sensations, in the philosophical sense. It is equally a problem for Hinton's disjunctive theory, but he does not seem to recognize this.)

We can now see why direct realism must include what I called "direct irrealism." Only thus can commitment to intermediaries be avoided even with respect to veridical perception. I suggested at the very beginning of this essay that direct realism is supported by common sense and phenomenological reflection. I can add that (as Price and Ayer recognized) it has this support even in the cases involving unreal objects: consider our natural descriptions of dreams and hallucinations as cases of seeing, tactually feeling, etc., and of our descriptions of their objects with predicates applicable to real material objects.[19] Of course, these are not our only natural descriptions of such cases: we sometimes describe them as cases of seeming to see, or to feel, etc., and this fact prompted me to describe what I call direct realism as constituting a regimentation of common sense. But the phenomenological evidence is overwhelmingly in favor of such regimentation, as the "no intrinsic difference" argument shows. If direct realism, so understood, did not face philosophical objections, such as that concerning perception of unreal objects, it would never occur to us to question it. This essay is devoted to meeting those objections, including the one just mentioned.

I shall limit my discussion to vision and tactual feeling, partly because hearing, smelling, and tasting, even though they can be given a direct realist account, require that the account be quite complex, but mainly because the philosophical implications of direct realism would be sufficiently demonstrated if it is true of seeing and tactual feeling.[20] Our conception of the material world is almost entirely that of the world of sight and touch.

I shall take perceiving to be expressed by statements of the form "x perceives y," not by statements of the form "x perceives that y is F" or of the form "x perceives y as F." The second kind of statement is usually understood as entailing knowledge that y is F and thus is unsuitable for a starting point in a discussion of direct realism, which inevitably raises the problem of skepticism. And statements of the third kind are ambiguous. They may mean "x perceives an F y," and then they would really belong to our first kind. Or they may mean "x perceives y and applies the concept F to y" or "x perceives y and is under the impression that y is F or resembles something that is F." Understood in either way, only the first conjunct, "x perceives y," would be a statement of perception.

II

At least five reasons have been given for the belief that direct realism is false, that we are never ("directly") aware of material objects: (1) the commonsense fact of perceptual relativity (I shall call it the objection from perceptual relativity); (2) the scientific facts about the circumstances (causal or not) in which states of perceptual awareness occur (I shall call it the scientific objection); (3) the phenomenological assumption that, if there are mental states or events such as direct perceptual awarenesses, they can only be "ghostly," occult, spooky, or in Hilary Putnam's word "magic" (I shall call it the phenomenological objection); (4) the assumption that direct realism commits us to the "being" of nonexistent objects in the cases of existentially illusory perceptual awareness, such as hallucinations and dreams (I shall call it the ontological objection); and (5) the assumption that direct realism cannot explain how we may distinguish between veridical and nonveridical perceptual awareness (I shall call it the epistemological objection).

The power of skepticism can now be understood without appeals to philosophical fantasies about deceiving demons or brains in vats; it seems to follow if direct realism is true, precisely for the reason mentioned in the epistemological objection, and it seems to follow if direct realism is false, for the familiar traditional reason that if our awareness is limited to the intermediaries mentioned earlier, to "our ideas and sensations," then we can never get outside their circle, behind their veil, because no deductive, inductive, abductive, coherentist, or any other known kind of inference can penetrate it. It is seldom recognized, perhaps because of the influence of Kant's "refutation of empirical idealism," that the mere acceptance of direct realism does not entail the rejection of skepticism.

The first three of the five objections to direct realism are related. (1), that from perceptual relativity, is often supposed to provide support for the relevance of (2), that from science, and (2) is often supposed to support (3), that from phenomenology. In this and the next section of this essay, I shall consider (1) only very briefly, (2) somewhat more fully, and will concentrate on (3) and (4), which together with (2) constitute what can be broadly called the *physicalist* (materialist) objection to direct realism. I shall have something to say about the epistemological objection in the final section.

Neither of the first two objections against the view that we can be directly aware of material objects is impressive. As to (1), from the fact that different qualities are perceived in objects in different situations even though there need not be, and often there is not, any intrinsic difference between perceived qualities the objects do have and perceived qualities they do not have, i.e., even though there is not an intrinsic difference between qualitatively veridical perception and qualitatively illusory perception, or indeed even between existentially veridical perception and existentially illusory perception, it does not follow that in the case of unqualifiedly veridical perception we are not directly aware of real material objects and of the qualities they really have. Direct realism is the view that in perception we *can* be, and perhaps often are, directly aware of real material objects and of their real qualities, not that we always are, or that it is only of real material objects and of their real qualities that we are directly aware in perception. It may be that we cannot *know* about any particular case whether or not it is one of veridical perception, but this is a different question; it is a part of the epistemological objection.

And as to (2), from the scientific fact that veridical perceptual awareness occurs only simultaneously with or after the last link in the physical causal chain that, say, begins with the object's reflecting light and ends in a specific event in the brain, whether further localized or not, it does not follow that the perceptual awareness that occurs simultaneously with or after that last event in the brain is itself somehow "in the head," rather than a direct relation to the object, i.e., a state that includes the object as a logical component, even if the object is earlier in time than the awareness. Analogously, the fact that I come to be 240 miles from Chicago as a result of a fairly long and complex causal process of driving does not entail that this end-result, my being 240 miles from Chicago, is not my being in a direct spatial relation to Chicago, which is neither in me nor in Chicago, but rather is a state that includes me and Chicago as *logical* components. My being 240 miles from Chicago is not at all the same as, nor even includes, the largely causal process of driving that led to it.[21] Moreover, the fact that I was in Chicago some hours ago is quite compatible with my being *now* 240 miles from Chicago. This suggests the obvious answer we should give to the so-called time-lag argument.

Of course, direct perceptual awareness, this peculiar relation of oneself to an external object, is not and perhaps cannot be acknowledged by the physical sciences. If direct realism is rejected just for this reason, then the real issue is the truth of physicalism, not the truth of direct realism. I cannot discuss in detail this global issue here, except insofar as it relates to direct realism, but the following observations are needed. If physicalism is not supported by argument, it deserves no discussion since it is hardly offered as a self-evident truth. (Avowals of commitment to "the scientific image of the world" are not arguments, they are expressions of faith. In this respect there is an analogy between recent Anglo-American philosophy and some parts of medieval philosophy). If it is supported by argument, this is likely to be the familiar phenomenological argument against there being "ghostly" events or things, in other words, what I have called the phenomenological objection. But our version of direct realism also rejects the existence of the ghostly events or things relevant to it, namely those I have called intermediaries. Therefore, if physicalism is incompatible with direct realism, this must be at a deeper level, or perhaps it is a mere appearance due to misunderstanding.

The widespread acceptance of physicalism is perhaps the most distinctive feature of contemporary Anglo-American philosophy. Why is physicalism so attractive today? Doubtless, part of the explanation is to be found in the pervasive influence of modern science, in the desire of philosophers to be "scientific," to conform to "the scientific image of the world," to be included, however vicariously, in the scientific community. But another part of the explanation is that the alternative to physicalism has seemed to be to accept a realm of being populated with such things as irreducibly and unequivocally mental images, ideas, thoughts, sensations, representations, an ego, perhaps even a soul, to say nothing of the ubiquitous "experiences," all in some, perhaps causal, relation to physical things, in particular the brain, but a relation which, unless confused with mere correlation between brain states and behavior, verbal or nonverbal, the physical sciences cannot study since *ex hypothesi* one of the relata falls under none of their distinctive concepts and principles (e.g., mass, motion, the conservation of energy). Impressed by this fact, the philosophizing scientist or the scientizing philosopher assumes that the only alternatives are either simply to deny that there is anything corresponding to ordinary psychological talk, or to identify what corresponds to it with certain physiological events and states, though perhaps only functionally described.[22] Although direct realism suggests that the former alternative is closer to the mark, it seems, on the face of it, just crazy, and so our philosopher-scientist is more likely to opt for the latter. He begins to talk about *neutral* representations that are identical with the alleged ghostly events, thus combining the structure of the theory of the ghost in the machine with a perverse application of the concept of identity, perverse because it accords with none of the paradigms of its application.

Now my present purpose is not to evaluate the merits of physicalism in general but to draw attention to the fact that as it is *usually* understood it ignores the general conception of consciousness in which direct realism is grounded, a conception familiar to phenomenologists and existentialists, versions of which I suggest were held by four of the most important twentieth-century philosophers: G. E. Moore, Ludwig Wittgenstein, Martin Heidegger, and Jean-Paul Sartre. None of them accepted the existence of the ghostly realm physicalists so abhor, but also none of them was a physicalist. I shall call it the direct realist conception of consciousness and contrast it with what I shall call the mental-contents conception.

It should be evident that Wittgenstein did not subscribe to the mental-contents conception.[23] One of his chief concerns was with getting "rid of the idea of the private object" generally,[24] with getting rid of what Sartre called "inhabitants of consciousness." His assertion that being in pain "is not a *something* but not a *nothing* either"[25] fits well with the views of the mental defended (at various times) by Sartre, Moore, and Heidegger.

In his revolutionary 1903 article "The Refutation of Idealism," Moore argued against what I have called the mental-contents theory, according to which "the object of experience is in reality merely a content or inseparable aspect of that experience," whether the experience be a sensation, a mental image, or a thought, and defended what has been called the act-object, or intentionality, theory, according to which the "peculiar relation . . . of 'awarenesses of anything' . . . is involved equally in the analysis of *every* experience . . . [and is] the only thing which gives us reason to call any fact mental."[26] And he described consciousness as something that seems to be "transparent,"[27] is "diaphanous," and thus seems to be "a mere emptiness."[28] He suggested that "many people fail to distinguish it at all," which "is sufficiently shown by the fact that there are materialists."[29] Applying this conception of consciousness to perception, he asserted: "There is, therefore, no question of how we are to 'get outside the circle of our own ideas and sensations'. Merely to have a sensation is already to *be* outside that circle."[30] He went on to say, "I am as directly aware of the existence of material things in space as of my own sensations . . . ."[31] Indeed, later, Moore accepted the sense-datum theory, but he interpreted it so as to allow for the possibility that the sense datum one senses is identical with the front surface of the material object one perceives, in which case of course one would be directly aware of the object.[32]

Heidegger wrote: "Let us take a natural perception without any theory . . . and let us interrogate this concrete perception in which we live, say, the perception of the window . . . . To what am I directed in this perception? To sensations? Or, when I avoid what is perceived, am I turning aside from representational images and taking care not to fall out of these representational images and sensations into the courtyard of the university building?" He insisted that perceiving, as well as representing, judging, thinking, and willing, are "intentionally structured," that they are by their very nature directed toward an object, whether real or not, but warned against the *"erroneous objectivizing"* of intentionality, against regarding it as "an extent relation between an extant subject and object," as well as against the *"erroneous subjectivizing"* of it, against regarding it as "something which is immanent to the so-called subject and which would first of all be in need of transcendence" (Heidegger's italics). He went on to say that "intentionality is neither objective, extant like an object, nor subjective in the sense of something that occurs within a so-called subject."[33] "Extant" (*vorhanden*) may be understood to mean "existing as a thing."

But the account both most detailed and clearest of the idea that seems common to Wittgenstein's, Moore's, and Heidegger's views was provided by Sartre. He held (1) that a consciousness (or, we may say, an act or a state of consciousness) necessarily has an object, it is always of, directed toward, something, and (2) that the consciousness has no contents, no intrinsic constitution, that everything it is it owes to its object. This view is strikingly similar to Moore's of the 1903, 1910, and 1925 articles mentioned in note 26. It is that if you try to consider the (act of) consciousness you do find something, but something that is entirely transparent, translucent, without any nature or character or content of its own. So a (an act of) consciousness may be said to be nothing, in the sense that it is not a thing that has a nature or intrinsic characteristics, yet it must also be said to be something, in the sense that it does exist. So, in Wittgenstein's words, if perhaps not meaning, consciousness is not something but neither is it nothing, and in Heidegger's words, it is neither objective nor subjective.

An immediate consequence of this conception is that a state of consciousness if considered in abstraction from its object is unequivocally *nothing,* since "all physical, psycho-physical, and psychic objects, all truths, all values are outside it . . . . There is no longer an 'inner life'."[34] "Consciousness does not have by itself any sufficiency of being as an absolute subjectivity . . . it has only a borrowed being."[35] Sartre's works abound with applications of this view. *"Representation,* as a psychic event, is a pure invention of philosophers."[36] "As soon as we abandon the hypothesis of the contents of consciousness, we must recognize that there is never a motive *in* consciousness; motives are only *for* consciousness."[37] "Such is the notion of *sensation.* We can see its absurdity. First of all, it is pure fiction. It does not correspond to anything which I experience in myself or with regard to the Other."[38] (Merleau-Ponty optimistically concurred: "It is unnecessary to show, since authors are agreed on it, that this notion [of sensation] corresponds to nothing in our experience."[39]) The phrase "material object" is the obvious sortal term for the usual objects of perceptual consciousness, for such things as trees, people, snakes, and rivers, whether they are real or not, just as "number" is the obvious sortal term even for numbers, the nonexistence of which can be proved.

I pointed out earlier that contemporary physicalists ignore the direct realist conception of consciousness and instead usually take themselves to be arguing against the existence of the mind as a ghostly realm, as a system of psychic, "spooky," entities, perhaps representations, a mental machine. But, as we have seen, the direct realist conception also rejects such a realm. To what extent would awareness by them of this conception influence their opposition to direct realism? It ought to have a major influence insofar as they are chiefly motivated by the thought that the existence in perceptual consciousness of a realm of ghostly things is sheer fantasy. For the perceptual consciousness, as understood, e.g., by Heidegger and Sartre, is no such realm, it is indeed not a thing at all. But insofar as their chief motive is the one I mentioned earlier, namely, their commitment to scientism, to the "scientific image of the world," obviously the direct realist conception of consciousness would not be acceptable to them. Consciousness, so understood, could hardly be a physical thing or property or relation, it has no place in the scientific image. Presumably, this is why Hilary Putnam writes that "postulating" that "the mind has a faculty of referring to external objects (or perhaps properties) [a faculty called "by the good old name 'intentionality'"] would be found by naturalistically minded philosophers (and, of course, psychologists) . . . unhelpful epistemologically and almost certainly bad science as well."[40] So, clearly, even the theory I have attributed to our four philosophers would not be acceptable to some physicalists. If this is the case, so much the worse for them, we may say, and dismiss what I called the physicalist objection to direct realism with just a sigh. For the direct realist conception of consciousness is hardly a postulate, whether scientific or nonscientific; it does not pretend to be science, good or bad. It is a straightforward acknowledgment of the most intimately known fact about ourselves. Nor is it intended as an explanation, which might be "helpful" to epistemology or to psychology, nor does there seem to be any prospect of finding an explanation, again whether scientific or nonscientific, of the fact of consciousness. In this sense Putnam is right in describing consciousness as mysterious[41] but wrong if he supposes that it is not completely familiar to us or that its existence is questionable. After all, the difference between being conscious and being unconscious or nonconscious is something we need to learn neither from science nor from philosophy.

Hilary Putnam is not a physicalist (now). In fact he expresses the opinion that "scientism . . . is one of the most dangerous contemporary intellectual tendencies," and that its most influential contemporary form is materialism.[42] He is chiefly interested in arguing against what he calls metaphysical realism, "the myth of comparing our representations directly with unconceptualized reality."[43] This theme is repeated in almost all of his recent works. I should note that he usually regards representations as linguistic entities, even if they occur in "mentalese." And the core of his argument is that we cannot even think of a unique relation of "correspondence" between any mental state and any external object or event because such a relation would itself be something external to the mind. Of course, the argument is fallacious: at most it follows that we cannot *know* any such relation. But for our purposes the argument is significant in that it displays particularly vividly the mental-contents theory's naive picture of the relationship between the mind and its objects. If there are no mental representations to begin with, if we are in direct touch with the objects of our perception and thought, then the belief, which is central to Putnam's reasoning, that any representations can be given an indefinite number of different interpretations, rests on what Ryle called "Descartes's myth," the myth of there being mental representations, a species of what I have called mental contents, a myth allegiance to which Putnam seems to manifest by saying that "we have no direct access to . . . mind-independent things."[44] He admits that "if the mind has direct access to the things in themselves, then there is no problem about how it can put them in correspondence with its 'signs'."[45] Putnam seems to have intellectual intuition in mind as the sort of direct access we do not have, but this merely shows that he takes for granted that perception cannot constitute such a direct access. I should note also that our acceptance of the direct realist account does not commit us to regarding the objects of perception as "unconceptualized," though neither does it give us reason for holding the opposite position. Direct realism is compatible with any view about this issue. Nevertheless, it is not hard to see what is wrong with Putnam's claim that we have no direct access to unconceptualized reality. As H. H. Price pointed out long ago, in *Perception* (the context was an argument against the earlier idealist position that Putnam's resembles), *of course* we must have direct access to *something* that is unconceptualized if we are to conceptualize it! On the other hand, the description of it as "reality" presupposes, trivially, that it has been conceptualized, at least by the application to it of the concept of reality. And if we say, as we should, that knowledge involves at least in part the application of concepts and that its general object is reality, we can agree also that we cannot have *knowledge* of something without conceptualizing it. But surely this is a tautology.

A judicious, non-ideological version of physicalism is compatible with the direct realist theory of *perception*. That would be a version which takes seriously the claim that perceptual consciousness involves no intermediaries and moreover itself is not a thing, or a property, or a relation, that it has no contents, that in a sense it is *nothing*. Whether such a version of physicalism would still deserve to be called physicalism is another, perhaps unimportant question. Of course, it would still be not compatible with any view that allows for the existence of irreducibly mental ("psychic") objects such as pains and itches, i.e., sensations in the ordinary sense of the term. These are not inhabitants, contents, of consciousness, and they are not intentional. But they are *objects* of consciousness. Perhaps they are not something, but certainly they are not nothing.[46] I shall not pursue here the question of their nature, since it is irrelevant to our topic, which lies squarely in the philosophy of *perception*. I shall only avow that I find eliminative materialism with respect to such objects obviously false, and the identity theory absurd.

III

But there is also the ontological objection to direct realism, and though it has far more general motivation, it might be eagerly embraced by the physicalist.

According to the direct realist conception of consciousness, some acts of consciousness have objects that are not real, that do not exist. And a physicalist may regard this as a *reductio ad absurdum* of direct realism. But whether this is so must be decided now on phenomenological grounds, not on the grounds appealed to by the simplistic physicalism, motivated by mere scientism, that we have already rejected. And when we do so we shall see that the ontological objection is based more on prejudice than on reason. (I shall use "existence" and "reality" as synonyms. The latter is actually preferable because it expresses the concept much more intuitively than the former does. On the other hand, much of the literature employs "existence," and so shall I occasionally. Saying that the dagger Macbeth saw did not exist may sound strange, but surely saying that the dagger Macbeth saw was not real does not; it is something we all readily understand and, unless we are philosophers, also readily accept.)

That some objects of consciousness are not real is a direct consequence of the thesis of the intentionality of consciousness: that all acts of consciousness are directed toward an object. One of the principles of phenomenology, indeed of all rational thought, is to accept the facts as they are given, and not to be swayed by preconceived ideas. It is obviously a fact that sometimes we think of things that do not exist, as Meinong pointed out. The things in question are ordinarily mountains, people, life situations; our thought is not directed toward some peculiar spiritual photographs of these "in our minds," or toward extraordinarily complex general ("quantified") states of affairs as implied by Russell's theory of definite descriptions. So, there are things that do not exist.

I described the ontological objection as based largely on prejudice, for it rests on two assumptions which have not been thought out and indeed are obviously false. The first is that to allow for nonexistent objects of consciousness is to allow for a special realm of being. The second is that to say that there are such objects is to say that there *exist* such objects, and thus to contradict oneself. The first assumption is explicitly rejected by anyone, e.g., Meinong, who has held the view against which the objection is directed. The second assumption fails to recognize that "there are" has a common use in which it is not a synonym of "there exist" (e.g., in "There are many fantastic things I dream about. Let me tell you about them"), and that in any case we can express the view simply by saying "Some things we are conscious of do not exist." It is worth noting that the synonymous expressions in German and French are, respectively, "*es gibt*" and "*il y a*," which do not contain forms of the German and French synonyms of the English verb "to be." Meinong's opponent, in denying that there are things that do not exist, is asserting the logically equivalent proposition that all things exist, that all things are real. It is incumbent upon her to tell us what she means by "exist" or "real" in making this startling claim. Anti-Meinongians have not offered an explanation. For example, Russell's account of existence as satisfaction of a propositional function[47] obviously presupposes a more fundamental notion of existence, which we would employ in deciding what to allow as arguments satisfying a function, e.g., whether to allow Secretariat but not Pegasus as an argument of "x is a horse"; but he never explained this notion, indeed seemed not even to notice that he presupposed it.

What then lies behind the two assumptions I have mentioned? Why are they made, if there is so little to be said in their favor? I think the answer is that it is natural to fail to distinguish between being conscious of nothing and being conscious of something that does not exist. This is natural because on the level of language the distinction is not clear, perhaps because it seldom needs to be made explicitly. It is, however, quite clear on the level of the facts to which we give linguistic expression. There is an obvious difference between not imagining anything and imagining something that is nonexistent. Anti-Meinongianism fails to take this difference seriously, and views such as the early Russell's (in *The Principles of Mathematics*) that ascribe being to all objects, existent and nonexistent, take it too seriously. Both are influenced by a picture of nonexistence as nothingness, as an undifferentiated darkness out of which emerge lit-up distinct objects, "beings." But the realm of nonexistence is not such an undifferentiated darkness, it is not sheer emptiness, nothingness, though it is easily confused with one. Once the confusion is made, we do indeed find it senseless to suppose that there are nonexistent things, for to suppose this would seem to be to suppose that the emptiness has occupants. But sheer nothingness is occupied by nothing. The realm of nonexistents is not sheer nothingness; it contains differentiable objects of thought, of imagination, of perception, etc., and seems to be impossible only if confused with sheer nothingness, which of course is not a realm of anything at all, whether dark or lit-up.[48]

How would the direct realist describe *qualitative* perceptual illusion, in which what is perceived is a material object that does exist but does not have some property that is perceived in it? I have already noted that the simplest proposal, one which I do not accept, but neither wholly reject, for ontological reasons I cannot go into here,[49] is to treat the qualities of particular things as themselves particulars, rather than universals, as G. F. Stout, Donald Williams, and more recently Keith Campbell have done. Then the account of qualitative illusion would be quite the same as that of existential illusion. The illusory quality, though perceived in the object, does not exist, is not real. Instead, some other, unperceived, quality exists in the object. The white book that looks blue exists, but the particular blue color that is perceived in it does not; rather a particular white color does.

But while this would be the simplest treatment of qualitative illusion, it is not the only one available to us. Let us suppose that the qualities of particular individual things are universals. But let us allow for nonexistent surfaces, for "disembodied" surfaces, for mere perceptual expanses.[50] The notion of a perceptual expanse is employed by H. H. Price[51] and by Frank Jackson[52] in explicating their (not to be identified!) notions of a sense datum. Price argues that a perceptual expanse cannot be identical with a surface of a body on the grounds that a surface is not a particular existent but an attribute.[53] But, as Price seems to recognize, we predicate of surfaces first-order attributes, e.g., colors and shapes, and therefore surfaces cannot be attributes, they must be particulars. Moreover, he introduces his term "sense datum" by giving a red *patch* as an example.[54] The idea of a perceptual expanse is in need of elucidation but it is not incoherent. Shadows, flashes of lightning, and rainbows provide a ready starting point for understanding it. Now in a case of qualitative illusion there is a real material object and one perceives a perceptual expanse, which could be and is perceived as being, but in fact is not, the front surface of the object or indeed of any real object. In effect, we allow for surfaces that may be surfaces of nothing. Needless to say, the notion of such a surface requires further explanation, which I shall not attempt here.[55] But neither do I need to, since I could also put my point by saying that in cases of qualitative illusion one perceives a perceptual expanse, not a surface, which is indistinguishable from a part of the surface of an object with respect to its perceived qualities, and could have been identical with such a part, but in fact is not.

Now the view I have suggested differs from Price's and any other sense-datum theory in allowing for nonexistent expanses. In effect, according to it, qualitative illusion is simply a kind of existential illusion. The much larger number of nonexistent, or better, not real, objects we would thus need to accept should not disturb us. If Ockham's razor has a legitimate function, surely it is to protect us from unnecessary multiplication of alleged existents, not of nonexistents. We do not overpopulate the universe by acknowledging a large number of nonexistent objects. We only hold that mere (i.e., illusory) perceptual expanses are not existent, real objects, and if we do hold this then the general defense of allowing for them would be like that of allowing for nonexistent material objects. If so, in addition to pointing out that the notion of a mere perceptual expanse does not entail that such expanses are private or mental, we should say that the question of whether they are or are not mind-dependent simply does not arise. A mere perceptual expanse, so understood, does not exist at all, and therefore is neither "dependent" nor "independent," though in every other respect is just like perceptual expanses that do exist, namely, the existent surfaces of existent material objects and perhaps objects such as shadows, flashes of lightning, and rainbows. That we make an appeal to nonexistent, unreal objects, viz. mere perceptual expanses, is no defect, if the appeal to such objects in the case of *existential* perceptual illusion is not a defect.

Such a view can be seen to incorporate the virtues of the sense-datum theory, indeed to coincide with a drastically revised version of it, a version compatible with direct realism as well as with any plausible phenomenology of perception. Sense data, according to this version, are what we perceive "directly." They are what could be but need not be the real facing surfaces of real material objects. If they are not, then they are nonexistent, not real, but nonetheless perceived perceptual expanses. If they are real, then to perceive them would be, of course, to perceive (as "directly" as it makes sense to say that we could) the real material objects of which they are the facing surfaces. We must not make the mistake of supposing that since we cannot perceive a material object without perceiving a surface of it, it is only the latter that is directly perceived. (As Thompson Clarke has pointed out, this would be like supposing that we cannot be eating a sandwich because we can do so only by chewing a part of it at any one time.[56])

This concludes my answer to the ontological objection. The reader may have noted that if understood as I have suggested, this answer need not be rejected by the physicalist. After all, why should she not admit that some things do not exist and still hold that all those that do are physical? In what way could this be incompatible with physicalism? Physicalism is incompatible with direct realism (with respect to perception, not ordinary sensations) only if it rejects the *general* direct realist conception of consciousness. But would it reject it if it understood it properly? Or would it rather acknowledge the limitations of physicalism as a metaphysical theory? I believe that a thoughtful physicalist would do the latter and thus in a sense cease to be a physicalist. But she would still be loyal to its chief motivation: the rejection of the myth of the ghost in the machine.

IV

For the sake of completeness, let us now briefly turn to the fifth, the epistemological objection to direct realism. While the direct realist conception of consciousness, like any of the competing conceptions, does not provide a solution to the problem of how we may know in a particular perceptual situation that there is a real material object before us, at least it renders the *possibility* of such a solution not obviously implausible. On the main opposing conception of consciousness, the mental-contents theory, we are encircled by our ideas and sensations, what we are aware of is only the contents of our minds. If so, our task is to explain how we may know that there is an external object in the first place, whether real or unreal, when no such object is given to perceptual consciousness at all, and this task is that of inferring that there is such an object from the contents of our minds. If it is suggested (e.g., by some adverbial theorists who have not thought through the *ontology* their theory presupposes) that no such inference is needed, then our knowledge of the external world becomes even more mysterious.

It may seem peculiar to speak of knowing that there is an unreal object. But let us recall that quantification over unreal objects is not only intelligible but common. And the knowledge in question need not result from a process of investigation. It could be, indeed ordinarily would be, direct, immediate, as for example knowing what one is thinking or imagining usually is. Of course, in speaking of knowledge here we are not begging the question against the skeptic. On any theory of perceptual knowledge that is at all plausible, there is something that is known directly and immediately, and on none so far offered that is defensible is what is so known the reality of a material object. The distinguishing feature of the direct realist theory is that what is known is that there is such an object, but not that this object is real. To know the latter is an additional item of knowledge. And it is a virtue of direct realism that it makes perspicuous the connection between the two steps required for arriving at this additional knowledge. It is an a priori, logical connection. The second step logically presupposes the first step. The two steps correspond to Stanley Cavell's distinction between "knowledge as the identification or recognition of things" and "knowledge of a thing's existence."[57] It is one thing to identify or recognize a thing as such and such, or to be able to call it by the right name, it is quite another to know that it exists. Yet if one could not do the former, one could not do the latter.

But if the reader still finds all this unpalatable, she might be satisfied with the assertion that the first step, i.e., knowing that there is an external, material object, even if that object is unreal, could be described just as the having of a clear conception of which and what is that particular thing the reality of which is in question. This makes the a priori status of the connection between the two steps explicit. We can also add Richard A. Fumerton's observation that "One ought to accept the responsibility of analyzing propositions about the physical world in such a way that one accounts for the fact that we believe them and believe we are justified in so doing."[58] And now one argument against the mental-contents theorist would be that she is unable to explain how such a conception and such beliefs would be arrived at. To just suppose that this can be done in some manner or other, and that then we can come to have knowledge of the existence of the object, would be to engage in empty speculation. It is worth remembering that Berkeley's chief argument against the existence of material objects was that we have no conception of such objects, indeed that the assertion that there are material objects is self-contradictory. This argument has no force against direct realism; if direct realism is true, then the conception of a material object is directly derived from the perceptual awareness of what it is a conception of, and of course there is not the slightest reason for thinking that such a conception is self-contradictory; moreover, it is quite obvious why we believe that there are real material objects and why we believe that we are justified in believing this: we *perceive* material objects, even if they turn out to be unreal. A realism that is based on a mental-contents theory, on the other hand, *is* faced with Berkeley's objection and I do not think it has an answer to it; nor do I think it can explain why we believe that there are real material objects and that we are justified in believing this.

First, there is the difficulty of making clear what the "contents" of our minds are supposed to be, and indeed that there are any such things at all. Appeals to vague ordinary notions, such as those of idea and sensation, or to technical notions of doubtful intelligibility, such as those of a sense datum and a way of being appeared to, are hardly helpful. Second, there is the difficulty of explaining why our mental contents should prompt us to believe, without any inference usually, that there are real *material* objects before us. Third, if as philosophers we attempt such an inference, presumably an appeal to "the best explanation," and if by a good explanation we mean in part a deep one, then it is not at all clear that the object, the existence of which we ought to infer from our mental contents, would be at all like what we ordinarily mean by a material object; the esoteric "objects" of quantum mechanics would seem far more suitable, but, as I shall point out presently, inferences to them appeal to facts about nonesoteric, ordinary material objects. And, fourth, the validity of the inference would be most questionable. The validity of ordinary scientific inferences to "the best explanation" is notoriously difficult to understand and defend, partly because of the extraordinary vagueness of the notion of "the best explanation" and indeed of the general notion of explanation. And, as we have seen, in the case under consideration we have the additional burden of being most unclear about the explanandum, since the explanandum is supposed to be such things as ideas and sensations, not familiar characteristics of material objects and events, such as readings of instruments, which are what we do appeal to in science. Scientific inferences to the best explanation proceed ultimately from what are taken to be facts about directly observable material objects and we have no conception of what these inferences might be like if they did not, if they proceeded from alleged facts about "mental contents." All four difficulties are familiar from the history of modern philosophy and do not need exploring here.[59]

Now the case with the direct realist conception is very different. According to it (again, I shall use G. E. Moore's vivid words), "Merely to have a sensation is already to *be* outside . . . the circle of our own ideas and sensations."[60] Moore continued this sentence by also saying, "It is to know something which is as truly *not* a part of *my* experience, as anything which I can ever know." I assume that Moore did not mean to deny that there could be hallucinations and dreams. I take his point to be that to have a sensation, in the sense he used this term, e.g., a sensation of blue, can only be to be in direct epistemic contact with something, an object, which is not a part of one's perceptual consciousness. But that object might not be a real object, and in the article from which I have quoted, Moore says nothing about how we can know that it is real. Nevertheless, on the direct realist view proper, we can be assured that *there is* an object we perceive, and the problem is how to find out the *further* fact about it, whether or not the object exists, is real. We may have no adequate philosophical solution of this problem, but at least in ordinary life we think we have a very clear idea of how to go about resolving it (in particular cases, with respect to which alone it is here relevant), and the general nature of the challenge is also clear—it is not such that it renders the possibility of our meeting it obviously implausible, as in the case of any mental-contents theory.

Our task is, in general, that of explaining how we may discover that a certain object before us has, in addition to the properties it is given as having, also another property or, better, characteristic or feature, namely, reality, which it is not (and probably, as Kant argued, cannot be) *given* as having. Presumably, the reason this feature is not given is not that it is somehow hidden. It might not be given simply because it is, very broadly speaking, a highly complex relational property which, at least to human minds, cannot be given as a whole. The relational property may be coherence with other objects, or, as I have argued elsewhere,[61] indefinite identifiability through time or by other people. We need not take a stand here on its exact nature; it suffices to point out that its not being given as some of the other characteristics of the object are given need not mean that there is something mysterious about it. This is why a view such as Sartre's or Moore's, though it does not answer the question whether we know, or even have evidence, in some particular perceptual situation, that there is a real material object before us, at least makes it not obviously implausible that an answer can be found. The mental-contents view, on the contrary, makes this quite implausible. To that extent the direct realist view is superior not only as a phenomenological account of the nature of perceptual consciousness. It is also superior from the standpoint of epistemology.[62]

NOTES

1. H. H. Price, *Perception* (London, 1932), 26–27 and chapter VI.

2. Ibid., 24–25.

3. A. J. Ayer, *The Foundations of Empirical Knowledge* (London, 1953), 21.

4. This conception of direct realism is very much like what Hilary Putnam interprets William James's theory of perception to have been. See Putnam, *Realism with a Human Face* (Cambridge, Mass., 1990), chapter 17.

5. In *Sensations: A Defense of Type Materialism* (Cambridge, 1991), Christopher S. Hill admits that we are not aware of visual sensations but argues that "the laws of folk psychology" make reference to them and that folk psychology is a well-confirmed theory (p. 191). Hill and I must have attended different schools of folk psychology! He is a type materialist, identifying types of sensations with types of brain events and the qualities of the former with qualities of the latter. He defends these identifications largely on grounds of ontological simplicity, but appears to regard the virtues of ontological simplicity as only aesthetic (p. 40).

6. Included in his *Philosophical Papers* (London, 1959), 48. See also Moore's "The Subject Matter of Psychology" (*Proceedings of the Aristotelian Society*, n.s., 10 [1910]: especially 51–52).

7. See Armstrong's *Perception and the Physical World* (London, 1961) and *A Materialist Theory of the Mind* (London, 1968); and Pitcher's *A Theory of Perception* (Princeton, 1971).

8. P. F. Strawson, "Perception and its Objects," included in *Perceptual Knowledge* edited by Jonathan Dancy (Oxford, 1988), 104–105. For a recent criticism of the view, see Paul Snowdon, "The Objects of Perceptual Experience," *The Aristotelian Society,* Suppl. vol. 64 (1990).

9. H. P. Grice, "The Causal Theory of Perception," *Proceedings of the Aristotelian Society*, Suppl. vol. 35 (1961).

10. An example of a philosopher who supposes this is Georges Dicker, in *Perceptual Knowledge: An Analytical and Historical Study* (Dordrecht, 1980). See also Robert Audi, *Belief, Justification, and Knowledge* (Belmont, Calif., 1988); John Pollock, *Knowledge and Justification* (Princeton, 1974) and *Contemporary Theories of Knowledge* (Totowa, N.J., 1986).

11. Roderick M. Chisholm, *Theory of Knowledge* (Englewood Cliffs, N.J., 1989), 67.

12. Ibid., 18.

13. Alvin Plantinga, *Warrant and Proper Function* (New York, 1993), 98.

14. Georges Dicker, *Perceptual Knowledge, seems* to hold such a view.

15. For some of them, see my "Adverbial Theories of Consciousness," *Midwest Studies in Philosophy* 5 (1980).

16. J. M. Hinton, *Experiences* (Oxford, 1973); John McDowell, "Criteria, Defeasibility, and Knowledge," *Proceedings of the British Academy* 68, 455–79, reprinted with omissions and revisions in Dancy; Paul Snowdon, "Experience, Vision, and Causation," also in Dancy. See also Snowdon's related "The Objects of Perceptual Experience" (mentioned above in

note 8) (in *Dancy*) and "How to Interpret 'Direct Perception'" in *The Contents of Experience*, edited by Tim Crane (Cambridge, 1992); and McDowell's also related "Singular Thought and the Extent of Inner Space," in *Subject, Thought, and Context,* edited by Philip Pettit and John McDowell (Oxford, 1986). Two very useful discussions of the view are John Hyman, "The Causal Theory of Perception," and William Child, "Vision and Experience: The Causal Theory and the Disjunctive Conception," both in *The Philosophical Quarterly* 42, no. 168 (July 1992). Not surprisingly, the view closest to our direct realism is Richard Routley's, in *Exploring Meinong's Jungle* (Canberra, 1980), chapter 8, #10.

17. Hinton, *Experiences,* 140.

18. "Sensation," in *Contemporary British Philosophy,* edited by H. D. Lewis, Third Series (London, 1956), 443–44.

19. Compare Frank Jackson, *Perception* (Cambridge, 1976), 72–77.

20. The most detailed philosophical discussion, known to me, of the other senses is in Moreland Perkins, *Sensing the World* (Indianapolis, 1983). Unfortunately, Perkins is an *indirect* realist.

21. It is the failure to make this distinction that gives rise to J. J. Valberg's puzzle about experience. See his important book *The Puzzle of Experience* (Oxford, 1992).

22. For an excellent account of these ways to physicalism, see Arthur W. Collins, *The Nature of Mental Things* (Notre Dame, Ind., 1987), especially the preface and chapter I.

23. On this general topic, P. M. S. Hacker, *Appearance and Reality* (Oxford, 1987), is especially instructive.

24. *Philosophical Investigations,* translated by G. E. M. Anscombe (Oxford, 1953), 207.

25. Ibid., #304.

26. "The Refutation of Idealism," *Mind,* n.s. vol. xii (1903), included in *Philosophical Studies* (London, 1922), 29. See also Moore's "The Subject-Matter of Psychology," *Proceedings of the Aristotelian Society,* n.s. 10 (1910), and "A Defense of Common Sense," included in *Philosophical Papers.*

27. Ibid., 20.

28. Ibid., 25.

29. Ibid., 20.

30. Ibid., 27.

31. Ibid., 30.

32. See "Some Judgments of Perception," included in *Philosophical Studies,* and "A Defense of Common Sense," included in *Philosophical Papers.* The extent to which Moore was attracted by direct realism is especially evident in his "A Reply to my Critics," in *The Philosophy of G. E. Moore,* edited by P. A. Schilpp (La Salle, Ill., 1942), 627–53.

33. *The Basic Problems of Phenomenology,* translated by Albert Hofstadter (Bloomington, Ind., 1982), 63–65.

34. *The Transcendence of the Ego,* translated by Forrest Williams and Robert Kirkpatrick (New York, 1951), 93. But what about pains? Sartre does not discuss the topic, but the natural view, which I have adopted, is that they too are objects of consciousness, not acts of consciousness, and therefore not intentional, albeit we may wish to call them mental. If so, Sartre would need to allow for such inhabitants of the mind, but not of consciousness. (He does not make the distinction.) Such a correction would not affect his views about other kinds of consciousness, such as perception and the imagination, which he can continue to hold to lack inhabitants, or his denial of the existence of an ego in consciousness. But it may well affect his general phenomenological ontology.

35. *Being and Nothingness,* translated by Hazel Barnes (New York, 1956), 618.

36. Ibid., 217.

37. Ibid., 34.

38. Ibid., 314.

39. Merleau-Ponty, *Phenomenology of Perception,* translated by Colin Smith (London, 1962), 3.

40. Hilary Putnam, *Realism and Reason. Philosophical Papers. Volume 3* (Cambridge, 1983), 14. See also his *Reason, Truth and History* (Cambridge, 1981), chapter 1.

41. Ibid., 15. Valberg is one of the very few recent Anglo-American philosophers acknowledging the mysterious nature of consciousness without embracing physicalism (see his *The Puzzle of Experience*), probably because of his acquaintance with the continental tradition. McDowell, in the articles cited previously, seems to be another such philosopher.

42. Putnam, *Realism and Reason*, 211.

43. Ibid., 143.

44. Ibid., 207.

45. Ibid., 225.

46. Cf. Laird Addis, "Pains and Other Secondary Mental Entities," *Philosophy and Phenomenological Research* 14 (1986): 59–74, and *Natural Signs* (Philadelphia, 1989).

47. See, for example, Russell, *Introduction to Mathematical Philosophy*, where he writes: "The notion of 'existence' has several forms . . . but the fundamental form is that which is derived immediately from the notion of 'sometimes true'. We say that an argument *a* 'satisfies' a function ϕx if ϕa is true. . . . Now if ϕx is sometimes true, we may say there are *x*'s for which it is true, or we may say 'arguments satisfying ϕx exist'. This is the fundamental meaning of the word 'existence'. Other meanings are either derived from this, or embody mere confusion of thought" (p. 164). The view had its origin, of course, in Frege, but it was Russell who forced it on contemporary Anglo-American philosophy.

48. I have discussed this topic in detail in *Being Qua Being: A Theory of Identity, Existence, and Predication* (Bloomington, Ind., 1979).

49. See my *Resemblance and Identity: An Examination of the Problem of Universals* (Bloomington, Ind., 1966), and *Being Qua Being*.

50. I explore this option in *The Concept of Knowledge* (Evanston, Ill., 1970), part three.

51. In Price, *Perception*.

52. Jackson, *Perception*.

53. Price, *Perception*, 106.

54. Ibid., 3.

55. I attempt such an explanation in *The Concept of Knowledge,* by arguing that the notion of a pure perceptual expanse can be derived from ordinary notions by analogy. For an argument against the possibility of such an explanation, and an extensive discussion of the concept of a surface, see Avrum Stroll, *Surfaces* (Minneapolis, 1988). But, in my opinion, Stroll is excessively impressed by some of the quirks of ordinary usage, e.g, that we (allegedly) do not speak of the surfaces of plants, animals, and people.

56. "Seeing Surfaces and Physical Objects," in *Philosophy in America*, edited by Max Black (Ithaca, N.Y., 1965).

57. Stanley Cavell, *The Claim of Reason* (Oxford, 1979), 224; see also pp. 51, 56. But Cavell's distinction is not intended to play the role mine does, nor is his view about skepticism at all like mine.

58. Richard A. Fumerton, *Metaphysical and Epistemological Problems of Perception* (Lincoln, Neb., 1985), 31. Fumerton is not a direct realist, however.

59. For an excellent criticism, though along lines somewhat different from mine, of abductive attempts to show the reliability of sense perception, see William P. Alston, *The Reliability of Sense Perception* (Ithaca, N.Y., 1993), chapter 4.

60. G. E. Moore, "The Refutation of Idealism," in *Philosophical Studies*, 27.

61. In *Being Qua Being*.

62. I offer positive arguments against skepticism in "Wittgenstein and Skepticism with Regard to the Senses," in *Wittgenstein and Contemporary Philosophy*, edited by Souren Teghrarian and Anthony Serafini (Wakefield, N.H., 1992), and in "The Untruth and the Truth of Skepticism," *Proceedings and Addresses of the American Philosophical Association*, January 1994.

Naturalism and Realism

FREDERIC SOMMERS

Whatever else realists say, they typically say they believe in a correspondence theory of truth.

Hilary Putnam

1

Ancient thought took knowledge in stride as just another topic in philosophy. But that was when a distinction between science and philosophy was undreamt of. In our own post-Cartesian, post-Kantian day, a move back to naturalism has been led by Quine who regards epistemology as continuous with other sciences engaged in reporting on what there is and what it does.

"Naturalism looks only to natural science"[1] which "tells us that our cognitive access to the world around us is limited to meager channels" including, especially, "the triggering of our sensory receptors by the impact of molecules and light rays."[2] The stimulations are processed and reported in "observation sentences" which have the "special epistemological status . . . of linking theory with outer reality."[3] Empirical knowledge (the only kind) is constituted as a "fabric of interlocking sentences [which] hooks on to the neural input at the observation sentences."[4]

In a typical protocol situation, a range of neural inputs, organically and socially processed as the perception of an object, will cause in X a belief he may express by the holophrastic observation sentence 'Rabbit.' Donald Davidson sees such situations as a source of shared meaning: "your utterance means what mine does if belief in its truth is systematically caused by the same events and objects."[5]

But, says Davidson, "a causal explanation of a belief does not show how or why the belief is justified." Rejecting a privileged status for observation sentences, Davidson opts for a complete coherentism[6] in which "nothing can count as a reason for holding a belief except another belief."[7] Because "[t]he distinction between beliefs justified by sensations and beliefs justified only by appeal to other beliefs is anathema to the coherentists," Davidson calls for the erasure of yet another seam in the fabric of knowledge: that "between observation sentences and the rest."[8] Popper, too, had denied that basic observation sentences are justified by experience. "Experiences can *motivate* . . . an acceptance or rejection of a statement, but a basic statement cannot be justified by them—no more than by thumping the table."[9]

Davidson claims that Quine's weak foundationalism is vulnerable to brain-in-vat skepticisms, something his own thoroughgoing coherentism avoids since any coherent body of actual beliefs is "intrinsically veridical." Quine's epistemology may indeed be susceptible to old skeptical worries, but Davidson's theory of presumptively veridical belief strikes many as too true to be good, engendering more skepticism than it claims to dispel.[10]

Davidson's principal and more serious objection to Quine's privileged sentences is that they lack the required evidential status since all we have to go by is the perception of the object of belief. Davidson points out that treating a perception of X as evidence that an X is there is to confuse, as Hume seems to have done, perceiving a green spot with perceiving that there is a green spot. And indeed Quine appears not to distinguish between these two kinds of "perceivings." The conflation, which does not seem to trouble Quine, is linguistic as well. Talking of expressions associated "holophrastically" with "certain ranges of neural input," Quine says: "I call these expressions observation sentences. Grammatically some indeed are sentences, e.g., 'it is raining', and some are nouns or adjectives, 'cat' or 'milk' or 'white'."[11] However, evidence is *sentential* and the *sentence* 'milk (is there)' must be based on an observation that milk is there.

2

In a recent article, Quine dismisses "objections to observation sentences as vehicles of evidence."[12] He points out that we normally ascribe 'seeing that' perceptions to children and even to animals. In teaching a child 'It's raining' or 'Milk', "the mother . . . must feel moved to assent to the observation sentence herself. I see this as her perceiving that *the child is perceiving that it is raining or that milk is there*" (my emphasis).[13] We are assured that assent to the observation sentences is "conditioned to distinctive ranges of sensory intake."

Unfortunately, this still appears to conflate seeing milk with seeing that milk is there. Michael Williams complains that Quine has not provided "even an explanatory, never mind a justificatory connection between stimulations . . . and assent to observation sentences."[14] That complaint is a bit unfair. After all, we lack an explanatory account even for object perception; current neuroscience offers only the barest explanation of how stimulations are synthesized as the perception of a cat. Nevertheless, Davidson and Williams are fairly pointing to a critical weak point in Quine's empiricism: sensory experience seems to reify objects (a cat, milk, a rabbit), but does not seem to synthesize something "seen" when we see that so and so. Put another way: we understand the research program leading to an explanatory account of object-perception like seeing a cat. What we do not understand is what it is we "see" when we see *that a cat is there*.[15]

2.1

All the same, we talk about "the evidence of our senses" and informally about seeing that a cat is there. Taking this at face value suggests that just as perceiving a cat (an object) causes in us the "idea" of a cat, so perceiving its being there (a state) causes in us the evidentiary belief that a cat is there; having "sensed" its presence we believe that the cat is there. Let us use *'perceive'* and *'see'* for this kind of perception. I perceive a cat and *perceive* that a cat is there. Though he may conflate object perception with state *perception*, Quine needs both: he needs to say, and does say, that *seeing* that there is a cat takes place when we see a cat. That *seeing* that a cat is there is nevertheless distinct from seeing a cat is evident when we consider that we often look and *see* that *no* cat is there. In either case, what we *see* or *perceive* is given through our sensory commerce with the world.

While not incorrigible, an observation sentence reporting a *perception* that a cat is there counts presumptively as part of "the evidence of our senses." Quine is in want of a theory of *perception*. But if countenancing states of affairs or facts is the going price, Quine won't pay it. *Perceiving* that a cat is there would be a case of *perceiving* a fact or state of affairs responsible for the truth of the observation sentence, 'Lo, there's a cat.' And Quine holds that physical objects are perceived but facts are not:

> There is a tendency—not among those who take facts as propositions—to think of facts as concrete. This is fostered by the commonplace ring of the word and the hint of bruteness, and is of a piece, for that matter, with the basic conception that it is facts that make sentences true. Yet what can they be, and be concrete? The sentences 'Fifth Avenue is six miles long' and 'Fifth Avenue is a hundred feet wide,' if we suppose them true, presumably state different facts; yet the only concrete or, at any rate, physical object involved is Fifth Avenue. . . . And surely [facts] cannot be seriously supposed to help us explain truth. Our two sentences are true because of Fifth Avenue, because it is a hundred feet wide and six miles long, because it was made that way, and because of the way we use our words.[16]

Quine is a realist about physical objects but not about facts. Truth is disquotational. 'Lo, rabbit' is not true because of a fact to which it corresponds. There are no such facts and, *a fortiori*, no such thing as *perceiving* them.

2.2

Quine's inveighings against facts would appear to be inconsistent with attributing to a child the perception that milk is there. If he did "countenance" facts, he could say that just as we are creatures that process our neural inputs objectually to see milk, so too do we process them factually to *see* that the milk is there. In both cases, the checks we write on a detailed account of "neural processing" are postdated to the future of neuroscience. Yet to suggest that a factual processing of experience could do service in a Quine-type empiricism is to presuppose that we have a reasonably clear conception of 'concrete fact'. And that is notoriously not at hand.

3

In repudiating concrete facts, Quine is on the well-beaten path of Frege, C. I. Lewis, Peter Strawson, and almost all other modern analysts who reject truth-making facts and correspondence theory. On this topic, Strawson speaks for most:

> That (person, thing, etc.) to which the referring part of the statement refers, and which the describing part of the statement fits or fails to fit, is that which the statement is *about*. It is evident that there is nothing else in the world for the statement itself to be related to. . . . The only plausible candidate for what (in the world) makes a statement true is the fact it states; but the fact it states is not something in the world. . . .
>
> Roughly, the thing referred to is the material correlate of the statement . . . the fact to which the statement "corresponds" is the pseudo-material correlate of the statement as whole."[17]

Strawson concludes that "the demand that there should be such [an objective] relatum . . . is logically absurd."[18]

Davidson has played with the idea of correspondence, but in the end he follows Quine in saying that "the idea of correspondence . . . is an idea without content."[19]

> The real objection is that such theories fail to provide entities to which truth vehicles (whether we take these to be statements, sentences, or utterances) can be said to correspond.[20]

The logical realists (as we may call the friends of facts and correspondence) accept facts as objective "truthmakers."[21] To them a fact like the presence of a rabbit is observable and no less real than the rabbit. They acknowledge that facts are not at all like objects. Indeed they are *very* unlike: it makes no sense to speak of the weight or color of a fact. But whatever facts may be, the logical realists accept them as real "objective nonlinguistic correlates" to true statements.

If I am right, Quine cannot afford the luxury of dismissing concrete facts. His grounded empiricism requires him to say that "the range of neural input" is processed to deliver facts as well as objects. In other words, he needs to assume that people "factify" as well as "entify." Without observable facts, Quine's empiricism lacks purchase. And Davidson, who follows Quine in rejecting facts, is right to draw the consequences.

The rare sight of Davidson at odds with Quine on a fundamental point of philosophy is to be explained as an effect of Quine at odds with Quine. On Mondays and Wednesdays, when Quine sits down to make out his list of entities invited to the feast of existence, he finds facts "entia non grata." But on Tuesdays and Thursdays, when he is discussing the foundations of his naturalized epistemology, he holds that observation via neural input delivers facts articulated in observation sentences like 'there is a rabbit' or 'milk is there'.

Which Quine is truer to himself? Is it the Quine skeptical about "concrete facts" or the Quine who argues for a weak foundationalist epistemology? I believe that Quine's doctrine of sensory evidence is more fundamental to his general philosophy than his "ontic" fastidiousness with regard to facts. If so, a sympathetic interpreter of Quine should put aside Quine's own pronounced disdain for concrete facts to seek a coherent notion of the facts observed and articulated in observation sentences.

In any case, and quite apart from what Quinians must do to buttress his empiricism, the fashionable repudiation of facts as "incoherent" or "non grata" has surely had its day. One wants an account of facts that makes sense of their observability, allowing for the *perception* of the fact that there is a rabbit. "Concrete facts" ought to have respectability in a naturalist epistemology. With such facts explicitly in the picture, it won't be Quine, but it will be something Quine can use to make repairs to his foundationalist doctrine if he so chooses.

4

In looking to make sense of facts, it helps to focus on the kind of protocol observational situation that Quine focused on—the kind that engenders a belief in the presence or absence of something and that may be reported in an observation sentence. The first thing to say about observational belief is that it is not necessarily "propositional." Quine reminds us that "beliefs can be ascribed even to dumb animals in the light of behavior,"[22] animals' cries being the counterpart to "holophrastic" observation sentences that express human beliefs. Since animals lack language, Quine considers ludicrous the hypothesis that their beliefs are propositionally encoded,[23] all of which suggests that entertaining a proposition is only incidental to believing something.

The second thing to say about observational beliefs is that they can be negative as well as positive. Aeschylus describes the despairing cry of a bird that has just discovered that her nest is empty and her anguished circling to find the missing fledglings. I think we may accept, in the light of the bird's behavior, that she believes her fledglings are not there. We may imagine she has come back from a hunt in which she had seen a rabbit and behaved as if she believed it was there (indeed we may imagine that she swooped down in an attempt to capture it). The belief engendered by her looking at the empty nest is worth attending to because here is a case of believing that something is *not there*. And this means that while the first neural input had been processed as a *perception* of rabbit presence, the second has been processed as a *perception* of fledgling absence.

In an attempt to give an account of the nature of facts, we are also helped by Quine's doctrine that all judgments (including singular judgments like 'Socrates is wise') are judgments of existence or nonexistence.[24] Then the third thing to say about any belief is that it is positively or negatively existential. In particular, an observational belief is a belief that something is present in or absent from the field of observation.

Finally, we bear in mind Strawson's challenge to the logical realist to show how a statement could possibly be like a term. Terms, says Strawson, denote or refer to things; statements do not. Strawson thought that the logical realist is committed to the doctrine that a true statement denotes the fact that makes it true. However, in meeting Strawson's challenge, we find that although statements do not denote facts, they do denote: just as a nonvacuous term signifies some property (e.g., wisdom or being wise) and denotes what has it (a wise person), so a true statement signifies a property (the fact that makes it true) and denotes the world that has that property.

We have replaced the question of what facts could be by the question of what it is we refer to when we use such phrases as 'the presence of a rabbit', 'the existence of elks', 'the nonexistence of elves'. In shifting over to existence, we have at least removed ourselves from one area of secular prejudice. Philosophers, trained to look askance on facts as *entia non grata*, are considerably more respectful when it comes to speaking of the existence of things like rabbits than they are in speaking of *that a rabbit is there* as a concrete fact or state of affairs. Quine himself is a paradigm example. He rashly jettisons concrete facts. Yet in allowing for "sensory evidence," he is allowing that our "neural inputs" are being processed as the *perception* of *P-presence* or *Q-absence*, as well as being processed as the perception of *P*-things. He continues to confuse state perception with object perception. He says: "When we want to check on existence, bodies have it over other objects on the score of their perceptibility."

In that characteristic remark, Quine errs doubly by failing to identify what should be identified and by failing to distinguish what should be distinguished. He can feel comfortable saying that the existence of the moon is observable while deriding the theory that "concrete facts" are observable, only by failing to see that the fact that the moon is there just *is* the existence of the moon (as concrete a fact as one could wish for). And he can feel comfortable saying that we check on the existence of the moon by perceiving the moon, only by failing to distinguish between perceiving the moon and *perceiving* the existence of the moon (sensing its presence, "seeing that it is there"). That the distinction is real is evident. A "check" can go either way: when Sartre checks on the presence of Pierre by looking at the bench of their customary rendezvous, he can see he is not there just as easily as he saw, the day before, that he was there.

But, now, having properly distinguished between the moon and its existence and having properly identified its existence with the fact that it exists, are we really any better off than before? Modern analytic philosophers, leery of facts, are equally leery (though more respectful) of existence. We are suggesting that such referring phrases as 'the existence of rabbits' and 'the absence of the teacher' refer to facts. But the grammar of 'existence' is notoriously deceptive and Strawson, Quine, and the other fact irrealists could turn out to be right after all.

4.1

We want to know what we are talking about when we talk about the presence of a rabbit. One answer is ruled out: as we have learned from Kant, despite the grammaticality of "its presence" or "their existence," the presence of a rabbit or the existence of elks is not a property of the rabbit that is present or the elks that exist. The question that Kant had left over is: If existence is not a property of a thing that exists, what is it a property *of*?

Frege's answer and its modern variants offer notions of existence and nonexistence that take them out of contention as observable or truthmaking facts. Alluding to Kant's negative thesis on what existence is not, Frege treats 'exists' as a "second level predicate," predicated of a concept denoted by a first level predicate. "Because existence is a property of concepts, the ontological argument for the existence of God breaks down."[25] For the logical realist, elk-existence is somehow a property of the world; for Frege it is the nonemptiness of the concept ELK.

According to Russell, "existence is essentially a property of a proposi-tional function" which, as he explained, "means that propositional function is true in at least one instance."[26] Thus, 'elks exist' asserts that 'x is an elk' is true in at least one instance or that it is "sometimes true." Russell's proposal was entirely in the spirit of Frege, but with the difference that Russell took propositional functions instead of concepts as the subjects for a predication of existence. Quine's proposal that to be is to be the value of a variable is an improved version of Russell's view that to exist is to instantiate an open sentence.

The Frege/Russell approach to predications of existence accommodates Kant's skeptical view that existence is not a property of things that exist and does so while keeping clear of "Plato's Beard." For in saying that centaurs do not exist, I am not talking about "what is not," but about something that exists, e.g., attributing to the concept CENTAUR the property of having nothing fall under it (characterizing it as an empty concept) or to 'x is a centaur', the property of being never true.

Despite some formal merits, the Frege/Russell way with the reference of phrases of form, 'the existence of P' offends against the robust sense of reality that Russell sought to accommodate in even the most abstract analysis. The existence of galaxies beyond the Milky Way must in some sense be a property of the external world; to speak of it in the Frege/Russell manner fails to do justice to the existence of such galaxies as a feature of the universe. Consider, too, what an animal perceives when it senses the presence of an enemy: formally the presence of an enemy is the nonemptiness of the concept ENEMY NEARBY, but is that what it perceives?

Nor do these formal conceptions of existence provide a conception of facts that serve as truthmakers. We want to say that the assertion 'there are galaxies beyond the Milky Way' is made true by the existence of galaxies beyond the Milky Way. That cries for an explanation, but we want to say it and go on to explain it. But if the existence of galaxies beyond the Milky Way is construed in the modern manner, we have the near circularity that 'there are galaxies beyond the Milky Way' is made true by the fact that the function 'x is a galaxy beyond the Milky Way' is satisfied or that it is made true by the fact that it denotes a nonempty concept or by the fact that it is "sometimes true." Only if you believe in "concrete facts" are you in a position to say—however darkly—that the existence of galaxies beyond the Milky Way is an observable, truthmaking fact. But then it is up to the logical realist to dispel the darkness by offering a coherent and "robust" conception of existence and the facts that make true statements true.

5

Elves do not exist, but elks do. Existence and nonexistence, as Kant rightly taught, are not properties of the things that are said to exist or not to exist. Of what else then? The logical realist's answer is that (the facts of) elk-existence and elf-nonexistence are properties of the world. How can we understand him?

In what follows "a world" or domain is the totality of things under consideration when a judgment is made, a question asked, a hope expressed, etc. It may consist of the objects in a visual field as when I say 'lo, an elk', or 'there's no elk here'. It may be as wide as the contemporary universe as when I say there are such things as red shifts and elks but no such things as elves or no such events as miracles. The totality under consideration need not be physical. The venue of the judgment that there is an even prime number is the domain of natural numbers. It may be mythological as when, speaking of the fauna of Greek myths, I say there was a flying horse but no flying kangaroo.

Any totality is *existentially* characterized by the presence of certain things and by the absence of certain things. The contemporary world is positively characterized by the existence of birds and snow and negatively characterized by the nonexistence of dinosaurs and phlogiston. The domain of natural numbers is characterized by the existence of an even prime number and the nonexistence of a greatest prime number. The presences and absences that characterize a domain are its existential properties. The nonexistence of dinosaurs is an existential property of the contemporary world. The existence of dinosaurs is a property or state of affairs that characterizes a past world. The nonexistence of a hammer is a negative existential property of the totality of objects in a drawer which may be the domain under consideration in the judgment 'there's no hammer here'.

In the case of an observation in which an object is seen and its presence sensed, we have two kinds of reality to consider. There are the "trees" and there is the "wood." There are the physical objects, situations, and events in the perceptual environment, and there is the environment itself, the Domain under Consideration (DC) which, for our purposes, is the totality of things (objects, situations, events) in the field of observation. The objects in a physical DC are perceived; the DC itself is "apperceived." Each type of reality has its characteristic properties. And just as in perceiving an elk we have sensory access to the attributes of the elk, so do we have sensory access to the attributes of the domain that we apperceive.

Let a domain containing (a) K (thing) be called $\{K\}$ish (pronounced "kayish") and otherwise, un$\{K\}$ish. The existence of (a) K is a property or state of the domain (its $\{K\}$ishness.) Looking at something in the domain, I may take it to be an elk. The *domain* itself I take to be $\{$elk$\}$ish. Thus two things occur: I see what I take to be an elk and I experience the visual field as characterized by the presence of an elk. When my wife tells me that I will find a hammer in the pantry drawer, the "world" under consideration is the totality of things in the drawer. I look for it there. Not seeing a hammer, I "apperceive" the DC as un$\{$hammer$\}$ish. I *see* that there is no hammer and announce my finding to my wife.

5.1

Epistemologists who focus solely on things perceived do not see the wood for the trees. The environment itself, the "field of observation"—distinguished by the presence of an elk—is experienced and taken to be $\{$elk$\}$ish, etc. In general, to believe there is a K is to take the domain to be $\{K\}$ish. We see the elk and *perceive* the fact that the elk is there. We see and we believe. Note that nothing has been said about propositions. Belief is "mondial," it is an attitude to the world or DC. Because the true object of belief is not a proposition but the domain under consideration, animals too can believe. For human beings, the domain need not be physical: to believe that there is an even prime number is to take the domain of natural numbers to be $\{$even prime$\}$ish. Even then belief is essentially propositionless.

5.2

Suppose there are K things but no J things. By construing K-existence and J-nonexistence as properties of totalities or domains, we take the decisive step to demystifying truthmaking facts.[27] To search for such "facts" in the world is indeed futile. Quine's presence is a fact but while Quine himself is present in the world, Quine's *presence* is not, no more so than Santa's absence. Quine's properties (e.g., his acumen, his pertinacity, his influence, etc.) may be thought of as being in the world, but to look in the world for the fact of his presence is to take a bite from Anselm's apple by thinking of Quine's existence as just another property of Quine.

The general consensus was that Strawson had the better of Austin in their debate over correspondence. I agree with that insofar as Strawson had decisively demolished all In-World Correspondence Theories (including Austin's). The existence of mangy cats in Maine is the "state of affairs" that makes 'there are mangy cats in Maine' true. But while Maine abounds in cats, their existence is not to be found in Maine. Strawson's Kant-like arguments convincingly showed that truthmaking states of affairs are *not situations*. To complete the picture, he *should* have added: "Though they are not states *in* the world, they are states *of* the world."

5.3

Rabbits are real and so are their properties. The world is real and so are its properties or states. The world's existential states are the facts, the "objective nonlinguistic correlates" of correspondence that "make true statements true." Not being *in* the world, states of affairs do not exist. But they are real and they "obtain." Elementary facts are positive or negative. The existence of elks makes 'there are elks' true, the nonexistence of an animal that eats no food is the elementary negative fact that makes 'every animal eats some food' true. The existence of elks and the nonexistence of animals that eat no food is the compound fact that makes the compound statement 'there are elks and every animal eats some food' true.

Strawson's challenge to the fact realist to show how statements are like terms is thus met. Just as a nonvacuous term such as 'mangy' signifies the characteristic of being mangy and denotes a thing that is mangy, so a true statement like 'some cat is mangy' signifies {mangy cat}ishness (the existence of a mangy cat) and denotes the {mangy cat}ish world. True statements signify facts and denote the world.

A nonvacuous term is traditionally said to have three modes of meaning. It *expresses* a sense or *characterization* (e.g., BEING WISE), it *signifies* a property or *characteristic* (e.g., being wise or wisdom) and *denotes* a thing (a wise person). (I use upper case for characterizations, lower case for characteristics.)

A true statement too expresses a (propositional) *characterization*; for example, 'some Athenian is wise' expresses the proposition SOME ATHENIAN BEING WISE, THE EXISTENCE OF A WISE ATHENIAN, or THAT SOME ATHENIAN IS WISE. It signifies a (mondial, existential) *characteristic* (a fact or state of affairs): some Athenian being wise, the existence of a wise Athenian, or that some Athenian is wise. And it *denotes* the world so characterized. And just as terms that signify different characteristics (being wise, being an Athenian) may denote one and the same person, so different true statements signify different facts but *all* true statements denote one and the same world.[28]

5.4

Characterizations are products of discourse. Just as a painting exists only when painted and not before, so a proposition exists only if a statement has been made, a question has been asked, etc. Though characterizations are language dependent, characteristics are not; the characteristics of gold existed before there was language, the existence of gold (a world characteristic) is language independent.

Unpossessed characteristics do not exist; since there are no centaurs, the characteristic of being a centaur does not exist. Though it neither signifies nor denotes, a vacuous term like 'centaur' is expressively meaningful; it expresses BEING A CENTAUR. No meaningful term or statement is vacuous with respect to being expressive.

False statements are like vacuous terms. 'There are elves' expresses THE EXISTENCE OF ELVES, THERE BEING ELVES, or THAT THERE ARE ELVES, but it is doubly vacuous since it fails to signify a (mondial) characteristic and fails to denote the world.

To sum up the logical realist's doctrine:

Every statement (asserted utterance) expresses a proposition and makes an existential claim about a domain under consideration—a DC—determined by the context of utterance or by explicit indices that specify it. A true statement denotes its DC, signifying a fact that existentially characterizes the DC. A false statement is expressive but that is all: it fails to signify a fact and it fails to denote the world it purports to characterize.[29]

6

Instead of construing belief as a "propositional attitude," the logical realist construes it as a "mondial attitude." To say of Teresa that she believes in God is to say of her that she experiences the world as {God}ish. Now anyone who takes the world to be {God}ish can *also* be said to have a pro attitude to the proposition THAT GOD EXISTS (taking it to be a FACT or true proposition). But to a "mondist," the proposition is only incidental to the belief and we need not bring it in at all. By contrast, anyone who rejects facts is not likely to construe x's belief in the existence of Y as x taking the world to be characterized by the fact of Y's existence. Turning from the world (a veritable "linguistic" turn), the fact skeptic thinks of belief as an attitude to a proposition.

"Mondists" have no problem ascribing belief to animals. Hearing a noise, the dog takes its domain to be {intruder}ish and gives a "holophrastic" bark. If the mondist is right, "propositional attitude" is a misnomer. In believing there is a K, one does not so much take a proposition to be true as take the world as {K}ish. The bereft kitten experiences its world as un{mother}ish without knowing the meaning of 'mother' in cat-language.

"Propositionalists," on the other hand, are not comfortable saying that a dog or cat has a propositional attitude and not good at explaining what it might be.

A more familiar difficulty facing the propositionalist is that it often seems right to ascribe to reasonable people a belief in contradictory propositions.

Kripke tells of Pierre, reading about London in his native Paris and coming across the sentence 'Londres est jolie'. He believes what it says. He later moves to London, which he finds ugly. Not knowing that 'Londres' and 'London' are names for the same city, he comes to believe the proposition expressed by 'London is not beautiful.' The puzzle is that, under the circumstances, it is reasonable for Pierre to take both propositions as true. The situation is the more acute because the sentences 'Londres est jolie' and 'London is beautiful' express the same proposition and that proposition is contradictory to the proposition expressed by 'London is not beautiful'.[30]

The mondist concedes to Kripke that the propositions expressed by 'Londres est jolie' and 'London is not beautiful' are contradictory and indeed that Pierre takes both propositions to be true. All the same, he points out that Pierre does not have contradictory *beliefs*. By hypothesis, Pierre takes the world to be characterized by the existence of a city known to him as Londres and which is distinct from the city he now lives in. Finding his new habitat ugly, he takes the world to be {ugly London}ish. But also, remembering the book he read in Paris, he still believes in the truth of 'Londres est jolie', thus also taking the world to be {jolie Londres}ish. He can reasonably take the world in both these ways because he mistakenly believes the world to be {London and non-Londres}ish.

David Kaplan has devised an example where the same proposition is believed but reacted to in different ways.

> If I see, reflected in a window, the image of a man whose pants appear to be on fire, my behavior is sensitive to whether I think 'His pants are on fire' or 'My pants are on fire', though the object of thought may be the same.[31]

The proposition, in either way of thinking of it, is that the pants of the man reflected in the window are on fire. But that proposition is "presented" differently by 'my pants are on fire' and 'his pants are on fire'. The difference in "character" makes for a difference in the "cognitive significance" of the proposition believed and this accounts for the different reactions.

So (ingeniously) Kaplan. The mondists take a different tack. I look at the window and react. Instead of regarding me as reacting to a proposition (presented in a certain way), the mondists regard me as reacting to the total situation (the DC or "world" under consideration). How I take the world to be is what I believe. Do I "*apperceive*" it as a world in which my pants are on fire or someone else's? Taking it as {my pants on fire}ish is the more galvanizing belief.

7

A statement or asserted sentence expresses a proposition whether or not it signifies a fact. The proposition is an *existential characterization*, true of the DC if and only if the DC has the corresponding *existential characteristic*. If there being a rabbit (the existence of a rabbit) is a characteristic of the DC and I assert 'there is a rabbit', then the characterization expressed—THERE BEING A RABBIT (THE EXISTENCE OF A RABBIT)—is true of the DC and is said to "correspond" to the fact that there is a rabbit. Just as the mondial characteristic is existential, so is the propositional characterization.

The view set forth—that propositions are existential—sharply limits propositional contents. In particular, because it contains none of the information that specifies the domain of the truth claim, the proposition is informationally incomplete. Merely knowing the propositional contents is not enough. 'There is a rabbit' expresses THERE BEING A RABBIT, but we are at sea until we know which domain is being characterized. Hearing the sentence assertively uttered by a speaker on January 1, 1993, we know that THERE BEING A RABBIT is being applied as a characterization of a domain in the vicinity of the speaker at that date. The domain specifying information supplied by the context thus completes our understanding of what was said, but that information is not incorporated into the propositional content which remains austerely existential. Sometimes tense or explicit time and place indices are used to specify the DC. If I say today there was a rabbit here yesterday, the statement specifies a past domain for characterization, but here too the proposition is still THERE BEING A RABBIT.[32]

Modern doctrine, deriving from Frege, preponderantly holds that the context of assertion contributes to propositional content by "completing its sense." Speaking of tensed utterances, Frege says: "The time of utterance is part of the expression of the thought." And more generally: "The knowledge of certain conditions accompanying the utterance is needed for us to grasp the thought correctly."[33] So if I say there was a rabbit here yesterday, the content expressed is understood to include a reference to the time and place. In effect, Frege and his followers hold that the content of a proposition or thought is informationally complete: THERE BEING A RABBIT AT TIME t AND AT PLACE p. This popular and conventional view of the proposition makes no reference to a DC of which the statement is true. It has no need of that since all the information conveyed by the statement is contained in the propositional content.[34]

7.1

Kaplan and his school regard indexical expressions like 'here' and 'now' as directly referring expressions. "Clearly" says Palle Yourgrau, " 'now' said at noon, refers to noon, said at midnight to midnight." On the "austere" view, the pure indexicals 'here' and 'now' are world indices that have no referential role at all. 'Now' specifies for us a contemporary domain, 'here' specifies a domain of things in the vicinity of the speaker; but neither index refers to anything in the domain that is specified.[35]

7.2

Context determines the DC and so do indexicals like 'now' and 'here' which fix the venue of the truth claim by determining it with respect to time and place. Other expressions determine the DC in a different way. Sometimes we want to make a claim about a particular thing and then we specify a domain that has *that thing* as a constituent. Two types of terms effect this kind of specification: demonstratives and proper names.

Pointing to an object, the speaker says 'that is an awl'. As usual, the context determines the spatial and temporal parameters of the DC: it is a contemporary domain consisting of things in the immediate neighborhood. But in addition, the use of the demonstrative further stipulates that the domain contains the demonstratum as a constituent. In that respect, 'that' differs from 'here'. A truly "pure" indexical like 'here' in 'there's no hammer here' is "syncategorematic"; it does not refer to or denote any constituent of the domain it helps to specify for the truth claim. By contrast, a demonstrative subject such as 'that' plays a *dual* role. Besides helping to specify the domain (as one containing the demonstratum), it also plays a role in the content as a term denoting something *in* the domain.

There is something paradoxical about this dual role since normally a term playing a denoting role may be vacuous. Thus 'The King of France is here' is false. But 'that thing is here' is true simply because the domain under consideration is being specified as a domain characterized by the presence of the thing designated. Proper names also have this dual character. Since my use of 'Quine' (unlike my use of 'Atlantis') normally stipulates a domain in which the bearer exists, the statement 'Quine exists' is incorrigibly true.[36] The exclusive use of domain specifying expressions like 'now', 'here', and 'I', in reporting on what there is makes for a safe bet. Thus, anyone who says 'I'm here now' has loaded the DC for an incorrigible truth claim. The most famous example of such contingent incorrigibility is 'I exist'.

8

It is recapitulation time. I have argued that logical realism fits in well with a naturalized epistemology. Traditional epistemologies focus too narrowly on the rabbits and their fluffiness and too little on the world qualified by their presence. One reason for the almost exclusive attention to objects is that facts or states of affairs are in so poor repute. The attitude of those who do not countenance facts and states of affairs is more posture than substance however; modern philosophy has never made a viable case for banishing truthmaking facts, let alone for counting them as "incoherent." The case against facts is based on several errors. First and foremost, the foes of facts err in not recognizing that a concrete fact like *that there is a rabbit* is nothing more and nothing less than the rabbit's presence. Second, thinking that the rabbit's presence is different from the fact that there is a rabbit, they snub the fact and treat the rabbit's presence as being in the world. (Most contemporary philosophers are guilty of this Anselmian lapse; it leads Quine to conflate perceiving rabbits with *perceiving* their existence or presence.) Third, they incorrectly assume that the logical realist is committed to the doctrine that truthmaking facts are *in* the world ("alongside" the rabbit and its fluffiness). Looking or pretending to look for such facts and finding no plausible candidates, they declare the ideas of concrete facts and correspondence to be incoherent. At the root of the posturing and confusion is the critical failure of modern philosophy to offer a "robustly" realist account of existence and nonexistence.

The logical realist would correct these mistakes. We occasionally find ourselves in a {rabbit}ish domain; its {rabbit}ishness (the presence of a rabbit) is something we *sense* although not as we sense the rabbit's fluffiness. Because the rabbit's existence, unlike its fluffiness, is not a property of the rabbit but of the domain, the existence of a rabbit cannot be represented in the way an object and its properties can be.[37] All the same we *perceive* that the rabbit is there. For just as the sensory data arriving through the "meager channels" are processed to give us the rabbit and its fluffiness, so are they processed to give us its presence. By construing the existence of the rabbit to be an observable state of the physical environment, the logical realist directs us to the concrete facts that constitute the basis of empirical knowledge.

NOTES

1. W. V. Quine, "Structure and Nature," *Journal of Philosophy* 89, no. 1 (1992): 9.
2. Ibid., 6.
3. Quine, "Let me accentuate the positive" in *Reading Rorty*, edited by A. Malachowski (Oxford, 1990), 119.
4. "Structure and Nature," 8.
5. Donald Davidson "A Coherence Theory of Truth and Knowledge" in *Truth and Interpretation, Perspectives on the Philosophy of Donald Davidson*, edited by Ernest Le Pore (Oxford, 1986), 318.
6. Ibid., 311.
7. Ibid., 310.
8. Ibid., 313.
9. Karl Popper, *The Logic of Scientific Discovery* (London, 1955), 105.
10. Susan Haack, who defends a Quine-type epistemology she calls "foundherentism" has convincingly deflated Davidson's claims to have answered the Cartesian skeptic. She also exposes internal weaknesses in Popper's view that basic sentences are unjustified. Susan Haack, *Evidence and Inquiry* (London, 1993), 60–72 and 98ff.
11. Quine, "Structure and Nature," 7.
12. Quine, "In Praise of Observation Sentences," *Journal of Philosophy* 90, no. 3 (March 1993): 108 and 112.
13. Ibid., 112.
14. In Michael Williams's review, "W. V. Quine: *Pursuit of Truth*," in *Journal of Philosophy* 99, no. 1 (1992): 50.
15. The distinction between seeing an object and *seeing* a state of affairs can be made out categorically. When we see a cat, we see something alive or dead, male or female. But what we see when we see that a cat is there is none of those things. Indeed to allow that a fact like the cat (not) being there as something we observe is to give up the idea that what we observe must have the features of physical objects.
16. *Word and Object*, (Cambridge, Mass., 1960), 247. See also, "Propositional Objects" in *Ontological Relativity and Other Essays* (New York, 1969), 145 where Quine echoes this in rejecting propositions, denying "that there are any such things as *that* the faces of the pyramid are equilateral along with there being such things as I and the pyramid and its faces."
17. P. F. Strawson, "Truth" in *Logico-Linguistic Papers*, (London, 1971), 194–95.
18. Ibid., 194.
19. Donald Davidson, "The Structure and Content of Truth," *Journal of Philosophy* 87, no. 6 (June 1990): 304.
20. Ibid., 304.

21. Not a fashionable doctrine: the sense of 'fact' now current is as a synonym for 'true statement' or 'true proposition'; that is, "facts" that are not themselves truth conditions or truthmakers but stand in need of them.

22. W. V. Quine, "Let me Accentuate the Positive" in *Reading Rorty*, edited by A. Malachowski (Oxford, 1990), 119.

23. See "Propositional Objects" in *Ontological Relativity and Other Essays* (New York, 1969), 117.

24. Indeed some judgments of existence and nonexistence, on masses and abstract objects (e.g., of things like snow, fun, or pollution) seem to be beyond the expressive resources of canonical languages. See my "Predication in the Logic of Terms" *Notre Dame Journal of Formal Logic* 31 (1990): 106–26.

25. G. Frege, *Die Grundlagen der Arithmetik*, published with English translation by J. L. Austin *en face* as *The Foundations of Arithmetic* (Oxford, 1952), 53.

For an excellent discussion of the doctrine that existence is an attribute of concepts, see C. J. F. Williams, *What is Existence?* (Oxford, 1981), chapter II.

26. Bertrand Russell, *Introduction to Mathematical Philosophy* (London, 1960), 164.

27. Nontrivial existence as an attribute of the world is always specified presence (elk-existence); non-trivial non-existence is specified absence (elf-nonexistence). Anything in a world under consideration is a thing, a mere "existent," in the uninformative sense that Kant derided. In the *informative* sense to exist or to fail to exist is to characterize the world by *specified* presence or absence.

28. Let '<p>' represent the world denoted by 'p'. Since all true statements denote one and the same world, propositional logic can be construed as a categorical monadic term logic in which 'p and q' is represented as 'some <p> is a <q>' and 'if p then q' as 'every <p> is a <q>' etc. See my article, "The World, the Facts and Primary Logic" in *Notre Dame Journal of Formal Logic* 34, no. 2 (spring 1993): 169–82.

29. The key elements in the logical realist account of statement meaning and realist truth conditions are:

's' (an asserted sentence or "statement")

[s] (the proposition THAT S; the proposition expressed by 's')

<s> (the fact, if any, that s)

W (the World)

In the favorable case,

[s] characterizes W (is true of W, "obtains", is a FACT or true proposition.)

<s> is a characteristic of W (is a fact, or state of affairs)

[s] corresponds to <s>

's' signifies <s>

's' denotes W

's' is true

In the unfavorable case, 's' merely expresses [s] but is otherwise unsuccessful.

30. Saul Kripke. "A Puzzle About Belief" in *Meaning and Use* edited by A. Margalit (Dordrecht, 1979), 239–83.

31. David Kaplan, "Thoughts on Demonstratives" in *Demonstratives*, edited by Palle Yourgrau (Oxford, 1991), 42.

32. A statement is an utterance that "says something." In the narrow and strict sense 'what is said' is simply the existential characterization; it is the proposition expressed by the utterance. In another sense it is information conveyed to one who fully understands what is said and in that wider sense, the domain figures in specifying "what is said" as a truth claim on that domain. Let [p] be what is expressed by 'p' and let D be the domain (as fixed by the context in which 'p' is asserted). Then to say that K said that p is to say that K claims that [p] characterizes D. Here "what is said" is a complex in which the context of assertion that fixes the domain has played a specifying role.

33. *Logical Investigations* translated by P. T. Geach and R. H. Stoothoff, (Oxford, 1977), 10 (cf. also 27–28).

In taking Frege as the standard bearer for the view that propositions are informationally complete, I omit consideration of assertions containing demonstrative subjects over which there is considerable dispute.

34. Though Quine does not hold with propositions as the meaning of sentences, he too says, that if one countenances them at all, it is as the meanings of eternal sentences (*Ontological Relativity*, 139).

35. 'Here,' 'now' and other "indexical" words are sometimes used referentially as demonstratives. Consider the difference between 'there's no hammer (here)' and 'here is a good place to look'. In the former, 'here' is a non-referential syncategorematic "pure" indexical that fixes the DC. In the latter, which *is* about a place, 'here' is not a pure indexical but a demonstrative that refers to *this* place in a DC that encompasses (alternative) locations as well as objects and events.

36. I may however use a proper name as a term for something or someone satisfying a definite description. In that use the name plays no indexical role. Thus, I do not stipulate that a bearer is in the DC, when I say that Homer did not exist or that (a city called) Atlantis did not sink into the sea.

37. Davidson says that because representationalism is false so is correspondence. "It is good to be rid of representations and with them the correspondence theory of truth." In fact, representationalism in any straightforward sense is false, because correspondence is *true*. Only things in the world (shaped, colored, textured, etc.) can be represented and the facts to which true statements correspond are not in the world. See Davidson, "The Myth of the Subjective" in *Relativism, Interpretation and Confrontation*, edited by Michael Krausz (Notre Dame, Ind., 1989), 165–66.

Naturalism: Both Metaphysical and Epistemological

HILARY KORNBLITH

Discussions of naturalism typically treat the metaphysics and epistemology of naturalism separately.[1] Indeed, it is often difficult to see why the metaphysical and epistemological theses characteristic of naturalism should bear a single name. That they do, however, is not an orthographic accident. In examining the views of the great figures in the history of philosophy, it is always illuminating to see how their metaphysical and epistemological views fit together. It is no less important or illuminating in the case of contemporary work. In this essay, I provide a sketch of a metaphysical project and an epistemological project, each of which is recognizably naturalistic. These projects present important constraints on one another. They also, if I am right, are mutually reinforcing. In the end, of course, I hope that the views I present are found to be attractive. My immediate goal, however, is not so much to argue for these views,[2] but rather to display the interaction between epistemological and metaphysical themes. We may understand naturalism better by seeing how a naturalistic metaphysics and a naturalistic epistemology fit together.[3]

Before I begin, however, I need to issue a brief disclaimer. I do not presume to speak for all naturalists. The metaphysical picture I present is not universally agreed upon by metaphysicians of a naturalistic turn of mind, nor is the epistemological picture I offer uncontroversial, even within the confines of naturalistic epistemologists. The motivations which attract philosophers to naturalism are many, and the views which arise from these motivations are no less diverse.[4] Naturalists who favor a different metaphysical view from the one offered here will likely have a different epistemology from my own as well. This is as it should be. One's metaphysics and epistemology should inform one another, and if I am very much in the wrong about either of these areas, I am probably at least as wrong about the other. I will thus be illustrating here how a particular naturalistic metaphysics interacts with a particular naturalistic epistemology. Those naturalists who have different ideas about these two areas will want to argue that their views too are complementary, that they too have metaphysical and epistemological views which are mutually illuminating and mutually supporting. But I will not be providing those arguments for them. That is work which they will need to do for themselves.

1. SKETCH OF A NATURALISTIC METAPHYSICS

In metaphysics, I believe, we should take our cue from the best available scientific theories. As Wilfrid Sellars so nicely put it, " . . . science is the measure of all things, of what is that it is, and of what is not that it is not."[5] Current scientific theories are rich in their metaphysical implications. The task of the naturalistic metaphysician, as I see it, is simply to draw out the metaphysical implications of contemporary science. A metaphysics which goes beyond the commitments of science is simply unsupported by the best available evidence. A metaphysics which does not make commitments as rich as those of our best current scientific theories asks us to narrow the scope of our ontology in ways which will not withstand scrutiny. For the naturalist, there simply is no extrascientific route to metaphysical understanding.

It is no surprise, of course, that anti-naturalists have defended metaphysical claims which are at odds with the best available scientific views. Well known are accounts of consciousness, human action, and mentality generally which appeal to occult entities or forces: immaterial stuff, agent causation, the "subjective ontology" of the mental. It is of little concern to defenders of such views that there is no more place for these things in contemporary scientific theory than there is for phlogiston, entelechies, or telekinesis. But theories postulating such occult entities are poor rivals for scientific theories; they are useless, or worse, in prediction, explanation, and technological application. The attempt to view appeal to the occult in some other way—not as a rival to scientific explanation, but as somehow insulated from it—is inevitably unsuccessful. Either the locus of incompatibility is simply shifted, in subtle or not so subtle ways,[6] or the occult claims are successively drained of cognitive content.[7]

More interesting, I believe, are attempts to contract, rather than expand upon, the ontology offered by science. Various forms of physicalism fall into this category when it is insisted, for example, that the ontology of microphysics gives us a complete account of what exists, or that physics and chemistry together provide us with a complete ontology, or, as some suggest, that physics, chemistry, and biology jointly provide us with a complete metaphysical catalog. Basic as these sciences are, they are not the sole arbiters of what exists. If we wish to know what the world is comprised of, we should look to successful scientific theories. Physics does not provide us with the only such theory, nor do physics and chemistry, nor physics, chemistry, and biology. The suggestion that (some of) these sciences are the sole determinants of what exists is a suggestion which does not derive from science itself.

Consider, for example, the widespread suggestion that mental phenomena need to be explained in physical terms if they are to be countenanced by a proper metaphysical theory. This suggestion seems to me to be deeply mistaken. It is as if there is antecedent reason to be suspicious of mental phenomena, reason to think that they are metaphysically guilty until proven innocent. But, indeed, our attitude toward the existence of mental phenomena should be nothing like this, and our attitude toward materialism should be nothing like this either. As regards mental phenomena, we have abundant reason to be realists about mentality in light of the important work which mentalistic terms perform in successful prediction and explanation. The fact that these terms capture important generalizations which cannot be captured in other vocabulary speaks to their ineliminability from psychological theory. And their ineliminability from a successful scientific theory gives us reason to believe that these terms genuinely refer. This is all the evidence one needs for holding that mental states and processes genuinely exist.

As a materialist, I also believe that mental states and processes are entirely physically constituted, but evidence for the physical composition of mental entities is importantly different from the evidence for their existence. If we should discover that mental states are not physically constituted, this would not be evidence of their non-existence, but evidence instead that materialism is false. Materialism should not be viewed as some kind of a priori constraint on theorizing about the mental. But the suggestion that mental phenomena can only earn their keep in our ontology by being appropriately connected with some privileged physical vocabulary does precisely that: it turns materialism into a doctrine which is held true independent of any evidence. On my view, that would be bad epistemology and bad metaphysics. It would be equally mistaken to insist that the claim that mental states exist should be held true independent of any evidence. My suggestion here does not do that, but ties it, instead, to evidence different from that for materialism.

Current scientific theory supports a number of interesting metaphysical claims. First, it is anti-reductionist, both about types and about tokens. We cannot, as I have been urging, simply presuppose some kind of reduction of the higher level sciences to the more basic sciences. If the claim of reduction is to be made, it must be supported by empirical evidence. But current evidence does not support an across-the-board reduction of higher to lower level sciences. In psychology, for example, mental state types are multiply realizable at the physical level, as has long been pointed out. This, by itself, is sufficient to defeat type-type reduction in psychology. But token-token reduction is no more plausible, for even token mental states are multiply realizable at the physical level. The criterion for sameness of mental state token in psychology does not make reference to the physical stuff which realizes the token, nor is there any kind of nomological relation guaranteeing that particular mental state tokens can only be physically realized in the very manner in which they are, in fact, realized. We are thus forced to acknowledge that the relationship between higher and lower level sciences need not involve any kind of identity of either types or tokens. The metaphysics of our current scientific theories does not support reductionism.

This is not to say, of course, that current scientific theory does not support materialism. I take materialism to be the view that everything is wholly physically constituted; current science gives us no reason to doubt this thesis.[8] Entities in higher level sciences are entirely constituted of physical stuff. Constitution, however, should not be confused with identity.

There has been a great deal of debate lately about whether genuine causal relations may obtain between events in the higher level sciences.[9] It has been urged by some that all causation is really microphysical causation, and thus events in the higher level sciences, if they cannot be identified with microphysical events, must be causally impotent. All of this is supposed to follow, somehow, from materialism. If we take our cue from the sciences themselves, however, rather than attempting to impose an a priori metaphysics upon our current scientific theory, we are led to just the opposite result. Our best current theories in psychology, economics, sociology, and so on, all are filled with causal claims. Mental states are said to interact; to cause behavior; to be caused by certain environmental conditions; and so on. These claims no more need to be reinterpreted or logically reconstructed than the causal claims to be found in the basic sciences. Because successful theories in the higher level sciences are currently committed to the existence of causal relations among the events over which they quantify, we too should be so committed.

This point about causal relations in the higher level sciences is a particularly important one because it is intimately related to a proper understanding of natural kinds. The view of natural kinds I favor, due to Richard Boyd,[10] identifies natural kinds with homeostatic property clusters: what is distinctive about natural kinds is that they involve clusters of properties which reside in a homeostatic relationship. Consider, for example, debates in psychiatry about the proper characterization of various mental disorders. When disagreements arise about which symptoms or syndromes are to be classified together as falling under a single diagnostic category, what is at issue is not merely a matter of convenience, but rather a question which ultimately turns on the causal relations among the various alleged characteristics of the disorder. If the disorder is properly characterized, then the symptoms cited must bear an intimate causal relationship to one another. They cannot be found together merely by chance. Instead, they must reside in a relationship which serves to promote their continued existence and interrelation. Proponents of various diagnostic categories seek to show that their preferred system of categorization answers to such a causal requirement. But this causal structure is not merely a feature of proper categorization in psychiatry. It is instead, I believe, a feature of proper categorization in the sciences generally. To claim that a group of properties constitute a natural kind just is to claim that they reside in such a homeostatic relationship.

The view that there are genuine causal relations operating in the higher level sciences is thus indispensable if one is to claim that there are natural kinds to be found at this level as well. One cannot on the one hand claim that there are real kinds to be found in psychology, for example, and then go on to deny that there are causal relations operating among the various events to which psychological theorizing commits one. Natural kinds and causal relations must stand or fall together.

Note as well that in taking this stand on the existence of genuine causal powers in the higher level sciences, one thereby commits oneself to a non-Humean account of causation. There cannot be exceptionless regularities outside the most basic sciences, since the operation of causal powers in higher level sciences is always subject to the possibility of interfering factors. It is thus that the higher level sciences are committed to the existence of *ceteris paribus* laws. But on a Humean account of causation, the very idea of causal laws which admit of exceptions is self-contradictory. The Humean account thus fails to square with our best current science.[11]

I thus draw five metaphysical lessons from contemporary scientific theory. (1) We should reject reductionism, both at the level of types and at the level of tokens. The higher level sciences do not simply reduce to more basic sciences. (2) Nevertheless, we should accept materialism. Everything is entirely physically constituted. (3) We should acknowledge the operation of causal powers not only in the basic sciences, but in the higher level sciences as well. (4) Natural kinds should be viewed as homeostatic clusters of properties. What is distinctive about the real kinds in nature is the way in which their constituent properties causally interact. (5) Our current understanding of causation requires that we view causal powers and causal laws in a distinctly non-Humean way. Causation need not, and cannot, be eliminated in favor of exceptionless regularities.

I now turn to the task of sketching a naturalistic epistemology which serves to complement these metaphysical theses.

2. SKETCH OF A NATURALISTIC EPISTEMOLOGY

A proper epistemological theory must explain how knowledge is possible. The achievements of the sciences make clear enough that human beings have indeed come to understand a great deal about the world. We should now be able to explain how we were capable of such an achievement. As a naturalist, I do not view this project as some kind of a priori exercise. We are not trying to respond to some imaginary skeptical opponent who doubts that knowledge of any kind is possible at all. Rather, in recognizing the achievements of the sciences, we are faced with a straightforward question which science itself may address. On the one hand, a scientific psychology characterizes the cognitive faculties of human beings. On the other, our current scientific theories give living proof of what those cognitive faculties are capable of. We must now try to explain how creatures with the faculties cognitive science tells us we have could have come to understand the kind of world which the sciences generally tell us that we inhabit. If all goes well, such an explanation should be possible.

Note that in trying to provide such an explanation, we allow our best psychological theories to put pressure on the theories in other sciences, and, by the same token, we allow the theories in the other sciences to put pressure on current psychological theorizing. We are thus simultaneously testing and refining our theories by allowing each to constrain the other. This is as it should be in science, where the application of theories in apparently different domains to a common question allows for greater understanding. Thus, for example, the great unifying power of Darwinism allowed work in ecology, microbiology, geology, and so on, to provide substantial constraints on one another, with rapid progress in each of these fields being the result. Similar progress can be made, I believe, by bringing the metaphysics of science and the epistemology of science to bear on a common question. The attempt to explain how knowledge is possible does just that.

I do not mean to suggest that this is the only question which a naturalistic epistemology should address. Epistemologists have traditionally occupied themselves with normative concerns, and a proper naturalistic epistemology should not abandon these. Instead, it must be shown how the normative concerns which have rightly moved epistemologists all along may better be addressed from within a naturalistic framework. In coming to understand how knowledge is possible, I believe, we will also come to see how best to refine and improve our cognitive practice. A naturalistic epistemology will not divorce itself from the project of giving epistemic advice. Rather, it will provide advice which is informed by the best current work in the sciences. The naturalistic approach may thereby show its superiority to traditional epistemology not only in its greater power to explain the phenomenon of human knowledge, but also in its practical application to the project of epistemic improvement. Epistemologists have long sought "rules for the direction of the understanding." Naturalistically minded epistemologists mean to take that idea seriously.

How is it then that our cognitive faculties allow us to understand the world around us? I will begin to answer this question by pointing out certain features of our perceptual faculties which allow for the possibility of knowledge, and then I will move on to discuss our native inferential tendencies. I will argue that there are deep analogies between these two kinds of cognitive equipment, and that our ability to reason well is best understood by way of the analogy with our perceptual faculties.

Our perceptual faculties are extraordinarily well suited to providing us with an accurate picture of the world around us. These faculties are, of course, fallible. The physical equipment of which they are made is subject to breakdown, and even when working properly, a certain pattern of error is typical as well. This equipment is not well suited to providing an accurate understanding of every logically possible or even every physically possible environment. Nevertheless, in the environment in which human beings tend to be found, our perceptual equipment works remarkably well.

Consider first, the physical machinery of which our perceptual equipment is constructed. While sensitive to a wide range of electromagnetic radiation, our eyes are useless outside of certain environmental conditions. When turned toward the sun, for example, we are unable to focus; prolonged exposure to such bright light will permanently damage the retina. Our eyes would be wholly unable to function in conditions regularly found on other planets. At temperature extremes found on Mercury or Pluto, the vitreous humor would boil or freeze. Our ability to detect bodily orientation, which depends on the motion of fluid in the semicircular canal, is impaired or absent in environments where gravitational forces differ substantially from those found on earth. As with all other mechanical devices, our perceptual equipment can only function in a restricted range of environments.

None of this, of course, is surprising, but these physical restrictions find interesting parallels at the psychological level. Just as the physical equipment of which our perceptual faculties are composed is subject to malfunction when placed in nonstandard environments, so too is the psychological dimension of perception deeply dependent on contingent features of standard environments. It is for this reason that the perceptual illusions are so revealing. By placing subjects in environments which are unusual or contrived, experimental psychologists may induce a characteristic pattern of error in unwitting subjects. Our natural tendency to misinterpret these nonstandard situations is revealing precisely because it alerts us to certain features of standard environments, features which we presuppose whenever we confront new situations. When the features are actually present, as they are in standard environments, we are able to recognize the environment for what it is, both quickly and accurately. When standard features are not present, our presuppositions are false, and the result is perceptual error or illusion. Our ability to get things right and our susceptibility to error and illusion are common products of a single underlying mechanism.

If we are properly to understand how perceptual knowledge is possible, we must recognize the presuppositions of our perceptual systems and, at the same time, the features of standard environments to which they correspond. The possibility of perceptual knowledge is dependent upon the truth, or approximate truth, of these presuppositions in standard environments. Just as the physical apparatus of which our perceptual systems are composed will not operate properly in every possible environment, our perceptual systems, viewed as information-processing devices, will not function effectively in every possible environment either. We should not think of our perceptual systems as devices for constructing the best possible hypothesis about any logically possible world which could conceivably present us with a given pattern of sensory stimulation. Instead, we must recognize that our perceptual systems provide us with largely accurate hypotheses about those portions of the world we tend to inhabit. The very same perceptual systems which work so well in standard environments would function very badly, or not at all, in environments which are sufficiently different from those to which we are accustomed.

A proper naturalism will view human inference in much the same way, and this, of course, is a very substantial break with traditional epistemology. It is definitive of deductive reasoning, on the traditional view, that its great importance lies in the fact that it is in no way dependent on contingent features of any particular environment; it will work equally well in any logically possible world. Even inductive inference, although not guaranteed of success, is, on the traditional view, a method which will work in any logically possible world in which accurate prediction is so much as possible. Proper statistical inference is not defended on the basis of contingent features of standard environments. Rather, it is thought to provide a constraint on inductive inference which, like deduction, would be appropriate in any logically possible world whatsoever.

But human inductive inference does not have these features, and it would not be a good idea for us to seek to reason in ways which would work in any logically possible world. Our ability to reason well, and our ability to understand the world around us, is deeply dependent upon reasoning in ways which presuppose certain contingent features of this particular world. The kind of reasoning we engage in, and which works so well for us, works well precisely because it makes certain presuppositions about the world around us, presuppositions which tend to be true in standard environments. The proper model for understanding good inductive inference is not deductive logic, but the deeply contingent and highly environmentally conditioned perceptual systems.

What this means is that if we are to understand how successful reasoning occurs, we must see it in its proper environmental perspective; i.e., we must see how it dovetails with pervasive features of the natural world. And this is where our epistemology must draw on the results of our metaphysics. I will use an illustration which I have discussed in greater detail elsewhere.[12]

Human beings have a natural tendency to draw inductive inferences from very small samples. Indeed, in many cases, people have a tendency to draw conclusions about an entire population on the basis of a single member of that population, thus violating the law of large numbers. Tversky and Kahneman thus remark,

> People's intuitions about random sampling appear to satisfy the law of small numbers, which asserts that the law of large numbers applies to small numbers as well.[13]

Because they hold human inference up to the standards of statistical reasoning, Tversky and Kahneman regard this tendency as deeply defective. It is the source of a "multitude of sins against the logic of statistical inference," and results in "a consistent misperception of the world."[14] If we wish to understand this natural tendency, however, and if we wish to evaluate it properly, the standards of statistical inference are inappropriate.

Our inductive inferential habits must be evaluated against the background of the environments in which they operate, and these environments are ones which are populated by natural kinds. Natural kinds, as I suggested earlier, are homeostatic clusters of properties. When our tendency to generalize from a single case operates on a member of a natural kind, the conclusion that other members of the kind will have similar properties will be an accurate one so long as we are sensitive to the relevant features of natural kinds. The tendency to draw conclusions about a population from a single case thus cannot be evaluated for its reliability without examining the extent to which we are tuned in, as it were, to the relevant features of natural kinds. The overly hasty conclusion here may perhaps have been drawn by Tversky and Kahneman, rather than by ordinary reasoners.

Indeed, we are appropriately sensitive to the relevant features of natural kinds, and we are natively disposed to recognize such features. Let me give one illustration of how this sensitivity operates. Because natural kinds consist of homeostatic clusters of properties, recognizing natural kinds requires a sensitivity to property covariation; we must be able to tell when a group of properties tend to be found together. The human ability to detect property covariation, however, has long been given a bad name. This bad name had been richly deserved, it seemed, as a result of some very striking work by Chapman and Chapman, in which subjects attempted to detect the covariation of pairs of properties, but failed miserably.[15] If subjects cannot accurately detect property covariation, it seems, they will surely be very poor detectors of natural kinds.

But natural kinds do not consist of a single pair of covarying properties. Instead, they consist of a cluster of properties which jointly covary. Our poor ability to detect the covariation of a single pair of properties when we inhabit a world which is populated by natural kinds is thus comparable to our inability to detect bodily orientation in a world with zero gravity when we inhabit a world with a substantial gravitational force. As it turns out, we are remarkably accurate detectors of covariation of clusters of properties, and with this ability goes the ability to recognize, and project, the relevant features of natural kinds.[16]

The way in which our inferential tendencies operate is thus sensitive to features of the environment in which we live. Our inferences achieve a high degree of reliability precisely because they are in tune with pervasive, though contingent, features of that environment. Because our inferential successes are achieved in this way, however, it is essential that we evaluate our cognitive faculties against the background of the environments in which they operate, rather than compare them to inferential techniques whose central virtue is that they would work in any conceivable environment at all. Our inferences do not live up to such standards,[17] but they are none the worse for that.

How does this kind of explanation of our cognitive achievements bear on the project of epistemic improvement? If the account I have offered is on the right track, what implications does it have for normative questions in epistemology? Here, I believe, are some of the most important potential payoffs of the project of naturalizing epistemology.

If we wish to offer constructive advice for improving our epistemic situation, we need to begin with an accurate assessment of our epistemic strengths and weaknesses. This requires an understanding of the extent to which our native cognitive equipment is well suited to the task of providing us with an accurate picture of the world around us. That this is an empirical project goes without saying. But it is an empirical project which is a precondition for offering useful epistemic advice. We need to know which of our native inferential tendencies are largely reliable as they stand, and which are terribly unreliable. Some of our natural tendencies may be so successful in providing us with an accurate picture of the world as to require no attention from us at all. Others may be in need of radical revision. A proper epistemology needs to begin with an inventory of our cognitive processes, and an assessment of the extent to which they tend to generate true belief.

Even those processes of belief acquisition and retention which are highly reliable, however, may need some attention. Since reliability is typically achieved, as I have been arguing, by processes specially tailored to standard environments, the very processes on which we are so dependent for a broad and accurate view of the world may at the same time be a source of misinformation when operating in nonstandard environments. This is not a reason to lament the operation of these mechanisms. Instead, it is reason to try to develop a sensitivity to the kinds of environments in which these generally reliable mechanisms are likely to mislead. What we need to do, in effect, is develop cognitive habits which alert us to the presence of nonstandard environments.

The extent to which we are able to do this is an open question, but it is an area on which attention needs to be focused. To what extent are our epistemic habits susceptible to training and development? Which kinds of training are most successful in developing the required sensitivities? Work is currently being done here which promises to offer the basis for empirically informed epistemic advice.[18] This is, to my mind, one of the more exciting developments in naturalistic epistemology, since the advice which rival epistemologies have offered has been of so little practical use.[19]

The conception of a naturalistic epistemology which I offer thus ties an understanding of how knowledge is possible to the very practical project of offering advice toward realizing the goal of epistemic improvement. This is not, by itself, a new thing.[20] Indeed, it is standard epistemological fare to tie these projects together. In traditional epistemologies, however, which construe the project of explaining the possibility of knowledge as one of responding to Cartesian skepticism, both the explanation of the possibility of knowledge and the epistemic advice which flows from this explanation are arrived at a priori. A naturalistic epistemology, on the other hand, seeks to offer a more substantive and satisfying explanation of how knowledge is possible, and a more constructive and productive set of epistemic prescriptions, through empirical investigation. Traditional epistemological concerns are not thereby ignored, but are now served in ways more likely to be successful.

It should also be pointed out that on this conception of epistemology, the relationship between the cognitive capacities of human beings and the causal structure of the environment bears an important resemblance to the relationship between some of the properties of animals, when they are flourishing, and certain structural features of their environment. What is at work in these adaptive relationships is a sensitivity and responsiveness to environmental factors. Cases of knowledge, on this view, constitute a natural kind, and epistemology is the empirical study which investigates its properties.[21] Indeed, the interest of knowledge as an object of theoretical study, for the naturalist, is precisely dependent upon its answering to just such a kind. If cases of knowledge did not exhibit some deep structural similarities, if there were no more theoretical unity here than in some random collection of objects, then naturalists would need to dispense with the notion of knowledge entirely, and with it, of course, the subject of epistemology.[22] By the same token, if cases of knowledge did exhibit some theoretical unity, but that unity consisted in nothing more than its playing a certain social role, as some social constructivists have urged, then the notion of knowledge would be an interesting sociological or anthropological object of investigation, but it would not hold the interest or importance which epistemologists have typically claimed for it. If epistemology is to be of any real significance at all, we must be able to locate knowledge as a real kind in nature. The program I have been urging here offers some hope that this can be carried out.

3. A UNIFIED NATURALISM

It is important that naturalistic themes be approached in the unified manner I have suggested, that we not have a compartmentalized metaphysics or epistemology. The history of philosophy well illustrates the dangers of allowing either an apparently sensible epistemological view simply to dictate the categories of our metaphysics, or an apparently sensible metaphysics simply to dictate the themes of our epistemology. Prima facie sensible views in either area may only fit well with views in the other which defy credibility. We should not allow ourselves to embrace such incredible views simply because they follow from ones which seemed so sensible at the outset. Instead, we must allow for a more holistic approach, one which allows the influence between our metaphysical and epistemological views to travel both ways. The route to reasonable views in metaphysics and epistemology allows neither to have absolute priority over the other.

What does have priority over both metaphysics and epistemology, from the naturalistic perspective, is successful scientific theory, and not because there is some a priori reason to trust science over philosophy, but rather because there is a body of scientific theory which has proven its value in prediction, explanation, and technological application. This gives scientific work a kind of grounding which no philosophical theory has thus far enjoyed. Only by making philosophy continuous with the sciences, as Quine has suggested, may we provide it with a proper foundation. This is what, I believe, the logical positivists hoped to do, but their desire to give philosophy such a foundation was frustrated by the a priori method which they employed, a method which succeeded only in insulating philosophical theorizing from the scientific results and scientific methods which the positivists so much respected.

The idea that philosophy must somehow be grounded in the sciences is not new, and indeed, has given rise to an extraordinarily diverse set of philosophical ideas. Descartes, Locke, Leibniz, Kant, Marx, Reichenbach, and numerous others sought to show that their ideas comported well with the best available science of their times. On anyone's account, this attitude toward science has frequently resulted in badly mistaken views. But this is not, I believe, reason to think that philosophers should not seek to develop views which are informed by the best available science. Rather, it is a reason for thinking that the project is not easy, and that it must be carried out with great care. Most of all, to my mind, we must be careful not to let an a priori conception of what science should be overrule the dictates of successful scientific theorizing. Attempts to allow philosophy to be informed by the sciences have all too often resulted in attempts to allow philosophy to dictate how science itself should be carried out. At this point in history, philosophy does not have the credentials to do that. Philosophers must be more modest, I believe, and attempt to construct philosophical theories which are scientifically well informed, rather than attempt to inform the sciences with some sort of extrascientific insight.[23]

NOTES

1. I myself have been part of the problem here. In the editor's introduction to *Naturalizing Epistemology* (Cambridge, Mass., 1985, 1993), I do very little to connect the epistemology of naturalism with its metaphysics.

2. This paucity of argument will, I'm afraid, give this essay the tone of a manifesto. This is, to my mind, regrettable, but it allows me to emphasize the interanimation of some large themes. I have, however, argued for these themes at length elsewhere. See *Inductive Inference and Its Natural Ground* (Cambridge, Mass., 1993), and Derk Pereboom and Hilary Kornblith, "The Metaphysics of Irreducibility," *Philosophical Studies* 63 (1991): 125–45.

3. I have been influenced here by the work of James J. Gibson, despite my many disagreements with his conception of perceptual psychology. Gibson's work on the psychology of perception is unique in beginning with a description of the environment in which the perceiver is found, thus vividly illustrating the importance of a proper metaphysics for an understanding of epistemological concerns. See *The Senses Considered as Perceptual Systems* (New York, 1966).

4. Approximately seventy-five years ago, Roy Wood Sellars wrote,

> . . . we are all naturalists now. But, even so, this common naturalism is of a very vague and general sort, capable of covering an immense diversity of opinion. It is an admission of a direction more than a clearly formulated belief. It is less a philosophical system than a recognition of the impressive implications of the physical and biological sciences. And, not to be outdone, psychology has swelled the chorus. . . . *(Evolutionary Naturalism* [New York, 1922], i)

This assessment of naturalism seems as apt today as it was then.

5. "Empiricism and the Philosophy of Mind," in *Science, Perception and Reality* (London, 1963), 173.

6. The debate over creationism is just one illustration of this. For a fine case study, see Philip Kitcher, *Abusing Science: The Case Against Creationism* (Cambridge, Mass., 1982).

7. One need not be any kind of verificationist to have this last worry, for everyone will have to allow that an otherwise meaningful claim may come to have little if any meaning at all when it continues to be uttered in circumstances which undermine its natural interpretation.

8. Tyler Burge disagrees. In his "Mind-Body Causation and Explanatory Practice," in *Mental Causation*, edited by John Heil and Alfred Mele (Oxford, 1993), Burge comments, "Materialism is not established, or even clearly supported, by science" (117). With the exception of this point, I am very largely in agreement with Burge's paper. Because his claim about materialism is not the main focus of the paper, it is not given much defense,

and thus I do not know quite what to say in response. It is surely clear that science does not currently offer any support to dualism, there being no research projects which make any reference to non-physical stuff. While it is also clear that current science is incomplete, this should give no comfort to dualists. One cannot draw conclusions about the existence of particular sorts of things from the fact of our present ignorance.

9. Some of the best discussion of this issue is collected in Heil and Mele's *Mental Causation*.

10. See "How to Be a Moral Realist," in *Essays on Moral Realism*, edited by Geoffrey Sayre-McCord (Ithaca, N.Y., 1988), 181–228; "Realism, Anti-Foundationalism and the Enthusiasm for Natural Kinds," *Philosophical Studies* 61 (1991): 127–48.

11. The fact that outside factors may always interfere with the operation of a causal power outside of the most basic sciences shows that, *at most*, exceptionless laws could be found to govern the ultimate constituents of matter. As it turns out, however, our best current theories do not even seem to indicate that exceptionless laws are to be found there. It thus turns out that there is nothing in the world at all that answers to the Humean notions of causation and of law.

12. In *Inductive Inference and Its Natural Ground*.

13. "Belief in the Law of Small Numbers," in *Judgment under Uncertainty: Heuristics and Biases*, edited by Daniel Kahneman, Paul Slovie, and Amos Tversky (Cambridge, 1982), 25.

14. Ibid., 31.

15. Loren Chapman and Jean Chapman, "Genesis of Popular but Erroneous Diagnostic Observations," *Journal of Abnormal Psychology* 72 (1967): 193–204; "Illusory Correlation as an Obstacle to the Use of Valid Psychodiagnostic Signs," *Journal of Abnormal Psychology* 74 (1969): 271–80; "Test Results Are What You Think They Are," in *Judgment under Uncertainty*, 239–48.

16. Dorrit Billman, Procedures for Learning Syntactic Categories: A Model and Test with Artificial Grammars, doctoral dissertation. University of Michigan, 1983; Dorrit Billman and Evan Heit, "Observational Learning from Internal Feedback: A Simulation of an Adaptive Learning Method," *Cognitive Science* 12 (1988): 587–625; John Holland, Keith Holyoak, Richard Nisbett, and Paul Thagard, *Induction: Processes of Inference, Learning and Discovery* (Cambridge, Mass., 1986), 200–204.

17. Indeed, it is not at all clear that they could. There are problems of computational complexity which arise when, for example, one attempts to apply statistical inference to large sets of beliefs. More than that, however, the whole project of learning simply could not get off the ground without deep native biases. Chomsky has made this argument in detail for the special case of language learning, but Goodman's work shows this to be a pervasive feature of the learning situation. See, e.g., Noam Chomsky, *Aspects of the Theory of Syntax* (Cambridge, Mass., 1965); Nelson Goodman, *Fact, Fiction and Forecast* (Indianapolis, 1955).

18. See, e.g., *Rules for Reasoning*, edited by Richard Nisbett (Hillsdale, N.J., 1993).

19. I have presented a case against both foundationalism and the coherence theory on this score in "Introspection and Misdirection," *Australasian Journal of Philosophy* 67 (1989): 410–22.

20. Some have, however, denied that naturalistic epistemology can do this. Thus, for example, Jaegwon Kim sees naturalistic epistemology as involving the rejection of normative concerns. See his "What is 'Naturalized Epistemology'?" *Philosophical Perspectives* 2 (1988): 381–405.

21. I thus subscribe to what Michael Williams calls "epistemological realism" (in *Unnatural Doubts* [Oxford, 1991]), although, like Williams, I reject the doctrine of epistemic priority.

22. This is another respect in which the naturalistic conception of knowledge contrasts with more traditional approaches. Many of those who seek a set of necessary and sufficient conditions for knowledge seem uninterested in the question of whether knowledge, on the

resulting account, displays any theoretical unity at all. (A similar point is made by Alvin Goldman, "What Is Justified Belief?" in *Justification and Knowledge*, edited by George Pappas [Dordrecht, 1979], 2.) The fact that many of the attempts to answer the Gettier problem have resulted in accounts which are badly lacking in such unity has driven many to despair, not only about answering the challenge posed by the Gettier problem, but that there is anything of interest to be found in the concept of knowledge. (See, e.g., Mark Kaplan, "It's Not What You Know That Counts," *Journal of Philosophy* 82 (1985): 350–63.) I believe that such worries need to be taken seriously.

23. I have received helpful comments on a draft of this essay from David Christensen and Derk Pereboom. A version of the essay was also presented at Carleton University, from which a number of changes have resulted.

Can Propositions Be
Naturalistically Acceptable?

JEFFREY C. KING

For all the talk about naturalism in philosophy today, there is a remarkable lack of consensus concerning precisely what it is. If you ask *n* philosophers what naturalism is, you receive *at least n* different answers. However, these answers very likely will contain some common threads. I wish to begin by disentangling and discussing three of these threads.[1]

On one way of thinking, to be a naturalist in philosophy is to employ the "scientific method" as a way of solving philosophical problems. One can imagine different versions of this view corresponding to different underlying reasons for advocating the use of the scientific method in philosophy. It might be claimed, for example, that the only way for human beings to secure knowledge is by employing the scientific method and that therefore, in so far as philosophy aims at securing knowledge, it must employ this method. Or it might be held that employment of the scientific method is merely the most effective way for humans to secure knowledge; so that the use of such method is recommended on practical grounds as the most efficient way to solve philosophical problems. Other reasons for endorsing the use of scientific method in philosophy can be imagined as well. Views of naturalism falling into this roughly characterized camp may differ in another respect: they may differ in terms of what they mean by "applying the scientific method in philosophy." On the one hand, they might intend by this phrase replacing traditional philosophical problems (deemed not well formed, insoluble, or merely too vague) with the scientific questions which are their nearest relatives by some measure or other.[2] Scientific method is then employed in attempting to answer the resulting questions. On the other hand, it might be thought that traditional philosophical problems as traditionally posed are themselves to be attacked using scientific method. Of course a given philosopher may adopt one of these views with regard to a certain philosophical problem, and adopt the other view with regard to another philosophical problem. Because the views of naturalism just characterized see it as a matter of employing a certain method in philosophy, let us call such views *methodological naturalism.*

The methodological naturalist has two burdens. First she must specify what counts as scientific method in a way that both is sufficiently general and has the bite she requires. The characterization of scientific method must be general enough so that botanists, cosmologists, molecular chemists, and perhaps mathematicians all count as employing it. But the characterization presumably must rule out at least some methods traditionally employed in philosophy. Second she must defend her underlying reason for advocating the use of the scientific method in philosophy (e.g., defend the claim that the method is the only or most efficient way of securing knowledge).

It is worth noting that methodological naturalism identifies *philosophers* as naturalistic or non-naturalistic: a philosopher qualifies as a naturalist in so far as she endorses the employment of scientific methods in philosophy. Methodological naturalism does not characterize philosophical *views* as naturalistic or not. Of course, it might be *expected* that the views taken with regard to specific philosophical issues (e.g., the nature of mental states, what it is for an action to be right, etc.) by a naturalist so construed would fall within a certain limited range. We might even imagine that some argument could be given which shows that the employment of scientific method would only allow a certain range of answers to philosophical questions. But in the absence of such an argument, that a philosopher holds a given view with regard to a given philosophical issue is neither necessary nor sufficient for the philosopher to be a naturalist. Moral: one cannot determine whether a philosopher is a naturalist in this sense by looking at his positions on specific philosophical issues. One needs to consider the methods the philosopher employed in reaching those positions. Because of the difficulty in characterizing scientific method and because I am interested in accounts of naturalism which directly apply to philosophical positions or theories rather than to philosophers, I shall set methodological naturalism aside.

A second way of characterizing naturalism holds that scientific theories, or certain well-established subtheories (e.g., physics) of "overall science," deliver a certain range of "privileged" entities: individuals, properties, and relations. Often additional individuals, properties, and relations which are related in specified ways to the privileged individuals, properties, and relations are allowed as well. It is then held that there is nothing in the world beyond these "natural" individuals, properties, and relations (i.e., privileged individuals, properties, relations, and the others related to them in specified ways). Hence any philosophical theory which requires for its truth the existence of additional individuals, properties, and relations is non-naturalistic and false. Let us call accounts of naturalism of this sort *ontological naturalism.*[3]

Accounts of ontological naturalism can differ along two dimensions. First they can differ as to which areas of science supply the "privileged" initial stock of individuals, properties, and relations. Some philosophers seem to think that only individuals, properties, and relations posited by physics should be allowed. Others may be more liberal. Second, they can differ in terms of how additional individuals, properties, and relations must be related to the privileged initial stock to be allowable. The extreme case is the one in which the relation in question must be identity: that is, only privileged individuals, properties, and relations are allowed. Other views might be that any individuals, properties, and relations that enter into *causal relations* with those that are privileged, or *supervene* on those that are privileged, are allowed. To defend a given version of ontological naturalism, a philosopher must explain why only the privileged individuals, properties, and relations and those related to the privileged stock in the specified manner should be thought to exist.

Note that it can be quite non-trivial to determine whether a philosopher's view on a specific philosophical issue is consistent with (a given version of) ontological naturalism. For this amounts to determining whether the philosopher's view requires for its truth individuals, properties, and relations beyond those that are either privileged or appropriately related to those that are privileged. And this is not a simple matter: a theory may require for its truth only individuals, properties, and relations posited by physics without it being obvious that this is so (e.g., the theory might be stated by means of linguistic expressions which are neither drawn from physics nor explicitly defined by means of terms drawn only from physics, though in fact this could be done in an extremely complicated manner unbeknownst to anyone). As a result, the ontological naturalist often takes philosophical theories to be guilty until proven innocent. To earn its naturalistic credentials, a theory must be *shown* to be consistent with (a given version of) ontological naturalism. This leads to a third way of thinking about naturalism.

A third way of characterizing naturalism is to say that a philosophical theory is naturalistic just in case the key terms of the theory (e.g., 'reference', 'mental state', 'morally wrong') are explicated by means of some "privileged" set of terms. Variations of this view differ regarding which set of terms is considered privileged and what is meant by "explication" of key terms, these differences mirroring the different versions of ontological naturalism resulting from different choices concerning the privileged individuals, properties, and relations, and the relation that other individuals, properties, and relations must bear to the latter to be acceptable. For example, some might require that the privileged terms be drawn only from physics. Others may allow terms from biology, the social sciences, or psychology, where there is no requirement that these terms have been, or could be, explicated in any sense by means of terms from physics. Regarding *explication*, some might require key philosophical terms to be explicitly defined by means of terms drawn from the privileged set (i.e., we must specify universally quantified biconditionals of the form:

$$(x) (Px \leftrightarrow Tx)$$

where P is the philosophical term (one place predicate) being explicated and Tx is a formula containing a single free variable x, all of whose non-logical simple expressions are drawn from the set of privileged terms). Others might require something weaker, again mirroring relations weaker than identity (e.g., causal interaction) that some ontological naturalists will allow between the privileged individuals, properties, and relations and the others that his version of ontological naturalism views as acceptable. We shall call characterizations of naturalism of the sorts just sketched *linguistic naturalism*.

As suggested at the end of our discussion of ontological naturalism, it may be misleading to think of linguistic naturalism as a way of characterizing naturalism. For it may be that no one thinks of linguistic naturalism as *constituting* naturalism. Rather, because of the difficulty of determining whether a philosophical theory satisfies the constraints of ontological naturalism (does the theory require for its truth more than privileged individuals, properties, and relations and those appropriately related to the former?), some suitable version of linguistic naturalism is adopted as a way of *showing* that a theory conforms to the constraints of a given version of ontological naturalism. On this way of thinking, then, satisfying the demands of linguistic naturalism does not constitute but demonstrates a theory's (ontological) naturalism.

Whether we construe linguistic naturalism this way depends on whether there are grounds other than those of the ontological naturalist for adopting the view. In any case, (a given version of) linguistic naturalism, construed as constitutive of naturalism or as a way of showing a view to be (ontologically) naturalistic, has the virtue that it is relatively easy to see when its constraints have been satisfied. For this reason I propose to adopt it as a criterion of a philosophical theory's being naturalistic. If a philosophical term such as 'reference' has satisfied the constraints of (a given version of) linguistic naturalism, we shall say that *reference (or the term 'reference') is naturalistically acceptable* (relative to that version). And if the key terms of a philosophical theory are naturalistically acceptable (relative to a given version of linguistic naturalism), we shall say that the theory is naturalistically acceptable (relative to that version).

Let us now turn to philosophy of language. In light of what was just said, to say that a certain account of propositions is naturalistically acceptable (relative to a given version of linguistic naturalism) is to say that the key terms used in providing the account are naturalistically acceptable (relative to that version). However because there are many versions of linguistic naturalism, the usefulness of showing that an account of propositions is naturalistically acceptable relative to any one version is unclear. Those philosophers who accept some other version of linguistic naturalism will remain unimpressed. Thus instead of attempting to show directly that an account of propositions is naturalistically acceptable relative to some version of linguistic naturalism, I propose to take a more indirect approach. Many philosophers of language seem to be reluctant to embrace propositions because they think that so doing renders it less likely that their semantic theory will be naturalistically acceptable (relative to a given version of linguistic naturalism). That is, many philosophers seem to think that a semantics which does not embrace propositions will be naturalistically acceptable relative to certain versions of linguistic naturalism, whereas the semantics resulting from adding a commitment to propositions to that semantics will fail to be naturalistically acceptable relative to the versions of linguistic naturalism in question. It is this claim I wish to challenge. I intend to argue that given plausible and fairly minimal assumptions about what a semantics needs to do, an additional commitment to propositions, as I shall construe them, results in a theory which is as naturalistically acceptable as its proposition-less predecessor. Hence we must briefly discuss things that must be explained by any semantic theory, with or without propositions.

A semantic theory for a natural language must assign meanings to the sentences of the language. Notoriously, there is significant disagreement about what meanings are, how they get assigned, and so on. However, I think there is a consensus that a semantics at least requires the recursive assignment of truth conditions to sentences of the language. As a starting point, then, let us ask what is required to produce a recursive assignment of truth conditions to the sentences of a language. To achieve this, a semantics must assign various features of the world to linguistic expressions of various categories. Names must be associated with appropriate individuals, predicates must be associated with appropriate properties/relations, and logical terms (determiners: 'every', 'most', etc.; connectives: 'and' 'not' etc.; and so on) must be associated with appropriate logical operations.[4] Henceforth we shall refer to these as the *semantic values* of names, predicates, and logical terms, respectively.

In the case of each sort of expression, an explanation must be given as to how expressions of that sort get associated with the particular semantic values they have. Presumably some relation between particular expressions of that sort and the particular individuals, properties/relations, and logical operations which are their semantic values must be posited. These relations are what explain why the expression has the semantic value it has. In the case of names, for example, we must suppose that there is some relation between a given name and its bearer which explains why the name has that bearer as its semantic value. Let us call this relation between a name and its bearer *N(ame) reference*. Similarly, a given predicate must bear some relation to the property/relation that is its semantic value which explains why that property/relation, as opposed to some other, is its semantic value. Let us call this relation *P(redicate) reference*. Similar remarks apply to logical words and the logical operations that are their semantic values. We shall call the relation between a logical term and the appropriate logical operation *L(ogical term) reference*.[5]

Having provided an account of the semantic values of various expressions and how they get these semantic values, a semantic theory assigns truth conditions to each sentence, presumably in part by making reference to the semantic values of the component parts of the sentence. Let us call any semantic theory possessing only these features and lacking propositions a *basic semantic theory*.

For any basic semantic theory to be naturalistically acceptable relative to a given version of linguistic naturalism, the terms 'N reference', 'P reference' and 'L reference' must be naturalistically acceptable relative to that version.[6] Any other terms employed or presupposed in the definition of truth must be naturalistically acceptable as well. In addition, the semantic values (individuals, properties/relations, and logical operations) which linguistic expressions N, P, and L refer to must be naturalistically acceptable. (However, it is in general not the job of the semanticist to worry about this. If we suppose that e.g., the predicate 'morally wrong' refers to the property of being morally wrong, to the extent that we are worried about the property of being morally wrong being naturalistically acceptable, we view it as the task of the naturalist in ethics to show this.)

Having said this much about basic semantic theories, we turn to propositions. There are many reasons for invoking propositions in the philosophy of language and I cannot recount them here. Among the various roles propositions play in the philosophy of language is that of being the primary bearers of truth and falsity. Sentences are true or false derivatively, in virtue of expressing true or false propositions. Among other things, this explains how the same sentence (e.g., 'It is snowing here now') can be true when uttered on one occasion and false when uttered on another. Further, propositions are the things we believe, assert, and doubt. They play a central role in the semantics of sentences ascribing so-called propositional attitudes.

Of course saying that propositions perform these functions leaves open the question of what sorts of things they are. I shall take propositions to be structured entities. More specifically, I take propositions to be complexes consisting of *constituents*, that is, individuals, properties, and relations, standing in a (possibly complex) relation, where it is the relation which provides the structure of the proposition. Thus, for example, I take the proposition expressed by

1. Mary hit Lisa

to have three constituents: Mary, Lisa, and the relation of hitting. The proposition is *structured* in that in the proposition Mary, Lisa, and the relation of hitting stand in a relation. We can represent this as follows:

1a. <Mary<<hitting>Lisa>>

where the brackets stand for the relation in which Mary, Lisa, and the relation of hitting stand in the proposition and which provides the structure of the proposition. I shall call such relations *propositional relations*. In the case of 1a, the propositional relation is *complex*. That is, that Mary, Lisa, and the hitting relation stand in it consists in Lisa standing in a certain relation (represented by brackets) to the relation of hitting, and Mary standing in a certain relation to the complex consisting of Lisa standing in the former relation to the hitting relation.

That propositions consist of constituents standing in propositional relations, and more generally that they are structured, are not theses I shall defend here, despite the fact that there are alternative conceptions of propositions.[7] For I am concerned with the question of the extent to which an account of propositions may be naturalistically acceptable. And I believe that propositions as I shall construe them have the best shot at naturalistic acceptability. To see this, however, we must be more explicit about our view of propositions. This in turn, will require us to say a bit about the syntax of natural languages.

The theories which presently dominate thinking in syntax, current versions of Chomsky's Extended Standard Theory, suppose that the syntactic representations which are the inputs to semantic interpretation are in general distinct from the surface structures of sentences. The idea is that certain syntactical transformations apply to surface structures (or something pretty close to surface structures) yielding syntactic representations which are distinct from the surface structures to which these transformations applied. These syntactic representations are then interpreted by the semantic component. It would be impossible to do justice here to the reasoning which has led syntacticians to suppose that the syntactic inputs to semantics are distinct from the surface structures of sentences.[8] However, I wish to emphasize that the view that the syntactic inputs to semantics (henceforth *SI's*) are distinct from surface structure is defended by syntacticians not on semantic grounds, but on independent syntactic grounds.

At this point we need to make clear what SI's are like and exactly how they diverge from surface structure representations. First, I assume that in SI's the internal structure of the sentence, including the internal structure of any phrase occurring in it, is represented. As is usual, we will use brackets to represent this structure. Thus, for example, we will assume that a sentence such as

2. Glen hastily left Los Angeles

has as its SI something like

2a. [[Glenn][hastily [left [Los Angeles]]]]

where the brackets capture the internal structure of the sentence including e.g., the internal structure of the verb phrase 'hastily left Los Angeles'. As is the case with propositions, to say that an SI has structure is to say that the lexical items in it stand in a certain relation which imposes this structure. In the case of 2a, the relation is complex. That is, for 'Glenn', 'hastily', 'left', and 'Los Angeles' to stand in this relation in 2a is for e.g., 'left' and 'Los Angeles' to stand in a certain relation (represented by the brackets around them) and for 'hastily' to stand in a relation to the complex consisting of 'left' and 'Los Angeles' standing in the former relation, and so on. We shall call the (possibly complex) relation in which lexical items stand in an SI underlying a sentence S the *sentential relation of S*.

The second assumption I make about SI's is that quantifier scope relations (as well as those of other operators) are explicitly represented and that quantifiers bind variables. This assumption is endorsed by syntacticians working within the Chomskyan tradition mentioned above. Indeed, they hold that the major difference between an SI (called an *LF representation* within this tradition) and the surface structure from which it was derived is that quantifier phrases are moved leaving "traces" behind which function as bound variables; and the movement results in explicit representation of quantifier scope. So for example, a sentence such as

3. Every philosopher admires some mathematician

has as SI's both of the following

3a. [[Every [x philosopher]] [[some [y mathematician]] [x admires y]]].

3b. [[Some [y mathematician]] [[every [x philosopher]] [x admires y]]].

The scope ambiguity exhibited by 3 is accounted for as a result of the transformations mapping 3 to an SI being able to apply in two different ways yielding 3a and 3b, which are then interpreted differently by the semantic component.

Because the view that SI's are distinct from surface structures and that e.g., quantifier scope is explicitly represented in SI's is defended by syntacticians on syntactic grounds, if the defense is successful, any semantic theory, even a basic semantic theory, is committed to this view. On a basic semantic theory, SI's will be the syntactic representations over which truth is defined.

For a semantic theory that employs propositions, the idea will be that there is a recursive assignment of propositions to SI's. On the view of propositions presupposed here according to which they are structured entities, this means that this recursive assignment will map one structured entity, an SI, to another, a structured proposition. The view taken here is that all this mapping does is to replace each lexical item in the SI with its semantic value, and that the mapping does nothing to the sentential relation. For a simple expression ε occurring in an SI, let ε* be its semantic value (for a name, its bearer; for a predicate, the appropriate property/relation; for a logical term, the appropriate logical operation). Then a sentence like 1, whose SI is as follows

1c. [[Mary [hit [Lisa]]]]

expresses a proposition like

1d. [[Mary*[hit*[Lisa*]]]]

3, which has the two underlying SI's 3a and 3b, expresses the following propositions:

3c. [[Every*[x philosopher*]] [[some*[y mathematician*]]
[x admires*y]]]

3d. [[Some*[y mathematician*]] [[every*[x philosopher*]]
[x admires*y]]][9]

where every* and some* are relations between sets (or properties).[10] As was suggested, the sentential relations in the SI's were not affected at all; the semantic clauses which map SI's to propositions simply "substitute" semantic values for lexical items. This means that on the present view, the sentential relation which obtains between lexical items in an SI *is identical to* the propositional relation which obtains between the constituents of the proposition that SI gets mapped to. Note that it is not *merely* that the proposition has the same structure as the SI which gets mapped to it. This is compatible with the claim that the propositional relation is distinct from the sentential relation, though these distinct relations impose the same structure on propositional constituents and lexical items, respectively. Rather it is being claimed that the *same relation* obtains between the lexical items in the SI as obtains between the propositional constituents in the proposition. This is what it means to say that in the mapping from SI to proposition, semantic values are substituted for lexical items and the sentential relation is not affected. We shall henceforth express this feature of our view of propositions by saying that *propositional relations are sentential relations.*

I have defended this view of propositions elsewhere.[11] My purpose here is not to defend the view, but to argue that a semantic theory which employs propositions thus construed is as naturalistically acceptable as a basic semantic theory. This means showing that if a basic semantic theory of the sort discussed earlier is naturalistically acceptable, then that semantic theory enhanced by our account of propositions is naturalistically acceptable. This, in turn, requires us to show that if the key terms employed in a basic semantic theory are naturalistically acceptable, then the key terms of our theory of propositions are naturalistically acceptable.

So suppose that the key terms of our basic semantic theory, including 'N reference', 'P reference', and 'L reference', are naturalistically acceptable. What are the key terms of our account of propositions? Our theory claims that propositions consist of *constituents* standing in *propositional relations.* Further, sentences *express* propositions. Thus we must show that the terms 'constituent', 'propositional relation', and 'express' (construed as standing for the appropriate relation between a sentence and a proposition) are naturalistically acceptable, given the naturalistic acceptability of N, P, and L reference. Constituents and propositional relations pose no difficulty. For our constituents are just the semantic values to which names, predicates, and logical terms N, P, and L refer on the basic semantic theory. In assuming that theory is naturalistically acceptable, we assume that these semantic values are naturalistically acceptable. Further, propositional relations pose no problems. For on the present view, these just are sentential relations. Recall that sentential relations are the relations in which lexical items stand in SI's. And as I suggested earlier, the claim that we need to posit SI's distinct from surface structures, with the sorts of sentential relations which we claim are identical to the propositional relations of the propositions expressed by those SI's, is defended on syntactic grounds. Thus any semantic theory which requires a syntax will be committed to SI's and hence to our propositional relations. Since we have shown that constituents and propositional relations are naturalistically acceptable (assuming our basic semantic theory is), it follows that propositions are naturalistically acceptable. For propositions just are these constituents standing in these relations.

Finally, what about the relation of *expression* between sentences and propositions? This relation will be specified by the various clauses in the definition of a sentence expressing a proposition. Those clauses will look like this (let α, β be names; and Π be a predicate):

A sentence of the form $[\alpha[\Pi[\beta]]]$ expresses the proposition $[\alpha^*[\beta^*[\Pi^*]]]$ where, as before, ε^* is the semantic value of the expression ε. Thus it appears that the only key term employed in the definition of the *expresses* relation which might be thought to require naturalistic legitimation is the term 'semantic value'. However, '*y* is the semantic value of *x*' is to be explicated by means of the terms 'N reference', 'P reference', and 'L reference'. And these terms we have assumed to be naturalistically acceptable! Thus our propositions and the semantic relation of expression between sentences and our propositions are naturalistically acceptable on the assumption that our basic semantic theory is.

It might be objected that we have failed to consider an important part of our account, indeed *any* account, of propositions. Propositions are supposed to represent the world. But we have not shown that the relation of *representation*, alleged to hold between propositions and the world, is naturalistically acceptable. Until this has been done, it cannot really be claimed that we have shown our semantic theory with propositions to be as naturalistically acceptable as the basic semantic theory. This objection is fair enough. In order to provide some response to it, we need to consider what it means to say that propositions represent the world.

To say that propositions represent the world is to say that they depict the world as being a certain way. This in turn means no more than that they impose conditions that the world must meet for the propositions to be true. That is, that propositions represent the world consists in their having truth conditions.[12] But then the question of whether the relation of representation is naturalistically acceptable reduces to the question of whether the terms employed in our assignment of truth conditions to propositions, that is, in our definition of truth (and falsity) for propositions, are naturalistically acceptable.

It is hard to see how terms in our definition of truth for propositions could fail to be naturalistically acceptable, while those occurring in the definition of truth for sentences are naturalistically acceptable. For consider how corresponding clauses in the definitions of truth for sentences and propositions will look (let α, β be names and Π be a two-place predicate; and let o,o' be individuals and R be a two-place relation):

A sentence of the form $[\alpha[\Pi[\beta]]]$ is true iff $<\alpha^*, \beta^*>$ belongs to the extension of Π^*

(where ε^* is the semantic value of an expression ε)

A proposition of the form $[o[R[o']]]$ is true iff $<o,o'>$ belongs to the extension of R.

As can be seen by the mention of semantic values in the clause for sentences, for a sentence to be true or false, certain relations must obtain between subsentential components and features of the world (N, P, L reference). A further and often neglected point is that for a sentence (or better, an SI) to be true or false, the relation which constitutes its structure also makes a contribution to the truth conditions of the sentence and so must stand in a certain relation to a feature of the world. For example,

4. [[David Letterman] [is rich]]

is true just in case David Letterman *instantiates* or *possesses* the property of *being rich*. While it is the lexical items in 4 which require David and the property of being rich to be configured or related in a certain way for 4 to be true, it is the *sentential relation* between the lexical items which requires that David and the property of being rich be related or configured by means of *possession* or *instantiation* for the truth of 4. That is, for *any* SI with this sentential relation to be true, the semantic value of the lexical item in subject position must possess or instantiate the semantic value of the lexical item following it. But then it appears that it must be the sentential relation itself which is responsible for the requirement in the truth conditions of sentences of the form of 4 that the semantic value of the lexical item in subject position *instantiate* the semantic value of the lexical item following it.

I am unsure how we should think of *instantiation/possession*. Is it a *relation* between individuals and properties (and between properties/relations and other properties)? This is at least suggested by the fact that 'to instantiate' (and 'to possess') is a transitive verb in sentences such as 'David Letterman instantiates the property of being rich'. However, one might worry that taking instantiation to be a relation will lead to trouble. For if o's having a property P requires that o stand in the relation of instantiation, R, to P, and if, similarly, for two things to stand in a relation requires them to bear a relation to that relation (presumably the relation expressed by ' . . . stands in _____ to /////' in 'o stands in R to P'), then it appears as though o's having P requires an infinite number of relations to obtain. It is unclear to me whether this *is* trouble and whether taking instantiation to be a relation leads to it. But it really does not matter. For surely 'to instantiate' has something as its semantic value, whether it is a relation or something else. And whatever this is, the sentential relation in 4 contributes it (or something very much like it) to the truth conditions of 4 by requiring that David *possess* the property of being rich for the truth of 4. Thus the assignment of truth conditions to 4 not only presupposes that the lexical items in 4 are associated with features of the world (David and the property of being rich), it presupposes that the sentential relation of 4 is associated with whatever is the semantic value of 'to instantiate' (henceforth I shall assume that instantiation is a relation, but the previous remarks should be borne in mind). Similar remarks apply to the sentential relations in sentences with different and more complex structures. In each case, sentential relations must be associated with relations like instantiation in such a way as to require the semantic values of lexical items to stand in those relations for the sentences to be true.[13] Thus sentential relations have a semantic significance and so the association between sentential relations and relations like instantiation must be some sort of semantic relation analogous to the relations of N, P, and L reference that hold between lexical items and their semantic values.[14] Let us henceforth call this association S(entential) R(elation) reference.

The important point from the standpoint of present interests is that assuming that the definition of truth for sentences is naturalistically acceptable amounts to assuming that N, P, L, *and* SR reference are naturalistically accept-able. But then the definition of truth for our propositions must be naturalistically acceptable as well. Since on our view propositional relations are sentential relations, the assumption that SR reference (the association between sentential relations and relations like instantiation), can be explicated naturalistically *just is* the assumption that the association between propositional relations and relations like instantiation can be cashed out naturalistically. And the only semantic relation presupposed by our definition of truth for *propositions* is the association between propositional/sentential relations and relations such as instantiation, that is, SR reference. For the definition of truth for propositions essentially says that a bunch of constituents standing in a propositional relation, that is, a proposition, is true iff the world is such that *those same constituents* stand in the relation to which the propositional relation SR refers.[15]

In a sense it should be obvious that the relation of expressing between sentences and propositions, and the relation of representing between proposi-tions and the world will both turn out to be naturalistically acceptable if our basic semantic theory is. For the definition of truth for sentences in the basic theory simultaneously exploits the N, P, L, and SR reference relations to yield truth conditions for sentences. Our theory of propositions differs only in that it does not exploit these relations simultaneously. It first exploits the N, P, and L reference relations in the definition of a sentence expressing a proposition (i.e., the relation of expressing obtains between a sentence and a proposition iff the sentence differs from the proposition only in having lexical items where the proposition has the entities those items N, P, or L refer to). It then exploits the SR reference relation in defining truth for propositions. Thus our theory of propositions simply does in two steps what the definition of truth for sentences does in one: instead of treating the semantic significance of lexical items and syntactic relations in one step, as the theory of truth for sentences does, our theory treats lexical items in one step and the syntactical relation in the next step. Propositions are the intermediaries resulting from the first step.

Thus we have achieved our goal of showing that our theory of proposi-tions is naturalistically acceptable if the basic semantic theory referred to earlier is. Of course, the claim that propositional relations are sentential relations played an important role in that argument. It may now seem as though that claim, in conjunction with certain plausible claims about the SR reference relation, will give rise to difficulties. For naturalistically minded advocates of the basic semantic theory will want to hold that sentential relations and relations like instantiation came to stand in the SR reference relation after natural languages came into existence and as a result of the activities of the users of the languages. That is, they will want to hold that just as the activities of users of English somehow resulted in English predicates standing in the P reference relation to certain properties/relations, so similarly activities of English speakers resulted in the sentential relation of 4 standing in the SR reference relation to the relation of instantiation. For surely had the activities of English speakers been somewhat different, so that English evolved in a somewhat different manner, a sentential relation other than that in 4 could have SR referred to instantiation; and the sentential relation in 4 might have SR referred to something other than instantiation.

Given the identification of propositional relations and sentential relations on the present view, it follows that propositional relations did not SR refer to other relations prior to certain activities of language users. But our propositions do not have truth conditions unless propositional relations SR refer to relations like instantiation. For the definition of truth for propositions says that a given proposition, consisting of constituents standing in some propositional relation R, is true iff those constituents stand in some relation R' in the world. Our explanation of why the constituents must stand in R' for the proposition in question to be true is that the propositional relation R SR refers to R'. If the propositional relation did not SR refer to another relation, there would be no relation which the constituents of the proposition must stand in for the proposition to be true and hence no truth conditions for the proposition. Thus adopting the claim that propositional relations (= sentential relations) came to SR refer as the result of the activities of humans entails that, prior to that, propositions did not represent the world, that is, did not have truth conditions and so were neither true nor false.

In order to secure the traditional view that propositions represent the world eternally, we would have to hold that propositional relations SR refer to relations like instantiation *eternally*. But then the argument we have given for the claim that our theory with propositions is as naturalistically acceptable as the basic semantic theory would not go through. From the fact that the SR reference relation can be understood naturalistically in our basic semantic theory it would not follow that the SR reference relation could be understood naturalistically in our theory with propositions. For a naturalistic explanation of SR reference in the basic theory, according to which things come to stand in this relation as the result of the activities of humans, would not allow us to say that propositional relations SR refer to relations like instantiation *eternally*. In effect we would have to give a different account of SR reference for our theory with propositions: it would be a different relation in the theory with propositions than it is in the theory without propositions. For to say that SR reference, as employed in our basic semantic theory according to which it comes to obtain between sentential relations and relations like instantiation as a result of the activities of language users, has been rendered naturalistically acceptable is to say that it has been "explicated," for example, by giving a sentence of the form

$$(x)(y)(x \text{ SR refers to } y = T(x,y))$$

where '$T(x,y)$' is a sentence containing only 'x' and 'y' free, all of whose predicates denote properties/relations which belong to the privileged set or are properly related to those in the privileged set. Since SR reference obtains as a result of the activities of humans, at least one of the predicates, say 'P', occurring in '$T(x,y)$' must have as its semantic value a property or relation which comes to be possessed or to obtain as the result of activities of humans. But then 'P' cannot occur on the right side of the quantified biconditional constituting the explication of SR reference given for our theory with propositions, if SR reference is to obtain eternally. Hence the SR reference relations will be different in the basic and the proposition-containing semantic theories. But then that the basic theory is naturalistically acceptable does not guarantee that our theory with propositions is. Let us henceforth call the SR reference relation in our semantic theory with propositions SR_p reference; SR reference shall be the relation between sentential relations and relations like instantiation, thought to obtain as the result of the actions of humans.

Given what has been said, in order to maintain that our semantic theory with propositions is as naturalistically acceptable as the basic semantic theory, we must either (i) maintain that SR reference and SR_p reference are distinct and show that SR_p reference, understood as eternally holding between propositional/sentential relations and relations like instantiation, is as naturalistically acceptable as SR reference in the basic theory, according to which it comes to obtain between sentential relations and relations like instantiation as a result of the activities of humans; or (ii) identify SR_p reference and SR reference, thus abandoning the claim that SR_p reference obtains eternally between propositional relations and relations like instantiation, and so abandoning the claim that propositions have their truth conditions eternally in favor of the claim that they only came to have truth conditions as a result of the activities of humans (i.e., in virtue of the activities of humans bringing it about that sentential/propositional relations SR refer to relations like instantiation).

It seems to me that the former task is hopeless. To accomplish this we would have to explicate SR_p reference by means of relations and properties which are as naturalistically acceptable as those used to explicate SR reference. Since SR_p reference is supposed to hold eternally, any relations and properties employed in the explication would have to hold or be possessed eternally! The combination of the requirements of naturalistic acceptability and holding eternally drastically restricts the relations and properties available for use in the explication of SR_p reference. Indeed, the requirement of holding eternally alone dramatically limits the properties and relations we can use. For example, since SR_p is a relation between relations, presumably some relations between relations would be employed in the explication of SR_p reference. But (assuming that relations themselves are eternal), think of which relations between relations plausibly might be held to obtain eternally. First, there are quasi-logical relations between relations: *being necessarily coextensive, strict entailment* (necessarily, if aRb then $aR'b$), *being necessarily isomorphic* (there is an f such that necessarily aRb iff $f(a)R'f(b)$), and so on. Next, assuming that relations can be complex and thus have constituents and internal structures, there are relations that hold between relations "because of the very nature" of the relations they hold between.[16] This would presumably include relations such as *having some/most/all/etc. of the same constituents, having the same internal structure, being of the same degree of complexity*, and so on. It seems to me hopeless to attempt to explicate SR_p reference by means of relations which hold eternally (and properties which are possessed eternally). SR_p reference, after all, is a semantic relation, a kind of representation. And given any purported explication consisting in a set of conditions specified in terms of properties and relations which hold eternally (and so are logical properties and relations, or properties and relations had by or obtaining between relations "because of their very natures"), it seems likely that pairs of relations would meet these conditions which are such that it would be implausible to claim that the one in any sense represents, or is semantically related to, the other.

Thus I think we ought to try the second strategy mentioned above for maintaining that our theory with propositions is as naturalistically acceptable as the basic theory. That is, we should identify SR reference and SR_p reference. As we have said, this requires abandoning the traditional view that propositions represent the world, and so have their truth conditions, eternally. Since SR reference obtains between a sentential relation and a relation like instantiation as a result of the activities of human language users, the identification of SR and SR_p reference entails that propositional relations (= sentential relations) come to SR refer to relations like instantiation as the result of the activities of humans. And since a proposition has truth conditions in virtue of its propositional relation SR referring, prior to the SR reference relation obtaining a "proposition" has no truth conditions and so no truth value.

Of course the "proposition," consisting of individuals, properties, and/or relations standing in the propositional relation, may exist prior to its propositional relation SR referring to a relation such as instantiation.[17] But it would not represent the world, that is have truth conditions, since its propositional relation would fail to SR refer. It would be like any other complex entity consisting of a certain number of individuals, properties, and/or relations standing in a certain relation. Such complex entities do not in general represent anything and do not have truth conditions. For example, suppose that Lytie admires humility. Then here we have an individual, Lytie, standing in a relation, admiration, to a property, humility. The complex entity, "fact" or "state of affairs" or whatever, consisting of this individual standing in this relation to this property is not true or false and does not represent anything. But a "proposition" whose propositional relation does not yet stand in the SR reference relation to anything is no different. So I think we ought not to call such things propositions at all (thus my use of scare quotes). For propositions represent the world. They are true or false. But constituents standing in a propositional relation prior to those relations SR referring do not do this: they are just some things standing in some relation. This no more merits the term 'proposition' than does some spatial arrangement of rocks. Hence I will say that prior to propositional relations SR referring, propositions did not exist (even if there were constituents standing in propositional relations such that once these propositional relations SR refer, these complexes do represent the world and are propositions).

To some, rejecting the traditional view that propositions exist and have truth conditions eternally will deem absurd. Some will claim that we must hold that true propositions are true at all times, and so must have truth conditions at all times.[18] Though many philosophers hold this view, it is surprisingly difficult to find explicit arguments for it. For the case of true mathematical propositions, Frege (1977) gave the following argument for the claim that they are true at all times:

> The astronomer can apply a mathematical truth in the investigation of long past events which took place when—on Earth at least—no one had yet recognized that truth. He can do this because the truth of a thought is timeless.[19]

I take Frege to be claiming that the only way we can explain how an astronomer can successfully apply a mathematical truth in determining, say, what events occurred seconds after the Big Bang is to suppose that the mathematical proposition was true then. But the same will be the case for *any* time we choose. Hence the mathematical proposition must be true at all times. I believe that Frege thought it obvious that the proposition must exist to be true. Thus, mathematical propositions exist and are true or false at all times.[20]

Now it is not clear that this line of reasoning can be generalized to show that all propositions are true or false at all times. For non-mathematical (and nonscientific) propositions, it might be thought that there is not any analogue of a mathematical truth being successfully applied at any given time and hence no compelling reason for holding that they are true at all times. Nonetheless, it does seem hard to deny that the proposition that no intelligent life existed in the universe one second after the Big Bang was true then. To summarize, then, there seem to be reasons for thinking that mathematical propositions (and perhaps those of other sciences) are true at all times; and it seems hard to deny that at least some non-mathematical propositions were true in the remote past prior to the existence of any conscious creatures.

In order to respond to these arguments, we must show that there is a way of explaining how mathematical truths can be successfully applied to times prior to the existence of humans without holding that they were true, and so had truth conditions, then; and we must provide an explanation of the intuition that some non-mathematical propositions were true prior to the existence of conscious creatures which does not commit us to the claim that they *were* true then. The rough idea behind the responses I shall provide is that now that propositional relations SR refer, so that propositions *now* have truth conditions, we can talk about whether those conditions obtained in the remote past or not. However, this must be distinguished from the claim that propositions *actually had* truth conditions, and so *actually were* true and false, in the remote past. By endorsing the former claim and denying the latter, we shall be able to provide the needed responses.

One way of articulating this rough idea behind our responses is to hold that truth is a three-place relation between propositions, the world, and times. To motivate this idea, let us begin by noting that it is plausible to claim that certain types of "semantic contents" ought to be thought of not as true or false *simpliciter*, but as true or false *for a given time*.[21] For example consider the sentence

'Sometimes, Glenn works.' The most natural account of the semantics of such a sentence is one according to which 'sometimes' is a sentential operator such that for a sentence S, 'Sometimes S' is true iff there is some time t such that S is true at t. Note that for the operator to have any effect, S must be "incomplete as to time." That is, in 'Sometimes, Glenn works on December 15, 1994' the operator is semantically superfluous. On a theory that invokes propositions as the bearers of truth and falsity, this means that in cases where the operator 'sometimes' is not semantically superfluous, S must express a proposition-like entity which contains no time or representation of a time.[22] Such as an entity has truth conditions that obtain or not at particular times (henceforth I shall call such entities *incomplete propositions*). That is, for incomplete propositions, we must view truth as a three-place relation between them, the world, and times. Certain sentences expressing propositions containing times (or representations of times), such a 'No intelligent life existed in the universe one second after the Big Bang', suggest the same idea. For it is natural to suppose that the *complete* proposition expressed by that sentence is true *simpliciter* iff the incomplete proposition expressed by 'No intelligent life exists in the universe' is true for the time: one second after the Big Bang.[23]

Indeed, once we adopt the view that truth is a three-place relation in certain cases, we should probably deny that there is anything like truth *simpliciter* and hold that truth is always (at least) a three-place relation between (complete or incomplete) propositions, the world, and times.[24] It is just that complete propositions take the same truth values for all times, and so this relatum of the truth relation ceases to be significant (i.e., a complete proposition stands in the truth relation to the world and a given time t iff it stands in the truth relation to the world and *every* time).

Let us suppose that everything we have said about propositions holds for incomplete propositions. In particular, their propositional relations are sentential relations and these propositional/sentential relations came to SR refer to other relations as a result of certain activities of humans. Thus, like complete propositions, incomplete propositions failed to have truth conditions prior to those activities. But notice that this does not affect the fact that a (complete or incomplete) proposition can be true for a time in the distant past when humans did not exist. *Now* that they have truth conditions, those conditions obtain or fail to obtain for any given time, including times when the proposition's propositional relation did not SR refer and so the proposition had no truth conditions. So *now* (incomplete or complete) propositions can stand in the relation of truth to (the world and) times at which they did not have truth conditions! In effect, we are distinguishing between *evaluating a proposition's truth conditions for a given time*—that is, the proposition's standing in the relation of truth (or falsity) to the world and a time, and *the proposition's having had truth conditions at that time*.

Armed with this distinction we can respond to the arguments previously given. Mathematical propositions are incomplete.[25] However, the result of evaluating mathematically true (incomplete) propositions for any time is always the same. They are true for any time. This is what allows the successful application of truths of mathematics to times prior to the existence of humans: *now* they stand in the relation of truth to the world and those times. We need not in addition hold that these propositions *had* truth conditions and *were* true in the distant past. On the present view, it is the fact that mathematical truths are true when evaluated for any time, including times in the very distant past, which gives rise to the illusion that they *were* true then.

We can also provide an explanation for the intuition that the proposition that no intelligent life existed in the universe one second after the Big Bang was true then. Presumably, now this proposition *is* true relative to the world and the present time. That is, now the proposition stands in the three-place relation of truth to the world and the present time. But then, because it is complete, now it stands in the three-place relation of truth to the world and *any time*. Thus, in particular, it now stands in the relation of truth to the world and the time one second after the Big Bang (or any other time in the distant past). But this does not mean that one second after the Big Bang, this proposition stood in the relation of truth to the world and that or any other time. It could not have, because its propositional relation did not SR refer at that time. Thus the "proposition" had no truth conditions at that time and so at that time did not stand in the relation of truth to the world and *any* time. As in the case of mathematical propositions, the fact that the proposition now stands in the relation of truth to the world and *any* time gives rise to the incorrect view that the proposition *was* true at times in the distant past.

Complete propositions such as that expressed by 'No intelligent life existed in the universe one second after the Big Bang' have a second feature which contributes to the false view that they were true in the distant past. Again, we suppose that this complete proposition now is true relative to the world and the present time. This is so iff the *in*complete proposition expressed by 'No intelligent life exists the universe' is true (relative to the world and) for the time: one second after the Big Bang. Presumably, that incomplete proposition *is* true for that time, and this is why the complete proposition is true. Thus that now the complete proposition is true for the present or any other time entails that the incomplete proposition expressed by 'No intelligent life exists in the universe' is true for the time one second after the Big Bang. This gives rise to the illusion that one second after the Big Bang, the incomplete proposition *was* true. But again, this does not follow. The propositional relation of the incomplete proposition *now* SR refers and so the incomplete proposition has truth conditions which can be evaluated for truth or falsity for the time one second after the Big Bang. But one second after the Big Bang, the propositional relation of the incomplete proposition did not SR refer and so the incomplete proposition had no truth conditions and was not true. As before, we hold that the incomplete proposition can be true *when evaluated for a time*, without having been true *at that time*.

To summarize, we have explained the successful application of mathematical truths to times in the distant past without holding they were true then. *Now* certain mathematical propositions stand in the relation of truth to the world and any time, including times in the distant past. Further, we have argued that the intuition that complete propositions such as that expressed by 'No intelligent life existed in the universe one second after the Big Bang' were true in the distant past has two sources. First, now such complete propositions stand in the relation of truth to the world and any time including times in the distant past. Second, that now the proposition stands in the relation of truth to the world and the present time entails that now the incomplete proposition expressed by 'No intelligent life exists in the universe' stands in the relation of truth to the world and the time one second after the Big Bang. But none of this requires us to say that any complete or incomplete proposition *was* true in the distant past.

At first, this suggestion might have an air of incoherence (or worse, antirealism!). "There *was* no intelligent life in the universe one second after the Big Bang. How can you say this wasn't true *then*?" This feeling stems from a failure to distinguish the question of *whether a proposition had truth conditions and was true* at such and such a time (relative to the world and that time) from the question of *whether things were a certain way* at that time. One second after the Big Bang, certain objects (particles and so on) stood in certain relations to each other, etc. But this claim, which I endorse, is quite distinct from the claim that *certain propositions were true then*, which I deny. And both of these claims are distinct from the claim that *now* a given complete or incomplete proposition is true when evaluated at that time, which, again, I endorse. For I believe that a version of the correspondence theory of truth is correct. As I have said, I take truth to be a relation between propositions, the world, and times. However, for propositions to stand in this relation, their propositional relations must SR refer to other relations. Yet as we have seen, they did not SR refer to other relations prior to the existence of conscious creatures. Thus at many times in the remote past, no things stood in the relation of truth. But clearly this does not mean that the world did not exist then and was not a certain way. Of course it was! So the claim that the proposition that no intelligent life existed in the universe one second after the Big Bang was not true at that time (though it is true now) is quite consistent with the claim that the universe was a certain way at that time—a way that included lacking intelligent life.[26] Though the universe was a certain way which included lacking intelligent life, nothing was *true* then because a necessary condition for the relation of truth to obtain (that the SR reference relation held between certain things) was not satisfied by anything. In short, no propositions *represented the world as being a certain way,* though of course *the world was a certain way.*

In conclusion, I believe that many philosophers would like to make use of propositions in their philosophizing, but are afraid to do so because they believe that invoking propositions requires a departure from a naturalistic way of thinking. I have tried to address this fear by sketching an account of propositions which no more departs from naturalism than does commitment to the basic semantic theory described earlier.[27] The central feature of our account of propositions which allows this result is the identification of propositional and sentential relations. I suspect that some will be skeptical about this feature of the view. They will wonder how propositional constituents, such as individuals, properties, and relations, can stand in sentential (= propositional) relations. How can things such as this stand in grammatical relations? One answer to this is that if I am right, sentential relations are not just grammatical relations, if by this one means relations that can hold only between linguistic items.[28] However, for those who, for whatever reason, cannot believe that propositional constituents can stand in sentential relations, I have a more "deflationary" account of propositions in the spirit of the present proposal. One could hold that talking of propositions is a way of talking about sentential relations and semantic values of lexical items, without going so far as holding that the semantic values actually stand in the sentential relations. On this view, to say two sentences express the same proposition is to say no more than that they have SI's whose sentential relations are the same, and which contain lexical items which have the same semantic values in all the same places. One does not hold that, in addition, each sentence expresses an entity consisting of those semantic values standing in the sentential relation of the SI. Thus proposition talk is just a device for talking about syntactic structure and semantic values, while abstracting from or ignoring the lexical items themselves. Though I am sympathetic to this view, careful investigation will be required to see whether it can bear the burden that philosophers want to place upon theories of propositions.

NOTES

I have benefited from discussions with David Copp, Michael Jubien, Michael Liston, Paul Teller, and Mark Wilson. David Copp provided helpful comments on an earlier draft of this essay.

1. For the most part, I do not discuss the various ways in which the three ways of thinking about naturalism I consider are related. This should not be taken as indicating that I think that there are no important connections among them.

2. Some versions of "naturalized epistemology" seem to be of this sort.

3. Some might object that a view worthy of the name 'ontological naturalism' shouldn't posit the existence of properties and relations at all, whereas I in effect define ontological naturalism as positing such things. I agree that a nominalist about property/relation talk should still be classifiable as an ontological naturalist, and in this sense my characterization of ontological naturalism is misleading and inaccurate. However, I deny that eschewing properties and relations is necessary for ontological naturalism. Many philosophers who are thought of as naturalists frame the question of naturalism by saying that it is the question of whether all properties are physical properties (a version of physicalism); and many philosophers whose views are considered to be naturalistic talk openly about properties and relations. For example Fodor (1984) characterizes the question of whether "representation can be naturalized" as follows "The worry about representation . . . is that the semantic/intentional properties of things will fail to supervene upon their physical properties" (p. 232); and in Fodor (1987) we find "If the semantic and the intentional are real properties of things, it must be in virtue of their identity with (or maybe their supervenience on?) properties that are themselves *neither* intentional *nor* semantic" (p. 97). Millikan (1984), described by herself and others as proposing a thoroughgoing naturalistic theory of meaning, also talks openly of properties, e.g., in defining reproduction (p. 19).

4. It might be objected that all that is needed is for a predicate to be associated with an appropriate *extension*, and not a property or relation. Though this is correct from the

standpoint of the theory of truth, many philosophers nonetheless pursue the course of directly associating the predicate with an appropriate property or relation, which in turn indirectly associates an appropriate extension with the predicate. One reason for this is that speakers have strong intuitions about the extensions of predicates in counterfactual situations. If predicates are associated in the first instance with properties/relations, these properties/relations deliver extensions in counterfactual circumstances and explain speakers' intuitions about extensions in such circumstances. A second reason for associating predicates with properties/relations is that it provides a reasonable explanation of how the (actual) extension gets associated with the predicate. Humans, so the story goes, are able to detect various properties and relations by means of their various perceptual organs and abilities (this doesn't mean we know anything about the nature of the property or relation; we simply are able to detect its presence or absence with some reliability). When a detectable property or relation plays a sufficiently important role in the lives of humans, we invent a word which we apply to things possessing the property or standing in the relation. Though the details of precisely how a given property or relation gets associated with a given predicate may not be entirely clear (e.g., is this process mediated by a mental representation becoming associated with the property or relation [and if so, how does that occur?] and the predicate becoming associated with the mental representation?), the outline of the story is clear enough.

Since the appropriate property/relation then associates the extension with the predicate, we can see how things never encountered by humans are in the extensions of predicates of human languages. For example, we can see how buried rocks never seen by humans are in the extension of 'rock'. Among other things, this in turn explains why when a geologist says 'All rocks are P' and rocks never seen by humans are unearthed which are not P, the geologist takes her claim to be refuted. It is hard to see how we could explain a predicate's having an extension which includes objects never encountered by humans without the detour through properties and relations. In any case, because it is common to hold that predicates get directly associated with properties/relations rather than extensions, I shall assume it henceforth.

5. In using the terms 'P *reference*', 'N *reference*', 'L *reference*' (and later 'SR *reference*') I in no way mean to suggest that these relations are similar in the sense that similar mechanisms result in the relevant items standing in these relations. They play a similar role in philosophical theory: they explain why something has something else as its semantic value.

6. Henceforth, I shall simply talk about a certain term (or relation or philosophical theory) being naturalistically acceptable, and shall suppress the qualification *relative to a given version of linguistic naturalism*. The qualification should be understood as still in force.

7. For example, there is the view that propositions are sets of possible worlds. Or see Michael Jubien's (1993) view. Scott Soames (1987) defends the view that propositions need to be thought of as structured.

8. See May (1985) for a defense of this view.

9. Some might object to variables occurring in propositions, as they appear to in 3c, d. The idea is really only that something in propositions must serve the placeholding role performed by variables.

10. Every* is something like the relation of *being a subset of*, so that 'Every A is B' is true iff the set determined by 'A' is a subset of the set determined by 'B'. I use the admittedly mushy locution 'the set *determined by* . . . ', because to cash this out precisely would require addressing a variety of issues which are tangential to the points I wish to stress here. See King (1994) for more detail.

11. See King (1994).

12. I am not claiming that in general representing consists in having truth conditions; I am claiming that in the case of propositions, their representing amounts to their having truth conditions. Note that on the present view propositions do not represent possible states

of affairs, so that true propositions represent existent states of affairs and false propositions represent merely possible states of affairs. Representation is a relation between propositions and the (actual) world. The relation obtains in virtue of propositions imposing conditions that the world must meet for the proposition to be true, whether the world meets these conditions or not. Thus both true and false propositions represent the (actual) world (this is not to say that one may not want to invoke counterfactual circumstances e.g., in formulating a semantics for modal operators and evaluate propositions for truth and falsity at these counterfactual circumstances). Of course, false propositions *mis*represent the world, but misrepresentation is a type of representation on this view.

13. This is actually slightly misleading. Recall that sentential relations are often complex in the sense that for lexical items to stand in the sentential relation is for a couple of those items to stand in some relation (represented by brackets), and for the complex consisting of these items standing in this relation to stand in some further relation to some other lexical item (or complex of lexical items standing in some relation). Thus for example the sentential relation of an SI such as:

[[Every [x philosopher]] [[some [y mathematician]] [x admires y]]]

is complex. It is the individual relations making up the complex sentential relation which are associated with relations like instantiation. Thus the "semantic significance" of the complex sentential relation as a whole reduces to the semantic significance of the individual relations making up the complex sentential relation. For the recursive definition of truth for sentences in effect cashes in the semantic significance of the individual relations making up the sentential relation one at a time. Indeed, it is precisely this that requires the definition to be recursive: it must apply repeatedly so that each of these individual relations is treated.

14. Again, these relations are analogous only in that they correlate a linguistic entity (a lexical item or syntactic relation) with the thing it contributes to truth conditions of sentences. See note 5.

15. This may not be obvious in the case of quantified propositions. But for quantified propositions to be true, certain properties and the relations which are the semantic values of determiners like 'every' must be configured in a certain way. For example, for the proposition expressed by 'Every human is mortal' to be true, the property of being human, the property of being mortal, and the relation (between sets of properties) expressed by 'every' must be configured in a certain way in the actual world. Of course these two properties and this relation will be so configured if and only if individuals possessing the property of being human possess the property of being mortal.

16. I have talked about the sense in which sentential/propositional relations are complex, so the idea should be tolerably clear. The Fregean reference relation may provide another example. For on Frege's view to say that a name n refers to an individual i is to say that there is a sense s such that n *expresses s* and *s determines i*. Thus some want to say that the relations of expression (between names and senses) and determination (between senses and individuals) are constituents of the Fregean reference relation, and thus that the latter is complex. If this sort of view is right, then it seems plausible to hold that (complex) relations may eternally stand in relations to other (complex) relations in virtue of features of their constituents and internal structures.

17. I am not claiming that constituents *did* stand in propositional relations prior to propositional relations SR referring. I have no view as to whether they did or did not.

18. Those who claim this presumably suppose that time, place, etc. somehow get in to (or are somehow represented in) propositions, so that the propositions expressed by sentences such as 'Glenn is hungry' don't change truth value over time. In any case some sentences express propositions which are complete with respect to time and place, such as 'There was no conscious life on Earth in two billion B.C.' Though mathematical propositions presumably do not contain times and places (or representations of times and places), their truth values are nonetheless held not to shift over time for other reasons. More on some of these issues below.

19. Frege (1977), 25.

20. I only discussed true mathematical propositions. However, presumably false mathematical propositions must be false at all times, since their negations are true at all times.

21. I use the term 'semantic contents' here, because for the moment I wish to remain neutral on the question of whether these contents ought to be called *propositions*.

22. Salmon (1989) gives this sort of account.

23. Kaplan (1977) suggests an account of this sort.

24. There are at least two reasons for holding that truth is always a three-place relation. First, it seems desirable to have a single notion of truth. Once we adopt the view that incomplete propositions stand in the three-place relation of truth to the world and times, if we are going to have a single notion, we are going to have to adopt the three-place notion. Second, and related to this point, adoption of a single three-place notion will result in a simpler semantics. For we must only provide a single definition of truth (relative to the world and a time) for both complete and incomplete propositions.

25. I assume here that mathematical propositions are like other propositions. On the present view that means that they contain constituents (mathematical individuals [if there are any], properties, and relations) which stand in propositional relations, etc. Should there be reason for thinking that mathematical propositions are significantly qualitatively different from other propositions, it may be that the present account doesn't apply to them at all and hence owes no response to the objection being considered.

26. When I say that the proposition "is true now" but "was not true at that time," I mean that *now* it stands in the relation of truth to any time, and that *then* it did *not* stand in the relation of truth to any time.

27. As mentioned earlier, I have not really defended the claim that propositions as I construe them are able to perform the roles in philosophy of language that propositions traditionally have been thought to perform. This claim is at least partly defended in King (1994).

28. A second answer is to note that the worry seems to presuppose a view of words that is not obviously correct. For I take it that the worry is that words and propositional constituents (individuals, properties, and relations) are so different, that it seems odd to think that both sorts of things could stand in sentential/propositional relations. However, it is far from clear what words are. It may be that words (types) are properties, so that sentences (types) are properties standing in sentential relations.

REFERENCES

Almog, J., J. Perry, and H. Wettstein (eds.) 1989. *Themes From Kaplan*. Oxford.

Fodor, Jerry. 1984. "Semantics Wisconsin Style," *Synthese* 59: 231–50.

Fodor, Jerry. 1987. *Psychosemantics*. Cambridge, Mass.

Frege, Gottlob. 1977. *Logical Investigations*, translated by P. T. Geach and R. H. Stoothoff. New Haven, Conn.

Jubien, Michael. 1993. *Ontology, Modality and the Fallacy of Reference*. Cambridge.

Kaplan, David. 1977. "Demonstratives," published in Almog et al. (1989).

King, Jeffery C. 1994. Structured Propositions and Sentence Structure, unpublished manuscript.

May, Robert. 1985. *Logical Form: Its Structure and Derivation*. Cambridge, Mass.

Millikan, Ruth G. 1984. *Language, Thought and Other Biological Categories*. Cambridge, Mass.

Salmon, Nathan. 1989. "Tense and Singular Propositions," in Almog et al. (1989).

Soames, Scott. 1987. "Direct Reference, Propositional Attitudes, and Semantic Content," *Philosophical Topics* 15: 47–87.

Autonomy Naturalized

MARINA A. L. OSHANA

What would it mean to view personal autonomy as a naturalized phenomenon? Suppose we understand "autonomy" to mean the condition of being self-governing; of facing minimal interference in one's actions and choices, where interference can be socially, or psychologically, or physically induced by means such as coercion and manipulation, neurosis, bodily impulse, or weakness of will. A more expansive, but, I think, no more controversial, claim is that the autonomous individual is able to meet her basic needs, and the needs of those who depend on her, without being dependent upon the judgements of others with regard to the satisfaction and importance of those needs.

I take ethical naturalism to be a theory about the epistemological status of moral claims. The view is that moral propositions (such as "torturing children is wrong") express facts about the natural world, which can be known *a posteriori* to be reasons for or against some action. Analogously, a naturalized view of personal autonomy will hold that claims about autonomy can be established *a posteriori* on the basis of natural facts. For example, the proposition 'Facing minimum interference is a condition for autonomy' will be knowable empirically; judgments about whether or not a person is autonomous will just be judgments about how persons are in the world, and the property of being autonomous will be an empirical property.

By contrast, a non-naturalized account will make the conditions for autonomy ones that cannot be known *a posteriori*. Kant's theory is avowedly non-naturalistic insofar as it links autonomy with a state of metaphysical freedom unobtainable in the empirical world. Equally non-naturalistic is a conception of autonomy that requires that a person's character be "self-made," such that the person alone bears responsibility for it.[1] And the traditional view, that self-government requires metaphysical or causal freedom of the will, is arguably non-naturalistic since it calls for a type of freedom which cannot obviously be known empirically. All three theories fail the criteria for naturalism since they all require something to be true of persons that cannot be known empirically or that is difficult to determine empirically.

I shall argue that a naturalized conception of autonomy must satisfy two conditions. The first condition is a consequence of the general account of naturalism that I have been explaining. This is that the properties which constitute autonomy must be natural properties, knowable through the senses or by introspection (or must supervene on natural properties).

If a naturalized theory is one that takes account of general empirical facts, then a second, and stronger, condition for a naturalized conception of autonomy exists. This is that the properties that constitute autonomy must not be restricted to phenomena "internal" to the agent. In addition, certain objective, "external" properties are required. After all, it is a natural, empirical fact of persons that they are socially situated, and that socially situated individuals are not self-governing unless they are free from interferences that are "external" in nature and origin. Thus a completely naturalized account will treat autonomy as, in part, a function of natural relations that are *extrinsic* to the individual.[2] By contrast, a theory which makes the psychological characteristics of persons decisive for autonomy—is non-naturalistic in this second sense.

Not every theory of autonomy is a naturalistic one. In particular, few are naturalistic in the sense that they satisfy the second condition above. But I think that a plausible theory of autonomy should meet both of these conditions and be naturalistic in both ways. Of course, not every naturalistic theory of self-government will be a good theory of autonomy. The sort of theory we should seek must satisfy our intuitions about naturalism while at the same time offering an attractive and tenable account of self-government.

Recently, a number of philosophers have offered thoughtful conceptions of personal autonomy that are naturalistic in the first sense. Among these are the hierarchical, the Platonic, and the historical views of Gerald Dworkin, Gary Watson, and John Christman, respectively. Though I will argue that none of their accounts of autonomy is adequate—in large part because they fail to satisfy the second condition for naturalism—I find their efforts refreshing and welcome. By naturalizing autonomy, they rid it of the metaphysical baggage that attaches to more traditional, Kantian-like conceptions. Doing so paves the way for understanding autonomy as a condition that can be had by persons in the world, subject to socialization and enculturation.

HIERARCHICAL THEORIES

Dworkin champions a conception of personal autonomy that centers on the hierarchical structure of an individual's psychology. He defines autonomy as "a theory about the presence or absence of certain psychological states,"[3] and claims that two conditions are necessary for autonomy. Persons are autonomous when, first, the lower-order desires that move them to act are ones they endorse subsequent to critical evaluation by desires of a higher order. Higher-order desires can be understood as meta-preferences, representative of the individual's considered convictions and values. On the basis of this evaluation, the person can accept, revise, or reject her lower-order desires, and ultimately come to identify with certain of these desires as those she wishes to make effective. Those she makes effective can be described as her "will." When a person identifies with the lower-order influences that motivate her, the influences become hers[4] and the individual acts "authentically."[5]

Second, autonomy requires that the critical evaluation of desires transpire in a "procedurally independent" manner. According to Dworkin,

> Spelling out the conditions of procedural independence involves distinguishing those ways of influencing people's reflective and critical faculties which subvert them from those which promote and improve them.[6]

Though Dworkin does not explain this condition in detail, procedural independence is meant to ensure that the faculties which an individual employs in evaluating his lower-order reasons for acting have developed in ways that are conducive to autonomy. When procedural independence is satisfied, the lower-order motivations with which a person identifies will be not merely "his," but "his own," even when they result from social and familial enculturation. In conjunction with the condition of authenticity or identification, procedural independence supplies "the full formula for autonomy."[7] Autonomous persons are those whose higher and lower-order desires are made coherent via a process of reflection that occurs in a procedurally independent fashion.

Violations to autonomy in the form of interferences with the ability of the agent to raise critical questions regarding her motives are ruled out as departures from procedural independence. These interferences may originate externally or internally to the agent. Dworkin focuses on external interferences. He contends that a failure of procedural independence occurs when the activity (or possibility) of higher-order reflection is hampered by manipulation, deception, hypnosis, or when

> the choice of the type of person he wants to be . . . [has] itself been influenced by other persons in such a fashion that we do not view [it] as being the person's own. . . . In this case his motivational structure is his, but [is] not his own.[8]

Presumably, internal interferences such as psychological neurosis, weakness of will, and the domination of the passions can also impair procedural independence.

Recently, however, Dworkin has modified his earlier view, and now claims that identification is not necessary for autonomy.[9] Instead, Dworkin says that what is crucial for self-government is not the act of identifying with lower-order desires, but the second-order *capacity* of an individual to evaluate, and if necessary, revise, her first-order motivations: "the capacity to raise the question whether I will identify with or reject the reasons for which I now act."[10] When this capacity is exercised, "persons define their nature, . . . and take responsibility for the kind of person they are."[11]

There are problems with Dworkin's capacity condition. I shall not pursue these here since they are not essential to my concern.[12] On either account, Dworkin's theory appears to satisfy the first of the above two conditions for a naturalistic theory of autonomy. The properties which constitute autonomy are knowable empirically; autonomy is a function of psychological states the existence of which can be investigated and reported upon by the subject. One promising feature of hierarchical theories is that they offer a way of understanding autonomy that bypasses the issues of free will and determinism. What is important for autonomy, they say, is not whether a person can do otherwise than she does, despite the possibility that her actions are determined, but whether the individual really wants to do what she does, and whether she identifies with (or, is capable of identifying with) her action in a procedurally independent (though not necessarily causally or socially independent) manner. On the hierarchical view, this is just a function of her assent or dissent to what may well be a causally determined situation.

However, Dworkin's theory fails as an adequate conception of self-government. In the first place, procedural independence and the capacity condition are not sufficient for autonomy. For the capacity condition is an even weaker condition for autonomy than we would have if we required the act of identification. A person may have the capacity to critically appraise her motives for action while failing to actually identify with the preference that moves her, as Dworkin's original thesis for autonomy demanded. Of course, a person can be autonomous without identifying with every desire that moves her. But she must identify with certain of these desires, and with sufficient frequency, to endorse them and to claim them as "her own." On Dworkin's earlier view, the addict who identifies, in a procedurally independent fashion, with her desire for heroin will qualify as autonomous. But making a capacity condition plus procedural independence sufficient for autonomy means that we will be permitted to count as self-governing the reluctant heroin addict who is moved by a desire with which she does not identify. Both addicts, of course, appear to lack the sort of control with respect to their desires that seems intuitively necessary for autonomy.

In the second place, even if a person does identify with a lower-order desire, and even if the person evaluates this desire in a procedurally independent fashion, the person might not have the power to make the desire she identifies with effective. For example, the heroin addict who identifies with a desire not to act on her addiction, but who is unable to be moved by this desire, lacks the self-control required of autonomy. The person who identifies with a desire to be healthy, but who cannot act on this desire given her overwhelming passion for chocolate, suffers in this fashion. Whether these persons are controlled by their passions, their physiology, or whether they suffer from weakness of will, none can act upon, or make effective, the preferences they do identify with. As a result, all experience diminished autonomy even though all may be self-governing in the manner Dworkin describes.[13]

I believe that autonomous persons can make the preferences they identify with effective in action. But capturing this ability calls for an account of self-government that is naturalized in the second as well as the first sense. It requires, in other words, a conception of autonomy that takes note of the circumstances external to the person and how they affect a person's ability to make her preferences actual. By "external" I mean to include the social and physical circumstances outside of an individual's psychology—among these circumstances would be a person's relationship to addictive substances. Such an account would be completely naturalized. Dworkin's hierarchical conception of autonomy is not naturalistic in this sense.

The problem is not that his conception of self-determination makes no appeal to the external environment. The condition of procedural independence, for example, stipulates that a person's autonomy depends on the absence of whatever factors—internal or external—would impair authenticity. The desires which are a part of an autonomous person's hierarchically structured psychology must be formed by procedurally independent processes of critical reflection. They must be the progeny of, say, non-coercive, non-manipulative circumstances. Thus Dworkin does introduce into his theory provisions regarding the environment external to the individual.

The problem is that Dworkin restricts these provisions to "a theory of internal psychological freedom."[14] His considered view appears to be the following. Self-determination is simply a matter of the fact that a person has the capacity to evaluate her lower-order desires and, perhaps, to identify with them, given procedural independence of the person's critical faculties. As long as this is the case, there is nothing to recommend the introduction of additional conditions specifying which external circumstances rather than others are suitable for autonomy.[15] Factors such as manipulation and hypnosis are deemed relevant for autonomy only to the extent that they affect a person's internal cognitive and dispositional states, and critical faculties; autonomy is just a matter of the internal character of a person's psychology.

But the idea that psychological freedom is sufficient for autonomy is one that I believe can be challenged as insufficiently naturalistic. A person who identifies with, and who acts on, a higher-order preference to live a life of consensual slavery, and who arrives at this preference in a procedurally independent fashion, can meet Dworkin's conditions for an autonomous psychology, in spite of the fact that this person's social standing relative to others does not allow him control over his life of the sort that, intuitively, is required for self-determination. Thus more must be said of the autonomous individual than that he possesses a certain kind of psychology, and that his desires originate in a certain way. At least as important for self-control is the external situation of the person, external, that is, to his psychology.

Given its failure to be naturalistic in the second, stronger sense, it is questionable whether Dworkin's hierarchical theory can provide us with an account of the kind of self-determination worth caring about from a moral perspective. It is commonly held (a) that self-government grounds moral responsibility, or moral agency, and (b) that violations of autonomy are among the starkest of moral violations to the person. Moreover, it seems plausible that we describe people as responsible moral agents because they are socially situated. And moral problems are, quite often, problems that refer to phenomena external to the structure of a person's psychology. As a result, the hierarchical theory appears inadequate to explain the implications of autonomy for a person considered as a moral agent. More generally, Dworkin's theory does not give us a sense of how autonomy may be of value to morality. What is the moral value of having a certain psychological hierarchy?[16] It seems likely that the resolution of many moral issues will call for a naturalized conception of self-determination in which conditions richer than those offered on desire-based hierarchical models are present.

PLATONIC THEORIES

"Platonic" theories understand autonomy as a property of persons whose actions are founded on reason-based, value judgment. Gary Watson argues for such a theory.[17] He contends that the hierarchical account, which analyzes autonomy exclusively in terms of desires, oversimplifies the motivational psychology of persons and so does not provide an accurate analysis of personal autonomy.

The Platonic view draws a contrast between valuing and desiring, as independent sources of motivation indicating different psychological systems of the agent. A person's valuational system consists in that set of ends and principles around which normative judgments are generated. A person who is free in the sense that she is able to follow certain desires is not necessarily free in the sense that she is able to do what she most *values*. The former variety of freedom takes as its subject matter what a person is moved to get as the object of her strongest desire, where the strength of this desire is gauged, in Humean fashion, by its effectiveness in motivating the person to action. But the intensity of a person's desire may not reflect the degree to which she values it; she may have less desire for what is, in fact, of greater value to her (say she *values* a low-cholesterol diet where she *craves* chocolate). What one wants most strongly is not always what one values most.[18]

The distinction between valuing and desiring does not concern the content of the values and the wants, respectively. This seems intuitively correct: if I value X because I believe X is good, or because I judge X to be worthwhile, then valuing is a cognitive activity involving propositions about which one can be mistaken. Thus one can be autonomous even where one makes mistaken or imprudent value judgments. Instead, the distinction deals with "the *source* of the want or with its role in the total system of the agent's desires and ends . . . [and] with why the agent wants what he does."[19]

Watson holds that the freedom to be motivated by what one values is the type of freedom necessary for free agency or autonomy. Doing what we *want* is not sufficient for autonomy, since we may find that we are doing what we like best when we are acting under the directives of another person. Nor is it always necessary for autonomy: we often are self-directing even while doing things we would prefer not to do. Moreover, to the extent that autonomy is important for ascriptions of responsibility, a theory of autonomy based on the values a person has is, Watson argues, more congenial to our intuitions about morality than is a theory framed solely in terms of the person's desires.

Two features mark the autonomous individual. One, she is someone who judges the value of alternative states of affairs by the use of reason rather than passion. This enables the individual to rank her preference for these states independently of the strength of her passion for them. Two, the autonomous individual is one for whom this ranking amounts to a recommendation that has motivational efficacy. Reason is able to motivate a person on the basis of this evaluation because, argues Watson, what a person values is what she most desires to obtain and will take the greatest pains to actualize.[20] To value an action is to desire that it be realized, and that other states of affairs not be achieved.

Watson contends that autonomy is forthcoming when the valuational and motivational systems of the agent are in harmony. The locus of autonomy is thus the coherence between two separate psychological systems of the agent. Should some antagonism occur between the desiring and valuing parts, the rational part enjoys the presumption of authenticity.[21] A failure of free action or autonomy arises when a person is

> motivated to do things that he does not deem worth doing. This possibility is the basis for the principal problem of free action: a person may be obstructed by his own will.[22]

Watson's view might offer certain advantages over Dworkin's. For example, Dworkin does not notice that a strong passion could be the catalyst for a coherent psychology, but as Haworth notes, "passion may prompt one to conclude that some motive is desirable, when the motive is such that on a calmer and more dispassionate moment it would be rejected."[23] Watson's bifurcation of the "systems" of motivations is an attempt to provide internal checks against the dominance of the passions.

Watson also contends that only an account of personal autonomy that respects the varied nature of the human motivational system can deal with the regress problem; the difficulty that hierarchical systems confront when they attempt to explain how the higher-order volitions that confer autonomy are themselves autonomous. The problem is that, unless the higher-order preference is itself arrived at in a manner that does not also require endorsement at a still higher level, an infinite regress ensues. And

> since second-order volitions are themselves simply desires, to add them to the context of conflict is just to increase the number of contenders; it is not to give any special place to any of those in contention. The agent may

not care which of the second-order desires wins out. The same possibility arises at each higher order.[24]

I do not think that Watson's view enjoys success in either of these two areas, however. It is not clear that the Platonic account bypasses the regress problem. Watson argues that, should conflict arise between the desiring and the valuing parts of a person's psychology, the rational part should be assigned the arbiter's role, and so should act as a point of termination for questions about identification. But this assumes that the deliberative, rational side of a person already has a greater claim to authenticity than does the desiring part, and this assumption can be challenged. Just as one's desires can be unauthentic, so too can one's values.

A person's rational abilities may not always be better equipped than the passions to render a person autonomous, nor do they of necessity speak for the "true self" of the individual. A strong passion might prove a better catalyst than reason for an autonomous, coherent psychology.[25] It is only where one's values are, in fact, reasonable, and succeed in overriding passions that, in fact, threaten personal autonomy that Watson's bifurcated view will appear more successful than Dworkin's.

Moreover, while people do experience psychological struggles between what they value or "most want," and what they desire, we need not characterize persons as lacking in autonomy as a result. Resolving psychological conflict is not plainly necessary for free agency. I might be frequently motivated to do what I do not deem worth doing; ambivalence or even weakness of will may, for example, cause me to choose what I desire (say, a slice of chocolate mousse cake) over what I value (a healthy cardiovascular system and a flat stomach). But this need not make me any less autonomous, or any less of a free agent, in my choice of cake. In numerous ways and to various degrees, an autonomous person can be alienated from her values.

Watson's view is naturalistic in the narrow sense; the claims he makes about a person's autonomy can be established by empirically examining certain (arguably natural) facts regarding the relation between a person's values and desires. The properties which constitute autonomy—coherence between a person's desires and values, and control over the former by the latter—lend themselves to empirical study.

But describing autonomy in terms of a coincidence between one's motivational and valuation systems gives us too little. It is not enough that the autonomous individual be one who acts from her values, for an individual can possess the sort of Platonic psychology Watson claims to be sufficient for autonomy even where her values emerge from situations where violations to autonomy are present, and even where she subsequently comes to face violations to her autonomy. The Watsonian criterion fails to ensure that the agent lives a life in which manipulative intervention is absent, a life that yields a system of values that have the mark of authenticity. In order to ensure that a self-governing person's values or desires are not generated against a background that is inhospitable to autonomy, and that the individual lives a life free of interferences to self-government, an account of autonomy must be sensitive to the circumstances in which the agent develops her desires and values, and carries them into action. Room must be made for standards of assessment beyond the testimony of an apparently coherent psychology. At the very least, Watson's account needs to be supplemented by something akin to Dworkin's condition of procedural independence.

HISTORICAL ACCOUNTS

John Christman argues that hierarchical theories of autonomy are incomplete and need to be supplemented with an account of the manner in which a person's preferences and values are formed. Autonomy, he contends, is a matter of the history of a person's psychological states and of the person's participation in, and attitude towards, this history. The salient component for autonomy is

> . . . the manner in which the agent *came to have* a set of desires rather than her attitude towards the desires at any one time. The key element of autonomy is . . . the agent's acceptance or rejection of the process of desire formation or the factors that give rise to that formation, rather than the agent's identification with the desire itself.[26]

Christman wishes to defend a hierarchical analysis of autonomy, and in fact, his historical approach recalls Dworkin's claim that autonomy requires procedural independence. But Christman does find problems with Dworkin's analysis of self-government. Christman's major concern stems from his belief that the phenomenon of identification might be interpreted to mean nothing more than that a person acknowledges a lower-order desire as her own. This interpretation is untenable, argues Christman, since a person might acknowledge as part of herself desires that have been engendered in ways that are intuitively incompatible with autonomy. In order for a strong sense of autonomy to obtain, reference must be made to the manner in which identification comes about.

I find it puzzling that Christman should entertain the idea that this interpretation of identification could be Dworkin's. Dworkin insists that a viable account of autonomy must be compatible with the fact that individuals are subject to a host of external influences. While this suggests a willingness to allow for autonomy even in the face of socialization, Dworkin is attentive to the kinds of influences consonant with an autonomous psychology. Moreover, Dworkin supplements the identification condition (or, the capacity-to-identify condition) with the condition of procedural independence. And Dworkin does this because he recognizes that evaluation and approval of a person's operative desires can be prompted by manipulation or by aberrant socialization, and he holds that these are not tenable origins for an autonomous psychology.[27]

Christman appears to overlook this. He charges that hierarchical theories lack the ability to distinguish between the person who "intuitively and pre-theoretically" lacks autonomy because the person's operative motives and choice of lifestyle result from *illegitimate* "socialization and fierce conditioning,"[28] and the person who genuinely is autonomous despite having chosen to conform his desires totally to the will of another.

To illustrate this, Christman invites us to consider the person who, in choosing to join the Marines, pursues a lifestyle that will compel him to have (or at least give expression to) desires that may stem from some source other than himself. The marine might make this choice under conditions that meet the hierarchical criteria for autonomy, and he might identify with a preference to conform to the will of another.[29] But the individual who consensually and happily opts for slavery can be identically described. Both can be said to possess the split-level psychology appropriate to evaluating and approving of those motives with which each allegedly identifies. Each opts for a way of life that subjects him to the directives of others. Why, then, are we inclined to characterize the marine, but not the slave, as autonomous?

Christman holds that autonomy must not be denied the slave on the grounds that his preferences are misguided where those of the marine are laudable. Doing so would suggest that autonomy may turn on the possession of certain desires rather than others. Like Dworkin, Christman wishes to defend the idea that people can be autonomous "despite having desires for subservient, demeaning, or even evil things."[30] Any preferences, no matter how outrageous, can be autonomous as long as there are good reasons for having it, and the agent is guided by those reasons in conceiving the desire.

Nor can we deny autonomy to the slave on the grounds that the desires he holds are the result of acculturation. As is true of all of us, both the slave and the marine are creatures of their environments, and the desires of both reflect the influence of socialization. An account of autonomy that demanded independence from the environment would be implausible: it would require that autonomous persons be unsocialized to the degree that their desires could be described as of their unique selection. Since this kind of material independence *from* the world is impossible for persons in and of the world to achieve, it is something that *both* the marine and the slave lack.

"What does matter for autonomy," Christman tells us, "is that [the agent] is not moved by desires whose genesis is outside of her control [and that she] was given, by the conditions present, the chance to approve of the manner by which [she] developed the desire."[31] Certain external factors act as "illegitimate external influences."[32] Illegitimate influences usually commence outside of the person and have causal force sufficient to direct a person's cognitive and judgmental abilities. When they do, something akin to a failure of procedural independence transpires. The result is that the lower-order desires that move the agent, and with which she identifies, are no longer her own; they are "non-autonomous." Recalling Dworkin, Christman contends that our intuition that the marine remains autonomous vis-à-vis his desire to become a marine turns on the fact that this desire is prompted by aspects of the social environment which do not "serve to subvert the autonomy of the desires, values, or character of [the] person."[33]

The influences which affect a person's reflection upon, and identification with, a desire can be illegitimate for two reasons. One reason, which turns on what I shall call the "revision" test, is that the agent would be moved to revise the relevant desire were she aware of the presence of the influence.[34] A second mark of illegitimacy is that the process of critical reflection, which takes place when the person identifies certain desires as his own, is brought on *only* because of the influence of these external factors. I will call this the "sole cause" test.[35]

For example, suppose that I desire to do volunteer work (X), and this is a desire with which I identify upon reflection. If I critically reflect about X *only* because certain influential persons have impressed me with their display of volunteerism (factor Y), or if, having become aware of factor Y, I want to revise or abandon X, then desire X is non-autonomous.

Having defined the manner in which external factors might subvert autonomy, Christman settles on three conditions for autonomy:

(1) A person is autonomous relative to some desire only if she does not resist, or would not have resisted, the development of the desire while reflecting upon the conditions that led to the having of the desire. In this manner, a person's motives for action are "transparent" to her; no external influences have "illegitimately" affected the development of her desires.

(2) "The lack of resistance to the development of the desire does not take place (or would not have [taken place]) under the influence of factors that inhibit self-reflection."[36]

(3) Adequate self-reflection calls for "normal cognitive functioning"; an autonomous person must be "minimally rational," and cannot form her preferences in a manner that involves self-deception.

The second condition recalls Dworkin's condition of procedural independence. Since both resistance to and acceptance of the development of a desire can be the products of manipulation, autonomy entails that "during the processes where [the agent] might have resisted these developing desires, the agent wasn't also under the influence of manipulating factors" that would interfere with a person's cognitive or reflective capacities.[37] Thus, Christman contends, it is not merely *that* a person does not resist the adoption of a desire or a value, but *why* the person does not do so that is important in determining autonomy with respect to that desire or value. This requirement is, I think, sound.[38]

But the first condition, which I shall call the "non-resistance" thesis, is questionable. This condition absorbs the revision test for illegitimacy and in effect claims that in order for an individual to be autonomous, it must be true that *had* the individual been fully aware of all the factors which contributed to her acceptance of a desire, she would not have resisted the development of the desire.

I believe that the non-resistance thesis does not state a necessary condition for autonomy. Consider the case of the reluctant careerist. The reluctant careerist develops a desire to leave her children in the care of another person so as to pursue full-time employment. This individual need not be studiously attentive to the formation of this preference, but let us assume that she is sufficiently attentive to note that her acceptance of it derives from her envious observations of other people engaged in lives of conspicuous, luxurious consumption. As a result of these observations, the woman resists the manner in which this desire develops, perhaps because she believes that desires of this sort—ones that will, after all, affect her life quite significantly—should never be prompted by such selfish yearnings. Her resistance to the development of this desire might also lead her to reject or revise it, but whether she does so is not decisive for autonomy, as I will now explain.

Christman must say that the reluctant careerist fails to be autonomous vis-à-vis her desire; her resistance to the manner in which her desire is formed signals the presence of a reflection-constraining factor. But I think this is incorrect. The reluctant careerist resists the manner in which her relevant desire occurs while remaining autonomous nevertheless. For, although she regrets the way in which her desire was formed, we may suppose that she nevertheless identifies with the desire and wants to sustain it.

We have no reason to think that the development of the reluctant careerist's desire involves a cognitive failure on her part. We can describe the situation of the reluctant careerist such that there are no factors at work that restrict her critically reflective attitude towards the manner in which the desire develops. Nothing about the scenario suggests that the woman is irrational, or misinformed, or under the influence of factors that inhibit self-reflection. Thus conditions two and three are satisfied. My suspicion is that the relationship a person bears to the development of her preferences is less important for autonomy than is the relationship the person bears to the world, or to a particular situation in the world. As long as she identifies with her desire, and has control over her desires and her actions, the autonomy of the reluctant careerist is preserved, in spite of the fact that she objects to the way in which her desire was generated.

Christman's third condition is meant to guarantee that autonomous persons are those who arrive at their preference in a manner that is at least minimally rational. This means that the person exhibits evidence of careful deliberation in her selection of preferences (the idea being that those who make decisions capriciously will be more inclined to resist that process when they attend to it). As Christman acknowledges, an autonomous person need not always be deliberative about her decisions and actions; not every decision that is capriciously and impetuously formed should be deemed non-autonomous, but the person must show evidence, for the most part, of rationality.

The less controversial element of the third condition states that the autonomous agent not be self-deceiving; she must be "self-aware" with regard to the processes by which she comes to hold her beliefs.

> Self-deception, or exposure to factors which make self-awareness impossible, will be inconsistent with autonomy, since it will rule out the possibility of effective *self*-government. If the "self" doing the "governing"

is dissociated, fragmented, or insufficiently transparent to itself, then the process of self-development sought for in a concept of autonomy is absent or incomplete.[39]

Since only severe instances of deception are excluded—for example, the sort of intense neurosis that disrupts a person's core cognitive capacities—this seems a fairly innocuous criterion. Clearly, not every case of deception renders a person incapable of critical reflection.[40]

The more controversial aspect of the third condition concerns Christman's contention that autonomy calls for rationality, where rationality is understood, somewhat narrowly, as a function of the consistency of a person's beliefs and desires. He argues that, in order to respect the idea that autonomy is a matter of being self-governing, a conception of autonomy can only make reference to the psychological states of the person. To make rationality a condition for autonomy, to say that an autonomous person is rational, is just to say that

> the autonomous agent does not act on the basis of mistaken inferences or violation of logical laws. If I believe that 'p' and I believe that 'if p then q,' but I desire something X which is based on the belief that 'not-q,' then the desire for X is not autonomous.[41]

To demand more—to require that rationality depends on the satisfaction of external criteria—would mean that even persons who acted for reasons which they took to be considered and well formed might fail to qualify as suitably autonomous. Christman rejects an *externalist* conception of rationality on the grounds that such a condition "fails to capture the idea of *self*-government that is the motivating concept behind autonomy,"[42] and in addition, "makes the property of being autonomous an open ended and vague characteristic."[43] An externalist conception leaves open the question of when a state of autonomy is actually met, since deciding that a person is rational, and so autonomous, will depend on the amount of evidence gathered in the person's favor. And it threatens self-government since judging a person's fitness for autonomy may become a matter for others to decide.

I do not wish to quarrel with the idea of an internalist conception of rationality. I will only remark that an internalist conception makes Christman's appeal to historical criteria less meaningful; minimizing the importance external factors have upon an individual's psychology means limiting the kind of historical factors relevant for autonomy.

It does seem to me, however, that logical consistency is more than we demand of an autonomous person. Suppose I am offered a job that I believe is beyond my level of ability. On the basis of this belief, I declare that "I would be a fool to accept this offer."

Nonetheless, I might still desire the job, and desire it because of the belief that I would be smart, and not foolish, to accept the job. I do not hold the latter belief because I have been misinformed or deceived, nor am I incapable of resisting the development of this belief as I might have been had I been misinformed. I have developed my desire for this job freely and thoughtfully, and might even value it, viewing it as a desire that reinforces my self-esteem and confidence, and thereby contributes to my autonomy. I see no need to view myself as non-autonomous in this scenario; consistency does not seem obviously necessary for autonomy. Let us call this "the problem of the job-seeker."

Christman modifies his account of rationality in response to an objection of Alfred Mele.[44] Mele claims that Christman's historical account of individual autonomy fails to capture the essence of self-government because it fails to explain how a person remains autonomous with regard to the continued possession of a desire, and with respect to the influence an autonomously engendered desire has on the person's behavior. For example, the individual who autonomously decides to develop an addiction to heroin seems plainly to lack continued control with respect to the influence the desire for the drug has upon her, and similarly appears non-autonomous with respect to her occurrent possession of that desire. Desires that were autonomously developed at t may no longer be ones the agent can be self-governing about at $t + 1$, if they are ones she cannot help but have and cannot help but feel influenced by.[45]

Christman cannot explain the failure of autonomy here by claiming that these desires are logically inconsistent, or that they are ones whose development the agent attempted to resist, or was unreflective with regard to. Richer criteria than consistency and rationality, non-resistance, and self-reflection thus appear necessary to explain self-determination with regard to occurrent desires and the persistent influence of desires.

Surprisingly, however, Christman thinks he can defeat Mele's objection merely by amending the rationality-consistency condition (hereafter RC). He proposes that the RC condition be modified to apply only to conflicting desires of the sort that significantly affect a person's behavior, and that are not subsumed under an otherwise rational plan of action.[46] More importantly, in an effort to remedy the problem a historical model of autonomy faces with respect to occurrent desires, Christman proposes the following: Rationality or consistency is satisfied when the agent—even one who cannot help but act upon the desires she has—fails to experience conflicts between the autonomously developed desire and her current preferences. If she does experience conflict, and is led to alter her original approval of the process by which the pertinent desire developed, then rationality is denied and so, of course, is autonomy.

To have desires that are rational and consistent, the agent must both anticipate that she will not experience, at some later date, conflict of the sort that will cause her to want to revise her desires, and she must not ever come to experience this sort of conflict. If, from a perspective free of reflection-constraining factors, the agent can foresee certain conflict, and yet she makes no attempt to alter these conflicts given this foresight, then the agent remains autonomous. The heroin addict who develops a desire for addiction with foresight, and with no sense of conflict, is autonomous even though she *cannot* control her life vis-à-vis this addiction. In this manner, claims Christman, the developmental model of autonomy is adequate to capture autonomy with respect to occurrent desires.

However, these revisions to the RC condition do not answer the objection raised by the case of the job-seeker. For the job-seeker may fail to anticipate conflict among her beliefs and desires, and may in fact come to experience such conflict. But she is, nonetheless, autonomous.

Additionally, revising the consistency criterion in this fashion does not minimize the deficiencies of Christman's historical account; if anything, it adds to the problem. For now, in order to capture autonomy with respect to the occurrent possession of a desire, and autonomy with respect to continued influence of a desire, the agent must be able to constantly reaffirm her approval of the original process by which the desire developed. Because she may, at any stage, rescind her approval, autonomy becomes an episodic phenomenon.

Christman intends the criteria for autonomy to show that we are autonomous only with regard to those desires whose development is epistemically accessible to us, where epistemic accessibility depends on a history in which illegitimate external influences and factors that constrain reflection are absent.[47] I agree that there are a host of factors whose presence might be sufficient to prevent the sort of control over one's mental states that is required for autonomy. Thus on some level, and to some degree, persons will require epistemic access to the influences that affect their decisions in order to be self-governing. Nevertheless, I do not believe that Christman's three conditions—of non-resistance, of freedom from factors that constrain reflection and of normal cognitive functioning (where this includes the requirement of consistency)—are jointly sufficient for autonomy.

Consider that an incarcerated person, or a citizen of a dictatorship, can meet Christman's conditions while finding themselves without the kind of political liberties, or the social institutions that ensure those liberties, that tend to accompany, and be necessary for, personal autonomy.[48] An enslaved person, or one who wishes to escape an oppressive domestic environment, might meet all three conditions, while lacking control over her life nonetheless. As Irving Thalberg noted, we would not describe as autonomous the person who, for reasons of prudence, desires to give up his wallet to a robber—even where his desire does not originate in illegitimate ways, and where the person recognizes, and does not resist, the development of this desire.[49]

The problem is that Christman's reluctance to incorporate external or objective criteria into the conditions for autonomy compels him to offer an account of personal autonomy that is restricted to the conditions under which a person's *desires* develop and become authentic. Only those factors that impede a person's cognitive and non-cognitive psychological functions are taken to endanger personal autonomy. But people are not psychological states, and their autonomy is a more complicated matter than that of their desires. Personal autonomy is not simply a function of a person's psychological history any more than it is simply a function of the structure of a person's psychology.

The theories of Dworkin, Watson, and Christman are naturalistic, at least in the first sense I described. The conditions given for personal autonomy—that a person's desires and values assume a certain hierarchical structure, or that one's desires cohere with one's values, or that the person has a certain psychological history—are susceptible to methods of explanation employed in the natural sciences. But independent of their success as accounts of autonomy sensitive to this general requirement of naturalism, and independent of the fact that the conditions each suggests might be desirable for self-government, I think that none of the three is a theory of self-determination that we would wish to adopt. Each theory is "internalistic" in character—each, that is, understands ascriptions of personal autonomy to depend only on the status of a person's psychological states and dispositions. Intuitively, however, a person's autonomy depends on the socio-relational environment in which she functions.

Obviously, more needs to be said concerning the nature of the external circumstances amenable to autonomy. My point is simply that the importance of the external realm is not restricted to the effect it has upon a person's desires. Just as it is unnatural to think of persons as epistemically isolated entities, doubtful as to the reality of anything but the contents of their own minds, so, too, it is unnatural to view autonomy as property that is true of persons in virtue of their inner psychological states, regardless of the circumstances they find themselves in. Until a fully naturalized account of autonomy is proffered, or until a more attractive internalist thesis arises, only a partial and indistinct sense of self-determination will be ours.[50]

NOTES

1. Among contemporary philosophers, Susan Wolf takes autonomy to mean that a person is "self-creating" and she rejects autonomy as a plausible condition for moral responsibility on this basis. (She also deems autonomy in undesirable condition insofar as it would grant persons the freedom not to act responsibly, rationally, and compassionately.) Wolf's view that moral responsibility requires that persons act for reasons that reflect "the true and the good" might itself be non-naturalistic depending on whether the true and the good are, as she believes, conditions that lend themselves to empirical investigation and discovery. See Wolf, *Freedom Within Reason* (Oxford, 1990).

2. The point is not that an external perspective is required in order to investigate personal autonomy, but that certain necessary conditions of autonomy are themselves external to and independent of the individual's "internal" character. In a similar vein, Michael Slote links externalism to naturalism in defending a naturalized virtue-ethics solution to the problem of moral luck. See his "Ethics Naturalized," *Philosophical Perspectives* 6, *Ethics* (1992): 355–76.

3. Dworkin, "The Concept of Autonomy," in *Science and Ethics*, edited by Rudolph Haller (Rodopi Press, 1981). Reprinted in *The Inner Citadel*, edited by John Christman (New York, 1989), 62. All references are to this text.

4. Or, "his." Dworkin, "Autonomy and Behavior Control," Hastings Center Report (February 1976), and "Concept of Autonomy," 60.

5. Dworkin, *The Theory and Practice of Autonomy* (Cambridge, 1988), 15.

6. Dworkin, *Theory and Practice*, 18, and "Concept of Autonomy," 61.

7. Dworkin, "Concept of Autonomy," 61.

8. Ibid.

9. Dworkin, *Theory and Practice*, 15.

10. Ibid.

11. Ibid., 20, 108. Three observations lead Dworkin to replace the identification condition with the capacity condition. First, he notes that it is not the experience of identification that is threatened by obvious interferences with self-government; one who is lobotomized, for example, does not have her identifications interfered with, but rather, suffers an interference with her *ability* to make authentic identifications. Additionally, Dworkin envisions autonomy as "a global rather than a local concept," a characteristic of an individual's entire life rather than a feature of the person at a particular juncture in time, or with regard to a particular event. A capacity condition better captures the global view of autonomy than does an episodic experience of identification. Third, Dworkin worries that a person might achieve the sort of coherent psychology required for identification merely by altering or rejecting her desires of a higher order. He contends that it is counterintuitive that "one becomes more autonomous by changing one's higher-order desires," presumably because these desires represent the individual's "authentic" wishes and thereby confer autonomy. Marilyn Friedman challenges this, arguing that autonomy may best be achieved by just such a revision at the higher levels of a person's psychology. See "Autonomy and the Split-Level Self," *Southern Journal of Philosophy* 24, 1 (1986): 19–35.

12. Lawrence Haworth discusses some of these problems in "Dworkin on Autonomy," a review of Dworkin's *The Theory and Practice of Autonomy*, *Ethics* 102 (October 1991): 129–39.

13. Haworth raises the same problem in his "Dworkin on Autonomy." In passing, Dworkin does question whether the drug addict who desires to be motivated by his addiction, and whose actions express his view of what influences he wants to motivate him, is autonomous since he cannot change his behavior. Dworkin states that "autonomy should have some relationship to the ability of individuals, not only to scrutinize critically their first-order motivations, but also change them if they so desire." Moreover, "The idea of autonomy . . . includes as well some ability both to alter one's preferences and to make them effective in one's actions and, indeed, to make them effective because one has reflected upon them and adopted them as one's own." (See *Theory and Practice*, 16, 17). The problem is that Dworkin only makes these remarks in passing and continues to present the capacity condition as his considered view.

14. Dworkin, "Acting Freely," *Nous* 9 (1970): 357–83.

15. Dworkin seeks a conception of autonomy as "a purely formal notion, (where what one decides for oneself can have any particular content)." He does this by concentrating on the inner, psychological circumstances of the individual. His desire for a purely "formal" account stems from his worry that a theory burdened by content or substance would be of little practical use. A content-laden theory might, for example, prove incompatible with moral obligation, or with a commitment to social standards and practices we value. See *Theory and Practice*, 12.

16. Dworkin does not raise the question whether autonomy itself is a moral good.

17. Watson, "Free Agency," *Journal of Philosophy* 72, no. 8, (April 24, 1975). I will use the terms free agency and autonomy interchangeably.

18. Watson, "Free Agency," 211. Additionally, what a person desires may be of no value or worth to him. Moreover, "agents frequently formulate values concerning alternatives they had not hitherto desired." Watson's view finds support from Thomas Hill, who points out that, on a conception of autonomy that emphasizes the capacity humans have for valuing, what an individual wants as an expression of her selfish interest may not be what the individual chooses as an autonomous being. What will color a person's self-determined selections will be what the person most values. See Hill, "Autonomy and Benevolent Lies," *Journal of Value Inquiry* 18, (1984): 251–267.

19. Watson, "Free Agency," 211.

20. Ibid., 215–16.

21. This does not mean that "appetitively motivated activities" cannot "constitute for a person the most worth-while aspects of his life" (ibid., 212–13). For example, eating is appetitively motivated; it fulfills a desire (hunger) that arises independently of what we value. But eating is nevertheless a worthy activity because it is good for us. Though his discussion is devoted to extolling the virtues of a value-based, versus a desire-based, theory of the human motivational system, Watson does not view *all* desires as ill equipped to inform a person of which course of action is most worth pursuing.

22. Ibid., 213.

23. Haworth, "Dworkin on Autonomy," 136.

24. Watson, "Free Agency," 218. Harry Frankfurt concedes that the regress problem illustrates the inadequacies of a hierarchy of desires theory, "for it appears impossible to explain, using the resources of this notion alone, in what way an individual with second-order volitions may be less wanton with respect to *them* than a wholly unreflective creature is with respect to its first-order desires." See his "Identification and Wholeheartedness," in *The Importance of What We Care About* (Cambridge, 1988), 165. (The term "wanton" is used by Frankfurt to characterize the individual who does not care about the desires that move her, and so is not a person in the true sense.) Dworkin attempts to bypass the threat of a regress by stating that it is the autonomy of *acts* which is vulnerable to the threat, where his concern is the question of what it means to be an autonomous person. But since the act of identifying (or the capacity to identify) in part confers autonomy, Dworkin must still explain what it is that conclusively makes *this* act "his own" in a way that does not call for endorsement of a higher order.

25. Marilyn Friedman, "Autonomy and the Split-Level Self," and Irving Thalberg argue along these lines. See Thalberg, "Hierarchical Analyses of Unfree Action." *Canadian Journal of Philosophy* 8, no. 2 (June 1978).

26. Christman, p. 2, "Autonomy and Personal History," *Canadian Journal of Philosophy* 20, no. 1 (March 1991): 1–24. Christman's approach leads him to reject a global conception of autonomy as a property of a person's whole life in favor of a more "localized" interpretation. As long as desire X develops autonomously it *is* autonomous, even if X becomes so much a part of the person that it cannot be modified or relinquished at a later date.

27. Christman concedes that the notion of identification may be understood differently, to mean that a person approves of her operative desire in light of evaluation by desires of a higher order. But he charges that this alternate view is also problematic for autonomy since it leads to the regress problem; it suggests that there is *something* authoritative about the higher-order desire that leads a person to identify with her lower-order desires, but fails to explain what this something is. Christman argues that authenticity is a function of the genesis of a person's psychology; all that is needed to stem the regress are stipulations regarding the history of higher-order, autonomy-conferring desires.

28. Christman, "Autonomy and Personal History," 6.

29. Christman, p. 288, "Autonomy: A Defense of the Split-Level Self," *Southern Journal of Philosophy* 25, no. 3 (1987): 281–93.

30. Christman, "Autonomy and Personal History," 22–23.

31. Ibid., 18.

32. Christman, "Autonomy: A Defense," 287.

33. Ibid., 289.

34. Ibid., 290–91.

35. Christman (ibid., 289–90) states, " . . . if the critical reflection that takes place as we identify certain desires as truly our own is induced from some outside source, then it would be correct to label the lower-order desire in question nonautonomous . . . we often have to know whether or not specific factors were the *major* causes of a person's action or desire," and this is a matter of empirical discovery.

36. Christman, "Autonomy and Personal History," 11.

37. Ibid., 19. Though weakness of will is not, strictly speaking, something that inhibits

reflection, presumably it, too, would be ruled out as compatible with autonomy by the second condition. A person who suffers from weakness of will may not be able to resist the development of a desire or revise it, even when she disapproves of the conditions under which she comes to accept the desire.

38. The conjunction of conditions #1 and #2 does allow the rather odd result that any method of developing a desire—be it manipulation, hypnosis, or drug consumption—will be consonant with autonomy as long as the individual is aware of, and does not register resistance to, this method while in a psychologically unimpaired state. Moreover, Christman seems to misapply his own conditions. He holds the view that a person who possesses false beliefs as the result of deliberate—and even malicious—misinformation on the part of another might nevertheless be autonomous with regard to whatever desires ensue from these beliefs, as long as the person does not find the manner in which she comes to have the beliefs unacceptable (and provided that she is sufficiently rational). But consider the lover who is deliberately misinformed about the fidelity of his beloved, and who falsely believes that he is the sole object of her affections. As a result, the lover may develop a desire to marry his beloved. If he is aware of the origin of his desire, but embraces it nonetheless, I would question whether he satisfies condition #3; whether, that is, he is not self-deceiving in an autonomy-undermining way. Moreover, misinformation is surely a factor that impedes self-reflection, and it is plausible that the very fact of being misinformed might cause the lover to lack resistance to the development of his desires. In consequence, it seems that misinformation threatens conditions #2 and #1.

39. Christman, "Autonomy and Personal History," 17.

40. For example, the person who tells himself that there is no element of danger in learning to drive—knowing that without this bit of self-deception, he would never take the first lesson—may be autonomous in spite of the fact that he deceives himself.

41. Christman, "Autonomy and Personal History," 15.

42. Ibid., 9, n. 18. Christman allows that "internalist" and "externalist" can be interchanged with "subjective" and "objective" p. 14, n. 23.

43. Ibid., 15.

44. See Mele, "History and Personal Autonomy," *Canadian Journal of Philosophy* 23, no. 2 (June 1993): 271–80.

45. Similar worries attend Christman's claim that a person can be autonomous while subjecting herself to processes that might restrain her choices. Hypnosis, for example, may induce a smoker to give up her habit, and the individual may critically assess this method of preference formation and may register approval of it. But if, at a later moment, she cannot help but be influenced by the hypnotic suggestion, how is she autonomous with respect to the desire not to smoke? That is, if she wishes to resist the resulting desire not to smoke, but cannot do so given the choice-restraining factor, then how is she autonomous vis-à-vis that desire?

46. Christman, "Defending Historical Autonomy: A Reply to Professor Mele," *Canadian Journal of Philosophy* 23, no. 2 (June 1993): 281–89.

47. There may, of course, be reasons other than the presence of illegitimate influences that prevent or inhibit a person from having access to and full knowledge of the genesis of her desires. We are beings possessed of a memory that is both selective and finite; our epistemic limitations need not depend on the presence of factors that illegitimately influence or restrain reflection.

48. One might object that these persons lack freedom but not autonomy. I disagree; if autonomy involves the ability to direct one's life, then it calls for social freedom, and the lack of such freedom ensures an absence of autonomy.

49. Thalberg, "Hierarchical Analysis of Unfree Action."

50. Thanks are due to David Copp for his comments on this essay.

Autonomy Reconsidered

SARAH BUSS

The most popular philosophical accounts of autonomy are variations on a single theme. Everyone seems to agree: whether a person acts autonomously has something essential to do with whether she endorses, or "identifies with," her action.[1]

The variations are quite numerous. On some accounts, a person's endorsements are a function of her higher-order desires;[2] other accounts assign a key role to the person's well-considered values.[3] There is further disagreement over whether a person's actual endorsement is necessary and sufficient to render her action autonomous. Some philosophers think that a person acts autonomously if and only if she endorses her behavior.[4] Others think that what counts is her *ability* to endorse her behavior.[5] Still others argue that an autonomous agent's endorsements must result from the sort of reasoning that would have yielded a different result under sufficiently different circumstances.[6]

In my view, no matter what the relative merits of these competing accounts may be, their common theme is ground for rejecting them all. *Autonomous* action, it is true, requires something more than the minimal self-direction intrinsic to mere *intentional* action. But the additional ingredient has nothing essential to do with an agent's *attitudes* toward her action, and, in particular, nothing essential to do with whether the agent endorses, identifies with, or is in any way "satisfied" with her action. Defenders of what we might call "endorsement-relative" accounts of autonomy are right to insist that an agent is truly self-governing—truly self-determining—only if her intention is truly her own. But a person's endorsements are irrelevant to whether her intentions are truly her own. Her attitudes toward her action make no difference to whether she is truly self-governing, except insofar as they make a difference to whether she does, indeed, act intentionally.

In the pages that follow I will try to defend this negative thesis. I will then propose an alternative theory of autonomy. According to this theory,

95

the difference between autonomous action and merely intentional action is a function of the different ways in which an agent can come to prefer one action over others.[7] When the *nonrational* influences on an agent's preferences are a function of her character or when they are compatible with her living a good life, then her intentions are truly her own. An autonomous agent not only governs herself in the sense that she directs her own behavior toward some preferred goal; she governs herself in the stricter sense that in setting the goal she expresses herself.

By clearly distinguishing self-satisfied action from self-determined action, my theory has several additional strengths. First, it reconciles our conviction that we are morally responsible for most of the things that we do with the fact that we are imperfectly rational agents who rarely, if ever, have access to the deepest psychic sources of our behavior.[8] Second, it does justice to the fact that the distinction between autonomous and merely intentional action is very difficult to detect: the genesis of an agent's preferences is never self-evident— not even to the agent herself.[9] Third, the theory helps make sense of the claim— made by feminists, Marxists, and many others—that a person's autonomy can be undermined by the ideology she shares with the other members of her community:[10] an ideology which someone wholeheartedly endorses can undermine her autonomy because it can influence her choices in a nonrational manner that is incompatible with human flourishing.

If my account is correct, then the metaphysician's inquiry into self-determination cannot be disentangled from the moral theorist's inquiry into the sort of life there is good reason to determine oneself to live; for the key metaphysical distinction between autonomous and nonautonomous action is parasitic on the ethical distinction between better and worse human lives. Whether someone's practical reasoning has the "purity" required to be truly her own may depend on whether it is the sort of reasoning compatible with living a good life. There are no strictly formal criteria of pure practical reasoning, no intrinsic features which distinguish it from reasoning of the "impure" variety. In order to distinguish autonomous from nonautonomous action, we must have a substantive conception of what reasons there are.[11]

DEFENDING THE IRRELEVANCE THESIS (I): ENDORSEMENT AS NECESSARY TO INTENTIONAL ACTION

In the first section I want to defend the negative thesis that the distinction between autonomous and nonautonomous intentional action has nothing to do with the relationship between what an agent does and what she prefers to do. Let us call this the "irrelevance thesis." My defense of the irrelevance thesis will rest on a distinction between two ways in which an agent can fail to "endorse" her action: (1) she can prefer to act otherwise, all things considered and (2) she can prefer to perform an action of a different type. I will argue that we cannot appreciate this distinction without at the same time appreciating the inadequacy of the most popular positive accounts of autonomy.

Everyone concedes that a person acts autonomously only if she acts intentionally. Accordingly, if there is some sense in which it is impossible for a person to do something intentionally while at the same tine preferring *not* to do it, then there is some sense in which a person's preferences are irrelevant to whether her intentional action is also autonomous. My first step in defending the irrelevance thesis will be to show that there is, indeed, an obvious and important sense in which no one can at *t* prefer *not* to do what at *t* she intends to do. Since this is a claim about the nature of practical rationality, I cannot defend it by appealing to an even more fundamental principle. My argument will thus take the form of painting as compelling a picture as possible of some conceptual relations I take to be constitutive of practical rationality. Since I have already attempted this task elsewhere,[12] my demonstration here will be rather brief.

Suppose, then, that it is a cold, blustery day. The teakettle is simmering. My refrigerator is well stocked. There is no place I have to be. Suppose further that, knowing all this, I *prefer* to stay at home, snuggled under a blanket, reading a good novel. Because I prefer to stay at home, I decide not to go out.[13]

Is it nonetheless possible for me to leave the house *intentionally*? Nothing, it seems, could be easier than to imagine all sorts of considerations that might cause me to do so. Thus, it might suddenly occur to me that I will not be able to concentrate on my book until I have gone for a jog. Or I might suddenly recall that I had promised to drop the car off for a tune-up. A friend might call with an invitation to lunch which I do not want to refuse. Or someone might threaten to blow up the house if I remain inside for one more minute. When I leave the house in response to these considerations, it seems that I leave the house intentionally. But notice that this is precisely because my behavior seems to reflect an *alteration in my preferences*. Given the new considerations that have come to my attention, I no longer prefer to remain at home. If we were to stipulate that these considerations had no effect on my preferences, we would have to deny that I left the house in pursuit of my own goals. So, we would have to deny that I left the house intentionally.

As long as I *prefer* to remain in the house, nothing can compel me to alter my intention to remain. Someone strong enough to overcome my resistance can, of course, push or pull my body outside. But nothing can push or pull *me* to *intend* to go outside as long as I prefer not to. This is impossible for two reasons. First, setting a goal for oneself and acting intentionally are interdefinable: one has not really set oneself the goal of doing *A* if one does not intend to do *A*;[14] and one does not really intend to do *A* if doing *A* is not one's goal.[15] Second, no agent takes herself to have sufficient reason for doing what she prefers *not* to do, all things considered. Accordingly, no agent sets herself the goal of doing what she prefers *not* to do, all things considered.

I am aware that this second claim is controversial; and I would like to say something in its defense. Let me begin by stressing that what a person *prefers* to do is distinct from what she feels *inclined* to do. Whereas a person *finds herself* with certain inclinations, her preferences are the product of her own comparative evaluations. If someone prefers to do *A* rather than *B*, then this can only be because *she* has compared the merits of doing *A* with the merits of doing *B*. To make such a comparison is to make a *judgment* about the relative desirability of the things compared. Accordingly, someone prefers to do *A* rather than *B* if and only if she believes that the considerations in favor of doing *A* outweigh the considerations in favor of doing *B*.

Could someone believe this while nonetheless also believing that she has sufficient reason for doing *B*? This is possible only if it is possible to believe that one has sufficient reason to do what one believes one has weightier (stronger, more compelling) reason *not* to do. And this is possible only if one can believe that one has sufficient reason to override the force of one's reasons. To override a consideration is to judge that it is not decisive; i.e., to judge that other considerations are at least as weighty. So to override what one takes to be one's weightiest consideration is to judge that this consideration does not outweigh all others, after all. This could either involve judging of a given consideration both that it is the weightiest consideration and that it is not, or it could simply involve altering one's earlier judgment as to which consideration is weightiest. Since only the latter possibility is coherent, it seems that one's views regarding which considerations are weightiest determine one's views regarding which considerations give one sufficient reason to act. Accordingly, whenever one does something because one takes oneself to have sufficient reason to do it, one does *not* do something one prefers *not* to do, all things considered.

From this it follows that one cannot do something intentionally if, all things considered, one prefers not to do it. For if, all things considered, one prefers not to do something, then one takes oneself to have insufficient reason for doing it. So, one does not regard doing it as a goal to be pursued.

This argument is, in effect, a defense of a restricted form of the principle of sufficient reason.[16] Again: if someone prefers to do *A* rather than *B*, then she prefers *not* to do *B*; if she prefers *not* to do *B*, then she takes herself to have overriding reason not to do *B*; if she takes herself to have overriding reason not to do *B*, then she takes herself to have insufficient reason to do *B*; and if she takes herself to have insufficient reason to do *B*, then if she does *B*, she does not *intentionally* do *B*. Finally, where doing *B* is performing a basic action, if she takes herself to have insufficient reason to do *B*, and if she is aware of doing *B*, then there is *nothing* she does intentionally: her behavior is merely the unintended effect of some motivating force at odds with her reasons.

It is important not to read too much into the principle that one cannot do *A* intentionally if one believes there are weightier reasons *against* doing *A*. In particular, it is important to note two things that are *not* implied by the principle. First, it does not imply that to do something intentionally, one must believe one has insufficient reason for doing otherwise. Someone engaged in the routine, habitual behavior of braking when the light turns red and accelerating when the light turns green cannot plausibly be characterized as having considered whether it might be a good idea to act otherwise, and so cannot plausibly be characterized as believing that she has *sufficient* reason for acting as she does; nonetheless, her behavior is intentional in the minimal sense that it is directed at a goal which she herself could identify if asked. Second, the principle does not imply that agents whose behavior is incompatible with their all-things-considered preferences *have no reason* for what they do. Someone who finds herself (unintentionally) doing something she believes she has insufficient reason to do may nonetheless believe there to be *some* consideration in favor of behaving as she does; indeed, it is difficult to imagine an action about which absolutely nothing can be said in its favor.[17]

This second observation calls attention to the relationship between the reasons in favor of performing a given action and the reasons *for which* the agent actually performs it: the fact that someone is keenly aware of various considerations for and against her action entails nothing whatsoever about the reason why she performs this action—nor, indeed, does it determine whether she acts for a reason. On the one hand, someone can recognize very strong reasons *in favor of* doing A, despite failing to do A for a reason. This is the much-discussed possibility of wayward causation.[18] On the other hand, someone can recognize very strong reasons *against* doing A, despite doing A for a reason. This second possibility brings me to the second part of my defense of the irrelevance thesis.

THE IRRELEVANCE THESIS (II):
ENDORSEMENT AS IRRELEVANT TO AUTONOMY

I have just argued that there is an obvious and important sense in which no one can intentionally do something she prefers *not* to do. I want now to call attention to an obvious and important sense in which someone who recognizes very strong reasons against her intentional action does, indeed, prefer *not* to act this way. More specifically, there is an obvious and important conception of preference according to which an agent prefers not to do something if she takes the considerations against doing things of this *type* to outweigh the considerations in favor of doing things of this *type*. In this sense, the agent does not endorse her own intentional behavior. But in this sense, her endorsement is irrelevant to whether she acts autonomously. Let me explain.

An action has many properties. Accordingly, it may be desirable in some respects and undesirable in others. Insofar as a person believes that her action is undesirable in some respects, she prefers to act otherwise. And the greater the significance she attributes to the undesirable aspects of her action, the more dissatisfaction she is likely to feel in performing it. Take, for example, someone who believes that, all else being equal, her life would be much better if it did not contain a daily routine of painful exercises. Insofar as she does the exercises anyway, she does something she would much rather refrain from doing; and this is true, even if she also believes that, since all else is *not* equal— since, for example, exercise is the only way to treat the terrible disease that is causing her muscles to degenerate—she has sufficient reason *not* to refrain. If, in addition, this person believes that there is something "wrong" or "unfair" about the circumstances that give her sufficient reason to do the exercises, then her frustration is likely to be especially keen. Under these circumstances, her actions fall short of her ideals—ideals which were not the stuff of fantasy, but which, on the contrary, she had every reasonable expectation of realizing. She had thought these ideals were "realistic" enough; she still thinks that they are. Yet reality has failed to cooperate. What could be more frustrating than this?

When reality falls short of our expectations, we have no choice but to adjust ourselves to this unfortunate fact. We would rather not do so. But this preference does not prevent us from making the adjustment, nor, indeed, from determining ourselves to make it. We are not prevented from acting autonomously, however bitterly we may mope, wail, or rage. It may flatter our self-conception to be told that, under such circumstances, our behavior is not "truly our own."[19] We may find comfort in endorsement-relative accounts of autonomy which assure us that we are "*helpless* in the face of a desire that [drives us] unwillingly, regardless of [our] preference for another action, to do what [we do]."[20] But when the moment of action is upon us, the soothing reassurances of talk show hosts and philosophers are impotent: we know that our next move is up to us.

Like a person's ideals and dreams, her preferences for one type of action over another are too *general* to determine a particular decision to perform a particular action. Accordingly, these preferences cannot possibly play a decisive role in whether the person determines her decision herself. In order for a person's decision to be her own, she must draw some conclusion about how her various *general* preferences relate to her actual circumstances. As Aristotle reminds us, "The things that in themselves are involuntary, but now and in return for these gains are worthy of choice, and whose moving principle is in the agent, are in themselves involuntary, but now and in return for these gains voluntary. They are *more like voluntary acts; for actions are in the class of particulars*, and the particular acts here are voluntary. What sort of things are to be chosen, and in return for what, it is not easy to state; for there are many differences in the particular cases."[21] In short, without failing to act autonomously, we can do things which, in an obvious and important sense, we would much rather refrain from doing. And this is possible, even when we do not display the characteristic irrationality of weakness of will.

My defense of the irrelevance thesis has, for the most part, remained at a pretty high level of abstraction. It is time to show that this thesis can withstand the test of concrete examples. I will now consider what is probably the most popular contemporary philosophical example of *non*autonomous agency: the case of the unwilling drug addict. This example appears to be a *counter*example to the irrelevance thesis because it appears to describe a case in which someone fails to act autonomously precisely because he does not identify with, or endorse, the desire that moves him to act. I will challenge this assumption by arguing that, for all the example shows, the unwilling drug addict takes his drugs *autonomously*. In the course of defending my own interpretation of the example, I will try to explain why so many people have been tempted to interpret it differently. The key to this temptation lies, I will argue, in the assimilation of the two distinct senses of 'preference', and 'endorsement'. This assimilation is closely tied to an equivocal use of the metaphors of 'passivity' and 'alienation'.

No one can thumb through the philosophical literature on autonomy without running into the addict who, "against his will," intentionally shoots himself up with heroin. This "unwilling addict" would really prefer not to act as he does; if he *could* resist his desire to act this way, he *would* resist it. Unfortunately, however, he is outmatched. His own desire simply overpowers him. Despite acting intentionally, he is the "helplessly violated" victim of the desire's conative force, a "passive bystander" to his own behavior.[22]

What are we to make of this story? If my earlier claims about practical rationality are correct, then the philosopher's unwilling addict is a conceptual impossibility. More specifically, since this addict intentionally injects drugs in his veins, he prefers to do so in the only sense in which preferences are relevant to autonomy. So, it seems, for all we are told, he is not a "passive bystander" to his own behavior, frustrated though he most certainly is.

Now, some will surely think that this interpretation represents a reduction to absurdity of my earlier claims about practical rationality. That is, it may seem that my claims about practical rationality do not force us to reinterpret the example, but that, on the contrary, the example is a damning counterexample to these claims. As a mere assertion, this objection has little force. But I think I understand the challenge that lies behind it:[23] why should we think that the unwilling addict takes himself to have sufficient reason for taking the drugs? What could this reason possibly be?

The answer to this question is missing from the example itself. Nonetheless, it is easy enough to discover. Since the addict is confident that his desire for drugs will soon so overpower him as to prevent him from acting intentionally, and since the struggle to remain drug-free is extremely painful, he decides to cease resisting his desire, and to take the steps necessary for satisfying it. There is an obvious sense in which he is the "helpless" victim of this desire. Yet rather than being compelled to take the drugs by an alien force, he acts on the conviction that, all things considered, he would rather ally himself with this force.[24] Strictly speaking, what moves him to act is not the *irresistibility* of his desire for drugs, but his *belief* that he would be foolish to put up a fight, since sooner or later resistance will prove impossible.[25] To be sure, he would rather not perform an act of drug-taking. Nonetheless, given his options, he would rather perform *this particular* drug-taking act.[26] What's more, this preference is quite sensible: in performing this particular drug-taking act, he avoids succumbing to a state in which his body trembles and writhes under the torture of withdrawal; he escapes a condition far worse than the condition of taking drugs and getting high—a condition in which deliberate, self-possessed, autonomous action is no longer possible.

Once we see this, we see that the unwilling addict of philosopher's examples is not a passive bystander to his behavior. Though he sincerely believes that it would be better if his effective desire were weaker, he does not thereby lose control over the fact that his body moves so as to satisfy this desire. The essential distinction between this addict and his willing counterpart is that the willing addict is far more contented with his inclinations, and hence, far more contented with his options. This difference may be relevant to what we think of the two addicts' characters. It may be relevant to whether we blame them for what they do. It is completely irrelevant, however, to whether they are autonomous agents.[27]

In sum, though the unwilling addict of philosophers' examples is "alienated" from his addiction, he is not alienated from its motivating power. He may curse his addiction. He may bitterly resent its effect on his options. But he knows that his dissatisfaction provides no grounds for disowning his behavior. Indeed, far from getting him off the hook, the unwilling addict's genuine *disapproval* of his addiction reflects the very *belief* that makes it possible for him to act autonomously. Were it not for his addiction, the unwilling addict would greatly prefer to refrain from taking drugs. So, he cannot acknowledge his addiction without disapproving of it. Only if he acknowledges his addiction, however, is it possible for him to conclude that he has a good reason to take the drugs. Hence, only under this condition is it possible for him to act autonomously. If his addiction had not figured among the things he considered in deciding what to do, then he would have tried to resist the desires associated with it.[28] And since these desires are, by stipulation, irresistible, they would have eventually overpowered him: his body would have become directly responsive to his drug craving; its movements would have become dissociated from his intentions.

The addict's desire to take drugs is "alien" in one sense, and not "alien" in another sense. And the sense in which it is not alien—viz., he endorses the desire's causal efficacy (because he believes that he is addicted)—depends on the sense in which it is alien—viz., he regards his addiction as an unfortunate, irremediable circumstance.[29] Discussions of autonomy in the philosophical literature are seriously flawed because they fail to distinguish between these two senses. If we fail to appreciate the distinction between attitudes toward an act-*type* and attitudes toward *tokens* of this type[30]—and more to the point, if we fail to distinguish between attitudes toward *having* a given desire and attitudes toward *being moved by* this desire under these very circumstances—then we will think it obvious that people can be forced to intend to do something they prefer not to do, all things considered. If, moreover, we believe that people can be compelled in this way, then we will find it quite natural to assume that the difference between autonomous action and merely intentional action is a function of the agent's attitudes toward what she does.

INTERLUDE: BAD FAITH AND RESIGNATION

One philosopher who seems to be sensitive to the relevant distinctions is Jean-Paul Sartre. In particular, Sartre insists that no person who does something intentionally can credibly protest that she really preferred to act otherwise, all things considered.[31] Sartre thus shares my belief that, for all we are told, the unwilling addict in philosophers' examples acts autonomously. At the same time, however, there is an important difference between Sartre's diagnosis of the unwilling addict and my own. Unlike Sartre, I do not believe that the unwilling addict is guilty of "bad faith" insofar as he attributes his action to the irresistibility of his desire.

More generally, Sartre's remarks about bad faith reflect a mistaken view of what follows from the impossibility of being a passive bystander to one's intentional action. It is *not* true, as Sartre suggests, that an agent is in bad faith whenever she regards some aspect of her so-called "motivational set" as both undesirable and impossible to prevent from influencing her behavior.[32] As the case of the unwilling addict shows, one can in good faith blame one's behavior on one's inability to refrain from behaving this way. An agent who believes she cannot acquire certain desirable dispositions may not be self-deceptively seeking to disown her behavior. To the contrary, she may intuitively recognize that taking a resigned attitude toward herself is the only possible means of making her behavior her own; and she may regard this as decisive grounds for resignation. Of course, a person could deceive herself into thinking that she disapproved of herself; and she could do this by deceiving herself into thinking that she was helpless to avoid behaving in the allegedly disapproved manner. My point is simply that the self-disapproval of an unwilling, autonomous agent need not reflect a self-deceiving effort to escape the burdens of autonomous agency. Resignation can be the attitude of last resort for someone who values nothing more dearly than her autonomy.

Not only is this possible; it is, in my view, quite typical. Agents may rarely be correct in ascribing to themselves irresistible inclinations of one sort or another. (This is, I take it, an empirical question.) But mistaken beliefs of this sort are less plausibly attributed to a bad faith desire to deny one's own autonomy than to the desire to remain autonomous. Rather than run the risk of suddenly discovering that they are no longer able to control their fate, agents will become the accomplices of fate. Rather than risk behaving in a manner that startles and confuses them, they will resign themselves to their "weaknesses"—for heroin, young boys, a life without "complications"; they will resign themselves to their inclinations—to gamble, to throw punches, to avoid crowds. This may be the coward's way out; it may be the way out taken by those whose fear is unjustified, or who could have behaved less ignominiously in avoiding the consequences they justifiably fear. But if so, it is the coward's escape from *un*freedom. In blaming their behavior on intractable weaknesses and inclinations, agents ensure that this behavior is their own response to these unfortunate conditions.

Nor need they be cowards to do so. The addict who has made many extremely painful, unsuccessful attempts to rid himself of his addiction may be correct to fear that this time he simply cannot hold out against his desire to take the drugs; the shy person who has made many extremely painful, unsuccessful attempts to overcome her aversion to speaking to strangers may be correct to fear that there is little she can do to escape the influence of this unfortunate character trait. Perhaps, these agents would be more virtuous if they refused to recognize the inevitability of their behavior. But this hardly means they ought to put up a fight. Where virtue threatens autonomy, to act virtuously is to go above and beyond the call of duty.

Spinoza seems to have thought that resigning oneself to one's inclinations is the inevitable consequence of the quest for truth, and that freedom from frustration is the inevitable consequence of resigning oneself to one's inclinations.[33] We need not go this far to acknowledge that there are occasions when a frustrated agent can transform herself into a contented agent by resigning herself to the unavailability of better alternatives. As our discussion of the unwilling addict indicates, such resignation is perfectly compatible with frustration. Nonetheless, an agent who resigns herself to her motives has taken the first step toward making peace with them.[34]

It is important to distinguish this road to contentment from the road of "sour grapes" described by Jon Elster.[35] Whereas sour grapes involves devaluing an action precisely because one does not believe it to be a genuine possibility, making peace with one's inclinations involves recognizing that, no matter how valuable the action, one would do better not to try to perform it. If this resigned attitude takes the form of accepting one's limitations without frustration, then one's desire to perform the valued action has, in effect, metamorphosed into the judgment that it would be nice to find oneself in circumstances in which it was possible to perform it. Despite this metamorphosis, one's values themselves remain unchanged. One still regards the unaddicted state as generally superior to the addicted state; when faced with two otherwise indistinguishable people, one still thinks more highly of the person who is comfortable speaking to strangers than of the person with inhibitions like one's own. In short, unlike sour grapes, the acceptance that often accompanies resignation enables the agent to adjust her expectations to her circumstances, without corrupting her values. The person who does this is not necessarily guilty of bad faith. She may well be manifesting an admirable ability to reconcile the demands of integrity with those of psychological health.

The burden of my discussion of the unwilling addict has been to show that this reconciliation is not a necessary ingredient of autonomy; autonomy, it must be confessed, is perfectly compatible with despair. To be sure, the addicts and kleptomaniacs who figure so prominently in the philosophical literature are less "free" than most other agents *insofar as their opportunities are far more limited*; and they act less "willingly" than others *insofar as their attitudes toward these opportunities are far more negative*. Nonetheless, for all we are told, they are autonomous agents; for all we are told, they determine their behavior themselves.

BEYOND ENDORSEMENTS

An agent's endorsements are not the key to a satisfactory account of autonomy. Having defended this negative thesis, I want now to offer a positive theory of autonomous action. To do this I must answer the question: what *is* the key to a satisfactory account of autonomy?

In attempting to answer this question I would like to begin by calling attention to two metaphors of nonautonomous action that occur frequently in Harry Frankfurt's deep and suggestive discussions of free will and moral responsibility. According to Frankfurt, a nonautonomous agent is a "passive bystander"[36] to her effective desire. That is, she is moved to do something by a desire from which she "holds herself apart."[37] At the same time, she can be conceived as having been "conquered" by this effective desire.[38] She is a victim who is "helplessly violated" by the desire's unwelcome assault on her will.[39]

Frankfurt takes the metaphor of the bystander and the metaphor of the conquered, violated victim to be two different ways of characterizing the same relation between an agent and her effective desire. It seems to me, however, that these two metaphors paint two very different pictures of the nonautonomous agent. Indeed, I believe they paint two *incompatible* pictures. Insofar as someone is truly a *bystander* to an activity, she is not *conquered* or *violated* by this activity; and insofar as someone is *conquered* or *violated* by an activity, she is not a *bystander* to it. Whereas a passive bystander is "left out" of the action, a helplessly violated victim is precisely someone who has *not* been "left alone." Whereas the first metaphor contrasts autonomous agents with agents who fail to cause their behavior themselves, the second metaphor contrasts autonomous agents with agents who cause their behavior in a nonautonomous manner.

It seems, then, that an adequate account of autonomy cannot do justice to both of Frankfurt's metaphors. We must choose between these metaphors. We must determine which of them provides the more accurate picture of the phenomenon we want a theory of autonomy to explain. This choice between metaphors represents the starting point of my own account. If my argument for the irrelevance thesis is sound, then only the second of Frankfurt's two pictures is coherent. For my argument entails that no one can be rendered a passive bystander to the formation of her own intentions.[40] True, my argument also seems to entail that no one can do *A* intentionally while *regarding herself* as having been "*helplessly* violated" by the inclination to do *A*: insofar as someone does *A* intentionally, she believes that it is up to her whether she does *A*. Nonetheless, my argument does not rule out the possibility that someone who does *A* intentionally may have been *unwittingly* assaulted by her inclination to do *A*; and it is this possibility I want to try to develop into a positive theory of autonomy.

I believe that this is the only strategy with any hope of yielding a satisfactory account of the distinction between autonomous and merely intentional action. No one, I have argued, can be prevented from acting autonomously by being forced to act as she prefers *not* to act, all things considered. So if it is possible for someone to be prevented from acting autonomously, then this must be because her *preferences* themselves can be the products of autonomy-undermining influences. A person's preferences, I have argued, are her judgments regarding the relative weight of the considerations for and against the alternatives she is comparing. So if it is possible for an agents preferences to be determined in an autonomy-undermining way, then it must be possible for something to interfere with an agent's ability to assess her reasons for action. That is, it must be possible for an agent to engage in practical reasoning that is not "truly her own"; it must be possible for her to become a helpless victim of the influences on her own reasoning. In order for this to occur, the agent herself cannot be aware of the interference. For if she were aware that her deliberations were not truly her own, then she could not regard the products of these deliberations as her own preferences; and so from her point of view it would be as if she had not yet decided what to do. it follows, therefore, that if it is possible for a person to be prevented from acting autonomously, then it must be possible for her to be a helpless victim of the influences on her practical deliberations *without believing herself to be either helpless or violated.* In short, it must be possible for her to be an *unwitting* victim of her own inclinations to prefer one thing rather than another.

This, then, is the key to a satisfactory account of autonomy: subversive influences on an agent's preferences. It is possible to act *non*autonomously (yet intentionally) if and only if it is possible to lose one's autonomy during the process of forming one's preferences. But if this is true, then it must be possible for autonomy to be undermined in a way that *interferes* with the process of preference-formation but does not cause this process to *break down* altogether. If we can make sense of this possibility, then we will have made considerable progress toward discovering a satisfactory account of autonomy.

There is in nature a model of what we are looking for. A virus prevents a cell from functioning normally, not by attacking the cell from without, but by invading, or "infecting," it. More particularly, a virus does its dirty work by incorporating itself into the cell's genome and thereby coopting the very activities essential to the cell's continued existence. To the best of its ability, the cell continues to perform its normal functions. But under the influence of the virus, its normal mode of maintaining itself is distorted into a process whereby it destroys itself.

Could something similar occur when an agent attempts to form her own preferences? I think the answer is clearly "yes." A strong desire or emotion—or even a physiological state like drowsiness—can sabotage an agent's attempts at self-determination by incorporating itself into her practical deliberations and thereby coopting the very activity essential to her capacity for self-determination. This is what happens, I believe, when the victim of a brutal rape is so overwhelmed with fear that she cannot give serious consideration to the possibility of fighting back. It is what happens when the victim of severe pain has such a strong desire to rid herself of this pain that she cannot appreciate the significant costs of doing so in the quickest, easiest manner possible.[41]

A person's desires, emotions, and physiological states can figure in her practical reasoning as some of the things she considers. Thus, the fact that someone strongly desires to do A can count for her as a reason in favor of doing A, and the fact that she is too sleepy to think clearly about whether to do A or B can count as a reason for postponing her decision. Sometimes, however, these very same states exert a *non*rational influence on a person's reasoning. Thus, a person's strong desire to take drugs can prevent her from paying attention to what she herself would admit to be good reasons for refraining; and a person's drowsiness can cause her to overlook considerations which she would otherwise take to be decisive reasons against her intended course of action. Like a virus in a cell, these nonrational conative forces undermine an agent's reasoning by surreptitiously forcing this reasoning to serve "their own ends." When this happens, the agent's practical conclusions are not truly her own. Hence, her self-directed behavior is not a genuine instance of self-expression. In short, she is prevented from acting autonomously.

NONREASONS AS SABOTEURS OF PRACTICAL REASON

If the preceding observations are correct, then the distinction between autonomous and nonautonomous action has something essential to do with the distinction between the influence of reasons and the influence of nonreasons. This is true, moreover, regardless of whether we conceive of practical reasoning as an actual episode of mental life. For even if people never *actually do* anything to form their intentions, their intentional actions can be plausibly characterized as the consequence of their reasoning; and the influences on this reasoning can be plausibly identified as either reasons or nonreasons.

Only nonreasons are capable of undermining a person's autonomy, for only nonreasons are capable of undermining a person's own contribution to her decisions. Insofar as a person's decision reflects her own reasons for action, it is something that she produces herself; she acts as she does because she herself believes she has sufficient reason to do so. Once we see this, we can also see the sense in which the nonautonomous agent is the victim of "alien," "external" forces. The influential nonreasons of the nonautonomous agent are external, not—as many have assumed—because she repudiates them, or wishes that they were weaker, or values something with which they are incompatible. Whatever her attitude toward these nonreasons may be, their status as external influences depends on how they relate to her practical reasoning. Rather than being *constituents of* this reasoning—*things considered* in the reasoning—they influence the reasoning from without. This is precisely the point of calling them "nonrational influences." Though they are "incorporated" into the agent's reasoning, they are not incorporated *as reasons*.

It is important not to think that because nonreasons are "external" in this sense, they are somehow "external" to the agent's "true self." Nor is my Kantian conception of autonomy as "the power so to act that the principle of our action may accord with the essential character of a rational cause"[42] incompatible with the very plausible belief that "we are our emotions as much as we are our reasons."[43] In denying that someone is truly self-governing when she fails to act for a reason, I am not claiming that a person is to be identified with her reason alone. Rather, I am claiming that regardless of whether a given nonreason is a constituent of an agent's "true self," if it causes her to act for no reason, then it causes her to act nonautonomously.

Though determination by reasons is a necessary condition of autonomy, and though nonreasons play an essential role in nonautonomous action, not every nonrational influence is autonomy undermining. Indeed, every deliberation is necessarily responsive to some nonrational influences: practical reasoning would be impossible if we did not simply find ourselves taking an interest in certain things, and if we did not simply find ourselves attributing greater significance to some of these things than we attribute to others.[44] This being the case, a plausible theory of autonomy must offer a plausible criterion for distinguishing between the nonrational *saboteurs* of practical reasoning (which prevent the "principles of our action" from "according with the essential character of a rational cause") and the nonrational *facilitators* (which do not prevent this accord). In the remaining pages of this essay I want to say something about this criterion.

As far as I can tell, there is no *intrinsic* difference between the two types of nonrational influence: independent of whatever status they may have as one of the things the person considers, each type of influence directly affects what gets considered, how carefully it gets considered, and how important this consideration is judged to be, relative to other considerations. If, then, it is possible to distinguish autonomous from nonautonomous action, there must be some *extrinsic* difference between nonrational facilitators and nonrational saboteurs. For if there is no such difference, then there are not really two different types of nonrational influence; and if there are not really two different types of nonrational influence, then either every episode of practical reasoning is sabotaged or no episode of practical reasoning is sabotaged—either no intentional action is an autonomous action or every one of them is.

Fortunately, there does seem to be a difference of just the sort we are seeking. In particular, the difference between the two types of nonrational influence seems to be a function of their content and of their relation to the agent's character. More particularly still, I wish to suggest rather tentatively that a decisive nonrational influence is autonomy undermining if and only if (1) it is *not* constitutive of the agent's character *and* (2) it is *not* the sort of influence that would be compatible with human flourishing if it regularly made itself felt under similar circumstances. Let me clarify these conditions with a pair of examples.

Consider, first, the difference between being overpowered by fear and being overpowered by good cheer. This difference is evident in the very descriptions themselves: though we are quite familiar with the possibility of being "overpowered" by fear, there is something funny about the idea of being "overpowered" by good cheer. Intense fear, we might say, is "presumptively autonomy undermining"; intense good cheer is not. The question is: what grounds this distinction? Like fear—and indeed, like anxiety and depression— good cheer, high spirits, joi de vivre can profoundly affect one's decisions by determining which options one recognizes, and how one evaluates these options.

A person's large donation to a beggar may be the manifestation of her joy to the same degree that her large donation to a mugger may be the manifestation of her fear. What distinguishes these two influences is neither their strength nor their manner. Rather, fear is presumptively autonomy undermining because we assume that people live less desirable lives under the influence of fear. When fear reaches a certain level of intensity its frequent influence in a person's life is "unhealthy"; its effects on human flourishing are like a virus' effects on a flourishing body.

It may well be that for every emotion there is an intensity beyond which its regular influence under certain circumstances would be detrimental to human flourishing.[45] If so, then for every emotion there will be circumstances in which the emotion is sufficiently intense to be presumptively autonomy undermining. If I am right, however, some emotions are much more likely than others to be presumptively autonomy undermining: whereas nonpathological fear can prevent an agent from determining her intentions herself, good cheer must approach mania before it can have a similar effect.[46]

Clearly, there is no systematic method for discovering which nonrational influences contributed decisively to an agent's decisions. But just as clearly, this poses no difficulty for my account. The account simply relies on the obvious fact that we are able to give plausible explanations of one another's choices in terms of a complex network of behavioral dispositions. If I am right, then in thus explaining an action in terms of its genesis, we are implicitly indicating whether we believe the agent acted autonomously.

An "unhealthy" nonrational influence is *presumptively* autonomy undermining. But not every *presumptively* autonomy-undermining influence is *actually* autonomy undermining. This brings me to the second example mentioned above. Consider the difference between a mild-tempered person who is overwhelmed by anger and a person whose anger reflects her irascibility. Even if we assume that the anger in the two cases has an equally decisive influence on the agents' decisions, and even if we assume that in each case this anger is sufficiently intense to render its frequent influence incompatible with human flourishing, the autonomy of the two agents seems to be differently affected. Whereas the irascible agent's anger is a form of self-expression, the mild-tempered agent's anger is something that "happens to" her. In each case, the anger is "external" to the agent, in the sense of being external to her reasons. But in the case of the irascible agent, this external influence on her reasoning is constitutive of who she is, whereas in the case of the mild-tempered agent, this same influence prevents her from reasoning in a manner that expresses who she is. It is, of course, possible for someone to act autonomously while acting "out of character." So, a nonrational influence can prevent someone from reasoning in her characteristic manner without preventing her from acting autonomously. Since, however, the mild-tempered person's anger is not only incompatible with her character but would (if it *were* part of her character) be incompatible with her living a good life, and since (like the rest of us) she believes that she has sufficient reason to live a good life, her anger undermines her ability to discover her own reasons for and against behaving as she does. That is, the anger subverts the proper functioning of her own practical reasoning. It prevents her from determining her action herself.

FIRST STEPS BEYOND A ROUGH SKETCH

I have stressed that there is no neat method for discovering the best explanation of why someone acted as she did, and that for this reason there is no neat method for distinguishing the autonomous from the nonautonomous, the more autonomous from the less autonomous. Nonetheless, the examples discussed above do raise many questions that must be answered if my account of autonomy is to be more than the merest rough sketch. In the limited space that remains, I would like to address a few of these questions. I want to say something about the intuitions behind the account; to bring the account to bear on the case of drug addiction; to offer one refinement of the account; to indicate how this account differs from a recent widely discussed theory of moral responsibility; and, finally, to call attention to some of the account's broad implications. Needless to say, even after these issues have been addressed, there will still be much work left to do.[47]

1. First, then, what lies behind my suggestion that someone acts autonomously as long as each decisive nonrational influence on her behavior satisfies either the "character" condition or the "human flourishing" condition? I hope the answer to this question is pretty obvious. The idea behind the first condition is simply that an agent's character is a very important aspect of her identity. This being the case, if a motivating reason can be attributed to the agent's character, then it can be attributed to the agent herself.

The idea behind the second condition is that every agent desires to live a good life (at least insofar as she desires to live at all), and that this desire underlies an agent's attempts to decide what to do. This being the case, a nonrational influence does not thwart an agent's attempts to set her own goals, as long as it is compatible with the agent's living a good life. As long as this condition is satisfied, the decisive influence of a nonreason is compatible with the agent's determining her action herself. (The point is not, I wish to stress, that the action itself is compatible with the agent's living a good life; nor is it that the agent performs the action willingly, or would perform it willingly if she reflected more carefully on its relation to her values and ideals. The point is simply that—character traits aside—no influence on her deliberations prevents these deliberations from being capable of serving their basic function of helping her discern her best options.[48]

2. What do these intuitions about autonomy suggest about the drug addict? Though I know very little about addiction, I suspect that the philosopher's caricature of the drug addict bears very little resemblance to the real thing. In particular, I believe that with respect to their drug-taking activities, most addicts are what Frankfurt calls "wantons": they rarely ask themselves whether they have sufficient reason to act as they do; it does not occur to them to

question the desirability of their habit.[49] Drug addicts may sometimes consider whether to buy now or later, from X or from Y; they may sometimes weigh the considerations for and against taking the drugs in a particular place, at a particular time; and some of them may frequently find themselves thinking quite deliberately about how to get the cash they need to support the habit whose desirability they do not think to question. For the most part, however, an addict's drug taking is just a routine; and the acts which constitute this routine are intentional in only the minimal sense that (like the acts of braking and accelerating discussed earlier) they are directed at a goal which the addict could identify if asked.

On my account of autonomy, an addict's indifference to his addiction is irrelevant to whether his intentions are truly his own. What counts, instead, is whether his intentional behavior is decisively influenced by nonrational factors which are *either* constitutive of his character *or* such that their regular influence under similar circumstances is compatible with human flourishing. If the addict takes drugs because his strong craving prevents him from seriously considering the alternatives, and if being governed by a strong craving for drugs is incompatible with living a good life, then the addict does not act autonomously when he takes the drugs. The same is true if his actions are decisively influenced by torpor or despair. If, on the other hand, no such influences play a decisive role in the addict's behavior, then, in taking the drugs intentionally, he also acts autonomously. In short, whether we regard an addict's intention as truly his own depends on which story we tell about the genesis of this intention and which genetic stories we take to be compatible with human flourishing. The addict's own conception of the good life and his own reports about what he is up to are relevant only insofar as they provide inconclusive evidence as to which causal story is the most plausible.

3. Like a person's drug addiction, a person's character can constitute a serious impediment to his pursuit of happiness. Thus, for example, someone's attempts to make friends or retain business partners can be impeded by his irascibility or sullenness. Given this possibility, it is important to insist that the human flourishing condition is not a *necessary* condition of autonomous agency.[50] Nonetheless, there do seem to be cases in which the influence of a person's character undermines her autonomy. These are cases in which the person's character is the product of "unhealthy," culture-wide indoctrination. If, for example, a young girl's meekness or lack of ambition reflects the pervasive sexism of her society, then the influence these traits exert on her choices is autonomy undermining. They represent her culture's interference with the attempt she makes every time she deliberates: the attempt to determine her next move herself.

To accommodate such cases, the character condition must be amended so as to include among the nonrational saboteurs those dispositions which reflect the fact that a person's society has pressured her to adopt a self-conception at odds with human flourishing. The reason why such cultural indoctrination is more detrimental to an agent's autonomy than the sort of indoctrination children often receive from their parents is that it effectively eliminates alternative role models. Here is one respect in which autonomy depends on opportunity— the liberty of spontaneity depends on the liberty of indifference. In short, if there is something about a culture that seriously undermines the capacity of certain types of people (e.g., women, blacks, fat people, etc.) to acquire certain character traits important to human flourishing (e.g., self-confidence), then when these people's preferences are decisively influenced by the absence of these character traits (or by the "opposite" character traits, e.g., self-doubt), their autonomy is thereby undermined.

At this essay's beginning I called attention to what I believed to be some strengths of my theory of autonomy. Among these strengths was the fact that the theory sheds light on various critiques of ideology. The remarks in the previous paragraph provide the material for illustrating my point. Thus consider the feminist claim that women are encouraged to adopt ideals and self-conceptions which prevent them from becoming autonomous agents. Those who make this claim concede that most girls "internalize" the relevant ideals as unconsciously, and with as little resistance, as they "internalize" their mothers' milk. They concede that many women endorse these ideals and profess to be contented with the roles they have been assigned on the basis of their gender. Yet the critics also insist that the choices made by these women are not really their own. Without experiencing the least disturbance, women, the critics charge, have been "infected," "violated," "contaminated" by something that sabotages their capacity for autonomous choice.[51]

How can we make sense of this charge? How can a noncoercive education, willingly received, undermine a person's capacity for autonomous choice? My suggestion is that the feminist critique is grounded in a particular conception of the good life for human beings: according to the critics, the considerations which women are less inclined to take seriously, the possibilities which they are more likely to discount, are the sort of considerations, the sort of possibilities, which most human beings must take seriously if they are to live full, flourishing lives. In the view of these critics, if it never occurs to someone with talent, intelligence, and sufficient means that she might be an astrophysicist or a political leader or a composer, then if her lack of vision can be attributed to the nonrational influence of certain cultural ideals, these ideals can be blamed for preventing her from determining her own fate—and so can the people who promote these ideals.

4. It is important to be clear about the role which substantive reasons play in my account of autonomy. To this end I want very briefly to contrast this account with Susan Wolf's well-known account of moral responsibility.[52] The two accounts resemble one another in one important respect: according to each, a person's accountability for her behavior is a function of her relationship to "the good." Nonetheless, there are important differences as well. First, my account does not evoke some underlying capacity for "tracking" the true and the good; and, indeed, a morally perverse agent could pass my test with flying colors.[53] Second, and relatedly, my account has a much less robust alternate

possibilities requirement: again, a person can act autonomously even though she has an evil character, and is thus incapable of doing the right thing for the right reasons; in refining the account, I suggested that the influence of an agent's character may be autonomy undermining if she belongs to a class of agents who have been systematically discouraged from acquiring alternative character traits; but this claim is far weaker than the claim that autonomous wrongdoers must have genuine alternatives to being influenced by their actual dispositions. Third, on my account, not only is the ability to track goodness an *unnecessary* condition of autonomous action, but it is an *insufficient* condition as well: an autonomy-undermining influence can cause someone to recognize the "right" reasons for doing something, as, for example, when drowsiness causes a person to forget her (unjustified) grudge against X and so, "without thinking," to offer him a drink because he looks very thirsty. In sum, whereas Wolf thinks that moral responsibility requires the *ability* to recognize the *"right"* reasons, I emphasize the importance of *how* someone *actually* becomes insufficiently sensitive to reasons: if a person's reasoning has not been sabotaged by nonreasons, then she acts autonomously, regardless of whether she might have done otherwise, and indeed, regardless of whether she could have recognized the true and the good.[54]

5. Again, there are many additional refinements which would have to be introduced into my account in order to render it satisfactory. But if the general contours of the account are correct, then it has some rather significant implications. I would like to bring this essay to a close by briefly identifying these implications.

First, if I have correctly identified the key to distinguishing autonomous action from merely intentional action, then there can be no purely formal account of pure practical reasoning; for if I am correct, then whether an episode of practical reasoning is "pure" depends, in part, on whether it is under the influence of the sort of nonrational force that tends to prevent human beings from living the sort of life they have good reason to live. Second, there can be no purely "metaphysical" account of autonomy, where by "metaphysical" I mean, minimally, an account that steers clear of appeals to human values. Third, since a satisfactory account of autonomy depends on an account of human values, and since human values display a variability across cultures, the line between autonomous and nonautonomous action may appear to fall in different places in different cultures. To take one example: in our own society, certain "tender" emotions were long deemed incompatible with manly virtue, and hence, with the virtues of rational agency; so we tended to think that a man's autonomy was threatened when he permitted these emotions to get the upper hand—and that women (who have always been encouraged to experience such emotions) were congenitally deficient in autonomy. As values change, however, so too does the conception of what counts as a "violation" of the self. What once appeared to turn human beings into "helpless victims" now appears to enhance their capacity to make the choices they have good reason to make.[55]

Finally, the account of autonomy I have defended here suggests that the task of constructing a disposition-dependent account of ethical value may be much more difficult than many philosophers have supposed. What I have in mind is this: If a person's deliberate, conscientious choice cannot be presumed to be an autonomous choice, then what is "good for a person" cannot be a function of what the person is disposed to choose deliberately; for we have no reason to regard the deliberate choice of a nonautonomous agent as indicating what the agent herself truly values. More importantly, we cannot fix things up by simply appealing to what a person would deliberately choose "under optimal circumstances"; for whether circumstances are optimal depends on whether they are circumstances in which the agent chooses autonomously; and if I am right, this depends—at least in some cases—on whether the nonrational influences on the agent's choice are compatible with her living a life whose "goodness" is not a function of her own dispositions to choose it.[56]

* * * * *

Throughout this essay I have taken pains to distinguish the value of acting autonomously from the value of acting as we would most like to act. Our intentions are truly our own, I have argued, insofar and only insofar as they can be attributed to practical deliberations that express who we are. We express ourselves in deliberating insofar as our reasoning reflects our character traits, and insofar as it reflects nonrational influences compatible with our fundamental desire to live a good life. Under these conditions, and only under these conditions, we not only act for a reason; but in acting for a reason, we govern ourselves. I have argued that we cannot deliberate about what to do without presuming that these conditions obtain. And I have tried to show why this presumption may nonetheless be mistaken.

NOTES

I would like to acknowledge many people who made helpful comments on earlier drafts of this essay. Julia Driver, John Fischer, Harry Frankfurt, Bob Hanna, Elijah Millgram, Cei Maslen, Dick Moran, Connie Rosati, Gideon Rosen, Raz Spector, and especially, Maggie Little, and William Buss.

1. Many of the philosophers to whom I refer do not use the term 'autonomy'. Nonetheless, the phenomenon that interests them is the phenomenon that interests me in this essay, viz., the sort of self-determination required for moral responsibility.

2. Harry Frankfurt is the chief spokesman for this view. See, e.g., "Freedom of the Will and the Concept of a Person," in *The Importance of What We Care About* (Cambridge, 1988), 11–25. Frankfurt elaborates upon and refines his view in "Three Concepts of Free Action," "Identification and Externality," and "Identification and Wholeheartedness." These essays are all in *The Importance of What We Care About.*

For a second presentation of this view see Gerald Dworkin, "Acting Freely," *Nous* 4, no. 4 (1970): 367–83.

3. See, for example, Gary Watson, "Free Agency," in *Free Will*, edited by Gary Watson (Oxford, 1989), 96–110.

4. See, e.g., Frankfurt, "Freedom of the Will and the Concept of a Person." In note 34 I cite a passage in which Frankfurt concedes that there may be cases in which a person "identifies with" a passion of which he disapproves. It is not clear to me what Frankfurt

has in mind when in this passage he distinguishes between (1) "disapproving" of a passion and (2) "feeling" that the passion is "alien" or "intrudes." In any case, my critique of endorsement-relative accounts of autonomy is meant to challenge the view that *some feeling* or *attitude* is *necessary* for autonomous action; and it is also meant to challenge Frankfurt's claim that *approval* is a *sufficient* condition of autonomy. (Regarding this last claim, see "Identification and Externality," 65; and the discussion of the willing addict in "Freedom of the Will and the Concept of a Person," 24–25.)

5. According to Watson, "It is part of our idea of autonomy that the fundamental determinants of our behavior are ones that we could endorse without delusion" (Gary Watson, "Free Action and Free Will," *Mind* 96 [April 1987]: 145–72).

6. The most careful articulation and defense of this view is presented in articles by John Martin Fischer. See, for example, "Responsiveness and Moral Responsibility," in *Responsibility, Character, and the Emotions*, edited by Ferdinand Schoeman (Cambridge, 1987), 81–106. The basic idea is that if, in a specified set of counterfactual conditions, the agent would act on what she takes to be good and sufficient reasons, then she is morally responsible for her action. I think such counterfactual analyses have insuperable difficulties. In particular, there will always be counterexamples in which autonomous agents are unresponsive to reasons under the allegedly relevant counterfactual conditions, or in which nonautonomous agents *are* responsive. David Shatz presents many such examples in "Compatibilism, Values, and 'Could Have Done Otherwise'," *Philosophical Topics* 14 (1988): 151–200.

7. To the extent that my account stresses the importance of the historical genesis of an agent's preferences, it is more sympathetic to incompatibilism than are most other compatibilist accounts of autonomy. (Very roughly, incompatibilism is the thesis that autonomous action is incompatible with causal determinism. For an extended discussion and defense of this thesis, see Peter van Inwagen, *An Essay on Free Will* [Oxford, 1983].)

8. Some philosophers seem to take a different view of the relationship between unconscious motives and autonomy insofar as they seem to suggest that an agent's autonomy depends on his at least being *capable* of discovering what motivates him. Thus Watson includes among the conditions of autonomy the capacity to "reflect . . . on the origins of [one's] motivations." (Watson, "Free Action and Free Will," 152.) And Frankfurt seems to assume that an agent's autonomy is transparent to him, inasmuch as he seems to assume (problematically, I think) that it is evident to an agent whether her failure to do what she has "made up her mind to do" is the effect of an irresistible desire with which she does not identify herself or whether it is, on the contrary, the effect of a desire with which she had unwittingly identified herself. (See Frankfurt, "The Importance of What We Care About," in *The Importance of What We Care About*, especially 83–88.)

9. The point is simply that the degree to which we are self-governing is not transparent to us. This does not mean that observers of an agent's behavior necessarily have an advantage over the agent when it comes to determining whether the agent acted autonomously. Someone may well suspect that her own intentional behavior is not autonomous.

10. See, for example, Sandra Bartky, *Femininity and Domination: Studies in the Phenomenology of Oppression* (New York, 1990).

11. Near the end of this essay I briefly indicate how this appeal to substantive reasons differs from the interesting and much discussed appeal in Susan Wolf's account of moral responsibility.

12. Sarah Buss, "Weakness of Will," unpublished manuscript.

13. The formation of the preference and the making of the decision need not be two distinct steps. Indeed, as I indicate later, they need not be actual events in the agent's mental life. The point is simply that the decision could be explained in terms of the preference. In other words, it could be characterized as *expressing* the preference.

14. As Mark Johnston notes, behavior can be goal directed without being *intentionally* directed toward the goal in question; it is possible to be unwittingly (and unintentionally)

doing something for a purpose of which we are also unaware. (Johnston offers the example of "running our eyes predominantly over the tops of printed words" in order to read faster (Mark Johnston, "Self-deception and the Nature of Mind," in *Perspectives on Self-deception*, edited by Amelie Rorty and Brian McLaughlin [Berkeley, 1988], 86). The sort of cases Johnston has in mind are not the sort of cases that interest me in this essay, since, *necessarily*, they are not cases in which one self-consciously acts for a purpose which one self-consciously repudiates. Nonetheless, I have been careful to speak here of "setting a goal for oneself" as opposed to "pursuing," or even simply "having," a goal.

15. There are good reasons to believe that one can do A intentionally without intending to do A. (See, for example, Michael E. Bratman, *Intention, Plans, and Practical Reason* (Cambridge, Mass., 1987).) One of these reasons is that it seems we can do something intentionally though we prefer *not* to do it (e.g., we can intentionally bring about certain side-effects of what we intend to do, even when we would much prefer that these side-effects did not occur). In the second section on the irrelevance thesis, I discuss the obvious sense in which we can intentionally do something we prefer *not* to do. In this section, however, I focus on all-things-considered preferences (i.e., preferences formed in light of everything the agent considers). My claim is that, no matter how indifferent or unhappy one may be about various side-effects of one's action, one prefers to perform this action, *all things considered*, if and only if one believes that, despite these unfortunate side-effects, the action has more going for it than any of the available alternatives.

16. In "Weakness of Will" I try to explain how this conception of practical rationality is compatible with the possibility of weakness of will.

17. Obviously, the principle is also compatible with the Humean thesis that one can judge it better to do A than B and yet be insufficiently motivated to do A. Since, moreover, the principle is silent about the *content* of an agent's preferences, it also allows for the possibility that a rational agent can prefer to have less of the very thing she deems most desirable. (In other words, it does not entail that someone is irrational whenever she fails to maximize her own satisfactions.) I discuss some alleged counterexamples to the principle in "Weakness of Will".

18. For a classic discussion of wayward causal chains, see Donald Davidson, "Freedom To Act," in *Essays on Actions and Events* (Oxford, 1980), 79–80.

19. Frankfurt, "Freedom of the Will and the Concept of a Person," 18.

20. Frankfurt, "Three Concepts of Free Action," 48.

21. Aristotle, *Nicomachean Ethics*, Book III, Chapter 1, 1110a8–10, translated by W. D. Ross, in *The Basic Works of Aristotle*, edited by R. M. McKeon (New York, 1941), 964–65. Aristotle offers the following example of a "mixed action": "Something of the sort happens . . . with regard to the throwing of goods overboard in a storm; for in the abstract no one throws goods away voluntarily, but on condition of its securing the safety of himself and his crew any sensible man does so." For a second example, see note 26.

22. For a classic discussion of the unwilling addict—and one which describes this addict as "helplessly violated" and a "passive bystander"—see Frankfurt, "Freedom of the Will and the Concept of a Person," 11–25.

23. I can think of an additional argument that might be offered in defense of the standard interpretation of the unwilling addict. It might be argued that though the addict takes the drugs intentionally, this is because he prefers to take the drugs *in a certain manner*, where this preference is compatible with his preferring *not to take the drugs*, all things considered. According to this argument, though the addict believes that, all things considered, it would be better to refrain from taking drugs, he acts intentionally because he believes there to be no better way to insert the needle. The idea here is that someone can be compelled to do something which he nonetheless does intentionally, since he can be compelled to do it without being compelled to do it *in a particular manner*. What could be better evidence of this possibility, it might further be urged, than the implausibility of claiming that the unwilling addict takes himself to have sufficient reason for doing what he has struggled so mightily to *refrain* from doing?

However plausible this argument may be, it cannot withstand careful scrutiny. For consider what is involved in deliberately executing such tasks as taking-drugs-*in-just-this-way* and inserting-the-needle-*in-just-this-way*. Since one's behavior in such cases is intentional, it is responsive to one's evaluations of one's options. That is, it reflects one's belief that, all things considered, it would not be better to behave otherwise. But if this is what one believes, then one does *not* believe that refraining from taking the drugs would be better than taking the drugs *in just this way*.

The point here is simply that if there is some act-token one *executes* deliberately, then there is some description of this act-token under which one performs *it* for a reason. Conversely, if one takes oneself to have insufficient reason to perform a given act, then one cannot contrive things so as to *execute* this particular act deliberately. The fact that one performs an act of a given *type* may be beyond one's control in virtue of some subset of this act's properties. But if one has insufficient reason to perform a particular act-token, then none of this act's properties renders it worth performing; so, in particular, the property of being executed in just this way gives one insufficient reason to perform it; so, if one executes it in just this way, one does not act for a reason; i.e., one does *not* act intentionally.

In sum, we cannot be passive with respect to the *what* of our acts, if we are active with respect to the *how*. We cannot deliberately let go gracefully, without deliberately letting go. The principle defended here is the converse of a principle defended by Leibniz: "a man never has a sufficient reason to act, when he has not also a sufficient reason to act in a particular manner; every action being individual, and not general, nor abstract from its circumstances, but always needing some particular way of being put in execution" (Gottfried Wilhelm Leibniz, fifth letter, in *The Leibniz-Clarke Correspondence*, edited by H. G. Alexander (New York, 1978), 60).

24. Contrast this claim with the following passage: "There is no reason to assume that an addict who succumbs unwillingly to his craving adopts as his own the desire he has tried to resist. He may in the end merely submit to it with resignation, like a man who knows he is beaten and who therefore despairingly accepts the consequences defeat must bring him, rather like someone who decides to join with or to incorporate forces which he had formerly opposed" (Frankfurt, "The Problem of Action," in *The Importance of What We Care About*, 77.)

25. Frankfurt claims that someone who lacks autonomy is moved by "an irresistible compulsion that originates within." "It is the irresistibility of [this agent's] inclination or desire that accounts for the action he performs." What's more, agents thus motivated include the person who "[believes] of himself that he cannot resist a certain desire, and therefore [proceeds] in calm resignation to satisfy it without experiencing the uncontrollable compulsive thrust that he might indeed encounter if he should attempt to refuse it satisfaction" (Frankfurt, "Three Concepts of Free Action," 49, 50).

This last claim is significant: where autonomy is concerned, Frankfurt does not seem to recognize a distinction between (1) doing something because one is overwhelmed by a desire's "compulsive thrust" and (2) doing something because one *believes* one *would be* overwhelmed if one did not resign oneself. Frankfurt himself acknowledges that we may alter our intentions when "we come to understand more completely what carrying [them] out would require us to do or to sacrifice doing" (Frankfurt, "Identification and Wholeheartedness," 176). As I argue, it seems quite likely that such a change of mind could account for what happens to the unwilling addict, whose appreciation of the costs of resisting his craving surely increases with every passing moment.

26. Frank Jackson makes a similar distinction in "Internal Conflicts in Desires and Morals," *American Philosophical Quarterly* 22 (April 1985): 105–14. We must, he argues, distinguish between the value of a *kind* of state of affairs and the value of a given *instance* of this kind. Thus, "Suppose lying is the only way to save John Doe from undeserved public disgrace, then I may want to lie. I want that a lying by me take place. But it will not be true that the state of affairs of saving John Doe from undeserved public disgrace is one I want to involve lying by me. I'd much rather that state of affairs were otherwise achievable" (111).

27. The intuition that unwilling agents are less blameworthy than their willing counterparts rests, I believe, on the further intuition that whereas the former are pressured, or coerced, by their circumstances, the latter are not.

28. Note that discussions of the unwilling addict often do not specify that he believes he is addicted. If, however, we do not make this (very reasonable) assumption, and if we acknowledge that he acts deliberately in taking the drugs, despite his awareness of certain strong reasons against doing so, then we will have to assume that, even if he believes he could refrain from taking drugs, he prefers to take them, given the price he will have to pay for abstaining.

29. In "Three Concepts of Free Action" Frankfurt does acknowledge that there is a sense in which an agent can act unwillingly without failing to act autonomously (47). But in his view, this possibility is limited to cases where the "circumstances" that disappoint the agent are not features of the agent's own motivational set.

30. If proattitudes are "propositional in character," then the object of a desire can only be a *type* of action. (This point has been stressed by Davidson. See, for example, "Freedom To Act," 77.) I am inclined to think that one can have attitudes toward the particular action one is presently performing. In any case, in distinguishing between an agent's attitude toward the *particular* action she performs and her attitude toward performing this *type*, or *kind*, of action, I am merely singling out a special instance of the key distinction between an agent's attitude toward some concatenation of act features and her attitude toward any one of these features.

31. Sartre claims that it is always up to the agent herself whether a given desire or character trait determines her action; for her various dispositions are causally efficacious only if she takes them to give her sufficient reason to act. ("In establishing a certain conduct as a possibility and precisely because it is *my* possibility, I am aware that *nothing* can compel me to adopt that conduct" [68]. "Motives are only *for* consciousness. And due to the very fact that the motive can arise only as appearance, consciousness is not subject to it because of the very fact that consciousness posits it; for consciousness has now the task of conferring on the motive its meaning and its importance" [71] [Jean-Paul Sartre, *Being and Nothingness*, translated by Hazel E. Barnes (New York, 1956].)

In my opinion, Sartre's view must be rejected, since someone's action can be self-determined even while being determined by motives of which she is not in the least bit conscious. Nonetheless, when the view is modified to accommodate this possibility, it reflects the very conception of practical rationality I defend earlier: in cases where someone is aware of reasons *not* to act as she does, she cannot act this way intentionally without concluding that she has sufficient reason for acting this way, after all.

32. "Bad Faith," *Being and Nothingness*, 86–116. In a typical characterization of bad faith Sartre writes, "Shall I uncover in myself 'drives' even though it be to affirm them in shame? But is this not deliberately to forget that these drives are realized with my consent, that they are not forces of nature but that I lend them their efficacy by a perpetually renewed decision concerning their value?" (106).

33. Benedict de Spinoza, *The Ethics*, in *On the Improvement of the Understanding, the Ethics, Correspondence*, translated by R. H. M. Elwes (New York, 1955). In "Of Human Freedom," for example, Spinoza writes, "The mind has greater power over the emotions and is less subject thereto, in so far as it understands all things as necessary" (250). One of the many subtleties of Spinoza's philosophy to which my passing remark does not do justice is his view that in accepting one's motives, one transforms them.

34. I take it that Frankfurt has something like this possibility in mind when he writes, "Perhaps, after long struggle and disillusioned with himself, a person may become resigned to being someone of whom he himself does not altogether approve. He no longer supposes that he is capable of bringing the course of his passions into harmony with his ideal concept of himself, and accordingly he ceases to reserve his acceptance of his passions as they are." "A person may acknowledge to himself that passions of which he disapproves are undeniably and unequivocally his; and he may then cease to feel, if he ever felt, that these

passions are in any way alien or that they intrude upon him" (Frankfurt, "Identification and Externality," 64, 65).

35. Jon Elster, "Sour Grapes—Utilitarianism and the Genesis of Wants," in *The Inner Citadel* edited by John Christman (Oxford, 1989), 170–88.

36. Frankfurt, "Freedom of the Will and the Concept of a Person," 22.

37. Frankfurt, "Identification and Wholeheartedness," 170.

38. Frankfurt, "Freedom of the Will and the Concept of a Person," 17.

39. Ibid.

40. Interestingly, there is one occasion on which Frankfurt himself seems to acknowledge the inappropriateness of describing someone as a "passive bystander" to her own action. "There can," he writes, "be no such thing as a passive willing. All of the movements of my will—for instance, my choices and decisions—are *movements that I make*. None is a mere impersonal occurrence, in which my will *moves without my moving it*. None of my choices or decisions merely happens. Its occurrence is my activity, and I can no more be a passive bystander with respect to my own choices and decisions than I can be passive with respect to any of my own actions. It is possible for me to be passive when my arm rises, but I cannot be passive when I raise it" ("Concerning the Freedom and Limits of the Will," *Philosophical Topics* 17, no. 1 [Spring 1989]: 177). I find it very difficult to reconcile this passage with the rest of Frankfurt's work. In conversation, he was sympathetic to the suggestion that he wishes to distinguish between two different degrees of passivity: (1) the passivity of one whose movements are unintentional and (2) the passivity of one whose intentional movements are not the movements he "really wants" to make. In arguing that (2) is irrelevant to autonomy, I am, in effect, challenging the notion that the "passivity" of "unwilling" agents is simply a *lesser degree* of the same relation that obtains between a person and her unintentional bodily movements.

41. In "Free Action and Free Will," Watson calls attention to the difference between constraints on "implementing one's will" and constraints on willing ("Free Action and Free Will," 162–63). Whereas in the first (critical) part of this essay, I challenge the assumption that an agent's intentional behavior could reflect a constraint on the agent's implementing her will, in the remaining (constructive) part of the essay, I am trying to articulate the conditions under which an agent's will may itself be constrained.

42. Immanuel Kant, *Groundwork of the Metaphysics of Morals*, translated by H. J. Paton (New York, 1964), 126.

43. Michael S. Moore, "Choice, Character, and Excuses," in *Crime, Culpability, and Remedy*, edited by Ellen Frankel Paul et al. (Oxford, 1990).

44. As Daniel Dennett writes, "The most rational course any finite, macroscopic intelligence could take (knowing itself to be finite) will have to involve 'heuristic' decision procedures, in which a risky, limited amount of analysis is terminated *in some arbitrary way* in the interests of conserving time on the game clock" (*Elbow Room: The Varieties of Free Will Worth Wanting* [Cambridge, Mass., 1984], 71).

45. This appears to be Aristotle's view. See his discussion of the "mean," *Nicomachean Ethics*, Book II, Chapter 6.

46. Like good cheer, hatred appears to be an emotion which must be abnormally strong in order to be presumptively autonomy undermining. This is obviously not because a life decisively influenced by hatred is a good life. Rather, it reflects the fact that in most cases where we attribute an action to the agent's hatred without thereby attributing it to her hateful character, we think that her hate is decisively influential in its capacity as one of her *reasons* for action (e.g., she killed him because she believed he was vile, had done her wrong, deserved to die, etc.). I say "most cases," for surely, there are at least in principle some cases where we want to say that a person was "blinded" by hatred and where this dim-sightedness cannot be attributed to a character flaw. For an interesting discussion of why determination by hatred is no excuse, see Peter Arenella, "Character, Choice, and Moral Agency," in *Crime, Culpability, and Remedy*, 77–83.

47. Among the many questions that still need to be addressed are these: How broadly or narrowly should we construe an agent's "circumstances" for the purposes of evaluating an emotion's impact on human flourishing? When are the distorting effects on an agent's perception of her options sufficiently great to be autonomy-undermining? Under what conditions does a nonrational influence count as an expression of character? What makes such an influence "decisive"? Exactly how are the character condition and the human flourishing condition related to one another? To what extent is the appeal to "the good life" compatible with moral relativism?

48. Note that though an agent's autonomy has nothing to do with whether she endorses, or would endorse, her action, it is nonetheless possible to express the human flourishing condition in terms of the agent's endorsements. Thus, under certain circumstances an agent's autonomy is undermined by an influence on her reasoning precisely because no rational person would endorse this influence *if she had a true conception of human flourishing*. According to the account I am proposing, if a given motive is not something an agent considers in deciding what to do, and if this motive is not constitutive of the agent's character, then it undermines her autonomy only if she would prefer not to be under its influence if she understood which motives were *really better* than others.

This view of autonomy should be contrasted with Robert Nozick's view that "a necessary condition, at least, of an act's being free it that is be in equilibrium," i.e., "withstand knowledge of its own causes" (Robert Nozick, *Philosophical Explanations* [Cambridge, Mass., 1981], 349–50). As Dennett explains, "[An act] withstands knowledge because the knowledge reveals the act to have been caused just as we would have wanted—by a clear view of reality and the best of intentions" (Dennett, *Elbow Room*, 65). Unlike Nozick, I do not believe that an act's being free depends on its being caused by a clear view of reality. Mine is the weaker view that *some* distorting influences on an agent's view of reality are autonomy undermining.

49. Frankfurt defines 'wanton' in "Freedom of the Will and the Concept of a Person," 16–17.

50. The character condition is not a necessary condition either, for the reason already mentioned, viz., that agents can act "out of character."

51. Watson seems to be sensitive to something like this possibility when he discusses the case of someone who "has been habituated to think that divorce is to be avoided in all cases" ("Free Agency," 104–105). In my view, Watson's discussion does not go deep enough. In contrasting the effects of "acculturation" with the judgments formed in response to critical reflection, he overlooks the fact that an agent's "acculturation" can undermine her autonomy by preventing her from even *recognizing* certain relevant options.

52. See Susan Wolf, "Asymmetrical Freedom," in *Moral Responsibility*, edited by John Martin Fischer (Ithaca, N.Y., 1986), 225–40; "Sanity and the Metaphysics of Responsibility," in *Responsibility, Character, and the Emotions*, 46–52; and *Freedom Within Reason* (New York, 1990). I focus on Wolf's account because it has received considerable attention in the recent philosophical literature. As I indicate in note 48, however, my chief disagreement with Wolf over the role of substantive reasons is a disagreement with anyone who claims that autonomy depends on a "clear view of reality." Thus, for example, I also reject Paul Benson's suggestion that "one's action is fully free only to the extent that one has the ability to appreciate the normative standards governing one's conduct and to make competent critical evaluations, in light of these norms, of open courses of action" (Paul Benson, "Freedom and Value," *Journal of Philosophy* 84, no. 9 (September 1987): 475.

53. One person who probably does fail to pass the test is the person who is morally normal (i.e., the person who is morally normal according to the standards of those determining whether she acted autonomously) and who would be morally perverse (according to these same standards) if she were regularly influenced as in the actual case. Such a person acts out of character, and if we assume that general confusion about right and wrong is incompatible with living a good human life, then she also acts in a way that would, if generalized, be incompatible with human flourishing.

54. Of course, Wolf's account also differs from mine in taking an agent's endorsement to be relevant to whether she is morally responsible for what she does.

55. As I mention in note 47, I need to explore the extent to which my account is compatible with moral relativism. Since I do not wish, at this point, to commit myself on this issue, I have been careful to speak of what "appears" to be the case.

56. Disposition-dependent accounts of value fall into two camps: reductive accounts which make no appeals to evaluative notions and nonreductive accounts which do appeal to evaluative notions. My point is that it looks as though a theory of value must appeal to substantive values which are neglected by even the nonreductive account. One example of a reductive dispositional theory of value is David Lewis, "Dispositional Theories of Value II" *Proceedings of the Aristotelian Society*, supplementary vol. 63 (1989): 113–37. For some examples of nonreductive theories, see Mark Johnston, "Dispositional Theories of Value III," *Proceedings of the Aristotelian Society*, supplementary vol. 63 (1985): 139–74; John McDowell, "Values and Secondary Qualities," *Morality and Objectivity*, edited by Ted Handerich (London, 1985), 110–29; and David Wiggins, "A Sensible Subjectivism," in *Needs, Values, and Truth* (Oxford, 1987), 185–211.

Naturalism and the Problem of Intentionality

MICHAEL TYE

In this essay, I shall argue that there is a fundamental confusion in much of the recent literature concerning naturalism and intentionality. One prominent view is that Brentano's Problem—the Problem of Intentionality—presents a serious challenge to the naturalist's position. This seems to me altogether mistaken. Brentano's Problem, at least as it is normally understood, is not a genuine problem for naturalism at all.

I begin my discussion by trying to get clear on just what the Problem of Intentionality is supposed to be, and I distinguish a number of different reductive strategies naturalists have developed for solving it. I then show that naturalism about intentionality does not require any of these strategies and I maintain that the challenge Brentano's Problem lays down for naturalism is best declined. In the final section, I consider what questions remain about intentionality and I make some remarks on the prospects for producing satisfying answers to them.

I. WHAT IS THE PROBLEM OF INTENTIONALITY?

The problem of intentionality is associated historically more with Franz Brentano than with any other philosopher.[1] Hence the name "Brentano's Problem." Brentano was struck by the fact that we can, it appears, undergo mental states which are about nonexistent objects. For example, I can hope for a life that lasts two hundred years, want a blue emerald, think that there are golden mountains, wonder whether unicorns ever have two horns, believe that Santa Claus lives at the North Pole, and seem to see a pink elephant, even though there are, in reality, no human lives of two centuries, no blue emeralds, no golden mountains, no unicorns, no Santa Claus, and no pink elephants.

Brentano believed that in each of these cases, while the relevant objects do not really exist, they nonetheless are presented in the mental states themselves.

He called this presentation "intentional inexistence." In Brentano's view, every mental state has its own intentionally inexistent object or objects, whatever reality itself is like. This, according to Brentano, is the basis of intentionality. It is found, he claimed, only in mental states and never in anything physical. He comments:

> Every mental phenomenon is characterized by what the Scholastics of the Middle Ages called the intentional (or mental) inexistence of an object, and what we might call, though not wholly unambiguously, reference to a content, direction toward an object (which is not to be understood here as meaning a thing), or immanent objectivity. Every mental phenomenon includes something as object within itself, although they do not all do so in the same way. In presentation something is presented, in judgement something is affirmed or denied, in love loved, in hate hated, in desire desired and so on. This intentional in-existence is characteristic exclusively of mental phenomena.[2]

Brentano's doctrine of intentional inexistence is deeply obscure. Brentano's student, Alexius Meinong, took Brentano here to be supposing that the objects of mental states have a special sort of existence, or subsistence, quite apart from their being in the real world.[3] Thus, on Meinong's interpretation, a thought about golden mountains is a thought which relates its subject to subsistent golden mountains. This regrettably amounts to explaining the obscure by the still more obscure. For the idea of a realm of objects which do not exist and yet which have being seems unintelligible.[4] Moreover, if intentional inexistence is the mark of the mind, then mental states which we normally suppose to be about real objects in the world, for example, my wish that I could afford a particular Ferrari I saw for sale yesterday, is not really about a real Ferrari at all but rather concerns a subsistent one. That, however, is not what I wish I could afford. Probably I can already afford one of *those*. It is the real thing that is beyond my means.

Brentano himself disavowed the interpretation Meinong adopted, seeing perhaps the difficulties mentioned above. But he offered no alternative characterization of intentional inexistence. So, his own view remains obscure. Still, Brentano did succeed in drawing to our attention an extremely interesting fact about a wide range of our mental states, namely their capacity to represent or be about things which do not exist. It is not at all obvious that this capacity extends to all mental states as Brentano supposed. Consider, for example, pain or the state of feeling depressed. These states do not *seem* to represent or be about anything at all.[5] But whether or not all mental states are representational—itself an interesting question—the property of representing what does not exist is, on the face of it, a very strange property quite unlike other relational properties which we can all agree are tokened in the natural realm. Apples fall from trees, rocks strike buildings, alkalis neutralize acids. In each of these cases, the properties are unproblematically physical. Moreover, the properties evidently cannot be instantiated unless the relevant objects exist. In a world in which there are no trees, for example, nothing falls from a tree. But intentionality seems different. The problem, then, for those who want to claim that the mind is part of the natural world is to explain how it is possible for a physical system to exhibit intentionality.

Although Brentano himself focused on the capacity of mental states to represent what does not exist, there are two other features of mental representation which have been much discussed by philosophers and which are also typically taken to be part and parcel of intentionality.

The first of these features is closely related to the capacity to represent mentally what does not exist. We can, it seems, think about, or imagine, or desire, or hope for a yacht or a house in the country, say, without there being any particular yacht or house which is being thought about or imagined or desired or hoped for.

By contrast, we can sometimes adopt these very same attitudes with respect to particular real things in the world. There may be some particular yacht, which I am thinking about or want. In some cases, then, the mind seems to 'reach out' into the world and 'latch onto' specific real objects.

Mental representation is also fine-grained. We have the capacity to think that all humans have hearts without thinking that all humans have at least one kidney, even though the property, having a heart is co-instantiated with the property, having one or more kidneys. This is true, moreover, even in those cases where the properties are *necessarily* co-instantiated. Thus, I can believe that some closed figure has three sides without believing that it has interior angles totalling 180 degrees. What is still more astonishing is the fact that we can, it seems, believe that P without believing that Q, even when 'P' and 'Q' are synonymous. For example, if I erroneously think that a fortnight is ten days, and I believe that Tom has gone away for a fortnight, I won't believe that Tom has gone away for fourteen days, even though the predicates "has gone away for a fortnight" and "has gone away for fourteen days" are synonyms.

The philosophical problem of intentionality, in its standard form, is presented as a problem which *must* be faced by any philosopher who wants to hold that mental states are part of the natural world. The problem is that of explaining how a physical system, something within the natural world, *could* exhibit states with all the above features. Here, for example, is how Robert Stalnaker lays out the problem:

> The problem of intentionality is a problem about the nature of representation. . . . For various familiar reasons, intentional or representational relations seem unlike relations holding between things and events in the natural world: causal interactions, spatiotemporal relations, various notions of similarity and difference. One can, it seems, picture, describe, or think about such things as gods and golden mountains even if they do not exist. And one can picture, describe, or think about a triangle or a sunset without there being any particular triangle or sunset that is pictured, described, or thought about. Some philosophers have used these

distinctive features of intentional relations to argue that they are irreducible to natural relations. From this conclusion it is argued that mental phenomena cannot be a species of natural phenomena. Any account of thinking things as natural objects in the material world, these philosophers argue, is bound to leave something out. The challenge presented to the philosopher who wants to regard human beings as part of the natural order is to explain intentional relations in naturalistic terms.[6]

In like manner, Jerry Fodor remarks:

> The worry about representation is above all that the semantic (and/or the intentional) will prove permanently recalcitrant to integration in the natural order. . . . What is required to relieve the worry is therefore, at a minimum, the framing of *naturalistic* conditions for representation.[7]

But what is supposed to follow, if no satisfactory naturalistic conditions for representation are forthcoming? Brentano clearly thought that such conditions could not be found, and he inferred from this that intentionality is a real but non-natural phenomenon. Fodor's own view is that if the project of naturalizing the intentional cannot be carried out—the project, that is, of specifying naturalistic conditions for representation—then there are no intentional states (in his terms "intentional irrealism" is true). For Fodor holds to the position that nothing exists outside the natural order. He says:

> the deepest motivation for intentional irrealism derives . . . from a certain ontological intuition: that there is no place for intentional categories in a physicalistic view of the world; that the intentional can't be *naturalized*.[8]

Both Fodor and Brentano, then, may be seen as subscribing to the following understanding of the problem of intentionality. The problem is one *for* the naturalist. It assumes, or presupposes, that if naturalism with respect to intentionality is true then an explanation must be *possible* of how a physical system can undergo intentional states. The challenge is to specify this explanation. Brentano seems to have thought that it is obvious that no satisfactory explanation is possible. So, he declined the challenge and accepted non-naturalism. Fodor accepts the challenge and proposes a naturalistic explanation.

Exactly what kind of naturalistic explanation is required to *solve* the philosophical problem of intentionality? Fodor, in one of his earlier articles on intentionality, puts the answer this way:

> what we want at a minimum is something of the form '*R represents S*' is *true iff C* where the vocabulary in which condition *C* is couched contains neither intentional nor semantic expressions.[9]

So, to naturalize intentionality, according to Fodor, we must provide reductionist necessary and sufficient conditions.

On this understanding of the problem of intentionality, the question: "How is it possible for a physical system to undergo intentional states?" will receive a satisfactory answer only if adequate reductionist necessary and sufficient conditions for a state's having an intentional content are adumbrated. So, the question effectively places a demand on the philosopher who maintains that intentionality is a natural phenomenon. The demand is to show how the intentional features of mental states can be reductively analyzed, to show that they have essences which are expressible in non-intentional, non-semantic language. Failure to meet this demand is seen as threatening the thesis that intentionality is a natural phenomenon.

The requirement Fodor lays down is one which has dominated work on the problem of intentionality at least until very recently. Important differences have existed, however, with respect to the issue of how to proceed.

Some philosophers have adopted a purely conceptual approach to the problem of intentionality. In other words, they have offered accounts of the essence of mental representation based upon *a priori* reflection on our intentional concepts rather than empirical investigation.[10] The test of a given proposal, within this approach, is whether it accords with what competent users of intentional vocabulary would say about its applicability in a variety of actual and counterfactual cases. For *a priori* discoverable essences are ones that match our concepts, and these concepts determine our categorizations of cases as involving tokens of the relevant types or not. This seems to be Fodor's view in the essay from which the last passage quoted above is taken, since he adopts there, albeit tentatively, on *a priori* grounds a version of the causal covariation account of mental representation.

Other philosophers have supposed that intentionality has an essence that cannot be completely described without scientific investigation.[11] In this case, the situation is more complicated. For the project of reducing the intentional can no longer depend on conceptual analysis alone. Instead it must be supposed that the philosophical task is to delineate *a priori* what *sort* of non-intentional, non-semantic essence intentionality has (for example, functional) and to indicate which sciences will tell the rest of the story (for example, cognitive psychology or biology). On this understanding, the problem of intentionality is only *partly* conceptual. For now it is held that any full specification of how it is that any physical state has any intentional content requires scientific knowledge. Naturalists who take this line typically hold that, under any acceptable account of the intentional, all or, at any rate, most of our ordinary everyday speech dispositions with respect to the use of language ascribing intentional contents in both actual and counterfactual situations must be preserved.[12] So, thought experiments about whether or not given creatures undergo mental states with given intentional contents are still very much relevant to the assessment of individual proposals.

There are, then, both wholly conceptual and partly conceptual strategies with respect to the problem of intentionality. In the former case, direct examination of our ordinary concepts, and the necessary and sufficient conditions that govern their application, is taken to yield *a priori* reductive analyses of the essence of intentionality. In the latter, scientific investigation, together with philosophical reflection regulated by our pretheoretical conception of intentionality, is needed to come to a full understanding of its essence.

I have suggested that the problem of intentionality demands that an explanation be given of how physical systems can undergo intentional states. But does it also implicitly demand that a reductive *analysis* be given of intentionality, as Fodor above and many other philosophers have supposed? Fodor himself no longer thinks so. In *Psychosemantics* he says the following:

> I suppose that sooner or later the physicists will complete the catalogue they've been compiling of the ultimate and irreducible properties of things. When they do, the likes of spin, charm, and charge will perhaps appear on their list. But aboutness surely won't; intentionality simply doesn't go that deep. It's hard to see, in face of this consideration, how one can be a Realist about intentionality without also being to some extent or other a Reductionist. If the semantic and the intentional are real properties of things, it must be in virtue of their identity with (or supervenience on?) properties that are themselves neither intentional nor semantic. If aboutness is real, it must really be something else.[13]

Here Fodor countenances the possibility that intentional properties are not identical with non-intentional, non-semantic properties but instead supervene on them. If this is the case, of course, then no *analysis* of intentionality in non-representational terms will be possible. In a later article, introducing his latest approach to intentionality, Fodor comments:

> this will have the form of a physicalist, atomistic, and putatively sufficient condition. . . . [14]
>
> [I]t's an attempt to solve Brentano's problem by showing that there are naturalistically specifiable, and atomistic, sufficient conditions for a physical state to have an intentional content. . . . [S]olving Brentano's problem requires giving sufficient conditions for intentionality, not *necessary* and sufficient conditions.[15]

So, now Fodor is prepared to accept that the problem of explaining how it is possible for a physical system to have intentional states demands only that appropriate *sufficient* conditions for intentionality be stated.

What sort of naturalistic sufficient conditions is Fodor now looking for? It is clear from his lengthy discussion of putative counterexamples that he is really after *conceptually* sufficient conditions, ones that may be discovered by *a priori* reflection (although Fodor himself would likely balk at this description). This switch from providing necessary and sufficient conditions for intentionality to providing just *a priori* sufficient conditions deserves further discussion.

If intentional properties are reductively analyzable then they are one and the same as properties that are themselves neither intentional nor semantic. Since the latter properties are assumed to be unproblematically physical, there is now no gap left in our understanding of how intentional properties can be tokened in physical systems. Once the right unproblematically physical properties are in place, the intentional properties are automatically present. Brentano's Problem is solved.

But suppose that intentional properties cannot be reduced, that is, that they have no non-intentional essences. Then, for any given intentional property I, there will be no physical property P which is such that necessarily P is tokened just in case I is tokened. Since I is evidently such that necessarily it is tokened just in case I is tokened, I and P differ in their modal properties. It follows, then, that I is not identical with P. So, if intentional properties do not have non-intentional essences then a gap opens up again between the intentional properties and the unproblematically physical ones. So, now, it seems, there is a puzzle again about how a physical system can have intentional properties. The Problem of Intentionality remains unsolved.

Suppose, however, through conceptual reflection, we manage to construct an *a priori* reductive sufficient condition for a state to have any given intentional content C. Then we will be able to see *a priori* that if the condition is met then a state with C must be tokened. So, a connection will have been made between the way in which we conceive of C and a certain physical state S, a connection which guarantees that the physical state S is sufficient for C. Now the gap between the intentional and the physical will apparently have been closed again. We will be able to say that a physical system can have a state with C by having a physical state S which our very concept of C guarantees is sufficient for C.

Let me now summarize this introduction to the Problem of Intentionality. The problem is presented as a puzzle for naturalism. It assumes, or presupposes, that if naturalism is true then it is possible to explain how a physical system can undergo intentional states. What it asks of those philosophers who want to view intentionality as a natural phenomenon is for a specification of this explanation. The question will be answered, the philosophical problem solved, on the usual interpretations, only if an account is given of what it is for a state to have an intentional content which either reveals the essence of the state's intentionality in unproblematically physical terms or, more modestly, specifies a conceptually sufficient condition of the same type for the state. Failure to produce such an account inevitably leaves a gap in our understanding, a philosophical mystery. This, in turn, seriously threatens the naturalistic view of intentionality.

II. 'NATURAL' AND 'PHYSICAL'

In this section, I want to make some general preliminary remarks about the meanings of the terms 'physical' and 'natural'. Let us begin with the term 'physical'.[16]

It is sometimes supposed that a general term is physical (that is, that it picks out a physical state or property or kind) just in case it occurs in some true theory of physics. This is evidently too narrow a definition, however; for terms like 'acid', 'alkali', and 'DNA' lie outside the domain of physics and yet they would normally be classified as physical. Perhaps we should say, then, that a general term is physical just in case it occurs in some true theory of physics, chemistry, molecular biology, or neurophysiology. But it is far from clear that this is a satisfactory way to characterize the physical. If 'gene' and 'neuron' are now classified as physical terms, then why not go further and classify 'tse-tse fly', 'crocodile', 'continent', and 'planet' (terms found in entomology, zoology, geology, and astronomy respectively) as physical too? The general problem here, of course, is that we have not been provided with any account of what physics, chemistry, molecular biology, and neurophysiology share in virtue of which they count as physical and the other sciences mentioned above do not.[17]

One way of avoiding this problem is to say that a general term is physical just in case it occurs in some true theory adequate for the explanation of the phenomena of nonliving matter. But there remain serious difficulties even here. Suppose that there are properties that are tokened only in the brains of certain living creatures, and that these properties figure in neurophysiological laws. It seems to me ad hoc to deny that such properties are physical.[18] Yet this is what we must do according to the final definition.

How, then, is the term 'physical' to be understood? If this question is taken to demand a fixed list of necessary and sufficient conditions for the application of 'physical', as it is ordinarily used, then I very much doubt that it has an answer. Necessary and sufficient conditions are hard to come by for any terms, let alone at this level of abstraction. Perhaps the best we can say is something like this: Physics is the paradigm or prototype for the physical sciences. A given science counts as physical, then, so long as it is sufficiently similar to physics, and a given term counts as physical so long as it occurs in a physical science. The notion of sufficient similarity at work here is vague and multi-dimensional. Thus, conflicts may arise about whether to count a given term as physical because different competent users of 'physical' may rely tacitly on different dimensions of similarity. I turn now to the term 'natural'.

There have been any number of different ways of understanding the term 'natural'. So, different philosophers have had very different conceptions of what it is to be a naturalist about a given domain, for example, the mental. The intuitive idea, I suggest, is simply that, on the naturalist view, the world contains nothing supernatural, that, at the bottom level, there are microphysical phenomena, governed by the laws of microphysics, and, at higher levels, phenomena that not only participate in causal interactions describable in scientific laws but also bear the same general ontic relationship to microphysical items as do the entities quantified over and referred to such higher-level laws as those which obtain in, for example, geology and neurophysiology. I want next to say something about what I take this relationship to be.

Consider Mount Everest. Suppose that t is one of the chunks of matter Everest would have lost had certain bombs been detonated at its top. Suppose also that the bombs are not in fact detonated. Then it is true that Everest might have existed without t. But the same is not true of the mereological sum of Everest's parts. Hence, Everest and the sum differ in a modal property. Hence,

Everest is not strictly identical with this sum. Rather, Everest is *constituted* by it. What is true here for Everest is true for other geological objects. A glacier, for example, is constituted by a massive chunk of ice. Indeed the same is true for higher-level natural objects and events generally. Each horse is constituted by a torso, four legs, a head, a tail. Each horse leg is constituted by a thigh, a calf, a hoof. Likewise, a predator's eating its prey is constituted by an action of chewing and swallowing. Each action of chewing is constituted by certain movements of the jaw, and each action of swallowing by certain movements in the throat. In all of these cases, modal considerations show that there is no strict identity.[19]

If higher-level tokens are viewed in this way, then it must be granted that each such token may vary in its constitution in different possible worlds. Something similar to this is true of higher-level types, I believe, if the naturalist perspective is adopted. Let me explain.

In general, higher-level natural types are not identical with lower-level ones. There are no types from chemistry and physics, for example, with which being a planet, being a continent, being an earthquake may plausibly be identified. Likewise, there is no single biochemical property with which the property of aging (in the sense of wear and tear) is identical. Plants and animals all age, and in aging their biochemical properties change. But there is no *shared* biochemical process which always goes along with aging. Similarly, gene types are not identical with chunks of DNA, contrary to what many philosophers have supposed. One and the same gene can be associated with different chunks of DNA. Moreover, some chunks of DNA redundantly repeat others within a single organism.[20]

The general relationship which obtains between higher-level and lower-level natural properties is one of *realization*. Higher-level properties typically have multiple lower-level realizations. Temperature, for example, is realized by mean molecular kinetic energy in a gas and by the blackbody distribution of electromagnetic waves in a vacuum.

Now, the realization relation is at least in part one of upward determination: the lower-level property, P, synchronically fixes the higher-level property, Q, so that the tokening of P at any time t by any object O necessitates the tokening of Q at t by O but not conversely. What sort of necessity is involved here? For natural properties, it is sometimes supposed that if P realizes Q, in all metaphysically possible worlds (even ones without our basic microphysical laws and facts), every instance of P is an instance of Q. However, it seems to me more plausible to assume something weaker, namely that, for properties in nature, in all possible worlds *sharing* our microphysical laws and facts, every instance of P is an instance of Q.

A second aspect to realization is that, again where natural properties are concerned, the determination of the higher-level property by the lower-level one is always mediated by a mechanism (or so it seems highly reasonable to suppose). I shall return to this point later.

The parallel between types and tokens on the above conception of naturalism should now be clear: higher-level types may be realized by more than one lower-level type within the actual world; higher-level tokens may be constituted by different lower-level tokens but only in different possible worlds.

We are now in a position to summarize how naturalistic phenomena in the actual world lying outside the microphysical realm are conceived within the above account:

> Higher-level naturalistic phenomena (both token and type) participate in causal interactions which fall under scientific laws, and are either ultimately constituted by, or ultimately realized by, microphysical phenomena.

The term 'ultimately' appears here, since, on the naturalist perspective, there is a hierarchy of constitution and realization relationships between higher-level and lower-level natural types which has as its foundation the microphysical realm.

So much by way of preliminary clarification. Let us return to Brentano's Problem.

III. HOW TO DISSOLVE BRENTANO'S PROBLEM

As I remarked earlier, Brentano's Problem is presented as a challenge to the naturalist. The challenge is to produce an acceptable explanation of how a physical system can undergo intentional states, that is, an explanation which either takes the form of reductive necessary and sufficient conditions (specifying the essences of intentional states in natural non-intentional terms) or else which consists of reductive sufficient conditions which are discoverable through armchair reflection alone.

Any naturalist who takes up the challenge and elaborates a reductive explanation of one of the desired sorts is thereby presenting a solution or putative solution to the problem. Any naturalist who declines the challenge and who attacks the presupposition that naturalism about intentionality requires that we articulate such an explanation is thereby dissolving or trying to dissolve the problem. The latter strategy is the one I favor: It aims to show that the problem is not real. This strategy, if it works, has all the advantages of theft over honest toil. For the constructive approach now becomes unnecessary as far as the defense of naturalism goes. So, in the present context, the attempt to solve Brentano's Problem should be eliminated. This is an application of the indolent philosopher's razor: Philosophical labor is not to be multiplied beyond necessity. Let us examine carefully, then, the negative or destructive approach.

The conception of naturalism sketched in the last section is consonant with our intuitive, pre-theoretical understanding of nature and the natural world. Given this conception, there is, I believe, a simple, but intuitively highly plausible, argument for the conclusion that intentional states are naturalistic. Here is the argument.

Some laws in science are basic and others are non-basic. This distinction can be drawn in a number of different ways, but it seems to me that one way in which our special science laws are non-basic is epistemic. An epistemically basic law is one for which there is no further explanation of *why* it obtains or *how* tokens of the property expressed in its antecedent cause tokens of the property expressed in its consequent. For the special sciences, as we normally conceive of them, it is never just a brute fact that the phenomena they study interact as their laws say: there is always some mechanism, or so we assume, which mediates or implements the transactions described in the laws, thereby explaining how those transactions take place. Consider, for example, the neurophysiological law that when a neuron reaches action potential, it fires.[21] The mechanism implementing this transaction is chemical. As positively charged sodium ions flow into the neuron from some prior stimulus, the negative electrical charge inside the neuron diminishes. Action potential is achieved at the base of the neuron at a certain threshold of depolarization. Once this threshhold is crossed, certain gates in the adjoining region of the post-synaptic neuron open, allowing further charged sodium ions to flow through. This process of gate opening and ion flow is repeated, region by region, in a chain reaction all the way down the axon, thereby generating an electrical impulse. When the process of conduction reaches the end of the axon, it causes the neuron to fire via the release, into the synaptic gap, of molecules of a neurotransmitter (one of several different chemicals), which have been stored in synaptic vesicles.

So, special science laws are implemented by lower-level mechanisms. Of course, these mechanisms will themselves be governed by the appropriate laws, and these laws, in turn, if they are special science laws, will require their own mechanisms. It follows that the epistemically basic laws lie outside the special sciences.[22] Where in particular? I suggest that the most reasonable view is that the epistemically basic laws are only to be found at the microphysical level.

So, we have the following premise:

(1) Our special science laws are ultimately implemented by microphysical mechanisms (the implementation being mediated by higher-level mechanisms which are governed by laws appropriate to their level).

But now if special science laws are ultimately implemented by microphysical mechanisms, it must certainly be true that the properties which their antecedents and consequents project themselves figure in bridge laws which connect them with the microphysical realm. At a minimum, these laws will be of the form: For any object x, if x has microphysical property P then x also has special science property S.[23] So (1) licenses

(2) For any property S projected in a special science law, there is an upward directed bridge law, the consequent of which projects S and the antecedent a microphysical property.

And once we appreciate that (1) requires (2), we may also draw out of (1) the following:

> (3) Bridge laws linking special science properties with microphysical properties are implemented by microphysical mechanisms.

One objection which might be raised at this stage is that premise (1) is now revealed as too strong, since (3) demands that the bridge laws themselves are epistemically non-basic, and this is not obviously true. Why not suppose that the bridge laws, like the microphysical laws, have no further explanations so that there are no implementing mechanisms?

I grant that this is a possibility. But it does not seem to me at all plausible. For there is an important difference between the bridge laws and the laws of microphysics which itself demands explanation, namely that the latter but not the former are *metaphysically* non-basic. This point deserves further elaboration.

It is widely accepted that once the microphysical laws are fixed and all the particular microphysical facts are in place, *all* the other laws are fixed too, including the bridge laws. As Jaegwon Kim puts it:

> we seem to share the conviction that . . . if God were to create a world, all he needs to do is to create the basic particles, their configurations, and the laws that are to govern the behavior of these basic entities. He need not *also* create tables and trees and refrigerators; once the micro-world is fixed, the rest will take care of itself.[24]

According to this intuitively very plausible view, there simply is no other possible world with all the same microphysical particles as the actual world, interacting in exactly the same ways according to the same microphysical laws, and yet having (via different bridge laws) different special science features—different ways of forming glaciers, different plant behavior, different combinations of genes, and so on.[25] The bridge laws, then, are not like the microphysical laws from a metaphysical perspective: they are derivative in a way that the microphysical laws are not. This disanalogy suggests that it cannot just be a brute epistemic fact that the bridge laws obtain, just as it is for the microphysical laws. Surely, there must be *some* explanation of how they are metaphysically determined.[26]

So, (3) is, I suggest, very reasonable. Given (3), together with my earlier comments on realization, we may conclude

> (4) Our special science laws project properties which are ultimately realized by microphysical properties.

Now cognitive psychology is, of course, one of the special sciences. Moreover, the causal interactions of intentional states lie in the domain of cognitive psychology. So, there are special science laws that advert to intentional content (for example, the law that believing that P and Q brings about believing that P, *ceteris paribus*, or the law that if people are asked questions about properties or aspects of things they have seen, and they have not thought about those properties or aspects much, then, *ceteris paribus*, they form images of the things before answering). We may add, then, the following premise:

(5) The intentional aspects of mental states figure in causal transactions that fall under special science laws.

From (4) and (5), along with the conception of naturalism sketched in the last section, we may infer

(6) Intentional states are naturalistic phenomena.

It follows that intentional states are *already* naturalistic, whether or not we manage to formulate appropriate defensible reductive analyses or *a priori* sufficient conditions for a state to have an intentional content. If such conditions are not forthcoming—and given the miserable history of philosophical attempts to produce reductive analyses which survive counterexamples, the prospects for successful *analyses* in the future are certainly not good—then, *that* is no more reason to deny that intentional state types are natural than it would be to deny that geological or seismological or palaeontological state types are natural in the face of corresponding failures at type reductions in those domains. Naturalism, on any plausible version of its commitments, simply does not require that we successfully articulate conceptual analyses or conceptually sufficient conditions or type identities.[27] So, there is really no point in trying to develop reductive theories of intentionality of these sorts, *if* our aim is simply to defend naturalism with respect to intentionality.

Note that I am not claiming here that intentional state types are unequivocally physical. These types, in my view, are certainly natural, and their tokens are certainly physical. But whether we count intentional types as physical depends upon whether we classify cognitive psychology as a physical science. Given my comments earlier, this is a matter which could be debated. After all, it certainly seems reasonable to count some special sciences as physical, for example, geology. However, I am inclined to hold that cognitive psychology is not a physical science, and that intentional state types are not physical.

Perhaps it will be objected that if we fail to explain, in non-intentional terms, how a physical system could have intentional states, then that failure itself undermines the claim that intentional properties are realized by non-intentional properties and hence upon the naturalist's position. For realization, as I have stressed, has an explanatory dimension.

This misses the point. While it is true that the realization of intentional properties by microphysical properties requires that there be an explanation, via intervening mechanisms, which links the two sorts of properties together, there is no *requirement* that this explanation be one which we will ever successfully formulate. Knowing *that* there is such an explanation is one thing, and this we do know, I claim, since we know, on the basis of the considerations adduced above, that intentional states are natural. Knowing *what* is the explanation is something quite different. Perhaps we will never know the real explanation. Perhaps we will destroy ourselves before we have the answer. Or perhaps the explanation is one which it is simply beyond our power to comprehend.[28]

With respect to the formulation of such an explanation, we *might* be in the same predicament as rats asked to find their way out of certain sorts of mazes or chimpanzees asked to identify correctly in a variety of cases which of three presented objects of varying magnitude is intermediate in size. Completion of the task might be beyond our cognitive capacities.

This suggestion may strike some philosophers as very strange. But if other creatures in nature can lack the capacity to understand some of the things we understand, we too surely, as products of nature ourselves, might not have the power to understand everything. In terms Colin McGinn has used, for each state with intentional content, it *could* be the case that there is an explanation which is *cognitively closed* to us of precisely how it is physically generated.[29] If this is so, then God knows wherein the answer lies, but for *us* the matter must remain an impenetrable puzzle. In the spirit of J. B. S. Haldane who is reported to have remarked: "The universe may not only be queerer than we suppose, it may also be queerer than we can suppose," we might say likewise: "Intentionality may not only be queerer than we suppose, it may also be queerer than we can suppose." In a sense, however, this comment is misleading. For on the above proposal, there is in the world itself no deep mystery, unfathomable even to a superbeing, about how intentionality is produced. There is no magic, no miracle involved. We are ourselves simply so constituted that we cannot grasp the explanation here.

Another objection which might be raised is that, without some further substantive account of the nature of ordinary intentional properties (for example, believing that there are black swans in Australia), the possibility that these properties involve intentional relations to Fregean propositions has not been ruled out. And Fregean propositions, as denizens of the world of sense, are certainly inimical to the naturalists' position.

I certainly accept that Fregean propositions are not themselves naturalistic items. This is the result delivered by my earlier comments on natural phenomena, since Fregean propositions are abstract entities which neither stand in causal relations nor are realized by microphysical phenomena. But it does not follow from this that intentional states and properties are not natural. To suppose otherwise is to commit a fallacy of composition along the following lines: the proposition that the leaves are falling is non-natural; this proposition enters into, or is a part of, the state of thinking that the leaves are falling. Therefore, thinking that the leaves are falling is not natural. So, naturalism with respect to intentional states is not *directly* threatened by the admission that these states take Fregean propositions as their contents.

Perhaps it will now be said that no state which contained a non-natural object as a part, indeed which involved a relation between a person and an abstract object that lacked any causal powers, could itself be natural. But why not? I am 74 inches in height, my temperature is normally 98.6 degrees Fahrenheit, my weight 160 pounds. Surely, it is a mistake to deny that the properties I have here are naturalistic.[30] These properties involve relations between persons and numbers, namely height in inches, temperature in degrees

Fahrenheit, and weight in pounds. And numbers intuitively are abstract entities without causal powers.

Moreover, even if it could be shown that the introduction of Fregean propositions *cannot* be reconciled with the thesis that intentionality is a natural phenomenon, this still would not threaten the thesis, even if no alternative proposal were forthcoming. For, I claim, we already know enough to know that intentionality is naturalistic, whether or not we can supply a further substantive account. So, what we should conclude in these circumstances is that intentional states do *not* involve relations to Fregean propositions.

There is a sense, then, in which the Problem of Intentionality, in its usual form, is a pseudo-problem. For it *demands* that the naturalist about intentionality produce a constructive account of how a physical system could undergo intentional states. Failure to meet this demand is seen as threatening the naturalist position. But, in reality, it does no such thing. The demand is misplaced. No constructive theory is needed to secure naturalism.

IV. INTENTIONALITY: WHERE THE REAL PUZZLES LIE

Suppose it is granted that intentional states are naturalistic. The physical states realizing them, for example, neural and environmental states, are not intentional. How is it that items which are realized by non-intentional items can be intentional? How can states in the brain mentally 'reach out' to specific objects in the world or be directed upon objects which do not exist? What is it about the neural nets in our heads, and their connection with the outside world, which is responsible for the production of states with an intentional character? These questions ask for a specification of the *mechanism* which underlies the generation of intentionality by non-intentional items in nature, and which closes the explanatory gap we feel intuitively between the two realms. I shall call the puzzle here "The Problem of the Mechanism of Intentionality."

One response which could be made to this puzzle is simply to deny that there is *any* mechanism which provides a link between the intentional and the non-intentional. On this view, it is simply a brute fact that certain non-intentional states, for example, such-and-such brain states standing in so-and-so causal relations to objects and properties in the environment, generate certain intentional states. The non-intentional states do not analyze the intentional ones. Nor is there any conceptual link between the two. Indeed, there is no explanation or further account of *how* the former give rise to the latter.

This position effectively assumes that there are epistemically basic bridge laws which link intentional states with lower-level non-intentional states. As I argued in the last section, such a position seems implausible. There is also at least one other reason, grounded in some well-established cases of realization, for thinking that there is an implementing mechanism.

Consider the realization of temperature in a gas or elasticity in a rubber band or brittleness in a thin glass sheet or liquidity in water or digestion in a human being. In each of these cases, there is a mechanism which explains how the higher-level natural property or process is generated from the lower-level one. In the case of liquidity, for example, once we appreciate that liquidity is a disposition, namely the disposition to pour easily, and we are told that in liquid water the H_2O molecules are free to slide past one another instead of being trapped in fixed locations, we have no difficulty in seeing how liquidity is generated from the underlying molecular properties. There is no explanatory gap.

A similar account is available in the case of brittleness. Like liquidity, brittleness is a disposition. Brittle objects are disposed to shatter easily. This disposition is produced in a thin glass sheet via the irregular alignment of crystals. Such an alignment results in there being weak forces between crystals holding them together. So, when a force is applied, the glass shatters. The generation of brittleness is now explained. Elasticity, and its production, can be understood in a parallel way.[31]

Digestion is a process whose function is to change food into energy. So, digestion is a functionally characterized process. It follows that digestion takes place in a given organism via any set of internal changes which performs the relevant function for that organism. In this way, digestion is realized in the organism. In human beings, for example, digestion is realized chiefly by the action of certain enzymes secreted into the alimentary canal. These enzymes cause the food to become absorbable and hence available as energy by dissolving it and breaking it down into simpler chemical compounds. Once one grasps these facts, there is no deep mystery about how digestion is generated. A structurally similar story can be told for temperature.

These cases strongly suggest that in the natural world the production of higher-level types by lower-level types is grounded in mechanisms which *explain* the generation of the higher-level types.[32] What, then, is the mechanism which provides the explanatory link between the intentional and the non-intentional? And how exactly are we to conceive of its operation? Let us take up the second question first.

Consider the case of hardness in a diamond. Hardness is a constitutional-dispositional property: something is hard just in case it is so constituted that it is disposed to resist penetration. This disposition is realized in diamonds by a certain crystalline structure in which the arrangement of crystals maximizes inter-crystal forces. Given such an arrangement, the crystals are very difficult to split apart and diamonds, therefore, resist penetration.

In this case, we understand the mechanism by which hardness is generated as operating in accordance with the following model: the higher-level property has a certain essence. This essence is of the sort: having a property that disposes its possessor to F. Given that as a matter of nomological necessity, the lower-level property disposes its possessor to F, it follows that once any individual has the lower-level property, it necessarily has *a* property that disposes its possessor to F and hence it necessarily has the higher-level one. Of course, the law appealed to here, namely that objects having the lower-level property are disposed to F itself demands explanation, if it is not microphysical. And further mechanisms and still lower-level laws will be relevant to *this* explanation.

This model provides an explanatory structure in terms of which the generation of hardness in diamonds can be understood. It should be noted, however, that it is not crucial to our understanding of how hardness is generated that hardness be taken to have the specified essence. For suppose that it is merely sufficient for an object to be hard in certain circumstances that it be so constituted that it is disposed to resist penetration in those circumstances. So long as this connection is a *conceptual* one, that is, one which we can see to obtain by reflecting on our concept of hardness, the explanation goes through in a parallel manner.

Likewise, if the higher-level property has a functional essence then a similar account can be given. Here the higher-level property is of the general type: having a property that plays functional role R in conditions C. So, the lower-level property determines the higher-level property in a corresponding manner to the dispositional case. The same is true, if the higher-level property has a functional sufficient condition which we can discover by conceptual reflection.

Now if the property of having some intentional content has a functional or dispositional essence or there are conceptually sufficient conditions of the same general sort for the tokening of this property, then the operation of the mechanism of intentionality is easily intelligible. But if it operates in some other way then, I suggest, we currently have no clear conception of what that operation might be. Of course, no one can eliminate *a priori* the possibility of a large-scale conceptual revolution that yielded new models that could be applied here. This abstract possibility is no help to us, however, in finding an actual solution to the Problem of the Mechanism of Intentionality.

It appears, then, that for us to solve the problem we should try to elaborate a reductive explanation of one of the types presented above. So, while it is not necessary for us to elaborate philosophical theories of intentionality of the sort I discussed in Section I in order to hold on to the view that intentionality is naturalistic, we do appear to need such theories in connection with the Problem of Mechanism.

I am not at all convinced that we will succeed in discovering a detailed essence for the property of having some intentional content by *a priori* philosophical reflection alone. After all, as I noted earlier, the history of philosophy is full of failed reductive analyses. Indeed there is not a single full-fledged reductive analysis which is generally accepted. So, why suppose that this case will be any different?[33] I am also not overly optimistic that a combination of scientific investigation and philosophical reflection will provide us with a fully articulated specification of the relevant essence. One worry here is that the accounts we develop will yield only (*a posteriori*) sufficient conditions, and not necessary *and* sufficient ones.

But do we really need to elaborate fully the essence of the property of having some intentional content in order to solve the Problem of the Mechanism of Intentionality? It is not clear that we do. For we may well be able to give some general argument which demonstrates that intentionality has *a* functional essence, for example, even though this essence is one which we will never be in a position to spell out in minute detail. If this is the case, then we will know enough about intentionality to understand the mechanism of its generation.

An alternative possibility is that we will succeed in finding a conceptually sufficient condition of the right sort. In general, conceptually sufficient conditions are easier to come by than analyses (since such conditions need not be necessary). Moreover, the idea that there is a conceptually sufficient condition here can be accommodated by recent work in cognitive psychology on categorization and concept possession which reveals that many concepts have very fuzzy boundaries. If, for example, the relevant concept has a prototype structure, then although none of the individual features of its prototypical instances is either necessary or sufficient for application of the concept, still, the conjunction of these features *is* sufficient. So, for prototype concepts, there is a conceptually sufficient condition.

As I noted earlier, the assumption that there is such a condition is one which Fodor accepts in his recent work on the Problem of Intentionality. This, I have suggested, is misguided. But it is, in my view, a reasonable hypothesis in connection with the Problem of the Mechanism of Intentionality.

So, there is certainly room to doubt that we will manage to solve the Problem of the Mechanism of Intentionality. But there is also room for hope. Unlike the original Problem of Intentionality, this problem is, I believe, a genuine one. If we fail to solve it, the conclusion I draw is that the property of having an intentional content is realized by lower-level non-intentional properties in a way that we do not properly comprehend. And if this is the case, it will not follow that there is no mechanism, only that we have failed to grasp what it is.

There is another related problem which deserves mention here, and which seems to me less difficult. I call this problem "the Problem of the Mechanism of Variations in Intentional Content" or "*PVC*" for short. What is it about the brain, and its location in the world, which is responsible for the production of variations in the intentional contents of particular intentional states, given that they have some intentional content or other in the first place?[34] Consider, for example, the *difference* between my mentally representing that snow is white and my mentally representing that grass is green. What is it about my brain, and its connection with the world, which is responsible for this difference? What is the mechanism which underlies it?

In trying to provide a solution to *PVC*, we are not attempting to explain how the phenomenon of mental 'directedness' is generated from the non-intentional facts. Instead, we are concerned with the more limited question of how *variations* in content arise in particular cases or ranges of cases.

One reasonable strategy to adopt here is that of trying to uncover a condition which we can see is sufficient (without also being necessary) for the differences in content in a certain range of cases, simply by reflecting upon our ordinary concepts of the contentful states in those cases. So, for example, one suggestion worth working out further is that it is causal covariation with different states of affairs, under normal conditions, which is conceptually sufficient for differences in the intentional contents of perceptual intentional states.[35] Another proposal deserving more amplification is that differences in teleofunctional roles of the type, bringing it about that P, are conceptually sufficient for differences in content in desires.[36]

I shall not attempt to adjudicate between these proposals here. My aim has been simply to lay out what are, I think, two genuine puzzles about intentionality, and to make some brief remarks on the prospects for success in solving them. These puzzles are not the only ones which should concern us, I might add. For there are other facts about intentional states which call for explanation. In particular, there is the systematicity and productivity of these states.[37] And there is also the way in which many causal interactions between intentional states seem characterizable in terms of logical inferences.[38] It is in this context, I suggest, that the hypothesis that there is a language of thought finds its primary home (and, in my view, explains the data remarkably well).[39]

So, there is much for philosophers to reflect on in connection with intentionality. And there is much which is not yet well understood. But Brentano's Problem—the classic Problem of Intentionality—can safely be ignored.[40]

NOTES

1. Franz Brentano, *Psychology from an Empirical Standpoint*, translated by A. Pancurello, D. Terrell, and L. McAllister (New York, 1973). Originally published in 1874.

2. Ibid., 88.

3. Alexius Meinong, "The Theory of Objects," reprinted in *Realism and the Background of Phenomenology*, edited by R. Chisholm (Glencoe, Ill., 1960). Originally published in 1904.

4. Indeed, the assertion that there are objects which do not exist is a contradiction if expressed in first-order quantification theory, its formalization being "$(\exists x)\sim(\exists y)$ $(x = y)$." One might, of course, deny that the assertion can be so expressed. But then the onus is upon one to spell out further just what is being asserted.

5. In my view, appearances are deceptive here, at least in the case of pain. See my "Do Pains Have Representational Content?" in *Philosophy and the Cognitive Sciences*, edited by B. Smith and R. Casati (Vienna, 1994). Also my "Does Pain Lie within the Domain of Cognitive Psychology?" in *Philosophical Perspectives, 9, AI, Connectionism and Philosophical Psychology*, edited by J. Tomberlin (Atascadero, Calif., forthcoming 1995).

6. Robert Stalnaker, *Inquiry* (Cambridge, Mass., 1984), 6.

7. Jerry Fodor, "Semantics, Wisconsin Style," reprinted in *A Theory of Content and Other Essays* (Cambridge, Mass., 1990), 32. Originally published in *Synthese* 59 (1984): 231–50.

8. Jerry Fodor, *Psychosemantics* (Cambridge, Mass., 1987), 97.

9. Fodor, "Semantics, Wisconsin Style," 32.

10. See, for example, D. Stampe, "Towards a Causal Theory of Linguistic Representation," in *Midwest Studies in Philosophy* 2 (1977); R. Stalnaker, *Inquiry*; F. Dretske, *Explaining Behavior* (Cambridge, Mass., 1988).

11. See, e.g., D. Dennett, *Content and Consciousness* (London, 1969); H. Field, "Mental Representation," reprinted in *Readings in the Philosophy of Psychology*, Volume 2, edited by N. Block (Cambridge, Mass., 1981); G. Harman, *Thought* (Princeton, N.J., 1973); also Harman, "Wide Functionalism," in *The Representation of Knowledge and Belief*, edited by R. Harnish and M. Brand (Tucson, 1986); R. Millikan, *Language, Thought, and Other Biological Categories* (Cambridge, Mass., 1984).

12. For an opposing view here, see W. Lycan, *Judgement and Justification* (Cambridge, 1988).

13. Fodor, *Psychosemantics*, 98.

14. J. Fodor, "A Theory of Content I," in *A Theory of Content and Other Essays*, 52.

15. J. Fodor, "A Theory of Content II," in ibid. 96.

16. This section draws heavily upon my "Naturalism and the Mental," *Mind* 101 (1992): 421–41.

17. This problem is discussed by Carl Hempel in his "Ontological and Linguistic Facts," in *Essays in Honor of Ernest Nagel*, edited by S. Morgenbesser, P. Suppes, and M. White (New York, 1970).

18. Compare Ned Block, "Introduction: What Is Functionalism?" in *Readings in the Philosophy of Psychology*, Volume 1, edited by N. Block (Cambridge, Mass., 1981), 296.

19. For more on constitution, see Richard Boyd, "Materialism without Reductionism: What Physicalism Does Not Entail," in *Readings in the Philosophy of Psychology*, Volume 1.

20. See here Kim Sterelny, *The Representational Theory of Mind* (Oxford, 1990), 203–206.

21. This law is, of course, *ceteris paribus* (as are special science laws generally).

22. I am indebted here to Jerry Fodor's discussion of special science laws in his "Making Mind Matter More" in his *A Theory of Content and Other Essays*, 144-46.

23. I assume here that the relevant microphysical property of x can be of the form: being constituted by microphysical entities having such and such microphysical features.

24. Jaegwon Kim, "Causality, Identity, and Supervenience in the Mind-Body Problem," in *Midwest Studies in Philosophy* 4 (1979): 40.

25. There are certain complications here. Perhaps it is possible that there is a world just like ours microphysically, but in which some further non-physical ectoplasms are to be found with their own biological properties, so that the biological laws there are not identical with ours. This complication is discussed by Terry Horgan. See his "Supervenience and Cosmic Hermeneutics," in *Southern Journal of Philosophy*, Spindel Supplement on Supervenience, 19–38. For present purposes, it suffices to stipulate that the only possible worlds which should be considered are those like ours microphysically *and* not having such extra 'alien' entities. A qualification of this sort is also needed in the previous sentence of the text.

26. Another reason for thinking that the bridge laws are metaphysically determined in the way I have described is that if they are not, then it becomes very hard to see how higher-level properties can be causally relevant, given the plausible hypothesis that for any particular causal sequence, there is a complete microphysical explanation of how the one event in the sequence causes the other.

27. Another philosopher who shares this view, and who has independently argued for it recently is Stephen Stich. See his "What is a Theory of Mental Representation?" *Mind* 101 (1992): 243–63. See also Stich and S. Lawrence, "Intentionality and Naturalism," this volume.

28. This could happen in two ways: the explanation might be too complex for us to comprehend fully or it might bring in new concepts of a sort we cannot grasp. I should stress here that I am *not* claiming that the explanation actually is of one of these sorts.

29. For more on cognitive closure, see Colin McGinn, *The Problem of Consciousness* (Oxford, 1991), essays 1 and 2. McGinn holds that we actually are cognitively closed to the property which explains intentionality and also to the property which explains phenomenal consciousness.

30. The analogy between numbers and propositions has been made by several philosophers. See, e.g., Paul Churchland, *Scientific Realism and the Plasticity of Mind* (Cambridge, 1979); Dan Dennett, "Beyond Belief," in *Thought and Object*, edited by A. Woodfield (Oxford, 1982), 1–85; Stalnaker, *Inquiry*.

31. For the details here, see my "Blindsight, the Absent Qualia Hypothesis, and the Mystery of Consciousness," forthcoming in *Philosophy and the Cognitive Sciences*, edited by C. Hookway (Cambridge).

32. Although I cannot pursue the matter in the present essay, I think that the constitution of higher-level tokens by lower-level ones also requires explanation and that implementing mechanisms are needed here.

33. The idea that concepts generally have *a priori* discoverable necessary and sufficient conditions also runs counter to recent work on categorization and concept possession in cognitive psychology. See here Eleanor Rosch, "Cognitive Representations of Semantic Categories," *Journal of Experimental Psychology: General*, 192–233; also E. Smith and D. Medin, *Concepts and Categories*, (Cambridge, Mass., 1981).

34. This problem is discussed by Colin McGinn in his " Consciousness and Content," in *The Problem of Consciousness*.

35. I should note that I myself reject this view at least for perceptual states across the board, since I hold that perceptual seemings have narrow contents. See here my "Qualia, Content, and the Inverted Spectrum," *Nous* forthcoming.

36. See here Millikan, *Language, Thought, and Other Biological Categories*.

37. For elucidations of systematicity and productivity, see Jerry Fodor and Zenon Pylyshyn, "Connectionism and Cognitive Architecture: A Critical Analysis," *Cognition* 28 (1988): 3–71.

38. See ibid.

39. See ibid. For a general discussion of the language of thought, see Jerry Fodor, *The Language of Thought* (New York, 1975).

40. I would like to thank Jerry Vision for helpful comments on an earlier version of this essay.

Emotions and Ethical Knowledge:
Some Naturalistic Connections

MICHAEL STOCKER

That something has the power to evoke favor on a true comprehension of what it is like [and is thus good] would depend partly on what it is like and partly on the affectivity of those who experience it or contemplate it for what it is like. . . . Nothing could conceivably have value except for those who can love or hate.[1]

So writes W. D. Falk, showing, among other things, that one need not be an emotivist to hold that there are important connections between emotions and value. The question for this volume should be, If there are such connections, are they naturalistic? To make the inquiry more manageable, however, I will restrict the essay to exploring some epistemological connections between emotions and value, which are at least largely naturalistic. Although these connections are naturalistic, or at least largely so, rather than entailment or conceptual ones, they are important. They are among the typical and important, deep and systematic, connections between evaluative judgments and having or lacking emotions.

It must be stressed that I am concerned to show that the connections, not what they connect, are at least largely naturalistic, as well as typical, important, deep, and systematic. In particular I am not concerned with the question of whether what they connect—emotions with value, evaluative knowledge, and evaluative judgments—do or do not admit of a naturalistic account.

It is a commonplace that certain emotions put us in a bad position to conduct inquiries and make sound decisions and judgments. This is part and parcel of, if not the ground for, the view that cool rationality is the best standpoint or state for all sorts of inquiry and knowledge, including evaluative inquiry and knowledge. What I want to do is call this view into question, by arguing that having certain emotions is often systematically connected with being epistemologically well placed to make good evaluative judgments, and more strongly that not having certain emotions is often systematically connected with being epistemologically ill placed to make good judgments. One way to put my claim is that hot judgments are, for quite systematic reasons, often better than cool ones.

Others have made this claim, of course. I take Aristotle as making it in the *Rhetoric*, e.g., when he argues that to secure an acquittal it is important to gain the jurors' friendliness towards a defendant, e.g., by convincing them of his good character. I do not take him as simply telling how jurors think, and thus how they can be led or misled. He is also reminding us that belief in another person and acceptance of what that person says is quite properly proportioned to how trustworthy we find that person. As Sartre notes in his discussion of bad faith, we are often epistemically lax in assessing views or people we like, and demanding in assessing views or people we dislike. We cannot judge on the basis of evidence without, somehow, assigning weight to the evidence. Proper assessments and decisions require proper epistemic demands, and thus proper trust and friendliness. So, if a witness or defendant is of good character, trust and its attendant friendliness are proper, and without proper trust and friendliness, a wrong decision is likely to be made.[2]

In many different ways, various contemporary philosophers have also argued that emotions are important for evaluation. There are, of course, the emotivists. As well, there are such anti-emotivists as W. D. Falk, Peter Strawson, Charles Taylor, Iris Murdoch, Larry Blum, Margaret Walker, Martha Nussbaum, and John McDowell.[3]

But rather than examine these positions, I now want to leave the confines of philosophy, to consider some claims made by various psychoanalysts. This is not an unmotivated choice on my part. For, of course, one of the central tenets of psychoanalysis is that there are systematic connections between emotions and epistemology, especially evaluative epistemology.[4]

Harry Guntrip and Joyce McDougall graphically describe two extreme ways of being affectless, and how each bears on epistemology, especially evaluative epistemology. Guntrip writes, "the ego of the schizoid person in consciousness and in the outer world is delibidinized and feels no interest in objects" (p. 30). And also,

> This state of emotional apathy, of not suffering any feeling, excitement or enthusiasm, not experiencing either affection or anger, can be very successfully masked. If feeling is repressed, it is often possible to build up a kind of mechanized, robot personality. The ego that operates consciously becomes more a system than a person, a trained and disciplined instrument for 'doing the right and necessary thing' without any real feeling entering in. Fairbairn made the highly important distinction between 'helping people without feeling' and 'love'. Duty rather than affection becomes the key word. (pp. 37–38)

And finally, "As a result of this lack of feeling, schizoid people can be cynical, callous, and cruel, having no sensitive appreciation of the way they hurt other people" [p. 44]. (The similarity between Guntrip and Falk is striking.)

Leading up to her discussion of *alexithymia*—literally, lacking words for emotions, and less literally, being unable to recognize one's emotions or that one is having emotions—McDougall writes,

> Freud came to refer to the *repression* of ideas and the *suppression* of affects. These metaphors suggest two quite different mental processes: ideas are said to be *pushed back* from consciousness and affects to be *squashed out* of the psyche.
>
> Where does affect go when it is rejected from the consciousness of the person in whom it has, if only momentarily, been mobilized? Freud provided a partial clue to the fate of unavailable affects. In *Studies on Hysteria* (Breuer and Freud 1895) as well as the papers on *Repression* (Freud 1915) and *The Unconscious* (1915), he speaks of the autonomous quality of affects and of their subsequent "transformations". The latter falls into three categories: the conversion of affects into hysterical symptoms; the displacement of an affect from its original representation onto another representation or set of representations, as in obsessional neurosis; and the transformation expressed in the actual neuroses, that is, anxiety neurosis, neurasthenia, and hypochondria.
>
> . . . It appears to me that we might also posit other transformations of the vicissitudes of affective experience. Certain people are capable of disavowing their affective experience, or segments of it, in such a way that it is radically repudiated or foreclosed from consciousness. (pp. 152–53, original emphasis)

Of these last people, who are alexithymic, she writes, "Instead of mentally elaborating their emotional states, they tended to discharge their feelings . . . often in inappropriate ways: through disputes, ill-considered decisions, or a series of accidents" [p. 155]. And also, "It is evident . . . that an inability to capture and become aware of one's own emotional experience must be accompanied by an equally great difficulty in understanding other people's emotional states and wishes" [p. 160].

Suggesting a comparison between alexithymics and psychotics, including schizophrenics, she says

> This comparison may seem incongruous: few individuals appear more bizarre in public than those dominated by psychotic thought processes, while few seem so well adapted to external reality, and to comply so readily with what the world demands, as those who suffer from alexithymic . . . symptoms. The latter have created a *false self-adaptation* to others and this wall of pseudonormality enables them to face the world in spite of the grave inner distress concerning contact with others. (p. 167, original emphasis)

And also

> Psychotics attribute to others their overwhelming affective pain and intolerable anxiety and proceed to create a neoreality in order to make

continued existence tolerable and understandable. With the same aim in mind, alexithymics attack their psychological capacity to capture affect and use it for thought or as a signal to themselves. But instead of creating a neoreality, they simply drain external reality and object relationships of their meaning. (p. 168)

At these extremes of affective pathology, then, there are clear—and clearly disastrous—connections between affect and evaluative epistemology. This holds especially in regard to the values involved in the experiences and relations that these very unfortunate people find so difficult.

Let us now turn to neuroses and neurotic formations. The connections here may be less disastrous, but they are still clear and important. As Anna Freud's *The Ego and the Mechanisms of Defense* and David Shapiro's *Neurotic Styles* show, neuroses and neurotic formations have constitutive and typical forms of epistemic-evaluative distortion.

I will here only mention several very simple examples. First, a depressed man, suffused by feelings of not being good or lovable, for that reason consistently does not even notice, much less take stock of, the ways his marriage is all-in-all a source of suffering for both him and his wife; and, indeed, when asked, sincerely claims that he is happy and that generally, the marriage is going pretty well. Second, a man in a manic state who feels invulnerable, denies his need of money, and gives away a considerable part of his savings—or is certain that his judgment is accurate and risks a good part of his needed savings on an extremely speculative stock. Third, a woman who because of grandiosity feels responsible for the well-being of the entire family to such an extent that she sees herself to blame for all unhappinesses suffered by her children or that occur between family members. Fourth, a man who was beaten as a child now, identifying with the aggressor, thinks that physical violence is an entirely proper way to settle family problems, and that when his eight-year-old son is bad he is asking for a beating and that he should give him one. Fifth, a woman who was sexually abused as a child, and accepted her abuser's account that this was done to her because she was bad, now continues to think that she deserves whatever harm and ill fortune, including bad treatment from her husband, happen to her. Sixth, that somewhat paranoid person who often sees the world as completely beyond his control pictures himself as victim. We have already encountered other examples, and still others will be given below.

As well as suggesting deep connections between emotions and evaluative knowledge, the quotes from Guntrip and McDougall raise a very serious question about recent philosophy. By this latter, I mean the work of those many philosophers, such as Pitcher, Solomon, Neu, and Sartre, who characterize emotions simply in terms of their non-affective content.

What I am referring to is quickly brought out: In his 1965 *Mind* article "Emotions," George Pitcher explicitly denies that emotions require, or often even have, feelings—or sensations, as he calls physical or mental sensations or feelings. Giving an account of hope, Pitcher writes, "If P hopes that she will come today, he simply believes that she might come and considers that her coming would be a good thing. He may also experience one or more sensations, but he need not; and even if he does it is doubtful that they will be part of his *hope*" [p. 338, original emphasis]. In "Emotions and Choice" Robert Solomon claims that "My anger [at John for stealing my car] *is* my judgment that John has wronged me."[5] Jerome Neu makes a similar point about jealousy: "the lover of a patient of a psychoanalyst may always raise the questions: 'What is missing?', 'What is the analyst providing that I cannot?,' 'Are there things that my lover can say to her analyst that she cannot say to me?,' and so on." He then adds what is here of importance to us, "To imagine the elimination of jealousy is to imagine the elimination of the possibility of these questions, for these questions *are* jealousy."[6] In his *Sketch for a Theory of the Emotions*, Sartre, similarly but more extensively, characterizes emotions in terms of ways of seeing the world—e.g., as magical as opposed to causal.

As can easily be seen, these characterizations of emotions can be satisfied without affect or emotion. So, contra Solomon, I might see that John has wronged me by stealing my car but not be angry at him: perhaps because I take such wrongs with shame, not anger, or perhaps because I do not mind his having wronged me. For anger, affect, not simply judgment, is needed. If I do not have affect, I cannot be angry at John but, as William James said, I can at most make "some cold-blooded and dispassionate judicial sentence confined entirely to the intellectual realm, to the effect that some person or persons deserve chastisement for their sins."[7] In Pitcher's case, all that is needed is that P has the beliefs that she might come today and that this would be good. And these beliefs can be cool, non-engaged, mere reflective musings. They can be affectless and non-emotional. In short, they are not, nor do they add up to, hope. Similar objections apply to Neu and Sartre.[8]

What has led these and other philosophers to present as conceptually true of people and emotions what, in fact, seems characteristic of those who dissociate and intellectualize, or suffer from schizophrenia or alexithymia? There is a simple, but to my mind unsatisfying, answer to this. It is that Pitcher and other Wittgensteineans were opposed to treating emotions as mental entities, especially private mental entities. And Solomon and other Sartreans were opposed to treating affectivity as bodily, and wanted to treat it rather as having meaning.

I find this answer unsatisfying because it simply raises the same question once again, but now about feelings: What has led philosophers to so misunderstand feelings? Why has it been thought that unless feelings are understood just in terms of beliefs, desires, and values, they must be understood as private entities or as bodily? Perhaps this is simply a philosophical mistake, a failure of philosophical imagination.

Or perhaps, as I suspect, it is something else. At the least, it is in remarkable agreement with our philosophical mistrust of emotions and feelings. To repeat, this is a mistrust that goes so far as seeming to prefer trusting what is central to dissociation and intellectualization, and even alexithymic and schizoid phenomena, to trusting emotions.

This mistrust, we might note, is found not only in philosophy. It is found even in psychoanalysis—of all places. I am thinking here of the view of many early psychoanalysts that the analyst's emotional reaction to the analysand, countertransference, was an obstacle to and interfered with the analysis. It was held that these emotional reactions show only problems of the analyst—e.g., unresolved conflicts indicating that analyst's need of further analysis—rather than an accurate, informed, and informative reaction to the patient. The ideal analyst was seen as a blank screen and emotionally detached, not an emotionally engaged person.[9]

Indeed, if Nancy Chodorow is right, we may see both how and why contemporary philosophers' mistrust of emotions expresses a deep aspect of our culture. For she argues that in our culture the moral world of boys, and subsequently men, tends to be at once, and for the same reasons, lacking in affect and also abstract, categorical, and positional:

> For boys, identification processes and masculine role learning are not likely to be embedded in relationships with their fathers or men but rather to involve the denial of affective relationship to their mothers. These processes tend to be more role-defined and cultural, to consist in abstract or categorical role learning rather than in personal identification.[10]

And, "Men, moreover, do not define themselves in relationship and have come to suppress relational capacities and repress relational needs. This prepares them to participate in the affect-denying world of alienated work" (p. 207).

Chodorow raises many issues, such as the connections between relational —i.e., interpersonal—capacities and emotions; and also about the role and priority of these emotions. For even if men in our society are, typically, deficient in interpersonal emotions, they do not seem deficient in all emotional engagements, e.g., about sports and professional success.[11] But, for the moment, I will not pursue these issues. Nor will I discuss how easy it is to parody or mischaracterize—or what may be worse, correctly characterize—certain ethical views by showing how they seem to incorporate into their favored philosophical accounts of thought and feeling what seem to be intellectualizing, or dissociative, or alexithymic, or schizoid forms of thought and feeling. Rather, I want to turn to some common, everyday ways in which, as we all know all too well, features of our emotional life, especially our not having emotions, are intertwined with our being epistemologically ill placed to make good evaluative judgments. So, let us return to Pitcher's man P and his hoping or not hoping that the visitor will come.

We can start by looking at someone whose "having of the emotion" is correctly described by one of the above-mentioned affectless accounts of emotions—e.g., someone whose "hoping that she will come" is nothing more than believing that she might come and that it would be a good thing if she did. As Pitcher has it, "If P hopes that she will come today, he simply believes that she might come and considers that her coming would be a good thing. He may also experience one or more sensations, but he need not; and even if he does it is doubtful that they will be part of his *hope*."

As suggested earlier, because this characterization does not include affect, then even if we know that it is satisfied, we still do not know whether P hopes that she will come. Indeed, if the full, relevant description of P is given by "P thinks that she might come and that her coming would be a good thing" then, because P lacks affect, P does not hope that she will come. P's thinking that she might come and that this would be good need not move P to care whether or not she comes, nor be pleased by the thought of her coming—in short, need not move P to hope that she does.

These thoughts need not move P to hope that she will come if P is not concerned with her coming, e.g., because as P sees and feels matters, it is not his business whether she comes or not. Here we might imagine that P has been told by neighbors that someone might be coming to visit them and that this will be good. Why, unless moved by concern for them, must P hope that she does come? Why must he take up any attitude toward his neighbors, even on their behalf?

Let us add to the story and say explicitly that P is involved with the coming of this person, since she is coming to visit someone in his family. Even so, despite thinking that she might come and that it would be good if she does, he still might not hope she does. Explanations for this are readily available: P is physically or emotionally tired, perhaps worn out; P does not like her; P is ambivalent about her coming—although thinking it overall good if she comes, her coming fits poorly with what he would really like to do, spend time alone; he thinks it would be good for the family if she came, but would be "too much" for him; he is suffering from depression; he is bitter at the world; he has little heart for company now.

These are just some non-exclusive and non-exhaustive reasons why P, despite satisfying the proposition-like content account of hoping, does not hope she will come. I want now to show that if those reasons hold, then for systematic reasons, P may well be, and is likely to be, ill placed to make evaluations—e.g., about her coming.

One explanation, mentioned above, of P's not hoping that she will come is that P is only a nodding-acquaintance neighbor of the people she is coming to visit. And not being a party to a goings-on—e.g., simply being such a neighbor—typically involves not being well positioned to see various evaluatively important details. This can be easily seen if we consider the case where P, despite being only a neighbor, does hope that their visitor will come.

My case has it that P is told by his neighbors that a visitor may be coming to visit them, and that it would be good if she does. I will suppose that P does not merely say, sincerely and politely, "I do hope for your sake that she comes," "Well then, let us hope that she does come," or even "I do hope she comes." Rather, P has a hope that "puts" him right into that family—a hope by means of which he obtrudes into the family. This would be a hope such that if the visitor does not come, P, too, can sincerely say that what he had hoped for, too, did not come about; perhaps that his hopes were not satisfied, even that they were dashed.

Here we might compare the assumptions—perhaps the presumptuousness —of a man who says to a neighboring woman he knows only by sight, "You know, when I saw you go out last night with that person, I was afraid for you." A gentle, friendly reply might be "Thank you for caring about me." A somewhat less gentle reply, by way of reproof perhaps, might be "I didn't know you cared so much for me." In certain cases, the rebuffing and chastising, "Who are you to care for me, to occupy yourself with me, to judge me and my situation?" might also be completely justified.

Some hopings, then, suggest that P has obtruded himself into the affairs of his neighbors, and has concerned or engaged himself with a family that he has only a nodding acquaintance with. I would draw three conclusions from these cases. First, that P believes that a visitor might come and that it would be good if she did is not sufficient to guarantee that P hopes she comes. Second, this may be a good thing—since it may well be wrong for P to hope that she comes. Third, turning now to the explicitly epistemological, in particular to the epistemological state of P who hopes improperly: It does not seem simply harsh and moralistic to think that the way he obtrudes into others' affairs, without being actively involved with them, suggests a willingness to make judgments without knowing the facts.

Somewhat similar situations of improper care also arise in families and other close relations. So, spouses and other family members may be *enmeshed* with each other—i.e., boundaries between them are porous, each is too caught up in the life of the other, too involved and overly concerned with that person. That people are enmeshed—how enmeshment is constituted by particular sorts of moral concern, attention, and understanding—explains why and how they are typically epistemologically ill placed or ill equipped to make good evaluative judgments of their situations.[12]

Here, as above, my point—now about those who are enmeshed—is not just the moral point that such people intrude into, even violate, others' privacy and autonomy. But even that is of some use in securing my epistemological claim. At the least, we should wonder whether we can trust their moral judgment about others after we have seen that they lack good moral judgment about others' privacy and autonomy.

To be sure, this question can be answered in favor of such people and their judgment. One can be lacking in one area of moral judgment without being lacking in all, and one's moral-epistemic judgment may be good even where one's behavior belies this. My epistemological claim could, thus, use further support. I will not offer—nor, for reasons sketched below, do I think there could be—an argument showing a necessary connection between the moral failure of being improperly concerned with others' affairs with making moral-epistemological errors. But I do have some more particular considerations, having to do with some actual characteristics of those who are enmeshed or otherwise over-concerned with others.

Frequently—even typically and characteristically—enmeshment involves a failure of empathy, at a deep evaluative level. The failure here is consistent with a full and fine-grained knowledge of the facts. It is a failure to appreciate the moral-emotional meaning of these facts. It is a failure to appreciate them from the standpoint of the other, to appreciate them in the way they are experienced by the other. Instead of appreciating them that way, the enmeshed person imposes or interposes a form of appreciation and evaluation something like "In those circumstances, I would be . . . ," or "That would make me feel . . . ," or "The normal way to feel here is . . ." and then to take those meanings and ways of feeling as how it is or should be for that person.

Here we might look at a parent who is embarrassed not only by, but also for, a child who "fails" to marry or to pursue a good profession, or in some other way violates family norms—even though the child is fully and reflectively content with that part of life. Often, it is as if the child has not made those contrary judgments and had those contrary experiences. This failure may be clearest in regard to the enmeshment itself. The enmeshed person often, even typically, fails to see how annoyed, even resentful, the "enmeshed upon" person finds the intrusiveness. Indeed, the enmeshed person may often believe that the intrusion—of course, not seen as such—is perfectly proper and even welcomed by the other: "Of course my children want to know what I think, I'm their parent after all." Even if the enmeshed person accurately sees how the other person feels, that feeling is, somehow, not taken seriously, not taken as giving the "correct" way to feel, or perhaps not even as how that person "really" feels.

Enmeshment, then, involves a failure to take the other person seriously— i.e., seriously as another and separate person, who has independent and separate forms of judgment, appreciation, and feeling. We should here note that these failures—which in a sense are other-regarding—are importantly like some self-regarding failures characteristic of lack of self-respect: e.g., not taking oneself seriously as a moral agent, turning over to others the power to make judgments, even about how things are for oneself.

If these brief descriptions of enmeshment are right, we see how the enmeshed person's moral failure of not respecting privacy and autonomy is deeply connected with moral-epistemological failures. So too, of course, for the moral and moral-epistemic failures characteristic of lack of self-respect.

Now, my point here is not that there must always be these connections. It is possible to violate another's autonomy and privacy in systematic ways and yet, in moral-epistemic ways, take them seriously as separate people. Indeed, this seems necessary if one is to do really well as a scam artist, confidence man, or police interrogator. And even when we restrict attention to those who improperly judge for or about others, enmeshment with its dual moral and moral-epistemic failures is not the only explanation. The man who improperly cared for his neighbor need not be enmeshed with her. Nor need the person who obtrudes into his neighbors' life by hoping with them be enmeshed with them. Nor, of course, need people—e.g., political, religious, or family leaders—who would arrogate all moral decisions to themselves and like-minded others be enmeshed with those they thus try to subjugate.

So, my claim is not that where there are moral failures like invasion of privacy, obtruding into others' affairs, there will also be moral-epistemic failures. Nor is my claim that where there are the first sorts of failures, or even both sorts of failures, there is always enmeshment. My claim, rather, is that, as in the case of enmeshment, these two sorts of failures are often deeply and systematically interconnected.

Let us turn away from these more interpersonal defects to more intrapersonal ones. Above, I listed some typical and non-controversial reasons why P might not hope that the visitor comes, despite thinking that she might and that it would be a good thing if she does: P is physically or emotionally tired; P does not like her; P is ambivalent about her coming; P wants to be alone; P is depressed or bitter. These "emotion-defeating" conditions often, even typically, put us in poor evaluative-epistemological positions: tiredness often, if not typically, decreases one's perceptiveness, as do ambivalence, depression, and bitterness.

It should be clear that, instead of describing generalities holding for all people, I am here describing generalities about certain sorts of people, or only certain sorts of people in certain sorts of conditions. Bitterness and ambivalence can dull attentiveness and perceptiveness. But they can do just the reverse—as they do for many who are given to resentment or revenge, as some people are quite generally, and as many are in certain conditions. When motivated by hate, those who are borderline or schizophrenic are famous for their ability to know just how to wound others.[13] So too, fear and anxiety can engender epistemic failures. But they can also engender epistemic success. Some people fail under stress because they cannot think clearly when afraid or anxious. But others respond well to stress, and some even need it to pay attention and succeed. Further, there is strong evidence that people in certain marginalized groups—such as women and blacks in the contemporary USA—are generally better at reading moods, e.g., interpreting facial expressions, than those in power, even when those in power are the very people being interpreted. Danger and need, here, seem to have engendered accuracy.

My point, then, is not that for all people there are general relations between emotion-defeating and emotion-engendering conditions, on the one hand, and epistemic success and failure, on the other. It is, rather, that there are such connections, and they are systematic and typical, even if this is so only when relativized to personality, character, social group, culture, circumstances, and so on. Thus, in describing conditions which aid or hinder a given person's understanding, we may well be describing, not people as such, but only that person's epistemic personality.

Philosophers have always had the materials to recognize this combination of systematic connections and lack of universality, even if, from time to time, we have failed to draw the conclusion. For even among philosophers, there are many intellectual styles, temperaments, and personalities.[14]

So far I have presented some aspects of *P*'s epistemic personality by giving conditions that may account for *P*'s not hoping that the visitor will come, despite believing that she might and that it would be good if she did. These and similar conditions may also account for *P*'s not even noting that she might come or that it would be good if she did. So, if *P* is very played out, or very bitter or depressed, or generally unable to make and sustain emotional connections, *P* may not even see that it would be good if she came. It may simply pass him by. These emotion-defeating conditions may, thus, explain a failure to see what is good or bad. They can also lead to false evaluations. So, *P* may be so "turned around" by those conditions—e.g., so filled with general, free-floating hostility, or with hostility to her or to others who would benefit from her coming—that he thinks that her coming will, in fact, be bad.

Here is a related point. Emotions often involve a focus or emphasis on certain people's values and not on others'. For example, according to Aristotle, if an unjustified slight is to get me angry, I must take it to be directed at me or mine [*Rhetoric* II.2, 1378a31 ff.]. This is so even though I see that undeserved slights are bad no matter to whom they are directed. Not surprisingly, then, some evaluative errors can be traced to focus.

So, *P* may be so self-absorbed that he does not hope that the visitor will come. For although he thinks that it would be a good thing if she came—good on balance, that is—he does not think it would be good for him if she does. His self-absorption, as well as explaining lack of hope that she will come, could also explain how he fails to see that her coming would be, on balance, good, where it would be this because of the way it would be good for his wife. Similarly *P* may be so concerned for his wife's welfare that he hopes the visitor does come, because it will be so good for his wife. His over-concern for his wife might also explain why he fails to note—or having noted, fails to be moved by—how disastrous the person's coming will be, on balance, because of the harm it will do his daughter. Here, we might say he is looking in the wrong places, or not looking at all the right places, for value. Here too, issues of enmeshment are to the point.

So too, one can be, or make oneself, emotionally disconnected and distant. Aristotle held that danger evokes fear if you or someone very close to you is endangered and that it evokes pity if the person at risk is not so close but still close enough. I extended this to hold that we might feel only sadness, rather than fear or pity, for those who are very far from us. And just as they are far from us—indeed, one of the ways they are far from us—we know less, both quantitatively and qualitatively, about them. So too, I can distance myself from you by not finding out about, not thinking about, and generally not attending to you.

Now, my claim is not that if one has defective or distorted emotions, or if one is emotionally distant, or at an extreme if one is affectless, one must make errors about value. Some emotions—e.g., some cases of excitement at the thought or experience of a roller-coaster ride—may not be tied in any way with evaluative judgments, nor therefore with evaluative correctness or error.[15]

And some emotional lacks may depend on a hardening of one's heart, closing oneself off emotionally—in ways which do not involve evaluative errors. In fact, various forms of emotional non-engagement and coldness depend on accurate evaluative views and judgment. In this way, anyway, hate can be as demanding as love.

Some emotions—or emotional defects—are, of course, typically and naturally connected with evaluative defects. But at least often, we can correct for those conditions. For example, knowing that I am played out, I pay special attention to sources of value that, in my state, I would otherwise be inclined to overlook. Or knowing that I do not much care about you, cannot warm to you, I take special pains to make sure I give your interests due weight.

But it is easy to overestimate how well, how easily, and how long we can correct for those conditions which at once impair our emotions and also our epistemological, judging relations with value. Our will, our attention, our vigilance are sooner or later all too likely to fail.

It might seem that this last argument shows, at most, that the epistemological relations emotions have with value and evaluation are only external or indirect. For it might seem that what helps or hinders the epistemological work is not emotions, but rather the various conditions which figure in having or not having emotions, with or without defect. Along these lines it could be held that if a self-absorbed person fails to see others' interests, or if having seen them fails to be moved by them, the real explanation would lie not in the emotions of self-absorption, but in the patterns of thought, attention, and desire that underlie self-absorption. Similarly—to turn now to a favorite example of a bad and disruptive emotion—it will be held that it is not anger that misleads, disrupts, and is destructive of proper thought and action, but rather what does this are its patterns of thought, attention, and desire, e.g., the short-sightedness that anger can involve, the restriction of attention to wrongs one has suffered, and the desire for revenge.

If something like this is right, the conclusion would not be that correct evaluative understanding comes from correct emotions, and incorrect evaluative understanding comes from incorrect emotions. Rather, it would be that typically and for systematic reasons correct evaluative understanding and correct emotions come together, as do incorrect evaluative understanding and incorrect emotions.

There may well be something to this move to focus on those patterns, rather than the emotions. But for several reasons, I am unsure. First, there is something bothersome about what was advanced in its favor: that someone who has self-absorbed emotions can take corrective epistemological action. This does seem right. But it is unclear how to stop it from showing too much. After all, someone who has self-absorbed patterns of thought, attention, and desire can also take corrective epistemological action. Should we—and those suggesting that those patterns, rather than the emotions, are epistemologically relevant—conclude from this that those patterns, too, are epistemologically irrelevant?

A further reason to be suspicious of this claim is that it strongly suggests that we should give primary importance to the non-affective components of emotions, or perhaps even that we can and should understand emotions non-affectively, e.g., in the ways Pitcher, Solomon, Neu, or Sartre do. What I mean is this: We can make the philosophical analytic distinction between emotions and the patterns of thought, attention, and desire which underlie emotions. And in fact we know that an emotion is not the same as this patterned thought, attention, and desire, and indeed that they are not even co-extensive: a person can have such thought, attention, and desire without having the emotion. (Variants of these considerations apply to Aristotle's discussion of pleasure at *NE* X.5.)

So, we can make a distinction between emotions and patterned thought, attention, and desire. But we should ask what sort of distinction this is. One question is whether in making this distinction we have carried philosophical analysis too far, to the point of misleading artificiality, or at least a mistaken psychology. As I have briefly indicated, this distinction, or its embodiment, points to, if it does not rest on, a possible but potentially worrisome, often undesirable and unhealthy, split. As argued by Anna Freud in her *The Ego and the Mechanisms of Defense*, it is, after all, part of the core of the common ego defense, and neurotic style, of intellectualization. And when it becomes general and typical of significant portions of a person's psychic life, this distinction typifies and is constitutively central to the "affect-denying world of alienated work," repression, delibidinization, dissociation, alexithymia, and more severe schizoid phenomena.

A closely related way to put my concern about this distinction has to do with why we call a process or relationship emotional. Earlier we saw that Chodorow talked of relational capacities and deficiencies in, so to speak, a dual way: as interpersonal and emotional. It was not that these are simply two characterizing features of those capacities and deficiencies. Rather, they are emotional because they are interpersonal. But how are we to understand 'are emotional' here? For it is also central to Chodorow's claims that men's interpersonal relations are deficient in, perhaps devoid of, emotions, and in that sense are not emotional.

My suggestion is that Chodorow can be understood as making something like the following claim. Such relations are emotional in the sense that this is what healthy or good relations are like: e.g., interpersonal relations will be emotional unless those relations have been deformed. This, I think, is clearly suggested in "Freedom and Resentment," when Strawson says,

> We should think of the many different kinds of relationship which we can have with other people—as sharers of a common interest; as members of the same family; as colleagues; as friends; as lovers; as chance parties to an enormous range of transactions and encounters. Then we should think in each of these connections in turn, and in others, of the kind of importance we attach to the attitudes and intentions towards us of those

who stand in these relations to us, and of the kinds of reactive attitudes and feelings to which we ourselves are prone.[16]

In this sense, family relations are emotional—and, perhaps, mathematics is not emotional. This is true even if, for certain people, those relations are not emotional—and mathematics is emotional. So, we may seek help if a child's relations with the family are, or seem, emotionless—and if a child is anguished by mathematics.

My overall conclusion, then, is not to deny that there can be distance between emotions and those patterns of thought, desire, and attention. Rather, it is to question the nature of that distance, and to suggest that it may not be the right sort of distance to sustain the claim that it is those patterns rather than the emotion that are epistemologically relevant.

I want now to raise a related worry about the distinction between emotions and emotionless patterns. The worry is not whether we can make the distinction, but whether, even if we can, it could help the claim that it is those emotionless patterns, not the affect, that play the epistemological roles in question. The worry can be put in terms of a twofold claim: First, the proper description of those emotionless patterns is that they are affectless. Second, affectlessness is not on all fours with affectfulness. Rather, affectlessness is to be understood in terms of affectfulness—e.g., as a privation or defect in regard to affect.

An example might help. To show that we can make the distinction between those patterns and the emotion, we might be referred to cases of repression. Here, there may be only emotionless patterns of thought, desire, and attention. But—and this is the problem—in at least some cases of repression what is repressed is affect, not just affectless content. Indeed, the repression involved in intellectualization would fail from the outset were only affectless content repressed. Here, and elsewhere, the repressed affect is poorly characterized as simply not being there. At the least, it is absent affect that should be and would be there but for the repression. And often, even though it is not there in usual ways, it is still there, but in special ways—e.g., in anxiety.

Further—as argued by Sigmund Freud and Harry Stack Sullivan, to name only two theorists—such emotions and emotional states as fear, anxiety, and distress explain both repression of affect but also such seemingly emotionless states as selective inattention. The significance of this for our concerns can be brought out as follows.

We might consider a case where my poor treatment of you seems not explained by my disliking you, or having any other hostile emotion toward you, but rather by my not knowing what you want or need. This might be a case where emotionless patterns of thought—mere inattention—not emotions, account for my moral evaluations and actions. But suppose further that I have not paid attention to you—that I have engaged in selective inattention—because I have been unwilling to engage emotionally with you, perhaps because such engagement is felt to be too dangerous. Here, too, then, emotions are at work.[17]

Now, I am not arguing that all morally significant patterns of emotionless thought, desire, and attention are really emotionally motivated. My being unaware of your desires may be morally significant—if only because of its effects. But it can be due entirely to your not telling me what you want, where you hide not only what you want but also that you have desires. Or we might consider young children in a racist society who use racist categories of thought without being emotionally moved by them, and without knowing their significance. These children have certain patterns of thought, desire, and attention not because of their emotions, but rather because they have been raised in a society or family that inculcates those patterns. It may be only later that those patterns gain emotional investment. But even before this, they can have moral significance.

So, I certainly accept the reality, and indeed the healthiness, as well as the moral importance of emotionless and emotionally unmotivated patterns of thought, attention, and desire. There is no need to deny these to show the importance, elsewhere, of emotions either as content or cause of our evaluations and action.

I do not think we now need go further into these tangled and complex issues. For we have seen that emotions—either emotions proper or the patterns that underlie them—play significant epistemological roles in helping and hindering us in noticing and appreciating value. We have yet to be sure about the conceptual relations between affect and those patterns. So too, we have yet to be sure about the exact nature of the relations between evaluative understanding and emotions. Nonetheless, we can be sure that, for reasons having to do with the nature of people, people who have correct emotions are, because they are such people, well placed to make correct evaluations, and people who have incorrect emotions are, because they are such people, poorly placed to make correct evaluations.

One last point. It might be suggested that my claim shows only that emotions are useful: they only help us notice and appreciate value and make evaluations. I would question the dismissive 'only'. For it is a well-established part of our ethical tradition, and most others, that being good at noticing and appreciating value—and, more widely, being a good judge—has instrumental value, but not only instrumental value. To be able to judge well, and to be a good judge, is, itself, an important internal part of what it is to live well and to be good.

NOTES

1. W. D. Falk, "Fact, Value and Nonnatural Predication" in *Ought, Reasons, and Morality* (Ithaca, N.Y., 1986), 120.

2. I have been greatly aided here by Eugene Garver, "Aristotle's *Rhetoric* II; Deliberative Rationality and the Emotions," unpublished.

3. Strawson, "Freedom and Resentment" *Proceedings of the British Academy* 48 (1962); Taylor, "Self-Interpreting Animals" in his *Human Agency and Language, Philosophical Papers, vol. 1* (New York, 1985); Murdoch, *The Sovereignty of Good* (London, 1970); Blum, *Friendship, Altruism, and Morality* (London, 1980), "Iris Murdoch and the Domain of the Moral," *Philosophical Studies*, (1986), and "Particularity and Responsiveness," in *The Emergence of Morality in Young Children*, edited by Kagan and Lamb (Chicago, 1987); Walker, "Moral Understandings: Alternative 'Epistemology' for a Feminist Ethics," *Hypatia*

(1989); Nussbaum, *Love's Knowledge* (Oxford, 1990); and McDowell, "Virtue and Reason," *The Monist* (1979). Walker's work situates this debate within a similar debate in feminist ethics: whether, as suggested by Carol Gilligan's *In a Different Voice*, emotions, especially those having to do with care, community, and nurturing are central to a desirable feminist ethics. My thanks are owed Walker for discussion of these and other issues.

4. Of the countless works on this, I have found especially useful Anna Freud, *The Ego and the Mechanisms of Defense* (London, 1937); David Shapiro, *Neurotic Styles* (New York, 1965); Harry Guntrip, *Schizoid Phenomena, Object Relations, and the Self* (New York, 1969); Joyce McDougall, *Theaters of the Mind: Illusion and Truth on the Psychoanalytic Stage* (New York, 1991), especially chapter 7, "Reflections on Affect: A Psychoanalytic View of Alexithymia"; and also Henry Krystal, "Aspects of Affect Theory," *Bulletin of the Menninger Clinic* 41 (1977): 1–26, "Trauma and Affect," *Psychoanalytic Study of the Child* 36 (1978): 81–116, and "The Hedonic Element in Affectivity," *Annual of Psychoanalysis* 9 (1981): 93–113, all collected in his *Integration and Self-healing: Affect, Trauma, and Alexithymia* (Hillsdale, N.J., 1988).

5. "Emotions and Choice" in *Explaining Emotions*, edited by A. O. Rorty (Berkeley, 1980), 257.

6. "Jealous Thoughts," also in *Explaining Emotions*, pp 431–32, original emphasis.

7. "What is an Emotion?" *Mind* (1884), reprinted in *The Emotions*, edited by K. Dunlap (New York, 1967), 17.

8. I have discussed and criticized these works in "Psychic Feelings: Their Importance and Irreducibility," *Australasian Journal of Philosophy* (1983): 5–26 and also in "Emotional Thoughts," *American Philosophical Quarterly* (1987): 59–69.

9. Two *loci classici* of this topic are D. W. Winnicott, "Countertransference," *British Journal of Medical Psychology* (1960): 17–21, reprinted in his *The Maturational Processes and the Facilitating Environment* (London, 1965) and Heinrich Racker, *Transference and Countertransference* (New York, 1968). See also Michael Gorkin, *The Uses of Counter-transference* (Northvale, N.J., 1987), which has a useful discussion and bibliography.

10. *The Reproduction of Mothering* (Berkeley, 1978), 177.

11. My thanks are owed to Laurence Thomas for discussion here.

12. I want to thank the philosopher and psychoanalyst Ernest Wallwork for many of the following points about enmeshment and for other help with this work. My thanks are also owed the psychoanalyst Elizabeth Hegeman for help on this issue and others throughout this essay.

13. My thanks are owed to the psychoanalyst Else First here.

14. See my "Intellectual Desire, Emotion, and Action," in *Explaining Emotions*.

15. For a discussion of near constitutional and non-value-based character differences which center around liking and disliking such activities, see Michael Balint, *Thrills and Regressions* (Madison, Conn., 1987).

16. As reprinted in *Free Will*, edited by Gary Watson (Oxford, 1982), 63–64.

17. My thanks are owed to the psychoanalyst Sandra Buechler for stressing the importance of being unwilling to experience certain emotions, in addition to the importance of not experiencing them.

Intentionality and Naturalism

STEPHEN P. STICH AND STEPHEN LAURENCE

> ... the deepest motivation for intentional irrealism derives
> not from such relatively technical worries about individualism and
> holism as we've been considering, but rather from a certain onto-
> logical intuition: that there is no place for intentional categories
> in a physicalistic view of the world; that the intentional can't be
> naturalized.
>
> (Fodor, 1987, p. 97)

1. CATASTROPHE THEORY

Intentional irrealism is the doctrine that meaning is a myth. A bit more precisely,
it is the claim that nothing in the world instantiates intentional properties—that
intentional predicates are true of nothing. If intentional irrealism is correct, then
it is not the case that

(1) 'Snow is white' means that snow is white.

or that

(2) George Bush often thinks about winning the next election.

or that

(3) Lincoln wanted to free the slaves.

Nor is it the case that

(4) Thinking about winning the election sometimes causes Bush to smile.

or that

(5) Lincoln's desire to free the slaves caused him to sign the Emancipation
Proclamation.

Obviously, intentional irrealism has some very startling consequences. If it is true then a very substantial part of what we read in our textbooks, teach our children, and say to each other is mistaken. Indeed, as Fodor has remarked, with only a bit of hyperbole,

> if it isn't literally true that my wanting is causally responsible for my reaching, and my itching is causally responsible for my scratching, and my believing is causally responsible for my saying . . . if none of that is literally true, then practically everything I believe about anything is false and it's the end of the world.[1]

Though we rather doubt that the world would come to an end, perhaps Fodor is closer to the mark in claiming that if intentional irrealism is correct and

> commonsense intentional psychology really were to collapse, that would be, beyond comparison, the greatest intellectual catastrophe in the history of our species. . . . The collapse of the supernatural didn't compare.[2]

Very well, then, let's agree that intentional irrealism is a very radical doctrine. But why on earth should anyone *worry* about it? Why does anyone think it is even remotely plausible? In the quote with which we began this essay Fodor maintains that the "deepest motivation for intentional irrealism" is the suspicion "that the intentional can't be naturalized." Viewed as a bit of sociology, it is our guess that Fodor is right. In recent years, many philosophers have put a very high priority on providing a "naturalistic" account of intentional categories.[3] Moreover, there is an unmistakable tone of urgency in much of this literature. Naturalizing the intentional isn't just an interesting project, it is vitally important. *Something dreadful* will follow if it doesn't succeed. And for many writers, we suspect, that dreadful consequence is intentional irrealism.[4] But this sociological fact raises a philosophical puzzle. *Why* would irrealism (or some comparably unsettling conclusion) follow if "the intentional can't be naturalized?" What is the connection between the existence or non-existence of a naturalistic account of intentional categories and the truth or falsehood of claims like (1)–(5)? These are the questions that motivate this essay.

To answer them, of course, it will be necessary to say just what is involved in "naturalizing" the intentional. And, as we shall see, there is no shortage of answers to choose from. But not just any answer will do. A satisfactory account of what it is to "naturalize the intentional"—an account that makes sense of what Fodor sees as "the deepest motivation for intentional irrealism"—will have to satisfy a pair of constraints. First, it will have to sustain an argument from the premise that intentional notions can't be naturalized to the conclusion that intentional irrealism or some other deeply troubling doctrine is true. Second, there must be some reason to think that, when "naturalizing" is unpacked along the lines proposed, it is in fact the case that the intentional can't be naturalized. For even if non-naturalizability entails irrealism, this is surely nothing to worry about if the claim that the intentional can't be naturalized is neither intuitively plausible nor supported by a convincing argument.

It is our contention that, while various accounts will satisfy one or the other of these constraints, there is no account of what it is to naturalize the intentional that will satisfy *both* of them. To support our contention, we will survey a number of proposals on what "naturalization" comes to and we will go on to argue that none of these candidates will satisfy both of the constraints. Obviously this strategy won't provide a conclusive case for our conclusion, since there may be some quite different account of naturalizing that does satisfy both constraints. But if so, we haven't a clue about what it might be.

If we are right, if there is no account that satisfies both constraints, then there is something deeply misguided about the urgency that imbues so much of the recent literature in this area. It may, of course, be perfectly reasonable to adopt one or another account of what it would be to naturalize the intentional, and to explore the possibility of bringing it off. A successful naturalization might well be an impressive and valuable accomplishment. But if it should turn out that intentional notions can't be naturalized, *no dire consequences will follow*. We will not have to rewrite history, or renounce intentional psychology, or revise the way we describe and explain people's behavior. It will not be the end of the world. It won't even be the beginning of the end.

Before launching into our survey of accounts of "naturalizing" a few words are in order on some of the other troubling consequences that might be thought to follow if naturalization does not succeed. In Fodor's writing, and elsewhere in the literature, the dominant worry is the one that has been center stage in this section: if the intentional can't be naturalized, then intentional irrealism will have won the day. But often enough one finds suggestions of other calamities that may ensue if naturalization fails. One of these is that intentional states might turn out to be causally impotent. In the passage quoted earlier, for example, Fodor frets that it's the end of the world if it isn't literally true that his wanting is causally responsible for his reaching, and his believing is causally responsible for his saying. In Fred Dretske's writing the worry that intentional states might turn out to be causally inert is frequently cited as a motive for seeking a naturalized account of these states. Indeed, Dretske sometimes suggests that if intentional states are causally impotent, then perhaps we should not include them in our ontology at all.

> If beliefs and desires are not causally relevant to behavior, I, for one, fail to see why it would be worth having them. . . . If reasons aren't causes, one of the chief—indeed (for certain people) the *only*—motive for including them in one's inventory of the mind, vanishes.[5]

Another, rather different concern is that if naturalization fails, then there could be no serious *science* of intentional psychology because there could be no *laws* that invoke intentional terms or intentional properties. We are no more impressed by these worries than we are about the concern over irrealism. For, as we shall argue in the sections that follow, on any reading of the claim that the intentional can't be naturalized which is even remotely likely to be true, neither of these calamitous consequences would follow.

2. NATURALIZING AND CONCEPTUAL ANALYSIS

Once upon a time something called "conceptual analysis" was all the rage in philosophy. The journals, back then, were filled with attempts to provide necessary and sufficient conditions for the application of a term or a concept. And, more often than not, when one philosopher published such an "analysis" another philosopher would describe a hypothetical situation in which we would intuitively say that the analysans applied and the analysandum did not, or vice versa. For people who remember those bygone days (only one of us does), much of the literature on naturalizing the intentional provokes a strong sense of *deja vu*. Consider, for example, the following quote:

> The worry about representation is above all that the semantic (and/or the intentional) will prove permanently recalcitrant to integration in the natural order. . . . What is required to relieve the worry is therefore, at a minimum, the framing of *naturalistic* conditions for representation. That is, what we want at a minimum is something of the form '*R represents S' is true iff C* where the vocabulary in which condition C is couched contains neither intentional nor semantic expressions.[6]

Of course, an interest in providing necessary and sufficient conditions is not, by itself, enough to convict a philosopher of engaging in conceptual analysis. For typically a conceptual analyst will not be happy with just any set of conditions that happen to be co-extensive with the predicate being analyzed. If a proposed analysis is to be acceptable, it has to be the case that the co-extension obtains not only in all actual cases, but in imaginary or hypothetical cases as well. The bi-conditional specifying the analysis must not only be true, it must be *necessary*. Moreover, the alleged co-extension in all possible worlds is supposed to be testable by consulting our linguistic intuition and determining what we would say about hypothetical cases. This method would seem to make the most sense if we suppose that the co-extension derives from the meaning of the concepts that underlie our predicates—the analysans (the right-hand side of the bi-conditional) unpacks the meaning of the concept expressed by the analysandum.

Is it the case that Fodor and others who worry about the possibility that the intentional can't be naturalized are actually worried about the possibility that the meaning of intentional predicates or intentional concepts can't be set out as a set of necessary and sufficient conditions which do not themselves invoke intentional terms? We're not at all sure. Indeed, it is our suspicion that these philosophers have *no* clear idea of what "naturalizing" amounts to, and that much of their anxiety can be traced to this confusion. But if it is not clear that these philosophers really want a conceptual analysis, it is clear that if "naturalizing" is understood in this way, it will not satisfy the first of our two constraints.

Indeed it is rather ironic that Fodor often seems to be troubled by the fact that our intentional concepts can't be analyzed in non-intentional terms. For among contemporary philosophers no one has been more adamant than Fodor in insisting that we should not expect our terms or concepts to be analyzable *at all*. Here is an example of the sorts of things he says when this mood is upon him:

> [I]t seems to me to be among the most important findings of philosophical and psychological research over the last several hundred years (say, since Locke first made the reductionist program explicit) that attempts at conceptual analysis practically always fail.
>
> Consider, for example, the failure of the reductionist program within the study of language. . . . [W]hat I'll call the *Definition Hypothesis* [is the claim that] (a, weak version) . . . many de facto lexical concepts are definable; and (b, strong version) that they are definable in a vocabulary of sensory-terms-plus-logical-syntax.
>
> It's simply notorious that the stronger version of this claim has proved to be untenable. . . . But what's equally true, and considerably more striking, is that the evidence seems to bear against the definition hypothesis even in the weak version; if there are no plausible cases of definition in a sensory vocabulary, there are also remarkably few plausible examples of definition in a *non*-sensory vocabulary, one indication of which is the striking paucity of working examples in the standard literature. There is 'bachelor', which is supposed to mean 'unmarried man'; . . . there are jargon terms, which are explicitly and stipulatively defined; . . . there is a handful of terms which belong to real, honest-to-God axiomatic systems; . . . and then there are the other half million or so items that the OED lists. About these last apparently nothing much can be done.[7]

On our view, there can be no serious quarrel with Fodor's assessment of the track record of conceptual analysis. Though lots of very clever people have tried very hard to produce them over the centuries, we still have no plausible definitions for 'knowledge' or 'cause' or 'law' or 'freedom,' or for any of the other terms that loom large in philosophical discussion. Moreover, as Fodor goes on to illustrate, it is no easier to provide definitions for more mundane terms like 'paint' or 'parent' or 'pig'. The more one plays the game of trying to provide exceptionless, intuitively acceptable necessary and sufficient conditions, the more one is inclined to accept Fodor's conclusion: "[W]hen it comes to definitions, the examples almost always don't work."[8]

What are we to make of this situation? Well, of course, it might be that conceptual analysis is just *hard*, and that if we keep at it we will ultimately succeed in producing a significant number of intuitively acceptable definitions. However, it is also entirely possible that we will never succeed—that the project of defining most common predicates is simply impossible.

If it *is* impossible, this will have important consequences for those parts of philosophy and psychology that deal with the structure of human concepts. There is a venerable tradition in this area which assumes that the concept or mental structure underlying the use of most predicates is actually a mentally represented definition—a set of necessary and sufficient conditions. In deciding whether or not a term applies to a given case, this "Classical View" maintains, we are either consciously or (more typically) unconsciously determining whether the case at hand satisfies the conditions of the definition. If it turns out that there just are no definitions for most terms, then obviously the Classical account of the structure and use of concepts will have to go.[9]

In recent years there has been a growing realization that the Classical account of concepts is in deep trouble, and a number of interesting alternatives have been proposed. Perhaps the best known of these are the prototype and exemplar accounts of concepts developed by Eleanor Rosch and her associates. On the prototype theory, concepts are weighted lists of features that are characteristic of the most typical members of the category that the concept picks out. The list will generally include lots of features that are not necessary for category membership. On the exemplar story concepts are, in effect, detailed mental descriptions of particular members of the category. Thus, for example, the concept underlying your use of the word 'dog' might include detailed descriptions of Lassie and Rin Tin Tin. In determining whether to categorize something as a dog, this theory maintains, you assess the similarity between the target and the various exemplars stored in semantic memory.[10] Fodor has proposed a very different alternative to the Classical account of concepts. On his view, the concepts that underlie most of our one-word predicates have no structure at all—or at least none that is relevant to the semantic properties of the concept. Of course if this is right it is very hard to see how these concepts might be learned. And that's just fine with Fodor, since he thinks they are all innate.[11]

This is not the place to elaborate the details of these various "non-Classical" theories of concepts, or to debate their virtues and shortcomings. Our reason for mentioning them was simply to make clear that there are lots of interesting theories about concepts on the market which are compatible with (and which might well explain) the finding that most of our concepts appear to have no intuitively acceptable definitions. So if it is indeed the case that most concepts have no definitions, there is nothing much to worry about. Rather, the appropriate response is to get busy and try to determine which of the various non-Classical theories of concepts is correct. It would, by contrast, be simply *mad* to think that if most of our concepts can't be defined, then the terms that express those concepts are not true of anything. The inference from *The predicate '_____ is a pig' cannot be defined* to *There are no such things as pigs* is simply perverse. Concern about porcine irrealism is not even a remotely appropriate reaction to the collapse of the Classical theory of concepts. But, of course, exactly the same can be said about intentional predicates. Perhaps there are good reasons to worry about intentional irrealism being true, but the fact that '*R* represents *C* ' can't be defined surely isn't one of them.[12]

What about the other two concerns that we sketched at the end of Section 1? If intentional terms can't be defined, does it follow that intentional states are causally impotent, or that there are no laws invoking intentional properties? In both cases, we maintain, the answer is clearly *no*. To see why, consider a few analogies. If the Classical theory of concepts is wrong, then there will be no way to provide necessary and sufficient conditions for predicates like '*x* shot *y*' or '*z* died'. But from this, surely, it does not even begin to follow that it is not literally true that being shot by John Wilkes Booth caused Lincoln to die. And, of course, if the Classical theory is wrong, then terms like 'force', 'mass', and 'gravity' won't be definable either. But it would be at best a bad joke to conclude, from this, that there are no laws that invoke these terms. If the Classical view of concepts collapses, it will not take all of physics with it. The situation seems entirely parallel for intentional terms. If it turns out that they can't be analyzed or defined, this would provide no reason at all to conclude that intentional states are causally impotent, or that there are no laws invoking them. So if "naturalizing the intentional" requires providing a Classical analysis of intentional concepts, then if the intentional can't be naturalized, we have found no reason to think that anything at all troublesome will follow.

3. NATURALIZING, NATURAL KINDS, AND ESSENTIAL PROPERTIES

To set the stage for our second account of what it might be to naturalize the intentional, we'll begin with a brief reminder of some very influential doctrines in the philosophy of language. Consider so-called "natural kind" predicates like 'water' or 'gold'. What is it that determines which parts of the world are in the extension of such predicates? According to the widely discussed causal/historical account of reference, the answer to this question must invoke the notion of "essential properties" of natural kinds—properties that everything in the extension of a natural kind term must have. A bit fancifully, the causal/historical story might be sketched as follows:

A kind term first acquires its referent when it is used to "baptize" or "dub" some newly noted samples of the stuff to which the term will refer. This process is sometimes described as "grounding" the predicate. Once the predicate has been grounded, it can be transmitted from one speaker to another in appropriate communicative settings. And those to whom the predicate is passed can pass it on again. The speakers who originally ground the predicate need have no deep understanding of the nature of the stuff they are dubbing; indeed, they may have all sorts of wildly mistaken beliefs about it. The speakers who acquire the predicate via reference preserving transmissions need never have come in contact with anything in the extension of the predicate. They too can harbor many false beliefs about the nature of the stuff to which the term refers.

Now obviously there is something missing in this tale. For a predicate like 'gold' gets grounded on just a few samples of gold. And yet the extension of the predicate must include *all* the gold that ever has or ever will exist in the universe. What is the relation between the dubbed samples and the rest of the gold in the universe, in virtue of which the dubbing succeeds in attaching the term to all gold, wherever it may be? It is here that the doctrine of *essential properties* is typically brought into play. The basic idea is that individual items are grouped into natural kinds in virtue of the possession of certain essential properties, and it is the job of science to discover what these properties are. Thus, for example, science tells us that having atomic number 79 is the essential property of gold, that being H_2O is the essential property of water, and so on. When a natural kind term gets grounded, the term comes to apply not only to the samples present at the dubbing but also to everything else in the universe that has the same essential properties.

How does all of this relate to the project of naturalizing the intentional? To see the answer, let's go back to the quote from Fodor near the beginning of the previous section. What was worrying Fodor was that intentional categories might "prove permanently recalcitrant to integration in the natural order." And what was required to relieve the worry was "a framing of naturalistic conditions for representation . . . something of the form '*R represents S*' *is true iff C* where the vocabulary in which condition C is couched contains neither intentional nor semantic expressions." Our first pass at unpacking this requirement was to view it as a demand for a conceptual analysis. But it could equally well be viewed as asking for a specification of an underlying essential property—the property in virtue of which the predicate '*R* represents *S*' applies to all and only those pairs of things in the universe such that the first represents the second. On this interpretation, the bi-conditional needed to naturalize the representation relation would have a status akin to the one Putnam and others have attributed to bi-conditionals like:

(6) (x) x is water iff x is H_2O.

It is a necessary truth, but its necessity has nothing to do with the structure of the concept that speakers invoke when they use the terms involved. It isn't known *a priori*, and it can't be discovered by probing intuitions or by doing psycholinguistics. The only way to discover it is to do the appropriate sort of science.

How likely is it that *this* is what philosophers want when they set about trying to naturalize the intentional. Well, there are some practitioners of the craft who offer accounts of representation that rely heavily on notions borrowed from science (typically evolutionary biology). Some of these writers go out of their way to explain that they are not trying to capture our intuitions about representation, and thus are not worried by the fact that their analyses have counterintuitive consequences.[13] All of this is compatible with the interpretation that these philosophers are seeking an account of the essential properties of representation. But we don't propose to press the point since, as we noted earlier, we rather suspect that most of the writers who worry about naturalizing the intentional have no clear idea of what "naturalizing" amounts to. What is clear is that if "naturalizing" is interpreted in this way, then once again it will not satisfy our first constraint.

One way of arguing for this claim would be to mount a head-on assault on the whole idea of scientifically discoverable essential properties, and on the account of the reference of natural kind terms that goes along with it. There is already a substantial literature pointing out the shortcomings of this rather trendy package of ideas, and we have considerable sympathy with the emerging critique.[14] But all that would make a very long argument, and we have a much shorter one to offer.

Suppose it is the case the doctrine of essential properties and the associated story about reference can survive serious scrutiny. Suppose further that when "naturalizing" is interpreted in the way we've just sketched, it turns out that 'R represents S' and other intentional predicates cannot be naturalized. Would this be enough to make intentional irrealism plausible? Surely the answer is *no*. To see the point, we need only note that there are endlessly many predicates for which no one would even dream of seeking scientifically discoverable essential properties. Yet it would be simply perverse to claim that these predicates can't be truly applied to anything. Nobody seriously thinks that anything remotely analogous to (6) will be available for such one-place predicates as 'couch', 'car', 'war', 'famine', or 'die', nor for two-place predicates like 'owns', 'kills', 'throws', 'mates with', 'fixes', or 'crushes'. But it would be preposterous to suggest that this entails there is no killing or war or famine, and that no one ever owns anything or dies. If natural kind terms are defined as those whose extension is determined by scientifically discoverable essential properties, then one way of putting our point is that there are many, many predicates that are not natural kind terms, and the fact that they are not natural kind terms is no reason at all to suppose that they cannot be truly predicated of anything. So if it turns out that nothing analogous to (6) is forthcoming for intentional predicates, the right conclusion is not that those predicates are true of nothing, but simply that, in the sense lately defined, they are not natural kind terms. And that would hardly be the end of the world.

Could it be that while intentional irrealism doesn't follow from the fact that intentional predicates aren't natural kind terms, something comparably unsettling does follow? Let's take a brief look at the pair of possibilities suggested at the end of Section 1. The first of them focuses on the causal efficacy of intentional states. Might it be the case that if intentional predicates aren't natural kind terms in the sense we've defined, then they can't be used to make causal claims that are literally true. This strikes us as a singularly implausible suggestion. For, as we noted earlier, it is literally true that being shot by John Wilkes Booth caused Abraham Lincoln to die, though neither 'shoots' nor 'dies' is likely to be the sort of term whose extension is determined by scientifically discoverable essential properties. So even if it turns out that intentional predicates are not natural kind terms in the sense we've defined, the causal efficacy of intentional states and processes might still be on a par with the causal efficacy of shooting, crushing, eating, or mating. And that should be efficacy enough for anyone.

A second possibility is that if intentional predicates aren't natural kind terms, then perhaps there could be no science of intentional psychology. For, it might be argued, such a science would have to include intentional laws, and laws can only be stated with natural kind terms. No kind terms, no laws; no laws, no science. Now as we see it, the problem here comes with the link between kind terms and laws. *Why* can laws only be stated with natural kind terms? One might view it as simply a stipulative definition: natural kind terms just are the sorts of terms that can occur in lawlike statements. But now we have a potential equivocation on our hands. For we have been assuming that natural kind terms are defined as those whose extension is determined by scientifically discoverable essential properties, and the current argument proposes a very different definition. Of course it might be claimed that these two definitions pick out the same class of terms—that all and only terms whose extension is determined by scientifically discoverable essential properties can be used in lawlike statements. But we find this a singularly implausible proposal. For in sciences far removed from psychology there appear to be lots of terms invoked in laws for which nothing much like (6) is in the offing. We see no reason at all to suppose there are scientifically discoverable essential properties that fix the reference of terms like 'inflation', 'fitness', 'mass', 'gravity', or 'electric charge', for example. If this is right—if there are lots of terms invoked in scientific laws whose extensions are not fixed in the way that the causal/historical theory claims the extensions of terms like 'gold' are fixed—then the putative threat to intentional psychology disappears.

Thus far we have been arguing that an account of naturalizing the intentional which requires producing something akin to (6) will not satisfy the first of our two constraints. Neither intentional irrealism nor any other catastrophic consequence follows if the intentional can't be naturalized, when naturalizing is interpreted in this way. But we are also inclined to think that if we take seriously the story about reference that serves as a backdrop for the current proposal on naturalizing, then our second constraint will not be satisfied either. For if that story is correct, then the usual arguments aimed at showing that the intentional can't be naturalized just don't go through.

Those arguments typically begin by describing some feature or cluster of features that are important or essential for intentional states, *on the commonsense account of these states*. The arguments then try to show that respectable scientific theories cannot accommodate states with the features in question. The conclusions the arguments draw are just the ones that Fodor feared: that the intentional "will prove permanently recalcitrant to integration in the natural order," and that "there is no place for intentional categories in a physicalistic view of the world." However, if the causal/historical account of reference is correct, then the conclusions of these arguments do not follow from the premises. For on the causal/historical account, the essential properties that determine the extension of natural kind terms are to be discovered by science, and our commonsense views about the things we are referring to with natural kind terms may be wildly, hopelessly wrong. Indeed, the fact that ignorance and error do not undermine reference is taken to be a major selling point of the causal/historical theory.[15] But if our commonsense views about the things we are referring to may be seriously mistaken, then the (alleged) fact that commonsense imbues intentional states with scientifically unacceptable features entails nothing at all about the scientific respectability of intentional states. For commonsense may just be *wrong*; our intentional terms may actually refer to states that do not have these scientifically unacceptable features. So if the causal/historical theory of reference is correct, there can be no serious argument from premises about the commonsense characterization of intentional states to conclusions about the role that the intentional states referred to by commonsense psychology might play in scientifically acceptable theories. Without some argument along those lines, however, it is hard to see why we would have any reason to believe that the intentional can't be naturalized.[16]

4. NATURALIZING AND SUPERVENIENCE

It's hard to see . . . how one can be a Realist about intentionality without also being, to some extent or other, a Reductionist. If the semantic and the intentional are real properties of things, it must be in virtue of their identity with (or maybe of their supervenience on?) properties that are themselves *neither* intentional *nor* semantic. If aboutness is real, it must be really something else.[17]

4.1. The Game Plan

Thus far we haven't done very well in finding interpretations of "naturalizing" that satisfy our two constraints. But in the passage just quoted, Fodor seems to be making a pair of suggestions that we haven't yet explored. To avoid irrealism, intentional properties must be *identical with* or *supervene upon* non-intentional properties. So perhaps naturalization should be explained in terms of property identity or supervenience. In the current section we'll consider whether either of *these* proposals satisfies our two constraints. Actually, we will focus almost entirely on supervenience, since on all plausible accounts of that notion, it is a weaker relation than identity. Indeed, on most accounts, property identity entails supervenience, and thus non-supervenience entails non-identity. So if nothing nasty follows from the fact that the intentional doesn't supervene on the non-intentional, then the fact that intentional properties are not identical with non-intentional ones will be no cause for worry.

In restricting our attention to supervenience we are not exactly making things easy for ourselves, however. For the literature on supervenience has blossomed profusely during the last few years, and this literature suggests a variety of different ways in which the idea that the intentional supervenes on the non-intentional may be spelled out.[18] These alternatives differ on a pair of dimensions. First, the notion of one class of properties supervening on another can be explicated in two different ways, one of which (so-called *strong supervenience*) entails the other (*weak supervenience*). Second, there are various options that might be proposed as the "supervenience base" for intentional properties—the class of properties on which intentional properties are expected to supervene. In the arguments that follow we will restrict our attention to weak supervenience. For, since strong supervenience entails weak supervenience, the failure of weak supervenience entails the failure of strong. Thus if we can show that no untoward consequences follow when weak supervenience does not obtain, the same conclusion will follow if strong supervenience fails.

Here's the game plan. We'll begin with a brief explanation of the two notions of supervenience. We'll then attend to three different candidates that might be proposed as the supervenience base for intentional properties. In each of these three cases we will argue that the constraints set out in Section 1 are not met. In the first two cases, it is the first constraint that isn't satisfied: Neither irrealism nor the other unwelcome consequences follow if supervenience fails. In the third case, it is the second constraint that isn't satisfied. For in this case it is wildly implausible that supervenience fails. We will follow all of this with a brief discussion of another notion of supervenience, so-called *global supervenience*, whose precise relation to the other two notions is a matter of some dispute. Here again, we will argue, nothing catastrophic follows if intentional properties fail to supervene on the various bases that have been proposed. End of game plan. It's time to get to work.

4.2. Two Notions of Supervenience

Supervenience is usually construed as a relation between two classes of properties. So to begin, let us adopt the following convention. Let B and S be two classes of properties (think of them as the Base class and the Supervenient class) whose members are $b_1, b_2, \ldots, b_i, \ldots$ and $s_1, s_2, \ldots s_i, \ldots$ respectively. Now the basic idea is that one class of properties, S, supervenes on a second, B, if the presence or absence of properties in the first class is completely determined by the presence or absence of properties in the second class. There are various ways in which this basic idea can be made more precise.

Perhaps the most intuitive way to proceed is to exploit the notion of a B- or S-doppelganger. A B-doppelganger of an object is an object that has exactly the same B properties as the original. An S-doppelganger is one which has exactly the same S properties. Thus, for example, if B includes only two sorts of properties, height and weight, then your B-doppelgangers are all and only those things that have the same height and weight that you do. One vivid way to explicate the various versions of the idea that B properties determine S properties is to use the picturesque language of possible worlds. If in all possible worlds, every pair of B-doppelgangers that exist in that world are also S-doppelgangers, then we will say that S *weakly supervenes on B*. So if S weakly supervenes on B, then in any possible world we select, if we know that a pair of objects in that world share the same B-properties, we know they share the same S-properties as well. And if a pair of objects in that world do not share the same S properties, we know that there must be at least one B property that one has and the other doesn't. We can build a stronger notion of supervenience if we relax the restriction that the B-doppelgangers are in the same world. We will say that S *strongly supervenes on* B if all B-doppelgangers of an object, no matter what possible world they inhabit, are also S-doppelgangers. Obviously, strong supervenience entails weak supervenience. Plainly there are lots of other distinctions that might be drawn by restricting attention to one or another special class of possible worlds. But we will leave all of that to the aficionados. Henceforth, when we use 'supervenience' we will mean weak supervenience, as characterized above, unless otherwise specified.

4.3. The Supervenience Base: Three Proposals

On what sorts of properties might it be thought (or hoped) that intentional properties should supervene? As we read the literature, there are at least three proposals for the Base class on which intentional properties must supervene if nasty consequences are to be avoided. We propose to consider each of these proposals, proceeding from the most restrictive to the least.

4.3.1. The first idea is that something untoward will follow if the intentional properties of an organism do not supervene on the *current, internal, physical properties* of the organism. These are the properties that organisms share with their Putnamian doppelgangers—the hypothetical particle for particle replicas that exist in some far corner of space-time.[19] And if intentional properties supervene on current internal physical properties then in any given world, organisms must have the same intentional properties as their Putnamian doppelgangers. What makes this proposal particularly interesting is that it is widely agreed that there are possible worlds in which organisms and their Putnamian doppelgangers *do not* share all of their intentional properties. Indeed, that's the main point that Putnam's famous thought experiment was supposed to establish. George Bush has many beliefs *about* Michail Gorbachev; he has no beliefs at all about Twin-Gorbachev, the atom for atom replica in some far-off corner of the universe. The situation is just the opposite for George Bush's doppelganger. Twin-Bush has lots of beliefs about Twin-Gorbachev, and none about the Gorbachev who leads his life in our part of the universe. But while there is considerable agreement about the fact that at least some intentional properties don't supervene on current, internal, physical properties, there is much less agreement on what unwelcome consequences this failure of supervenience is supposed to entail. Let's consider the options.

First on our list, as always, must be the specter of intentional irrealism— the thesis that intentional properties aren't "real properties of things." But surely intentional irrealism would be a preposterous conclusion to draw from the fact that intentional properties don't supervene on current, internal, physical properties. For there are *lots* of properties of objects that don't supervene on their current, internal, physical properties—often, it would appear, for much the same reason that intentional properties do not. And it would be quite absurd to suggest that non-supervenience entails irrealism in *all* these cases. To see the point, consider a few examples. There are lots of copies of Picasso paintings in the world. And some of them are astoundingly accurate. Let us imagine that someone produces a "perfect" copy—a canvas that is an atom for atom duplicate of the original. Of course, the perfect copy would still be a *copy*, it wouldn't be the original. For to be an original Picasso, a canvas must have the right *history*—it must actually have been painted by Picasso. Much the same point can be made about real $100 bills. A master counterfeiter might produce a bill that is an atom for atom replica of one produced by the Bureau of Engraving and Printing. But it would still not be a *real* $100 bill. Indeed, as Fodor has noted, not even *God* can make a real $100 bill. Only a branch of the U.S. Treasury can do that.[20] It follows, then, that neither the property of being an original Picasso nor the property of being a genuine $100 bill supervenes on the current, internal, physical states of an object. So if a property's failure to supervene on current, internal, physical states were sufficient to show that nothing has the property, then it would follow that there are no genuine Picassos or real $100 bills. But that, of course, is just silly. The idea that intentional irrealism follows from failure to supervene on current, internal, physical states is equally silly.

Before pushing on, it will be useful to mention a rather different sort of example. Both genuine Picassos and real $100 bills are artifacts. And it might be thought that natural properties or categories are not linked to history in this way. But this is almost certainly a mistake. To see the point, consider the classification of organisms into species. Regardless of how similar a pair of organisms are, it is plausible to suppose that they will not count as members of the same species unless they also share the appropriate sort of evolutionary history. If there are creatures in Australia that evolved from birds, then they do not count as members of the same species as Stich's cat, Eggplant, no matter how similar their current, internal, physical states and Eggplant's current, internal, physical states may be. And if scientific explorers on Mars should come upon a macro-molecule that is an atom for atom replica of an HIV virus isolated on Earth, it would not be an HIV virus unless it shared a common evolutionary ancestry with HIV viruses found on Earth. If this is right, then the property of being a cat and the property of being an HIV virus do not supervene on the current, internal states of the entities that have those properties. But here again, it would be simply absurd to conclude that there are no such things as cats or HIV viruses.

What we have been arguing in the last two paragraphs is that intentional irrealism does not even begin to follow from the fact that intentional properties do not supervene on the current, internal, physical states of organisms. Let's now ask whether one of our other discomforting conclusions follows from the failure of the intentional to supervene on this sort of Base. Does it, perhaps, follow that intentional states, though they exist, must be causally impotent— that believings can't cause sayings, that wantings can't cause scratchings—and thus that the end of the world is near? It seems clear that the answer is no. To see why, consider an analogy. Suppose some poor fellow, call him Henry, is crushed to death when an original Picasso sculpture falls on him. Being crushed by an original Picasso caused Henry to die. In some possible world in which Henry exists, we may suppose that he has a Twin who is crushed to death by an atom for atom identical statue, but one which was not made by Picasso. So being crushed by an original Picasso does *not* cause Twin-Henry to die. Nonetheless it is "literally true" that being crushed by an original Picasso caused Henry to die. Consider now the case of intentional causation. Suppose that both Bush and Twin-Bush say, "Gorbachev is bold." Only Bush believes that Gorbachev is bold, however; Twin-Bush believes that Twin-Gorbachev is bold. Does this difference somehow entail that it could not be "literally true" that Bush's belief caused his utterance? Since it appears that this case is entirely parallel to the previous one, it's hard to see why we should be skeptical about one causal claim and not about the other.

Another worry that one might have at this point focuses on the causal efficacy of *properties* rather than *states*. The concern might be put like this:

> Though it is true enough that Bush's belief state causes his utterance despite its failure to supervene on his current, internal, physical properties, it isn't true that this state causes his utterance *in virtue of being the belief that Gorbachev is bold*. What is worrisome about this sort of failure to "naturalize" the intentional is that it makes intentional properties causally irrelevant.[21]

Now we are none too clear about how one goes about determining the causal efficacy of properties. But, for argument's sake, let us grant that if intentional properties do not supervene on the current, internal, physical properties of organisms, then intentional properties are not causally efficacious. Would this be a major catastrophe? So far as we can see, it would be no catastrophe at all. For given any intentional property, it is easy to find a "narrow" surrogate of that property which *does* supervene on the current, internal, physical state of the organism. Following Stich (1991b), we can take the property of believing that [p] to be the narrow surrogate of believing that p. The extension of the expression, "_____ believes that [p]" is just the class of all possible individuals who believe that p along with all of their current-internal-physical-property doppelgangers.[22] Similarly, we could construct a "narrow" surrogate for the property of being an HIV virus. The extension of this surrogate property would be the class of all possible entities that have the property of being an HIV virus, along with all their current-internal-physical-property doppelgangers. Here, again, the narrow surrogate *will* supervene on the current, internal, physical states of the entities in question. Thus even if we grant that intentional properties (and properties like being an HIV virus) are not causally efficacious, there is no reason to fear that the end of the world is near. In both cases, the properties fail to be causally efficacious because they have historical or relational components "built in." But it is easy enough to characterize narrow surrogates that factor out the historical or relational components. And we see no reason at all to suppose that these narrow surrogates are not causally efficacious. It's hard to think that even Fodor's Granny could ask for more.[23]

Let's turn to the worry about laws. Does the fact that intentional properties don't supervene on current, internal, physical states indicate that they cannot play a role in laws? There are, in the literature, a number of arguments aimed at establishing some sort of link between laws and properties that supervene on the current, internal, physical states of systems. But we don't propose to tackle these arguments head-on, for, if the truth be known, we are not at all sure we really understand them.[24] But we are sure that when one starts looking at cases, the proposed link seems very implausible. Consider the HIV virus. Though the details are still to be worked out, it is plausible to assume there is a lawlike connection between infection by the HIV virus and the death of certain cells that play an important role in the immune system. Thus something like the following might well turn out to be a law:

> For all x, if x is infected by the HIV virus (and certain further conditions are met), then most of x's T-cells will be destroyed.

But if the current worry were correct, then there could be no such law, because being infected by the HIV virus is not a property that supervenes on an organism's current, internal, physical state. For a rather different example, consider Greshem's Law which claims that bad money drives good money out of circulation. Plainly, neither the property of being money nor the properties of being good and bad money supervene on the current, internal, physical state of coins, banknotes, wampum, and the like. But this is no reason at all to suppose that Greshem's Law is mistaken. Analogously, the fact that intentional properties do not supervene on the current, internal, physical states of organisms does not entail that intentional properties cannot play a role in laws. So the reading of "naturalizing the intentional" which requires showing that the intentional supervenes on the current, internal, physical state of the organism, fails to satisfy our first constraint. If the intentional can't be naturalized (in this sense) nothing on our list of unwelcome consequences will follow.

4.3.2. A second proposal for a supervenience base widens the base class by dropping the restriction to *current, internal* states. On this proposal, intentional properties will be naturalized if we can show that they supervene on *physical* properties of the organism. Though it is not entirely clear which properties to count as physical properties, a natural way to construe the current proposal is to take the physical properties to be those that might be invoked in physical laws. When the proposal is construed in this way, however, just about everything we said in the previous section can be repeated with minor modifications. More specifically:

i) Intentional properties do not supervene on physical properties. The crucial difference between Bush and Twin-Bush is that the former has had appropriate causal interactions with Gorbachev, while the latter has had completely parallel interactions with Twin-Gorby. But having had appropriate causal interactions with Gorby (rather than Twin-Gorby) is not the sort of property that is likely to be invoked by a physical law.

ii) Being a genuine Picasso or a real $100 bill doesn't supervene on physical properties either. Thus

iii) If the fact that a property, P, does not supervene on physical properties is sufficient to establish that nothing has P, then we would have to be irrealists about genuine Picassos and real $100 bills. And that's absurd.

iv) So the failure of the intentional to supervene on the physical will give no support at all to intentional irrealism.

v) The properties that differentiate people who are crushed by original Picassos from their Twins who are crushed by perfect copies are not properties that will be invoked in physical laws. But it may still be literally true that Henry's death was caused by being crushed by an original Picasso. Analogously, the fact that Bush believes that Gorbachev is bold, while Twin-Bush believes that Twin-Gorbachev is bold, does not entail that Bush's utterance was not caused by his belief. And finally,

vi) The properties that distinguish real HIV viruses from their atom for atom duplicates on Mars are not properties that physics is likely to invoke. Nonetheless, it may well turn out to be a law that if a person is infected by HIV, then most of his or her T-cells will die. So the fact that a property does not supervene on physical properties does not preclude it from being invoked in a law. Thus the failure of the intentional to supervene on the physical would not entail that intentional properties can't be invoked in laws.

We conclude that the second proposed base does no better than the first. If naturalizing the intentional means showing that the intentional supervenes on the physical, then if the intentional can't be naturalized, none of our catastrophic consequences will follow.

4.3.3. The final proposal for a supervenience base that we will consider is the one that Fodor seems to be urging in the quote with which we began this section. If semantic and intentional properties are real properties of things, he urges, they must be identical with or supervene on "properties that are themselves neither intentional nor semantic." So let's ask whether our constraints are satisfied if we construe naturalizing the intentional to require that intentional properties weakly supervene on the class of all non-intentional and non-semantic properties. The answer we would urge is no. But in this case the problem is with the second constraint not the first. For when naturalizing is understood in this way, the claim that the intentional can't be naturalized is extremely implausible—indeed it may be incoherent. To see the point, we need only remind ourselves of what has to be the case if one class of properties, S, does not supervene on another, B. For supervenience to fail, there must be a possible world in which there are B-doppelgangers that are not S-doppelgangers. That is, there must be objects, x and y, in some world that share all of their B-properties but do not share all of their S-properties. On the current proposal the B-properties are *all* non-intentional and non-semantic properties. So the B-doppelgangers, x and y, must share their physical properties, their relational properties, their spatial location, their temporal location, and their history. But surely if x and y share *all* of these properties, then x and y are *identical*. And if x and y are identical, then they share all their properties, including their intentional properties.

On the current reading of what naturalizing comes to, it would indeed be a catastrophe if the intentional could not be naturalized. For if this happened then in some possible world there would be a single object which both did and did not have a certain property, and logic itself would crumble.[25] Fortunately, there is not the slightest reason to take this prospect seriously.

4.4. Global Supervenience

Before bringing this essay to a close, we propose to take a brief look at a third strategy for spelling out the idea of one class of properties supervening on another, the one that goes by the label *global supervenience*. In defining both weak and strong supervenience, the notion of *objects* that were B- or S-doppelgangers of one another played a central role. But, as the name suggests, in global supervenience the central notion is that of *worlds* that are doppelgangers of one another. A pair of possible worlds are doppelgangers of one another with respect to a given property if and only if the total distribution of the property in one of those worlds is the same as the total distribution of the property in the other. So, for example, a possible world which is exactly like our world except for the fact that Stich's cat, Eggplant, has a black nose rather than a pink one would be a shape- and size-doppelganger of the actual world. But that world would not be a color-doppelganger of the actual world. With this notion in hand, we can define global supervenience as follows: A class of properties, S, *globally supervenes* on a class of properties, B, if and only if all possible worlds that are B-doppelgangers are also S-doppelgangers. So if S globally supervenes on B, then if a pair of worlds are indistinguishable with respect to the properties in B, they will also be indistinguishable with respect to the properties in S.

In the previous section, we considered three proposals for the base class on which it might be thought that intentional properties should supervene. The first of these, the class of current, internal, physical properties of an object, has no obvious application when global supervenience is at issue. But the other two, the class of physical properties and the class of all non-intentional properties, might both be proposed as a global supervenience base for the class of intentional properties. Let's consider each of them in turn.

Recall that, as we proposed to unpack the notion, a physical property is one that might be invoked in a physical law. Do intentional properties globally supervene on physical properties, when physical properties are construed in this way? The answer, we think, is clearly no. For it seems extremely plausible to suppose that there is a possible world, W_1, that is a physical doppelganger of the actual world as it exists right now, but which has no history at all. W_1

is one of those worlds that Russell often worried about. It was created just a few seconds ago, fully stocked with phony fossils and light waves racing toward earth just as they would be if they had been emitted by stars millions of years ago. But if W_1 has no history, then, according to many philosophers, the distribution of intentional properties in W_1 must be very different from the distribution of intentional properties in our world. For in our world, Laurence has lots of beliefs about Julius Caesar; he is connected to Caesar in just the right way to have these beliefs, whatever that way is. But in W_1, Laurence has no beliefs about Caesar. There was no Caesar to have beliefs about in W_1, so Laurence couldn't be connected to him in the right way.

Very well, then, intentional properties do not globally supervene on physical properties. What follows? Nothing terribly troublesome, so far as we can see. The arguments here are pretty much the same as those in 4.3.2. There are *lots* of properties that do not globally supervene on physical properties—the property of being a genuine Picasso, for example (there are no genuine Picassos in W_1), and the property of being a real $100 bill. But from the fact that these properties do not globally supervene on the physical, it surely does not follow that there are no real Picassos and $100 bills in our world. Analogously, from the fact that the intentional doesn't globally supervene on the physical, it does not follow that intentional properties are not instantiated in our world. The property of being an HIV virus doesn't globally supervene on the physical either. But from this we cannot conclude that this property can't be invoked in laws, nor, alas, can we conclude that being infected by HIV doesn't cause people to die. And here, again, the situation for intentional properties looks to be exactly the same.

What about the broader base, the class of all non-intentional properties. Do intentional properties globally supervene on this base? Once again, so far as we can see, the answer is no. For it certainly seems to be logically possible for there to be a world, W_2, that is a non-intentional doppelganger of the actual world, but in which trees or cars or dead people have beliefs or desires or some other intentional states. And it also seems logically possible for there to be a world, W_3, that is a non-intentional doppelganger of the actual world, but in which Dan Quayle has no thoughts at all—he's just a mindless organic robot. The sorts of worlds we are imagining are, near enough, the sorts that some property dualists suppose the actual world might be. And whatever problems one might think this sort of property dualism confronts, it certainly does not seem to be a logically incoherent view. If it is not logically incoherent, if worlds like W_2 and W_3 really are possible, then intentional properties do not globally supervene on non-intentional properties. But it is hard to see why anyone would think that catastrophic consequences follow. Surely the logical possibility of a world like W_2 or W_3 does not entail that intentional properties are not instantiated in the actual world. Nor, so far as we can see, does it even begin to entail that *in our world* intentional states are causally impotent or that they cannot be invoked in laws of nature.

At this point, we fear, a resolute opponent might begin fiddling with the notion of *possibility* that is embedded in the definition of global supervenience. Such an opponent might suspect that problems will arise if there are pairs of *nomologically possible* worlds or *metaphysically possible* worlds that are non-intentional doppelgangers but not intentional doppelgangers. The path on which our imagined opponent has embarked is not one we're tempted to follow, for we suspect that it leads directly to a metaphysical swamp. Moreover, even if unwelcome consequences really do follow in these cases—and we see no clear reason to suppose that they do—we are inclined to think that both of them violate our second constraint. It is certainly not *intuitively* plausible that there are pairs of nomologically or metaphysically possible worlds that *are* non-intentional doppelgangers but *are not* intentional doppelgangers. Most people, including many who seem to have exquisitely subtle metaphysical intuition, have no intuitions at all about matters like this. So until someone presents a plausible argument that such world pairs are nomologically or metaphysically possible, we see no reason to take the prospect seriously.

5. CONCLUSION

It's time to sum up. We began with Fodor's observation that "the deepest motivation for intentional irrealism derives . . . from a certain ontological intuition: . . . that the intentional can't be *naturalized*." But we have had no success at all in making sense of this motivation. If the motivation is to stand up to scrutiny, there must be some account of what naturalizing the intentional comes to which satisfies a pair of constraints. First, the account must sustain an argument from the premise that the intentional can't be naturalized to the conclusion that nothing satisfies intentional properties (or perhaps to the conclusion that intentional states are causally impotent, or to the conclusion that there can be no intentional laws). Second, the claim that the intentional can't be naturalized must not turn out to be utterly implausible. None of the accounts we have been considering satisfy both of these constraints. Of course, it is always possible that there is some other account that will satisfy the constraints. But at this point we think the ball is in the other guy's court. Until some account of naturalizing is given that satisfies both constraints, the most plausible view is that the motivation that Fodor recounts is simply confused. There may be good reasons to take the prospect of intentional irrealism seriously, but the worry that the intentional can't be naturalized is not one of them.

NOTES

We are grateful to Brian McLaughlin for many hours of helpful discussion. Versions of this essay have been presented at CUNY Graduate Center, Notre Dame University, the University of North Carolina–Greensboro, the Australian National University, and the University of Virginia. Comments and criticisms from those audiences are acknowledged with thanks. After completing work on this essay, early in 1992, we were delighted to discover that Michael Tye (1992; this volume) had independently arrived at a very similar view.

    1. Fodor (1990a), 156.

2. Fodor (1987), xii.

3. See, for example, Block (1986), Devitt (1990), Dretske (1981; 1988), Field (1978), Fodor (1984; 1987; 1990a; 1990b), Loar (1981), Lycan (1988), Millikan (1984), Papineau (1987), Schiffer (1982), Stalnaker (1984).

4. Schiffer provides a characteristically forthright illustration of this attitude. On his view, the question of how the semantic and the psychological are related to the physical is "an urgent question" since "we should not be prepared to maintain that there *are* semantical or psychological facts unless we are prepared to maintain that such facts are completely determined by, are nothing over and above, physical facts" (1982, p. 119).

On Fodor's view, the urgency of the issue reaches to the very core of contemporary academic life. For if the intentional can't be naturalized, then lots of people who work in cognitive science should no longer get government-sponsored research grants.

> If it turns out that the physicalization—naturalization—of intentional science . . . is impossible, . . . then it seems to me that what you ought to do is do your science in some other way. . . . [I]f you really can't give an account of the role of the intentional in the physical world. . . . [then] by Christ . . . we should stop spending the taxpayer's money. (Fodor, 1990c, pp. 202–203)

5. Dretske (1989), 1. See also Dretske (1988), 80, and Dretske (1990), 6.

6. Fodor (1984), 32.

7. Fodor (1981), 283–84.

8. Fodor (1981), p. 288.

9. For a useful discussion of the Classical View, see Smith & Medin (1981), chapter 3.

10. See Smith & Medin, chapters 4–6.

11. For Fodor's view see Fodor (1981).

12. In the passage from Fodor (1984) quoted at the beginning of this section, he insists that "what we want at a minimum is something of the form *'R represents S' is true iff C.* . . ." But in later papers Fodor is prepared to accept a lot less. In the following passage, for example, he no longer insists on necessary and sufficient conditions. Rather, he tells us, merely sufficient conditions will do.

> I want a *naturalized* theory of meaning; a theory that articulates, in nonsemantic and nonintentional terms, sufficient conditions for one bit of the world to be *about* (to express, represent, or be true of) another bit. (Fodor, 1987, p. 98; see also Fodor, 1990, pp. 51–52)

But as noted by Jones, Mulaire & Stich (1991), if we read him literally this is just too easy. Here are two sufficient conditions that seem to meet Fodor's requirement.

> If R is Fodor's most recent utterance of "Meaning Holism is a *crazy* doctrine" (or the thought that underlies it) then R is *about* Meaning Holism, and R is true iff Meaning Holism is a crazy doctrine.

> If R is Laurence's most recent utterance of "Madonna is daring" (or the thought that underlies it) then R is about Madonna and expresses the proposition that Madonna is daring.

Obviously, it would be an easy task to produce indefinitely many more. But perhaps this reading is uncharitably literal. Perhaps what Fodor requires in a naturalized theory of meaning are sufficient conditions which follow from the meaning of the terms involved. It is easy enough to provide intuitively plausible sufficient conditions of this sort for many non-intentional terms. Here's one:

> For all x, if x is a sow, then x is a pig.

But, of course, examples like this are cheating. In the spirit of Fodor's requirement that sufficient conditions for representation or aboutness be stated in *nonsemantic* and *nonintentional* terms, we should require that the sufficient conditions for being a pig be stated in *nonporcine* terms. Once *this* requirement is imposed, however, providing meaning-based sufficient conditions for being a pig looks to be just about as intractable as providing a full-blown definition. If it is impossible to provide such sufficient conditions, that will be an interesting result in lexical semantics. But it will *not* entail that there are no pigs. Similarly, if it turns out that meaning-based sufficient conditions cannot be given for intentional locutions, it will not follow that meaning is a myth.

13. See, for example, Millikan (1989), 290–91.

14. Canfield (1983), Donnellan (1983), Leplin (1979; 1988), Shapere (1982).

15. See, for example, Devitt & Sterelny (1987), Secs. 4.2 & 5.2.

16. For some elaboration on the argument set out in the last two paragraphs see Stich (1991a & in preparation).

17. Fodor (1987), 98.

18. Haugeland (1982), Horgan (1982), Kim (1978; 1982; 1984; 1987), Lewis (1983), Petrie (1987), Teller (1984).

19. This idea, or something like it, is suggested in Stich (1978; 1983) and in Fodor (1980; 1987; 1991). For the original account of Putnamian doppelgangers, see Putnam (1975).

20. Fodor (1987), 45.

21. For a vivid illustration of this worry, see Dretske (1988), 79–80.

22. Alternatively, if the reference to possible individuals is problematic, we can take the extension of "_____ believes that [p]" in a given possible world to be the class of all individuals in that world who believe that p, and all their current-internal-physical-property doppelgangers in that world, and all individuals in that world who are current-internal-physical-property doppelgangers of individuals in other possible worlds who believe that p. (The account in Stich [1991b] neglects this last conjunct.)

23. For more Fodor's Granny and her views, see Fodor (1987), passim, and Loewer and Rey (1991), ii.

24. One of these arguments is to be found in Fodor (1987), chapter 2. Another is to be found in Fodor (1991). Fodor himself no longer claims to understand the first of these. For a critique of the second, see Christensen (forthcoming).

25. This argument will not work if naturalizing is unpacked in terms of *strong* supervenience, since in that case the B-doppelgangers might be in different possible worlds. Our view about the account of naturalizing that requires *strong* supervenience on *all* nonintentional properties is much the same as our view—set out at the end of 4.4—about the account that requires *global* supervenience on those properties.

REFERENCES

Baker, L. 1987. *Saving Belief.* Princeton.

Block, N. 1986. "Advertisement for a Semantics for Psychology." *Midwest Studies in Philosophy: Studies in the Philosophy of Mind.*

Canfield, J. 1983. "Discovering Essence." In *Knowledge and Mind,* edited by C. Ginet and S. Shoemaker. Oxford.

Christensen, D. Forthcoming. "Causal Powers and Conceptual Connections." *Analysis.*

Devitt, M. 1990. "A Narrow Representational Theory of the Mind." In *Mind and Cognition,* edited by W. Lycan. Oxford.

Devitt, M. and K. Sterelny. 1987. *Language and Reality.* Cambridge, Mass.

Donnellan, K. 1983. "Kripke and Putnam on Natural Kind Terms," in *Knowledge and Mind,* edited by C. Ginet and S. Shoemaker. Oxford.

Dretske, F. 1981. *Knowledge and the Flow of Information.* Cambridge, Mass.

———. 1988. *Explaining Behavior.* Cambridge, Mass.

———. 1989. "Reasons and Causes." *Philosophical Perspectives* 3.

———. 1990. "Does Meaning Matter?" In *Information, Semantics and Epistemology*, edited by E. Villanueva. Oxford.

Field, H. 1978. "Mental Representation." *Erkenntnis* 13.

Fodor, J. 1980. "Methodological Solipsism Considered as a Research Strategy in Cognitive Psychology." *Behavioral and Brain Sciences* 3.

———. 1981. "The Present Status of the Innateness Controversy." In *Representations*, edited by J. Fodor. Cambridge, Mass.

———. 1984. "Semantics, Wisconsin Style." *Synthese* 59. Reprinted in Fodor (1990a). Page references are to Fodor (1990a).

———. 1987. *Psychosemantics*. Cambridge, Mass.

———. 1990a. *A Theory of Content and Other Essays*. Cambridge, Mass.

———. 1990b. "Psychosemantics, or: Where Do Truth Conditions Come From?" In *Mind and Cognition*, edited by W. Lycan. Oxford.

———. 1990c. "Roundtable Discussion." In *Information, Language and Cognition*, edited by P. Hanson. Vancouver.

———. 1991. "A Modal Argument for Narrow Content." *Journal of Philosophy* 88.

Haugeland, J. 1982. "Weak Supervenience." *American Philosophical Quarterly* 19.

Horgan, T. 1982. "Supervenience and Microphysics." *Pacific Philosophical Quarterly* 63.

Jones, T., E. Mulaire, and S. Stich. 1991. "Staving Off Catastrophe: A Critical Notice of Jerry Fodor's *Psychosemantics*," *Mind and Language* 6, no. 1.

Kim, J. 1978. "Supervenience and Nomological Incommensurables." *American Philosophical Quarterly* 15.

———. 1982. "Psychophysical Supervenience." *Philosophical Studies* 41.

———. 1984. "Concepts of Supervenience." *Philosophy and Phenomenological Research* 45.

———. 1987. " 'Strong' and 'Global' Supervenience Revisited." *Philosophy and Phenomenological Research* 48.

Leplin, J. 1979. "Reference and Scientific Realism." *Studies in History and Philosophy of Science* 10.

———. 1988. "Is Essentialism Unscientific?" *Philosophy of Science* 55.

Lewis, D. 1983. "New Work for a Theory of Universals." *Australasian Journal of Philosophy* 61.

Loar, B. 1981. *Mind and Meaning*. Cambridge.

Loewer, B., and G. Rey, Eds. 1991. *Meaning in Mind: Fodor and his Critics*. Oxford.

Lycan, W. 1988. *Judgement and Justification*. Cambridge.

Millikan, R. 1984. *Language, Thought and Other Biological Categories*. Cambridge, Mass.

———. 1989. "In Defense of Proper Function." *Philosophy of Science* 56.

Papineau, D. 1987. *Reality and Representation*. Oxford.

Petrie, B. 1987. "Global Supervenience and Reduction." *Philosophy and Phenomenological Research* 48.

Putnam, H. 1975. "The Meaning of 'Meaning'." In *Language, Mind and Knowledge: Minnesota Studies in the Philosophy of Science* 7.

Schiffer, S. 1982. "Intention Based Semantics." *Notre Dame Journal of Formal Logic* 23.

Shapere, D. 1982. "Reason, Reference and the Quest for Knowledge." *Philosophy of Science* 49, no. 1.

Smith, E., and D. Medin. 1981. *Categories and Concepts*. Cambridge, Mass.

Stalnaker, R. 1984. *Inquiry*. Cambridge, Mass.

Stich, S. 1978. "Autonomous Psychology and the Belief-Desire Thesis." *The Monist* 61.

———. 1983. *From Folk Psychology to Cognitive Science*. Cambridge, Mass.

———. 1991a. "Do True Believers Exist?" *Aristotelian Society*, Supplementary Volume 65.

———. 1991b. "Narrow Content Meets Fat Syntax." In *Meaning in Mind: Fodor and His Critics*, edited by B. Loewer and G. Rey. Oxford.

———. In preparation. *Deconstructing the Mind*.

Teller, P. 1984. "A Poor Man's Guide to Supervenience and Determination." *Southern Journal of Philosophy*, Supplement to Volume 22.

Tye, M. 1992. "Naturalism and the Mental." *Mind* 101.

———. This volume. "Naturalism and the Problem of Intentionality."

MIDWEST STUDIES IN PHILOSOPHY, XIX (1994)

What Is a Mind?

ARNOLD ZUBOFF

THE REPLACEMENT ARGUMENT

Let's imagine that a chunk of your brain was to be replaced by a wire and transistor gadget that, as we shall just stipulate, will keep precisely the same causal relationship with the rest of the brain that the replaced chunk had. We can know, based merely on this stipulation of the sameness of the gadget's effects on the rest of the brain, that you will behave and speak exactly as you would have done if the circumstances were otherwise the same but no such replacement of a chunk of the brain had been made. For the parts of the brain responsible for speech and behavior must, according to the stipulation, be affected by the gadget in all ways as they would have been by the normal brain chunk.

But think about this: it would be absurd for us thus to be assured that you would go on behaving and speaking the same after the replacement if it were possible for us to think that your experience might have been different from what it would have been with the chunk of brain unreplaced. If the replacement by wires and transistors in that part of brain activity could have made you see or hear or feel or think any differently, how could we have the assurance our stipulation must give us that you would not do or say anything different? (Anyone who is not startled by this step in the argument is probably not understanding it.) A gadget that saves the pattern of mental functioning must, surprisingly, therein have saved the experience too.

So we can know *a priori* that the preservation of nothing more than that brain chunk's extrinsic causal role within the rest of the mental system also perfectly preserved all the nature of any experience to which that chunk of brain had made a contribution. The radical change of intrinsic properties, from those of the brain chunk to those of the gadget, was necessarily irrelevant to what the experience was like. For only the extrinsic causal role could have shaped the speech and behavior and other mental functions whose sameness was sufficient to make it absurd that the experience be different. Anything that maintained that role must maintain that contribution to experience, regardless of its intrinsic properties and, I could add, regardless of the presence or absence of any epiphenomena that might have been thought to have depended on those intrinsic properties.

And we can argue that this brain chunk, which was standing for any, is also standing for all the chunks of the brain at once. For, since the replacement of one chunk of the brain by something that maintained its causal role within the mental system kept experience the same, a further such replacement of an additional chunk must also preserve experience, and then, by the same reasoning, any more replacements after that as well. If the whole brain was replaced by gadgets, or anything else, that maintained the same causal pattern, the mind would be unaffected. So, it seems, we have discovered what makes the mind what it is in an ordinary brain: the causal pattern of that brain's parts in relation to each other and behavior and speech.

This is, I think, an immensely powerful argument for the view of the mind called functionalism, and more specifically for that form of functionalism called the causal role identity thesis. But the argument has proceeded too quickly here, and some of what I have said will need some qualification. So let's start again and take things more slowly.

THE GADGET REPLACEMENT OF THE VISUAL CORTEX

I would like us to begin afresh by thinking carefully about sight. The initial processing of the stimulation of the eyes leads from the eyes to the visual cortex, at the back of the brain. The visual cortex is in turn connected by networks of neurons to parts of the brain that are involved in speech, movement, and other functions that are responsive to vision.

The significance of these connections is brought out in a case of aphasia where one set of them breaks down. Someone with a lesion between the visual cortex and the speech-center that prevents the speech-center's receiving impulses from the visual cortex cannot speak about what he is seeing. He will either say that he is blind or say that he is seeing something that is actually very different from what is there.[1] The philosophically unsettling thing is that, since the visual cortex is still properly connected to movement and other functions, much of the same person's conscious behavior apart from speech is based on vision. The same person who sees where to move and how to handle things will honestly say he is seeing something different or not seeing at all. Later we will discuss the challenge that this strange disagreement of functions poses to our usual thinking about experience. But what concerns us now is that the aphasia case suggests that speech will be informed by vision if and only if a speech center receives the proper pattern of impulses.

Now we may consider an imaginary case in which the visual cortex has been replaced by a gadget of wires and transistors that is caused by the stimulation of the eyes to send to the speech center and the rest of the brain exactly the same pattern of impulses as they would have been receiving from the replaced chunk of brain. And, with no more than this, I think we are now in a position to draw a powerful conclusion about the nature of a mind.

We can know that, with our gadget in place, speech and behavior will be, *must* be, exactly like the speech and behavior that would have occurred if the visual cortex were there. This is not speculation. It follows immediately from our stipulation of the character of our imaginary gadget. So long as the stipulated gadget is one with the same input/output relationship with the rest of the brain as the replaced visual cortex, all the rest of the brain can do no other than everything it would have done with the normal visual cortex.

The crucially instructive conclusion we may next draw from this is that the visual, and other, experience of the person with the gadget must be exactly the same as it would have been in the normal case. If things looked different or if vision disappeared altogether, surely a person would, or at least might, say "things look different" or "I am blind" and behave accordingly instead of carrying on as though with the normal vision he was not having. If there could have been any change at all in the experience of the person with the gadget, it things could have looked different, we could not have the assurance we do have that speech and behavior would be the same.

FUNCTIONAL PROPERTIES

Soon we will consider more fully whether this result I am claiming, that the gadget preserves experience, is correct. But if it is correct, what does that say about the role of the visual cortex in vision? It will help answer this if we define what I shall call the "functional" property or character of the visual cortex. Among the many properties of the visual cortex, neural, chemical, and computational (and let me also mention the imagined property of generating epiphenomena), there is the functional property of the visual cortex, its purely extrinsic property of causing a particular pattern of effects in the various mental functions. But the visual cortex possesses this extrinsic functional character only because its intrinsic neural and other properties have combined to produce the required pattern of external effects. Let's briefly explore an example of the same kind of relationship of functional and other properties in the workings of the eye.

Retinene is a light-sensitive chemical in the retina of the eye. When this chemical reacts to light it triggers impulses in associated neurons. After a processing of these impulses in the visual cortex, the original retinene reactions are finally translated into effects in the mental functions. In this way the functions are made responsive to the light and the object emitting it.

Now, the functional character of this retinene depends on, but is not equivalent to, its chemical character. Another light-sensitive process that could replace the retinene with no change in the ultimate effects in the mental functions would therein possess the same functional character as the retinene, even though the replacement's non-functional characterization might have been radically different. If the laws of nature were so unaccommodating to such substitution as to have made it impossible for anything but retinene to play its role, it would still have been solely the pattern of effects in the mental functions and not the intrinsic chemical character itself that defined what we are calling the retinene's functional character; and it must be this alone that counted in the character of experience. Similarly, if nothing like our gadget replacement of the visual cortex were in any way possible, we still would have shown, merely by invoking it, that visual experience is logically determined by purely the functional character of the visual cortex, that sameness in the effects of its output is equivalent to sameness in the experience.

Let me take a moment to repeat our important gadget replacement thought experiment in a somewhat more dramatic form. In humans the right half of the visual cortex processes the left side of the visual field while the left half processes the right side. Imagine that one night, without your knowing it, a mad surgeon of remarkable powers replaced only the left half of your visual cortex with a gadget of wires and transistors that would have all the same input/output relationship to the rest of your brain as the removed part.

We can know, given the stipulated character of the gadget, that all the next day you would have been treating things as though they were looking the same on both sides of your visual field. But would they actually be looking the same? Well, there is no reason things seen on the side of your visual field processed by the normal half of the visual cortex should look anything but normal. But what of your experience of the other side, processed by the gadget? Would the part of this page to the left of center in your vision look normal, while the part to the right look different because of the enormous difference of intrinsic properties between the gadget and the brain tissue? But just try to imagine that there was a radically abnormal look to anything seen on the right, a look that was different from that of even the same thing when seen on the left, while you just went on thinking, talking, and acting as though things looked the same, and the same as usual, on both sides of your vision. That's absurd. If your experience were affected by the intrinsic difference of the gadget, how could it be that it is impossible you ever say, do, or think anything about there being any difference?

MUST THE EXPERIENCE BE THE SAME?

Of course one and the same pattern of speech and behavior, as described from the outside, might be produced by very different psychological states, as when sincerity is replaced by pretending. It is this consideration that seems to defeat the behaviorist attempt to define the mind purely in terms of behavioral dispositions. But in our case we know that the pattern of psychological responses to vision remains the same; it is impossible that anything like pretending be introduced by the gadget as stipulated. For the parts of the brain that would be involved in pretending, or in any other psychological complication that could have produced the same speech and behavior despite a difference in the experience, are necessarily unchanged by the gadget and therefore unadjusted to any change in experience. So the speech and behavior, it seems, must simply be responsive to an unchanged experience.

But there may be a way we can think of even the psychological pattern remaining the same despite important differences in the quality of experience. It seems I can easily imagine myself as experiencing red objects with the same phenomenal quality with which I now experience blue objects and vice versa. And it seems I can also easily imagine myself as having experienced color differently in this way from birth (which is essentially, of course, the tale often told by philosophers about such a difference of experience between two people). It seems I could further imagine that, despite that private difference in experience, I was still taught to say a fire was "red" and the sky was "blue" and, whichever qualia I regularly experienced with them, I still formed the same patterns of practical, intellectual, emotional, and irrational associations and reactions regarding the colors of fire and sky. It seems that the pattern of my psychological responses, not just my behavioral dispositions, could have been the same as now in such an imagined case of qualia inversion, while my experience of red and blue was different. Moreover, it seems I can imagine an automaton, with something like my pattern of mental functioning in its mechanism, but with no qualia, no experience, at all.

But just as it is impossible that anything like pretending be introduced by the gadget, it is impossible also that anything be introduced like the sort of sweeping qualia inversion or absence that might be imagined to allow experience to change while the pattern of mental functioning stayed the same. For, once again, it is impossible for the remainder of the mental system to adjust in any way to any change in the experience processed by the gadget, since the remainder of the mental system is, due to the stipulation, necessarily unchanged.

An inversion that might seem to be without functional implications would have to be both systematic and total; it would have to occur consistently across the whole of the experience involving the relevant qualia, and therefore, in this case, in the qualia of visual memories and imaginings as well as in those of all of immediate vision. (And an absence of qualia that might seem to be without functional implications would have to be a total absence of all the qualia, an absence, that is, of all consciousness.) But our gadget replacement was of only the left half of the visual cortex. So if this replacement somehow resulted in an inversion or absence of qualia in the vision processed by the gadget, this inversion or absence on the right side of vision would clash with the necessarily unchanged qualia of visual memories and associations, as well as with the unchanged qualia of the other side of the visual field. Such a clash would make it absurd, in the now familiar way, that the pattern of mental functioning could not be reflecting a clash. So qualia inversion or absence cannot be what is happening in the gadget replacement. The experience must simply be the same.

Anyway, even if we did still entertain the idea I have been attacking, that visual qualia are changed by the gadget replacement, we would surely not have expected that this change would be a systematic inversion of the qualia. For in the wires and transistors of the gadget there is nothing resembling a systematic inversion of intrinsic properties of the replaced left visual cortex. We would surely have expected, in the vision processed by the gadget, not a neat inversion but rather a weird new wiry and transistory quality or, perhaps because of the lifelessness of the materials of the gadget, an absence of qualia on that side of vision. Let's examine a bit these very natural thoughts. They take us, I believe, to the heart of the error I am hoping to expose.

It misleadingly seems to us that the intrinsic nature of our quale of red cannot be determined by something as extrinsic to our visual processing as the external pattern of the gadget's causal relations with the surrounding brain. And this seems aptly illustrated by the ease with which one can imagine color qualia reversing their roles in one's psychology, as we earlier did with red and blue. Impressed by the apparent non-relational immediacy of qualia and their seeming interchangeability, we want to link them intimately to non-relational, interchangeable intrinsic properties of the brain. And we can then seem to understand the possibility of qualia inversion as the possibility of a role reversal in brain activity, between, say, "chemical x" and "chemical y."

But what can prevent our imagining a reversal of the roles of such functionally interchangeable chemicals between the right and left visual cortex of the same person? And then, according to this assignment of qualia to such intrinsic determinations, red and blue things on one side of the visual field would look the other way around from how they looked on the other side; yet they would be treated and thought of, in all the activities of the rest of the brain in which they were compared, as looking the same on both sides. And this would be absurd.

If we are to imagine that qualia can be totally inverted or absent without functional implications, this requires that we think that qualia depend on interchangeable non-functional properties of a sort that *could* thus be inverted or absent without functional implications. But that means it must also be possible that these non-functional properties, and therein qualia, could be changed unsystematically, and that there could be merely partial inversions or absences of qualia, without any functional implications. And this, of course, is absurd.

(Let me just point out here that the anti-functionalist thought experiment of inverted qualia and the pro-functionalist thought experiment of the gadget replacement both require us to be thinking of non-functional properties that can be changed without functional significance. The difference is that the non-functionalist maintains that qualia are dependent on such properties while the functionalist maintains that qualia must be independent of them.)

The gadget replacement swept away the specifically brain-like intrinsic properties. With the gadget there would no longer be anything at all like a chemical x and chemical y in visual processing to account for the difference between the look of red and the look of blue. Yet with the gadget in place you would be treating red and blue and the difference between them just as you usually do; and in fact, as we earlier concluded, it must be that you would still be experiencing them as you usually do. Any attempt to identify mental determinations with such intrinsic determinations of perceptual processing as these chemicals must be misguided.

Let me mention a further couple of closely related considerations against taking qualia to depend like this on internal details of visual processing. We speak about, think about, and otherwise respond to qualia. How would non-relational, interchangeable details of the workings of the visual cortex, such as the presence of chemicals x and y, be communicated in a distinctive fashion across the brain to the speech center and the areas involved in the other functions?

Our visual cortex emerged from evolution shaped by the requirement that it contribute to the kind of ordered responses to the world that allowed us to survive. Our responses to the world that are based on vision depend on the extrinsic causal character of the visual cortex, on how it affects the rest of the brain. There would have been no evolutionary pressure for neatly differentiating and organizing non-relational, interchangeable chemical or other details of visual processing. If the red and blue qualia within immediate vision, within imagination, and within memory all depended on the presence of chemicals x and y, by what hand would these have been distributed appropriately across the relevant brain activities? Evolution would have been blind to all but how we functioned. Any qualia that were determined by non-functional detail would have been overwhelmingly likely to end up anarchic or perhaps undifferentiated rather than ordered as they are in our experience. We would be dealing with the world as though through orderly vision, but the qualia would be in a mess, as clearly they are not. Experience and functioning cannot be put into the merely contingent relationship that these intrinsic properties have to functioning without absurd results. We must rather understand everything of experience including qualia as defined by its relation to the functions of the mind.

But, one might think, there may yet be a way to resist this conclusion. What about the very aphasia case I described earlier? We would naturally regard it as absurd that a person could at once be moving based on vision and honestly reporting he is not seeing that scene in which he is moving. This case of mental inconsistency seems impossible, yet it exists. So maybe what we rejected, a gadget replacement in which experience changed with no effect on mental functioning, is like aphasia, and only seemingly impossible. But the cases are crucially different.

We try to imagine what it is like for the aphasia patient to move around and deal with objects based on vision that he honestly says he is not having. We then realize that the state of vision on which the movement is based and the very different state of vision on which the speech is based must each be experienced as though it did not belong to the same person who is in the other state. But surely both states must really belong equally to the patient. If only one of them had existed, it would undoubtedly have been his experience. How can the mere existence of the other have changed that ownership? The solution to this puzzle, then, is that it must just be *seeming* to the patient that he is in only one of these visual states. He is really in both states at once, but with an illusion in each that he is not in the other. *Being* in both is not the same as *knowing* that one is. This confusion between metaphysical and merely epistemic boundaries is what makes such a break between the functions of a single person's mind seem impossible though it really is not.[2]

Notice that this case of aphasia, unlike that of the gadget replacement, has functional implications, which are essential to it. It consists in a disharmony between functions, those of speech and movement, which corresponds, we must suppose, to an alienation between the visual experiences on which these functions are based.

But while such a break between functions is possible, a break between a function and the experience on which that function is based is a different matter. Honestly reporting that one did not see based on an experience of seeing, or moving about based on seeing when one did not see, really is an impossibility, a contradiction. Both honestly speaking about and behaving towards colors as though they looked the same on both sides of the visual field based on an experience of them as radically different is an impossibility, a contradiction. These are the sorts of genuine impossibilities that made it impossible that our gadget did not preserve experience; for if, as given by our stipulation of the gadget, the same mental functions had to be there, then we could know *a priori* that the same experience had to be there as well.. The sameness of function must logically determine the sameness of experience. But how? Let me try to explain.

THE FUNCTIONAL ANALYSIS OF EXPERIENCE

Please make yourself alternate between seeing transparent cube *A* as being oriented like cube *B* and like cube *C*. There should be a dramatic shift in the look of the picture of *A* as you change from one way of regarding it to the other. How are we to understand your experience in this shift?

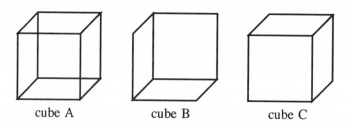

cube A   cube B   cube C

A naive view is that the shift is an event in the object, in the picture on the paper, and you are simply open to this in your perception of it. If it were not for the special obviousness in this case of a reason for rejecting it, this naive view would be by far the most natural one. After all, that view agrees with how things look. The phenomenal properties of the picture are changing, and it can only look to us as though the picture in itself is changing.

What makes it so obvious in this case that the natural view is wrong is that you are controlling the shift. Which way the picture looks is decided by you, not by anything in the object. So you know that what changes is not the object but something in you, your way of seeing it. As philosophers we are lucky here. Since in the struggle for survival either way of seeing such a cube (called a "Necker cube" in perceptual psychology) could be useful, in this special sort of case nature has allowed us not only a rare power over our own perception but with it also a rare opportunity to see beyond our usual naivety. In most cases we simply take our perception as a passive openness to the object, which is thought of as in itself just as we see it. But now we may learn that seeing anything requires an activity in us, of seeing it as something.

The Necker cube can, I think, suggest strongly to us the secret of what this visual experience is. Is it not plausible that the shift in your experience of the cube be nothing but a shift between two systematic patterns of potential psychological and behavioral responses, the responses that you would make if called on to describe the cube, trace its front side, imagine objects resting upon it, etc.? When you are shifting from one way of seeing to the other, and the object is looking as though it is changing in its properties, the various ways you would function regarding that object are shifting. The suggestion is that the change of look in the object is nothing but the shift in the functions, from an appropriateness of function to one orientation of the cube to an appropriateness of it to the other orientation. In that change in the functions, and logically inseparable from it, the look of the object is changing. The object could not now look like that without such a shift in the functions and there could not be such a shift in the functions without it now looking like that. The shift in functions and in look are necessary and sufficient conditions of each other. And this that the Necker cube so strongly suggests is that which our consideration of the gadget replacement had already proved. Experience is logically determined by function.

Someone who straightforwardly saw an object would be therein fixed to say, do, and think things appropriate to it having a look; that would be its having that look for him. A lesion between the visual cortex and the speech center could, in robbing him of some but not all of that appropriateness of function, make us say he both does and does not see. Further such lesions, between the visual cortex and more functions, would rob him of more ways in which he was seeing till finally, cut off from having any functional character, the visual cortex would have lost its significance for vision and he would be straightforwardly sightless.

The appropriateness of potential responses to an orientation of the cube would not be a consciousness of the potential responses themselves. No, rather the existence of the pattern of potential responses would be the consciousness of the orientation of the cube. And one must not imagine lots of distinct structures and determinations in the brain, each designed to deal explicitly with another circumstance in which another appropriate response would be implied by the existence of the mental state. Thus if an appropriate response is that I would, with the right motivation, describe cube *A* as seeming to have the orientation of cube *B*, one must not expect the function of speech to include an explicit, spelled-out determination that I would be so describing it to a circus clown named Bozo to whom I was honestly reporting my experience or that I would be ready to say the appropriate thing in some particular ancient lost language if I had learned to speak it. These implications would be there, in my function of speech, if it was fixed in a way appropriate to my seeing that orientation of the cube; but they would be there only implicitly.

Let's now examine more closely what happens when we see. Light from the object strikes the retinas. In the retinas light-sensitive chemical reactions trigger an immediate pattern of impulses in associated neurons. Specialized cells are so connected with this immediate stimulation that they are stimulated only by various abstract features of it. For example, one specialized neuron will receive impulses when, and only when, lines lie at a certain angle, no matter where on the retinas they are registered. This will finally be translated into functional responses to that angle of line as an abstraction. Much of the processing in the visual cortex carries on like this, with more and more general features of the scene being registered in specialized neurons. But none of this is vision if it is considered only at this stage. None of it ever would be vision if it did not issue in functional effects that fixed the look of the object of vision by their appropriateness to its being that way.

A pawn in a game of chess may be a piece of stone or a piece of wood. Its being stone or wood is an intrinsic property not importantly related to its being a pawn. That the piece of stone or wood is also a pawn is logically determined by its extrinsic property of possessing a role in a game. Without the context of the game it makes no sense to call this a pawn. Yet the pawn still is the piece of wood or stone. It has intrinsic properties too, intrinsic properties which must be consistent with its role if it is to be a pawn. It would be a crude mistake to want to identify the pawn somehow with the wider game and not the piece of stone or wood simply because it is the wider game that makes the stone or wood also a pawn.

Seeing the angle of a line is something caused by the relevant stimulation of the eyes, something that in its turn then causes the various appropriate functional determinations of talking, thinking, and behaving, the ones that go with the line being seen as at that angle. I do not want to say that seeing the angle is the determination of the functions any more than I would want to say that a pawn is a game of chess. It is the stimulation of the specialized cell in the visual cortex that is the seeing of the angle, but only because of its effects in the functions. Without those effects the seeing would be bereft of its phenomenal character, as well as its behavioral and internal psychological implications, and then it would be no seeing. I am here endorsing a view called "the causal role identity thesis"; I am endorsing it, that is, if it includes my understanding of phenomenology. A mental item has its mental nature purely through playing the causal role of that item; but its playing that role, I would insist, is to be understood, as we proved through our gadget replacement case, to be fixing any phenomenal character the mental item may have. This is crucial because a phenomenal character is essential to much of the mental. What would a pain be without it?

And, speaking of pain, let me reinforce this analysis of vision with a consideration of another mental item, a pain in my right hand. The naive view that is directly suggested by the way the thing seems is that an unpleasant substance or quality is actually occupying an area of my physical hand, just as some injected material would be doing. But no physical investigation of my hand will turn up that substance or quality. Furthermore, someone who had lost an arm could be genuinely encountering an object just like this one, as a phantom limb pain, without the hand even being there.

The naive view is that if the area of the pain then shrinks two causally connected events are occurring. The pain itself is shrinking, and this shrinking of the pain is causing my experience of it to change accordingly. But there are not here two causally connected events. It would be absurd, a contradiction, for the pain to shrink while my experience failed to reflect this. My experience of the pain logically determines the entire existence and nature of the pain itself. This is not to say that the pain as mental object somehow is the experience of it. This also would be absurd. The pain and the experience of it are correlatives. For a purely phenomenal object like a pain, to be is to be perceived. Its whole existence and nature is logically determined by the existence and nature of the experience of it. In a sense only the experience exists, since in its existence alone does the pain exist; but then in that other sense, of course, that it is perceived, the pain does exist. And all its phenomenal properties, of location, intensity, unpleasantness, are determined utterly in the experience of them.

But what makes the experience an experience of just such a pain? Try to think of my feeling that pain in my right hand while I was in all ways fixed to respond to it as a tickle on the sole of my left foot. How could it have the properties of a pain in my right hand then? How could it fail to be instead a sensation of a tickle on the sole of my left foot?

The pain or the tickle, the phenomenal object, exists only in there being an experience of it. This experience is the brain process, or whatever else, that plays the psychological causal role of the experience of the pain or the tickle. And this experience possesses its phenomenological character, and therein the pain or tickle possesses its apparent character, solely through the experience's functional character, through the way it affects the mental functions that would deal with the pain or the tickle.

Yet much of the mental is partly or wholly unconscious. The conscious mental activities, speech, imagination, voluntary movement and so on, are, as it happens, in the upper part of the brain. They typically are highly integrated with and reflective of each other, though, as we saw in the case of aphasia, they are not necessarily so. When a child learns to use a spoon, at first it is the conscious mind that awkwardly deals with it. As the child practices, however, neurons lower down in the brain are firing sympathetically with the conscious brain activity and also averaging out the mistakes and clumsiness. Such actions, once learned, are far better performed unconsciously. Soon it will not be the conscious mind that deals with the spoon. The conscious mental activities will be free for those things done better by them.

In the view I am urging consciousness is not an occult quality but rather a certain area and style of activity. Consider for a moment some things that lie on the borderline of consciousness. Some detail of your peripheral vision or the sensations in your toes, were you really conscious of these before I mentioned them? That may be hard to say. But they were brought very definitely into consciousness when I did mention them. In your becoming more conscious of the toes they became much more influential in the conscious mental activities; you then were ready to talk about them, think about them, perform voluntary actions in response to them. My view, of course, is that this much fuller occupation of your conscious functions with the state of your toes just was your more definite consciousness of them.

FURTHER GADGET REPLACEMENTS

Anyway, this is the sort of understanding of experience consistent with the logical dependence of experience on function discovered in contemplating a gadget replacement of part or all of the visual cortex. And if we now simply followed that successful replacement of the visual cortex with similar replacements of additional chunks of brain, one might have supposed that we would continue to find that experience could not have been changed after any such replacement. Finally, could not the whole brain be imagined as replaced with no possibility of a loss to the original mind?

But it is not that simple. With the visual cortex all that turned out to matter was the sameness of its ultimate effect on the functions. Soon I shall be stressing just how little of the normal visual cortex that required. But when our additional imagined replacements are in the areas of the brain associated with the mental functions themselves, we do not want to end up inadvertently replacing them by other functions that combine to yield the same effects or even with no proper functions at all, if the effects may be maintained without them. To preserve the original functions, and therein the experience, we must, in our replacements, be respectful of the character and the boundaries of the functions.

I believe it will help our thinking about the meaning of gadget replacements in the rest of the brain if we first deal with that business I mentioned of just how little of the visual cortex is required for experience. We should consider a case of the replacement of the visual cortex by a gadget that feeds merely random impulses into the rest of the brain. This could be just a shell with energy randomly playing on its surface and flowing into the surrounding nerves. It may seem that the result for the state of the functions in this case would be chaotic. But let's also imagine that this substitution has been tried in countless different cases, and we are now attending to a case in which the pattern in the rest of the brain ended up accidentally precisely as the normal visual cortex would have produced it. We may not want to say that the subject is properly seeing an object, since the connection between his visual experience and the object is not reliable. But surely the visual experience must still be phenomenologically the same as it would have been with the reliable gadget or the visual cortex. The subject would speak and do the same; so it must all be seeming the same to him.

Could the experience be continued if there were replacements of other parts of the brain by other such accidentally successful shells? First let's take this random gadget case to an extreme. Imagine that the whole brain is replaced by a shell that uselessly receives impulses from nerves that had previously led into the brain and also randomly stimulates the nerves that had led out of the brain. The resulting movement of the body will both seem and be mindless. But we are interested in just one among countless such experiments, one in which the external forms of the speech and behavior of a normal person were perfectly, accidentally, matched. Would there be a mind there?

I remarked earlier that behaviorism failed in its attempt to define mental states purely in terms of behavioral dispositions because the same pattern of behavior, as described from the outside, might have been produced by very different psychological states, as when sincerity is replaced by pretending. Any set of behavioral dispositions, no matter how complex and precisely specified, will be consistent with virtually unlimited numbers of psychological states in which beliefs, perceptions, and motives have been so adjusted to each other that they would be producing such behavior. Not to mention all the logically possible cases of random neural firings or random gadgets that forever, accidentally, would remain consistent with the given set of dispositions. The point is not whether these states are at all likely. That more than one of them would be logically consistent with that same set of dispositions is what destroys the behaviorist attempt actually to define logically any one of the psychological states, or any mental item in one, by way of such dispositions alone. Any set of dispositions must logically underdetermine the psychological state that accounts for it.

I think our shell-brained creature, despite its impressive pattern of external movements and sounds, precisely those of a proper person, would have no psychological state at all. The operation of this thing involves no mental functioning. With no functions there is no experience, no mind, only show. Even unconscious mental states could only seem to be there. For it has no unconscious functioning; and, besides, something that is never capable of consciousness cannot have a mind and therefore cannot have desires or beliefs, even ones that are unconscious.

Let's next consider the replacement by a shell of just one hemisphere of the brain. This, I think, would be like a case of aphasia. In the remaining normal hemisphere there would be mistaken impressions of normality in the whole, while in the shell there would really be no functions and no experience.

It is vital to remember that the absence of the half of the visual cortex that belonged to the shell-replaced hemisphere is not going to result in a missing side of the visual field for the remaining functions. As we have established repeatedly, the visual field exists through the functions, not in the immediate visual processing. The remaining functions will be equally responsive to both sides of vision, since the pattern that is caused in them by the shell is the same as would have been caused by the replaced hemisphere. In our earlier case of aphasia the function of speech was blind while the functions of movement were visual: in this case a hemisphere's functions are gone altogether while the functions of the remaining hemisphere are responsive to the whole of the visual field.

Finally let's think of a neat shell replacement of a complete function, for example some aspect of movement. If what I said earlier about the Necker cube, and the gadget, is correct, then how one is ready to move in relation to an object is part, along with the other visual functions, of what determines how the object looks. Since the shell would, even though accidentally, be fixing that the person move in ways appropriate to the object as seen in the normal case, perhaps this would be sufficient for the same experience to be occurring in this case too. Or is this a bit of a shell game? Do we think there is experience in this shell when nothing of experience is there? Is this another case like aphasia, as was the recent hemispheric shell replacement, with an illusion of complete normality in the other, proper functions but no real experience in what is only a shell of a function?

Let's try to think a little more deeply about how the look of the Necker cube was logically determined by the ways we would respond to it. When I am looking at the cube, there is an enormously complex set of forces, of tensions, in me, that would, in conjunction with those tensions that are my motives, have me talking and behaving in ways appropriate to one orientation of that cube rather than the other. The point is not at all that I am directly aware of the tensions themselves; I am not. It is rather that in the mere existence of the psychologically pertinent tensions, those that shape my responses, exists my experience of the cube.

The explanation of the existence of these tensions would be irrelevant to their phenomenological character. It seems to me therefore that the shell that neatly replaced a function could be properly participating, even though only accidentally, in the set of tensions that is experience. The shell that replaced the whole brain, however, would be doing no more than accidentally matching an external pattern of movements that any number of combinations of such tensions might have produced; but this would be without the tensions, without experience.

But can we understand qualia this way? Could the look of red, like the look of a Necker cube, be plausibly derived from nothing but how I would respond to that look, when in a lifetime's qualia inversion I would have responded in all the same ways, but to my current look of blue?

An alternative might again seem to be to associate or identify qualia with intrinsic brain properties, this time not of the visual cortex, however, but rather of the parts of the brain that embody the functions themselves. But I think we may counter this temptation with a careful new program of imagined replacements.

This must be careful because we must remember the danger of inadvertently introducing the sort of aphasia that occurred when we replaced an entire hemisphere by a shell; when replacing chunks of brain that embody the functions we must care for preserving the nature and boundaries of those functions if we wish to be sure of preserving the experience. But it would seem there is no danger if we imagine the replacement, by a tiny gadget, of only a single neuron among all those involved in some function informed by vision. And any further replacements of individual neurons, no matter how many we may make, could also carry none of that risk of either fusing or losing functions that would be incurred if a replacement straddled the boundaries of functions in the manner of the hemispheric shell.

So we have confidently replaced some neurons by tiny gadgets that maintain the input/output relations of those neurons to the rest of the function they are in and to the brain in general. Let's say this function has me slowing in response to the color of a warning signal. If something in the experience to which this function is the response, namely the quale of red, is to be understood as dependent on the presence of chemical x in the intrinsic properties of the function, then replacements by tiny gadgets of neurons that contain chemical x will have robbed the experience of that quale, while the function remained unaffected. But this would be the familiar absurdity. Nothing can in this way come between a function and the experience that is its basis. If I am slowing in response to the signal, the quale that has me doing this is there for me.

We can be confident that a replacement by tiny gadgets of all the neurons in the brain could have preserved the mind perfectly, if, as I believe, we can be confident that this replacement could have preserved the nature and boundaries of all the brain's functions. But if we were to worry that even such replacements on the level of neurons might somehow interfere with the functions, that is of no matter to our real thesis. The important point is that we know *a priori* that whatever did preserve the functions would therein preserve the mind. We know, then, what the mind is. Even if, because of natural laws that were strangely unaccommodating to such substitutions, any replacement of the brain would somehow upset its pattern of functioning, this would leave our thesis untouched. If we extend our meaning of "functional property" beyond the earlier *property of affecting a function* to include now also *property of being a function*, we may say that experience is logically determined by only the functional properties of the brain.

Earlier I made a point about how the evolution of the visual cortex would not have organized qualia if qualia depended on its non-functional properties. We can apply this point to the idea of qualia depending on non-functional properties of the functions. If the quale of red, whenever it occurred within the various experiences of speech, movement, imagining, and memory depended on the presence of chemical x, by what hand would this have been distributed consistently across all these functions? Evolution would have been blind to all but functional properties, since survival would be hanging on these alone.

In rejecting the non-functional account of qualia we are rejecting two popular views of the mind. One is a physicalism that would simply identify qualia with non-functional physical properties. The other is epiphenomenalism, a form of dualism. The epiphenomenalist balks at identifying a quale with something so obviously unlike it as a physical property of the brain. But he is so impressed by the indications in brain research that the physical character of the brain and its environment is sufficient to explain the physical activities and interactions of the brain, that he describes the qualia, and all mental occurrences, as mere epiphenomena, non-physical epiphenomena, of brain activity, each caused by some particular physical occurrence in the brain but not itself having any causal powers. So instead of identifying a quale with a chemical x he will say that the presence of something like chemical x in the relevant brain activity is the immediate physical cause of an epiphenomenal non-physical experience of that quale.

Both the non-functional physicalist and epiphenomenalist must believe that a gadget replacement changes experience, since with it all the non-functional properties would have changed. But we know such a change in experience without a change in function is absurd. If an epiphenomenalist untypically decides to make his mental epiphenomena causally depend instead on functional properties, he is still out of luck, since the sameness of functions could not establish with logical necessity the sameness of experience if experience is a logically contingent effect of the functions. No, the logical impossibility of the change in experience requires the logical determination of experience by function. It requires the truth of functionalism.

THE REPLACEMENT ARGUMENT AND INTERACTIONISM

But there is a second form of dualism that might seem to have escaped these problems. This is substance dualism, interactionism. The interactionist agrees with the epiphenomenalist that the mental is obviously not physical. But unlike the epiphenomenalist he is not impressed by the indications of brain research that the physical properties of the brain and its environment are sufficient to account for all the physical activities and interactions of the brain. For he thinks the brain's activities are caused in part by an interaction with something that is not physical, the mind. The mind's creativity and will are a non-physical kind of causation. The brain is merely the mind's mechanistic instrument. The brain mechanically processes sensory stimulation; but if there is to be any experience at all, the result of this processing must somehow be apprehended by the immaterial mind, in which all the actual consciousness of perception occurs. In response to this consciousness, the mind may engage in the peculiar, non-mechanistic activities of thought, decision, and willing; and the willing can somehow trigger the brain to pass impulses through nerves to muscles that move the body in a way that was willed.

The interactionist might seem to have avoided the absurdity that arises from identifying or associating qualia with non-functional physical properties of the brain. But till we know where he stands on qualia inversion, we cannot say whether he has really escaped the absurdity.

The problem is that we have not yet specified whether this interactionism is a functionalist or a non-functionalist one. Does the immaterial mind have its mental character because of its functional or its non-functional properties? If the interactionist believes that my quale of red could, with no functional implications, be interchangeable with my quale of blue in a total systematic qualia inversion, then the interactionist is committed also to the absurdity that these qualia could be partially and unsystematically changed with no implications for the functions. That this contingent relationship of functional and non-functional properties occurred within an immaterial substance could make no difference. The problem would be merely reproduced in an exotic medium.

In our gadget replacements we were imagining a physical brain and its mechanical interactions. But the point that it would be absurd for me to be carrying on functionally the same if my experience changed partially and unsystematically, the point against the contingent relationship of qualia and functioning, is independent of this material setting. The claim that if any physical replacement maintained the function it would therein preserve the experience would still be true and relevant if in fact no physical replacement, because no material thing, could actually maintain the function. The argument did not at all depend on the replacement being physical; it depended only on the replacement maintaining the function. If any non-physical replacement maintained the function, it too would preserve the experience. And if it happened that there could be no replacements within a mental substance (as before we imagined there might be allowed no physical substitution because of unaccommodating natural laws), the point would remain (as before), that the functional properties logically determined the experience.

Of course, the interactionist who is a functionalist must allow that if ever it is shown that the physical brain actually does embody our mental functioning then the physical brain would have completely accounted for the mind. And although as a functionalist he really has avoided the absurdity of identifying or associating qualia with non-functional properties, he has the same problem as any functionalist in explaining the seeming possibility of qualia inversion.

A FUNCTIONAL ANALYSIS OF COLOR QUALIA

So what should a functionalist say about qualia inversion? It is not surprising that colors are experienced as systematically interchangeable on the most obvious level of functioning. For colors serve, quite literally, as mere placeholders in our spatial experience. It must be that one color could easily appear in the place of another. Yet colors must be distinguishable; something in how we experience them makes red look different from blue. Anyone who embraces functionalism because of the *a priori* reasoning of this essay must say that, since only functional properties determine the experience of qualia, when we imagine an inversion of that experience without any obvious functional change we are actually imagining an inversion of certain subtler functional properties that give the colors their particular looks. But what could these subtler functional properties be?

At one time it was popular to talk about the "red-green paradox," that two people might be experiencing red and green qualia that were inverted between them with no sign of this difference in their speech or behavior. But philosophers have largely been won over instead to talking about an inversion of the whole spectrum (with which my earlier inversion of red and blue is roughly in line). This is because the qualia of red and green are not in every way interchangeable after all; they are differently related to the qualia of the other colors.

For example, green will be produced by a blending of blue and yellow. This looks right to us. But if your quale of green was replaced by that of red, the unchanged blue and yellow qualia would be rather unconvincing in producing the former red quale instead of the green when they blended. This would look wrong, even if experienced that way from birth. It was thought that standing the qualia of the rainbow upside down, an inverted spectrum, would preserve the pattern of blending. But this has been challenged. I think the truth is rather that each color quale is in a unique relationship with all the others. For then we may be able to understand a quale as logically determined by the set, appropriate only to that quale, of one's potential responses to its potential blendings and contrasts.

There is a feature of color experience that perceptual psychologists call "color constancy." I once looked at my familiar brown briefcase lying on a couch and was surprised to discover that a spot on its surface had turned pink. My first thought was that perhaps some strong bleach had been splashed on it. But after a while I realized that a circle of bright, unusually focused sunlight was shining on the briefcase through a small opening in a curtain across the room. As soon as I recognized this fact the color constancy in my perception changed the look of the color of that spot from pink-in-the-shade to a lighted-up brown. I was able then to make myself move back and forth between seeing one color and the other, just as you were able to do between the two orientations of the Necker cube.

I think that when my experience of that color changed what was crucially changing was a set of implicit potential responses to relationships of colors and light, to how this color would blend and contrast with others, in sunlight or out of sunlight. To see this color as pink-in-the-shade was to be ready, implicitly, with all those responses appropriate to its looking pink-in-the-shade; and the change to seeing the color as lighted-up brown was a change to an alternative state of readiness and appropriateness that was dramatically different. If a color has any look for us we must be in a state of appropriate response to that look.

And the *a priori* assurance that functions preserve all experience requires that the color having its look just is our being in such a functional state.

The functions of speech and behavior that we are tempted to think would remain unaffected in a systematic qualia inversion are those based on extrinsic relationships of qualia, such as being associated with certain names or objects. The functions that I am arguing logically determine the qualia are based rather on qualitative relationships that are inherent in the qualia and inseparable from their natures.

The number nine has extrinsic relationships with its name and with the planets of the solar system, which happen to be nine in number but might not have been. But its inherent relation to three, considered as its square root, logically determines that the number is nine. Nothing that has nine's relationships with three, or with five hundred and four, could fail to be nine. Just so, nothing could fail to be a certain quale that had its inherent relationships with the other qualia. And an expression of those same inherent relationships in the higher functions, in the implicit potential responses to the look of a color, could not fail to be an experience of that quale.

But the main point for me is not that such an account of our experience of qualia is in its own right persuasive. It is rather that something like this account must be correct because functionalism can be established as necessarily true by the reasoning of our replacement argument.

I confess that the combination of the replacement argument for functionalism and the inverted spectrum argument against it has sometimes appeared to me to represent an unresolvable paradox at the heart of the mind-body problem. On the one hand it seemed easy to conceive of total systematic inversions or absences of qualia that were functionally irrelevant. On the other hand the proposition that such functionally irrelevant changes in qualia were possible would have had to imply that the qualia depended on non-functional properties; and this in turn would have had to imply that there could also be partial, unsystematic changes in qualia that were functionally irrelevant. We have seen that such non-functional disturbances of experience would be absurd. They would be far more clearly absurd, I have been arguing, than the determination of qualia by purely functional properties.[3]

If I find myself insisting that my experience of red is uncapturable by any functional analysis, I can stop myself by reflecting that if God were playing a trick on me, of fiddling with the character of whatever was causing me to speak, as long as God preserved just its functional implications for speech, I would go on talking in exactly this way about the absurdity of functionalism. Until, of course, this reflection stopped me. Functionalism seems to me by far the lesser of two apparent absurdities.

ONE LAST REPLACEMENT STORY

At the relatively unimportant risk of seeming repetitious, I would like to end by telling again a replacement story, though this time in a way that may summarize the debate in a manner not earlier possible.

Imagine that I am frozen soon after my death and that after many decades I am finally thawed and revived. The doctors explain to me that, though I was in good shape otherwise, they decided to replace the damaged left visual cortex (where my fatal injury occurred) with a device that would maintain the normal relationship of inputs and outputs with the rest of my brain. I begin to express fears that this will affect the character of the relevant half of my visual field; but then they explain further that the replacement has been carried out already. Well, I can detect nothing unusual about my vision. So I exclaim how pleased I am that, despite the replacement, my vision has the same old character it always had on both sides of my field of vision; and I thank them very much.

What I have told, of course, is a functionalist story. Only functionalism could allow, not to mention require, experience to go unaffected by a replacement of the left visual cortex that preserved all and only its functional properties and none of its non-functional ones.

It is essential to an understanding of this whole debate to be clear that a proper skeptic about functionalism would not be concerned about whether it was possible to make such a replacement. In his own stories of inverted or absent qualia such replacements are made; non-functional properties are changed systematically with no functional effect. The debate is entirely about what is logically establishable about the mental *if* such a change is imagined.

For both views are concerned with conditionals. Functionalism can be expressed as the conditional statement, "*if* and *only if* the functional properties of a mind are preserved, its mental character is preserved." Skepticism about functionalism can be expressed as, "*if* there is a preservation of functional properties with a change of the non-functional ones, we are not logically forced to think that the mental character has not been changed." What any skeptic about functionalism needs to show, then, is that we are not forced logically to tell my story in the functionalist fashion.

But there are just two non-functionalist ways to try to reconstruct this story. That neither way is coherent is the doom of non-functionalism.

In one attempted reconstruction, on being revived I am struck by a great difference in the quality of the right side of my visual field and I complain of this. The doctors apologize; they should have listened to the warnings of the skeptics about functionalism. This is the sort of effect on experience the skeptics had feared.

Such a reconstruction of the story is impossible, however. If the gadget replacement about which the skeptics had warned was the one relevant to the issue, the one, that is, that actually did preserve the input and output relationship of the left visual cortex with the rest of the brain, then it would have been impossible for me honestly to complain that my vision was any different from normal. For the pattern of neural activity in my speech center, and hence the pattern of my speech, must then have remained the same as with the normal brain. So if I complained like this the doctors would need to be apologizing not for having put their faith in functionalism but for having failed to install a true functional equivalent.

But there is one other attempt at a non-functionalist reconstruction of my story to examine. In this one the stipulated effects of the gadget on speech have not been forgotten, as they were in the first non-functionalist attempt, so I am revived and say exactly what I did in the functionalist story. I exclaim sincerely how pleased I am that, despite the replacement, my vision has the same old character it always had on both sides of my field of vision; and I thank the doctors very much. But the right side of my vision is actually a mess. The vision is metallic or missing; it is not normal at all. Yet not only do I go on thanking the doctors for their great preservation of my vision, there is not as much as a possibility that I could honestly do otherwise. And not only in speech but in memory, imagination, and any other faculty dependent on the rest of my brain, there is not a jot of difference from the normal.

Skepticism about functionalism is based on the claim that preserving only the functional character of the parts of the brain that are involved in experience at least might not be sufficient to guarantee the sameness of the mental. It is impossible to make any sense of this claim.[4]

APPENDIX: A NON-INTERACTIONIST ACCOUNT OF THE INDETERMINACY OF SELF-PREDICTION

Imagine that a computer, with a complete description of its own current state and the rules for the development of this state and shielded from or else informed fully about any future external influences on it, has been given the job of predicting precisely what it will be like in one of its own future states. And imagine this to be a future state whose exact character the computer could calculate only by taking fully into account the precise development of the states leading up to it. Unfortunately, then, one of those states it would have to take fully into account before it could reach the prediction is the predicting state itself, which must, to be a prediction, be only part way along towards the state that it is predicting. So the predicting state would be one of those that would have to be represented before *it*, the very prediction towards which we are supposedly working, can have been arrived at.

Let me try to make more evident the absurdity of this requirement. The prediction could not be made until states that follow the predicting state had been calculated, and that could not happen till the predicting state itself had been determined. But it, the prediction, could not be determined till after those states following it had been calculated. Precise self-prediction of the sort described would always thus require determining the prediction before determining the prediction and always be impossible.

But, leaving prediction aside, there was already a difficulty, of a sort raised by Popper, Ryle, and others, in asking at the start that the computer contain a complete description of its own current state, since the state included the description itself. Therefore the description would not only have had to describe itself and its relations with the rest of the state but also that describing of itself and its relations and so on to infinity.

Notice that these are problems only for *self*-prediction and *self*-description. *Another* computer could predict in detail our computer's future states and entertain a detailed description of our computer's current state. But then that other computer would face the same impossibilities when it attempted to predict its own future or describe its own present state. A computer *could*, however, describe with precision its own *past* states and calculate their development, as long as this remained past. And a computer *could* predict its own future and describe its own current state if this is done with a measure of uncertainty and incompleteness. In particular, it must leave out any detailed account of the nature or effects of its own self-description or self-prediction. But this is not due to any exotic metaphysics; another computer, as we have said, could capture everything.

Each of us strongly feels the impossibility of ever knowing fully or with certainty what he is or what he will do. If I try to grasp what I am or will be, something of that which tries to grasp, the grasping itself, must remain outside the grasp. We are inclined to take this epistemic indeterminacy of self-prediction and self-description for a metaphysical indeterminacy of what we are. The resulting illusion is, I believe, an inspiration for both interactionist dualism and our retributive judgments of desert (in which we must misperceive ourselves as impossibly responsible for our own natures).

(A future state of our computer might be available to precise self-prediction, let me just add, if its detailed character would not be differentially dependent on, and therefore calculable only from, the precise character of the predicting state. For example, from a mere indication that the batteries were running down a computer might predict with precision its own future dormant state.)[5]

NOTES

1. See Norman Geschwind, "Anatomy and the Higher Functions of the Brain," *Boston Studies in the Philosophy of Science* 5 (Dordrecht, 1966/68), esp. pp. 354–55.

2. I say much more about this in "One Self: The Logic of Experience," *Inquiry* 33, no. 33 (1990): 39–68.

3. In his well-known paper "Functionalism and Qualia," which can be found in his book *Identity, Cause and Mind* (Cambridge, 1984), 184–206, Sydney Shoemaker commits the odd mistake of treating the possibilities of qualia absence and qualia inversion unevenly. He rejects the possibility of there being an absence of qualia without functional implications because he considers only a case of partial absence, in which there being no functional implications is, indeed, absurd (as he strangely does not notice would be true also of a partial inversion); and then he accepts the possibility of there being an inversion of qualia without functional implications because he considers only a case of total inversion, in which there being no functional implications is, indeed, plausible (as he strangely does not notice would be true also of a total absence).

His conclusion based on this arbitrary selectivity is that the presence of qualia can be functionally defined, since he thinks absence without functional implications is absurd, but the rigidly predicated character of the qualia cannot be functionally defined, since he thinks inversion without functional implications is possible. I think that his conclusion if he had treated absence and inversion even-handedly would have been the same as mine, that while both absence and inversion of qualia without functional implications seem possible, such a possibility would require that qualia depended on non-functional properties, those that could be absent or systematically inverted while the functional properties stayed the same. And this in turn must require that there be possible partial absences and partial inversions, systematic or haphazard, of such properties, and therein of qualia, without functional implications, which is clearly absurd. The only way of avoiding that clear absurdity is to accept functionalism as the full account of not just the presence but also the character of qualia.

4. The closest thing I know to this essay's replacement argument for functionalism is Gilbert Harman's discussion of the replacement of a pain center, in his book *Thought* (Princeton, N.J., 1973), 38–40. The person who most influenced my thinking about the mind-body problem was, indeed, Gilbert Harman. I had wonderful conversations on this topic with him and with Thomas Nagel when they supervised me in my graduate studies. (It is a bit tempting to describe what I have arrived at as a blend of Harman's functionalism and Nagel's insistence of fidelity to the subjective character of experience.) I am very grateful for advice and encouragement regarding this essay from Tim Crane, G. A. Cohen, Thomas Nagel, Margaret Gullan-Whur, Anne Wagstaff, Alison Ray Fenton, and Myung-Ok Shim.

5. I would like to thank G. A. Cohen and Peter Smith for valuable suggestions regarding this appendix.

Animal Minds

JOHN R. SEARLE

I.

Many species of animals have consciousness, intentionality, and thought processes. By "consciousness" I mean those subjective states of sentience and awareness that we have during our waking life (and at a lower level of intensity in our dreams); by "intentionality" I mean that feature of the mind by which it is directed at or about objects and states of affairs in the world; and by "thought processes" I mean those temporal sequences of intentional states that are systematically related to each other, where the relationship is constrained by some rational principles. Examples of conscious states are such things as feeling a pain or hearing a sound. Examples of intentional states are such things as wanting to eat food or believing that someone is approaching. Examples of thought processes are such things as figuring how to get a banana that is out of reach or monitoring the behavior of prey who is on the move and is trying to escape. Though these three phenomena—consciousness, intentionality, and thought processes—overlap, they are not identical. Some conscious states are intentional, some not. Some intentional states are conscious, many are not. For example, my current thought that it is unlikely to rain is conscious, my belief when I am asleep that Bill Clinton is president of the United States is unconscious. All thought processes, as I have defined them, are intentional; but not every intentional state occurs as part of a thought process. For example, a pang of undirected anxiety, though conscious, is not intentional. A sudden desire for a cold beer is both conscious and intentional. An animal who has a sudden pang of hunger can have that pang without it being part of any thought process.

I have said that many species of animals have consciousness, intentionality, and thought processes. Now why am I so confident about that? Why, for example, am I so confident that my dog, Ludwig Wittgenstein, is conscious? Well, why is he so confident I am conscious? I think part of the correct answer, in the case of both Ludwig and me, is that any other possibility is out of the question. We have, for example, known each other now for quite a while so there is not really any possibility of doubt.

Philosophically speaking the interesting question is why in philosophy and science we have so much trouble seeing that such sorts of answers are the correct ones? I will come back to this point later. Now I want to turn the original question around and ask, why have so many thinkers denied what would appear to be obvious points, that many species of animals other than our own have consciousness, intentionality, and thought processes? Think for a moment how counterintuitive such denials are: I get home from work and Ludwig rushes out to meet me. He jumps up and down and wags his tail. I am certain that (a) he is conscious; (b) he is aware of my presence (intentionality); and (c) that awareness produces in him a state of pleasure (thought process). How could anyone deny either a, b or c? As his namesake might have said, "This is how we play the language game with 'certain'." I now turn to consider some of these denials.

II.

In the seventeenth and eighteenth centuries, in response to the Cartesian revolution, it made sense both philosophically and theologically to wonder whether animals had minds. If, as Descartes had taught us, there were two kinds of substances in the universe, mental substance whose essence was thinking or consciousness, and physical substance whose essence was extension, then the question becomes pressing: Which of the animate extended substances had minds? Which of the living substances contained consciousness?

The basic Aristotelian dichotomy between the living and the non-living was transcended by an even more fundamental dichotomy between those things that had minds and those that did not. The question became even more pressing when people reflected on the theological implications of any philosophical answer that they might care to give. The commonsense view that higher animals are conscious in exactly the same sense that human beings are conscious has the result that every such animal possesses an immortal soul. This is because the Cartesian theory of the nature of the mental, and of the distinction between the mental and the physical, has the implication that consciousness is indestructible. Any mental substance is indivisible and so lasts eternally. But if animals have consciousness, then it follows immediately that they have immortal souls, and the afterlife will, to put it mildly, be very much overpopulated. Worse yet, if consciousness extends very far down the phylogenetic scale, then it might turn out that the population of the afterlife included a very large number of the souls of fleas, snails, ants, etc. This is an unwelcome theological consequence of what seemed a plausible philosophical doctrine.

Another problem that arose even for theologians who were not Cartesians is this: If animals are conscious then they can suffer. But if they can suffer then how is their suffering to be justified, given that they do not have original sin and presumably do not have free will? The arguments that were used to reconcile the existence of an omnipotent and beneficent God with a suffering human population do not seem to work for animals.

We now regard these ways of thinking about the problem of animal minds as completely implausible, and the Cartesians gave an equally implausible solution: On their view, animals simply do not have minds. Animals are unconscious automatons and though we feel sympathy for the dog crushed beneath the car wheel, our sympathy is misplaced. It is just as if a computer had been run over.

Ridiculous as this view now seems to us, I believe it is an inevitable consequence of the rest of the Cartesian system. If every mind is an immortal soul, then only beings that can have immortal souls can have minds. The natural way out of this puzzle is to abandon dualism, both property dualism and substance dualism. And if one abandons dualism, if one really abandons it, then one must also abandon materialism, monism, the identity thesis, behaviorism, token-token identity, functionalism, Strong Artificial Intelligence, and all of the other excrescences that dualism has produced in the nineteenth and twentieth centuries. Properly understood, all these absurd views are forms of dualism.[1]

If one thoroughly abandons dualism, what is the result as far as animal minds are concerned? Before answering that, I want to consider some other more recent attempts to show that animals do not have certain sorts of mental phenomena.

III

Very few people today would be willing to argue that animals lack consciousness altogether. But several thinkers, both philosophers and scientists, have argued that animals either lack intentionality in general or at least that animals cannot think, that is they cannot have thought processes in my sense. I am frankly extremely suspicious *a priori* of any argument of this form because we know in advance that humans do have intentionality and thought processes and we know that humans are biologically continuous with the rest of the animal kingdom. Whatever its surface logical form, any argument against animal intentionality and thinking has to imply the following piece of speculative neurobiology: the difference between human and animal brains is such that the human brain can cause and sustain intentionality and thinking, and animal brains cannot.

Given what we know about the brains of the higher mammals, especially the primates, any such speculation must seem breathtakingly irresponsible. Anatomically the similarities are too great for such a speculation to seem even remotely plausible, and physiologically we know that the mechanisms that produce intentionality and thought in humans have close parallels in other beasts. Humans, dogs, and chimpanzees all take in perceptual stimuli through visual, tactile, auditory, olfactory, and other sensory receptors, they all send the signals produced by these stimuli to the brain where they are processed, and eventually the resultant brain processes cause motor outputs in the forms of intentional actions such as socializing with other conspecific beasts, eating, playing, fighting, reproducing, raising their young, and trying to stay alive. It seems out of the question, given the neurobiological continuity, to suppose that only humans have intentionality and thoughts.

However let us turn to the actual arguments against the possibility of animal thinking. The form of the arguments is and has to be the same: humans satisfy a necessary condition on thinking which animals do not and cannot satisfy. Given what we know of the similarities and differences between human and animal capacities, the alleged crucial difference between humans and animals, in all of the arguments I know, is the same: the human possession of language makes human thought possible and the absence of language in animals makes animal thought impossible.

The Cartesians also thought that language was the crucial differentiating feature that distinguished humans from animals. But they thought the significance of language was epistemic. The possession of language was a sure sign that humans are conscious and its absence a sure sign that animals are not conscious. This view has always seemed very puzzling to me. Why should linguistic behavior be epistemically essential for the presence of consciousness? We know in the case of human beings that children are conscious long before they are able to speak a language and we know that many human beings never acquire the ability to speak a language, but we do not for that reason doubt that they are conscious.

More recent thinkers concede that animals are conscious but think of language as somehow playing a constitutive role in thought, such that beings without language could not have thoughts.

The major premise, then, of these arguments is always that humans have language in a sense in which animals do not have a language, and so far that premise seems to me to be correct. Even those of us who would be willing to describe the waggle dance of the bees as a language and the achievements of the chimpanzees, Washoe, Lana, and others, as genuinely linguistic would still grant that such symbolizing behavior is vastly weaker than any natural human language. So let us grant that, in some important sense of "language," humans have language, and as far as we know, no other species does. What follows about the mind? Well one thing follows immediately: If there are any intentional states whose possession requires a language, animals cannot have those states, and *a fortiori* they cannot have thought processes involving those states. Clearly there are such states. My dog can want me to take him for a walk but he cannot want me to get my income tax returns in on time for the 1993 tax year. He can want to be let out but he cannot want to write a doctoral thesis on the incidence of mononucleiosis among American undergraduates. To have these latter sorts of desires he would have to have, at the very least, linguistic abilities that he lacks. Is there a principle? How do we decide which intentional states require language and which do not? I think there are several principles involved, and I will come back to this question later. Right now I want to continue to follow the arguments against the possibility of any intentionality and thought among linguistically deprived beasts. The argument that there are some intentional states that animals cannot have does not show that they can have no intentional states. Here are some arguments for the stronger thesis.

One argument is that in order to attribute beliefs to a system we have to have a way of distinguishing cases where the system genuinely believes that *p* from cases where the system merely supposes that *p*, hypothesizes that *p*, reckons that *p*, has a hunch that *p*, is certain that *p*, or is merely inclined to think that on balance, all things considered, that *p*.[2] But we cannot make these distinctions for a being that cannot make them for itself, and a being can only make them for itself if it has the relevant vocabulary. The vocabulary need not be the same as or translatable exactly into English, but there must be some vocabulary for marking the different types of intentional states within the range or there is no sense to the attribution of the states.

What are we to make of this argument? Even if we grant the premise that such discriminations require a language it does not follow that we need to be able to make fine-grained distinctions before we can make any attributions of intentional states at all. In fact this premise just seems wrong. Very general psychological verbs like "believe" and "desire" are often used in such a way as to allow for a slack, an indeterminacy, as to which of the subsidiary forms of the general attitude are exemplified by the agent. Thus I may believe that it is going to rain, without it being the case that I myself could say without reflection whether it is a strong or weak belief, a hunch, a conviction, or a supposition. And even if I can answer these questions on reflection, the reflection itself may fix the relevant attitude. Before I thought about it there simply may not have been any fact of the matter about which kind of belief it was, I just believed that it was going to rain. So I conclude that the fact that fine-grained discriminations cannot be made for animal beliefs and desires does not show that animals do not have beliefs and desires.

A related argument has been considered by Davidson (I am not sure if he accepts it).[3] The fine discriminations we make about the propositional content of beliefs and desires cannot be made for the alleged intentional attributions to animals. We say that the dog believes his master is at home, but does it believe that Mister Smith (who is his master) is at home or that the president of the bank (who is that same master) is at home? Without an answer to such questions we cannot attribute beliefs to the dog.

This argument is parallel to one mentioned earlier. According to that argument, unless there is a determinate fact of the matter about *psychological type*, there is no intentional state; according to this argument, unless there is a determinate fact of the matter about *propositional content* there is no intentional state. The argument is subject to the same objection we made to the earlier one. The premise seems to be false. Even if we assume that there is no fact of the matter as to which is the correct translation of the dog's mental representations into our vocabulary; that, by itself does not show that the dog does not have any mental representations, any beliefs and desires, that we are trying to translate.

Davidson mentions this argument only in passing. An argument he presents more seriously against animal thoughts goes as follows. In order that an animal have a thought, the thought must occur in a network of beliefs. His example is: in order to think the gun is loaded I must believe that guns are a type of weapon, and that a gun is an enduring physical object. So in order to have a thought there must be beliefs. But, and this is the crucial step, in order to have beliefs a creature must have the concept of belief. Why? Because in order to have a belief one must be able to distinguish true from false beliefs. But this contrast, between the true and the false, "can only emerge in the context of interpretation" (of language).[4] The notion of a true belief or a false belief depends on the notion of true and false utterances, and these notions cannot exist without a shared language. So, only a creature who is the possessor and interpreter of a language can have thoughts. The basic idea in this argument seems to be that since truth is a metalinguistic semantic predicate and since the possession of belief requires the ability to make the distinction between true and false beliefs, it seems to follow immediately that the possession of beliefs requires metalinguistic semantic predicates, and that obviously requires a language.

This argument is not as clear as it might be, and one might object to various of its steps. The feature on which I want to concentrate here is what I take to be the central core of the argument: In order to tell the difference between true and false beliefs one must have a linguistically articulated concept of belief.

Only within a language can one distinguish correct from incorrect beliefs. I agree with the first part of this claim: having an intentional state requires the capacity to discriminate conditions which satisfy from those that do not satisfy the intentional state. Indeed, I wish to generalize this point to all intentional states, and not just confine it to beliefs. In general, in order to have intentional states one must be able to tell the difference between satisfied and unsatisfied intentional states. But I see no reason at all to suppose that this necessarily requires a language, and even the most casual observation of animals suggests that they typically discriminate the satisfaction from the frustration of their intentional states, and they do this without a language.

How does it work? Well the first and most important thing to notice is that beliefs and desires are embedded not only in a network of other beliefs and desires but more importantly in a network of perceptions and actions, and these are the biologically primary forms of intentionality. We have all along in this discussion been talking as if perception and action were not forms of intentionality but of course they are; they are the biologically primary forms. Typically, for animals as well as humans, perception fixes belief, and belief together with desire determines courses of action. Consider real-life examples: Why is my dog barking up that tree? Because he *believes* that the cat is up the tree, and he wants to catch up to the cat. Why does he believe the cat is up the tree? Because he *saw* the cat run up the tree. Why does he now stop barking up the tree and start running toward the neighbor's yard? Because he no longer believes that the cat is up the tree, but in the neighbor's yard. And why did he correct his belief? Because he just saw (and no doubt smelled) the cat run into the neighbor's yard; and *Seeing and Smelling is Believing*. The general point is that animals correct their beliefs all the time on the basis of their perceptions. In order to make these corrections they have to be able to distinguish the state of affairs in which their belief is satisfied from the state of affairs in which it is not satisfied. And what goes for beliefs also goes for desires.

But why do we need to "postulate" beliefs and desires at all? Why not just grant the existence of perceptions and actions in such cases? The answer is that the behavior is unintelligible without the assumption of beliefs and desires; because the animal, e.g., barks up the tree even when he can no longer see or smell the cat, thus manifesting a belief that the cat is up the tree even when he cannot see or smell that the cat is up the tree. And similarly he behaves in ways that manifest a desire for food even when he is neither seeing, smelling, nor eating food.

In such cases animals distinguish true from false beliefs, satisfied from unsatisfied desires, without having the concepts of truth, falsity, satisfaction, or even belief and desire. And why should that seem surprising to anyone? After all, in vision some animals distinguish between red-colored from green-colored objects without having the concepts vision, color, red, or green. I think many people suppose there must be something special about "true" and "false," because they suppose them to be *essentially* semantic predicates in a metalanguage. Given our Tarskian upbringing, we tend to think that the use of "true" and "false" to characterize beliefs must somehow be derived from a more fundamental use to characterize linguistic entities, sentences, and statements, for example. And then it seems to us that if a creature could tell true from false beliefs it would first have to have an object language to give any grip to the original metalanguage distinction between truth and falsity, now being applied by extension to something nonlinguistic.

But all of this is a mistake. "True" and "false," are indeed metalinguistic predicates, but more fundamentally they are *metaintentional* predicates. They are used to assess success and failure of representations to achieve fit in the mind-to-world direction of fit, *of which statements and sentences are a special case*. It is no more mysterious that an animal, at least sometimes, can tell whether its belief is true or false, than that it can tell whether its desire is satisfied or frustrated. For neither beliefs nor desires does the animal require a language; rather what it requires is some device from recognizing whether the world is the way it seemed to be (belief) and whether the world is the way the animal wants it to be (desire). But an animal does not have to have a language in order to tell true from false beliefs, any more than it has to have a language to tell satisfied from unsatisfied desires. Consider the example of the dog chasing the cat, for an illustration.

IV.

I conclude that the arguments I have seen which deny mental phenomena to animals, ranging from Descartes to Davidson, are without force. I now turn to a remaining question: How do we distinguish those intentional states that require a language, and hence are impossible for animals, from those that do not? I believe the best way to answer this question is to list some of the categories of intentional states which require a language and explain the reasons why they require a language. I doubt that I have thought of all of these, but here are five for a start.

1. *Intentional states that are about language.* For example, a creature cannot think that "eat" is a transitive verb or wonder how to translate "Je n'aurais pas pu" into English if it does not possess the capacity to speak a language.

2. *Intentional states that are about facts which have language as partly constitutive of the fact.* For example an animal cannot think that the object in front of it is a twenty-dollar bill or that the man it sees is the Chairman of the Philosophy Department at the University of California, because the facts represented, facts involving human institutions such as money and universities, require language as a constitutive element of the facts.

3. *Intentional states that represent facts that are so remote in space and time from the animal's experience as to be unrepresentable without language.* For example, my dog might think that I am now eating good food, but it cannot think that Napolean ate good food.

4. *Intentional states that represent complex facts, where the complexity cannot be represented without language.* This is a very large class. Thus my dog can fear a falling object, but he cannot believe the law of gravity even though the falling object instantiates the law of gravity. He can probably have some simple conditional thoughts, but he cannot have subjunctive counterfactual thoughts. Perhaps he can think: "If he gives me that bone I will eat it," but not "If only he had given me a bigger bone I would have enjoyed it more!"

5. *Intentional states that represent facts where the mode of presentation of the fact locates it relative to some linguistic system.* For example, my dog can believe that it is warm here now, but he cannot believe that the 30th of April, 1993 is a warm day, because the system of representing days is essentially linguistic.

No doubt this list could be continued. What it shows so far is that the reasons that an intentional state essentially requires a language for its existence fall into two classes. Either the state has conditions of satisfaction that are essentially linguistic or the mode of representing the conditions of satisfaction is essentially linguistic. Or, quite commonly both. A third type of reason would be that the type of the state requires language for the very possession of a state of that type. I have seen it claimed that there are such types of state—perhaps hope and resentment would be examples—but I have never seen a convincing argument.

V.

I now return to the question: How should we think of animals' mental phenomena in a philosophy purged of dualism? The answer is a form of what I have elsewhere called biological naturalism. Consciousness and other forms of mental phenomena are biological processes occurring in human and certain animal brains. They are as much a part of the biological natural history of animals as are lactation, the secretion of bile, mitosis, miosis, growth, and digestion. Once we remind ourselves of what we know about the brain and we forget our dualist upbringing, the general outline of the solution to the so-called mind-body problem, whether for humans or animals, is quite simple. Mental phenomena are caused by lower-level neuronal processes in human and animal brains and are themselves higher-level or macro features of those brains. Of course, we do not yet know the details of how it works, how the quite specific neurobiology of human and animal nervous systems causes all the enormous variety of our mental lives. But from the fact that we do not yet know *how* it works it does not follow that we do not know *that* it works.

From the fact that human and animal brains cause consciousness it also does not follow that only human and animal brains could do it. Perhaps one could create consciousness of the sort that exists in us and other animals using some artificial device, perhaps one might be able to create it in systems not made of carbon-based molecules at all. And for all we know, consciousness may have evolved among beasts in other galaxies, or other solar systems within our own dear galaxy, that do not have our local obsession with carbon, hydrogen, nitrogen, and oxygen. But one thing that we know for certain: any system capable of causing consciousness and other mental phenomena must have causal capacities to do it equivalent to the biological capacities of animal brains, both our own human brains and the brains of other kinds of animals. From the fact that brains do it causally, it is a trivial logical consequence that any other system capable of doing it causally, must have causal powers to do it equivalent to brains. If that sounds trivial, it should. It is, however, routinely denied by any amount of confused contemporary philosophy of mind that tries to treat consciousness as some purely formal abstract phenomenon independent of any biological or physical reality at all. Contemporary versions of this view are sometimes called 'Strong Artificial Intelligence'.[5] They are expressions of one of the major tenets of traditional dualism, the view that where the mind is concerned the specific neurobiology of the brain is of little importance.

So far, we have not the faintest idea how to create consciousness artificially in some other medium, because we do not know exactly how it is created in our own brains. Some of our best contemporary theories tell us that it is a matter of variable rates of neuron firings relative to certain specific neuronal architectures. But what is it exactly about the peculiar electrochemistry of neurons, synapses, transmitters, receptors, etc., that enables them to cause consciousness? At present, we do not know. So, the prospects of artificial consciousness are extremely remote, even though the existence of consciousness in brains other than human brains is not seriously in doubt.

Well, what about the special problems having to do with animal minds? I have so far been talking as if humans and animals are in the same boat, but what about the special features of animal minds? Problems in this area can be divided roughly into two categories and it is important to keep them separate. First, *ontological* problems which have to do with the nature, character, and causal relations of animal mental phenomena, both what causes them and what they in turn cause. Second, *epistemic* problems which have to do with how we find out about animal mental states, how we know that animals have mental states, and how we know which animals have which sorts of mental states. It is a consequence of the views that I have enunciated so far, that there are not very many interesting philosophical questions about the ontology of animal mental life in general and animal consciousness in particular. The most important questions in this are largely questions for animal psychologists, biologists, and especially neurobiologists. Specifically, if we know that our brains cause consciousness, and we know therefore that any other system capable of causing consciousness must have the relevant causal powers equivalent to our own brains, then the question becomes a factual empirical question: which sorts of animal brains are capable of causing and sustaining consciousness?

Often however in this area epistemology and ontology are confused. The Turing Test tempts us to precisely such a confusion, because the behaviorism behind the test leads to arguments like the following: If two systems behave the same way we have the same grounds for attributing mental states to one as we do to the other. For example, both snails and termites are capable of exhibiting what appears to be goal-directed behavior, so what sense could be attached, for example, to the claim that snails had consciousness and termites did not have it? In fact, since the appearance of goal-directed behavior seems to be a feature of all sorts of artifacts, mouse traps and heat-seeking missiles for example, if we are going to attribute consciousness to snails or termites on the basis of the appearance of goal-directed behavior, why not to any system that appears to be goal directed, such as mouse traps or heat-seeking missiles?

But if, as I am claiming, this approach confuses epistemology and ontology, what is the right way to look at such questions? How, for example, would we test the hypothesis that snails had consciousness and termites did not? Well, here is one possible way. Suppose we had a science of the brain which enabled us to establish conclusively the causal bases of consciousness in humans. Suppose we discovered that certain electrochemical sequences were causally necessary and sufficient for consciousness in humans. Suppose we knew that humans that had those features were conscious and humans that lacked them lacked consciousness. Suppose we knew, for example, in our own case, that if we knocked out these specific features through anaesthetics, we became unconscious. We may suppose that this is an extremely complicated electrochemical phenomenon, and following a long philosophical tradition, I will simply abbreviate its description as XYZ. Suppose that the presence of features XYZ in the otherwise normal human brain are causally both necessary and sufficient for consciousness. Now, if we found XYZ present in snails but absent in termites, that would seem very strong empirical evidence that snails had consciousness and termites did not. If we had a rich enough theory so that we could identify XYZ as causally both necessary and sufficient for consciousness, then we might regard the hypothesis as definitely established, pending, of course, the usual hesitations about the ultimate falsifiability in principle of any scientific hypothesis.

VI.

If the ontological questions are mostly for specialists, what about the epistemology? Here we find plenty of opportunities to clear up philosophical confusions. I have said that contrary to Descartes we are absolutely confident that the higher animals are conscious; but what are the grounds for our confidence? After all, we can design machines that can behave in some areas just as intelligently as animals, perhaps more so, and we are not inclined to ascribe consciousness to these machines. What's the difference? What other than biological chauvinism would lead us to ascribe consciousness to animals but not, for example, to computers?

The standard answer has been that we know of the existence of other minds in animals in the same way we know it in humans, we infer from the *behavior* of the human or animal that it has consciousness and other mental phenomena. Since the behavior of other humans and animals is relevantly similar to my own, I infer that they have conscious states just like mine. On this view, if we could build a mechanical animal out of tinker toy parts that behaved like real animals, we would have to say that it too had consciousness.

In response I want to say that I think this view is hopelessly confused and that behavior by itself is simply irrelevant. Even if we confine ourselves to verbal behavior, as Descartes did, it is important to point out that my car radio exhibits much more intelligent verbal behavior, not only than any animal but even than any human that I know. Furthermore, it is capable of extremely intelligent verbal behavior. It will on demand provide me with predictions of the weather, reports of the latest news, discussions of the Stock Market as well as Western songs and rock and roll music, and it will display a large number of other forms of verbal behavior, even some where the same radio speaks with a whole lot of its different voices at once. But I do not for a moment suppose that my radio is conscious, and I have no doubt that my dog is conscious. The reason for the distinction is that I have a theory. I have a theory about how radios work and I have a theory about how dogs work. By 'theory' I do not mean anything fancy, I just mean a kind of commonsense theory. I know that a radio is a machine designed for the purpose of transmitting the voices and music produced by people a long way away in such a fashion that I can hear it in my living room or my car. I know that my dog has a certain inner causal structure that is relevantly similar to my own. I know that my dog has eyes, ears, skin, etc., and that these form part of the causal bases of his mental life, just as similar structures form part of the causal bases of my mental life. In giving this answer, I am not trying to "answer skepticism" or trying to "solve the other minds problem." I do not think there is any such problem and I do not take skepticism seriously. Rather, I am explaining what are in fact, in real life, the grounds for our complete confidence that dogs are conscious and radios are not. It is not a matter of behavior as such. By itself, behavior is irrelevant. Behavior is only interesting to us to the extent that we see it as the expression of a more ontologically fundamental causal structure. The principle by which we "solve the other minds problem for animals" is not that intelligent behavior is proof of consciousness but rather the principle is that if the animal has a causally relevant structure similar to our own, then it is likely to produce the similar mental states in response to similar stimuli. The "behavior" is simply evidence that it is so responding. Nothing more.

Contrary to the whole epistemological tradition I am suggesting that the grounds on which we found our certainty that animals are conscious is not that intelligent behavior which is the same or similar to ours is proof of consciousness, but rather that causal structures which are the same or similar causal structures to ours produce the same or similar effects. Behavior, even linguistic behavior, is only relevant given certain assumptions about structure. That is why we attribute consciousness to humans and animals, with or without language, and we do not attribute it to radios.

But even saying this seems to me to concede too much. It will almost unavoidably give the impression that I think there really is an other minds problem, that there are tests that a system must pass in order to have a mind, and that dogs and baboons are passing the tests and computers as well as chairs and tables are failing. I think that is the wrong way to see these matters and I will now try to explain why.

The worst mistake that we inherited from Cartesianism was dualism, together with all of its idealist, monist, materialist, physicalist progeny. But the second worst mistake was to take epistemology seriously, or rather to take it seriously in the wrong way. Descartes together with the British empiricists and right up through the Positivists and the Behaviorists of the twentieth century have given us the impression that the question: "How do you know?" asks the fundamental question, the answer to which will explain the relation between us as conscious beings and the world. The idea is that somehow or other we are constantly in some epistemic stance toward the world whereby we are making inferences from evidence of various kinds. We are busy inferring that the sun will rise tomorrow, that other people are conscious, that objects are solid, that events in the past really occurred, etc. In this case, the idea is that the evidence that we have that other people are conscious is based on their behavior, and since we see relevantly similar behavior in dogs and primates, we may reasonably infer that they, too, are conscious. Against this tradition, I want to say that epistemology is of relatively little interest in philosophy and daily life. It has its own little corner of interest where we are concentrating on such things such as how to understand certain traditional skeptical arguments, but our basic relationships to reality are seldom matters of epistemology. I do not infer that my dog is conscious, any more than, when I come into a room, I infer that the people present are conscious. I simply respond to them as is appropriate to respond to conscious beings. I just treat them as conscious beings and that is that. If somebody says, "Yes, but aren't you ignoring the possibility that other people might be unconscious zombies, and the dog might be, as Descartes thought, a cleverly constructed machine, and that the chairs and tables might, for all you know, be conscious? Aren't you simply ignoring these possibilities?" The answer is: Yes. I am simply ignoring all of these possibilities. They are out of the question. I do not take any of them seriously. Epistemology is of very little interest in the philosophy of mind and in the philosophy of language for the simple reason that where mind and language are concerned, very little of our relationship to the phenomena in question is epistemic. The epistemic stance is a very special attitude that we adopt under certain special circumstances. Normally, it plays very little role in our dealings with people or animals. Another way to put this is to say that it does not matter really *how* I know whether my dog is conscious, or even *whether* or not I do 'know' that he is conscious. The fact is, he is conscious and epistemology in this area has to *start* with this fact.

There are indeed grounds for my certainty in the cases of dogs, chairs, tables, baboons, and other people, and I tried to state some of those grounds earlier, but the important thing to see is that I am certain. When I state the grounds for my certainty I am not trying to answer philosophical skepticism or "prove" that animals have minds and tables and chairs do not.

However, though the general or philosophically skeptical form of the "other animals' minds problem" seems to me confused, there are quite specific questions about specific mechanisms the answers to which are essential to scientific progress in this area. For example, how are cats' visual experiences similar to and different from that of humans'? We know quite a lot about this question because we have studied the cat's visual system fairly extensively, and we have an extra motivation for wanting to answer it because we need to know how much we can learn about the human visual system from work done on cats. Furthermore, we currently suppose that certain species of birds navigate by detecting the earth's magnetic field. And the question arises, if they do this, do they do it consciously? And if so, what are the mechanisms for conscious detection of magnetism? In the same vein, bats navigate by bouncing sonar off solid objects in the dark. We would like to know not only what it feels like to do this but what the mechanisms are that produce the conscious experience of detecting material objects by reflected sound waves. The most general question of all is this: What exactly are the neurobiological mechanisms by which consciousness is produced and sustained in animals and humans? An answer to this question would give us solid epistemic grounds for settling the issue as to which animals are conscious and which are not.

Such epistemic questions seem to me meaningful, important, and indeed crucial for scientific progress in these areas. But notice how different they are from traditional philosophical skepticism. They are answered by doing specific work on specific mechanisms, using the best tools available. For example, no one could have said in advance, just on the basis of philosophical reflection, that using PET scans and CAT scans would prove crucial in studying human and animal minds. To these genuine epistemic questions the answer is always the same: Use your ingenuity. Use any weapon you can lay your hands on and stick with any weapon that works. With this type of epistemology we have the best chance of understanding both human and animal minds.

NOTES

1. See John R. Searle, *The Rediscovery of the Mind* (Cambridge, Mass., 1992) for arguments to substantiate this claim.

2. This was an argument popular during my student days at Oxford in the 1950s. I first heard it in lectures and seminars by Stuart Hampshire. I do not know if he ever published it.

3. D. Davidson, "Thought and Talk" in *Truth and Interpretation* (Oxford, 1984), 155–70.

4. Ibid., 170.

5. Cf. John R. Searle, "Minds, Brains and Programs," *Behavioral and Brain Sciences* 3 (1980): 417–24.

Some Remarks on Logical Truth:
Human Nature and Romanticism
RICHARD ELDRIDGE

What makes a truth of logic true? It is difficult not to ask this question. There is a natural puzzle here. The propositions of logic seem "fashioned from the hardest materials, a hundred times stronger than concrete or steel."[1] And we are able to know them. But how? What makes them so strong? They seem to describe nothing that we can sense. What then makes it the case that "$[(p \lor q) \& \sim p] \supset q]$" must be true? What is the nature of this *must*? Is it somehow grounded in the nature of negation as an abstract logical operation on propositions, or perhaps in the very nature of the proposition itself? Or is it rather the product of a decision we have somehow (implicitly) made to use symbols in a certain way, to keep to certain rules? Or is it that we just cannot help (at least ignoring interference and distraction) taking such propositions to be true, that that is how we are?

These are deep questions that ask about the interrelations of abstract objects, conventions of usage, and innate human tendencies and endowments. Behind these questions lurks the even deeper wish somehow to separate the natural and the real from the conventional clearly and sharply. It is as if we wish to locate and describe exactly what we must be responsible to and for in our linguistic, communicative, descriptive, and theoretical practices. We wish as it were to know where and what we must obey—real abstract entities, implicit conventions, decisions, and rules, or human mental-biological nature, as may be—and where and how we might be free, improvisatory. What confines us in our practices as they stand, and where and how might we be free within them?

For all that these questions are deep and natural, however, there may very well be no general philosophical answer to them, no general philosophical conception of the distinct natures of the abstract, the conventional, and the natural that will enable us to sort and circumscribe our responsibilities finally and definitely. Our wish to do so may go perennially unsatisfied (human reason has this peculiar fate), thus emerging as itself more haltingly definitive of our nature as it is displayed in practice than any conception of ourselves that is rooted in a theory of ultimate realities—abstract, voluntaristic-conventional, or psycho-physical—that are taken somehow to lie behind or beneath or above our practice. That, at any rate, is what a reflective survey of the virtues and vices of Platonism, conventionalism, and naturalism in the philosophy of logic may suggest.

PLATONISM

Logical truths seem to be objective, in that they seemingly hold true independently of any subject's inclinations, tendencies, decisions, or beliefs about particular subject matters. They are put to use in deriving some propositions from others (logic as the topic-neutral language of proof). As Frege urged, "to make a judgment because we are cognizant of other truths as providing a justification for it is known as *inferring*. There are laws governing this kind of justification, and to set up these laws of valid inference is the goal of logic."[2] That some truths do justify other truths seems to be a matter of fact, but a matter of fact that is not a matter of physical or psychological nature. Since what happens in nature is, even if physically necessary, nonetheless contingent on the way matter and energy happen to be, while logical truths are fully necessary, are even the paradigms of the necessary, it follows that "the subject-matter of logic is therefore such as cannot be perceived by the senses."[3] Nor do logical truths describe psychological processes; "what is true is true independently of our recognizing it as such."[4] Since logical truths—that one judgment does deductively justify another, that these relations of justification seem to be relations that objectively obtain and seem to be described by logical truths—are neither physical nor psychological, "it would perhaps not be beside the mark to say that the laws of logic are nothing other than an unfolding of the content of the word 'true'."[5]

This Platonist-Fregean view has considerable motivations. The history of logic is generally stable, in that new developments in logic (e.g., quantificational logic out of propositional logic) are generally conservative extensions of existing logical systems. Though there is some debate about some issues, most of the simplest truths of propositional logic that are, upon reflection, usually accepted seem not to change. New truths are added, and debate continues in certain regions, but there are, seemingly, few or no wholesale revolutions or disenfranchisements of the well enfranchised. The formal language of proof and deductive inference that is used in a variety of subject areas seems not to change much.

Platonism offers a ready explanation of these facts (to the extent that they are facts). The rough, reflective consensus that obtains about logical truths is the result of discovery of abstract objects (propositions, concepts) and functions (negation, quantification). The hardness of the logical is grounded in the natures of these abstract objects and functions, which subsist independently of the vagaries of time, space, and contingency. Logic is in this respect different from the empirical sciences that investigate empirical phenomena, but it is no less cognitive. The boundary between logic (and perhaps mathematics) and the empirical sciences is the boundary between the abstract and the concrete. Reflection or intuition affords genuine discoveries of the natures of abstract things. Failure to acknowledge logical truths is a failure to have reflected well on the abstract, on what must be so no matter what. As Russell urged, "it is obvious that the knowledge of logical forms is something quite different from knowledge of existing things. The form of 'Socrates drank the hemlock' is not an existing thing like Socrates or the hemlock, nor does it have even that close relation to existing things that drinking has. It is something altogether more abstract and remote."[6] Such abstract and remote things as logical forms, and the relations among logical forms that are described in formal logical truths, seem to be the subject matter of logic. Philosophical logic, by distinguishing between the surface and deep grammars of sentences, finds these forms. "Some kind of knowledge of logical forms, though with most people it is not explicit, is involved in all understanding of discourse. It is the business of philosophical logic to extract this knowledge from its concrete integuments and to render it explicit and precise."[7] Logic proper then describes certain relations among these forms: some contain others, or are necessarily usable (so far as information is concerned) whenever others are. These descriptions are the truths of logic.

Despite the attractions of this view, it also faces considerable and well-known difficulties, particularly for anyone with empiricist scruples. Logical Platonism requires the postulation of some special cognitive faculty—usually logical intuition or reflection—that gives us access to abstract, non-spatiotemporal objects and their properties. Such a faculty may well seem mysterious to anyone in the grip of either a materialist metaphysics or an empiricist epistemology. It treats logic as a scientific investigation of the properties of abstract objects, with the consequence that at least in principle our logic could be wrong[8] (science could be in error). Logic should thus be open to radical revision based on new discoveries just as physics is, yet this seems to undermine the claim that certain logical truths are both necessary and known to be necessary. There are no criteria for ascribing a correct grasp or intuition of abstract objects apart from the display of logical competence in one's practices of inferring, so it seems forced to say that an intellectual grasp undergirds and explains one's competent practice (a general liability of Platonism). And perhaps the truths of logic do or could change more than logical Platonism suggests: there are proposals for non-bivalent logics, logics that admit restricted contradictions, logics that deny the logical rule that permits the addition of a disjunct to any sentence, modal logics, and so forth.

It is possible to meet some of these worries by moving more in the direction of Aristotle, locating logical truths as truths that are fully immanent in our practice as it stands, rather than as practice-independent, eternal, abstract objects of logical intuition. This position, a kind of "Platonism without (logical) objects"[9] is arguably the position of Wittgenstein in the *Tractatus* and is arguably suggested by Russell's remark about extracting our knowledge of forms "from its concrete integuments." "Logic," as the *Tractatus* puts it, "pervades the world."[10] "[T]here are no 'logical objects' or 'logical constants' (in Frege's and Russell's sense)."[11] *All* logical truths are instead built into the structure of *any* thought about objects in the world. Hence no thought could record a new *discovery* of logical truths or logical objects, in the way that we might discover that there are polar bears on Baffin Island. "Propositions cannot represent logical form: it is mirrored in them. What finds its reflection in language, language cannot represent."[12] "The 'experience' that we need in order to understand logic is not that something or other is the state of things, but that something *is*: that, however, is *not* an experience."[13]

While this Tractarian view responds to certain epistemological difficulties that trouble logical Platonism, it also faces further difficulties of its own. A non-empiricist 'logical intuition' of objects is replaced by an equally non-empiricist quasi-awareness of 'confinement' by 'structures' that 'show themselves' in thought and language. These structures are not objects of discovery (so no logical intuition is required). But this undercuts the view that higher 'nontrivial' truths, such as those of metalogic (e.g., the Lowenheim-Skolem theorem) *are* discovered. Since the ontological and epistemological commitments of Tractarian philosophy of logic with regard to 'immanent structures' are at least as murky as those of logical Platonism, since it seems implausibly to undercut the possibility of logical discoveries, and since Tarski has shown how to characterize the semantic properties of sentences in certain artificial languages clearly and precisely, recent philosophies of logic in the Platonist style have reverted to more classically Fregean stances. Thus Hao Wang observes that "philosophy should pay more attention to what we, the human species, know and believe (and feel) at present. . . . Both [Carnap and Quine] fail to take logic and mathematics seriously as clear representatives of our conceptual knowledge. . . . [In order to refute 'empiricism in the sense of Carnap or Quine'] it is enough to exhibit some basic aspect of [mathematics] that is unaccountable by empiricism. The examples of modus ponens and the integers are a very solid part of what we know, and philosophy has an obligation to do justice to what we know." This obligation requires us to accept the existence of knowledge by logical and conceptual *intuition*.[14] Similarly, Jerrold Katz urges that "if one acknowledges genuine necessity in these areas [logic, mathematics, and semantics], then one ought to accept the one account of the meaning of logical, mathematical, and linguistic statements and of the reality such statements are about on which they can be necessary. The Platonist *explains* the necessity in logic, mathematics, and grammar on the grounds that the statements in these subjects are about abstract objects" that are atemporal, aspatial, objective, cohesive, and known by intuition.[15]

Such Platonist views have considerable charms. They seem to explain the nature of what we seem to know with such definiteness and certainty. But exactly how does intuition enter into logical or mathematical practice? What difference to our practice does the claim to have intuited something make? Certainly it does not strengthen a proof in logic or mathematics to append to

any line "I know this by intuition on the basis of the foregoing." The appeal
to intuition of logical objects hangs in the air, does no work. Does logical
Platonism somehow reassure us that our practice is in order? Does it provide
'philosophical understanding' of our practice? The best arguments in favor of
Platonism are arguments that nothing else explains our knowledge, particularly
not empiricism. But Platonism's own explanation of our logical knowledge
seems to provide more heat than illumination. The formula that nothing else
besides intuitions of logical objects could explain our logical knowledge is
simply repeated. And could our present logical intuitions really be wrong, open
to correction through subsequent intuition and argumentation? And if they could
be wrong (as Wang and Katz concede in holding that they are correctable and
admit of argumentation), then are they, even when (we think) correct, so clearly
intuitions *of* necessary properties of abstract objects? Just what does the appeal
to intuition explain or elucidate? It is as though that philosophical formula—we
have logical intuitions of the natures of abstract logical objects—by itself had
the power to show what circumscribes our will: the natures of abstract things.
But is this circumscription of our will by abstract entities really illuminated
by Platonism? Perhaps we would be better off to conceive of logical truths in
another way.

CONVENTIONALISM

Not all true sentences are made true by existing objects possessing certain
properties and standing in certain relations. Only a fetishistic substantialism
and referentialism pushes us to think otherwise. But surely the sentence "two
pints are equal to a quart" is both true and not in the first instance about
existing objects and their properties and relations. It is instead in the first
instance about *our* conventions or procedures for measuring liquids. And of
course the sentence *is* true. Why should not the truths of logic be like this
sample truth, or, as Russell put it (in criticizing the view), might it not be that
"mathematical knowledge is all of the same nature as the 'great truth' that there
are three feet in a yard?"[16]

The view that logical truths are made true in virtue of our adoption of
certain procedures and conventions that govern our practice and talk has obvious appeals. The truths of logic become less mysterious. No talk of insight into
'third realms' of abstract entities need be introduced. The relative immunity of
logic from change is explained by the fact that the conventions and procedures
that govern our talk presumably change less quickly than do the particular
observations about the world that we make after empiricial investigation. But
the existence and intelligibility of alternative logics is also accounted for by
the fact that different procedures or conventions can be useful for carrying out
different tasks in different times and places, just as talk of miles may be natural
and useful in certain places while talk of kilometers may be useful in others.
That people by and large know logical truths is explained as resulting from the
prosaic fact that people get trained in and become competent at certain ways of

measuring and talking about things. No appeal to logical intuition is required in order to explain our possession of logical knowledge.

This conventionalist account of logical truths is appealing not only in virtue of its prosaicness and simplicity. It also is consistent with positivist and pragmatist suspicion of traditional metaphysics and regard for the more substantial cognitive achievements of the modern, mathematical natural sciences. Expressing positivist attitudes toward science and metaphysics, Hans Hahn observed that "the idea that thinking is an instrument for learning more about the world [e.g., about its forms or structures] than has been observed, for acquiring knowledge of something that has absolute validity always and everywhere in the world, an instrument for grasping general laws of all being, seems to us wholly mystical."[17] Since logic and mathematics can neither be dismissed as useless and unintelligible nor given foundations in sense experience (as Mill had hoped), "We must look out for a different interpretation of logic and mathematics."[18]

Conventionalism lies ready to hand. "Logic," we may hold, "does not by any means treat of the totality of things, it does not treat of objects at all but *only of our way of speaking about objects*; logic is first generated by language."[19] Certain sentences are true by definition. The sentence "every snow rose is a helleborus niger" "merely expresses a convention concerning the way we wish to talk about the plant in question."[20] "The same is to be said of all the other principles of logic."[21] Everything is on the surface. A person who does not acknowledge a truth of (our) logic is not failing in logical insight or making a mistake about the nature of Platonic logical objects. Such a person is simply playing a different game, using different conventions. "A person who refused to recognize logical deduction would not thereby manifest a different belief from mine about the behavior of things, but he would refuse to speak about things according to the same rules as I do. I could not convince him, but I would have to refuse to speak with him any longer, just as I should refuse to play chess with a partner who insisted on moving the bishop orthogonally."[22]

A similar stance arises in C. I. Lewis's pragmatic empiricism. Lewis too divides "the sources of knowledge" into "on the one hand data of sense and on the other hand our own intended meanings."[23] While he held that "intended meanings" are the results of mental acts that are conceptually prior to their linguistic expression ("Linguistic *expression . . .* is the dependent and derivative phenomenon"[24]), Lewis, like Hahn, treated logical truths as matters of convention, for him primordially mental and derivatively linguistic. "*Information* in logic can be only verbal or concern the logician's conventions of classification and formulation."[25] Again, everything is on the surface. Recourse to the epistemological and metaphysical obscurities of Platonism is avoided. Logical knowledge is explained as knowledge of conventions, not of substances. The history of logic is elucidated as consisting in (motivated) changes of conventions, with at present a central core of conventions and contending candidate conventions at the edges. Here, it seems, we know what we are to be responsible to and for in our logical practice: certain ways of talking. As Carnap urged the view, "the question, whether a certain proposition is an inference (entailment) of certain other propositions or not, is therefore completely analogous to the question whether a certain position in chess can be played from another or not. This question is answered by chess theory, i.e., a combinatorial or mathematical investigation which is *based on the chess rules*."[26] Where once logical truths were taken to be descriptions of how abstract objects necessarily are, they are now taken to derive from rules, conventions, or procedures.

Such rules, conventions, or procedures need not, however, be entirely free-floating or the products of arbitrary decision. Choices of conventions can be motivated by interests and constrained by how the world to one degree or another enables the effective pursuit of those interests. Thus Carnap observes that "A proposal for the syntactical formulation of the language of science [a proposal for employing certain formal conventions in scientific discourse] is, when seen as a principle, a proposal for a freely choosable convention; but what induces us to prefer certain forms of language to others is the recourse to the empirical material which scientific investigation furnishes."[27] In his later writings, Carnap mentions that "efficiency, fruitfulness, and simplicity of the use" of a language or set of conventions "may be among the decisive factors" motivating our decision to employ it.[28] But whether certain conventions— among them the conventions that hold certain forms of expressions to be always intersubstitutable for others and that thus make the truths of logic true— are efficient, fruitful, and simple to use is always a matter of degree. "These questions cannot be identified with the question of realism. They are not yes-no questions but questions of degree."[29] Because these are matters of degree, it is misbegotten to take our stances on them to rest on a response, intuitive or reflective, to the nature of Platonic logical entities, any more than we can have an intuition of how many feet there are in a yard apart from the existence of any human practices. "The acceptance of a linguistic framework must not be regarded as implying a metaphysical doctrine concerning the reality of the entities in question:" "neglect of this important distinction" is a principal, and ill-founded, source of Platonism.[30] The important question about logical truths, and about other syntactical and semantical conventions, "is a practical, not a theoretical question."[31]

A similar view has recently surfaced in some feminist accounts of logical truth. In many ways, these feminist accounts are sharply at odds with positivism and pragmatism, since they tend to be substantially less impressed by the autonomy and authority of the mathematical natural sciences and substantially to urge the importance of certain interests in rearranging political life, rather than interests in understanding and controlling physical nature. But just because a certain feminist account of the interests that do or ought to motivate the adoption of certain conventions diverges so sharply from the picture of our technological interests that underlay positivism and pragmatism, in a curious way that feminist account of logic supports a conventionalist account of the nature of logical truth quite similar to the kind of account found in Hahn, Lewis, or Carnap.

Thus Andrea Nye has asked "What is it that Aristotle is saying? Or Frege? And how is it possible to know without knowing the 'genesis' of their words, without knowing the situation and concerns out of which logicians spoke, without hearing in their words who they were, what sort of 'men' they were?"[32] One traditional, Platonist answer to these questions would be that the genesis of logic is obvious: it rests in rational intelligence or in logical intuition of logical objects, disinterestedly exercised. To Nye, however, this answer seems patently ideological, in that it advances certain interests that are misrepresented as objective and suppresses other interests that Nye herself favors. "It is only when the claim of logic to be reason and truth and knowledge is accepted that the anarchical chaos of purely personal expression is the only alternative to masculine rationality."[33] But that claim, Nye argues, is false. "At logic's very birth, Parmenides made clear this purpose: to leave the world of women, the world of sexual generation and fertility, the world of change, of the emotions, of the flesh."[34] Traditional logic, that is to say, serves distinctively masculine interests.

> It is the will of the Fuehrer that creates the world of objects that can be integrated in logic. It is his sense of himself as an object, projected onto history, that creates a world with a common will. Only in this way can there be the self-consistency and the hard-edged concepts necessary for logic, only if it is spun out from one man's will, a lonely man, someone who had been wounded, someone whose family has rejected him living or dead, someone who has never felt at home in the world of objects shared by others, someone whose thoughts must replace the thoughts and the actions of others because that is the only way there can be any understanding, someone whose will has become law.[35]

Once we abandon Platonism, however, we can see that it is possible to adopt new logics, new sets of conventions, that reflect different experiences and subserve different interests. "It becomes possible to undertake a new feminist study of thought and language free from the logicist assumptions that dominate contemporary linguistics and epistemology."[36] It should then be both possible and desirable to create a new logic, reflecting the experiences of embodied, fleshed, communal beings, where not all objects have hard edges, where not everything that is worth talking about either definitely has a definite property or definitely lacks it. If logic is to reflect our patterns of reasoning about indefinite objects, it too will have to become less hard-edged and formal. And this will be a matter of what (motivated) conventions it is now in our interest to adopt, just as in Carnap.

The conventionalist view thus has considerable appeal. It seems naturally to surface when there are deep interests in conflict, whether in the positivist and pragmatist interest in control of nature achieved through the mathematical natural sciences set against the claims of Idealist or religious metaphysics or in the feminist interest in creating and honoring certain political-communal spaces and structures set against a bureaucratic-scientific interest in order, control, and exactness. When one is seeking to pursue an emerging, radically new direction of interest and seeking to develop and sustain certain patterns of reasoning connected with that interest, then logic will seem conventional, and it will seem to be time for new conventions.

Conventionalism thus sets commitment to logical truths firmly in the web of human practical life. It avoids epistemological obscurities. It accounts for changes in the history of logic as motivated by changes in human interests that are effectively pursued in practice, and it accounts for continuities in logic by appeal to continuities of interest (whatever account of our interests as either stable in part or shifting in part turns out to be the right one).

But can it be right? Despite its appeal, conventionalism, like Platonism, faces considerable objections. The most common criticism, and one often held to be devastating, is due to Quine. There is an infinite number of logical truths. But only a finite number of truths is specifiable in a list of propositions that are held true by convention. The remainder of the infinity of logical truths will have to be derived from the original list, and these derivations will have to proceed in accordance with logical rules that are based on logical truths not appearing on the original list (e.g., $\sim\sim\sim(p \ \& \sim p)$ will have to be derived from $\sim(p \ \& \sim p)$ by double negation). So not all logical truths can simply be listed. Knowledge that the rule of double negation embodies a logical truth (viz. $\sim\sim\emptyset \equiv \emptyset$, for all forumlae $\emptyset$) over an infinite range of cases must be taken for granted. So the conventions of holding true certain sentences formally defined will not themselves yield the class of logical truths. 'Logical knowledge' in some sense above and beyond knowledge of conventions is needed. "In a word, the difficulty is that if logic is to proceed *mediately* from conventions, logic is needed for inferring logic from the conventions."[37]

One way to meet this difficulty would be to adopt the full-blooded or radical conventionalism that Dummett has ascribed to the later Wittgenstein: all logical truths are "the *direct* expression of a linguistic convention. That a given statement is necessary consists in our having expressly decided to treat *that very statement* as unassailable; it cannot rest on our having adopted certain other conventions which are found to involve our treating it so."[38] But while this position avoids the difficulty for conventionalism posed by Quine, it also undoes all of conventionalism's charms. Conventionalism had sought to describe to what our wills in accepting logical truths are and ought to be responsible: our past decisions. But in radical conventionalism (arguably not properly ascribable to Wittgenstein), our wills are responsible to nothing. All decisions to accept a logical truth are directed at this particular sentence (type?: but how are sentence-types to be recognized?). This has the consequence that the very possibility of describing our behavior with regard to logical truths as evincing rational willing disappears. Everything becomes arbitrary, surely not a happy result.

Second, as A. N. Prior noticed, *if* logical connectives are completely defined by the inference rules governing their use, and *if* our decisions about which inference rules to employ are matters of arbitrary convention, then it is possible to devise a perfectly legitimate logical connective "tonk," the meaning of which is given in arbitrary rules, and which enables us to derive any proposition whatsoever from any other. After describing this possibility, Prior mordantly concludes his essay by looking forward to the day when "more enlightened views will surely prevail at last, especially when men consider the extreme *convenience* of the new form, which promises to banish *falsche Spitzfindigkeit* from Logic forever."[39] Arbitrary conventionalism thus threatens to destroy the very contrast between valid and invalid inference: all inferences become valid. If we then wish to avoid this consequence and to reject one of the conventionalist assumptions, then we are implicitly accepting, Prior's concluding wit suggests, the thought that our decisions about which inference rules to employ *cannot* be arbitrary. We must employ rules that ensure that our inferences are (in the order of things?) *valid*. But this in turn seems to force us to rely on non-conventional knowledge of following-from relations, non-conventional knowledge of logical truths. Conventionalism can accommodate the point that conventions of inference and of accepting logical truths may not be arbitrary, but must instead be motivated, but it is hard to see how it can accept the point that these conventions must themselves reflect logical truths.[40]

Conventionalism at the hands of the positivists and pragmatists promised to avoid epistemological obscurities and to make logical knowledge unproblematic. Logical knowledge is understood as knowledge of conventions that we keep to in the courses of our practical (including scientific practical) lives. It accounts for the possibility of motivated change in logical systems and logical truths as flowing from changes in interests that are pursued in practices. Like Platonism, however, conventionalism seems in the end to provide more heat than illumination. Like Platonism, conventionalism seeks to circumscribe what we must be responsible to and for in our practice: the decisions to speak in certain ways that we have either implicitly taken or that we are prepared to stand responsible for now. But in actual practice conventionalism oscillates between the view that conventions are matters of free, albeit motivated, decision and the view that conventions must respect what we already recognize as valid inferences in our practice. The best arguments in favor of conventionalism are the claims that logical Platonism is epistemologically obscure and that there are (or might be) changes in our practices of inferring. But these arguments are mostly negative. They do not elucidate the nature of our commitments to our practices of inferring or of the changes we might make in that practice. The formula that these are matters of convention is simply repeated, as though we had understood the circumscription of our wills now not by nature, but instead by our wills themselves, simply through this phrase. Perhaps we might better conceive of the nature of logical truths in another way, setting them even more firmly in the courses of our practices, where these practices are themselves understood as reflections not of the abstract, and not of our choices of conventions, but of what we ourselves naturally are.

NATURALISM

The view that our commitment to logical truths is an outgrowth of our more or less biological nature, as that nature has developed through evolution and undergirded our practices, has obvious appeal. It seems readily to avoid the difficulties faced by both Platonism and conventionalism. No appeal to logical intuition of abstract entities is required, but also no appeal to acts of will that mysteriously bind future acts of will. Yet there is a kind of necessity to logical truths—natural necessity, or the claim that (our) nature being (contingently) what it is, things just could not be otherwise: we could not have any other logic. Mistakes in inferring are then ascribed to some failure of a natural inferential system. Perhaps the natural inferential system has not yet matured, just as three year olds cannot yet run a mile in eight minutes. Or perhaps there is some interference in the operation of a natural system from some other natural phenomena, say distraction of attention by immediate sensation or bodily phenomena. The existence of a rough consensus regarding valid inferences and logical truths is explained as resulting from our possession of a common biological nature, itself expressed and developed in practice, just as we are all, after sufficient maturation and training, able to speak grammatical sentences in a natural language. Logical truths are responsive to no mysterious abstract entities and no oddly compelling acts of will, but instead are responsive to facts of nature, our nature as it confronts the physical things around it.

It is the rejection of both metaphysical necessity and obscure acts of will that clearly lies behind Quine's initial rejection of conventionalism and reconceiving of the truths of logic as on a par with other truths of the natural sciences as pieces of the cognitive equipment that we have developed over time for confronting nature. For Quine, commenting on conventionalism, "Meaning is what essence becomes when it is divorced from the object of reference and wedded to the word."[41] That is to say that Carnapian, positivist conventionalism, wherein truths of logic are matters of linguistic convention, is no better off, no less obscure, than traditional metaphysical essentialism. Against traditional metaphysics, with its limnings of categories of reality that are putatively deeper, more fundamental, than any categories used in any local practice, we ought to set the more fruitful tracings of reality that are used in the mathematical natural sciences. Logical truths are simply among the useful products of these sciences. "My countersuggestion . . . is that our statements about the external world face the tribunal of sense experience not individually but only as a corporate body."[42] There are no categorial distinctions among kinds of truths, with some grounded in observation and experimentation and others grounded in either intuition or convention. All truths, logical and otherwise, are best regarded as tools human nature has developed in its efforts, biological and practical (where the biological and the practical are inextricably intermixed), to cope with its environment. "As an empiricist I continue to think of the conceptual scheme of science as a tool, ultimately, for predicting future experience in the light of past experience. . . . The myth of physical objects is epistemologically superior to most in that it has proved more efficacious than other myths as a device for working a manageable structure into the flux of experience."[43] Just so, too, with the truths of logic. Behind the development of these tools there is nothing more—nothing more exalted or more mysterious—than nature. "In principle, therefore, I see no higher or more austere necessity than natural necessity. . . ."[44]

In developing his naturalist program in the philosophy of logic in particular, Quine articulates a subtle sense of the intermixing of facts of practice and facts of biological nature, while avoiding appeal to either abstract entities or conventions and will. We might, Quine suggests, "defin[e] logical truth more abstractly, by appealing . . . to whatever grammatical constructions one's object language may contain. A logical truth is, on this approach, a sentence whose grammatical structure is such that all sentences with that structure are true. . . . *A logical truth is a truth that cannot be turned false by substituting for lexicon.*"[45] Immediately one wonders why this should be so. Are certain forms Platonically forms that must embody truth, no matter how filled in? Or are certain forms privileged, immune from embodying falsehoods, as a result of the voluntary adoption of certain conventions? No; the grammatical forms that embody logical truths are simply written into our languages as we have developed them and as we study them. We cannot separate out what in our languages and their forms is responsive to an abstract reality, what reflects voluntary convention, what reflects the pressures of nature, or even what is read into them through our procedures of studying them. We can only note what is there in our languages as we reflect on them. Nothing in particular—not abstract entities, conventions, or physical reality in itself—but instead everything, undecomposably, stands behind the claim that certain truths are truths of logic. "The definition [of logical truth] is still not transcendent. It hinges on the notion of a grammatical construction, or, in the complementary phrasing, the notion of lexicon. We have no defensible transcendent notion of construction or lexicon, but only a loosely related family of immanent notions. One and the same language . . . can of course be generated by different constructions from different lexical beginnings. Our proposed abstract notion of logical truth depends not only on the language but on how we grammatize it."[46] Our nature, confronting natural circumstances, and expressing itself in certain languages useful for prediction and in certain ways of reflecting on those languages, leads us to regard certain forms we see in languages as embodying truths no matter what predicates or referring terms they contain. Logical necessity is analyzed into natural necessity (whatever that turns out to be).

One difficulty attaching to Quine's version of naturalism in the philosophy of logic, however, is that it yields no program for critically sorting through which are the genuine truths of logic. It provides no basis for arguing for or against one or another alternative logical system. Instead it provides more reassurance than anything else: our acceptance of logical truths is somehow grounded in our nature as it has manifested itself in practice as we have pragmatically, naturally, reflected on it. Here too there seems more heat than light. In order to develop a naturalist program for critical reflection on logic, one would need a more richly developed and specific theory of human nature, an actual psychology of how natural patterns of thought make themselves felt in practice.

This is exactly what Chomsky aims to provide. Against Quine's vaguer, and vaguely more instrumentalist-biological naturalism, Chomsky is concerned to describe the natural mental reality that underlies both our linguistic performances and our language-embedded acceptances of certain logical truths. "To know a language," Chomsky tells us, " . . . is to be in a certain mental state, which persists as a relatively steady component of transitory mental states. . . . To be in such a mental state is to have a certain mental structure consisting of rules and principles that generate and relate mental representations of various types."[47] That is to say, there is a steady state of knowing, consisting of having certain rules and representations 'in mind,' that naturally underlies our linguistic performances. On the basis of poverty of stimulus arguments and claims that similar structures and categories (noun phrase, verb phrase, physical object, property, cause) are to be found embedded in all languages, Chomsky hypothesizes that there is a natural level of understanding—knowledge of universal grammar, of the most basic principles and categories that must inform any language—that pre-exists and constrains our learning of any public natural language. Thus he observes that

> The child approaches language with an intuitive understanding of such concepts as physical object, human intention, volition, causation, goal and so on. These constitute a framework for thought and language and are common to the languages of the world. . . . Though words may not match precisely across languages, the conceptual framework in which they find their place is a common human property. The extent to which this framework can be modified by experience is a matter of debate, but it is beyond question that the acquisition of a vocabulary is guided by a rich and invariant conceptual system, which is prior to any experience.[48]

Once this thought is accepted, it becomes an immediate possibility that there are certain truths to which we are committed simply in virtue of having the natural conceptual structure that we have. Perhaps, for example, "all objects occupy space" is one of them; perhaps "$\sim(p \ \& \ \sim p)$" and "$(p \supset q) \equiv (\sim q \supset \sim p)$" are also. Moreover, which truths we accept naturally, in virtue of having the biologically evolved conceptual structures that we have, will be something that admits of empirical study. We can hope to figure out by empirical inquiry into that conceptual structure what the logical truths and other truths of meaning are—for example, by seeing just which truths are accepted in all languages as immune from disconfirmation. Chomsky draws these consequences straightforwardly from his views about the existence of an innate conceptual structure in human beings.

One conclusion that seems quite well established on the basis of considerations such as these is that some statements are known to be true independently of any experience. They are what is called truths of meaning, not truths of empirical fact. Without knowing anything about the facts of the matter, I know that if you persuaded John to go to college, then at some point he intended or decided to go to college; if he did not, then you did not persuade him. The statement that to persuade John to do something is to cause him to intend or decide to do that thing is necessarily true. It is true by virtue of the meaning of its terms, independently of any facts; it is an 'analytic' truth in technical jargon. On the other hand, to know whether the statement that John went to college is true, I must know certain facts about the world. . . . Furthermore, empirical inquiry can help clarify the status of a statement as a truth of meaning or of empirical fact, for example, inquiry into language acquisition and variation among languages. Thus the distinction between truths of meaning and truths of empirical fact is an empirical issue, not to be decided merely by reflection or, certainly, by stipulation.[49]

Chomskyan naturalism, unlike Quinean naturalism, hence does promise us the possibility of determining empirically, through systematic inquiry, which are the genuine truths of logic. Rather than providing idle reassurance, it points toward a program of linguistic and psychological study. Unfortunately, however, it faces considerable difficulties of its own.

There are, to begin with, epistemological problems. What ground could we have for deciding that we have *discovered* something about the innate conceptual structure of human subjects rather than simply *projecting* our own casual and uncritical sense of what categories we (think we) use onto those we study? As Quine notoriously urges in arguing the thesis of the indeterminacy of translation, it is unclear that we *could* have any evidence that would show that in theorizing about categories we were *not* projecting "our sense of linguistic analogy unverifiably" onto the minds of subjects. "There is no telling how much of one's success with analytical hypotheses [correlating others' conceptual structures with 'our own'] is due to real kinship of outlook on the part of the natives and ourselves, and how much of it is due to linguistic ingenuity or lucky coincidence. I am not sure that it even makes sense to ask."[50] The effort to get beneath our nature as it is manifested in practice to our nature as it is, innately, prior to practice, seems to founder epistemologically. To be sure, Chomsky regards such epistemological difficulties as practical, scientific problems to be overcome, not in principle difficulties, but in the absence of furnishing a criterion for distinguishing what we project from what is really there, this view seems more a matter of faith than results. The mere claim to have results, in the absence of an epistemological criterion of discovery, seems hollow.

More serious yet, however, are the ontological difficulties attaching to Chomskyan naturalism. As Anthony Kenny has argued, Chomsky confuses the *criteria* for the ascription of an ability (knowledge of a concept) with *symptoms* of a natural condition or event.[51] Measles have symptoms (spots) that tend strongly to accompany the disease according to laws of nature. Knowledge that something is an iguana, however, has as its *criterion*, not its mere, typical, accompaniment, the ability under normal conditions to say that that is an iguana when queried in the presence of iguanas. The connection is logical, not causal. Nothing, in particular no inquiry into psychological or biological states, could make us in normal conditions ascribe knowledge of a concept in the absence of the ability to apply it aptly. Nothing, no inquiry into psychological or biological states, could make us withhold that ascription in the presence of apt performance. Possession of an ability may require a biological vehicle, but it is logically of a different order from possession of the vehicle alone. It is something which in principle can only be displayed and established in actual practice under normal conditions. So there is something—possession of an ability—which is criterially connected with actual performance under normal conditions, which, as it were, has its essence there. Here too, then, the effort to get beneath our practice to facts of our nature that determine that practice founders. When one finds biological or physical vehicles of abilities, one is finding a different sort of thing ontologically from the ability itself.

Thus Quinean naturalism offers empty reassurance, without critical examination of our interests or of the mental reality that underlies our practice. Our logical practice is 'grounded' in our nature as it is manifested in our practice as we reflect on it. Chomskyan naturalism offers a critical, empirical theory of how our nature, our 'conceptual framework,' issues in commitment to certain logical truths, but its techniques for studying that nature, that conceptual framework, founder on conceptual difficulties, epistemological and ontological. In neither case is the explanation of our commitment to certain logical truths and of a partial consensus concerning relations of valid inference really forthcoming. Logical necessity is not clearly reduced to natural necessity that admits of empirical study. The attempt to reconstrue the normativity of logic as a matter of the normal operation of a logic module in mind, sometimes interfered with by other modules or modalities, goes nowhere, for the characterization of *how* the logic module normally operates is in fact derived from a prior characterization of our commitments to certain logical truths and valid inferences, rather than vice versa.

Here too, as in Platonism and conventionalism, the temptation of naturalism is its promise to sublime away the practical problem of what in our practice of inferring we are ready, in context, to take responsibility for. Naturalism offers us the promise of a final demarcation of what we must do in inferring. Not Platonic entities, not conventions rooted in will, but instead, somehow, our nature makes us infer as we do and accept certain logical truths. Here too, the best arguments for this view are chiefly negative. Platonism and conventionalism are mysterious; it is unclear how abstract entities or acts of will could of themselves bind us in our logical practices. But it is, again, equally unclear how our biological-psychological nature could do this. We are left either with empty reassurances that it must or with confused programs for the study of that nature regarded as like in kind, but deeper than, our overt possession of abilities.

What remains, then, is the thought that the wish for a philosophy of logic, the wish to circumscribe finally our responsibilities in inferring by reference to something deeper or more primordial than our inferring itself, is a standing feature of our nature as it manifests itself in practice. Human reason, it seems, may have this peculiar fate: as it gives birth to reflections on practice, it contains the wish to be free of the dangers and difficulties of particular responsibilities in context, the wish to know once and for all how we must 'go on.' This wish, it seems, persists in, is legible in, each of the accounts of logical truth that have been surveyed. Here is a view of what we are that may well be worth some elaboration as it bears on the philosophy of logic.

WITTGENSTEIN AND ROMANTICISM

What, we have asked, lies behind our commitment to various logical truths? Is it abstract reality, convention and will, or human biological-psychological nature? Surely, it seems, we must be able to say something about the roots of our practices of inferring and how best to go on in them. What makes us infer as we do, or controls how we ought to infer?

Nothing. "You can't," Wittgenstein tells us, "get behind the rules, because there isn't any behind."[52] That is to say that there is nothing behind our practice of inferring that admits of philosophical scrutiny, yielding a general explanation of how and why that practice is or must be thus-and-so. A thousand particular things—knowledge of the world, facts about our size and perceptual abilities, the manifold things in which we have taken an interest, convenience in being able to substitute symbols for one another—but nothing in general governs our practice. Yet we think there must be something deeper.

> But still, I must only infer what really *follows*! —Is this supposed to mean: only what follows, going by the rules of inference; or is it supposed to mean: only what follows, going by *such* rules of inference as somehow agree with (some sort) of reality? Here what is before our minds in a vague way is that this reality is something very abstract, very general, and very rigid. Logic is a kind of ultra-physics, the description of the 'logical structure' of the world, which we perceive through a kind of ultra-experience (with the understanding, e.g.).[53]

But it is not like this. There is no ontological order—not Platonic reality, not will, not biological-psychological nature—decisively standing behind our norms of inferring. "The steps which are not brought into question are logical inferences. But the reason why they are not brought into question is not that they 'certainly correspond to the truth'—or something of the sort,—no, it is just this that is called 'thinking', 'speaking', 'inferring', 'arguing'."[54] Philosophy can at best survey and describe (some of) our norms as we appeal to them in certain contexts, as part of thinking, speaking, inferring, and arguing. Any attempt to go deeper leads nowhere. Neither explanation nor justification of our inferring practice in general is possible. As Gordon Baker and Peter Hacker observe, on Wittgenstein's view,

> Philosophy is purely descriptive. It clarifies the grammar of our language, the rules for the construction of significant utterances whose violation yields nonsense. Explanation would be possible only if it made sense to get behind these rules and supply a deeper foundation. But there is no behind, and rules are not answerable to reality in the currency of truth. Any deeper explanation would simply be another rule of grammar standing in the same relation to the use of expressions as the rules it allegedly explains. Therefore philosophy must be flat. This insight shapes the whole of Wittgenstein's philosophy.[55]

The rules of inference and the logical truths that embody them are not just natural facts about the disposition of objects in space. They are norms. Somehow we use them and appeal to them in practice in the world, when we act and speak in space and time. How can this be so? What gets the norms into the practice?[56] (How easy should it be to solve the mind/body problem?)

Perhaps it is like this. As we grow up we are trained in certain practices. We learn to add, to sing songs, to observe natural phenomena, to build with blocks and bricks, to calculate costs per ounce, to care for children, to promise and apologize and argue, to prepare food and eat it, to watch television programs, to play games, to work at a job, and to tell and laugh at jokes. We are able to do any of these things only in virtue of our natural endowments. No other animals do any of them in the ways that we do. But we are also able to do such things only because we are taught and trained to do them. Absent a practice of building with bricks and training in that practice, one will not build with bricks. No one does all these things all the time; some people rarely if ever do some of them. Our natural endowments do not force us to do these things. As we learn to do all these particular things, we are told rules for being effective in the practice. "Breathe at the end of a phrase." "Turn the pancakes when the edges are brown and the bubbles don't disappear." "Carry tens to the next column." "Tell your brother you're sorry."

As we grow into our practices by coming to conform to these norms, we are also capable of becoming conscious of them, articulating them, reflecting on them, and passing them along to others. Children do this from a very young age. "Don't hit." "Use your words."

Certain practices are more widely shared in than others. Relatively few people in America prepare Ethiopian injera. Many people tell jokes. Most people add and subtract numbers regularly in the course of daily life.

Among the practices that are most widespread is inferring. "Your school bag must either be in your room or somewhere else; have you looked all through your room? Well, where else could it be?" "You can go to the pool only if you practice; no practice, no pool." Many of the inferences we make embody patterns $[Fa \lor \sim Fa); (p \supset q) \equiv (\sim q \supset \sim p)]$ that are also evident in other inferences that we accept. Generalizations about patterns that range across topics are available and often useful. But not invariably: it might be both raining and not raining; or the United States might both be democratic and undemocratic. Formal logical truths that reflect patterns of inferring are hence among the most general, but still not absolute, norms of human life. Nothing—not Platonic forms, not conventions, not our biology—stands behind them except the fact that we do often, but not invariably, infer according to certain patterns without regard to subject matter. In doing formal logic, we can describe and reflect on these facts of practice, but can never discover what our practice must be according to some order of reality (abstract reality, will, or biological-psychological nature). There is good reason to reflect on these patterns or norms of inference and to articulate and teach them, just as there is good reason to reflect on, articulate, and teach norms of food preparation, without, however, regarding them as absolute. Certain patterns of inferring may be followed very widely throughout many practices, yet without embodying all the valid inferences that there are. (Does "you should take an umbrella if you go outside" follow from "it's raining"? According to what norm or pattern, how laid down by abstract reality, will, or nature?)

Suppose this view of the priority of logical practice to any order of reality that might constrain it absolutely is right. How should we then regard the business of logical theory? We should, first of all, be suspicious of any exhaustive or absolute distinction between formal logic and the substantive logic of a given practice. Patterns of inferring that can be abstracted and generalized nonetheless have their life in the varieties of things that people do. Or, as Hegel put it,

> [Thought] becomes the unconscious power to take up the previous multiplicity of sciences and the elements of knowledge into the rational form, grasping them in their essential character, eliminating the external and thus extracting out the Logical in them—or, which comes to the same thing, of filling in the abstract fundament of the Logical, which was arrived at previously by Logical study, with the content of all that is true.[57]

But we should not, second, expect this abstraction or filling in (whichever it is) of "the abstract fundament of the Logical" to be complete or completable. The sciences *are* multiple, and inferring is a practice that extends well beyond the sciences. There will be certain patterns of inferring that will be more or less central in our inferring practice, certain logical truths that we will hold true no matter how filled in, but others that will be somewhat more domain specific, with the boundaries between what is necessarily true as a norm no matter what we talk about and what we are prepared to abandon in taking up a new subject remaining essentially unclear and contested. Hence we will have natural occasions to wonder what, in a given domain, our logical practice ought to be, which norms of inferring, which logical truths, ought to have pride of place. Hence we will further be prompted to wonder what facts—abstract, volitional, or biological-psychological—might tell us which norms to prefer. But we will be disappointed. The patterns of inferring appropriate to a given domain of practice must show themselves to be appropriate within that practice. Their appropriateness cannot be guaranteed by the way things are somewhere else.

This view is in a certain way perhaps a variety of naturalism. We have norms of inferring, some of them involving formal patterns of very wide use in many practices, that have proven their worths *to us* within those practices. But it differs markedly from the cruder, more physicalist versions of naturalism found in Quine or Chomsky. It is, one might say, a sort of Romantic naturalism, in seeing our practices as both partly autonomous and partly reflective of our nature and circumstances, where what rests in nature alone cannot be pried apart from what rests in will and decision. Thus room is left for us to worry over which logical truths to accept where. There is a natural temptation to wonder about the foundations of our practice, a natural temptation for human reason to reflect on the conditions of its own emergence and exercise, but a temptation that is doomed, it seems, to disappointment. "Romanticism" is one reasonably accurate name for the sense that human beings are thus perennially between the aspiration to establish the ultimate terms of human responsibility and that aspiration's disappointment.

Neither our neurophysiology nor our conceptual structure alone determines our acceptance of logical truths. They are, rather, immanent in our practices, which are facts of culture, where culture flows out of human nature but is not determined by it. As Baker and Hacker put it, in characterizing Wittgenstein's views, "going on thus [for example, to infer according to pattern] is not *correct* because it is natural for us, in our culture. Rather, it is because we find it natural that we *make it correct.* . . ."[58] Variations of logical practice, across cultures or across domains, are possible, even if many patterns of inferring are in fact commonly accepted. "If anyone believes that certain concepts are absolutely the correct ones, and that having different ones would mean not realizing something that we realize—then let him imagine certain very general facts of nature to be different from what we are used to, and the formation of concepts different from the usual ones will become intelligible to him."[59] Nothing can fully and finally circumscribe our acceptance of certain patterns of inferring, certain logical truths. We will have to see what we will be ready to be responsible for, and we will be tempted to wonder about how we are prepared to be responsible where and when. "We have a colour system as we have a number system. Do the systems reside in *our* nature or in the nature of things? How are we to put it?—*Not* in the nature of numbers or colours. Then is there something arbitrary about this system? Yes and no. It is akin both to what is arbitrary and to what is non-arbitrary."[60]

Conformity to certain formal patterns of inference and appeal to logical truths are woven through a great range of our practices. We teach such patterns and can articulate and reflect on the logical truths that display them. Such teaching, articulation, and reflection can be useful in sustaining forms of activity in culture into which inferring and appeal to logical truths are woven. It is difficult to imagine that we will cease assigning properties to objects, making generalizations, noting relations, and inferring according to patterns that appear in sentences that record such descriptions. Patterns of inferring are likely to continue to be used across different subject matters, though they are also unlikely to describe exhaustively the valid inferences we make in all subject matters. Logical truths "are norms or reflections of norms of representation and of reasoning which form the network of concepts and transitions between concepts and propositions in terms of which we describe the world. A form of representation is the product of human activity throughout history. It is moulded by the nature of the world around us, conditioned by human nature, focused and directed by human, historically determined, interests and concerns."[61] Nothing more or less stands behind our commitment to logical truths than this.

Or perhaps it is like this. The laws of harmonic composition in music are highly stable. It is useful to teach performers and composition students the circle of fifths, to show them how, in our practice, what we hear as tension increases as the key center of a piece moves away from the home key. It is difficult to imagine that pieces written in classical harmony will cease to be dominant paradigms of musical organization and sense. Almost everything small children are taught to sing and play resolves on the tonic chord of the key center of the piece. The practice of classical harmonic composition has spread widely throughout the world, partly through commercial media, but partly also because commercial media make use of patterns of musical organization that make sense to people. But there are alternatives. The appeal of classical patterns of composition may wane, as we become bored with them and as our other practices evolve. Or they may not. Modal systems of composition lack the idea of an organizing key center altogether. Behind the dominance of classical harmonic composition there rests a complicated and undecomposable mixture of human nature, awareness of patterns, particular historical decisions to use certain patterns (decisions that could have been otherwise and that can be departed from), and a sense of temporality—of effort and resistance and resolution in time—that is present in other activities and expressed in classical harmonic music. It is tempting to ask whether classical harmonic music is natural or conventional or based on patterns of musical sense that simply exist on their own. But this question, while nearly inevitable, is misbegotten, is based on a wish to deny and overcome the complexities of musical practice and the risks of responsibility within that practice by appeal to something deeper or more primordial. We will have to see what patterns of musical organization and sense we will be prepared to urge on others and stand responsible for as embodiments of sense, and which ones will be taken up widely within musical practice by listeners and performers.

Perhaps then it is like this with logical truths and the laws of inferring according to formal patterns, although it is unlikely also to be exactly like this either.

NOTES

1. J. Lukaziewicz, quoted in G. P. Baker and P. M. S. Hacker, *Wittgenstein: Rules, Grammar and Necessity* (Oxford, 1985), 307.

2. Gottlob Frege, "Logic," *Posthumous Writings*, edited by H. Hermes, F. Kambartel, F. Kaulbach, translated by Peter Long and Roger White (Oxford, 1979), 3.

3. Ibid.

4. Ibid., 2.

5. Ibid., 3.

6. Bertrand Russell, "Logic as the Essence of Philosophy," in *Our Knowledge of the External World* (London, 1914), 42–69; reprinted in *Readings on Logic*, 2d. ed., edited by I. Copi and J. Gould (New York, 1972), 80B.

7. Ibid., 80b.

8. Gordon Baker makes this criticism of Platonism in *Wittgenstein, Frege and the Vienna Circle* (Oxford, 1988), 160-61.

9. Baker suggests this phrase characterizes "one important aspect" of Wittgenstein's views in the *Tractatus*, as does the phrase "conventionalism without options," and he emphasizes important continuities between Wittgenstein's early and late philosophies of logic, centering around the idea that logical truths do *not* admit of (quasi-scientific) discovery. Ibid., 255.

10. Ludwig Wittgenstein, *Tractatus Logico-Philosophicus*, translated by D. F. Pears and B. F. McGuinness (London, 1961), 115; Remark 5.61.

11. Ibid., 5.4.

12. Ibid., 4.121.

13. Ibid., 5.552.

14. Hao Wang, *Beyond Analytic Philosophy: Doing Justice to What We Know* (Cambridge, Mass., 1986), 36, 18, 19–20.

15. Jerrold J. Katz, *Language and Other Abstract Objects* (Totowa, N.J., 1981), 1985–86. Emphasis added. Katz describes the nature of logical, mathematical, and grammatical intuition on pp. 192–216.

16. Russell, *History of Western Philosophy* (1946), 860. Cited in Wang, *Beyond Analytic Philosophy*, 13.

17. Hans Hahn, "Logic, Mathematics, and Knowledge of Nature," in German (Vienna, 1933), reprinted in *Logical Positivism*, edited by A. J. Ayer (New York, 1959), 151.

18. Ibid., 152.

19. Ibid.

20. Ibid.

21. Ibid., 153.

22. Ibid., 156.

23. C. I. Lewis, "The Modes of Meaning," chapter III of *An Analysis of Knowledge and Valuation* (LaSalle, Ill., 1946); reprinted in *Readings in the Philosophy of Language*, edited by Jay F. Rosenberg and Charles Travis (Englewood Cliffs, N.J., 1971), 15–16.

24. Ibid., 17.

25. Ibid., 17n1.

26. Rudolf Carnap, "On the Character of Philosophic Problems," *Philosophy of Science* 1 (1934); reprinted in *The Linguistic Turn*, edited by Richard Rorty (Chicago, 1967), 57B.

27. Ibid., 62B.

28. Carnap, "Empiricism, Semantics, and Ontology," *Revue Internationale de Philosophie* 4 (1950); reprinted in *Meaning and Necessity*, 2d. ed., (Chicago, 1956), 208.

29. Ibid.

30. Ibid., 214–15.

31. Ibid., 214.

32. Andrea Nye, *Words of Power: A Feminist Reading of the History of Logic* (New York, 1990), 174.

33. Ibid., 179.

34. Ibid., 177.

35. Ibid., 170.

36. Ibid., 179.

37. W. V. O. Quine, "Truth by Convention," in *Philosophical Essays for A. N. Whitehead*, edited by O. H. Lee (New York, 1936); reprinted in Quine, *The Ways of Paradox and Other Essays*, 2d. ed. (Cambridge, Mass., 1976), 104. See also Quine's "Carnap and Logical Truth," in *The Ways of Paradox*, p. 115: "the point is that the logical truths, being infinite in number, must be given by general conventions rather than singly; and logic is needed then to begin with, in the metatheory, in order to apply the general conventions to individual cases." Quine in both cases mentions Lewis Carroll, "What the Tortoise Said to Achilles," *Mind*, N.S. 4, 14 (April 1895): 278–80, as making this same point.

38. M. A. E. Dummett, "Wittgenstein's Philosophy of Mathematics," *Philosophical Review* 68 (1959); reprinted in Dummett, *Truth and Other Enigmas* (Cambridge, Mass., 1978), 170. Second emphasis added.

39. A. N. Prior, "The Runabout Inference-Ticket," *Analysis* 21, no. 2 (December 1960): 39.

40. Ian Hacking, "What is Logic?" *Journal of Philosophy*, 76, no. 6 (1979) has proposed a sophisticated syntactic or proof-theoretic characterization of logical systems and of logical truth. Hacking recognizes, however, that this *characterization* is *not* a *definition*, in that it presupposes both certain semantic intuitions about what is logically true and a commitment to bivalence, which likewise has semantic motivations or seems to rest on logical intuition. For a full discussion of Hacking's views, see Pascal Engel, *The Norm of Truth* (Toronto, 1991), 240–49.

41. Quine, "Two Dogmas of Empiricism," *Philosophical Review* (January 1951); reprinted in Quine, *From a Logical Point of View*, 2d. ed. (Cambridge, Mass., 1961), 22.

42. Ibid., 41.

43. Ibid., 44.

44. Quine, "Necessary Truth," in *The Ways of Paradox*, 76.

45. Quine, *Philosophy of Logic*, 2d. ed. (Cambridge, Mass., 1986), 58.

46. Ibid., 60.

47. Noam Chomsky, *Rules and Representations* (New York, 1980), 48.

48. Chomsky, *Language and Problems of Knowledge: The Managua Lectures* (Cambridge, Mass., 1988), 32.

49. Ibid., 33–34.

50. Quine, *Word and Object* (Cambridge, Mass., 1960), 72, 77.

51. Anthony Kenny, "Language and the Mind," in *The Legacy of Wittgenstein* (Oxford, 1984), 141–45, esp. p. 144. Chomsky has responded to this argument in *Language and Problems of Knowledge*, 9–11, where he attempts to distinguish possession of an ability from possession of knowledge, something deeper which underlies the ability. Here, however, he misconstrues Kenny's remarks about abilities as remarks about either actual performances or dispositions to behave, and he reintroduces the same considerations about aphasia to which Kenny had responded with more care in his article.

52. Ludwig Wittgenstein, *Philosophical Grammar*, edited by Rush Rhees, translated by Anthony Kenny (Oxford, 1974), Part II, Section I, p. 244.

53. Wittgenstein, *Remarks on the Foundations of Mathematics*, edited by G. H. von Wright, R. Rhees, and G. E. M. Anscombe; translated by G. E. M. Anscombe (Oxford, 1956), Part I, Section 8, p. 6e.

54. Ibid., Part I, Section 155, p. 45e.

55. Baker and Hacker, *Wittgenstein: Rules, Grammar and Necessity*, 22.

56. Pascal Engel, *The Norm of Truth*, 309–320, touches on this question in discussing what he calls "the paradox of the norm." "On the one hand, a norm or an ideal is abstract, and would cease to be so if it were to describe real situations, or be inductive generalisations from these situations. On the other hand, a norm or an ideal cannot be totally abstract, up to

the point where it could not be said *of what* they are norms or ideals" (p. 310). His solution to this paradox—viz. that it disappears once we see that logic is a matter of motivated conventions with respect to which "total irrevisability . . . is impossible" (p. 289), rather than something responsive to either Platonic entities or facts of nature—is an interesting effort to be coy about whether logic stems from will or human nature. Logical truths are norms, rules, or conventions, as Wittgenstein urged. But there are, following Davidson, certain necessary conventions of minimal rationality. This seems to me to be on the right track, but perhaps still too confident of the topic-neutrality of valid formal inference as the necessary core of all inferential practice. Perhaps it is the core, I will say, but not the necessary core, even if grand deviations from it are not readily imaginable.

57. G. W. F. Hegel, *Science of Logic*, cited in Michael Rosen, *Hegel's Dialectic and its Criticism* (Cambridge, 1982), 65, Rosen's translation. The passage cited appears in Hegel, *Science of Logic*, translated by A. V. Miller (London, 1969), 59.

58. Baker and Hacker, *Wittgenstein: Rules, Grammar and Necessity*, 237.

59. Wittgenstein, *Philosophical Investigations*, 3d. ed., translated by G. E. M. Anscombe (New York, 1958), 230e.

60. Wittgenstein, *Zettel*, edited by G. E. M. Anscombe and G. H. von Wright, translated by G. E. M. Anscombe (Berkeley, 1970), Sections 357–58, pp. 65–6e.

61. Baker and Hacker, *Wittgenstein: Rules, Grammar and Necessity*, 318.

Quine and Naturalized Epistemology

RICHARD FOLEY

M ovements to naturalize are dominant in almost every area of contempo-rary philosophy. In philosophy of mind, the dominant project is to show either that intentional attitudes are scientifically respectable or that they can be made so; in philosophy of language it is one of how to naturalize content; and in moral philosophy it is one of how to naturalize moral concepts.

In each of these areas, the idea is to make sure that our philosophical theories are compatible with science. Put roughly, and it may be that it cannot be put any other way, this means that in our philosophical theories we are to make use only of those properties that are either reducible to or supervene upon properties that science countenances.

Of course, as science countenances stranger and stranger properties, phi-losophy is correspondingly free to make use of them. But the guiding idea remains the same. Science constrains philosophy. Philosophical theories, on this view, must be naturalistic, and it is science, ultimately, that will tell us what this amounts to.

Not everyone accepts this view of philosophy, needless to say. Moreover, when the view is stated as vaguely as I have stated it, it is far from clear what its implications are. But for the discussion here, which will concern the naturalization movement in epistemology, I am not going to worry about the plausibility of the view, nor am I even going to try to identify its implications. It is not necessary to do so, since naturalized epistemology cannot be understood as just one more instance of the movement in philosophy to naturalize. In particular, it cannot be understood as an attempt to naturalize the concept of justified belief and other concepts that are central to epistemology. Almost all contemporary epistemologists are engaged in this project, and yet many of these epistemologists are not thought of as doing naturalized epistemology. So, this way of thinking about naturalized epistemology does not succeed in capturing what is supposed to be distinctive about it.

For example, coherentists are not ordinarily regarded as doing naturalized epistemology. Yet they understand epistemic justification in terms of such notions as belief, consistency, and simplicity, and these notions, most would agree, are compatible with a scientific picture of world. Or consider Bayesians who understand epistemic rationality in terms of probabilistic coherence among one's degrees of beliefs. Once again, most would agree that these notions either are or can be made scientifically respectable, and yet ordinarily Bayesians are not thought of as doing naturalized epistemology. Or consider Roderick Chisholm, who is usually thought to be as distant from the naturalized tradition as any contemporary epistemologist. The notion of epistemic justification, says Chisholm, is ultimately to be understood in terms of an ethical requirement to prefer. To say you are more justified in believing a proposition than withholding on it is to say, roughly, that you have a *prima facie* obligation to prefer believing it to withholding on it. But Chisholm then goes on to say that these ethical requirements supervene on non-normative states, most importantly your beliefs and your sense experiences.[1] So, if the movement to naturalize epistemology is thought of simply as a movement that aims to show how epistemic properties are scientifically respectable, then even Chisholm's epistemology is a naturalistic one.

Admittedly, there are those who argue that the notions of belief and sense experience cannot be made compatible with a scientific picture of the world and that, thus, neither the coherentist nor the Bayesian nor Chisholm has succeeded in formulating an acceptably naturalistic epistemology. But in order to be a naturalized epistemologist, one does not have to abandon the notions of belief and sense experience. Indeed, very few of the epistemologists who are most closely associated with naturalized epistemology do so. Think, for example, of W. V. Quine, Fred Dretske, D. M. Armstrong, Alvin Goldman, and Donald Campbell, none of whom altogether discard the notion of belief or sense experience.

But the issue of whose epistemology is, or is not, scientifically respectable is a side issue. The main point I am making is that the program to naturalize epistemology aims at something stronger than merely ensuring that epistemology is compatible with science. It is interested in proposing a stronger, more positive role for science in shaping epistemology. The question is, what exactly is this stronger role?

A number of philosophers have attempted to answer this question. Among the most interesting attempts are those of Jaegwon Kim, Alvin Goldman, Philip Kitcher, Hilary Kornblith, and Hilary Putnam.[2] There is much to be learned from these attempts, but it is also worth noting that these philosophers do not agree on which epistemologists are doing naturalized epistemology, much less on what naturalized epistemology is. I think that there is an explanation for this other than the standard one of philosophers having a special talent for disagreement. Namely, those who see themselves as practicing naturalized epistemology are in fact engaged in different kinds of projects. Thus, it is not surprising that we have trouble agreeing on who is doing naturalized epistemology, and likewise it is not surprising that we have trouble finding any one thesis or set of theses that definitively characterizes it.

In any event, I am not going to try to provide a general characterization of naturalized epistemology or even try to say who is doing it. I am going to look only at Quine's view of epistemology. After all, if anyone is a naturalized epistemologist, it had better be the case that he is.

Unfortunately, in addition to being one of our most important philosophers, Quine is also one of our most exasperating philosophers. He is legitimately regarded as a great stylist, but in spite of this, indeed in part because of it, he is often difficult to decipher. When faced with the choice of expressing his views with great elegance or maximum clarity, he rarely chooses the latter. And nowhere is his penchant for the stunning phrase more on display than in his epistemology. The result, over the years, is a collection of maxims, mottos, and pronouncements that are none too easy to fit into a coherent whole.

Of course, Quine's broad themes are clear enough. It is clear, for example, that he rejects the analytic-synthetic distinction. This in turn has implications for his epistemology, the most important of which is his rejection of the idea that epistemology can be done *a priori*. But problems begin to crop up when we try to go beyond these familiar Quinean themes to see how his more specific recommendations fit with one another. Indeed, I do not think that they do fit. More specifically, I think that some of Quine's most famous pronouncements on epistemology conflict with what seem to be his settled views.

My aim, however, is not so much to reveal conflicts among the various things Quine has said about epistemology. Nor is it even to evaluate the plausibility of what he has said. Primarily, I just want to get as clear as possible about his epistemology and to get clear also about whether he is doing epistemology in some new and distinctively naturalized way.

The best place to begin is "Epistemology Naturalized." There Quine gives his most famous characterization of naturalized epistemology. He says that its defining mark is that it makes epistemology into a chapter of psychology.

> Epistemology, or something like it, simply falls into place as a chapter of psychology and hence of natural science. It studies a natural phenomenon, viz., a physical human subject. This human subject is accorded a certain experimentally controlled input—certain patterns of irradiation in assorted frequencies, for instance—and in the fullness of time the subject delivers as output a description of the three-dimensional external world and its history. The relation between the meager input and the torrential output is a relation that we are prompted to study for somewhat the same reasons that always prompted epistemology; namely, in order to see how evidence related to theory, and in what ways one's theory of nature transcends any available evidence.[3]

If this passage is taken at face value, Quine is suggesting that we altogether replace epistemology with a psychology. More specifically, we are to replace it with the project of describing the relationship between our sensory input and our theoretical output. Within this project, questions of justifying the theoretical output do not arise.

The above passage occurs in the context of a discussion in which Quine argues that a certain kind of project in epistemology has failed—the project of validating science on the basis of sense experience, where validation means proof by logic and set theory. Since theory is underdetermined, it is not possible to validate science. Still, in itself this does not force Quine to give up questions of justification unless he thinks that validation is the only kind of justification worth having. But why would he think that? He never explicitly endorses this position, and he certainly does not give an argument for it.

Nevertheless, the passage suggests that Quine does want to give up epistemology. It suggests that he is an eliminativist when it comes to epistemic justification. Apparently, his idea is not to naturalize this notion. Rather, the idea is to jettison it as unuseful. Or perhaps more accurately, the recommendation is to jettison it as part of the scientific picture of world. Justification has no place in the science game, it seems.

If there is a standard interpretation of Quine's view, this is it. For example, Jaegwon Kim, Alvin Goldman, and Hilary Kornblith all insist that what is distinctive about Quine's view, and for that matter what is also most objectionable about it, is that he is asking us to give up the notion of epistemic justification and with it the normative element in epistemology. Here are some representative passages, the first from Kim, the second from Goldman, and the third from Kornblith:

> . . . it is normativity that Quine is asking us to repudiate. Although Quine does not explicitly characterize traditional epistemology as "normative" or "prescriptive", his meaning is unmistakable. Epistemology is to be "a chapter of psychology", a law-based predictive-explanatory theory, like any other theory within empirical science; its principal job is to see how human cognizers develop theories (their "picture of the world") from observation ("the stimulation of their sensory receptors"). Epistemology is to go out of the business of justification. . . . Quine is urging us to replace a normative theory of cognition with a descriptive science.[4]

> . . . on W. V. Quine's naturalistic conception, the epistemologist would study how the human subject responds to certain input; how, in response to various stimulus patterns, the subject delivers a description of the external world and its history. In studying the relation between this "meager input" and "torrential output," epistemology "simply falls into place as a chapter of psychology and hence of natural science."
> . . . But this approach, though perfectly tenable, neglects the evaluative strain pervading most of historical epistemology. Epistemologists have traditionally been interested in whether beliefs about the world are justified or warranted; whether we are rationally entitled to these beliefs. Epistemologists seek to discover or invent proper methods of inquiry

and investigation, often dismissing established procedures as irrational. Clearly, 'justified', 'warranted', and 'rational' are evaluative terms; and the advocacy of particular methods is a normative activity. So traditional epistemology has a strong evaluative-normative strain. I aim to preserve that strain.[5]

. . . according to Quine, foundationalists were asking the wrong question. Once we see the sterility of the foundationalist program, we see that the only genuine questions there are to ask about the relation between theory and evidence and about the acquisition of belief are psychological questions. In this view question 2 [How do we arrive at our beliefs?] is relevant to question 1 [How ought we arrive at our beliefs?] because it holds all the content that is left in question 1. The relation between these two questions is much like the relation atheists believe to hold between questions about God's act of creation and questions about the details of, for example, the big bang; the latter questions exhaust all the content there is in the former questions.[6]

I do not think that this standard view of Quine will ultimately do, but undeniably it is a natural interpretation. The above passage from "Epistemology Naturalized" seems not just to suggest this interpretation but to demand it. Moreover, there are numerous other passages in Quine's work that seem to support the standard interpretation. For example, from *Theories and Things*:

Naturalism does not repudiate epistemology, but assimilates it to empirical psychology. Science itself tells us that our information about the world is limited to irritations of our surfaces, and then the epistemological question is in turn a question within science, the question how we human animals can have managed to arrive at science from such limited information. Our scientific epistemologist pursues this inquiry and comes out with an account which has a good deal to do with the learning of language and the neurology of perception. . . . Evolution and natural selection will doubtless figure in this account, and he will be free to apply physics if he sees a way.[7]

And here is another passage from "Epistemology Naturalized":

But why all this creative reconstruction, all this make-believe? The stimulation of his sensory receptors is all the evidence anybody has had to go on, ultimately, in arriving at his picture of the world. Why not just see how this construction really proceeds? Why not settle for psychology? Such a surrender of the epistemological burden to psychology is a move that was disallowed in earlier times as circular reasoning. If the epistemologist's goal is validation of the grounds of empirical science, he defeats his purpose by using psychology or other empirical science in the validation. However, such scruples against circularity have little point once we have stopped dreaming of deducing science from observations. If we are out simply to understand the link between observations and science, we are all well advised to use any available information, including that provided by the very science whose link with observation we are seeking to understand.[8]

Despite the seemingly unambiguous intent of these passages, there are two devastating problems for the standard interpretation. The first is that Quine has explicitly rejected it. In his most recent defense of naturalized epistemology, he says he has no quarrel with those critics who object to his retaining the word 'epistemology', since he agrees that the "repudiation of the Cartesian dream is no minor deviation." But then he immediately adds that "they are wrong in protesting that the normative element, so characteristic of epistemology, goes by the board."[9] The matter-of-fact tone with which he announces this looks a little disingenuous in light of the above quotations, but nevertheless he does deny that this was ever his view.

The second devastating problem for the standard view is that at approximately the same time Quine was writing "Epistemology Naturalized," he co-authored *The Web of Belief* with Joseph Ullian, and this book is paradigmatically a work of normative epistemology. Here is a passage from the early pages of the first edition:

The story of the origins and intensities of our beliefs, the story of what happens in our heads, is a very different story from the one sought in our quest for evidence. Where we are rational in our beliefs the stories may correspond; elsewhere they may diverge. The former story is for psychology to tell. On the other hand, our present concern is with grounds, with reasons, with the evidential relations that hold among beliefs.[10]

There is nothing in this passage to suggest that Quine is jettisoning the normative element in epistemology, and likewise nothing to suggest that epistemology is merely a chapter in psychology. On the contrary, he is distinguishing the task of the epistemologist from that of the psychologist and moreover distinguishing them in an altogether traditional way. The psychologist is to tell us what happens in our heads that results in our believing what we do, while the epistemologist is to tell us what we have reasons to believe. And it is the latter project that Quine and Ullian are pursuing in *The Web of Belief.*

So, the standard interpretation will not do. Quine's settled view is not one that simply turns epistemology into a chapter of psychology. Indeed, his own practice illustrates that he thinks that there is something for epistemologists to do other than merely describe the relation between experiential input and theoretical output. They can also be concerned, as always, with what it is rational for us to believe as opposed to what we actually do believe. This is what Quine himself is concerned with in *The Web of Belief.*

Why, then, does Quine say that epistemology is to be a chapter of psychology? Part of the answer, no doubt, is Quine's fondness for shocking aphorisms. But it is not just that. He sees epistemology as continuous with science in general. Indeed, it is not an exaggeration to say that he sees epistemology as a part of science, or if you prefer, a chapter of science. On the other hand, it is an exaggeration to say, as he does, that epistemology is a chapter of one particular science, viz., psychology. This might seem to be a minor distinction, but in fact it is far from minor. It is crucial for understanding how epistemology can be normative in Quine's view.

To explain why, I need first to discuss Quine's view of normativity in epistemology. Then I will return to the distinction between epistemology as a chapter of science in general and epistemology as a chapter of psychology.

Quine thinks that the normative element in epistemology is ultimately a matter of identifying effective means to a valued end, where in epistemology the relevant valued end is truth, or more cautiously, accurate predictions. He never defends the idea that the ability to predict observations has value. He apparently takes it as obvious that it does, and thus he also takes it as obvious that whatever helps us to make more accurate predictions likewise has value—instrumental value. So, put crudely, the view is that we are justified in using a certain method insofar as it helps us to generate theories that accurately predict. In effect, this means that the norms operative within the domain of epistemology are ones with which we can "engineer" our way to accurate theories. But then, insofar as science gives us information about which methods are reliable and which are not, it is providing us with the information we need to solve this engineering problem. In so doing, science itself has normative import.

Here are a couple of relevant passages:

> There is no question here [in epistemology] of ultimate value, as in morals; it is a matter of efficacy for an ulterior end, truth or prediction. The normative here, as elsewhere in engineering, becomes descriptive when the terminal parameter has been expressed.[11]

> . . . normative epistemology gets naturalized into a chapter of engineering: the technology of anticipating sensory stimulation.[12]

These passages, which emphasize the normative element of epistemology, contrast with those passages in "Epistemology Naturalized" where Quine seems to be recommending that we replace epistemology with psychology. But it is also important to remember that in that same article, Quine deplores what he takes to be the epistemic nihilism of Kuhn, Polanyi, and Hanson. He seems to be complaining that these philosophers repudiate traditional epistemology and its normative notion of justification without replacing it with anything else. By contrast he sees himself as extracting and thereby salvaging the scientifically respectable part of normative epistemology—what he later calls the 'engineering' part.

But exactly where and how does this normative element, understood as the engineering of accurate theories, enter into Quine's epistemology? I do not think there is an easy answer to this question, but Quine's most recent words on epistemology may help provide at least the beginnings of an answer. On the very first page of *Pursuit of Truth*, Quine says that in looking at the relation between sensory stimulation and scientific theory, we can separate out some things to do without paying much attention to neurology or psychology.

> Within this baffling tangle of relations between our sensory stimulation and our scientific theory of the world, there is a segment that we can gratefully separate out and clarify without pursuing neurology, psychology, psycho-linguistics, genetics, or history. It is the part where theory is tested by prediction. It is the relation of evidential support.[13]

This sounds exactly like traditional epistemology. It sounds as if Quine is going to tell us about the relation of evidential support, and he is going to do so from his armchair, without relying on the findings of science. In other words, it sounds as if he is going to be doing epistemology in an *a priori* manner. He would no doubt insist that it is not really *a priori*. On his view, even armchair theorizing draws upon a large background of empirical information. So, it is not truly *a priori* even if it is not truly neurology, psychology, psycho-linguistics, genetics, or history either. But it is the Quinean counterpart of *a priori* theorizing.

In any event, after having announced that he is going to tell us about the relation of evidential support, he never does. He says nothing at all about this relation, although he does spend quite a bit of time on the notion of evidence, or at least its surrogate within the Quinean system, observation.[14]

Quine's struggles with the notions of observation and observation sentences are legendary, but for purposes here it is another question that is more pressing. Namely, why is it, after telling us that we can clarify the relation of evidential support without doing science, that Quine does not tell us anything about how observation evidentially supports theory?

There is a simple answer to this question. There is nothing to tell. There is nothing to tell because in Quine's system observation does not support theory; it only tests theory. Or expressed another way, observation is capable of generating only negative evidence. Quine is a Popperian: strictly speaking, observations can only refute theories; they cannot support them.[15]

The qualification 'strictly speaking' is needed because Quine need not deny that within a theory there are relations of positive evidential support. He can say, for example, that the litmus turning pink is evidence for, or confirms, that the liquid is an acid. But this sense of confirmation is theory-relative for Quine. The pinkness confirms acidity relative to our best overall theory of the world, and that theory is not confirmed by our observations; it is only tested by them.

> It is clearly true, moreover, that one continually reasons not only in refutation of hypotheses but in support of them. This, however, is a matter of arguing logically or probabilistically from other beliefs already held. . . . Some of those supporting beliefs may be observational, they contribute support only in company with others that are theoretical. Pure observation

lends only negative evidence, by refuting an observation categorical that a proposed theory implies.[16]

So, according to Quine, there is no theory-independent relation of positive evidential support between observation and theory. Accordingly, one cannot appeal to such a relation in order to introduce a normative element into epistemology. For example, the normative element cannot be a matter of having an obligation to believe only those theories for which we have adequate, positive empirical evidence. Locke thought this was the way in which epistemology became normative. In *An Essay Concerning Human Understanding*, he talks of our duty as rational creatures to conform our beliefs to the evidence.[17] Moreover, the view also has distinguished contemporary adherents, e.g. Laurence BonJour and Roderick Chisholm.[18]

But if this is not how the normative element enters into Quine's epistemology, how and where does it enter? One natural answer is that it enters with the testing of theories. After all, Quine does think that theories can be tested by observations even if they are not positively supported by them, and antecedently one would think that the testing of theories must involve normative elements.

But surprisingly, this is not Quine's view. He is explicit that it is not in the testing of theories that the normative element enters into epistemology. Here is the crucial passage:

> I have been treating the testing of a theory after it has been thought up, this being where the truth conditions and empirical content lie; so I have passed over the thinking up, which is where the normative considerations come in.[19]

And shortly after this passage, Quine adds:

> . . . when I cite prediction as the checkpoints of science, I do not see that as normative. I see it as defining a particular language game, in Wittgenstein's phrase: the game of science, in contrast to other good language games such as fiction and poetry.[20]

I say that this view is surprising, because there is a tradition in epistemology and philosophy of science that insists that the distinctively normative element of epistemology is not concerned with the context of discovery but rather the context of justification. In effect, Quine reverses this, although he prefers to talk not of the context of justification and the context of discovery but rather of the process of testing theories and the process of thinking them up. But he does say that the former is not normative whereas the latter is.

More specifically, Quine's view is that insofar as we are doing science, we have to make predictions that are testable. Moreover, if the predictions are not as we say they will be, something has to be revised. There is no choice in this and nothing at all normative about it. It is just part of the science game that when things do not turn out as we have predicted, something has to give. There is, of course, a normative issue as to whether to do science at all, but once we have agreed to do science, it is the constitutive rule of the game that something has to give when our predictions go wrong. Normative considerations come in with respect to what is to give. We have choices about what to revise when our predictions do not come out as we expect. It is here that there is room for norms. The norms govern what Quine calls 'the thinking up of theories', only it is important to realize that as he uses the phrase, the thinking up of theories can be a matter of either inventing altogether new theories or revising existing ones in the face of unsuccessful predictions.

Moreover, Quine identifies the normative considerations that in his judgment should govern this process of thinking up new theories and revising old ones. In *The Web of Belief*, Quine and Ullian listed five virtues to seek in a new or revised hypothesis: conservatism, generality, simplicity, refutability, and modesty. In his latest work, *Pursuit of Truth*, Quine has pared the list down to two fundamental norms: the maximization of simplicity of our hypotheses and the minimalization of the mutilation of old hypotheses.[21]

Of course, often enough these two overarching norms will be at odds with one another, in which case they must be balanced in some appropriate way. Quine tells us nothing about how to go about doing this, even though his view commits him to regarding this as one of the most fundamental normative issues in epistemology. Perhaps he thinks that there just is not anything specific to say about how an appropriate weighting can be achieved. We just have to muck around and do the best we can.

By way of contrast, Quine does think that at a lower level it is possible to generate specific advice about how to conduct our theorizing, but to do so we need to draw upon the detailed findings of our various sciences. We need these findings, because, as I pointed out before, Quine thinks that the norms that govern our theorizing are engineering norms, and in engineering, we are free, indeed required, to draw upon the findings of science. Here is a relevant passage, a portion of which I cited earlier:

> Naturalization of epistemology does not jettison the normative and settle for indiscriminate description of the on-going process. For me normative epistemology is a branch of engineering. It is the technology of truth-seeking, or, in more cautiously epistemic terms, prediction. Like any technology, it makes free use of whatever scientific finding may suit its purpose. It draws upon mathematics in computing standard deviation and probable error and in scouting the gambler's fallacy. It draws upon experimental psychology in exploring perceptual illusions and upon cognitive psychology in scouting wishful thinking. It draws upon neurology and physics, in a general way, in discounting testimony from occult and parapsychological sources. There is no question here of ultimate value, as in morals; it is a matter of efficacy for an ulterior end, truth or prediction. The normative here, as elsewhere in engineering, becomes descriptive when the terminal parameter has been expressed.[22]

So, if we are looking for specific intellectual advice, we must look at mathematics, cognitive psychology, neurology, statistics, and any other relevant science. Notice that the point is not that these are the places to look if what we want are philosophical criteria for justified belief or rational belief. The point, rather, is that these are places to find one of the other things that epistemologists have traditionally wanted—namely, concrete advice about how to get at the truth, or more cautiously accurate predictions.

Notice also that psychology is just one of the sciences that we look to for advice. If naturalized epistemology were simply in the business of explaining how we get from observation to theory, then psychology would be the only, or at least the principally, relevant science. But naturalized epistemology, Quine insists, is normative, and precisely because of this psychology has no privileged position with respect to it. Epistemology is not simply a chapter of psychology. Any science that is relevant to the technology of truth seeking is *ipso facto* relevant for epistemology.[23]

This link between epistemology and science explains why Quine thinks he is not jettisoning the normative in epistemology, but on the other hand it cannot be this that makes his epistemology distinctively naturalistic, since it is not even controversial that science is linked in this way with epistemology. Neither Descartes nor Locke nor any other non-naturalized epistemologist need deny that the particular sciences are capable of providing us with information that is relevant to what Quine calls 'the technology of truth seeking'. They would have no trouble agreeing, for example, that probability theory can warn us about the gambler's fallacy, psychology about perceptual illusions, and physics about testimony from the occult. What they will deny is that science is capable of telling us anything interesting about the most fundamental epistemological norms—for example, the norms that guide us in doing science itself.

This suggests that if we are to find something distinctively naturalized in Quine's epistemology, we must look at the status of the most general epistemological norms within his system. According to Quine, these norms are ones that tell us to maximize simplicity and minimize mutilation in thinking up theories. So, the crucial question to ask is, what on Quine's view makes these norms the correct ones?

Regrettably, Quine never says. In fact, he never even tries to cite considerations in favor of these norms. He simply posits them from his philosophical armchair, much as Descartes posited his method of doubt and Locke his way of ideas from their armchairs. The appearance, in other words, is that at the most basic level, Quine's way of doing epistemology is not different in kind from the traditional way of doing epistemology. He is proposing general norms of inquiry and he seems to be doing so *a priori*.

But of course, this cannot be right. If Quine stands for anything, he stands for the rejection of *a priori* epistemology. So, there is a puzzle here. Quine's official pronouncements on epistemology make it sound as if he sees himself doing epistemology in a radically new way, and yet his actual practice in doing normative epistemology looks altogether familiar.

One way of solving the puzzle would be to insist that Quine is merely saying that when scientists revise their theories and think up new ones, they in fact try to maximize simplicity and minimize mutilation. This reading has the advantage of making Quine's claim about simplicity and mutilation straightforwardly empirical. Of course, it also makes it incumbent upon him to cite some empirical evidence indicating that scientists do act in this way. However, he neither cites such evidence nor even displays much interest in empirical studies of science. Besides, on this interpretation, his epistemology would once again lose its normative force. It would be simply reporting how scientists go about their theorizing, while remaining neutral on whether this is a desirable way to theorize. But as we have seen, Quine sees himself as doing normative epistemology.

How, then, are we to interpret Quine's recommendation that we maximize simplicity and minimize mutilation? The only interpretation consistent with Quine's rejection of *a priori* epistemology is one that has the recommended norms as themselves being engineering norms. They too are part of the technology of truth seeking, and as such they are the products of science, broadly construed. To be sure, Quine never tries to show that this is so. He simply posits the norms without defense. Nonetheless, he has no choice but to regard them as conclusions of science, albeit ones with normative import for the technology of truth seeking.

A good way to see how this might work within the Quinean system is to look at what he says about another norm. In addition to the norms that tells us to maximize simplicity and minimize mutilation, Quine also defends an empiricist norm, which he identifies using the Latin phrase: *nihil in mente quod non primus in sensu*. He also expresses the norm in a less refined way by putting the motto of the Sherwin-Williams paint company to his own use: save the surface and you save all. Saving the surface is here equated with saving observation sentences.

According to Quine, empiricism is a position that tells us where to look for the content and truth conditions of our theories—we are to look at observation sentences. But in addition, Quine thinks of empiricism as a normative position that tells us to do science insofar as we are interested in truth. What this means, most generally expressed, is that we are to formulate hypotheses that are empirically testable, and if these hypotheses together with our other beliefs generate faulty predictions, we are to change something. The overarching norms then tell us how to make the changes. We are to maximize simplicity and minimize mutilation.

So, in addition to the simplicity and non-mutilation norms, Quine also endorses an empiricist norm, which he conceives to be identical with the scientific method broadly conceived. This then is one of the senses in which Quine's epistemology can be regarded as a scientific epistemology: the norms of rational belief, as he sees it, just are the norms of science broadly conceived.

There are many questions that can be raised about this view, chief among them are whether empiricism can be plausibly identified with the scientific method, even broadly construed, and whether empiricism, so conceived, is really a plausible candidate to be a fundamental norm of rational belief. But I am going to glide over these questions, since my main concern is not so much the content of Quine's recommendations as his way of doing epistemology. The objective is to identify something distinctively naturalistic about his way of doing epistemology, and this objective is not met by pointing out that on Quine's view the norms of rational belief are identical with the norms of science broadly conceived. This only shows that the content of Quine's normative recommendations is different from the content of, say, Descartes's and Chisholm's recommendations, not that his way of doing epistemology is distinct in some interesting way. The interesting conception is one that makes his epistemology a part of science, but this requires that even his most fundamental norms—the empiricist norm as well as the simplicity/non-mutilation norms—be products of science. We have seen that Quine thinks that psychology, statistics, physics, and other sciences provide us with information that we can use to fashion a technology of truth seeking. In so doing, they provide us with lower-level epistemic norms. What is not yet so clear is how psychology, statistics, physics, or any of the other sciences could generate the most fundamental norms. It is not clear, in other words, in what sense these norms are engineering norms.

As a way of trying to get an answer to this question, let's ask another one—how, if at all, are these norms revisable? This question is a pressing one given Quine's rejection of the analytic-synthetic distinction and his endorsement of epistemological holism. These positions may not quite entail that all of our opinions are in principle revisable, but they do make the view hard to resist. And of course, it is a view that Quine accepts. Thus, it had better be the case the most fundamental parts of his epistemology are revisable.

And indeed, Quine says precisely this about the empiricist norm. He says the norm is itself a finding of science and hence revisable. In particular, it is a finding of science that our information about the world comes from our five senses, but this point, he adds, is normative, since it warns us against any purported source of information that is not rooted in observations. It warns against telepathers and soothsayers, for instance.[24]

But can it really be the case that empiricism is a finding of science? Science, in Quine's view, is defined by its empirical methods. It is essentially a matter of constructing theories that can be refuted by observations. But then, isn't empiricism a presupposition of science rather than a finding of it?

Quine does not explicitly address this question, but it is clear what he should say. He should say that empiricism is both a presupposition and a finding of science. It is a presupposition in that science is defined, on Quine's view, by its empirical methods, but it is also a finding of science in that science, according to Quine, tells us that our most reliable information about the world comes to us through our senses. It tells us that we are not telepathic and that we are not clairvoyant and that we do not have any other reliable, non-observational access to the world.

But isn't it inevitably question begging to make use of empirical methods to argue that empirical methods are our most reliable ways of gaining information? Perhaps, but we should expect question begging when the issue concerns our most fundamental methods of inquiry. If a method is not fundamental, it can be defended employing methods that are more fundamental than it. But epistemology is most centrally concerned with our fundamental methods of inquiry, and our fundamental methods, if they are to be defended at all, must be defended using those very methods. We can say that this begs the questions, if we so wish, but some questions need to be begged, if they are to be answered at all, and questions about the reliability of our most fundamental methods of inquiry are just such questions.

Besides, it is no trivial matter for a method to beg the question in its own defense. Not every proposed method in every situation will be able to do so, since it is possible for a method to generate evidence that undermines its own reliability. Indeed, it is just this that accounts for the revisability of the empirical norm, in Quine's eyes. To be sure, he thinks that at the current, relatively advanced stage of inquiry, it would take an extraordinary turn of events to convince us (or at least most of us) that we have a faculty of clairvoyance and that this faculty is a more reliable source of information about the world than our eyes, ears, and other senses. But it is at least thinkable for things to go this way, and if they did, Quine admits, even the empiricist norm could be rejected. This norm is derived from science, and like the rest of science it is fallible. This is the price of Quine's rejection of epistemology as a first philosophy, and it is a price that Quine thinks we have no choice but to pay. There simply is no helpful *a priori* intellectual advice to be given.[25]

Having said this, it is also important to see that Quine is proposing something that is very, very close to an *a priori* epistemology, a kind of Quinean counterpart to it. To be sure, Quine is clear about his rejection of *a priori* epistemology. For him there is no difference in kind between the truths sought in philosophy (and hence epistemology) and those sought in science. But he is also well known for pointing out that some opinions are more central to the web of our beliefs than others and that we will be more reluctant to give up these beliefs. Since they are so central, we will and should do everything we can to protect them. It is this that gives some of these beliefs the appearance of being necessarily true. We shield such beliefs from revision by exercising our freedom to reject other beliefs in the web instead, and this creates the appearance of necessity.[26] We do this in mathematics, and we can do it in epistemology as well. We can shield the opinion that undergirds the empiricist norm—viz., the opinion that insofar as we are interested in truth, it is best for us to look for hypotheses that can be tested empirically—and this can create the appearance that we are treating it as a necessary truth that we know *a priori*.

As a devout empiricist, this is precisely the appearance that Quine creates. He talks about the empiricist norm almost as if it were a necessary truth known *a priori* and that as such it is beyond dispute. In turn, this creates the appearance that he is doing epistemology pretty much as usual. Indeed, for all practical purposes he *is* doing epistemology as usual. In practice, he is no more concerned with the empirical support for his empiricist norm than Descartes was concerned with the empirical support for his method of doubt. However, unlike Descartes and unlike a good many other traditional epistemologists, Quine is committed to the view that this norm, and the belief upon which it is based, are revisable. But this really is not much more than a bare possibility. The sense in which they are revisable is the same as the sense in which elementary truths of mathematics are revisable, which is just to say that for all practical purposes, they might as well not be revisable at all.

Exactly the same must be said about Quine's other fundamental norms, the ones that tell us to maximize simplicity and minimize mutilation. Although Quine never explicitly says so, they too had better be based on findings of science and hence revisable. In particular, they must correspond to an empirical claim about the technology of truth seeking—viz., that a policy of maximizing simplicity and minimizing mutilation helps us in our engineering task of constructing theories that accurately predict observations. Quine apparently takes it as utterly obvious that this is the case. So, he never tries to marshal empirical evidence in defense of the claim. And no doubt he would be prepared to shield it from revision at almost any cost, thus creating the appearance of necessity. But again, he is committed to its revisability in principle, even if this does not have much effect on his practice of epistemology.

This, then, is the overall structure of Quine's epistemology. The various norms he endorses correspond to various beliefs he has, and he hopes that the rest of us have as well, about the technology of truth seeking. Since these beliefs are revisable, the norms that are derived from them are also revisable. However, we will exhibit different degrees of stubbornness with respect to different norms.

It is relatively easy to imagine circumstances in which we would give up norms that are derived from specific findings in the sciences; we need only imagine circumstances in which we would abandon or revise the findings on which they are based. For example, currently our best theory of dreaming takes REM as the most reliable indicator of dream activity, and our epistemic norms reflect this theory. We tend to discount first-person negative testimony about dreaming; even if in the morning I do not remember dreaming, you are entitled to conclude that I dreamed if I displayed REM during the night. Even so, it is not all that difficult to imagine dream research developing in such a way that our best future theory will imply that REM produces dreams only in conjunction with some other factor F, and, surprisingly, subjects almost always remember dreaming when REM + F are present. If so, our epistemic norms will be correspondingly revised; first-person negative testimony about dreaming will be taken more seriously.

By contrast, it is much harder to imagine our giving up the empiricist norm, since on Quine's view it is constitutive of the scientific method as we know it. Still, he is committed to the position that science could generate evidence that undermines science as we know it. More accurately, it could generate evidence that make the costs of hanging on to science unacceptably high, where the costs here would be a matter of decreased simplicity and increased mutilation of our web of beliefs.

Similarly, Quine is also committed to saying that the policy of maximizing simplicity and minimizing mutilation might generate evidence that undermined this very policy. Again, it would take a remarkable turn of events for this to happen, but it is at least thinkable that in maximizing simplicity and minimizing mutilation we worsen, or at least do not help, our abilities to predict observations. Hence, it is at least thinkable that we will come to believe that moderately unstable and complex belief systems serve us as well or better in predicting the course of observations as maximally stable and simple ones. Indeed, in the worst case scenario, we might become convinced that every available way of conducting inquiry, whether it be one that emphasizes simplicity and non-mutilation or any other, will be met with widespread predictive failures, in which case we might well resign ourselves to skepticism. If so, then no way of conducting inquiry would be rational for us.

So, where does this leave us in our attempt to identify a sense in which Quine is a naturalized epistemologist, whereas Descartes, Locke, Carnap, and Chisholm are not. It leaves us, I think, with two possible ways of doing so, although one, I have argued, is not especially interesting.

First, the uninteresting way: within Quine's system, the most fundamental norms are identical, as Quine sees it, with the norms of natural science. So, the canons of rational belief just are the canons of science, broadly conceived. But all this means is that the content of Quine's recommendations is different from other epistemologists, not that his way of doing epistemology is different.

The second and more interesting way: Quine rejects the analytic-synthetic distinction and with it any distinction between *a priori* knowledge and *a posteriori* knowledge and any distinction between necessary and contingent truths. So, the fundamental epistemic norms in his system cannot be known *a priori*, nor are they necessary. Rather, they are continuous with science. They are part of our overall theory of the world, and like any other part of that theory, they are revisable in principle. Any appearance to the contrary is to be explained by our freedom to make revisions elsewhere in our web of belief when things go wrong, thus shielding these norms from revision.

Still, what is remarkable is how little difference this second point makes to Quine's practice of epistemology. Admittedly, it does make some difference. The rejection of the analytic-synthetic distinction leads Quine to endorse holism, and one implication of his holism is that the primary objects of epistemic justification are not individual beliefs but rather our overall theory of the world—in effect, our overall web of beliefs. So, this becomes the focus of his epistemology. But once it is settled that the primary epistemological norms are to be ones that govern the revision of our overall theory, Quine proceeds in the usual manner. The specific norms Quine favors are ones that he recommends from his philosophical armchair, with little or no concern for an empirical defense of them.

So, Quine's practice as a naturalized epistemologist is not discernibly different from that of any other famous epistemologist in the history of the subject. His rejection of the analytic-synthetic distinction does make for a significant difference when we are thinking about the metaphysical status of his claims, but it has little relevance when Quine is actually doing epistemology.

An interesting final question is whether something analogous is true of other philosophers who are regarded as doing naturalized epistemology. I think that it is. More specifically, I think that insofar as their concerns are normative and fundamental, their practice, like Quine's, will not be discernibly different from that of other epistemologists in the history of the subject. But to establish this would require a case by case examination of their views. So, for the time being, I will be content with limiting my claim to Quine, who is widely recognized as the founder of naturalized epistemology: he is not doing epistemology in a fundamentally new way.

NOTES

1. Roderick Chisholm, *Theory of Knowledge*, 3rd ed. (Englewood Cliffs, N.J., 1989).

2. Jaegwon Kim, "What Is Naturalized Epistemology?" in *Philosophical Perspectives*, edited by J. Tomberlin vol. 2 (Atascadero, Calif., 1988), 381–405; Alvin Goldman, *Epistemology and Cognition* (Cambridge, Mass., 1986); Philip Kitcher, "The Naturalists Return," *Philosophical Review* 101 (January 1992): 53–114; Hilary Kornblith, "Introduction: What Is Naturalized Epistemology?" in *Naturalizing Epistemology*, edited by Hilary Kornblith (Cambridge, Mass., 1985), 1–14; and Hilary Putnam, "Why Reason Can't be Naturalized," *Synthese* 52 (1982): 3–23.

3. Quine, "Epistemology Naturalized," in *Naturalizing Epistemology*, 25.

4. Kim, "What Is Naturalized Epistemology?" 389.

5. Alvin Goldman, *Epistemology and Cognition*, 3. But also see footnote 5, where Goldman admits that it is not always clear whether Quine wants to repudiate altogether the normative element of epistemology, but he does insist that Quine's "actual characterizations of naturalized epistemology do not expressly introduce this dimension."

6. Kornblith, "Introduction: What is Naturalized Epistemology?" 4.

7. Quine, *Theories and Things* (Cambridge, Mass., 1981), 72.

8. Quine, "Epistemology Naturalized," 19.

9. Quine, *Pursuit of Truth* (Cambridge, Mass., 1990), 19.

10. Quine and J. S. Ullian, *The Web of Belief* (New York, 1970), 7. The second and significantly revised edition (1978) does not contain this passage.

11. Quine, "Reply to White," in *The Philosophy of W. V. Quine*, edited by L. A. Hahn and P. A. Schilpp (LaSalle, Ill., 1986), 663–65.

12. Quine, *Pursuit of Truth*, 19.

13. Quine, *Pursuit of Truth*, 1.

14. Quine does not define evidence in terms of observations. He talks rather of observations, or more exactly observation sentences, as being "the vehicle of scientific evidence." See, e.g., *Pursuit of Truth*, 5.

15. See *Pursuit of Truth*, 12–13.

16. Ibid., 13.

17. Locke, *An Essay Concerning Human Understanding*, edited by P. H. Nidditch (Oxford, 1975); see especially IV, xvii, 24.

18. See Chisholm, *Theory of Knowledge*, 3rd ed., and BonJour, *The Structure of Empirical Knowledge* (Cambridge, Mass., 1985).

19. *Pursuit of Truth*, 20.

20. Ibid.

21. This was also the way he expressed the point in *Word and Object*, which was written ten years before *The Web of Belief*: "The last arbiter is the so-called scientific method, however amorphous . . . a matter of being guided by sensory stimuli, a taste for simplicity in some sense, and a taste for old things" (Quine, *Word and Object* [Cambridge, Mass., 1960], 22).

22. "Reply to White," in *The Philosophy of W. V. Quine*, 663–65.

23. Susan Haack makes a similar point. See Haack, "Two Faces of Quine's Naturalism," *Synthese* 94 (1993): 335.

24. *Pursuit of Truth*, 19.

25. "I admit to naturalism and even glory in it. This means banishing the dream of a first philosophy and pursuing philosophy rather as a part of one's system of the world, continuous with the rest of science" (Quine, "Reply to Putnam," in *The Philosophy of W. V. Quine*, 430–31).

26. See, e.g., Quine, *Pursuit of Truth*, 15.

Quine's Naturalism

PETER HYLTON

In a broad and loose sense, naturalism has commanded wide philosophical support. If phrased generally as the claim that the methods and techniques of natural science are the source of knowledge about the world, it would certainly be accepted by, for example, Carnap, and even perhaps by Kant.[1] Quine's naturalism, however, is another matter. In the context of Quine's predecessors it is, as I shall try to indicate, a revolutionary philosophical doctrine, especially in its view of the status of philosophy itself.

My discussion of Quine's naturalism will not focus on his explicit statements of the doctrine which may, in some cases, be misleading. I shall concentrate, rather, on two points. First, how Quine *uses* his naturalism. In particular, Quine appeals to naturalism to defend the claim that his philosophy is a form of realism against charges that his view leads to idealism or instrumentalism or skepticism. Seeing how naturalism is supposed to defeat or deflect these charges will give us an idea of what naturalism, in Quine's hands, must come to. Second, how Quine's naturalism can be defended from within his philosophy. This matter is complicated. There is, I shall claim, no real attempt in Quine's work to justify naturalism, and the idea of a justification which does not itself presuppose naturalism in some form is quite problematic. We can, however, construct an illuminating argument for Quine's version of naturalism which does draw on features of Quine's view which are themselves, in some ways and to some extent, naturalistic. Such an argument will not, of course, serve to convince those who hold strongly non-naturalistic opinions, but may have some force against those who hold a form of naturalism more moderate than Quine's. The argument will also serve to give us some insight into the crucial features of Quine's naturalism—especially the role played in that doctrine by observation and prediction.

Quine's philosophy exhibits a dichotomy that many critics have found puzzling, or incoherent. On the one hand, his epistemology emphasizes the gap between theory and evidence; on the other hand, his ontology is unqualifiedly realistic. Epistemologically, he is concerned to investigate "to what extent science is man's free creation; to what extent . . . it is a put-up job,"[2] and his conclusion is that to a very considerable extent it *is* a put-up job. The disparity between the evidence we have for our knowledge and the knowledge itself is a recurrent theme in Quine's work. Thus he speaks of the epistemologist's question as "how it is that man works up his command of . . . science from the limited impingements that are available to his sensory surfaces" (p. 3), and, again, he speaks of studying "[t]he relation between the meager input and the torrential output . . . in order to see how evidence relates to theory, and in what ways one's theory of nature transcends any available evidence."[3] The most striking manifestation of this disparity between theory and evidence is the doctrine of the underdetermination of theory by evidence: more than one theory is compatible with the totality of observational truths (not only the known observational truths, but all of them).[4] While this view has proved difficult to formulate precisely, Quine has consistently maintained the crucial point: that there is no reason to think that our theory of the world is the only one compatible with the observational truths, even given constraints of simplicity and so on. Thus in his latest word on the subject he says: "What the empirical under-determination of global science shows is that there are various defensible ways of conceiving the world."[5] On the one hand, then, Quine holds that our theories far outrun the evidence that we have for them, and that more than one theory is compatible with that evidence. On the other hand, however, he maintains that his view is "a robust realism,"[6] that he fully accepts the reality both of ordinary objects and (a little more tentatively) of the objects whose existence is asserted by accepted scientific theories. In response to the idea that these two views are incompatible, Quine invokes what he calls "naturalism"; his naturalism, he claims, can reconcile the two.

Quine's ontology, then, asserts an unqualified realism; his epistemology, however, argues for a wide disparity between evidence and theory, and thus seems to many to suggest skepticism or instrumentalism, or at any rate to make considerable qualification to the realism. It is not hard to see why these two views should be thought of as *prima facie* incompatible—and thus in need of reconciliation if both are to be maintained. If our theory of the world—not only our scientific theory but even our commonsense beliefs in trees and rocks and people and other medium-sized objects—is to a large extent a put-up job, a theory to which there are equally good alternatives, then why should we accept it as true? It may be convenient, even indispensable, since we do not in fact have any of the other equally good theories, but can it be more than that? To say that all the evidence is compatible with either of two theories is normally to suggest an agnostic position, that neither should yet be taken as true. So in this case: what answer has Quine to the charge that on his own account, we have no compelling reason to accept that our theory tells us how the world really is? However well our theory of the world works, however efficiently it enables us to predict and deal with experience, still on Quine's view it is only one of a number of equally good theories: so what reason do we have to take it as more than an efficient instrument? Quine claims that all objects are theoretical, and thus have a status no firmer than that of our theory of the world (see, e.g., *T&T*, p. 23). In that case, again, if the objects whose existence that theory asserts are merely theoretical, why should we accept them as real? It is in answer to questions of this sort that Quine invokes naturalism. In his reply to Harold Lee, in the Schilpp volume, Quine says: "Perhaps he [Lee] was misled by my realism, not appreciating that it is consistent with recognizing man's creative role in science. The reconciliation lies in my naturalism."[7] Similarly, in "Things and Their Place in Theories," Quine raises the question of how his realism is to be reconciled with the paucity of evidence that we have for our theories, and he says: "The answer is naturalism . . ." (*T&T*, p. 21).

How does naturalism play this role? Or, perhaps a better way to angle the question, what is Quine's naturalism that it can play this role? In Quine's explicit statements, naturalism is often identified with the abandonment of the ideal of a 'first philosophy' prior to science. Thus the statement quoted immediately above continues like this: "The answer is naturalism: the recognition that it is within science itself, and not in some prior philosophy, that reality is to be identified and described" (*T&T*, p. 21); and in the Schilpp volume Quine says: "I admit to naturalism, even glory in it. This means banishing the dream of a first philosophy and pursuing philosophy rather as part of one's system of the world, continuous with the rest of science."[8] But, again, how exactly does this help? The answer must be something like this: if we are always within our 'system of the world', then there is no position from which the apparently threatening philosophical questions can be asked; it is only if one has an external perspective on that system—such as might be afforded by a philosophical view independent of ordinary knowledge—that those questions can be raised.

This point emerges perhaps most explicitly in one of Quine's discussions of relativism. Quine raises the possibility of empirically equivalent systems of the world, i.e., different global theories of the world which lead to all of the same observational predictions. It might seem natural to draw relativist conclusions from this possibility: if there are two distinct theories, each of which leads to the same observational predictions, then surely we have no empirical basis on which to say that one is right and the other wrong. So should we not say that each is correct in its own way, on its own terms—recognizing that truth in such a case is relative to theory or culture? Quine's conclusion is different: "Truth, says the cultural relativist, is culture-bound. But if it were, then he, within his own culture, ought to see his own culture-bound truth as absolute. He cannot proclaim cultural relativism without rising above it, and he cannot rise above it without giving it up."[9] It is explicit here that what is at stake is the sense of the relativist's claim, or the sense of the terms in which the challenge to Quine is issued. From what standpoint does the cultural relativist speak? Not simply from within a given culture, for in that case no issue of relativism would arise. So the relativist must occupy a standpoint which is not within any of the theories that he is talking about—a standpoint from which he can talk about all such theories evenhandedly, as it were; but it is just that sort of standpoint which, according to the relativist himself, does not exist. So, in Quine's view, there simply is no standpoint from which relativism can be advocated, or even coherently stated. What is the relevance of this to the idea of 'first philosophy', i.e., philosophy independent of our substantive theory of the world? Just this: that if there were such a philosophy it would provide a standpoint from which the question of relativism, or the question of the reality of the objects our theory speaks about, could be raised.[10]

A different kind of example may bring out slightly different issues within our basic theme. In considering the *prima facie* tension between Quine's epistemology and his ontology, we suggested the following question: our theory of the world may work well in enabling us to predict and deal with experience, but what reason have we to accept that it is *true*? Quine's response, again, is to raise the issue of the standpoint from which the critic speaks. The critic's standpoint is not, evidently, that of our ordinary system of the world, since the truth of the whole of that theory is being cast in doubt. But neither, in asking the question, does Quine's critic have in mind another system of the world which can underpin her use of the notion of truth; in that case we would simply have a conflict of theories, to be settled on the ordinary sort of scientific grounds. So Quine's critic seems to speak neither from within our current theory of the world, nor from within an alternative. But for Quine the point of naturalism is that we are always within a system of the world, and that our talk of truth is tied to that system. As Quine says: "Truth is immanent, and there is no higher. We must speak from within a theory, albeit any of various. . . . What evaporates is the transcendental question of the reality of the external world—the question whether or how far our science measures up to the *Ding an sich*."[11]

Now it may be said that the realism that Quine defends in this way is anemic rather that robust, that it at most deserves Putman's name 'internal realism', or Kant's 'empirical realism', or even that it is tantamount to instrumentalism. The use of pre-existing labels to characterize a philosophical position is always dubious, especially in the case of a philosopher such as Quine, who shifts the ground on which philosophy is being done. And certainly Quine is no respecter of such labels. The point is that Quine is a realist in the only sense that he holds there is to that term. For him there are no different senses of being or reality; there is a single univocal notion.[12] Concomitantly, he holds that there are no distinctions to be made between kinds of realism: he is a realist in the only sense that there is. Indeed the point of the discussion of the past few pages could be phrased by saying that it shows that for Quine there is no other form of realism, stronger than his: on his view, he is a realist in the only sense that there is to that idea. It is, however, a crucial fact that Quine himself does not contrast his form of realism with another. Once one begins to argue against the coherence of some form of realism—external or transcendental realism, say—it is almost too late to deny that there is any sense to such an idea: if there is no sense to it, how can one be arguing against it? And if there is sense to it, of however dubious and attenuated a kind, then any other form of realism is in danger of looking second-best. The passage quoted at the end of the previous paragraph is as close as Quine ever comes to saying that there might be a form of realism that is stronger than his, that there might be a sense of the question of the reality of the external world in which his realism does not answer that question—and even then he acknowledges such a question only to say that it evaporates.

It is worth noting in passing that Quine's view does not exclude the fact that our theory of the world is constantly criticized, revised, and improved. From within our theory of the world, we can question the empirical adequacy of that theory—how far it in fact succeeds in predicting the course of experience. But in Quine's view it is crucial that this questioning takes place either within the theory we are considering (perhaps using the less contentious parts of it) or from the standpoint of some proposed new theory. In this latter case, it is the proposed new theory that provides a standpoint from which our current theory can be judged, and it is the new theory that provides a standard of truth. But at that point it is the new theory which is 'our theory', and it is its conformity to the world that is in question. Criticizing our present beliefs by our present standards, and replacing some of those beliefs by improved versions, must be legitimate. What is not legitimate, on Quine's account, is criticism of the whole theory which does not offer to replace it by a better, but which simply stigmatizes it (and, by extension, anything else of the same kind) as untrue. In that case, Quine claims, the notion of truth which the critic relies upon has no force; it floats free of any theory that could anchor it.

The crucial aspect of Quine's naturalism, as it emerges from the above discussion, is that we always speak from within a theory, a system of the world. There is no neutral or presuppositionless position from which we can make judgments about the world and our theory of it: all of our judgments must be evaluated as being part of a substantive theory of the world. In particular, our philosophical remarks are made from within such a theory. Quine's own doctrines are quite general and abstract, and in some cases speculative. On that account, he thinks, they are correctly called "philosophical": but this word does not mark out any special status. Quine's critics, on his view, do not sufficiently acknowledge or think through the fact that their remarks, too, are made from the standpoint of a substantive theory of the world. They attempt to speak transcendentally, i.e., as if independent of any system of the world. This preliminary understanding of Quine's naturalism raises two closely related questions: First, where are we when we are "inside a system of the world"? Second, how can we elaborate the metaphor of "inside" so as to make the issues more concrete?

Quine's view, as we have already seen, is that to be inside a system of the world is to be within science; his view is that we always speak from within a scientific theory. Taking this as literally as possible, it might seem false. Sometimes I am concerned about the truths of science, but often I am not. If I want to know what time the meeting begins, or where I left my copy of *Word and Object*, what I am concerned with is very oddly described as a question of "science." Quine accepts this oddity, however. It is a crucial part of his doctrine that there is no break between science and common sense: "science is itself a continuation of common sense."[13] Thus he describes science as "self-conscious common sense,"[14] and equates "common-sense about bodies" with "[r]udimentary physical science."[15] It is, he stresses, the same notion of evidence that is used everywhere: "The scientist is indistinguishable from the common man in his sense of evidence, except that the scientist is more careful. This increased care is not a revision of evidential standard, but only the more patient and systematic collection and use of what anyone would deem to be evidence."[16] This amounts to an assertion of one sense of the idea of the unity of knowledge, and also of the idea that the paradigmatic form of knowledge is that of what are sometimes called the "empirical sciences."[17] All of our knowledge, or attempts at knowledge, are subject to standards of evidence and justification which are most explicitly displayed, and most successfully implemented, in (empirical) science in the ordinary sense of that word. In particular, it is Quine's view that success in the prediction of observations (and so of stimulations: see *Pursuit of Truth*, p. 2) is the ultimate test not only of science in the narrow sense but for all attempts at knowledge (the second half of this essay will perhaps give some idea of why Quine holds this view).

These considerations help also with our second question: how to make more literal sense of the idea that we are always inside our system of the world. What does "inside" mean here? Presumably it must mean something like this: that every claim we make—everything we say that aims at being true—is answerable to the same sort of standards of evidence and justification. One immediate implication of this, which will surprise no reader of Quine, is that there is no real *a priori* knowledge, for that would be a sort of knowledge which is not subject to the same standards of evidence and justification as the ordinary claims of (empirical) science, or which is even exempt from any question of justification and evidence at all. Mathematics, in particular, must be seen as in some sense answerable to evidence, though no doubt in a very remote and indirect way. The denial of the *a priori* is a fundamental Quinean doctrine, integral to his version of naturalism; for Quine, this doctrine is based on (what he takes to be) the inadequacy of Carnap's conception of analyticity, but that may be thought to beg the question of other conceptions of the *a priori*.

Beyond the denial of the *a priori*, however, the view that all our knowledge is subject to the same standards of evidence may seem abstract and hard to pin down. There is not must in common to the way we settle, on the one hand, the mundane question of what time the meeting is and, on the other hand, the most abstruse questions of the nature of elementary particles, or of the structure of space-time. Quine's view is that all such questions—i.e., all genuinely factual questions[18]—are in principle of the same sort, i.e, answerable to what are in principle the same standards of evidence and justification. As a positive account of scientific method this is, at the least, weak; what is in common to all attempts at knowledge, what is 'in principle the same', will be at best very thin. If Quine's point is understood as purely negative, however, it seems more plausible. If Quine's thesis is not about the uniformity of method but rather about the lack of sharp dividing lines, lack of clear differences in principle, between the most mundane questions and the most abstruse, then it may be hard to find a basis for disagreement. In that case Quine need not show a clear sense to the idea of "difference in principle": he need merely deny that there is such an idea which is correctly applied in this case. It is, I think, the negative point that Quine needs. In particular, as we saw, Quine asks us to consider our own philosophical perspective, the position from which we raise philosophical questions about Quine's work. It is intrinsic to his view that in doing philosophy we do not occupy an epistemological position which is fundamentally different in kind from that which we occupy when we are concerned with other sorts of knowledge; no substantial convergence of method is implied. Thus to defuse the threat of the question whether our scientific system of the world, even if completely successful in predicting observations, might nevertheless fail to be true, Quine must insist that the questioner cannot occupy a position which is wholly outside our system of the world. Nothing more than this negative point seems to be required.

Let us summarize our discussion of Quine's naturalism to this point. We could phrase naturalism by saying that all of our knowledge has, in principle, the same status as our knowledge of scientific theories. The crucial point of Quine's naturalism, as it emerged from our discussion, is that this principle is explicitly and self-consciously applied to philosophy itself. One can of course question the truth of a scientific theory as a way of suggesting a replacement; the undiscriminating question of the truth of our theories in general, however, the question whether they are even the right sort of thing to give an account of the way of the world really is, looks like a distinctively philosophical question. Such a question is not asked in a way which takes for granted the correctness of the bulk of the developing body of theory, or some likely successor; it purports rather to be asked from a different perspective entirely. Quine's deepest move is to deny that there is any coherent alternative theoretical perspective.[19] And when Quine says that, he takes it that he is himself also speaking from the perspective afforded by our global theory of the world. A number of philosophers have raised the question whether Quine's naturalized epistemology really is a form of epistemology.[20] For Quine such worries are beside the point: for him there is no other sense of epistemology.

Naturalism is sometimes thought of as simply the view that it is permissible to use the results of science within philosophy.[21] As a statement about *Quine's* version of naturalism, that would not be incorrect, exactly, but it would be misleading. What is crucial to Quine's naturalism is the negative point, that there is no theoretical perspective other than the general perspective of natural science—and, in particular, no distinctively philosophical perspective. The permissibility of using the results of science within philosophy follows from this shift, for there simply ceases to be a difference in principle between philosophy and natural science. I began this essay by saying that in a broad and loose sense even figures as diverse as Carnap and Kant could be thought of as naturalists. But clearly Quine's form of naturalism, the conclusion that philosophy is not different in any principled way from natural science, would have been repugnant to them. It is this conclusion, however, that underlies all of Quine's philosophy; and it is in his embracing it, and rigorously following out its consequences, that much of Quine's interest lies.

Further progress with understanding Quine's naturalism, and the questions that it raises, can be made by considering what arguments might be offered for it. Quine's overt statements on this score do not seem to me to amount to an argument for naturalism, and the first part of our discussion will be spent on this point. Quine's most explicit statement of the bases for his naturalism occurs in "Five Milestones of Empiricism."[22] Quine says there: "Naturalism has two sources, both negative. One of them is despair of being able to define theoretical terms generally in terms of phenomena, even by contextual definition. A holistic or system-centered attitude should suffice to induce this despair. The other negative source of naturalism is unregenerate realism, the robust state of mind of the natural scientist who has never felt any qualms beyond the negotiable uncertainties internal to science" (*T&T*, p. 72). This passage may be accurate as a statement of Quine's reasons for adopting naturalism: that he always took a form of realism for granted, and so took the failure of radical reductionism as showing that we must begin with the findings of science, since they cannot be reconstructed on the basis of a more primitive experiential language. As a statement of the reasons for naturalism, as a defense of the view against those not sympathetic to it, however, the passage seems to me quite evidently inadequate.[23] Let us first take the second of the two sources cited in the passage. Quine states that "unregenerate realism" is a source of naturalism. Yet we have seen that in defending his realism he emphasizes the role of naturalism. Which comes first? The two doctrines, as Quine interprets them, are so alike that to cite each in support of the other can hardly be taken as progress—if we are indeed looking for reasons and justification rather than merely for the explanation of an attitude.

Quine's other point is that holism, or the failure of radical reductionism, i.e., the failure of the enterprise of translating all our scientific discourse into logic and observation terms, leads to naturalism. This is closely related to the idea, which Quine also advances, that naturalism can be equated with the failure of foundationalism. This point requires more extensive discussion, but is in the end no more satisfactory as an argument for naturalism. Quine discusses the failure of radical reductionism in the essay "Epistemology Naturalized," which sets out his own alternative, naturalistic, approach to knowledge. I shall quote one passage at length. Quine is discussing Carnap's project of radical reductionism in *Der logische Aufbau der Welt*.[24] He asks:

> But why all creative reconstruction, why all this make-believe? The stimulation of his sensory receptors is all the evidence anybody has to go on, ultimately, in arriving at his picture of the world. Why not just

see how this construction really proceeds? Why not settle for psychology? Such a surrender of the epistemological burden to psychology is a move that was disallowed in earlier times as circular reasoning. If the epistemologist's goal is validation of the grounds of empirical science, he defeats is purpose by using psychology or other empirical science in the validation. However, such scruples against circularity have little point once we have stopped dreaming of deducing science from observations. If we are out simply to understand the link between observation and science, we are well advised to use any available information, including that provided by the very science whose link with observation we are seeking to understand.[25]

For Quine the failure of radical reductionism—essentially, the failure of Carnap's program in the *Aufbau*—means that we should give up the goal of *justifying* science on the basis of observation and logic: the goal simply cannot be reached.[26] When we replace it by the more modest goal of understanding the link between observation and science, we see that there is nothing in this new goal that prevents us from using the results of empirical science in our pursuit of it. We give up the idea that the relation between theory and evidence is to be understood from a distinctively philosophical point of view, and settle instead for a naturalistic perspective: so naturalism seems to emerge from the failure of radical reductionism. But of course this is only one among various possible reactions to the failure of radical reductionism. Another would be to say that since the goal of justifying science on the basis of observations and logic cannot be met, science is therefore unjustified, or is justified merely as a useful instrument which does not attempt to give us the truth about the world. What reason has Quine for the view that his reaction is to be preferred to this latter? "Epistemology Naturalized" contains no answer; nor is it easy to see how there could be an answer that does not presuppose naturalism in substantially the same form as that in which we wish to find a justification for it. Quine, in particular, would argue that there is no standpoint from which one can pronounce science as a whole to be untrue or unjustified; this answer, however, presupposes the crucial feature of Quine's naturalism. So the failure of radical reductionism, which Quine cites as a source of naturalism, is not compelling as a *reason* for naturalism that will carry any weight with those who do not already accept the doctrine.

Quine's explicit statements of the sources of his naturalism thus seem to me not to be reasons of the sort that could justify naturalism. For Quine, I suspect, naturalism has always seemed too obvious to require, or admit of, justification; in his earlier work, indeed, it is not even explicitly stated (although always presupposed), for Quine there does not seem to take it as a *doctrine*, as a view to which there might be alternatives.[27] In one sense this lack of argument, in Quine's work, for naturalism is no more than consistency demands. We saw that for Quine a crucial part of naturalism is the view that there is no perspective other than the naturalistic perspective of common sense and natural science: in particular, there is no distinctively philosophical perspective. But then it seems to follow immediately from this that there is no perspective from which we might argue for naturalism which does not already presuppose naturalism. A consistent naturalist could hardly hope to base naturalism on a wholly independent view, a first philosophy. That sort of ultimate grounding for naturalism would be in fact a denial of it: one can hardly attempt to occupy an Archimedean point in order to argue that all arguments must begin *in medias res*.

In saying that there can be no ultimate grounding for naturalism, however, I do not wish to suggest that there can be no arguments which are relevant to our understanding of the doctrine and of its place in Quine's philosophy as a whole.[28] In particular there is, as I shall indicate, an argument for naturalism that can be constructed which draws largely on Quine's view of language. That this view is itself naturalistic, and the argument to some extent circular is, as we have noted, inevitable. If we conceive of naturalism fairly broadly, then the argument is internal to naturalism. This may be of some interest on its own account: to show how a naturalist can justify naturalism is not a trivial endeavor. More than this, it may also suggest that there is serious difficulty with attempts to hold a naturalist position without embracing the radical consequence which we saw to be central to Quine's form of that doctrine, namely that philosophy itself must be thought of as simply part of our theory of nature, with no claims to a special status. Finally, the argument will, I hope, offer insight into the structure of Quine's version of naturalism.

Let us begin by contrasting Quine's views on language with those of Carnap. According to one statement of Carnap's, a language is "a system of sounds, or rather of the habits of producing them by the speaking organs, for the purpose of communicating."[29] Although he says this, however, all of Carnap's serious discussion of language is carried out in terms of the more precise notion of a semantical system, i.e., "a system of rules, formulated in a metalanguage and referring to an object language, of such a kind that the rules determine a **truth-condition** for every sentence of the object language" (p. 22). Note that the rules of the system—i.e., in Carnap's view, of the language—will determine truth-values (as opposed to truth-conditions) only for the so-called analytic sentences of the language; this is constitutive of the notion of analyticity. Such sentences are, relative to the language, empty: they convey no factual content. On the other hand, disagreement about such a sentence indicates misunderstanding, i.e., that one or both parties is either speaking a different language or is simply confused (speaking no coherent language). Now while the notion of analyticity here is language-relative, we would expect the analytic truths of a well-behaved language to be more or less those that we might informally recognize as nonempirical: the truths of logic and mathematics, together with statements that might plausibly be construed as definitions. In particular, we would not expect those truths which we informally recognize as being flat-out empirical to count as analytic.[30] In this picture it is the rules, and the analytic sentences which follow from them, that constitute the language: two people who have the same rules have the same language, whatever else they may disagree on.

What does this picture of language, as constituted by a set of semantical rules, have to do with the picture of language as a system of habits of producing sounds? Quine exploits the gap between these two pictures in his criticism of Carnap. I shall, in particular, focus on one point in Quine's essay, "Carnap and Logical Truth."[31] Quine is considering a view which he attributes to Carnap, and calls "the linguistic doctrine of logical truth," which seeks to explain the status of logic by saying that it is true in virtue of language. In an attempt to find a definite content for this vague doctrine—to assign it, as he (ever the naturalist) says, "an experimental meaning"—Quine suggests the following version of it: "Deductively irresoluble disagreement as to a logical truth is evidence of deviation in usage (or meanings) of words" (p. 112). The difficulty that Quine finds with this is that what it says of logical truth in fact holds of all *obvious* truths, regardless of whether we might informally classify them as empirical or as non-empirical. The linguistic doctrine of logical truth, which was to explain the obviousness of logical truth, is in danger of amounting to no more than the repetition of the statement that such truths are indeed obvious. The truth, at a given time, of the sentence "There is a table here" is not due solely to language; yet under the right circumstances disagreement over that truth may be just as strong evidence for deviation in meaning as is disagreement over a logical truth. As Quine says: "there can be no stronger evidence of a change in usage than the repudiation of what had been obvious, and no stronger evidence of bad translation than that it translates earnest affirmations into obvious falsehoods" (p. 113). To put the point another way: that sort of fluency and harmony in discourse and in non-verbal interaction which may be taken as a criterion of a shared language will fail if each person finds the other to be asserting absurdities, or denying trivialities. To restore fluency, we resort to an alternative translation which comes closer to translating obvious truths into obvious truths, and absurdities into absurdities.

I focus on this criticism because it indicates a crucial point: that it is not only agreement about the supposedly non-empirical sentences which is constitutive of the language. If someone disagrees with us over elementary truths of logic, this is evidence that she is speaking a different language from ours, and we do well to cast around for an alternative way of understanding her. But equally so if someone disagrees about, say, attributions of tablehood under favorable circumstances. Now a crucial point is that for Quine there is no gap in principle between what is *evidence* of someone's being a user of a given language and what is constitutive of that fact. Sufficient fluent discourse and interaction is not merely evidence for the fact that two people speak the same language, as if there were a fact on the one hand and on the other hand evidence quite distinct from the fact. Fluency of discourse and interaction between two people is, rather, constitutive of their sharing a language.[32] So in this case: sufficient disagreement over obvious truths is not merely evidence for deviation in meaning or of misunderstanding—it *is* misunderstanding. In short: for two people to speak the same language they must agree over a whole range of judgments, the intuitively empirical just as much as the intuitively non-empirical.[33] One way to put this is by invoking Quine's technical notion of an observation sentence. Such a sentence is, very roughly, one which is dependent on current stimulation, in the sense that some current stimulations will prompt a speaker to assent, and others to dissent (and yet others, perhaps, to give no verdict), and which any two speakers of the language will give the same verdict on, given the same stimulations. Thus an observation sentence is immediately answerable to current stimulation, and, given the same stimulations, will receive the same verdict from all members of the linguistic community.[34] Thus we can say: for two people to speak the same language, they must share a wide range of observation sentences—meaning not only that each speaker counts the sentences as part of his or her language, but also that in any given stimulus conditions, each gives the same verdict on each of the sentences.

The implication of this is that we cannot think of a language, as Carnap did, as a wholly neutral framework, which one may speak with no commitment to any empirical fact (i.e., no commitment to any fact which counts as empirical relative to that language). On the contrary: to be a speaker of a given language is to accept a wide range of substantive judgments; or, more accurately, it is to be disposed to assent to any one of a wide range of judgments, under the conditions appropriate for assenting to that judgment (in what follows I shall sometimes employ the less accurate formulation for convenience). There is no given judgment over which two speakers of the same language may not disagree, but if they disagree over too many such judgments then communication between them breaks down: they cease to be speakers of the same language.

Now in the previous paragraph I have assumed that two people who share a body of observation sentences also agree on a wide range of substantive judgments, i.e., agree on many facts. It might be thought, however, that observation sentences do not yet encapsulate facts (even if they are true), and so cannot amount to a theory of the world in any sense, since an observation sentence taken holophrastically is a mere response to stimulation, and has, in particular, no ontological commitments (so it cannot say that there are such-and-such objects arranged in such-and-such a fashion, since it makes no claims about any particular objects at all). This reaction, however, seems to me mistaken. The distinction between taking an observation sentence analytically and taking it holophrastically is relevant to translation, but does not arise if we are simply within a single language, if we are "acquiescing in our mother tongue and taking its words at face value ("Ontological Relativity," in *Ontological Relativity*, p. 49). From within the language issues having to do with ontological relativity do not arise: "Ontological relativity," Quine says, "is just an adjunct of translation" (*The Philosophy of W. V. Quine*, p. 367). The possibility of construing observation sentences holophrastically in the initial stages of translation does not rule them out as stating facts, just as the possibility of alternate translations does not. That observation sentences are responses to stimulation, again, does not rule them out as stating facts, for *all* language is a response to stimulation (by a sufficiently complex animal). As Quine says: "One is taught so to associate words with words and other stimulations that there emerges *something recognizable as talk of things*, and *not to be distinguished from truth about the world" (Word and Object*, p. 26; my emphases). One might think that sharing observation sentences is simply sharing the propensity to make certain noises, and certain concomitant non-verbal actions, in response to certain stimulations, and that this is not yet agreeing on any *facts*. But from a Quinean perspective it seems that there could be no more than this to agreeing on facts.

A language, for Quine, is thus not a neutral framework; to speak a language is implicitly to accept a theory of the world, at least of a very rudimentary sort (hence for Quine, and to the confusion of some of the commentators, "theory" and "language" become more or less interchangeable terms in many contexts[35]). To speak a language is thus to have implicitly accepted a large body of doctrine—a large body of sentences which cannot, on any plausible account, be thought of as analytic or as non-empirical. The relevance to naturalism of this shift in the conception of language is, I hope, apparent. We cannot coherently think of ourselves as remaining neutral on all questions of fact, since to think thoughts of any complexity requires a language, and to speak a language at all is to accept a body of doctrine. If we are bound to accept a body of doctrine, we should surely accept the best that we know of. As Quine says: "we can never do better than occupy the standpoint of some theory or other, the best we can muster at the time" (*Word and Object*, p. 22). Hence we should not "imagine for the philosopher a vantage point outside the conceptual scheme he takes in charge." The philosopher "cannot study and revise the fundamental conceptual scheme of science and commonsense without having some conceptual scheme, whether the same or another no less in need of philosophical scrutiny, in which to work" (*Word and Object*, pp. 275–76).

This argument for naturalism is not flatly circular, as I think the argument which appeals to realism is. It does, however, presuppose an approach to language which, if it need not be naturalistic in Quine's sense, is at least naturalistic in some broader and looser sense. Let us elaborate on the comparison between Carnap and Quine. In some ways, to some extent, Carnap, like Quine, takes a naturalistic attitude towards language. As we saw a couple of pages back, he refers to language as "a system of habits," and in his "Autobiography" he endorses the view "that language phenomena are events *within* the world, not something that refers to the world from outside. Spoken language consists of sound waves; written language consists of marks of ink on paper. . . ."[36] He goes on, however, to make what are from his point of view crucial qualifications. In particular, he argues for the possibility of what he calls "pure syntax" and "pure semantics." These are to be subjects which are not answerable to the use of any actual language. Rather, they set up rules for the syntax (semantics) of a possible language, and proceed to derive, from these rules, theorems about those languages. The idea that this endeavor makes significant qualification to a thorough-going naturalism about language presupposes that pure syntax (semantics) has the same epistemological status as mathematics, and that this is not that of our ordinary empirical knowledge. Clearly on this point there is a disagreement between Carnap and Quine. More pressingly, however, Carnap's pure syntax (semantics) raises the question: how do the syntactic or semantic rules that one may formulate when doing pure syntax or pure semantics relate to the actual use of a language? An avowed anti-naturalist might say that the rules give the structure of language, or of thought, and that it is only insofar as our actual speech embodies those rules that it is real language at all. No such dogmatic view is in Carnap, however; fundamentally his view of language is naturalistic. As he compares pure syntax (semantics) with pure mathematics, so he compares the application of those subjects to actual language with applied mathematics: the justification for appealing to the rules in consideration of an actual language must, ultimately, be based on the empirical—naturalistic— study of that language. Having accepted this much naturalism, Carnap cannot convincingly hold out against Quine's view of language. Quine's argument against Carnap is effective in part because Carnap has already granted Quine's view of language. Quine's argument against Carnap is effective in part because Carnap has already granted Quine his crucial premise.[37]

If, by contrast, one compares Quine's view with a Fregean view of language, then a different picture emerges. Quine takes absolutely seriously the idea that language is a system of habits, or dispositions. According to that view, what endows our noises with meaning is that we live in a community of speakers who use such noises in ways that systematically relate to their environment (or, to be more accurate, to the ways in which their environment impinges upon them). On this picture, as Quine says, language is first and foremost a social art (see *Word and Object*, p. ix); its use in solitary silent thinking is derivative, and dependent on its use as a means of communication. What gives meaning to the individual utterance is—to speak very loosely— the fact that it is the utterance of sounds each of which would be made in combination with various other sounds under such-and-such circumstances.[38] In particular, some utterances are tied to circumstances—or rather to stimulations, in Quine's formulation—in such a way as to be observation sentences. Only this can ensure that the language has empirical content, and is learnable. Thus Quine says that one of the tenets of empiricism that remains "unassailable" is "that all inculcation of meanings of words must ultimately rest on sensory evidence."[39] The fact that what guarantees the language empirical content is also what makes it learnable should not surprise us. What gives the language empirical content is the constant and enduring relation that some of its sentences have to the stimulations that impinge on the speaker; and the relations in which those sentences stand to other sentences of the language. This is also what makes the language learnable: a language lacking that feature, in which there were no sentences standing in such relations to stimulations, would not be learnable. The presupposition here is that learning theory is empirical, at least in a rudimentary sense—so that it would not count as an explanation of how the language is learned to say: and then at some point, with luck, the pupil's mind simply comes into contact with the right *Sinn*, and so on. It is this largely unarticulated requirement that the learning theory be empirical that results in learnability coinciding with having empirical content. This point is fundamental for Quine, and underlies the claim that there must be a broad measure of substantive agreement between two people who are speakers of the same language.

For a Fregean, at least a Fregean of a platonistic stripe, what endows our words with meaning is, by contrast, that we associate each with an abstract entity, a *Sinn*. Nothing in this situation requires that language be social in any sense at all. The paradigmatic situation, indeed, seems to be that of the individual speaker or thinker, associating his words with appropriate *Sinne*. If two people associate the same words with the same *Sinne* then they speak the same language; their agreement or disagreement in judgments may be evidence for this, but it is not constitutive of it (for Quine, as we saw a few pages back, there is no fundamental contrast between what is evidence here and what is constitutive of the fact that two people share a language). This sort of approach to language is so remote from Quine's that none of his arguments will have any grip on it, since their basic assumptions are not granted.[40]

So Quine's approach to language—and hence the argument for naturalism that we have constructed—does at least presuppose that one is not willing to accept the sort of strongly non-naturalistic approach characteristic of the Fregean view. Many philosophers, however, Carnap among them, have attempted to avoid both Quine's thoroughgoing naturalism and also the strongly non-naturalistic approach to language. One might see the argument we constructed as posing a challenge: how, short of the strongly non-naturalistic view, can one think about language without opening the way for a form of naturalism as strong as Quine's?

Near the beginning of this essay we saw that Quine appeals to (his version of) naturalism to reconcile his epistemology with his ontology. The epistemology suggests that our theory far outruns our evidence, that it is to a large extent a put-up job; the ontology is nevertheless unqualifiedly realistic. Quine's naturalism was to reconcile these positions, essentially because according to that view there is no perspective, no standpoint, except that of some theory, from which our theory can be judged to conform or not to conform to reality. We can now reformulate this idea. To speak a language at all—and hence, at least on Quine's view, to think thoughts of any significant complexity—is to accept a large though ill-defined body of judgments. In particular, it is to accept the reality of at least some of the objects that our theory of the world talks about. Hence there is no coherent position from which the reality of all such objects—or the truth of all such judgments—can be denied: the attempted denial undercuts the language in which it is made, and hence leaves us with no coherent statement at all. Now if we think of Quine's naturalism as justified more or less as we have suggested over the last few pages, how persuasive does this use of naturalism look? In other words, does Quine's use of naturalism fit with the justification that we have found for it? (One might say: is it a single doctrine that is on the one hand used in these ways, and on the other hand defended like this?)

One source of doubt about the fit is as follows. The argument for naturalism seems to show that to speak a language is to have s substantive body of theory. It is consistent with that argument, however, to suppose that that theory is of the most rudimentary kind. To count as having the same language, two speakers must agree on a vast range of statements, but it is entirely possible that these statements are all of a very low-level, commonsensical kind. Thus two people may both count as English speakers if they agree, in appropriate circumstances, on statements about the presence of medium-sized physical objects; but clearly this is compatible with one of them having possession of a very detailed and sophisticated physical theory whereas the other has none, or even has a quite bizarre, or perhaps supernatural, explanation of all the physical events around him. *Complete* agreement is very far from necessary: a foundation of agreement about the most elementary judgments—those that usually pass without mention—is sufficient, and allows for all sorts of disagreement elsewhere. We might note in passing that it does not seem as if the opposite idea—agreement in sophisticated physical theory but disagreement in all ordinary commonsense judgments—is fully coherent. We have already appealed to the idea that what is needed for two speakers to be speaking the same language is agreement on (a sufficient number of) observation sentences, i.e., sentences to which every language-user, nearly enough, will assent under the same stimulus conditions, and dissent under the same stimulus conditions. Only this basis of agreement can make it clear that what looks like a case of two people having the same high-level physical theory is not, rather, a case of mistranslation. (This point may be clearer if one emphasizes that the observation sentences function not only as the way into language, but also as the ultimate evidence for physical theory.)

These considerations suggest that while the speaking of a language may carry with it some substantive commitments, these may be very low-level and rudimentary: they may amount simply to the observation sentences of the language. Thus one might ask whether these low-level judgments do not amount to a perspective from which the rest of our theory might be judged and perhaps found wanting; perhaps one could coherently argue that only those judgments really reflect the way the world is, while others have a merely instrumental status. Does this possibility threaten Quine's defense of his realism? From his point of view it does not. Two different lines of criticism may be distinguished here. On one hand, Quine's critic may adopt exactly our current theory of the world, but argue that only its observation sentences should be interpreted realistically. This line of argument, however, looks quite unpromising: from a Quinean perspective there is no reason at all why the distinction between observation sentences and others should correspond to a distinction between those sentences which are to be interpreted realistically and those which are not. The two sorts of sentences play the same sort of epistemological role, and are answerable to evidence in just the same sense.[41] On the other hand, Quine's critic may take the more drastic step of arguing that we should adopt a theory consisting *only* of observation sentences. Here again, however, the critic appears to be on shaky ground. If once the critic accepts that her criticism is made from a substantive point of view—a standpoint that carries with it substantive commitments—then Quine can engage with her on internal grounds: let the best theory win. He and his critic both have theories of the world, however rudimentary. Quine can be content to let the decision between them be made on ordinary scientific grounds—the more powerful, accurate, and simple theory being the winner. The contentious issue is the same as that involved in Quine's insistence that science is continuous with common sense, for it is the question whether our most rudimentary judgments are to be construed as a theory of the world, in Quine's sense, as a beginning of the enterprise with which science is continuous.

The point here, then, is that for Quine, to speak a language is not simply to have substantive commitments, but also to have at least a rudimentary scientific theory, where the crucial fact about such a theory is that it is tested by its ability to predict experience.[42] This may appear to be a further step, in need of further justification, for there are, after all, many uses of language other than that of making the sort of factual claims that can be confirmed or disconfirmed by experience. For Quine, however, no further step is needed. Consider again the role of what Quine calls observation sentences. Any language must contain such sentences, for only thus is it possible to learn a language. And the observation sentences will be of just the sort wanted, for they are sentences which are justified or not precisely on the basis of current experience. This is enough to say that such sentences embody factual claims, claims which for Quine thus count as scientific, however low-level they may be. While there may, of course, be cultures which have no interest in scientific theory or scientific explanation, every culture must be in the business of making some factual claims about the world. Quite apart from issues of survival, a language which contained no such statements would not be learnable or usable. Thus the fact that every culture speaks a language containing observation sentences may be enough for Quine's purposes here.

Our construction of an internal argument for naturalism has a number of implications. One is perhaps to clarify the options for a form of naturalism more moderate than Quine's. Many philosophers have advocated naturalism but have explicitly or (more often) implicitly resisted the idea that philosophy too can be no more than part of our theory of nature. Perhaps there is here a difficulty intrinsic to philosophical thought: that it is hard not to think of one's own thought as detached from that about which one is theorizing, and thus hard to be a thorough-going naturalist. Whatever the reason, our discussion may help to suggest the options open to such a would-be moderate naturalist. One crucial consideration which emerged from the argument is how one thinks of language. A naturalistic view of language—which sees it as a subject to be studied and explained empirically—at least opens the way for the form of argument we gave. Other prerequisites included the denial of the *a priori*, the insistence of the continuity of all knowledge, from the most rudimentary to the most abstruse, and the neglect of the idea of a practical, as opposed to theoretical, standpoint. Any of these are points at which the argument for Quine's absolutely thorough-going naturalism might perhaps be resisted.

Another implication concerns the role of experience and prediction in Quine's version of naturalism. Quine's emphasis on science may seem to be lacking in content, for he advocates no particular ontology, and no particular scientific method: on his account there are no methodological principles that are not themselves subject to change as science progresses. This might seem to leave the notion of science, so crucial to Quine's naturalism, floating free of all but institutional ties—so that if universities and grant-giving agencies began to favor astrology at the expense of physics a Quinean naturalist would have no recourse but to fall in line. But in fact Quine's notion of science, and hence of naturalism, is crucially tied to prediction. In *Pursuit of Truth* he remarks that understanding is the chief aim of science, but prediction "is what decides the game, like runs and outs in baseball" (p. 20). He goes on to say:

> Even telepathy and clairvoyance are scientific options, however moribund. It would take some extraordinary evidence to enliven them, but, if that were to happen, then empiricism itself—the crowning norm, we saw, of naturalized epistemology—would go by the board. For remember that that norm, and naturalized epistemology itself, are integral to science, and science is fallible and corrigible. (*Pursuit of Truth*, pp. 20–21)

The point here is that for Quine science, and thus naturalism, are not tied to any particular epistemology, still less to any particular metaphysics. Unlike the French eighteenth-century naturalists to whom the word is due, Quine is not concerned to advocate materialism or deism or atheism or any other ontology. His view is rather that the truth about the world is to be found in science, and that the central feature of science is that it is the best method of obtaining predictions about experience: whatever performs this function will count as science for Quine. The burden of the second half of this essay has been that this version of naturalism can be understood as a consequence of an approach to language which, at least on the surface, has rather weaker and vaguer naturalistic presuppositions.

A further moral to be drawn concerns the role of argument in philosophical thought. It is often simply assumed that the only role, or at least the primary role, of argument is to induce conviction, but about philosophical argument at least this is, I think, a mistake. My point here is not, or not only, that philosophical reasoning cannot be reconstructed in logical terms. More important, I think, is the fact that the content of an interesting and controversial philosophical claim is seldom straightforward or clear-cut. The role of interesting philosophical arguments is not, or not only, to induce conviction in one who accepts the premises but does not accept the conclusion (in the case of interesting arguments I suspect that that happens quite rarely). Argument also plays the role of refining and revealing the content of the claim that is the conclusion of the argument and, very often, simultaneously of the premises of the argument. To understand why one holds, or why someone else might hold, a certain position is to obtain insight into what that position is. This is not, of course, to deny that the process of articulating one's thoughts in this way may change them: on the contrary. It is, however, to deny that such changes will generally take the form of new inferences straightforwardly drawn from already accepted premises. The case in hand, I think, illustrates this complexity. It is unlikely, I suspect, that many people will be persuaded by the argument that I have put forward, and will accordingly adopt a more extreme form of naturalism. But I hope that the argument succeeds in shedding light on Quine's view, and on the role of observation and prediction in that view.[43]

NOTES

1. Philip Kitcher includes Descartes, Leibniz, Locke, Kant, and Mill among the naturalists ("The Naturalists Return," *Philosophical Review* 101, no. 1: 53–114; see especially p. 54). He would disagree with me about Carnap, but then I am here deliberately using the word "naturalism" in a loose and vague sense.

2. W. V. Quine, *Roots of Reference* (La Salle, Ill., 1973), 3–4; Quine takes the phrase "a put-up job" from Eddington's *The Nature of the Physical World* (New York, 1948), e.g., 143, 147, 238–39. See Burton Dreben, "Putnam, Quine—and the Facts," *Philosophical Topics* 20, no. 1 (1992): appendix 2.

3. W. V. Quine, "Epistemology Naturalized," in *Ontological Relativity* (New York, 1969), 69–90; the passage cited is on p. 83.

4. See e.g., "On Empirically Equivalent Systems of the World," *Erkenntniss* 9 (1975): 313–28.

5. W. V. Quine, *Pursuit of Truth* (Cambridge, Mass., 1992), 102.

6. W. V. Quine, "Things and Their Place in Theories," chap. 1 of *Theories and Things* (Cambridge, Mass., 1981), 21. This work hereafter cited in the text as *T&T*.

7. W. V. Quine, "Reply to Harold N. Lee," in *The Philosophy of W. V. Quine*, edited by Lewis Edwin Hahn and Paul Arthur Schilpp (La Salle, Ill., 1986), 316.

8. "Reply to Hilary Putnam," in *The Philosophy of W. V. Quine*, 430.

9. Quine, "On Empirically Equivalent Systems," 327–28.

10. If 'first philosophy' simply means philosophy independent of our substantive theory of science, then we may identify naturalism, as Quine seems to, with the abandonment of first philosophy. At times, however, Quine seems to think of 'first philosophy' as Cartesian foundationalism, or the reduction of all knowledge to the sensory given (see, for example, *Pursuit of Truth*, 19). On that understanding the identification of naturalism with the abandonment of first philosophy is tendentious, since there appear to be positions which are neither foundationalist nor naturalistic in anything like Quine's sense. See Graciela de Pierris, "The Constitutive A Priori," *Canadian Journal of Philosophy*, suppl. vol. 18 (1992): 179–214.

11. *T&T*, 21. For Kant, too, this question is illegitimate. He (usually) speaks of such questions as "transcendent" (*tranzendent*), reserving "transcendental" (*tranzendental*) to describe the status of his own investigations. It is, however, not surprising that Quine should feel free to ignore this Kantian distinction: for Quine, as we shall see, it is crucial that philosophy has no special status, distinguished from that of ordinary common sense and natural science. The transcendental, if that is thought of as picking out such a special status, is thus for Quine no more legitimate than the transcendent. As so often in Quine, the apparently casual, or even apparently mistaken, choice of word in fact encapsulates central doctrine.

12. Quine has stressed the harmlessness, even the triviality, of his notion of ontological commitment (see e.g., "Responding Further to Kripke," *T&T*, 174–75). Behind that harmless

idea, however, lies the extremely controversial metaphysical thesis that being is only of one kind: that there are no Orders of Being, no distinction between the sort of existence that objects have and the sort that concepts have, or between the sort that concrete objects have and the sort that abstract objects have, no differing types of objects with differing types of existence.

13. W. V. Quine, "The Scope and Language of Science," in *Ways of Paradox* (Cambridge, Mass., 1976), 233.

14. W. V. Quine, *Word and Object* (New York, 1960), 3.

15. W. V. Quine, "The Nature of Natural Knowledge," *Mind and Language*, edited by Samuel Guttenplan (Oxford, 1975), 67–81; the phrase quoted is on p. 67.

16. Quine "The Scope and Language of Science," 233. Note that "the scientist" here must include the mathematical physicist and even the mathematician: this indicates the strength of the commitment that Quine has at this point.

17. There are complex issues around Quine's advocacy of the unity of knowledge. The Vienna Circle, and other scientifically minded German-speaking philosophers of the same era, advocated this view in conscious opposition to the idea that the *Naturwissenschaften* and the *Geisteswissenschaften* are separate branches of knowledge, with separate standards and techniques—an idea embodied, for example, in Brentano's thesis that knowledge requiring intentional idioms is different in kind from others. Quine, however, accepts a version of Brentano's thesis. This might seem to be in direct contradiction with the thesis of the unity of knowledge; what saves consistency is that for Quine 'knowledge' requiring intentional idioms is not in fact real knowledge; this view in turn seems to rest on the thesis of the indeterminacy of translation. See *Word and Object*, 219–22.

18. This phrase is of course the location of a problem: exactly what constitutes a genuinely factual question? Quine's answer here is far from straightforward.

19. I say *theoretical* perspective here because Quine's attention is confined to the theoretical. He does not consider, and therefore does not deny, the Kantian idea that there is a practical perspective which must also be taken into account. For a recent articulation and development of this idea, see Christine M. Korsgaard's Tanner Lectures, forthcoming from Cambridge University Press.

20. See, e.g., Jaegwon Kim, "What is 'naturalized epistemology?" chap. 12 of his *Supervenience and the Mind* (Cambridge, 1993), especially 226–27. The issue of normativity, which is crucial to Kim's discussion, is one that I have not space to raise in this essay.

21. I take this statement to be in general agreement with Kitcher, who characterizes "naturalistic epistemology" in terms of its rejection of two closely related ideas: first, that epistemology be pursued in an apsychologistic fashion; second, that philosophy result in claims that are *a priori*. See his "The Naturalists Return," especially pp. 57–59.

22. Chap. 7 of *Theories and Things*.

23. Roger Gibson, by contrast, seems to take this passage as stating an argument for naturalism, and to attempt to defend it on that basis; see chap. 2 of *Enlightened Empiricism* (Tampa, Fla., 1988).

24. Rudolf Carnap, *Der logische Aufbau der Welt* (Berlin: 1928); translated by Rolf A. George as *The Logical Structure of the World* (Berkeley, 1967).

25. Quine, "Epistemology Naturalized," 75–76.

26. Note that the view of the *Aufbau* as concerned with the justification of knowledge is Quine's; as a statement of Carnap's motivation this is, at least, oversimplified. See e.g., Michael Friedman, "Carnap's *Aufbau* Reconsidered," *Nous* 21: 521–45; Alan Richardson, "How not to Russell Carnap's *Aufbau*," *PSA* 1990, vol. 1, 3–14; and Thomas A. Rykman, "Designation and Convention: A Chapter of Early Logical Empiricism," *PSA* 1990, vol. 2, 149–57.

27. In Quine's earliest substantial published philosophical essay, "Truth By Convention," the doctrine is presupposed by Quine's attempt to make sense of the distinction between the *a priori* and the *a posteriori* "behavioristically and without reference to a metaphysical

system" (*Ways of Paradox*, 102). Not until much later, however, does Quine seem to become aware that relative to the views of other philosophers this is a radical step.

28. That argument has no role to play is a summary, or caricature, of a view both about philosophy in general and about Quine in particular associated with the name of Burton Dreben (see, e.g., his essays "Putnam, Quine, and the Facts," and "Quine," in *Perspectives on Quine*, edited by Robert Barrett and Roger Gibson, [Oxford, 1990], 81–95). I should say that I do not take myself to be disagreeing with Dreben, exactly, except in matters of emphasis: it seems to me of crucial importance that philosophy is worked out and articulated in argument. See the final paragraph of this essay.

29. Rudolf Carnap, *Introduction to Semantics* (Cambridge, Mass., 1942), 3.

30. This point is complicated, since I can of course choose a language in which any arbitrary sentence is analytic; by Carnap's principle of tolerance (p. 247), my choice may be unwise or even perverse, but it cannot be *wrong*. But the crucial point for us is that there should be languages in which only sentences informally recognizable as non-empirical are analytic.

31. Originally written, according to Quine's note, early in 1954; first published in *Rudolf Carnap*, edited by Paul A. Schilpp (La Salle, Ill., 1963), reprinted in Quine's *Ways of Paradox*. I quote from the latter of these sources.

32. This point is connected with Quine's assertion that "Language is a social art" (this is the first sentence of the Preface to *Word and Object*, p. ix). See also Quine's explanation of why behaviorism is optional in psychology in general, but mandatory in linguistics: "Each of us learns his language by observing other people's verbal behaviour and having his own faltering verbal behaviour observed and reinforced or corrected by others. We depend strictly on overt behaviour in observable situations. As long as our command of our language fits all external checkpoints, where our utterance or our reaction to someone's utterance can be appraised in the light of some shared situation, so long all is well. Our mental life between checkpoints is indifferent to our rating as a master of the language. There is nothing in linguistic meaning beyond what is to be gleaned from overt behavior in observable circumstances" (*Pursuit of Truth*, 38).

33. Compare Wittgenstein: "If language is to be a means of communication there must be agreement not only in definitions but also (queer as this may sound) in judgments" (*Philosophical Investigations*, translated by G. E. M. Anscombe [Oxford, 1953]), section 242. A similar fundamental idea, drawn from Quine, underpins the work of Donald Davidson on the philosophy of language.

34. Although Quine speaks this way in *Word and Object*, he comes to see that we cannot in fact compare the stimulations of two people, since there is no reason to expect their nerve endings to be isomorphic. For his response to this issue see *Pursuit of Truth*, sections 15 and 16; these subtleties do not appear to affect the present line of thought.

35. See for example Quine's reply to Chomsky in *Words and Objections*, edited by D. Davidson and J. Hintikka (Dordrecht, 1969), 301–11, especially p. 310. Note that Quine stretches the word "theory" in two ways. Besides the blurring of the ordinary distinction between language and theory, he also uses the word "theory" of even the most straightforward commonsensical beliefs. The ordinary distinction between fact and theory is thus also blurred. In each case, of course, Quine has reason to think that the distinctions are mistaken.

36. Rudolf Carnap, "Autobiography," in *The Philosophy of Rudolf Carnap*, 29.

37. I hope it is unnecessary to add that I am not here attempting to do full justice to Carnap's philosophy. I think that a more detailed examination would have the same upshot as my cursory remarks, but obviously I cannot defend this point here.

38. This is not to say that the solitary speaker is ruled out by the Quinean view. Such a speaker may have a set of habits, extended over time, which suffice to give meaning to her utterances. What one might think is ruled out is the idea that a solitary speaker could exist just for a moment of time (and still count as speaking a language, i.e., her sounds count as meaningful).—This whole line of thought, however, perhaps does not do sufficient justice

to the fact that Quine does not take the notion of possibility seriously: in his view there is no serious question as to what *could* be; the serious questions are only about what is. And the fact is that language *is* social.

39. "Epistemology Naturalized," see 75. In this context note also the emphasis on language learning in the passage quoted in note 3 above.

40. Quine says that the motivation of his doctrine of the indeterminacy of translation "was to undermine Frege's notion of a proposition or *Gedanke*," "Comment on Hintikka" in *Perspectives on Quine*, 176. The most that Quine's discussion could show, however, is that Frege's notion requires a strongly non-naturalistic view of language; there seems to be no reason to think that Frege himself would have been discontented with such a requirement.

41. Quine argues just this point in "Posits and Reality": that there is no reason to draw an ontological distinction between "common-sense bodies" on the one hand and "molecules and their ilk" on the other. Neither sort of object is "given in sensation"; "[t]he positing of either sort of body is good science insofar merely as it helps us formulate our laws—laws whose ultimate justification lies in the sense data of the past, and whose ultimate vindication lies in anticipation of sense data of the future." See *Ways of Paradox*, chap. 23; the passages cited are on p. 250. This does not imply that we could not have reasons to be less than fully realistic about the entities posited by some branch of science (quantum mechanics, say). But it does imply that those reasons would be internal to that branch of science, rather than relying on very general considerations about observability.

42. For this view of what science amounts to, see Quine's *Pursuit of Truth*, sections 1 and 8.

43. A version of this essay was read at Northwestern; I am grateful both for the invitation and for the discussion that ensued. I am also indebted for comments on an earlier version by Christine Korsgaard and T. A. Rykman, and by my colleagues, Graciela DePierris, Dorothy Grover, Michael Friedman, and Bill Hart; and to the members of my seminar at the University of Illinois, Chicago, in the fall of 1993. In addition, I am greatly indebted to Burton Dreben both for his comments on an earlier version of this essay and for many conversations over the years.

Against Naturalized Epistemology

LAURENCE BONJOUR

My aim in this essay is to examine and criticize the idea of *naturalized epistemology*, understood as embodying the idea that traditional epistemology is fatally flawed and hence should be replaced by a properly naturalistic successor discipline.[1] My thesis is that while the idea of naturalized epistemology reflects some genuine, albeit modest insights that need to be recognized and preserved, there is no interesting sense in which epistemology either can or needs to be naturalized. A thoroughgoing naturalization of epistemology strikes me as wrongheaded and ultimately self-destructive, and I will try to show here why this is so.

Unfortunately, however, like many fashionable positions, naturalized epistemology is a rather diffuse and uncertain target, and considering all of the things that have been understood by this phrase would obviously go well beyond the allowable scope of the present essay. Thus I will focus here primarily on the accounts of naturalized epistemology offered by its original proponent, namely W. V. O. Quine, and by the philosopher who has offered the most complete and systematic recent account, namely Philip Kitcher.[2] After an initial examination, in section I, of Quine's original introduction of and rationale for the idea that epistemology should be naturalized, I will turn, in sections II and III, to an examination of the two main ingredients of the idea of naturalized epistemology, as identified by Kitcher, together with the arguments in support of them that he discusses: (i) the rejection of "apsychologistic" epistemology; and (ii) the rejection of the idea of *a priori* justification, especially but not only as it applies to the theses of epistemology itself (58). I will argue that while there are insights of value in the area of (i), their significance is much more limited than Kitcher and others have taken it to be. Ingredient (ii), on the other hand, seems to me to be almost entirely a mistake. I will then conclude the essay by trying to show, in section IV, why the idea of naturalized epistemology, especially as it involves the rejection of *a priori* justification, is not only inadequately supported but inherently self-destructive.

Two other preliminary issues require brief consideration. One of these is the nature of the epistemological project itself. Here I am forced to be at least mildly dogmatic. I will assume here that at least one central aim of traditional epistemology is: (a) to decide whether or not we have good reasons for thinking that our various beliefs about the world are true; and (b), if the answer to this first question is affirmative, to say what those reasons are and to explain *why* they are good ones. I take this to be *the* central issue, the common thread that connects the concerns of Descartes, Locke, Hume, Reid, and others with twentieth-century epistemology. But it is enough for my purposes if it is one central issue, and it is on this issue, the issue of *critical epistemology*, that my discussion will focus.[3]

Second, while a good part of my discussion will take Kitcher's account of naturalized epistemology as its main target, it is important to acknowledge at the outset that my conception of the main dialectical alternatives is importantly different from his, in a way that means that I am approaching his arguments somewhat obliquely, rather than head on. For Kitcher, the main alternative to naturalized epistemology on the more conservative side[4] is the analytic approach to epistemology, reflecting the so-called "linguistic turn," that is characteristic of the logical positivists and their contemporary progeny. His thesis, very roughly, is that this view is an ill-grounded aberration ("an odd blip in the history of philosophy" [56]) and that naturalized epistemology represents a return to the "restrained" version of naturalism exemplified by "Descartes, Locke, Leibniz, Hume, Kant, and Mill" (54). My own view, in contrast, is: first, that while the great early moderns certainly did not feel any need to fastidiously eschew the use of psychological concepts, there is no very interesting sense in which their philosophical claims depended on anything like empirical results from psychology and the other sciences, and thus no very interesting sense in which they were naturalists;[5] and, second, that while the explicit methodological theses of positivism and analytic epistemology were indeed an ill-grounded aberration (one for which I suspect that I have substantially less regard than does Kitcher), these were largely superficial window dressing, beneath which there was very substantial continuity with a *rationalistic* approach to epistemology in particular and philosophy in general that extends back through the early moderns to much earlier times. (The defining thesis of rationalism, as I intend it here, is that *a priori* justification and knowledge genuinely exist and are not confined to claims that are in any useful sense merely conceptual or linguistic or "analytic" in character.[6]) An adequate consideration of these historical issues would far exceed the allowable bounds of the present essay. But it is important to be clear that when I oppose naturalized epistemology in favor of traditional epistemology, it is the older and deeper tradition of rationalistic epistemology that I mean to be defending. (As this suggests, it is the issue pertaining to *a priori* justification and knowledge, rather than that pertaining to psychologism, that is in my judgment by far the more fundamental.)

I

It was Quine who first introduced the idea that epistemology should be naturalized, and it will be useful to begin by examining his case for this claim, as presented in his essay "Epistemology Naturalized."[7] Quine's introduction of this idea can, I believe, be plausibly viewed as an attempt to defend and make sense of his own epistemological position. Though elaborated somewhat in later works, Quine's main epistemological view seems to be essentially that suggested by the final section of "Two Dogmas of Empiricism": what we believe is a huge, interconnected "web" or "fabric" of sentences, a web that "impinges on experience only along the edges."[8] We revise this web or fabric more or less continuously in an effort to keep the edge "squared with experience," and the results of these revisions represent our best epistemic efforts at any particular moment.

Many questions can be raised about this familiar but still undeniably fuzzy picture. But the central issue is what bearing it has or is supposed to have on the epistemic justification of our beliefs, i.e., with whether we have any *reason* to think that they are *true*. Quine's predominant view seems to be that the web picture is merely a psychological description: we simply do treat some sentences as more relevant or "germane" to a particular experience than others and some as generally less open to revision than others, and we do revise or modify our system of sentences accordingly. But the problem at this point is obvious: merely from the psychological fact that we do operate in this way, it does not follow in any obvious way that the beliefs that result are epistemically justified or rational, ones that we have any good reason for thinking to be true, so that, if true, they would constitute knowledge. Why, it may well be asked, should Quine be taken to have even offered an epistemology?

In response to this pretty obvious question, Quine offers a radical reinterpretation of what epistemology itself is all about. In "Epistemology Naturalized," he argues that epistemology, "or something like it," should be reconstructed as "a chapter of psychology," an empirical study of the relation between "a certain experimentally controlled input—certain patterns of irradiation in assorted frequencies, for instance" and an output consisting of "a description of the three-dimensional external world and its history" (*EN* 83–83). His claim, in first approximation, is that while such a naturalized epistemology admittedly falls short of achieving the goals of traditional epistemology, it goes as far in that direction as turns out to be possible, and far enough to constitute a reasonable, albeit less ambitious substitute. The rationale offered by Quine for such a reconstrual is basically that the epistemological project, as traditionally conceived, has failed more or less irredeemably and hence must be replaced by a more viable substitute. This view depends in part on a fairly narrow conception of traditional epistemology, roughly that put forward by positivistic empiricism, according to which epistemology (or at least the part of epistemology that is concerned with "natural knowledge," i.e., knowledge of the physical world) involves two correlative goals: (i) to explain the relevant concepts, e.g., the concept of a physical body, in sensory terms ("the conceptual side of epistemology"); and (ii) on the basis of this explanation, to justify claims about the physical world on the basis of sense experience ("the doctrinal side of epistemology") (*EN* 71). It is obviously these goals that motivate phenomenalism, as advocated by Hume, Ayer, Lewis, and many others. But, argues Quine, it is clear by now that neither of these goals, at least as traditionally conceived, can be achieved. The attempt to reduce physicalistic concepts to phenomenal ones fails to yield genuine translations; and, since sensory generalizations at least would be required, the attempt to prove physical statements on the basis of sensory evidence is defeated in any case by the problem of induction. What is left, once these goals are abandoned as hopeless, is the attempt "simply to understand the link between observation and science," and there is no reason not to appeal to psychology in achieving this end. In particular, the worry that an epistemological appeal to the results of natural science would be circular no longer applies once we abandon the goal of justification (*EN* 75–76).

There are many problems with this line of argument. A relatively minor one is that Quine's picture of "the conceptual side" and "the doctrinal side" of traditional epistemology as more or less equally important vastly exaggerates the importance of the former. Construed in the reductive way in which Quine construes it, "the conceptual side" of epistemology is a feature only of the narrowest and most implausible versions of empiricism, and even there is motivated primarily by the attempt to satisfy "the doctrinal side." Thus the failure to achieve the aim of "the conceptual side," to which Quine devotes most of his attention in "Epistemology Naturalized," does very little to show that traditional epistemology has failed and hence needs to be replaced by the suggested Quinean surrogate.

More importantly, Quine's discussion seriously muddies the waters by failing to distinguish a stronger and a weaker conception of "the doctrinal side" of traditional epistemology. According to the stronger conception, deriving from Descartes, the goal is to achieve *certainty* in our beliefs about the world, to establish that they are infallibly and indubitably true. For the weaker conception, on the other hand, the goal is the more modest one of showing that there are good reasons for thinking that our beliefs are at least likely to be true; complete certainty, while of course still desirable, is not essential. Though his discussion of "the doctrinal side" is too sketchy to allow much confidence on this point, Quine seems to slide illegitimately from the relatively uncontroversial claim that the stronger, Cartesian goal cannot be attained for "natural knowledge" to the much less obvious claim that the more modest goal is not achievable either. Thus we are told that statements about bodies cannot be "proved" from observation sentences, that "the Cartesian quest for certainty" is a "lost cause," that claims about the external world cannot be "strictly derived" "from sensory evidence" (*EN* 74–75); and on this basis it is apparently concluded that the entire "doctrinal side" of traditional epistemology, which Quine characterizes in one place as concerned with "the justification of our knowledge of truths about nature" (*EN* 71), must be abandoned. But this, of course, simply does not follow.[9]

What might cast doubt on this reading of Quine's argument is his employment of the term 'evidence' to characterize even the project of naturalistic epistemology. Thus he claims that despite the failure of traditional epistemology, it remains unassailable "that whatever evidence there is for science is sensory evidence" (*EN* 75). And further on we are told that the goal of naturalistic epistemology is "to see how evidence relates to theory, and in what ways one's theory of nature transcends any available evidence" (*EN* 83); and also that "observation sentences are the repository of evidence of scientific hypotheses" (*EN* 88). I do not see any way, however, to take these remarks at face value, for surely the standard normative concept of evidence, i.e., the concept of a reason, perhaps of a certain restricted sort, for thinking that some claim is true, is not a concept of empirical psychology. Psychology can describe the causal relations between sensory stimulations and beliefs of various sorts, but it cannot offer any assessment of the rational acceptability of any such transition. Perhaps there is some other, naturalistically acceptable conception of evidence that Quine has in mind, but if so this would not count against the conclusion that Quine has entirely abandoned "the doctrinal side" of traditional epistemology.

It thus seems clear that at least Quine's version of naturalized epistemology has nothing whatsoever to say about whether we have any reason to think that our beliefs about the world are true. And hence, if Quine is right that this sort of naturalized epistemology is the best we can do, the result is a thoroughgoing version of skepticism: we have a set of beliefs, i.e., we accept a set of sentences, that describe the external world;[10] part of that set of beliefs describes how the beliefs are caused by observation, i.e., by sensory stimulation; but we have no cogent reason of any sort for thinking that *any* of these beliefs are true. And if knowledge necessarily involves the possession of such reasons, as most philosophers would still insist, then we also have no knowledge.[11] This may indeed, as Quine suggests at one place, be "the human predicament" (*EN* 72). But it is surely extremely unsatisfactory and also intuitively implausible from both a theoretical and a practical standpoint.[12]

To see how Quine would respond to this sort of objection, we need to look at his conception of skepticism:

> Scepticism is an offshoot of science. The basis for scepticism is the awareness of illusion, the discovery that we must not always believe our eyes. Scepticism battens on mirages, on seemingly bent sticks in water, on rainbows, after-images, double images, dreams. But in what sense are these illusions? In the sense that they seem to be material objects which they in fact are not. Illusions are illusions only relative to a prior acceptance of genuine bodies with which to contrast them. . . . The positing of bodies is already rudimentary physical science; and it is only after that stage that the sceptic's invidious distinctions can make sense.[13]

Thus skepticism, in Quine's view, arises only from within science; "sceptical doubts are scientific doubts," and hence can best be answered by science itself:

> Retaining our present beliefs about nature, we can still ask how we can have arrived at them. Science tells us that our only source of information about the external world is through the impact of light rays and molecules upon our sensory surfaces. Stimulated in these ways, we somehow evolve an elaborate and useful science. How do we do this, and why does the resulting science work so well? These are . . . scientific questions about a species of primates, and they are open to investigation in natural science, the very science whose acquisition is being investigated.[14]

Thus, Quine claims, naturalized epistemology is in principle quite adequate to deal with skepticism.

But this view of the skeptical challenge is seriously inadequate in two distinct ways. In the first place, while it is of course true that skeptics have often appealed to various sorts of illusions to motivate their doubts, such an appeal is in no way essential to the basic thrust of skepticism. The fundamental skeptical move is to challenge the adequacy of our reasons for accepting our beliefs, and such a challenge can be mounted without any appeal to illusion. A prominent example of such a challenge is Hume's skepticism about induction, mentioned in passing by Quine himself (*EN* 71–72), but there are many, many others. Such a challenge can in principle be raised against any alleged piece of knowledge: is the reason or justification that is available for the belief in question adequate to show that it is (at least) likely to be true? To the difficult issues raised by these other versions of skepticism, Quine's version of naturalized epistemology has nothing at all to say. This is a very serious deficiency if one takes the project of traditional epistemology at all seriously, and the point is that Quine has offered no reason for not taking it seriously.

Moreover, even if we restrict our attention to the more limited versions of skepticism that essentially involve an appeal to illusions, the sort of response that is offered by naturalized epistemology totally misses the main issue—which is, of course, reasons or justification. What the skeptic questions is whether, once the possibility of illusion is appreciated, our sensory experience any longer constitutes a good reason for accepting our various beliefs about the world. Such a skeptic need not doubt that our beliefs are caused in some way, nor still less that an account of how they are caused can be given from within our body of beliefs about how the world operates. What he doubts is whether we have any reason for thinking that any of our beliefs about the world, including those that are involved in such an account, are true, and to this issue of justification, the Quinean version of naturalized epistemology once again has nothing at all to say.

Another, quite different way to appreciate the irrelevance of this conception of naturalized epistemology to traditional epistemological issues is to consider its application to bodies of belief where a substantial degree of skepticism seems warranted, e.g., to religious beliefs and beliefs in occult phenomena of various sorts. For just as naturalized epistemology can say nothing positive about the justification of science and common sense, and is thus impotent in the face of skepticism, so also it can say nothing distinctively negative about the justification of these less reputable sorts of belief. There is, after all, no reason to doubt that occult beliefs are caused in *some* way by the total sensory experience of the individual, and thus no reason to doubt that psychology can offer an empirical account of how they are produced.[15] Such an account would no doubt differ in major ways from that which would be given for more properly scientific beliefs, but the differences would not, within psychology, have any justificatory significance. Thus the only epistemology that is possible on Quine's view apparently cannot distinguish between science and occult belief in any way that would constitute a reason for preferring the former to the latter.

I conclude that at least Quine's original version of naturalized epistemology is both inadequately defended and extremely unsatisfactory in light of its radically skeptical implications. It should not be assumed, however, that all those who have followed Quine's lead (or at least adopted his slogan) are guilty of the same mistakes. (Kitcher, in particular, makes abundantly clear that he wants to preserve the normative dimension of epistemology.) Thus I want to examine, in the next two sections, the two main ingredients of naturalized epistemology, as identified by Kitcher, together with the arguments that allegedly support them.[16] Following that, I will return in the final section to the question of whether any version of naturalized epistemology involving these components can avoid the skeptical consequences that we have seen to follow from Quine's version.

II

I turn then to the first of Kitcher's two main ingredients, the rejection of "apsychologistic" epistemology. Here there are a number of issues that need to be carefully sorted out. My main claim will be that while there are a number of ways, all of them pretty obvious, in which psychological concepts and psychological theorizing are relevant to epistemological issues, none of them are even approximately central enough for their recognition to constitute an interesting psychologizing or naturalizing of epistemology.

We may begin with what is probably the most widely discussed recent argument for some degree of psychologization. In Kitcher's presentation, it runs as follows:[17]

... By the mid 1970s a powerful argument for psychologistic epistemology had emerged. Take any set of favored logical relations among propositions that a subject believes. It is nonetheless possible that the subject lacks knowledge and lacks justification because the *psychological* connections among her states of belief have nothing to do with the logical relations. Thus, to take an extreme example, assume that a subject justifiably believes that p, justifiably believes that $p \rightarrow q$, and believes that q. It might seem that the belief that q must be justified because there is an elementary logical inference to q from propositions that are believed. Nonetheless, it is easy to understand that the causes of the subject's belief may have nothing to do with this elementary inference, that she fails to make the inference and believes that q because of some thoroughly disreputable generative process. . . . (60)

If a powerful argument is one whose conclusion is hard to resist, then almost anyone will agree that this argument is indeed powerful. Unfortunately, however, as is indeed the case with many powerful arguments, its importance might well be questioned on the ground that its conclusion is something that it is hard to believe anyone has ever disputed. Has there ever been a significant epistemologist, or indeed philosopher of any kind, who seriously (as opposed to inadvertently[18]) advocated the view that the mere presence of a logical relation among a person's beliefs might yield justification, even if it went entirely unnoticed by the individual in question? I at least can think of no remotely plausible candidate for such a dubious honor. Thus, I suggest, the degree of psychologism that follows from this argument, which we might for obvious reasons call *minimal psychologism*, is entirely uncontroversial. But also, as Kitcher himself seems to acknowledge (62), minimal psychologism involves at most a quite minor departure from traditional epistemology, if indeed it involves any departure at all.

There is a second kind or level of psychologism that is equally undeniable, but also, I believe, equally innocuous from the standpoint of traditional epistemology. As Kitcher points out, various philosophers have made the logical or conceptual point that perception depends on causal relations, e.g., "that one can see that p only if there is some lawful dependency between one's belief that p and p" (61).[19] Analogous points could obviously be made about introspection and memory and, in a somewhat different way, about logical inference itself. It follows that the philosophical consideration of such concepts and, especially, the application of the philosophical results to actual cases will have to make reference to psychological facts about, e.g., the causation of belief. But this does nothing to show that the distinctively philosophical content of such discussion depends on empirical psychological results in any interesting way. Thus, as Kitcher seems again to acknowledge (62), this second kind of psychologism, which we may term *conceptual psychologism*, again represents no significant advance toward the naturalist's main conclusion in this area, viz. that epistemology must appeal in important and thoroughgoing ways to empirical psychological results.

There is yet a third kind of psychologism that must be acknowledged, one which, while in a way more substantive than those discussed so far, still poses no real threat to traditional epistemology, as understood here. Consider again Kitcher's idea of the *meliorative* epistemological project, the project of improving the reliability and success of human cognitive functioning. It is once more obvious and something that it is hard to imagine anyone denying that serious attempts in this direction must at some point take notice of the human cognitive behavior in question and especially of human cognitive limitations. Thus, for example, it does no good *for this purpose* to describe a complicated schema for, e.g., inductive or explanatory inference, however logically impeccable it may be in itself, if it is one that human beings are for some psychological reason incapable of conforming to or a least reasonably approximating. And, to take the other side of the coin, it is presumably an important part of this general meliorative effort to provide critical assessments of inferential patterns and other modes of cognitive behavior that are actually exemplified in practice, for which purpose some knowledge of the relevant facts about such practice, psychological and otherwise, is clearly needed. All of these points, however, have to do again with *applying* epistemological assessments to actual practice, not with how those assessments are themselves arrived at and justified. And thus there seems to be nothing about what we may call *meliorative psychologism*, understood in the way just indicated, that has any serious bearing on the nature of epistemological criticism and argument when considered in itself—and thus once again, nothing that supports any significant kind of naturalization.

The question is whether, once minimal, conceptual, and meliorative psychologism are set aside as essentially irrelevant to the main issue between traditional epistemology and the proposed naturalistic successor discipline, there is any argument left in this area in favor of the latter, any reason for thinking that epistemology needs to be psychologized in some deeper, more fundamental way. Kitcher's response to this question consists mainly of a critique, primarily within the context of the meliorative project, of an *a priori* epistemology that construes its claims as "analytic" or "conceptual" truths pertaining to our concepts of justification or rationality. To this sort of view, exemplified perhaps most clearly in the ordinary language solution to the problem of induction advanced by Strawson and others,[20] "an appropriate challenge is always, 'But why should we care about these concepts of justification and rationality?'" (63)—or, more specifically, why should we think that seeking beliefs that are justified or rational according to these concepts is likely to lead us to the truth?

But while it is easy to agree that *a priori* claims, when construed in this moderate way, appear to have little significance either for the meliorative project or for the central epistemological project as explained above, Kitcher seems to me to conclude much too quickly that the only alternative to an appeal to merely analytic or conceptual truths is the sort of appeal to empirical scientific and especially psychological results that is characteristic of naturalism. In addition, he seems to me not to worry enough about whether and how such an empirical epistemology could stand on its own, without being grounded on at least some *a priori* principles. Both of these issues can be restated in terms of the traditional rationalist conception of *a priori* justification (and knowledge) alluded to above: Is there any argument that the naturalist can give for excluding the very possibility of such justification? And is there any way that either the empirical results that the naturalist depends on or the naturalist epistemological theses themselves can be justified without such an *a priori* appeal? These questions will be the concern of the final two sections of this essay.

III

The foregoing discussion suggests one clear way (though not, I believe, the only way) in which the issue of *a priori* justification is apparently prior to and more fundamental than that of psychologism: when relatively innocuous versions of psychologism have been set aside, the argument for anything stronger in this direction depends on rejecting the idea that significant epistemological principles or premises can be established on an *a priori* basis, since this would represent an obvious alternative to naturalism. It is time to ask whether the proponents of naturalism can offer any compelling arguments for such a rejection.

Unfortunately, however, as already briefly suggested above, the arguments of the naturalists are mainly aimed, not at the central conception of *a priori* justification itself, but instead at the rather idiosyncratic form that the idea of *a priori* justification took within the context of analytic epistemology. The specific target is the view that I have referred to elsewhere as *moderate empiricism*: the thesis that the only claims or propositions that can be justified *a priori* are those which are *analytic* (in *some* sense of this exceedingly flexible term).[21] One consequence of this focus is that the resulting case for naturalized epistemology is seriously incomplete, in that a significant alternative is not adequately considered. But a more subtle problem, as I will explain, is that the kinds of arguments that Quine and others have mounted against moderate empiricism, if successful, have the consequence that there was never any good case for a moderate empiricist (as opposed to a rationalist) conception of *a priori* justification in the first place. The naturalists are thus in the dialectically embarrassing position of concentrating almost entirely on a view that, if their own arguments are any good, is not the main alternative.

As I have suggested elsewhere,[22] and as Kitcher's account of Quine also amply corroborates, Quine's arguments against the idea of *a priori* justification tend to assume what amounts to a hypothetical version of moderate empiricism: the view that if there *were* any *a priori* justified claims, they would have to be analytic. It is this implicit premise that makes his arguments against analyticity into arguments against *a priori* justification. But why should such a premise be accepted? What Quine does not seem to realize is that the case for moderate empiricism, especially in the face of the numerous counterexamples offered by recalcitrant rationalists, rests almost entirely on the claim that the account of *a priori* justification that can be given using the concept of analyticity is clear and unmysterious in a way that the general concept of *a priori* justification is not, so that only the moderate empiricist reduction of apriority to analyticity can make clear sense of how *a priori* justification is possible. It is, I suggest, this moderate empiricist argument, and not the idea of *a priori* justification itself, that is defeated by Quine's arguments (assuming that they are otherwise successful). This is most conspicuously true for the central argument of "Two

Dogmas of Empiricism":[23] the argument that the very idea of analyticity cannot be defined or explicated in an intelligible way. For obviously, if the very idea of analyticity is unintelligible, there can be no warrant for the claim that the appeal to analyticity provides a clearer and less problematic account of the possibility of *a priori* justification than that offered by the rationalist.

The upshot is that the naturalist cannot justify the rejection of the idea of *a priori* justification by arguing against moderate empiricism, for the claim that moderate empiricism is the preferred account of such justification, superior to that of the rationalist, will not survive such arguments, if they otherwise have any force. What naturalism needs, then, is a direct objection to rationalism—or, more of less equivalently, an argument that the idea of *a priori* justification is untenable even when not construed in a moderate empiricist way. Once the issue is posed in this way, arguments of the sort required are anything but thick on the ground. In the present essay, I will limit myself to the two possibilities for such an argument mentioned by Kitcher, one from Quine that Kitcher alludes to but does not really discuss in any detail and one that he rather tentatively attributes to Kuhn.[24]

First. If Quine's arguments against analyticity are set aside as essentially irrelevant to the main issue, only one very clear possibility remains within Quine's own writings for an argument against *a priori* justification: the argument, at the end of "Two Dogmas of Empiricism," that depends on the thesis that any claim can be (rationally) given up.[25] The idea, apparently, is that an *a priori* justified claim would have to be one which could never be (rationally) given up, so that if no claim has this status, then nothing is justified *a priori*.

There are many problems with this strangely influential line of argument.[26] But the central one pertains to the way in which Quine defends the thesis that any claim can be (rationally) given up. He appeals to an extended (or perhaps exaggerated) version of the celebrated thesis of Duhem concerning the way in which background assumptions are relevant to the assessment of an observation or experiment that conflicts with and apparently refutes some particular claim or thesis. Duhem's argument is that the claim or thesis in question can always be retained by abandoning instead one of these background assumptions. Quine generalizes this by arguing that in principle *any* element of the system or "web" of belief could be such that modifying or abandoning it would help to resolve the conflict with experience, so that such modification or abandonment might well be the most rational course. But whether or not Quine's hyperbolically holistic view of our accepted body of beliefs is correct, the present line of argument is in fact clearly and utterly question begging. For the most that Duhem's thesis, in however extreme a form, could show is that it might be rational to give up any claim in the web *if the only consideration relevant to rationality were how best to accommodate such conflicting experience.* But to assume that this is so is obviously tantamount to assuming, rather than showing, that *a priori* considerations have no independent rational force.

Second. The Kuhnian or a least Kuhn-inspired argument is formulated by Kitcher as follows:

. . . Kuhn's passing remarks about the details of earlier accounts of scientific methodology stress the mismatch between the deliverances of methodology and the reasoning that scientists actually employ. Unless one can show that attention to the historical record will close the gap between philosopher's methodologies and scientific practice . . . , methodologists are confronted with a dilemma. Either they can continue to insist that philosophers know *a priori* the principles of confirmation and evidence, concluding that the actual reasoning of scientists is cognitively deficient, or they can abandon the *a priori* status of methodological claims and use the performances of past and present scientists as a guide to formulating a *fallible* theory of confirmation and evidence. Since the first option has an uncomfortable air of arrogance, it is hardly surprising that most responses to Kuhn have followed the latter course. (73)

How exactly the latter, preferred alternative is supposed to go is less than clear, at least to me, though some of the discussion of the final section will be at least relevant. But if it is interpreted in the seemingly obvious way as involving a total rejection of any *a priori* appeal, then there is the more immediate problem that the alternatives posed in the alleged dilemma fail to be exhaustive. For in addition to the alternatives of (i) sticking stubbornly and perhaps dogmatically to one's initial, allegedly *a priori* precepts or (ii) adopting what may seem to amount to an abandonment of philosophy altogether in favor of a kind of psychology or sociology of scientific practice, there is the seemingly obvious further alternative of (iii) reconsidering one's initial *a priori* assessment in light of what scientists seem to be doing, while still insisting that any acceptable mode of scientific reasoning must ultimately be able to be seen or shown to be rationally cogent in an *a priori* way that transcends the mere fact that it is employed in practice.

Here it may be useful to briefly consider an example, and fortunately there is a relatively perspicuous and pivotal one available, though not perhaps one that Kuhn himself would be entirely happy with. Consider what is often referred to as *theoretical reasoning:* reasoning that moves from observational premises to a conclusion about objects or processes that are not directly observable, the rationale being that such objects or processes provide the best *explanation* of the observational evidence. Notoriously there were generations of philosophers who denied, allegedly on *a priori* grounds, that such reasoning could be rationally cogent, or perhaps even intelligible, unless the conclusion were so reinterpreted as to no longer pertain to genuinely observation-transcendent entities, but instead to amount simply to a redescription of the observations themselves. This was of course the rationale for instrumentalism or fictionalism in the philosophy of science, behaviorism in the philosophy of mind, phenomenalism in the philosophy of perception, and other less important but basically similar views. But in spite of the philosophers' admonitions, both scientists and ordinary people continued to make the inferences in question and to construe the conclusions in the supposedly unacceptable way.[27] What eventually happened, of course, was not an abandonment of *a priori* epistemology in favor of psychology or sociology, but rather the realization of a gradually increasing group of philosophers, beginning with Peirce, that the initial philosophical view was seriously oversimplified and that an *a priori* case (or at least apparent case) could be made for the kind of reasoning in question (what has come to be called "inference to the best explanation"). I do not mean to suggest that such reasoning is now entirely unproblematic or that the issues in question have been fully resolved. The point for now is just that this case illustrates a third alternative to the two mentioned in Kitcher's alleged dilemma.

If this third alternative is indeed available, then Kuhn's historical argument fails to establish the strong thesis that the ideas of *a priori* justification and *a priori* epistemology should be abandoned, as opposed to the much weaker thesis that an apparent conflict with scientific practice can and should provoke a reconsideration of the specific *a priori* results in question, possibly but certainly not inevitably leading to their correction or abandonment. All this assumes, of course, that it makes sense to speak of correcting or abandoning *a priori* claims, i.e., that *a priori* justification need not be construed as incorrigible or infallible. My view is that a conception of *a priori* justification as both corrigible and fallible is quite tenable (and is indeed easily seen to be unavoidable in the face of various kinds of apparent mistakes). But a full discussion of this issue is beyond the scope of the present essay.[28]

My conclusion is that at least the main naturalist arguments against the possibility of *a priori* justification are rather spectacularly unsuccessful, so that the case for the second main element of the idea of naturalized epistemology has not been made out. It is possible, of course, that there are other, better arguments that the naturalist might invoke instead, but a consideration of whether this is so will have to await another occasion. For now, I want to turn in the final section to an argument that naturalized epistemology in general and the rejection of *a priori* justification in particular leads directly to epistemological disaster.

IV

The argument in question depends on a distinction between two classes of beliefs: those which report the results of direct observation or experience; and those whose content transcends the results of direct observation or experience. It might be thought that such a distinction has been shown to be highly problematic or even completely untenable by the extended controversy in the philosophy of science concerning the observational/theoretical distinction, but this would, I believe, be a mistake. That discussion indeed shows that it is hard to be sure precisely where the observational/non-observational line is to be drawn, and in particular that many claims that it is initially plausible to count as direct observations may be infected with background theory in a way that renders their status as observations at least uncertain. But none of these considerations provides the slightest reason for doubting that there are many, many beliefs that we confidently hold which cannot be construed as strictly observational or experiential in any sense that has the slightest plausibility: beliefs about the remote past, beliefs about the future, beliefs about present situations where no observer is present, beliefs about general laws, the vast majority of the beliefs that make up theoretical science, and perhaps others. (Any belief whose status in this respect is seriously uncertain may for present purposes simply be consigned to the observational or experiential side of the ledger.)

I will assume here, without worrying about the details, that the fact that a belief is a report of direct observation or experience constitutes an adequate reason for thinking it to be true. But what about the non-observational or non-experiential beliefs? If we are to have any reason for thinking these latter beliefs to be true, such a reason must apparently either (i) depend on an inference of some sort from some of the directly observational beliefs or (ii) be entirely independent of direct observation. A reason of sort (ii) is plainly *a priori*. And a reason of sort (i) can only be cogent if its corresponding conditional, a conditional statement having the conjunction of the directly observational premises as antecedent and the proposition that is the content of the non-observational belief as consequent, is something that we in turn have a reason to think to be true. But the reason for thinking that this latter, conditional statement is true can again only be *a priori*: if, as we may assume, all relevant observations are already included in the antecedent, they can offer no support to the claim that *if* that antecedent is true, then something further is true. Thus if, as the naturalist claims, there are no *a priori* reasons for thinking anything to be true (or, as Kitcher sometimes seems to suggest, none of any epistemological importance), the inevitable result is that we have no reason for thinking that any of our beliefs whose content transcends direct observation are true.[29]

This is epistemological disaster in itself, but a further consequence is that the vast majority of the claims about the nature of the world, the nature and reliability of human psychological processes, etc., upon which naturalized epistemology so lovingly focuses, are things that we have no reason at all for thinking to be true—as, indeed, are the very theses that epistemology must be naturalized or that traditional epistemology is untenable (together with all normative claims of any sort). In this way, naturalized epistemology is *self-referentially inconsistent*: its own epistemological claims exclude the possibility of there being any cogent reason for thinking that those claims are true.[30]

The foregoing argument seems to me as obvious and compelling as any in the whole of philosophy, so much so that it would be embarrassing to advance it in print were it not so often ignored. The question is whether there is anything that the proponent of naturalized epistemology can offer in reply. Here I will focus on some remarks of Kitcher's, in the essay under discussion here, which while not aimed at precisely the argument formulated above, are at least enough in the same general vicinity to be worth considering. While I do not believe that the response that I will extrapolate from Kitcher is adequate, I know of no one who has done any better.

Kitcher's immediate target is a skeptic who challenges a naturalistic defense of principles of "cognitive optimality" on grounds of circularity, but his response has wider application:

The demand is for synchronic reconstruction of beliefs: take the totality of things you believe, subtract this claim and everything that you cannot defend without assuming it, and now show that the claim is correct. With respect to some claims, synchronic reconstruction is possible. . . . Traditional naturalists, however, cognizant of the history of mathematics, science, and methodology, should know in advance of skeptical embarrassments that some forms of the problem of synchronic reconstruction are solvable and others are not. On their account there is no substantial body of *a priori* knowledge, so that successful synchronic reconstructions must always appeal to empirical findings. . . . On naturalism's own grounds, there are bound to be unanswerable forms of skepticism.

Traditional naturalists should therefore decline blanket invitations to play the game of synchronic reconstruction. . . . (90)

And in his recent book on the philosophy of science, he remarks that "Skeptics who insist that we begin from *no* assumptions are inviting us to play a mug's game,"[31] the suggestion being that *of course* this sort of skeptical problem cannot be solved because it is unreasonably posed in the first place.

But it does not seem to me that this response will do. While this sort of answer may be appropriate for some skeptical problems, the issue of whether and why we ever have any reason to think that a conclusion that goes beyond observation is true is far too fundamental and inescapable to be dismissed as some clever dialectical trick. Nor does the appeal to the synchronic/diachronic distinction seem to help, since the same issue can of course be raised for our ancestors, however remote, and it is hardly reasonable to say that the fact that something was accepted at some earlier point despite there being no reason to think that it was true somehow gives a reason now to think that it is true. It is quite true, of course, that it is part of the naturalist's own position, or so immediate a consequence as to make no difference, that the skeptical problem posed above cannot be solved, but their explicit adoption of this consequence does nothing to make it less catastrophic or less self-defeating. Thus it is the naturalists who are asking us to play a "mug's game"—an invitation that, I suggest, should be firmly declined.

Summarizing, I have argued, first, that Quine's original argument for naturalizing epistemology fails either to show that this is necessary or to establish a viable alternative; second, that the various reasons offered by Kitcher and others fail to show the need for psychologizing, and so naturalizing, epistemology in any important sense; third, that the main arguments of the naturalists fail to show that a traditional, rationalist conception of *a priori* justification is untenable; and, fourth, that the abandonment of any sort of *a priori* justification leads directly to epistemological disaster and also undercuts the very premises used to argue for it.

I will conclude with two further remarks. First, one thing that it is important to bear in mind about the issue of *a priori* justification is how easy it is to rely on *a priori* insights without explicitly acknowledging them, even to oneself. This is particularly easy where such insights pertain to fundamental patterns of reasoning and argument. Thus it becomes fatally easy for a proponent of naturalized epistemology to rely on the intuitively obvious rational credentials of logic, induction, and explanatory reasoning, while at the very same time denying the very possibility of the only sort of non–question-begging justification which such reasoning could have. The argument offered at the beginning of this section can serve as a useful antidote to this kind of mistake.

Second, it is important to emphasize that I have not attempted to say anything here about the *scope* of *a priori* justification, in particular about how specific and numerous *a priori* epistemological principles may be. Nothing about the argument advanced here excludes the possibility that such principles might be few in number and very general in character, perhaps even limited to logic (including probability theory) and general principles of inductive and explanatory reasoning.[32] Thus it might be that such principles do not take us very far—and in particular that much of the job of "meliorative epistemology" must be done empirically. This would mean that while the general thesis of naturalism is false, many specific naturalistic results may be correct and valuable. But it would still remain the case that the *a priori* underpinning is indispensable to the rational acceptability of these more specific results, so that naturalized epistemology, as Kitcher understands it, would be unacceptable.

At one point in his essay, Kitcher speaks of a "broader vision" that underlies naturalism, one part of which is the following:

. . . How could our scientific understanding of ourselves—or our reflections on the history of the sciences—support the notion that answers to skepticism and organons of methodology (or, indeed, anything very much) could be generated *a priori*?(58)

To this, my response is that unless some general answers to skepticism can be justified *a priori* (even if these may not add up to anything that deserves to be called a methodology), we will have no reason for thinking that "our scientific understanding of ourselves" (or, indeed, *anything* else beyond the results of direct observation) is true.[33]

NOTES

1. I have no wish to deny that some of the things that are or might be done under the rubric of naturalized epistemology might have independent value of their own, so long as they are not intended as a replacement for traditional epistemology. But an exploration and assessment of this possibility is beyond the scope of the present essay.

2. Philip Kitcher, "The Naturalists Return," *Philosophical Review* 101 (1992): 53–114. Otherwise unspecified references in the text are to the pages of this article.

3. This is not to deny that epistemologists have had other aims as well, in particular that many of them have also sought to advance what Kitcher calls the "meliorative epistemological project"(64f.), i.e., the project of improving the reliability of human cognitive efforts. Indeed, as we will see further below, the relevance of psychology to this second project is a good deal clearer than it is for critical epistemology. But it seems obvious that no appeal to a further project of this sort provides any reason for abandoning critical epistemology, which is where I shall argue that naturalization would in effect lead.

4. There are also more radical alternatives that would take naturalization farther than Kitcher wants to go, e.g., by abandoning any idea that epistemology has a normative dimension. But apart from Quine's own view, which seems to have such a consequence, I will not be concerned here with these other views, which seem to me to be even further from the truth.

5. A partial exception is the explicitly psychologistic accounts that Hume offers of inductive reasoning, the apparent inference to the external world, etc. But these are precisely the parts of Hume's philosophy, I submit, that have the least value in relation to the philosophical issues in question and indeed which are the hardest even to recognize as even constituting philosophy.

6. For a fuller characterization, see my paper "A Rationalist Manifesto," *Canadian Journal of Philosophy*, Supplementary Volume 18 (1993): 53–88.

7. Reprinted in Quine, *Ontological Relativity and Other Essays* (New York, 1969), 69–90. Further references in the present section to the pages of this article will use the abbreviation "*EN*," and will be placed in the text.

8. Quine, "Two Dogmas of Empiricism," reprinted in Quine, *From a Logical Point of View*, 2nd ed. (Cambridge, Mass., 1961), 42.

9. Though this is by no means apparent from the actual texts, it is possible that Quine would want to argue that the goal of even the more modest construal of "the doctrinal side" is rendered unachievable by the complete intractability of the problem of induction. I do not think that such a pessimistic view of the problem of induction is warranted, but a discussion of that issue is impossible here. See my "A Reconsideration of the Problem of Induction," *Philosophical Topics* 14 (1986): 93–124.

10. Or rather we believe that (accept a sentence saying that?) we have such beliefs or accept such sentences.

11. It is important, however, to see that the main issue here does not turn on the term 'knowledge'. Even if, as some believe, the ordinary meaning of 'knowledge' does not require epistemic justification in the sense advocated here, but only something like reliable or truth-conducive causation of belief, it would remain true even for beliefs that constitute knowledge in this sense that we have no reason at all for thinking them to be true, and that result is enough in itself to constitute a very deep and intuitively paradoxical version of skepticism.

12. Notice also in passing that the belief that this is the best that we can do, that naturalized epistemology is all that is possible, is obviously not itself a psychological claim and thus cannot be part of the content of such an epistemology.

13. Quine, "The Nature of Natural Knowledge," in *Mind and Language*, edited by Samuel Guttenplan (Oxford, 1975), 67–81; the quoted passage is from p. 67.

14. Ibid., p 68.

15. Of course, some sorts of occult beliefs may stand in conflict with the sort of psychology that Quine has in mind. It is, however, not clear why such a conflict poses any problem once issues of justification are set aside; and in any case, there will be or could be other, occult versions of psychology that Quine can offer no reason for not taking just as seriously as the scientific brand.

16. The second component and some of its supporting arguments also originate with Quine and were almost certainly influential in leading him to advocate the naturalization of epistemology, even though they are not mentioned in any very explicit way in "Epistemology Naturalized" itself.

17. For further discussion of this same argument, see Hilary Kornblith, "Beyond Foundationalism and the Coherence Theory," *Journal of Philosophy* 72 (1980): 597–612; reprinted in Hilary Kornblith (ed.), *Naturalizing Epistemology* (Cambridge, Mass., 1985), 115–28, esp. pp. 118–19.

18. I am not denying that people may have sometimes carelessly said things that might suggest the view in question, partly due to the grip of the analytic methodological preconceptions briefly alluded to above and partly because the precise sort of case that

Kitcher describes had not occurred to them (though it no doubt should have). What I am denying is that there has ever been a significant philosopher who, once clearly presented with the argument, would have rejected the conclusion or who would have felt that it was a significant emendation of his views to accept it. Ironically enough, a good part of the motivation for the formulations that might suggest the contrary was a reluctance to formulate matters in terms of intentional mental states, states which were thought to be philosophically suspect for reasons that are quite close to some of those that often motivate naturalists.

19. Kitcher, of course, does not accept the category of logical or conceptual truth, and so places descriptions of the quoted point as logical in scarequotes. But this issue, to be discussed later, is irrelevant here.

20. See P. F. Strawson, *Introduction to Logical Theory* (London, 1952), chap. 9, Part II. For a critique of Strawson's account from the standpoint of traditional epistemology as understood here, see "A Reconsideration of the Problem of Induction," pp. 100–104.

21. For a detailed discussion of the vicissitudes of the concept of analyticity, see "A Rationalist Manifesto," 62–69; and also Appendix A of my book, *The Structure of Empirical Knowledge* (Cambridge, Mass., 1985).

22. See "A Rationalist Manifesto," 71–72.

23. Quine, "Two Dogmas of Empiricism," 20–37. Oddly enough, Kitcher does not mention this argument.

24. For a discussion of other arguments against rationalism, see my book *In Defense of Pure Reason*, forthcoming (eventually).

25. "Two Dogmas of Empiricism," 37–46, especially pp. 42–46. A second possibility worth noting is the argument for the indeterminacy of radical translation, which some have taken to be an argument against the *a priori*. Both this argument and its relevance to the *a priori* seem to me too uncertain and problematic to be worth discussing here. But see "A Rationalist Manifesto," 76–79.

26. See "A Rationalist Manifesto," 72–76, for a fuller discussion.

27. At least this is true for the cases of instrumentalism or fictionalism and behaviorism. Whether the same thing is true in the case of phenomenalism (or instead whether something like "direct realism" is true in a way that avoids the need for such an inference) is an issue that I cannot go into here.

28. Kitcher has argued elsewhere in effect that the only way to make sense of the concept of *a priori* justification is to construe it as guaranteeing truth and so ruling out fallibility. See his "A Priori Knowledge," *Philosophical Review* 86 (1980): 3–23; and *The Nature of Mathematical Knowledge* (New York, 1983), chaps. 1–4. I believe that this claim is mistaken, but an adequate consideration of it is impossible here.

29. I have formulated the argument in terms of a reason for thinking that the belief is true, rather than in terms of the belief's being (epistemically) justified, because I do not want to enter here into the somewhat vexed controversy between externalist and internalist conceptions of justification. My view is that the result arrived at in the text is enough to constitute epistemological disaster whether or not the beliefs in question may be said to be justified in some other sense of justification that does not involve our having a reason to think that they are true.

30. I owe my appreciation of the fundamental importance of the issue of self-referential consistency or inconsistency to the teaching, long ago and far away, of Richard Rorty. Unfortunately, however, Rorty's own philosophical views seem to me to have long since ceased to reflect any concern for this kind of issue.

31. Philip Kitcher, *The Advancement of Science* (New York, 1993), 135.

32. Many philosophers have suggested that enumerative or instantial induction may be justified by appeal to explanatory reasoning. For my own version of this idea, within a general rationalist context, see "A Reconsideration of the Problem of Induction," 114–21.

33. I am grateful to Ann Baker and Larry Colter for helpful comments on earlier drafts of this essay.

Naturalistic Epistemology and Reliabilism

ALVIN I. GOLDMAN

1. GOLDMAN'S GUIDE TO EPISTEMIC NATURALISM

Naturalistic epistemology (NE) has become a popular program in recent years, but how it is conceived varies widely. This section of the essay charts the major positions that have been or might be subsumed under this label.[1] At the highest level of abstraction, we may distinguish three types of NE: (I) *meta-epistemic naturalism*, (II) *substantive naturalism*, and (III) *methodological naturalism*.

Naturalism is epistemology might be expected to be a close cousin of naturalism in ethics. In ethics, naturalism is primarily a meta-ethical position, which addresses the ontological status of moral properties or the nature of our thought and language concerning morals. Analogously, one might expect epistemic naturalism to be a meta-epistemic position concerning the ontological status of epistemic properties or the nature of our thought and language about epistemic matters. A typical thesis of meta-epistemic naturalism might then be the thesis that (normative) epistemic properties are analyzable, or reducible, to natural properties. In fact, this is not the principal sort of position that has been denoted by "naturalistic epistemology." If we mean by "natural property" what G. E. Moore meant, viz., any sort of descriptive or factual property, then many epistemologies might qualify as naturalistic under the foregoing characterization which would not be so labeled by working epistemologists. Traditional forms of foundationalism or coherentism, for example, might so qualify.[2] I shall continue to treat meta-epistemic naturalism as one type of NE, though we should recognize that other, more restrictive, senses of "naturalistic" are usually intended. These latter are best articulated not as meta-epistemic positions but rather as positions within one of the other two categories: a substantive position about knowledge, justification, or rationality, or a methodological position about the way to study these topics.[3]

What sorts of substantive positions are commonly referred to as "naturalistic"? At a first approximation, they are ones that invoke physico-causal processes of the epistemic agent, or perhaps relations that obtain between the cognizing agent and its environment. Substantive epistemic non-naturalism, by contrast, is typified by the view that knowledge, justification, and rationality arise primarily from evidential relations between sentences or propositions, abstract subject matter than can be studied by logic and probability theory rather than the study of biological or psychological systems in the natural (physical) world.[4]

The substantive views standardly considered naturalistic are closely associated with the third conception of epistemic naturalism, the methodological conception. The latter holds that epistemology is (or should be), in whole or part, a scientific or empirical discipline rather than an a priori one. Methodological epistemic naturalism maintains that the study of epistemology coincides with portions of certain empirical sciences, such as cognitive psychology, evolutionary biology, or the history and sociology of science; or at least it must exploit the findings of such empirical sciences rather than conduct its business in pristine isolation from these sciences.

Let us now examine these three broad categories in more detail, beginning with meta-epistemic naturalism (MEN). MEN is best viewed as a thesis about normative epistemic properties such as justifiedness, warrant, or rationality. (Knowledge, on the usual accounts, is a mixture of normative and non-normative properties, and hence will not be discussed under this heading.) Although we initially identified MEN with the view that (normative) epistemic properties are *reducible* to natural properties,[5] several other theses could also be subsumed under MEN. For example, the thesis that epistemic properties *supervene* on natural ones is readily classified as a form of naturalism; and even the *elimination* of normative epistemic properties in favor of natural ones (epistemic nihilism, or the "error theory") might count as a species of MEN. Admittedly, eliminativism in meta-ethical theory is not consistently regarded as a form of naturalism. In ethical theory, "naturalism" is commonly reserved for reductionist theories, which countenance the existence of moral properties. But at least one writer, Harman (1985, pp. 29–30), explicitly uses the term "naturalism" (in ethics) to include eliminativism or nihilism. And in philosophy of mind the elimination of contentful states, leaving only purely neural states, or other states not characterized semantically, is commonly regarded as a naturalistic program. Analogously, elimination of normative epistemic properties in favor of purely descriptive ones might be viewed as a form of MEN.

Finally, MEN could assume the form of a naturalistic theory of our *thought* or *concepts* of the epistemic, without endorsing an ontological theory about the reduction of epistemic norms to natural facts, or the supervenience of the former on the latter. This would be analogous to the meta-ethical strategy of embracing non-cognitivism or expressivism about moral language but trying to fashion an evolutionary or psychological account of the uses of this language, as exemplified by Gibbard (1990). On one variant of this approach, the epistemic naturalist would not try to give a reductive analysis of, e.g., justification, but would offer a psychological account of when epistemic evaluators judge a belief to be justified. This approach is pursued, for example, in Goldman (1992). It is analogous to Gibbard's approach to rationality, which omits any explicit definition thereof but offers an account of what it is for a person to believe that something is rational.[6]

Returning to ontological versions of MEN, is there anything that would count as a specimen of non-naturalism or anti-naturalism in this domain? Presumably, a thesis to the effect that normative epistemic properties (or relations) are unique, primitive, or *sui generis*, would qualify as anti-naturalism. Such a position seems to be implied by Chisholm (1977), when he offers definitions of various epistemic expressions in terms of the relation of comparative reasonableness but leaves comparative reasonableness undefined in non-epistemic terms. Chisholm does provide synonyms for "more reasonable than," but these synonyms are themselves normative epistemic expressions, viz., "epistemically better than" and "epistemically preferable to" (1977, p. 7). This suggests that comparative reasonableness is not naturalistically reducible.[7] Lehrer (1990) also appears to take this position. He initially treats the notion of reasonableness as "primitive" (1990, p. 127), and goes on to reject the only candidates he considers for a naturalistic reduction of reasonableness. So endorsement of MEN is by no means universal.

We turn next to substantive epistemic naturalism (SEN). Here perhaps the leading examples of NE are causal, counterfactual, and reliabilist accounts of knowledge or justification.[8] Such theories say that knowledge is the product of a causal connection between the world and the believer, or that knowledge is the product of "information flow" from the world to the cognizer, or that justified belief is belief caused by reliable belief-forming processes, and so on. Various biological and/or teleological accounts of these concepts are also readily classed as naturalistic. For example, Lycan (1988) proposes to "reduce the evaluative notions of epistemology to the teleological notions of the theory of organ systems" (p. 144). Plantinga (1993) analyzes warrant in terms of the proper functioning of a creature's cognitive faculties, where proper function *may* be interpreted in evolutionary terms (though this is not his preferred interpretation).

What feature of features of these theories invite the "naturalism" label? I doubt that there is a single such characteristic, just a family of overlapping themes. One theme is to treat the epistemic agent as a physical or biological system, causally interacting with the external ("natural") world. This conception of the epistemic agent is nicely epitomized by Churchland's (1979) phrase "epistemic engine." Goldman's (1967) early causal theory clearly instantiates this theme, as does Dretske's (1981) information-theoretic approach, which resonates with an engineering-based image of the knower. When a cognizer is compared to a thermometer (Armstrong 1973) or a gasoline gauge (Dretske 1981), he is clearly viewed as part of the physical world, and a user of physical mechanisms to acquire his knowledge. Similarly, when knowledge and justification are viewed as products of psychological processes operating on sensory or doxastic inputs (Goldman 1986), the outlook is distinctly organismic and hence naturalistic.[9]

It is noteworthy that all of the preceding examples of NEs are externalist theories. But this is not an essential feature of SEN. For example, Pollock (1986) offers an internalist form of justification theory which is nonetheless quite naturalistic. It is naturalistic, first, because it views the epistemic agent as a "cognitive machine." Second, it says that "[a] person's belief is justified if and only if he holds it in conformance to his epistemic norms" (1986, p. 168), where conformance with norms consists in reasoning being *causally guided* by the norms. Pollock's theory is internalist because his norms or rules are required to cite "internal" factors, i.e., factors directly accessible to the agent. This is because the rules are intended to have a first-person reason-guiding, or belief-guiding, function, which is feasible only if the cited factors are directly accessible. This is a perfectly legitimate form of SEN, despite its internalist character.

It is worth remarking that many so-called externalists could cheerfully accept much of what Pollock says, because the difference between Pollock and these externalists comes at the level of the *criterion of rightness* for norms or rules, not at the level of norm *contents* (as Pollock supposes). In Goldman (1986), for example, a rule framework is employed, and the sorts of rules invoked there are just as internalist as Pollock's rules (although this is not emphasized). These rules permit certain cognitive processes and by implication forbid others. Since the processes would be picked out internalistically, the cognitive system would not have to appeal to external factors (such as truth) to apply these processes, once the proper ones were identified.[10] The difference between Pollock and externalists like myself would come at the level of the criterion for norm correctness. Whereas Pollock says, "it is a necessary truth that our actual epistemic norms are correct" (1986, p. 168), I maintain that only a proper subset of the cognitive processes we natively use are correct (in the sense of being justification-conferring). My own criterion of correctness is reliability, an externalist criterion. Pollock's criterion is actual, de facto possession of a norm by human beings, a non-externalist criterion.[11] The problem with the latter criterion, however, is that there seem to be many cases of reasoning, e.g., reasoning driven by wishful thinking or a desire to preserve a favorable self-image, that produce (epistemically) unjustified beliefs. Pollock would have to claim that these specimens of reasoning violate our actual norms, i.e., are not expressive of any actual norms. But what would be the grounds for this claim? Since we do in fact reason in these ways, at least some of the time, we appear to have cognitive procedures that guide such reasoning, and such procedures are precisely what Pollock means by "epistemic norms." Pollock is not unaware of this difficulty; in a later passage (p. 170) he points out that we do not always reason correctly. But how can this be accommodated within his theory? Apparently, he has to maintain that the mere fact that we use a procedure does not entail that it is a "norm." But then he needs to place additional constraints on what counts as a norm, which he does not do. What might these constraints be? Perhaps he would say that a procedure is a norm only if it is used in a certain way, viz., reflectively, to correct our behavior. But couldn't even reflective corrections of our behavior be erroneous? Why would reflectiveness *per se* guarantee correctness?

Another theme in SEN is descriptive realism as opposed idealization. Traditional (twentieth-century) epistemologists often theorized about ideal epistemic agents. Theories of rationality, in particular, have posited normative principles like deductive closure, which it is doubtful that real human beings can instantiate. By contrast, naturalists commonly plead for closer attention to actual or realizable cognitive procedures. Quine (1969) writes: "Better to discover how science is in fact developed and learned than to fabricate a fictitious structure to a similar effect" (p. 78). Goldman (1978) endorses the principle that "ought implies can," claiming that suitable epistemic norms are ones to which human beings are capable of conforming. Harman (1980) argues against Bayesianism on grounds of computational complexity, and Cherniak (1986, chap. 4) similarly argues against logic-based rules of rationality of a familiar sort by appeal to considerations of computational complexity.

Let us turn next to the third category of epistemic naturalism: methodological naturalism (MDN). This is probably the most discussed dimension of NE, especially since Quine (1969) was responsible for the label "epistemology naturalized," and his own version of the idea is predominantly methodological.[12] MDN claims that epistemology should either consist in empirical science, or should at least be informed and beholden to the results of scientific disciplines. This invites two questions: (1) *which* scientific disciplines are relevant to epistemology?, and (2) *how* are they relevant? Quine himself has emphasized psychology, and to a lesser extent evolutionary biology; but other practitioners of NE emphasize the history and sociology of science. Concerning the *mode* of relevance, a number of assorted answers have been offered. Let us begin with the second question, answers to which will provide smooth lead-ins to the first.

Quine's answer to the second question is direct: NE is simply *part of* empirical science, or natural science. He asserts this in numerous passages: "Epistemology, or something like it, simply falls into place as a chapter of psychology and hence of natural science" (1969, p. 82); "Our liberated epistemologist ends up as an empirical psychologist, scientifically investigating man's acquisition of science" (1974, p. 3); "Epistemology is best looked on, then, as an enterprise within natural science" (1975, p. 68); "Naturalism does not repudiate epistemology, but assimilates it to empirical psychology." (1981, p. 72).[13] Quine's incorporation of epistemology within natural science is made possible, at least in these sorts of passages, by his assignment to epistemology of the task of answering a purely *explanatory* question, viz., "how we human animals can have managed to arrive at science from such information" (viz., irritations of our surfaces). His focus on this explanatory mission has led many commentators to interpret his brand of NE as spurning normative questions,[14] although in later writings Quine disclaims any intent to jettison the normative (Quine 1986, p. 664, and 1990, pp. 19–21).

Other exponents of MDN, however, place greater weight on the normative dimension than Quine, and it is worth exploring the precise ways in which they expect natural science to bear on normative epistemic questions. I shall distinguish three types of contributions that science might make to questions about epistemic normativity. (1) A different (non-scientific) methodology should first be used to identify proper cognitive conduct; then science should be used to determine whether people have the wherewithal to instantiate such normatively appropriate conduct, or whether and how they can be taught or trained to instantiate it. (2) Another (non-scientific) methodology should first be used to identify the goals and values of cognition, or the criterion of proper cognitive conduct; then science should be used to identify the specific methods of processes that (best) promote these goals, or that satisfy the criterion. (3) Science itself should be used to identify the goals and values of cognition (the goals tacitly embedded in epistemic norms), or the criterion of proper cognitive conduct. This gives us three grades of normative involvement.

Consider the first and lowest grade of normative involvement. This approach assumes that epistemic norms can be identified through some methodology other than natural science, perhaps logic, probability theory, or statistics. The question then arises whether people have the psychological capacities to conform with these norms. For example, what kinds of deductive tasks are they capable of executing? Do they appreciate principles of probability theory such as the conjunction rule? And so forth. These are topics to which much research in the psychology of reasoning has been devoted.[15] Second, to the extent that naive cognizers are not innately equipped to execute certain inferential tasks, what modes of instruction can best train them or facilitate normatively proper inference?[16]

The second grade of normative involvement is illustrated by my own epistemological program in Goldman (1986). There I contended that identifying the criterion of rightness for justificational rules is not a province of empirical psychology, but that the choice of certain rightness criteria would invite contributions from scientific psychology. My favored rightness criterion specified that a system of justification rules is right just in case these rules authorize selected cognitive processes within the human repertoire, cognitive belief-forming processes that would yield a high ratio of true beliefs. In short, a "J-rule" system is right just in case the belief-forming processes it authorizes are highly reliable. Given such a criterion, scientific psychology has two jobs: (A) to identify the cognitive processes that are in the human repertoire and hence potentially authorizable by J-rules, and (B) to help identify the levels of reliability of these sundry processes. So this approach vindicates the role of scientific psychology at the second grade of normative involvement.

Another example of the second grade of normative involvement is the theory of scientific methodology offered by Boyd (1984; 1985). Boyd claims that proper methods of science, including methods for suitable experimental controls, essentially depend on contingent scientific theories. In short, there is no body of specific epistemic methodology that can be certified as correct prior to, or in abstraction from, substantive empirical theory. For example, the sorts of controls that are methodologically required for a given type of experiment is a function of established background theory. It is impossible to control for all possible experimental artifacts, of which there is an infinite number. Instead we rely on established theory to indicate the sorts of artifacts that should be suspected and the sorts of experimental controls which will permit us to avoid or discount for their effects.

A third specimen that exemplifies the second grade of normative involvement is that of Laudan (1987); he invokes the history of science as the relevant empirical science. It is not the task of history of science, says Laudan, to determine appropriate cognitive aims for science (especially since the cognitive aims of past scientists are said to differ significantly from ours). Hence Laudan's view does not exemplify the third grade of normative involvement. We should, however, use the history of science to inform us which methods have promoted, or failed to promote, various sorts of cognitive ends in the past. We should then use this empirically determined past track record to select those methods that have (and will continue to have) the best means/ends connections for the realization of cognitive ends that most of us *now* hold to be important and worthwhile (for science).

Finally, let us turn to approaches that advocate the third and highest level of normative involvement. These approaches claim that science is essential either to epistemic axiology (the task of identifying epistemic goals or ends) and/or to the selection of criteria or standards of epistemic evaluation. This corresponds roughly to what Maffie (1990) calls "unlimited naturalism."

One scientific approach to epistemic axiology is an evolutionary approach. This assumes that our proper cognitive aims are specified by the biological function of our cognitive faculties (that for which they were selected), and this function is often said to be the promotion of reproductive fitness (see Lycan 1988, p. 145). Alternatively, it might be contended that cognitive faculties, at least some of them, have been selected for their true-belief promoting properties (Plantinga 1993, Nozick 1993; see Stich 1985 for a competing view).

A second approach at the third level of normative involvement is one that appeals to cognitive science, including psychology and linguistics, to help elucidate our normative epistemic standards. This approach presupposes that the way to get at our epistemic standards or criteria is to illuminate the nature of our normative epistemic concepts. To this extent, it resembles "analytical" philosophical methodology. This approach claims, however, that the nature of mental concepts is a problem for psychological science, and that psychological theories of concepts may be instructive in illuminating (normative) epistemic concepts such as justification and rationality. In other words, the theory of epistemic norms invokes scientific psychology not to study the epistemic agent but to study the concept(s) of the epistemic judge or evaluator. This is my (more recent) approach in Goldman (1992). Appealing partly to an "exemplar" or prototype theory of concepts that appears in the psychology literature, I offer a two-stage account of the concept of justification which is reliabilist (only) at the deepest level.[17] I shall return to this approach toward the end of the essay.

A variant of this use of psychology is to place constraints on the psychological complexity of a theory of epistemic concepts. A theory about the concepts of knowledge, justification, and/or warrant presumably has implications about the mental representations associated with these concepts, and about the inferences that a deployer of these concepts needs to make in applying them to concrete cases. But certain philosophical theories of these epistemic concepts involve such complexity that it seems psychologically implausible that naive cognizers in fact have any corresponding mental representations, or engage in the requisite computations (in real-time applications).[18] If a theory of knowledge or justification is an ontological theory about kinds in nature, perhaps there are no bounds of psychological plausibility. These kinds just have their properties, whether or not they are grasped by human beings. But if theories of knowledge and justification are, fundamentally, theories of how ordinary speakers (tacitly) understand and deploy the language of knowledge and epistemic justification, then any theory of this subject-matter needs to be psychologically or cognitively realistic. Cognitive science will clearly be relevant to the assessment of candidate theories.[19]

Our discussion of MDN, like our discussion of the other categories of naturalism, has focused on the epistemology of individual cognizers. Many of the same points apply, *mutatis mutandis*, to the epistemology of groups or communities (social epistemology). At the second grade of normative involvement, for example, empirical (or theoretical) science can help identify the forms of social organization that would optimize the chances of obtaining epistemic ends. Optimal ways of amalgamating individual judgments into group judgments (Goldman 1987), for example, or optimal ways of distributing a scientific community's research activity (Kitcher 1990; 1993) may be chosen with the help of scientific (or mathematical) analyses. Thus, the social sciences should play a role in social epistemology that is somewhat (though not totally) analogous to the role psychology should play in individual epistemology.

By way of summary, I present the following outline of the varieties of epistemic naturalism that we have distinguished.

I.   Meta-epistemic naturalism
     A. Ontological
        1. Reduction
        2. Supervenience
        3. Eliminativism (nihilism)
     B. Conceptual-linguistic
II. Substantive epistemic naturalism
     A. Physicalism/organicism
     B. Causalism
     C. Descriptive realism; realizability

III. Methodological naturalism
  A. Explanatory relevance
  B. Normative relevance
    1. Science should determine our capacity for norm instantiation;
    2. Science should determine the specific methods or processes that satisfy the criteria of epistemic rightness;
    3. Science should (help) determine the goals, values, or general criteria associated with epistemic norms.

2. RELIABILISM AND META-JUSTIFICATION

As noted above, reliabilism—especially process reliabilism—is usually viewed as a standard example of NE. In the second half of this essay, I shall address one problem that has been raised for earlier versions of reliabilism, and I shall discuss how a recent reformulation of reliabilism can resolve this problem. No attempt is made to survey or meet all types of problems raised against reliabilism. This specific problem is selected because of its relevance to issues in epistemic naturalism and to the debate over internalism and externalism.

The topic for discussion is reliabilism about justification, not reliabilism about knowledge. For present purposes I shall start with a fairly simple formulation of justificational reliabilism, which will help us concentrate on certain core features of the approach without distracting complications. Let us consider, then, formulation (R1):

(R1) S's belief in p is justified IFF it is caused (or causally sustained) by a reliable cognitive process, or a history of reliable processes.[20]

The causal dimension of (R1) is a crucial and good-making feature of the theory. It allows the theory to handle cases properly in which a cognizer *possesses* fully adequate evidence in support of his belief that p but where that evidence is causally inert or isolated from the belief. Detective Dennis, for example, may possess strands of evidence that collectively make it highly probable that X committed a certain crime, but this evidence is entirely inert vis-à-vis Dennis's belief that X is guilty. Dennis does not appreciate how these disparate strands of evidence can be woven together to show X's guilt. They play no role in initiating or sustaining his belief in X's guilt. Instead, Dennis is moved to believe this because of X's unsavory appearance, because of his vague resemblance to a certain famous gangster. Dennis's belief is clearly unjustified because of its improper (unreliable) mode of production, despite the fact that Dennis's credal corpus contains strong evidential support for the believed proposition.

Not only is the mere possession of adequate evidence not sufficient for a belief's justifiedness, as the detective case shows, but it also is not necessary. Consider the case of Stanley who *once* had excellent evidence for p (he read it in an encyclopedia), but no longer recalls what the evidence was. He retains his belief in p, but not in any evidence that provides adequate support for p.

Nonetheless, so long as he has not meanwhile acquired evidence against *p* (or evidence that undermines the encyclopedia's authoritativeness), our intuitive judgment is that Stanley's belief in *p* is justified (and a good candidate for knowledge). This is consonant with (R1), since his original acquisition of the belief in *p* involved a reliable inferential process, and his continued recollection of *p* also features a reliable memory process. So historical reliabilism correctly captures the intuitive judgment that his belief is justified, while theories requiring *concurrent* possession of adequate evidence—traditional foundationalism and coherentism—would get this case wrong.

Let us now consider an objection to reliabilism to the effect that (R1) does not provide a sufficient condition for justifiedness. Lehrer writes: "a person who has no idea that her beliefs are caused or causally sustained by a reliable belief-forming process might fail to know because of her ignorance of this" (1990, p. 162); and again, "a person totally ignorant of the reliability of the process producing his belief would not know that what he believes is true" (1990, p. 165). In other words, Lehrer seems to imply, for a person to have first-level knowledge (knowledge that *p*), she would have to have higher-order knowledge, viz., knowledge that her belief was reliably caused. Lehrer generalizes this problem to all forms of externalism, writing: "All forms of externalism fail to deal with this problem adequately" (1990, p. 164). He supports this objection with the help of the following example. Suppose that a surgeon invents a small device which is both a very accurate thermometer and a computational device capable of generating thoughts. The device, call it a tempucomp, is implanted in Mr. Truetemp's head so that the very tip of the tiny device sits unnoticed on his scalp and acts as a sensor to transmit information about the temperature to his brain. This yields a very reliable belief-forming process, regularly giving him correct temperature thoughts, although he has no idea that the tempucomp has been inserted in his brain nor how he happens to get his temperature thoughts. He just unreflectively accepts them, without checking a thermometer to see whether these thoughts are usually correct. Intuitively, Truetemp does not have first-order knowledge, e.g., knowledge that the temperature on a particular occasion is 104 degrees. The trouble, says Lehrer, is that Truetemp has no idea whether his thoughts about the temperature are reliable.[21]

Although Lehrer's discussion is formulated in terms of "knowledge," he presumably intends it to apply to justification as well. Without substantial change, the point can then be expressed as follows. Externalist theories of justification that merely require of a belief that it have some "external" property, such as being caused by a reliable process, are inadequate. First-order justification requires in addition that the agent *justifiably believe* that the first-order belief has this external property. We may call this requirement the "higher-level justification requirement" (HLJR). It is similar to BonJour's (1985) requirement of a "metajustification." If a reliabilist were to adopt (HLJR), he would then replace simple reliabilism, (R1), with a strengthened version of reliabilism, (R2):

(R2) S's belief in p is justified IFF
    (A) S's belief in p is caused by a history of reliable processes, and
    (B) S believes justifiably that his belief in p is caused by a history of reliable processes.

There are a number of problems associated with the proposal that (R2) be substituted for (R1).[22] First, recall our earlier example of forgotten evidence. Stanley may not currently be justified in believing that he originally formed his p-belief by reliable inference from authoritative sources, so he does not justifiably believe that his p-belief was caused by a history of reliable processes. But this does not keep his p-belief from being (intuitively) justified.

Second, according to (R2), first-level justification requires second-level justification about reliability. But when this theory is applied to the second-level belief, it will similarly require third-level justification about reliability; and so on ad infinitum. (R2) evidently requires an infinite hierarchy of reliability beliefs, and this may well be impossible for human beings with finite belief resources. This plays unnecessarily into the hands of the skeptic.[23]

Some might retort that human beings do have resources for infinitely many beliefs, where beliefs are construed dispositionally.[24] So let us pass on to a further problem. Consider supervenience, perhaps the most attractive version of MEN. Avoiding more technical formulations of supervenience, we may follow Van Cleve (1985) in the following general definition:

A-properties supervene on B-properties IFF necessarily, for any item x and A-property F, if x has F then there is a B-property G such that (i) x has G, and (ii) necessarily, whatever has G also has F.

Where A-properties are some sort of normative properties and B-properties are natural properties, the supervenience thesis says that the instantiation of any normative property must be in virtue of some natural property. Normative properties, in other words, cannot float freely; they must be "anchored" to natural properties. Applying this to the epistemic case, supervenience would imply that the instantiation of normative epistemic properties must be anchored to the instantiation of natural, non-epistemic properties.

How does (R1) sit vis-à-vis the supervenience thesis? Very comfortably. The conditions for justifiedness presented in (R1) only involve natural, non-epistemic subject matter: causation, psychological processes, and reliability (the last involves truth, which is not an epistemic notion). So the property of being caused by a history of reliable processes—call it the CRP property—is a natural property. Hence, if (R1) is correct, justification supervenes on a natural property. How does the new principle, (R2), sit vis-à-vis the supervenience thesis? Not comfortably at all, since clause (B) of (R2) requires the satisfaction of a non-natural condition, which seems to rule out the possibility of (first-order) justification being necessitated or guaranteed by CRP *alone*, or by any other natural property.

We should not be too hasty here, however. Perhaps supervenience could still be satisfied, for example, if (first-order) instantiation of the CRP property itself necessitated satisfaction of clause (B). But how could this transpire? First-level satisfaction of the CRP property would have to necessitate possession of an ascending hierarchy of higher-order beliefs, and it would have to necessitate that each of these has the CRP property. Clearly, however, no such necessitation does obtain. If it did, the original Truetemp case would be impossible, because the CRP property of Truetemp's temperature belief would guarantee that he justifiably believes that it has the CRP property. But the very possibility of the Truetemp case, as described, indicates that no such guarantee obtains.

Is (R2) compatible with some *other* natural property (not plain CRP) being the supervenience basis of justification? What about the conjunction of CRP plus possession of a meta-belief (which is a natural condition)? (R2) implies that both of these are necessary for (first-order) justification; maybe they are sufficient as well. But for this to work, the conjunctive condition would have to guarantee that clause (B) is satisfied, in other words, that the meta-belief is *justified*. Applying clause (A) to the meta-belief, however, the conjunction condition would have to guarantee that the meta-belief has CRP. But there can be no such guarantee. It is certainly possible for someone to have a meta-belief that lacks CRP. So (R2) does appear to violate the supervenience thesis.

These problems could be avoided by replacing (R2) with a weaker, purely natural, higher-order condition, for example, requiring only a meta-belief about the reliable production of the first-order belief. This would yield (R3):

(R3) S's belief in p is justified IFF
    (A) S's belief in p is caused by a history of reliable processes, and
    (B) S believes that this belief in p is caused by a history of reliable processes.

But is (R3) any better than (R1) for the purposes at hand? Not at all. For one thing, it may still be too strong for the forgotten evidence case, since Stanley may not believe that his first-order belief was caused by a history of reliable processes; yet his first-order belief may nonetheless be justified. Second, (R3) can be satisfied even if S's belief in the higher-order proposition is very *un*reliably caused, e.g., by idle conjecture. It is doubtful that this should confer justification on the first-order belief if mere possession of CRP is insufficient for justification.

This might tempt us to substitute a still stronger, higher-order principle, viz., (R4):

(R4) S's belief in p is justified IFF
    (A) S's belief in p is caused by a history of reliable processes,
    (B) S believes that his belief in p is caused by a history of reliable processes, and
    (C) this meta-belief is caused by a history of reliable processes.

It is not clear that (R4) is satisfactory. On the one hand, if (R3) is too strong for the Stanley case, (R4) will be too strong as well.[25] On the other hand, it may not be strong enough to satisfy the critics who urge HLJR. After all, if they are right in thinking that the simple CRP property does not suffice to generate justification, why should (merely) reliably formed meta-beliefs suffice? However, if (R4) *is* deemed acceptable by such critics, at least we will have a reliabilist condition that is *sufficient* for justification, which could be viewed as a substantial victory for reliabilism. (But I doubt that its opponents would acquiesce in [R4].)

At this point, however, I want to turn the tables on the critics. The problems raised by HLJR are not confined to reliabilism. Lehrer, we recall, insists on something like HLJR (or HLKR) as a condition required for all forms of externalism.[26] But coherentism itself, I suggest, is (in its main forms) a brand of externalism! So if all externalisms must incorporate HLJR, then coherentism will share the problems it poses.

To elaborate on these points, let us introduce the property of *cohering with one's background system (of beliefs)*, and assume that this is a natural, non-epistemic property.[27] We shall abbreviate this property as "CBS." We can then formulate simple coherentism as follows:

(C1)   *S*'s belief in *p* is justified IFF *S*'s belief in *p* has the CBS property.

If we now adopt the popular definition of "internal" (illustrated in our earlier discussion of Pollock) according to which a property or relation is internal if and only if its satisfaction is (directly) "accessible" from a first-person perspective, then the CBS property is *not* an internal property. To appreciate this point, let us be clear on what is meant by a property being "accessible." Presumably this means that an agent (any agent, even a naive one) can always determine correctly whether or not that property or relation holds of his belief. This requirement is certainly not satisfied by the CBS property. Any adult person's background system of beliefs is enormous in size, even if conservative criteria are used for belief attribution. Any such system would have thousands, tens of thousands, or more, of beliefs, most of them stored in long-term memory. Clearly, nobody can retrieve *all* these beliefs and survey them at a given moment to check whether a target proposition or belief, *p*, coheres with them all. A single member of the system might sharply conflict with *p*; but if the agent fails to retrieve that member (and notice the conflict), he will erroneously judge *p* to possess the CBS property. Furthermore, the relation of coherence may well involve comparisons of probabilities (as detailed formulations of coherence, like Lehrer's, commonly specify), and where these probabilistic requirements pertain to a very large set of propositions, coherence may be mathematically quite difficult to determine. Only an extremely proficient probabilist would be able to determine whether a given proposition *p* coheres with his entire background system.[28] Hence the CBS property is not generally accessible, certainly not to the ordinary epistemic agent, any more than a fact about the reliability of a belief's production is generally accessible. So (C1) is as much an externalist theory as (R1)! If Lehrer and BonJour are right to require any externalist theory to be strengthened by adding a HLJR, they will need the revised formulation (C2):

(C2) S's belief in p is justified IFF
   (A) S's belief in p has the CBS property, and
   (B) S justifiably believes that his belief in p has the CBS property.

But this encounters the very same problems as (R2), including an infinite hierarchy of beliefs and violation of supervenience.[29]

My suggestion is that HLJR must be abandoned; it is simply a misguided idea. However, although we may abandon HLJR, we cannot duck the problem cases the HLJR was introduced to solve, e.g., the Truetemp case. If we do not add HLJR to simple reliabilism, we still need to modify simple reliabilism in some way to cope with such examples.

One simple solution is suggested by Alston (1989a; 1989b). Perhaps it should be required that the production of a belief should involve a "ground" or "basis"—either a premise belief, or a perceptual appearance, or the like—that is either a conscious state or a state readily brought into consciousness. If we add this requirement to (R1), it would adequately handle the Truetemp and clairvoyance cases, in which the epistemic agents lack conscious grounds or bases for their beliefs.

Unfortunately, this may be too strong a condition. Justified *memory* beliefs do not standardly seem to have a conscious or potentially conscious ground. Similarly, in the case of justified inductively based beliefs, it is implausible that the entirety of the ground (all of the background premises) are conscious or even potentially conscious.

A variant of Alston's idea, however, may be found in the context of a recent version of reliabilism to which I alluded earlier, the version contained in Goldman (1992). This approach to reliabilism is in the framework of a conceptual-linguistic theory of epistemic evaluators, rather than an ontological approach to epistemic properties, i.e., category (B) rather than (A) under meta-epistemic naturalism. It aims to provide a psychologically plausible explanatory theory of how epistemic evaluators make their epistemic judgments, without necessarily identifying the "property" of justification itself. This explanatory theory has two components (somewhat analogous to rule utilitarianism). One component is the theory of representation and judgment. It says that epistemic evaluators mentally store certain prototypes of good and bad belief-forming processes (epistemic virtues and vices). Virtue prototypes would include various perceptual processes, memory processes, and "good" inferential processes. When a question arises concerning the justificational status of a target belief, the evaluator (more precisely, the evaluator's cognitive system) considers what he knows about the process(es) that produced the target belief and tries to "match" this information to the virtue prototypes. If he finds a sufficiently close match, the target belief is judged to be justified; if no sufficiently close match is found, or if its processes match those of vice prototypes, then the belief is judged to be unjustified. The second component of the theory addresses the question of how the virtue and vice prototypes are selected or acquired in the first place. This component appeals to reliability: virtue prototypes are chosen for their (judged) reliability, vice prototypes for their (judged) unreliability.

How does this theory ("Two-Component Reliabilism." or "Virtue Reliabilism") handle the Truetemp example? It suggests that when confronted with the Truetemp case, an evaluator tries to match the belief-forming process of Mr. Truetemp to the processes associated with one of the virtue prototypes. The closest prototypes, presumably, would be prototypes of perceptual processes: vision, audition, etc. But although the temperature-detecting process has certain points of similarity with these, such as sensitivity to environmental information, it saliently lacks another feature possessed by each of these prototypes, viz., sensory awareness or feeling in some distinctive perceptual modality. This lack of a match, according to the present theory, accounts for the evaluator's judgment of unjustifiedness, or at any rate, in a certain measure of reluctance to judge that the belief is justified. The theory would acknowledge that other virtue prototypes, such as the memory prototype, might lack the element of sensory awareness or feeling, but Truetemp's belief-forming process has no prospect of matching *those* quite dissimilar prototypes. So we have an explanation of evaluator judgments (or intuitions) in the Truetemp case without appeal to anything like HLJR (or even a higher-level *belief* requirement).

A question inevitably raised by this two-component theory is the following. Assuming the correctness of this explanatory story, what follows about whether an agent's belief really *is* justified? Suppose, for example, that evaluators have made mistakes in estimating the reliabilities of certain processes. Suppose they have assigned "virtue" status to certain processes in the mistaken belief that those processes are reliable. If a belief is (known to be) caused by one of these processes, then the evaluators will *judge* it to be justified. But is it *really* justified? This sort of "ontological" question is one I am not currently prepared to answer, although I acknowledge that it is the most prominent question in standard epistemological inquiry. Methodologically, however, I think that the preferable way to proceed is to try to get as good a handle as we can on the concepts, conceptual apparatus, and concept-deploying procedures that are utilized by epistemic evaluators (however messy or logically unsatisfactory these concepts and procedures may turn out to be). The ontological ramifications of our findings can be postponed for a later juncture.

NOTES

1. For other recent surveys of naturalistic epistemologies, see Maffie (1990) and Kitcher (1992).

2. If coherentism is defined as the view that a belief is justified if and only if it coheres with the cognizer's corpus of beliefs, and if coherence is defined in factual (non-normative) terms, e.g., as logical consistency, then it would qualify as a specimen of naturalism.

3. My distinction between meta-epistemic and methodological naturalism parallels a similar distinction drawn (in slightly different form and terminology) by Steup (1992).

4. Kitcher, for example, suggests that epistemological naturalism can be characterized negatively by its rejection of post-Fregean approaches that reduce epistemological issues to questions of logic, conceptual analysis, or "grammar" (Kitcher 1992, p. 56).

5. Different kinds of reduction might be distinguished here, e.g., definitional reduction versus weaker forms of reduction. See Maffie (1990). My discussion neglects some of these possible distinctions.

6. My own approach, however, is not in the service of (epistemic) expressivism, nor is it avowedly committed to any form of anti-realism about epistemic properties. I say a bit more about this approach later in this essay.

7. In the third edition of *Theory of Knowledge* (Chisholm, 1989), however, Chisholm expressly endorses the supervenience of epistemic normative facts on non-normative facts (see pp. 42–43).

8. On causal theories, see Goldman (1967), and Dretske and Enc (1984); on counterfactual theories, see Dretske (1969; 1971; 1981); Goldman (1976; 1986), and Nozick (1981); on reliabilist theories, see Armstrong (1973), Goldman (1975; 1979; 1986), Boyd (1980), Alston (1989a), Sosa (1991), Swain (1981), Talbott (1990), and Schmitt (1992).

9. For a similar treatment of rationality, see Nozick (1993), especially chaps. 3–4.

10. Of course, I do not suppose that cognitive processes can all be applied or executed at the "personal" or conscious level of cognition; many, if not most, can only be executed at the "sub-personal" level. But Pollock does not differ with me on this, since his norms are equally "tacit," and presumably available only at the sub-personal level.

11. On reflection it is questionable whether this criterion is really non-externalist, since which norms human beings actually possess may not be "directly accessible" to ordinary people. Pollock seems to concede this since he views epistemic norms as pieces of "proceduralized knowledge," and assigns the task of describing such knowledge (and hence the possession of these norms) to scientific psychology.

12. Although Quine introduced the phrase "epistemology naturalized," certain substantive versions of NE in fact antedated Quine's article, e.g., Goldman (1967), as did historically oriented versions of methodological naturalism, e.g., Kuhn (1962). Moreover, as Kitcher (1992) and Goldman (1985) emphasize, the dominant epistemological tradition before Frege was heavily naturalistic, especially psychologistic.

13. Haack (1993) identifies an ambiguity or ambivalence in Quine's writings on NE, which she explains by distinguishing "scientistic" and "modest" naturalism. In scientistic naturalism, "science" refers to the natural sciences exclusively; in modest naturalism, "science" refers to our empirical beliefs generally, including common sense and history. I shall not try to observe her distinction, though most of what I say is consonant with the stronger, "scientistic" interpretation.

14. E.g., J. Kim (1988).

15. See Wason and Johnson-Laird (1972), Evans (1983), Holland, Holyoak, Misbett, and Thagard (1986), Cosmides (1989), Johnson-Laird and Byrne (1991), Rips (1993), Kahneman, Slovic, and Tversky (1982), Tversky and Kahneman (1983), Gigerenzer, Hell, and Blank, (1988), Osherson (1990), and, for an introductory overview, Goldman (1993a).

16. On this topic see Holland, Holyoak, Nisbett, and Thagard (1986, chap. 9), Cheng, Holyoak, Nisbett, and Oliver (1986), and Fong, Krantz, and Nisbett (1986).

17. This essay, then, goes beyond the more limited naturalism of *Epistemology and Cognition* (Goldman 1986), which denied the necessity of using cognitive psychology at the purely "conceptual" level of the theory of justification, i.e., at the level of the criterion. For this earlier position I was criticized by Taylor (1990) and Maffie (1990).

18. For example, consider Lehrer's (1990) theory of knowledge and justification. Knowledge is defined in terms of the notion of justification and undefeated justification, and the latter are defined in elaborate ways, using the notions of competition, beating, and neutralizing, and the fairly rarified notions of an acceptance system, a verific system, and an ultrasystem of beliefs (see Lehrer 1990, esp. pp. 147–49).

19. In Goldman (1993b) I endorse an analogous argument about the meanings of mentalistic expressions. For example, I claim that functionalist theories of mind, construed as theories about how ordinary speakers understand or represent mental terms, are implausible because of the excessive computational complexity that would be required for their application.

20. (R1) is close to the basic formulation of reliabilism in Goldman (1979). There, however, I introduce the distinctions between conditional and unconditional reliability and between belief-dependent and belief-independent processes. Readers familiar with these distinctions and the uses to which they were put may substitute for (R1) an appropriately modified formulation.

21. This example is quite similar to BonJour's (1985) earlier example of clairvoyance.

22. Several of these problems, including the regress and supervenience problems, are discussed by K. Kim (1992).

23. The problem is not merely the sheer number of beliefs required for justification, but the increasing complexity of their propositional contents as one ascends the hierarchy. This is pointed out by K. Kim (1992).

24. E.g., see Foley (1978) and Klein (1993). Personally, I have never found purely dispositional accounts of belief plausible, but I shall let this pass for the sake of argument.

25. I have therefore tended to favor a weaker, merely negative additional condition, e.g.: S does not believe that his belief in p is caused by unreliable processes. Of course, that would not handle the Truetemp case (as Lehrer notes), because Truetemp is assumed to have no beliefs about the reliability of his temperature belief's production.

26. Actually Lehrer does not explicitly formulate either HLKR or HLJR. But he strongly hints at HLKR when he writes: "[M]ore than the possession of correct information [in Dretske's sense of information possession] is required for knowledge. One must have some way of knowing that the information is correct" (1990, p. 164). BonJour, moreover, explicitly favors a "meta-justification" condition (although his precise formulation of this condition does not match mine).

27. Lehrer's own definition of coherence with a background system does not seem to be natural and non-epistemic, for it is defined in terms of the epistemic relation "more reasonable than." So his approach already faces the problem of failing to meet the supervenience constraint.

28. Even the mere logical consistency of a given belief with the background system may not be determinable, as Kornblith (1988), following Cherniak (1986), points out.

29. BonJour is aware of certain aspects of this predicament. He recognizes, to begin with, that a simple version of coherentism would be a form of externalism insofar as it does not require the coherence property to be "accessible" to the cognizer (1985, p. 101). Since he does not want his own coherentism to be externalist, he recognizes that he needs some additional conditions. He does not quite recognize, however, that his meta-justification requirement leads to the problems we have identified. Instead, he introduces the "doxastic presumption," which incorporates the requirement (and postulation) of a suitable meta-belief, but denies that the meta-belief needs to be justified in a coherentist fashion (1985, pp. 102–103). This "doxastic presumption" is problematic in several ways; among other things, it seems to constitute an abandonment of coherentism in favor of foundationalism, as noted by Brueckner (1988) and Goldman (1988).

REFERENCES

Alston, William. 1989a. *Epistemic Justification*. Ithaca, N.Y.
———. 1989b. "Goldman on Epistemic Justification." *Philosophia* 19: 115–31.
Armstrong, David. 1973. *Belief, Truth and Knowledge*. Cambridge.
BonJour, Laurence. 1985. *The Structure of Empirical Knowledge*. Cambridge, Mass.
Boyd, Richard. 1981. "Scientific Realism and Naturalistic Epistemology." In *PSA 1980*, *vol.2*, edited by P. D. Asquith and R. N. Giere. East Lansing, Mich.

————. 1984. "The Current Status of Scientific Realism." In *Scientific Realism*, edited by Jarrett Leplin. Berkeley.

————. 1985. "Lex Orandi est Lex Credendi." In *Images of Science*, edited by Paul Churchland and Clifford Hooker. Chicago.

Brueckner, Anthony. 1988. "Problems with Internalist Coherentism." *Philosophical Studies* 54: 153–60.

Cheng, P. W., K. J. Holyoak, R. E. Nisbett, and L. M. Oliver. 1986. "Pragmatic Versus Syntactic Approaches to Training Deductive Reasoning." *Cognitive Psychology* 18: 293–328.

Cherniak, Christopher. 1986. *Minimal Rationality*. Cambridge, Mass.

Chisholm, Roderick. 1977. *Theory of Knowledge*, 2nd edition. Englewood-Cliffs, N.J.

————. 1989. *Theory of Knowledge*, 3rd edition. Englewood-Cliffs, N.J.

Churchland, Paul. 1979. *Scientific Realism and the Plasticity of Mind*. Cambridge.

Cosmides, Leda. 1989. "The Logic of Social Exchange: Has Natural Selection Shaped How Humans Reason? Studies with the Wason Selection Task." *Cognition* 31: 187–276.

Dretske, Fred. 1969. *Seeing and Knowing*. Chicago.

————. 1971. "Conclusive Reasons." *Australasian Journal of Philosophy* 49: 1–22.

————. 1981. *Knowledge and the Flow of Information*. Cambridge, Mass.

Dretske, Fred and Berent Enc. 1984. "Causal Theories of Knowledge." In *Midwest Studies in Philosophy IX: Causation and Causal Theories*. Minneapolis.

Evans, Jonathan, ed. 1983. *Thinking and Reasoning*. London.

Foley, Richard. 1978. "Inferential Justification and the Infinite Regress." *American Philosophical Quarterly* 15: 311–16.

Fong, G. T., D. H. Krantz, and R. E. Nisbett. 1986. "The Effects of Statistical Training on Thinking about Everyday Problems." *Cognitive Psychology* 18: 253–92.

Gibbard, Allan. 1990. *Wise Choices, Apt Feelings*. Cambridge, Mass.

Gigerenzer, G., W. Hell, and H. Blank. 1988. "Presentation and Content: The Use of Base Rates as a Continuous Variable." *Journal of Experimental Psychology: Human Perception and Performance* 14: 513–25.

Goldman, Alvin. 1967. "A Causal Theory of Knowing." *Journal of Philosophy* 64: 357–72.

————. 1975. "Innate Knowledge." In *Innate Ideas*, edited by Stephen Stich. Berkeley.

————. 1976. "Discrimination and Perceptual Knowledge." *Journal of Philosophy* 73: 771–91.

————. 1978. "Epistemics: The Regulative Theory of Cognition." *Journal of Philosophy* 75: 509–23.

————. 1979. "What Is Justified Belief?" In *Justification and Knowledge*, edited by George Pappas. Dordrecht.

————. 1985. "The Relation between Epistemology and Psychology." *Synthese* 64: 29–68.

————. 1986. *Epistemology and Cognition*. Cambridge, Mass.

————. 1987. "Foundations of Social Epistemics." *Synthese* 73: 109–44.

————. 1988. "BonJour's *The Structure of Empirical Knowledge*." In *The Current State of the Coherence Theory*, edited by John Bender. Dordrecht.

————. 1992. "Epistemic Folkways and Scientific Epistemology." In *Liaisons: Philosophy Meets the Cognitive and Social Sciences*, by Alvin Goldman. Cambridge, Mass.

————. 1993a. *Philosophical Applications of Cognitive Science*. Boulder, Colo.

————. 1993b. "The Psychology of Folk Psychology." *Behavioral and Brain Sciences* 16: 15–28.

Haack, Susan. 1993. "The Two Faces of Quine's Naturalism." *Synthese* 94: 335–56.

Harman, Gilbert. 1980. "Reasoning and Explanatory Coherence." *American Philosophical Quarterly* 17: 151–57.

————. 1985. "Is There a Single True Morality?" In *Morality, Reason and Truth*, edited by David Copp and David Zimmerman. Totowa, N.J.

Holland, John, Keith Holyoak, Richard Nisbett, and Paul Thagard. 1986. *Induction: Processes of Inference, Learning, and Discovery.* Cambridge, Mass.

Johnson-Laird, Philip, and Jane Byrne. 1991. *Deduction.* Hillsdale, N.J.

Kahneman, Daniel, Paul Slovic, and Amos Tversky, eds. 1982. *Judgment under Uncertainty: Heuristics and Biases.* Cambridge.

Kim, Jaegwon. 1988. "What Is 'Naturalized Epistemology'?" In *Philosophical Perspectives, 2, Epistemology,* edited by James Tomberlin. Atascadero, Calif.

Kim, Kihyeon. 1992. "The Defense Activation Theory of Epistemic Justification." Doctoral dissertation, University of Arizona, Tucson.

Kitcher, Philip. 1990. "The Division of Cognitive Labor." *Journal of Philosophy* 87: 5–22.

———. 1992. "The Naturalists Return." *Philosophical Review* 101: 53–114.

———. 1993. *The Advancement of Science.* New York.

Klien, Peter. 1993. "Human Knowledge and the Infinite Regress of Reasons." Paper presented at the NEH Summer Institute on Knowledge, Virtue, and Teaching. Berkeley.

Kornblith, Hilary. 1988. "The Unattainability of Coherence." In *The Current State of the Coherence Theory,* edited by John Bender. Dordrecht.

Kuhn, Thomas. 1962. *The Structure of Scientific Revolutions.* Chicago.

Laudan, Larry. 1987. "Progress or Rationality? The Prospects for Normative Naturalism." *American Philosophical Quarterly* 24: 19–31.

Lehrer, Keith. 1990. *Theory of Knowledge.* Boulder, Colo.

Lycan, William. 1988. *Judgment and Justification.* Cambridge.

Maffie, James. 1990. "Recent Work on Naturalized Epistemology." *American Philosophical Quarterly* 27: 281–93.

Nozick, Robert. 1981. *Philosophical Explanations.* Cambridge, Mass.

———. 1993. *The Nature of Rationality.* Princeton.

Osherson, Daniel. 1990. "Judgement." In *Thinking: An Invitation to Cognitive Science, vol. 3.* Cambridge, Mass.

Plantinga, Alvin. 1993. *Warrant and Proper Function.* New York.

Pollock, John. 1986. *Contemporary Theories of Knowledge.* Totowa, N.J.

Quine, Willard V. 1969. "Epistemology Naturalized." In *Ontological Relativity and Other Essays,* by Williard V. Quine. New York.

———. 1974. *The Roots of Reference.* La Salle, Ill.

———. 1975. "The Nature of Natural Knowledge." In *Mind and Language,* edited by Samuel Guttenplan. Oxford.

———. 1981. "Things and Their Place in Theories." In *Theories and Things,* by Willard V. Quine. Cambridge, Mass.

———. 1986. "Reply to White." In *The Philosophy of W. V. Quine,* edited by L. Hahn and P. Schilpp. La Salle, Ill.

———. 1990. *Pursuit of Truth.* Cambridge, Mass.

Rips, Lance. 1993. *The Psychology of Proof.* Cambridge, Mass.

Schmitt, Frederick. 1992. *Knowledge and Belief.* London.

Sosa, Ernest. 1991. *Knowledge in Perspective.* Cambridge.

Steup, Matthias. 1992. "Epistemological Naturalism and Naturalistic Epistemology." Paper read at Pacific Division meeting of the American Philosophical Association. Portland.

Stich, Stephen. 1985. "Could Man Be an Irrational Animal? Some Notes on the Epistemology of Rationality." *Synthese* 64: 115–35.

Swain, Marshall. 1981. *Reasons and Knowledge.* Ithaca, N.Y.

Talbott, William. 1990. *The Reliability of the Cognitive Mechanism: A Mechanist Account of Empirical Justification.* New York.

Taylor, James. 1990. "Epistemic Justification and Psychological Realism." *Synthese* 85: 199–230.

Tversky, Amos, and Daniel Kahneman. 1983. "Extensional Versus Intuitive Reasoning: The Conjunction Fallacy in Probabilistic Reasoning." *Psychological Review* 90: 293–315.

Van Cleve, James. 1985. "Epistemic Supervenience and the Circle of Belief." *Monist* 68: 90–104.

Wason, P. C., and P. N. Johnson-Laird. 1972. *Psychology of Reasoning: Structure and Content*. London.

MIDWEST STUDIES IN PHILOSOPHY, XIX (1994)

Skepticism and Naturalistic Epistemology

RICHARD FUMERTON

In this essay I am primarily interested in exploring the implications of contemporary versions of naturalistic epistemology for the way in which one
should address traditional skeptical arguments. My interest goes beyond this,
however, for I remain convinced that once one understands clearly the full
implications of such views, one should find their approach to *philosophical*
epistemology implausible.

NATURALISM

Before we proceed, however, a few comments about the concept of naturalism
as it relates to such fields as epistemology, philosophy of mind, ethics, mathematics, and the like, might be in order. A common rhetorical technique of
philosophers involves the attempt to seize a terminological high ground. Thus,
the philosopher who succeeds in getting an opponent's theory of perception
called "naive realism" has the battle half won. And if one's philosophical
opponents manage to get their views labeled "naturalistic" it might appear that
one is left with the unenviable task of defending "unnatural" or "nonnatural"
views. But it is obviously important right from the start to remember that we are
dealing with technical philosophical debates framed in technical philosophical
vocabulary. And it is more than a little difficult to see what is so "natural"
about naturalistic philosophical views.

What does make a view naturalistic? What is the contrast that is intended
to be drawn? Generally speaking, the naturalists are on the side of what
they take to be *scientifically* respectable views. Naturalists typically analyze
the properties with which they are interested into natural properties. And
what makes a property natural? That it is the kind of property with which
science feels comfortable. Of course, the concepts which scientists take to
be unproblematic vary depending on the nature of the science, and thus
"respectable" naturalism is relative to the science with which the naturalistic

philosopher identifies. Thus historically prominent naturalists in ethics include among the natural properties such psychological properties as being desired. But the philosopher of mind who wants a naturalistic account of mental states might well reject the "folk science" vocabulary of desire as unsuited to a philosophically perspicuous reduction of mental states. That philosopher might feel more comfortable with an analysans that employs the concepts of contemporary cognitive science.

Why do so many contemporary philosophers want philosophical analyses provided in the vocabulary of science? The most obvious answer, I suppose, is that science has enjoyed extraordinary success. Television sets, computers, and microwave ovens convince many that whatever they are doing, scientists are doing it effectively. The terms they employ in their scientific reasoning must unproblematically refer to kinds of things that really exist. If we as philosophers want to piggy-back on the success of science then we ought to make sure that we can reduce traditional philosophical disputes to terms that make the relevant questions scientifically respectable. Typically, the "harder" the science, the more impressive has been its successes, and consequently if we can reduce familiar concepts of mental states to the concepts of physics, we will be better off than if we stay with the concepts employed by the relatively soft science of psychology. Psychologists, after all, are hopeless when it comes to offering the kind of explanations that offer the possibility of lawful prediction. Indeed, they are hopeless when it comes to offering anything that looks like a genuine law of nature.

There is, of course, a real irony in the fact that so many philosophers yearn to provide philosophical analyses employing the "respectable" concepts of contemporary science. One of the concepts most eagerly embraced by naturalists for use in naturalistic analyses is the concept of causal and lawful connection. Thus many naturalists seek to understand intentionality and representational capacity in terms of complex causal connections that obtain between the thing represented and the entity or event doing the representing.[1] Many naturalistic epistemologists seek to understand knowledge and justified belief by understanding the relation that exists between knower and known as like that obtaining between thermometer and the temperature it registers.[2] Others embrace the view that justified belief is essentially reliably produced belief where the concept of reliability is clearly to be understood in terms of lawful (probabilistic or universal) connections between the conditions that produce the belief and the truth of the belief produced. But while the concept of causal and lawful connection does seem to be presupposed by scientific inquiry, it is, from a certain perspective, one of the least respectable concepts for use in philosophical analyses.

The history of philosophical attempts to provide illuminating analyses of the concept of lawful connection, causal connection, or the relation expressed by contingent subjunctive conditionals is hardly a history distinguished by its glowing success. It would be a gross understatement to suggest that there is no philosophically received view about the correct way to understand any of these problematic concepts. Many still embrace Humean regularity theories as the most promising attempt to get at the heart of causal or lawful connection, but no one has offered a plausible account of the distinction between lawful and accidental regularity within the framework of a Humean analysis. Recently, a number of philosophers have suggested that we think of lawful connection as a kind of sui generis relation obtaining between universals,[3] but again, it is a distinct minority of philosophers who can convince themselves that they are either phenomenologically acquainted with such a relation or have dialectically defensible reasons for positing its existence. Possible worlds accounts of lawful connection, causal connection, or the truth conditions of counterfactuals are almost comical. The interpretation of the relevant possible worlds semantics inevitably requires an understanding of the very modalities one seeks to illuminate.

With the embarrassing lack of success that philosophers have had arriving at enlightening accounts of lawful and causal connection, it is a little odd to find so many philosophers scrambling to make philosophical accounts of intentionality and epistemic concepts "respectable" by reducing the relevant intentional and epistemic properties to nomological properties. And it is more than a little bit hard to listen to such philosophers bemoaning the philosopher of mind who appeals to a "mysterious" sui generis capacity of mental properties to constitute "natural" signs of the states of affairs they represent, or the equally "mysterious" relations of acquaintance to facts that is said by some philosophers to partially constitute the foundations for empirical knowledge.

It is worth remembering that given an epistemic perspective that was virtually taken for granted for hundreds, if not thousands, of years, it is facts about mental states that have been taken to be conceptually and epistemically more secure than any of the complex facts that form the subject matter of contemporary science. The traditional problem of perception, after all, just is the problem of getting philosophically respectable access to the physical world with which science *begins* its investigation. In the heyday of logical positivism at least one goal was to reduce *scientific* talk into an analytically equivalent vocabulary of sense data, precisely because sense data were taken to be conceptually and epistemically less problematic than physical objects. Furthermore, even if these philosophical theories about what is and is not conceptually and epistemically unproblematic are not defensible, it is worth remembering that the sciences studying the mind can get nowhere without presupposing in the course of their investigations that people have unproblematic access to their mental life. If people do not know when they are in pain, for example, the cognitive psychologist will have to wait until the cows come home to make any discoveries about the state of the brain responsible for pain.

Now it is obviously unprofitable to continue at length this rather abstract (and somewhat polemical) discussion of the relative merits of naturalist as opposed to nonnaturalist accounts of philosophically interesting concepts. It is, however, worth emphasizing one of the initial motivations behind naturalistic *epistemology* that goes beyond any of the factors mentioned above. Specifically, the naturalistic epistemologist seems moved, in large part, by the conviction that it is only by taking a naturalistic turn that the epistemologist can avoid massive skepticism. Quine's famous injunction to naturalize epistemology seemed largely based on the alleged impossibility of refuting the skeptical challenge from within traditional foundationalist frameworks.[4] In the remainder of this essay I want to examine more precisely how naturalizing epistemology in the manner of contemporary externalists would affect the way in which we respond to traditional skeptical arguments. Again, as I see it, contemporary externalists are naturalistic epistemologists because of their commitment to analyzing fundamental epistemic concepts into "natural" nomological properties and because of the fact that their views allow them to follow Quine's advice to use the methods of natural science to answer epistemological questions (more about this later).[5] For much of the discussion I will take as my paradigm naturalistic epistemology the kind of reliabilism that Goldman first defended in Goldman (1979). What I say will apply *mutatis mutandis* to other paradigm naturalistic/externalist accounts of epistemic concepts such as Armstrong's conception of basic knowledge (1973) and Nozick's much discussed "tracking" analysis of knowledge and evidence (Nozick, 1981).

SKEPTICISM AND NATURALISTIC EPISTEMOLOGY

Let me very briefly sketch the kind of skepticism with which I am concerned and what I take to be the classic form of the skeptical challenge. First, it might be helpful to emphasize that the problem of skepticism is primarily a problem in what I call normative epistemology. The contrast is to metaepistemology. Metaepistemological questions concern the philosophical analysis of fundamental epistemic concepts. Normative epistemological questions ask to what the epistemic concepts apply.[6] As I understand it, naturalism in epistemology is best construed as a metaepistemological position.[7] Claims that we are or are not justified in believing something are part of normative epistemology.

The skepticism I am most interested in is skepticism with respect to justified or epistemically rational belief (rather than knowledge). Furthermore, I am primarily concerned with what we might call "local" rather than "global" skepticism. The global skeptic maintains the highly suspicious (because it is epistemically self-refuting[8]) position that we have no justification for believing anything. The local skeptic puts forth arguments designed to establish that we have no justified beliefs with respect to a certain *class* of propositions. The history of local skepticisms includes skeptics with respect to the possibility of justifying beliefs about the physical world, the past, other minds, the future, and so on. The traditional skeptic virtually always presupposed some version of foundationalism, i.e., presupposed that we do have noninferentially justified belief in at least some propositions. To be sure the presupposition was seldom explicitly stated, but one cannot read any of the important historical figures concerned with either advancing or refuting skepticism without reaching the conclusion that they took some propositions to be epistemically unproblematic, where their unproblematic character seemed to stem from the fact that one did not need to *infer* their truth from any other propositions believed.[9]

The first step, then, in advancing an argument for skepticism with respect to some kind of proposition is to establish that our access to the relevant truth is at best *indirect*. Skeptics with respect to the physical world deny that we have noninferential "direct" access to physical objects. The standard skeptical claim is that if we have justification for believing anything about the physical world, that justification reduces to what we can legitimately *infer* about the physical world from what we know about the character of our past and present sensations. The skeptic about the past claims that we have no direct (i.e., noninferential) access to truths about the past. What we know or reasonably believe about the past is restricted to what we can legitimately infer about past events from what we know about the *present* state of our minds. The future is known to us only through our knowledge of the past and present. Other minds are known to us only through what we know about the physical appearance and behavior of bodies.

NATURALISTIC EPISTEMOLOGY AND
NONINFERENTIAL JUSTIFICATION

As many of its proponents would be quick to point out, paradigmatic naturalistic (and externalist) accounts of justification actually allow a distinction that parallels the classic distinction between noninferentially and inferentially justified beliefs. The reliabilist, for example, can distinguish reliable belief-producing processes that take as their input *belief* states from reliable belief-producing processes that take as their input something other than belief states. And it would be natural to describe justified beliefs produced by the latter as noninferentially justified beliefs. Their justification, after all, would not depend on the having of any other different justified beliefs. Belief-dependent processes can generate justified beliefs only when they take as input beliefs that are already justified.[10]

Now one of the primary advantages that paradigmatic naturalistic accounts might seem to have in the battle against skepticism is the ease with which they can deny the crucial first premise of skeptical arguments. The class of noninferentially justified beliefs is likely to be much larger given a reliabilist or "tracking" account of justified belief. Notice, I say "likely" to be much larger. As far as I can see, virtually all naturalistic epistemologies entail that it is a purely contingent question as to which beliefs are justified noninferentially and which are not. On the reliabilist's view, for example, the question of whether or not one is noninferentially justified in believing at least some propositions about the physical world is a question about the nature of the processes that yield beliefs about the physical world and the nature of their "input." If we have been programmed through evolution to *react* to sensory stimuli with certain representations of the world, and we have been lucky enough to have "effective" programming, then we will have noninferentially justified beliefs about the physical world. If Nozick (1981) is right and our beliefs track facts about the physical world around us, and this tracking does not involve inference from other propositions, we will again have noninferentially justified beliefs about the physical world. If our beliefs about the physical world are acting like that reliable thermometer that Armstrong (1973) uses as his model for direct knowledge, if we are accurately registering the physical world around us with the appropriate representations, then again we have noninferential, direct knowledge of the world. Whether or not we have such noninferential justification for believing propositions describing the physical world, on any of these naturalistic ways of understanding noninferential justification, is a purely *contingent* matter.

Now that it is a contingent fact is not in itself surprising, nor is it a consequence peculiar to naturalistic epistemology. It is certainly a contingent fact on a classic "acquaintance" foundationalist theory[11] that I am acquainted with the fact that I am in pain. It is a contingent fact that I am in pain and so obviously contingent that I am acquainted with it. It is less obvious on traditional foundationalisms that it is a contingent fact that we are *not* acquainted with certain facts. It might seem, for example, that one *could* not be acquainted with facts about the distant past, the future, or even the physical world if it is understood as a construct out of actual or possible experience or as the cause of certain actual and possible experience.[12] But even here it is difficult to claim that it is necessarily the case that conscious minds are not acquainted with such facts. There may be no God but it is not obvious that the concept of a consciousness far greater than ours is unintelligible. If the concept of a specious present makes sense, such a consciousness may have the capacity to directly apprehend a much greater expanse of time than can finite minds. In any event it is not *clear* that the class of facts with which *we* can be acquainted exhausts the facts with which all possible consciousness can be acquainted.

But even if the scope of noninferentially justified belief is contingent on both classic foundationalist views and contemporary naturalistic (externalist) versions of foundationalism, there are crucial differences. On traditional versions of foundationalism, philosophers are at least in a position to address reasonably the question of the content of noninferentially justified belief. The philosopher is *competent*, at least as competent as anyone else, to address the questions of whether or not we have noninferentially justified beliefs in propositions about the physical world, for example. There are two sources of knowledge as to what we are noninferentially justified in believing. One is dialectical argument. The other is acquaintance itself. One can be directly acquainted with the fact that one is directly acquainted with certain facts.

According to paradigm naturalistic epistemology, the facts that determine whether one is noninferentially justified in believing a proposition are complex nomological facts. Given such views, it is not clear that a philosopher *qua philosopher* is even in a position to speculate intelligently on the question of whether or not we have noninferentially justified belief in any of the propositions under skeptical attack.[13] Because the naturalist has reduced the question of what is noninferentially justified to questions about the nature of the causal interaction between stimuli and response, and particularly to the processes of the brain that operate on the stimuli so as to produce the response, the search for noninferential justification would seem to be as much in the purview of the neurophysiologist as the philosopher.[14] In the last two hundred years, the vast majority of philosophers simply have not had the training to do a decent job of investigating the hardware and software of the brain. But without this training, it hardly seems reasonable for philosophers to be speculating as to what is or is not a reliable belief-independent process. To be sure, some contemporary epistemologists are trying to "catch-up" with developments in cognitive science and even neurophysiology, but I cannot help worrying that the experts in such fields will quite correctly regard these philosophers as simply dilettantes who, having tired of their *a priori* discipline, now want to get their hands dirty in the real-life world of science.

Given the above, it is ironic that so many philosophers find naturalistic epistemology attractive precisely because it can more easily capture the prephilosophical intuition that there *is* something direct about our knowledge of the physical world through sensations. Critics of traditional foundationalism complain that it is only through sheer repetition of the positions that many philosophers got used to talk about *inferring* the existence of a table from propositions about the character of sensation, or *inferring* propositions about the past from propositions describing present consciousness. Such critics have correctly pointed out that if these claims are intended to be phenomenologically accurate descriptions of our epistemic relation to the world they are hardly credible. Anyone who has tried to paint knows that it is very difficult to distinguish the world as it appears from the world as it is. That there is a conceptual distinction between phenomenological appearance and reality seems to me obvious. If the difficulty of artistic representation shows that we rarely reflect on appearances (as opposed to reality) it also seems to show that there is such a thing as appearance. But whether or not one can introduce an intelligible "noncomparative"[15] use of "appears," it does not alter the phenomenological fact that we do seldom, if ever, consciously infer propositions about the physical world from propositions describing the character of sensation.

We also seldom consciously infer propositions about the past from anything we might call a memory "experience." The very existence of memory "experience" is far from obvious. We might also observe, however, that our commonplace expectations about the future are often not formed as a result of careful consideration of premises describing past correlations of properties or states of affairs. When I expect my next drink of water to quench my thirst instead of killing me, I do *not* first consider past instances of water quenching thirst. It is useful to reflect carefully on this fact for even most naturalists will view this kind of knowledge as involving inductive *inference*. We must, therefore, be cautious in reaching conclusions about the role of phenomenology in determining whether a *justification* is inferential or not. We must distinguish questions about the causal origin of a belief from questions about the justification available for a belief.

We must also distinguish between occurrent and dispositional belief. It may be that I have all sorts of dispositional beliefs that are causally sustaining my beliefs when I am completely unaware of the causal role these dispositional beliefs play. In introducing this discussion I suggested that it was ironic that naturalists would find attractive the fact that their naturalistic epistemology can accommodate the apparent phenomenological fact that far less commonsense belief involves inference than is postulated by traditional foundationalism. The irony is that phenomenology should have no particular role to play for our paradigm naturalists in reaching conclusions about what is or is not inferentially justified. According to these naturalists, the epistemic status of a belief is a function of the nomological relations that belief has to various features of the world. These nomological facts are complex and are typically not the kinds of facts which have traditionally been thought to be under the purview of phenomenology. I suppose a reliabilist, for example, can define some belief-producing process as "phenomenological." But again, even if one can describe such a process it will be a contingent question as to what beliefs such a process might justify, a contingent question that goes far beyond the competency of most philosophers qua philosophers (and certainly most phenomenologists qua phenomenologists) to answer.

But perhaps I am being unfair in suggesting that our paradigm naturalistic epistemologists have no particular *credentials* qualifying them to assess the question of whether the skeptic is right or wrong in denying the availability of noninferential justification for beliefs under skeptical attack. The skeptics, after all, had arguments in support of their conclusion that we have no noninferentially justified beliefs in propositions about the physical world, the past, the future, other minds, and so on. The naturalists can at least refute those arguments based on their *a priori* reasoning about the correct metaepistemological position. The most common way of supporting the conclusion that we do not have noninferentially justified beliefs about the physical world is to point out that we can imagine someone having the very best justification possible for believing that there is a table, say, before him, when the table is not in fact there. A person who is vividly hallucinating a table can have just as good reason to think that the table exists as you do. But we can easily suppose that there is no table present before the victim of hallucination. If *direct* epistemic access to the table is anything like a real relation, then it cannot be present when the table is not present. But if the victim of hallucination does not have direct access to the table, and the victim of hallucination has the same kind of justification you have for thinking that the table exists (when you take yourself to be standing before a table in broad daylight), then you do not have direct access to the table either.

The reliabilist will deny the association between noninferential justification and direct access to the table. To have a noninferentially justified belief about the table's existence is to have a belief about the table produced by an unconditionally reliable belief-independent process. The victim of hallucination has (or at least might have) a belief in the table's existence produced by an unconditionally reliable belief-independent process. It depends in part on how we define the relevant process. But if we think of the stimuli as something like sensations (which the hallucinator has), and the process as what goes on in the brain when sensation is assimilated and turned into representation, there is no reason why someone hallucinating cannot satisfy the conditions for having a noninferentially justified belief, assuming of course that the process in question really is unconditionally reliable. The reliabilist's metaepistemology allows at least a conditional response to the skeptic's attack. More precisely, the reliabilist can point out that a reliabilist metaepistemology entails that the skeptic's conclusion about the noninferential character of belief about the physical world does not follow. And, of course, everything the reliabilist says about the physical world applies to the past, other minds, and even the future. The reliabilist probably would not claim that beliefs about the future are noninferentially justified but the reliabilist should claim that there is no reason in principle why they could not be, and should continue to assert that the skeptic has no argument for the conclusion that we have no direct, i.e., noninferentially justified, beliefs about the future.

Interestingly, not all naturalists will reject the skeptic's claim about noninferential justification in the same way. Consider again the reliabilist's response to the argument from hallucination as a way of establishing that we have no noninferentially justified beliefs about the physical world. The crucial move for the reliabilist was to deny that we are forced to regard the hallucinatory situation as one in which the subject lacked a noninferentially justified belief. A causal theorist about direct knowledge, like Armstrong, might admit that in hallucinatory experience we lack noninferential knowledge, but continue to assert that in veridical experience we have such knowledge. This naturalist is more likely to deny the skeptic's presupposition that we should say the same thing about the nature of the justification available to the victim of vivid hallucination and the person who has *qualitatively* indistinguishable veridical experiences. On one version of internalism, the internalist holds that the conditions sufficient for justification are always states internal to the subject. If sensations are not themselves relations (a controversial claim to be sure), and the sensory evidence of S and R is indistinguishable, and there is nothing else "inside their minds" to distinguish their epistemic states, then this internalist will insist that if the one has a certain kind of justification for believing something, then so does the other. But a causal theorist thinks that the relevant question that determines the nature of the justification available for a belief involves the *origin* of the belief. The internal, i.e., nonrelational, states of S and R can be qualitatively indistinguishable but S's internal states can result in S's having a noninferentially justified belief by virtue of their being *produced* in the appropriate way. R's internal states might produce the very same belief, but because they were not caused by the appropriate facts, they will not result in the having of a noninferentially justified belief. In short the hallucinator's belief cannot be traced via sensation back to the fact about the world that would make the belief true. The person lucky enough to have veridical experience typically has a belief that can be traced back to the fact that makes the belief true. This is a perfectly clear distinction, and there is nothing to prevent an epistemologist from arguing that this just is the distinction that determines whether or not someone has a justified or rational belief. Furthermore the question of whether the justification is inferential has only to do with the kinds of links in the causal chain leading to the relevant belief. If the causal connection goes directly from some fact about the physical world, to the occurrence of sensory states, to representations about the physical world, there are no other *beliefs* that crucially enter the story. The justification that results will be justification that does not logically depend on the having of other justified beliefs.[16] It will be noninferential justification. So again, we can see how naturalistic metaepistemology can put one in a position to claim that the skeptic has not established the crucial premise concerning the inferential character of our belief in the propositions under skeptical attack.

Even if naturalism allows one to point out that the skeptic has not established the crucial first premise of the argument, it does not follow, of course, that the naturalist has given any positive reason to suppose that the skeptic is wrong in claiming that the propositions under skeptical attack are not the objects of noninferentially justified belief. If skeptics and nonskeptics are to play on a level playing field, there is no "burden of proof" when it comes to fundamental issues in epistemology. If the philosopher wants to claim that we have noninferentially justified belief in certain propositions, then the philosopher can give us good reasons to think that such justification exists. The skeptic who wishes to deny that we have such justification can give us good reasons to think that it does not exist. The skeptic, however, also has a fall-back position. Without arguing that we have no noninferentially justified beliefs in propositions about the physical world, the past, other minds, and the future, the skeptic can move "up" a level, and deny that we have any good reason to believe that we have noninferentially justified belief about the existence of noninferential justification for these beliefs. An "access" internalist[17] can move from the proposition that we have no justification for believing that we have a noninferentially justified belief that P to the conclusion that we do not have a noninferentially justified belief that P. But the externalist rejects just such an inference. Even if we abandon strong access internalism, however, we might find skepticism that maintains that we have no justification for believing that we have a justified belief that P just as threatening as skepticism that concludes that we are unjustified in believing P. Before we consider the question of whether skepticism will arise at the next level up within naturalistic epsitemology, let us briefly discuss the naturalist's approach to skeptical issues involving inferential justification.

SKEPTICISM, NATURALISTIC EPISTEMOLOGY, AND INFERENTIAL JUSTIFICATION

Most of the general observations made about the naturalist's response to skeptical challenges concerning the class of noninferentially justified beliefs will apply as well to inferential justification. If the skeptic were to suc-ceed in convincing the naturalist that we are not noninferentially justified in believing propositions about the physical world, for example, the naturalist will presumably argue that such beliefs are inferentially justified. The reliabilist, for example, would argue that if our beliefs about the external world result from input that includes beliefs about the internal and external conditions of perceiving, or even beliefs about the qualitative character of sensation, the relevant belief-dependent processes are conditionally reliable and therefore produce (inferentially) justified beliefs *provided that the input beliefs are themselves justified.* The proviso is crucial, of course, and reminds us that to establish that first-level skepticism is false, the reliabilist who concedes that the justification is inferential in character must establish the existence of at least one unconditionally reliable process and at least one conditionally reliable process.

We noted in discussing the naturalist's views about noninferentially justified belief that the naturalistic epistemology has a potentially significant advantage in dealing with skepticism precisely because there are no restrictions on how large the class of noninferentially justified beliefs might be. As I indicated, there is no *a priori* reason for the naturalist to deny even that we have noninferentially justified beliefs about the past and the future. Evolution might have taken care of us rather well when it comes to reaching true conclusions about the world, and evolution might have accomplished this end without burdening our brains with too many conditionally reliable belief-forming processes. Nozick's tracking relations can in principle hold between any fact and any belief, and the tracking relations *need* not involve any intermediate beliefs.

Just as the naturalist's class of noninferentially justified beliefs can be very large in comparison to those recognized by traditional foundationalists, so the class of inferences recognized as legitimate by the naturalist can be equally large. Consider again the reliabilist's position. There are no *a priori* restrictions on how many different kinds of conditionally reliable belief-dependent processes there might be. Valid deductive inferences are presumably the paradigm of a conditionally reliable belief-dependent process. Classical enumerative induction may satisfy the requirements as well provided that we find some suitably restricted characterization of the inductive "process" that succeeds in denoting and that takes care of grue/green riddles of induction.[18] I suspect most naturalists will be reluctant to include perceptual beliefs among the beliefs produced by belief-dependent processes, but there is no reason why a reliabilist could not be a sense-datum theorist or an appearing theorist who holds that we do have at least dispositional beliefs about the qualitative character of sensation and who further holds that such beliefs are processed by conditionally reliable belief-dependent processes that churn out commonsense beliefs about the physical world. In short, take any kind of inference that people actually make and the reliabilist could hold that it is a conditionally reliable belief-dependent process. All one needs to do is to formulate a description of the process that takes the beliefs one relies on as premises (the input) and produces the beliefs that constitute the conclusion (the output). The description will have to be such that we succeed in picking out a *kind* of process that does play the causal role described, but it will not need to involve any reference to the "hardware" of the brain. Indeed we can try to *denote* the relevant process by directly referring only to the kind of premises and conclusion with which it is associated. Roughly the idea is that we can try to denote a belief-dependent process *X*, for example, using the description "the process (whatever it is) that takes premises like these and churns out conclusions like this." Of course, such a description is probably too vague to do the trick. The locution "like these" can hardly be said to characterize precisely enough a class of premises. One would need to characterize the relevant points of similarity to have a well-defined class of premises which could then enter into the definite descriptions denoting the process that takes them as input.

If we consider any argument someone actually makes there will be indefinitely many classes of propositions to which the premises and the conclusion belong, and that will enable us to formulate any number of different descriptions of belief-forming processes. This is *not* a difficulty for the reliabilist, for as long as we have a locution that succeeds in denoting a process playing a causal role, we can use counterfactuals to define conditional reliability. The fact that a single inference might be subsumed under a number of different reliable belief-dependent processes is hardly a problem. If the inference can be subsumed under the description of both a reliable and an unreliable process, the crucial question will be the process that is causally determining the production of a belief. Thus if someone trustworthy tells me today that it rained in New York, I can describe this as a case of processing testimony to reach a conclusion about the truth of what is testified to, or I can describe it as a case of taking a statement I hear involving the name "New York" and believing all of the noun clauses containing that name. The former, let us suppose, is a reliable belief-dependent process while the latter is not. But you will recall that in formulating descriptions of processes appealing to kinds of premises and conclusions we are merely *hoping* to denote some process (presumably a complex brain process) that does take input and causally produce output beliefs. It does not follow, of course, that every definite description we formulate will succeed in denoting. In the hypothetical situation we are discussing, it may be that there is no programming in the brain that takes the "New York" input and processes it in the way described. If there is nothing denoted by the description playing the relevant causal role then we do not need to worry about the fact that such a process *if used* would be unreliable. And we do not need to worry about the fact that we describe the inference in question *as if* it involved a belief-forming process of the sort described. If someone is programmed in such a way that he sometimes makes the legitimate "testimony" inference and sometimes makes the bizarre "New York" inference, the justificatory status of the resulting belief will be a function of the process that was causally operative in this case. If both processes are operating simultaneously the reliabilist will probably need something like Nozick's conception of one method outweighing another. The justificatory status of the belief will depend on which belief-forming mechanism would have prevailed had they conflicted.

To emphasize the point made earlier, according to paradigm naturalists there are indefinitely many candidates for legitimate inferential processes. There are no *a priori* restrictions on how many conditionally reliable belief-dependent processes might be operating in normal human beings. There are no *a priori* restrictions on how many belief-dependent tracking relations might exist between beliefs and the facts that they track. Furthermore, just as in the case of the noninferential justification, the question of which inferential processes generate justified beliefs for the naturalist will be a purely contingent fact of a sort inaccessible to most philosophers. The existence of conditionally reliable processes, tracking relations, and the like, is something that could be discovered only as a result of empirical investigation into causal relations. Philosophers are not trained to engage in this sort of empirical investigation.

NATURALISM, NORMATIVE EPISTEMOLOGY, AND THE LIMITS OF PHILOSOPHY

Based on the observations above, I would argue that if paradigm naturalist/externalist metaepistemologies are correct, then normative epistemology is an inappropriate subject matter for philosophy. Philosophers as they are presently trained have no special *philosophical* expertise enabling them to reach conclusions about which beliefs are or are not justified. Since the classic issues of skepticism fall under normative epistemology, it follows that if naturalism were correct, philosophers should simply stop addressing the questions raised by the skeptic. The complex causal conditions that determine the presence or absence of justification for a belief are the subject matter of empirical investigations that would take the philosopher out of the easy chair and into the laboratory.

The realization that a good part of the history of epistemology becomes irrelevant to contemporary philosophy if we become metaepistemological naturalists might cause a good many philosophers to reconsider the view. I have always found the skeptical challenge to be fascinating and it has always seemed to me that I can address the relevant issues from my armchair. If I had wanted to go mucking around in the brain trying to figure out the causal mechanisms that hook up various stimuli with belief I would have gone into neurophysiology.

To rely on the philosopher's interest in skepticism and penchant for armchair philosophy as a rhetorical device to recruit wavering naturalists, however, might be viewed as a new low in the art of philosophical persuasion. The mere fact that philosophers have been preoccupied with a certain sort of question does not mean that they were qualified to answer it. There are all kinds of perfectly respectable candidates for misguided philosophical investigations. Many philosophers, for example, have taken the question of whether every event has a cause to be a deep metaphysical issue in philosophy. As a good Humean, I would be the first to argue that it is a purely contingent question and if one wants to know the answer to it, one should not go asking a philosopher. I am also sympathetic to the less popular view advanced by the positivists that metaethics exhausts the appropriate domain for philosophical investigation into morality. If a consequentialist analysis of right and wrong action is correct, for example, questions about what kinds of actions, or particular actions, we ought to perform are very complicated causal questions. Even if philosophy gives us some special insight into what is intrinsically good and bad (a thesis that is itself highly dubious), the question of which action would maximize that which is intrinsically good and minimize that which is intrinsically bad is the kind of question that philosophers are not particularly competent to address. The kind of person who is good at figuring out the consequences of actions if the kind of person who has extensive "worldly" experience and good common sense. Perhaps philosophers of the past who were so preoccupied with normative issues in ethics had that kind of experience, but without denigrating my profession, I would humbly submit that today's academic is not the kind of person to whom one should turn for advice in dealing with real-world problems. The ivory towers of the philosophy professor are anathema to the kind of experience one needs to reach reasonable conclusions about what the world would look like if we behaved one way rather than another.

The question of whether normative ethics is a legitimate area of philosophy is far too controversial to settle with a few glib remarks. My only interest here is to point out that the history of philosophy need not constrain us when it comes to reaching conclusions about the appropriate subject matter of philosophy. Philosophers have worried about fundamental normative questions of ethics for well over two thousand years. That need not stop a philosopher from presenting a respectable argument for the conclusion that philosophical concern with ethics ends with the successful analysis of the subject matter of moral judgments. If one wants to do normative ethics in addition to metaethics, one will need to do the kind of empirical work that contemporary philosophers have not been trained to do. Analogously, the fact that philosophers have been preoccupied with the skeptical challenge for literally thousands of years should not stop contemporary epistemologists from entertaining the thesis that the appropriate subject matter of epistemology ends with metaepistemology. After the metaepistemological analysis is complete, the naturalist might argue, the only way to answer normative questions in epistemology is to engage in the kind of empirical investigation that contemporary philosophers have not been trained *by philosophy* to do.

I suggested in some of my introductory comments that contemporary metaepistemological debate has the potential to change the very face of the philosophical study of epistemology. Specifically, I want to argue that if any of the paradigm naturalistic accounts of knowledge and justification are correct, we should dismiss all skeptical inquiry as irrelevant to the subject matter of philosophy. If the naturalist is right, philosophers should stop doing normative epistemology.

In reaching this conclusion I should be careful to admit that the naturalistic epistemologist can, of course, embed normative epistemological conclusions in the consequents of conditional assertions. One can talk about what one would be justified in believing were certain conditions to obtain. But these conditionals are still part of metaepistemology. Indeed, such conditionals are merely a way of illustrating the consequences of metaepistemological positions as they apply to particular hypothetical situations. A Nozick can, for example, discuss what one would or would not know about the external world *if* a tracking analysis of knowledge were correct and *if* our beliefs about the physical world track the facts that would make them true. Nozick's analysis of knowledge also has the interesting feature that we can apparently determine *a priori* that we do *not* know certain things, for example, that we do not know that there is no evil demon deceiving us. But there will be no positive normative claim with respect to empirical knowledge that Nozick is particularly competent to make *qua philosopher*. As we shall see in a moment, naturalism does not prevent a philosopher from reaching rational conclusions about what one is justified in believing. My conclusion is only that a philosopher's philosophical expertise is nothing that would help in reaching such conclusions. To illustrate this claim more clearly, let us turn to the question of whether naturalistic epistemology suggests that one should be a skeptic about whether or not one has justified belief.

SECOND-LEVEL SKEPTICISM, AND THE FUNDAMENTAL PROBLEM WITH NATURALISM

It is tempting to think that naturalistic analyses of justified or rational belief and knowledge simply remove one *level* of the traditional problems of skepticism. When one reads Quine, Goldman, Nozick, Armstrong, or Dretske one is surely inclined to wonder why they are so sanguine about their supposition that our commonsense beliefs are, for the most part, justified, if not knowledge. When Nozick, for example, stresses that interesting feature of his account allowing us to conclude consistently that we know that we see the table even though we do not know that there is no demon deceiving us, we must surely wonder *why* he is so confident that the subjunctives which on his view are sufficient for knowledge are true. Perception, memory, and induction *may* be reliable processes in Goldman's sense, and thus given his metaepistemological position we *may* be justified in having the beliefs they produce, but, the skeptic can argue, we have no reason to believe that these processes *are* reliable and thus even if we accept reliabilism, we have no reason to conclude that the beliefs they produce are justified.

In the previous section I have emphasized that if naturalistic epistemology is correct then philosophers *qua philosophers* may not be particularly competent to answer normative questions in epistemology. I did *not* assert that if the view is true we have no reason to believe that we have justified belief in commonsense truths about the world around us. According to naturalistic epistemologies it is a purely contingent question as to what kinds of beliefs are justified. The existence of justified beliefs depends on nomological features of the world—facts about the reliability of belief-producing processes, the existence of tracking relations, causal connections between facts and beliefs, and the like. There are no *a priori* restrictions on what one might be justified in believing. But it *follows* from this that there are also *no a priori* restrictions on second-level knowledge or justified belief. It will also be a purely contingent question as to whether we have knowledge of knowledge or justified beliefs about justified beliefs. If we accept the naturalist's metaepistemological views it *may* be true that not only do we know what we think we know, but we know that we know these things. Similarly we may have not only all the justified beliefs we think we have, but we might also be justified in believing that we have these justified beliefs. The processes that yield beliefs about reliable processes may themselves be reliable. The beliefs about the truth of the subjunctives that Nozick uses to define first-level knowledge might themselves be embedded in true subjunctive conditionals that, *given the metaepistemological view,* are sufficient for second-level knowledge. My belief that my belief that P tracks the fact that P might track the fact that my belief that P tracks the fact that P. And there is no greater problem in principle when we move up levels. A reliable process might produce a belief that a reliable process produced the belief that my belief that P was produced by a reliable process. There might be a tracking relation tracking the tracking relation that tracks the fact that my belief that P tracks the fact that P. To be sure the sentences describing the conditions for higher levels of metajustification might look more like tonguetwisters than metaepistemological analyses but, as ugly as they are, they are perfectly intelligible, and there is no *a priori* reason why the conditions required for higher-level justified belief and knowledge might not be satisfied.

It is also important to note that, according to most naturalists, in order to be justified in believing that I have a justified belief that P I need not know anything about the *details* of the nomological connections sufficient for knowledge. Consider again reliabilism. In order to be justified in believing that my belief that P is produced by a reliable process, I do not need to know the physiological details of the brain states linking stimuli and belief. I would need to believe that there is *some* process producing the belief and I would need to believe that the process is reliable, but I would not need to know very much about what that process is. As I indicated earlier, one can denote the processes that produce beliefs using definite descriptions that refer directly only to the kinds of premises and conclusions that are linked by the process. Of course the definite descriptions might fail to denote, and the beliefs in propositions expressed using such definite descriptions will either be false or meaningless (depending on what one does with the truth value of statements containing definite descriptions that fail to denote). But the descriptions might be successful, and in any event the belief that there is a reliable process taking stimuli S and resulting in belief P might itself be produced by a reliable process.

All this talk about what would be in principle possible given a naturalistic metaepistemology is fine, the skeptic might argue. But *how* exactly would one justify one's belief that, say, perception or memory are reliable processes? The rather startling and, I think disconcerting, answer is that *if* reliabilism, for example, is true, and *if* perception happens to be reliable, we could *perceive* various facts about our sense organs and the way in which they respond to the external world. Again, *if* reliabilism is true, and *if* memory is reliable, we could use memory, in part, to justify our belief that memory is reliable. You want a solution to the problem of induction. There is potentially no difficulty for the naturalistic epistemologist. If reliabilism is true, and if inductive inference is a conditionally reliable belief-dependent process, then we can inductively justify the reliability of inductive inference. Our inductive justification for the reliability of inductive inference might itself be reliable and if it is that will give us second-level justification that our inductive conclusions are justified. A solution to the problem of induction will be important because with induction giving us inferentially justified conclusions, we can use inductive inference with the deliverances of perception and memory to justify our belief that those processes are reliable. I can remember, for example, that I remembered putting my keys on the desk and I can remember the keys being on the desk. If memory is an unconditionally reliable belief-independent process, then both my belief that I remembered putting the keys on the desk and my belief that I put the keys on the desk will be justified. I now have a premise that can be used as part of an inductive justification for memory being reliable. The more occasions on which I can remember memory being reliable the stronger my inductive argument will be for the general reliability of memory.

The skeptic could not figure out how to get from sensations to the physical world. Assume that perception is itself a belief-independent uncon-ditionally reliable process. Assume also that whatever perception involves its specification involves reference to sensation, and assume further that we have "introspective" access to sensation. Introspective access might itself be another belief-independent, unconditionally reliable process. Given these suppositions, if reliabilism is true, then introspection can give us justified belief that we are perceiving, and perception can give us justified belief that a physical object is present. The two reliable processes together can furnish a premise that when combined with others generated in a similar fashion give us inductive justification for believing that perception is reliable. So if both introspection and perception happen to be reliable there seems to be no great obstacle to obtaining justified belief that they are reliable. Second-level justified belief is not much more difficult to get than first-level justified belief.

The above is quite in keeping with Quine's original injunction to natu-ralize epistemology.[19] Quine suggested that we give ourselves full access to the deliverances and methods of science when it comes to understanding how we have knowledge of the world around us. Contemporary naturalists have simply given us more detailed metaepistemological views which allow us to rationalize following Quine's advice. If the mere reliability of a process, for example, is sufficient to give us justified belief, then *if* that process is reliable we can use it to get justified belief wherever and whenever we like.

None of this, of course, will make the skeptic happy. You cannot *use* perception to justify the reliability of perception! You cannot *use* memory to justify the reliability of memory! You cannot *use* induction to justify the reliability of induction! Such attempts to respond to the skeptic's concerns involve blatant, indeed pathetic, circularity. Frankly, this does seem right to *me* and I hope it seems right to *you* but *if* it does then I would suggest that you have a powerful reason to reject naturalistic epistemology. I would suggest that, ironically, the very ease with which these naturalists can deal with the skeptical challenge at the next level betrays the ultimate implausibility of the view as an attempt to explicate concepts that are of *philosophical* interest. If a philosopher starts wondering about the reliability of astrological inference, the philosopher will not allow the astrologer to read in the stars the reliability of astrology. Even if astrological inferences happen to be reliable, the astrologer is missing the point of a philosophical inquiry into the justifiability of astrological inference if the inquiry is answered using the techniques of astrology. The problem is perhaps most acute if one thinks about first-person philosophical reflection about justification. If I really am interested in knowing whether astrological inference is legitimate, if I have the kind of philosophical curiosity that leads me to raise this question in the first place, I will not for a moment suppose that further use of astrology might help me find the answer to my question. Similarly, if as a philosopher I start wondering whether perceptual beliefs are accurate reflections of the way the world really is, I would not dream of using perception to resolve my doubt. Even if there is some sense in which the reliable process of perception might yield justified beliefs about the reliability of perception, the use of perception could never satisfy a *philosophical curiosity* about the legitimacy of perceptual beliefs. When the philosopher wants an answer to the question of whether memory gives us justified beliefs about the past, that answer cannot possibly be provided by memory.

Again, if one raises skeptical concerns understanding fundamental epistemic concepts as the naturalist does, then there should be no objection to perceptual justifications of perception, inductive justifications of induction, and reliance on memory to justify the use of memory. If we are understanding epistemic concepts as the reliabilist suggests, for example, then one can have no objection in principle to the use of a process to justify its use. After all, paradigm naturalists are access externalists and explicity deny the necessity of having access to the probabilistic relationship between premises and conclusion in order to have an inferentially justified belief. The mere reliability of the process is sufficient to generate justified belief in the conclusion of an argument. There is no conceptual basis for the reliabilist to get cold feet when epistemological questions are raised the next level up. Either reliability alone is sufficient or it is not. If it is, then it is sufficient whether one is talking about justification for believing *P* or justification for believing that one has a justified belief that *P*.

The above objection to paradigm naturalistic epistemologies can be easily summarized. If we understand epistemic concepts as the naturalist suggests we do, then there would be no objection in principle to using perception to justify reliance on perception, memory to justify reliance on memory, and induction to justify reliance on induction. But there is no philosophically interesting concept of justification or knowledge which would allow us to use a process to justify the legitimacy of using that process. Therefore the naturalist has failed to analyze a philosophically interesting concept of justification or knowledge.

The objection is by no means decisive. Obviously, many will bite the bullet and happily embrace Quine's recommendation to naturalize epistemology. If the argument convinces anyone it will be those who were initially inclined to suppose that paradigm naturalists and externalists will inevitably encounter skepticism at the next level up. Maybe we have knowledge or justified belief as the naturalist understands these concepts, some would argue, but we would never be in a position to know that we have knowledge or justified belief if the naturalist is right. The only reason I can see for granting the first possibility, but denying the second, is that one is implicitly abandoning a naturalistic understanding of epistemic concepts as one moves to questions about knowledge or justification at the next level. But if when one gets philosophically "serious" one abandons a naturalist's understanding of epistemic concepts, then for philosophical purposes one should not even concede the naturalist's understanding of epsitemic concepts at the first level. Once you concede that according to the naturalist we might have knowledge or justified belief about the past and the external world, you have also implicitly conceded that we might have knowledge that we have such knowledge, justified belief that we have such justified belief. And we might also have knowledge that we have knowledge that we have knowledge, and have justified beliefs that we have justified beliefs that we have justified beliefs. It seems to many of us that naturalistic epistemology is simply missing the point of the philosophical inquiry when their analyses of epistemic concepts continue to be presupposed as the skeptical challenge is repeated at the metalevels. But the only explanation for this is that the naturalist's analysis of epistemic concepts never was adequate to a philosophical understanding of epistemic concepts.

NOTES

1. I refer, of course, to causal theories of reference which take the items capable of referring to include both linguistic and mental entities.

2. Armstrong (1973).

3. See, for example, Armstrong (1983) and Fales (1990).

4. Quine (1969).

5. I am trying to avoid here a detailed characterization of either naturalism, externalism, or the relation between the views. I have argued elsewhere (Fumerton, 1988 and 1993) that one should distinguish a *number* of quite different versions of externalism, but that it is plausible to simply identify one sense of externalism with a commitment to the kind of nomological analyses of epistemic concepts that I have called here naturalistic. Other senses of externalism have more to do with "access" requirements for the conditions that constitute knowledge and justified belief.

6. By characterizing normative epistemology this way I hope that I make it clear that the label "normative" is not meant to imply that the questions can be reduced to questions of value theory. I have argued that it is a serious mistake to think that epistemology has much in common with ethics (see Fumerton 1993).

7. As I indicated above, naturalistic epistemology could be understood in terms of the vaguer suggestions that we use science to answer traditional epistemological questions. But

I think it best to reserve the term for the analysis of epistemic concepts that allows one consistently to follow the suggestion.

8. An epistemically self-refuting position is one which if true would entail that one has no reason to believe that it is true.

9. In both the realist and empiricist tradition, at least some propositions about the content of one's current mental states were taken to have this unproblematic, noninferential character.

10. On Nozick's tracking analysis of knowledge (1981), beliefs can clearly track facts without relying on any intermediate beliefs and we can again call these beliefs noninferentially justified. Armstrong (1973) explicitly distinguishes basic beliefs from other sorts of justified beliefs.

11. For a defense of such a view see Fumerton (1985) and (1993).

12. For a detailed defense of this last view see Fumerton (1985).

13. I stress "*qua* philosopher" for there is a real danger that I will be misunderstood on this point. I will argue that the kind of naturalism discussed here is perfectly compatible with philosophers (and anyone else) having justified beliefs and having justified beliefs about whether or not they have justified beliefs. It will not, however, be their philosophical competence that yields such justification.

14. As I shall argue shortly, this claim might be misleading. In one sense the detailed character of belief-forming processes would be best discovered by neurophysiologists. But there is another sense in which anyone can form beliefs about such processes even without any detailed knowledge of how the brain works.

15. The terminology is, of course, from Chisholm (1957), 50–53.

16. It should go without saying that there may be causally necessary conditions for the existence of such noninferential justification having to do with the capacity to form other beliefs. The dependency that concerns us, however, is logical. Justification is noninferential when no other belief is a *constituent* of the justification.

17. By "access" internalist, I mean a philosopher who holds that X can constitute S's justification for believing P only if S has access to the fact that X obtains. Most naturalists will reject access internalism (although I have argued that it is not obvious that their naturalism prevents them from accepting the view—see Fumerton [1988]).

18. The allusion is, of course, to the problem discussed in N. Goodman (1955), chap. 3.

19. Quine (1969), chap. 3.

REFERENCES

Armstrong, David. 1973. *Belief, Truth and Knowledge*. London.
———. 1983. *What is a Law of Nature*. London.
Chisholm, Roderick. 1957. *Perceiving*. Ithaca, N.Y.
Fales, Evan. 1990. *Causation and Universals*. London.
Fumerton, Richard. 1985. *Metaphysical and Epistemological Problems of Perception*. Lincoln, Neb.
———. 1988. "The Internalism/Externalism Controversy." In *Philosophical Perspectives 2: Epistemology*, edited by Toberlin. Atascadero, Calif.
———. 1993. *Metaepistemology and Skepticism*. Unpublished manuscript.
Goldman, Alvin. 1979. "What is Justified Belief?" In *Justification and Knowledge*, edited by Pappas. Dordrecht.
Goodman, Nelson. 1955. *Fact, Fiction and Forecast*. Indianapolis.
Nozick, Robert. 1981. *Philosophical Explanations*. Cambridge, Mass.
Quine, W. V. 1969. *Ontological Relativity and Other Essays*. New York.

Epistemology Naturalized and "Epistemology Naturalized"

RICHARD E. GRANDY

The phrase "epistemology naturalized" is habitually associated with Quine's (1969) essay of that title, though the concept of naturalism is very explicit and thorough in Ernest Nagel, Morris R. Cohen, John Dewey, and other earlier philosophers. In fact, if I were a historian of an earlier period, rather than the 1960s, I would perhaps argue that Locke was attempting to naturalize epistemology as he understood it, or, more accurately as he would have understood it if he had the concept of epistemology.

The most famous passage of Quine's essay deserves to be quoted in full for my main topic is the relation between epistemology, psychology, and the other cognitive sciences. I shall argue for a much broader construal of epistemology naturalized than that in "Epistemology Naturalized."

> Carnap and the other logical positivists of the Vienna Circle had already pressed the term "metaphysics" into pejorative use, as connoting meaninglessness; and the term "epistemology" was next. Wittgenstein and his followers, mainly at Oxford, found a residual philosophical vocation in therapy: in curing philosophers of the delusion that there were epistemological problems.

> But I think at this point it may be more useful to say rather that epistemology still goes on, though in a new setting and a clarified status. Epistemology, or something like it, simply falls into place as a chapter of psychology and hence of natural science. (1969, p. 82)

Which chapter of what psychology does epistemology become? Kornblith (1985, p. 1) structures the discussion around three questions:

1. How ought we to arrive at our beliefs?
2. How do we arrive at our beliefs?
3. Are the processes by which we arrive at our beliefs the ones by which we ought to arrive at our beliefs?

Kornblith then distinguishes two theses about the relation between epistemology and psychology, which he calls strong replacement and weak replacement. On the strong replacement thesis, unemployment is inevitable for epistemologists since "psychological questions hold all the content there is in epistemological questions. On this view psychology replaces epistemology in much the same way that chemistry has replaced alchemy" (6).

One question I want to press is which chapter of what psychology epistemology is to become. Quine's answer was Skinnerian behaviorism. "This human subject is accorded a certain experimentally controlled input—certain patterns of irradiation in assorted frequencies, for instance—and in the fullness of time the subjected delivers as output a description of the three-dimensional external world and its history" (82–83). Personally, I doubt that anyone, except Carnap in *Der Logische Aufbau der Welt* (1928), has ever delivered as output a description of the external world and its history.

To put things into clearer perspective, let us consider some of the questions epistemology currently asks: For example, if we consider the Gettier/Goldman cases about knowledge in a case where George sees a red barn, but unknown to him there are many fake barns in the neighborhood, and his traveling companion was about to tell him about the fake barns. So instead of consulting our intuitions imagine that we send over to the psychology department the question whether George knows there is a red barn. I do not know of any department that is currently researching this kind of question. Or imagine asking the psychology department whether I am a brain in a vat—in this case the answer would be a plain, but unhelpful, "No." And if we ask instead how I know I am not a brain in a vat, the answer is likely to be a referral to psychiatry.

Perhaps this parody is unfair. But this strongly suggests that on whatever version of convergence or elimination one adopts, not all of epistemology is naturalizable, a point that was made by Stroud (1981). If epistemology is really at root all about skepticism, then none of the core will be naturalizable. I do not want to argue over the history or the core of epistemology, but hope to show that there are enough philosophically interesting problems in naturalized epistemology that it is worth pursuing regardless of how one ultimately delineates the historical connections.

Let us return to the questions Kornblith posed, with my editorial emphasis:

> How *ought* we to arrive at our beliefs? How *do* we arrive at our beliefs? How well do the processes by which we *do* arrive at our beliefs match the ones by which we *ought* to arrive at our beliefs?

I do not think that contemporary cognitive psychology is yet prepared to provide much information beyond fairly elementary domains about how we do arrive at our beliefs. Consider my colleague's belief that the sun will rise on July 4, 1994. He has lived long enough that a straight induction would not be unreasonable, and he is a philosopher of science so he knows what the straight rule of induction is. He also has sufficient knowledge of astronomy that he could give a theoretical backing to the claim, as well as an unpacking of the mistaken, or misleading, semantics of "sunrise." But he almost certainly formed the belief long before any of these was the case. And, of course, we are abstracting from the fact that although he would undoubtedly assent to this statement, it has almost certainly never occupied his conscious attention yet.

The fact is that psychologists, having practical goals such as publishing, have a strong preference for answerable questions—whereas philosophers generally, and epistemologists in particular, are prone to be concerned with questions which do not have direct experimental answers. They tend very much, therefore to pay attention to beliefs that have been formed in the recent past in situations that they have (attempted to) experimentally control and about which the subject had no prior beliefs. As part of the design, typical experiments eliminate any doubt in the experimenters' mind about what is true *ab initio*.

I agree with Quine that there are no natural boundaries between philosophy and psychology, but at present there is a largely uninhabited and unexplored area where the two interact only minimally, though there is potential for considerably more cooperation. Some philosophical pioneers in this regard are Goldman (1986) and Bach (1984). The main reason that I believe that epistemology would have much to learn from psychology if psychologists knew more about belief formation is that I believe that in epistemology as in ethics ought implies can. Epistemic agents cannot and ought not be faulted on the grounds that they did not follow epistemic strategies which are not cognitively possible for them. Among the older injunctions which fall into this category is "Make sure your beliefs are consistent," for there is no general decision procedure for consistency. Thus the simple natural division of labor in Kornblith's scheme which assigns problem (1) to psychology and (2) to philosophy does not work because of the empirical elements of (2).

We are natural creatures, and the process of belief formation, knowledge acquisition, etcetera, are natural processes and can be studied by scientific methods. Note that I intend "scientific methods" to be taken broadly and I believe that one of the major tools of science is mathematics. Many naturalists are physicalists, but I regard it as an open question how naturalism will ultimately deal with questions in the philosophy of mathematics. Certainly Quine's view that (some proper subset of) extant mathematics is to be accepted because it is necessary for physics is a matter of rational construction of our overall view, and does not bear, nor is it intended to bear, any connection to the way we form our mathematical beliefs.

As natural creatures, we have some continuities with other species, though there are evidently very significant discontinuities too. This is yet one more angle from which to argue for the importance of images and other non-linguistic processing, as well as the centrality of non-conscious processing. Many of our intuitive natural language judgments about epistemic matters tend to be too coarse grained. For example, we tend to dichotomize remembering and not remembering. But there is an extensive literature on 'implicit memory', the characteristic of which is that subjects show evidence in various ways of previous exposure to material even though they cannot recall it on request.

For example, subjects may be shown a list of words to remember. At a suitably later time they are asked to recall as many as they can. The important task though consists of subsequently completing word fragments. Subjects show a consistently higher ability to complete word fragments with words which they have seen on the list but could not recall in comparison to fragments which can only be completed with words not on the list. For example, if "donkey" was on the list (but not remembered) while "rabbit" was not on the list, then more subjects successfully complete the word fragment "d__k_y" than complete "r__b_t" (Kolers and Roediger, 1984). The conclusion seems to be that memory is not a unitary phenomenon, but is dependent on the kind of task required as well as the kind of original exposure.

The cognitive perspective tends to be that we are information processors, which tends to overlook, or at least to deemphasize, the fact that we are ambulatory and goal directed. I regard it as preferable instead to think of us as information hunters, gatherers, and processors. Since computers have been the dominant model in most of cognitive science, it is not surprising that there is a very strong emphasis on the processing of information, to the neglect, I argue, of the importance of how we acquire the information and what we do with it.

This point may suggest a strong affinity with evolutionary epistemology. While something of importance may yet emerge from this general line of thought, almost all of the arguments which have been produced thus far under that rubric make little or no real use of the fact of evolution. At a conference on the topic at the University of Pittsburgh in 1989, an analysis of the papers seemed to show that the arguments about the appropriateness of our beliefs or our belief-forming mechanisms were only slightly diminished if one substituted the supposition that our species had survived intact in an indifferent environment for six millennia rather than several hundred thousand years.

Returning closer to our opening line of discussion, Quine's own formulation of the argument for naturalizing epistemology is flawed, in my opinion, by his insistence on identifying evidence with a class of sentences. This is related to an objection by Jonathan Dancy (1985) specifically to Quine's claim that there is a contrast between "the meager input and torrential output" (83) of the subject.

> there is no contrast between meagre and torrential. The input is (together with other things) sufficient to cause the brain states which are its effects, and in following this causal story we are not any more studying a gap between input and output, if that gap is thought of as analogous to the gap between evidence and theory. (238)

This is an important issue for understanding Quinian epistemology, for his full remark ("The relation between the meager input and the torrential output is a relation that we are prompted to study for somewhat the same reasons that always prompted epistemology; namely in order to see how evidence relates to theory") certainly suggests a conflation of causal and evidential relations. A neo-Quinian might respond that the output depends on brainstate, or on the previous history of the subject as well, and one can discuss Duhemianism in the brain.

Rather than explore Quinian options here, I want instead to contrast the cognitivist point of view which construes information more broadly. From this perspective the *input* is vast, and the perceptual systems discard most of the information before it moves very far toward the central processing system. From a vast amount of information about what is currently happening at, e.g., the retinal surface, we get (sometimes) a modest amount of information about what is currently happening at a distance, or even about what has or will happen. The function of the perceptual systems is to process the information—since a great deal is redundant or irrelevant, the first level of processing is primarily a matter of finding changes, i.e., edges, motion or color change.

Looked at this way the process is a causal one, but it is the causal embodiment of an information-processing algorithm. There are assumptions about the world, e.g., of continuity and some underlying invariances, a few of which are hardwired and some of which are acquired through early experience. Having interposed this level of explanation in terms of the physical embodiment of algorithms which process the physical representations of information, one can then ask questions about optimality of the algorithms. The most forceful development of this approach is Marr's Vision, and although many details of his specific conclusions may be faulted, the overall approach seems very promising for naturalizing epistemology beyond the perceptual.

Traditional epistemologists may well still be unimpressed, for the conclusions one reaches tend to be hypothetical or conditional—if one has the following goals and these cognitive capacities, then the best you can do is. . . . But I am not certain that we have ever had anything better than such conclusions in traditional epistemology. Notice here that there is a shift in emphasis from questions about formation of individual beliefs to emphasis on the methods by which beliefs are formed in general. Thus the assessment seems to shift somewhat from the product (the belief) to the process (the process by which beliefs of this kind are formed).

Although few psychologists have addressed the questions posed by Kornblith, some, most notably or notoriously Tversky and associates, have addressed the issues and concluded that we often do not form our beliefs as we ought. Having emphasized that epistemology could learn from psychology, I want to raise the, probably unnecessary, caution that we ought not to believe everything our colleagues tell us.

In one experiment, subjects were confronted with two lights, and in each trial one of the two would light. The mechanism was set to randomize whether the left or right light went on, but with a bias so that (depending randomly on the subject) one light went on 70 percent of the time. On average subjects tended in the long run to guess that the more frequent light would be the next to light about 70 percent of the time. This means that they will correctly guess that light .7x.7, or 49 percent of the time; guessing the other light 30 percent of the time will produce a correct response 9 percent (.3x.3) giving a total of 58 percent correct responses. The simpler strategy of *always* guessing the light which had been lit most frequently up to that point would give 70 percent correct and the authors conclude the subjects perform suboptimally (Kahnemann and Tversky 1972).

While this is true, it only shows irrationality or suboptimality if one assumes that the subjects knew, which they did not, that the sequence was random. If one is simply confronted with a sequence without knowing it is random then it is far from clear what is the optimal strategy. Before we can make our judgment as to what strategy for belief formation ought to be used we need to know not only which strategies we can use, but what the set of problems is, what the time constraints for solutions are, what the acceptable error rate is, and the relative value of different answers.

I suspect, and have argued elsewhere (Grandy, 1987), that the many observations that subjects significantly misestimate with very low probabilities may have to do with survival value of not underestimating some risks. On the other hand, I do intend to argue that we are always optimal in our belief formation. The strongest example I know of to the contrary is the conjunction fallacy. In the most familiar example subjects make inconsistent probability judgments about a feminist lawyer. This example, however, allows some explaining away in terms of conversational implicatures or contextual features.

The example I prefer is one in which subjects were given the following task (in early 1981).

> Suppose Bjorn Borg reaches the Wimbledon finals in 1981. Please rank the following outcomes from most likely to least likely.
> Borg will win the match.
> Borg will lose the first set.
> Borg will win the first set but lose the match.
> Borg will lose the first set but win the match.

In this study (Kahnemann and Tversky [1982], 96) 72 percent of the subjects ranked the conjunction "Borg will lose the first set but win the match" as more likely than its first conjunct. It could be argued, of course, that "but" is not interpreted as a simple conjunction in this case, but I find that line of argument much less persuasive in this case than in some others.

Returning to my theme of several pages ago that we are information hunters and gatherers, as well as processors, I would also argue that we are also social animals. Thus the goals of the epistemic process can be dependent on social questions as well as individual ones. It has probably not been sufficiently appreciated that even Quine's behavioristic characterization of observation sentences, the repository of all evidence, has a social dimension.

This is explicit in the formulation in Quine (1969), "an observation sentence is one on which all speakers of the language give the same verdict when given the same concurrent stimulation. To put the point negatively, an observation sentence is one that is not sensitive to differences of past experience within the speech community" (86–87). While it is less obvious that the equivalent definition in *Word and Object* incorporates reference to a community, Quine thinks it worth remarking on the contrast between the concepts of stimulus meaning and of observation sentence. "[T]he notion of stimulus meaning itself, as defined, depends on no multiplicity of speakers. Now the notion of observationality, in contrast, is social" (1962, 44–45).

An alternative way of phrasing what Quine's concept of an observation sentence captures is that those are the sentences where disagreement must come to an end within the linguistic community. The fact that a sentence is in that set is, however, something that is perhaps only known to an outside observer. A different, more usefully internal conception of an observation sentence can be given if we eschew the allegedly austere vocabulary of behaviorism and give a griceful twist to the idea. We can define an observation sentence instead as one about which everyone in the linguistic community believes that everyone in the linguistic community will give the same verdict given the same concurrent stimulation. These sentences and the relevant stimulations could be sought by members of the community as paths to resolving disputes.

It is important to note from a naturalistic perspective, and in this instance perhaps the evolutionary one is helpful, that goals of groups and goals of individuals can be at odds with one another. Survival, or thriving, of a group may be best served by individual behavior which is not optimal for the individual. Here epistemology naturalized may have much to learn from the literature on such topics as prisoner's dilemma.

A natural metaphysical question that arises at this point is whether one sees the group or the individual as the basic unit of analysis and explanation. Two fairly representative but extreme positions are the following:

> What I propose . . . is a much more thoroughgoing contextualism than the one which urges us to remember that scientific inquiry occurs in a social context, or even that scientists are social actors whose interests drive their scientific work. What I urge is a contextualism which understands the cognitive processes of scientific inquiry not as opposed to the social, but as themselves social. This means that normativity, if it is possible at all, must be imposed on social processes and interactions, that is, that the rules or norms of justification that distinguish knowledge (or justified hypothesis-acceptance) from opinion must operate at the level of social as opposed to individual cognitive processes. (Longino, 1992)

In contrast

> The conclusion is simple. The most promising approach to a general theory of science is one that takes individual scientists as the basic units of analysis. It follows that we must look to the cognitive sciences for our most basic models, for it is these sciences that currently produce the

best causal models of the cognitive activities of individual human agents. (Giere, 1989)

The view I am advocating accepts neither model, but sees the continuing dynamic interaction between group and individuals as critical. It is essential to see that although a group is in a sense constituted at a given time by a set of individuals, as a group changes over time members are attracted to the group or become part of it because of the properties of the group as a whole. The group, and the perception of the group, shape the cognitive behavior of those who join it. Moreover, epistemic evaluation seems appropriate for both individual and group processes, although the units and the measure of evaluation differ.

Let me emphasize again that from a naturalistic perspective true beliefs are not necessarily an end in themselves but a means to the ends of the agent. For some agents true beliefs about a subject, e.g., prime numbers, may be an end in itself. But for many agents the beliefs are instrumental to some other end. Thus the goal is not necessarily maximizing the number of true beliefs, that could be done by correctly identifying blades of grass or calculating whether numbers are prime, but to maximize the usefulness of beliefs. True beliefs, or perhaps even probable beliefs, about important issues may be more important than more probable beliefs about less important issues.

This point leads to one criticism I would make of the fine survey "The Naturalists Return" by Kitcher (1992). While I agree with most of his delineation of recent naturalists, I have reservations about his list of basic theses of naturalized epistemology. His third principle is:

(3) The central epistemological project is to be carried out by describing processes that are reliable in the sense that they would have a high frequency of generating epistemically virtuous states in human beings in our world. (75–76)

I do not see why a naturalist needs to be committed to this narrow sense of virtue—less reliable beliefs about necessities may be more important than highly reliable beliefs about other matters. The central epistemological project would rather, on my account, be one of finding the most reliable methods of providing the important information at a reasonable cost in time and effort. In some circumstances, e.g., at the frontiers of new subjects, or in the difficult regions of old ones, there may be no strategies that are very reliable, but some may still be judged epistemically preferable![1]

NOTE

1. Earlier versions of this essay were read to the Philosophy Department Colloquium at Rice University and as the 1983 George Myro Memorial Lecture at UC-Berkeley. I am indebted to members of both audiences for helpful comments.

REFERENCES

Bach, K. 1984. "Default Reasoning: Jumping to Conclusions and Knowing When to Think Twice." *Pacific Philosophical Quarterly* 65:37–58.

Carnap, R. 1928. *Der Logische Aufbau der Welt*. Berlin.

Dancy, J. 1985. *Introduction to Contemporary Epistemology*. Oxford.

Giere, R. 1989. "The Units of Analysis in Science Studies." In *The Cognitive Turn*, edited by S. Fuller et al. Dordrecht.

Grandy, R. 1987. "Information-based Epistemology, Ecological Epistemology and Epistemology Naturalized." *Syntheses* 70:191–204.

Goldman, A. 1986. *Epistemology and Cognition*. Cambridge, Mass.

Kahnemann, D., and A. Tversky. 1972. *On Prediction and Judgement*. ORI Research Monograph.

Kahnemann, D., P. Slovic, and A. Tversky. 1982. Eds. *Judgment under Uncertainty: Heuristics and Biases*. Cambridge.

Kitcher, P. 1992. "The Naturalists Return" *Philosophical Review* 101:53–114.

Kolers, P., and H. Roediger, III. 1984. "Procedures of Mind." *Journal of Verbal Learning and Verbal Behavior* 23:425–49.

Kornblith, H. 1985. Ed. *Naturalizing Epistemology*. Cambridge, Mass.

Longino, H. 1992. "Essential Tensions–Phase Two: Feminist, Philosophical and Social Studies of Science." In *The Social Dimensions of Science*, edited by E. McMullin. Notre Dame, Ind.

Quine, W. V. 1962. *Word and Object*. Cambridge, Mass.

———. 1969. "Epistemology Naturalized." In *Ontological Relativity and Other Essays*. New York.

Stroud, B. 1981. "The Significance of Epistemology Naturalized." *Midwest Studies in Philosophy* 6:455–71.

Tversky, A., and D. Kahnemann. 1982. "Judgements of and by Representativeness." In *Judgement under Uncertainty*, edited by D. Kahnemann et al. Cambridge.

MIDWEST STUDIES IN PHILOSOPHY, XIX (1994)

Epistemology Denatured

MARK KAPLAN

I

If it was not already obvious from the reception of Alvin Goldman's work on justification in the last fifteen years or so,[1] if it was not already patent in the success of *Naturalizing Epistemology*, Hilary Kornblith's collection of papers (now in its second edition),[2] then the appearance of Philip Kitcher's "The Naturalists Return," in the centenary issue of the *Philosophical Review*[3] has made it abundantly clear: naturalist accounts of epistemic justification are very much in vogue.

That this should be so is doubtless due in part to Quine's influence—but by no means entirely. Most of the work on justification that has made its way under the naturalist banner has been quite un-Quinean in its commitments, full of unreconstructed talk of belief and yoked to the enterprise of conceptual analysis in a manner much more reminiscent of Chisholm than of Quine.[4] What seems to have done the most to animate the re-emergence of naturalism in the theory of justification is the influence of one particular criticism that has been leveled at the theories of justification naturalism has sought to displace.

Those theories hold that a person's belief in p is justified just if there is a good argument for p that can be constructed from propositions she already believes.[5] This much granted, the task of the theory of epistemic justification is clear: it is to specify what is required for an argument to count as good. The debates that task has spawned are familiar enough. For example, foundationalists maintain that there is a special class of self-justifying propositions such that an argument can count as good only if it has ultimate premises that belong to that class. Coherentists counter that no self-justifying premises are available or necessary: an argument counts as good so long as it establishes that p bears the appropriate relation of coherence with the person's system of beliefs.

But while naturalists tend to have sympathy for certain of the positions that have been defended in the course of the debate (they tend, for example, to endorse the coherentists' denial that justification admits of the sort of foundations upon which foundationalists insist), it is what is *not* under dispute between foundationalists and coherentists that has most bothered naturalists. What bothers the naturalists is the idea that the mere fact that there is a certain sort of argument for p constructible from propositions she believes should suffice to render a person's belief that p justified. It is an idea Kornblith has called *the arguments-on-paper thesis*.[6]

After all, suppose the person in question repudiates that argument. Worse still, suppose she believes p only because she likes the sound of one of the sentences that expresses p. Surely, say the naturalists, we are not going to say in such circumstances that she is justified in believing p! And why? Because, they suggest, it is to the etiology of her belief that p that we are going to look to assess whether that belief is justified. When we look at its etiology, we see that the constructibility of the argument for p from her beliefs is in no way causally responsible for her harboring her belief that p. And we reckon that the process that *is* causally responsible is not the sort that confers justification on the beliefs it produces and sustains.[7]

The moral the naturalists draw is that what determines whether a person's belief that p is justified is not the constructibility of a good argument for p from her beliefs. What determines (at least in large part) whether her belief is justified is, rather, the process by which her belief was caused and is sustained. The theory of epistemic justification thus has no particular call to concern itself with the anatomy of good argument. Its task is, rather, to specify the features a process must have in order for the beliefs it causes and/or sustains to count as justified and to identify the processes that have these features.

The idea (quite plausible so long as the arguments-on-paper thesis was in place) that one might determine from the comfort of one's armchair the epistemic propriety of a principle or rule of inference, is (the naturalists conclude) fundamentally mistaken. Determining how justified beliefs are arrived at is a thoroughly empirical matter. It is only through the scientific study of the processes that cause and sustain our beliefs that we can determine by what means we can and do acquire justified beliefs.[8] In particular, we must be open to the possibility that this scientific study will reveal that principles of inference that seem compelling in our armchairs set the wrong standards for appraising the inference of actual human beings.[9]

Now, I hold no brief for the arguments-on-paper thesis and I am no friend of foundationalism or coherentism. But it seems to me that the foregoing critique of the arguments-on-paper thesis, so widely disseminated and apparently so influential in naturalist circles, is itself fundamentally mistaken, that the moral drawn from it is fundamentally misguided. My purpose here is to explain why.

II

First a confession. I believe that Abraham Lincoln was assassinated. I believe that the sun does not orbit the earth. I believe that Walter Mondale would not have defeated Ronald Reagan in 1984 even if he (Mondale) hadn't promised at the nominating convention that he would raise federal taxes. I harbor all these beliefs but I have not the slightest idea what the etiology of any of them is. I cannot even remember when, or in what circumstances, I first came by these beliefs. Nor can I be said to have done anything resembling serious scientific research into the matter of what causal processes sustain the beliefs now. Whatever the features are that a causal process must have in order to produce justified beliefs, I find myself in no position to say whether any of the three beliefs to which I have just confessed was caused (or is causally sustained) by a process that has these features.[10]

Now, I expect that few naturalists will find my confession remarkable or disturbing. It is no part of the naturalist credo that I should be able casually to tell which of my beliefs are justified. Nor is it any part of the naturalist credo that only such beliefs whose fortunate causal provenance I am aware of can count as justified. But, in the light of the naturalist credo, it seems to me that my confession should count as very disturbing indeed.

For, insofar as I find myself in no position to say, of any of the three beliefs to which I have confessed, whether it enjoys the sort of fortunate etiology required for it to count as justified by naturalist lights, then I cannot but conclude that, should I embrace the naturalist credo, I will find myself in no position to say, of any of these beliefs, whether that belief is justified. That is, I will find myself in no position to say, of any of these beliefs, that its propositional object is any more worthy of my belief than the propositions reported as news on the front page of the *National Enquirer*—in no position to say why I should not do what I can to divest myself of these beliefs.

But this is methodological madness. It is madness to suppose that I should be trying to divest myself of these beliefs. And that is because it is madness to suppose that I *need* to be in a position to say that a belief of mine enjoys a happy etiology before I can feel that it is intellectually respectable to harbor the belief. If the naturalist conception of justified belief is suggesting otherwise, then it is surely mistaken.

I suspect that few naturalists will be worried. Their response will be that their conception of justification suggests no such thing. The outline of this line of thought is fully present in Goldman's writings. "Evaluative, or normative, discourse appears in different styles," he writes. And one

> division of styles distinguishes *regulative* and *nonregulative* normative schemes. A regulative system of norms formulates rules to be consciously adopted and followed, for example, precepts or recipes by which an agent should guide his conduct. A nonregulative system of evaluation, by contrast, formulates principles for appraising a performance or trait, or assigning a normative status, but without providing instructions for the

agent to follow, or apply. They are only principles for an *appraiser* to utilize in judging.

He goes on to say that,

> [f]or the most part, my evaluative approach will be non-regulative. . . . This non-regulative style will be adopted even in talking about justificatory rules.[11]

My argument against the naturalist account of justification, the naturalist can thus claim, is a product of a mistake. I have mistaken the naturalist's nonregulative account of when a belief is justified for a regulative one. Having made that mistake, I have gone on to complain that this account has outrageous methodological consequences. But, once the mistake is exposed, my complaint about the naturalist account of justification collapses. For that account means only to capture what we are saying when, taking a nonregulative approach to epistemic appraisal, we say a person's belief is justified. And such an account cannot have outrageous methological consequences. Being an account of the nonregulative use of "justified," it has no methodological consequences at all.

But this response to my complaint is problematic—and in two ways. The first problem lies in the way Goldman distinguishes between regulative and nonregulative systems of evaluation. The importance of a regulative system of evaluation is clear, and made clear, by Goldman: it provides rules for agents to follow in the conduct of inquiry. And what does a nonregulative system of evaluation provide? The only answer offered is: "principles for an *appraiser* to utilize in judging" a performance or trait "without providing instructions for the *agent* to follow or apply." But to what end, in what interest, is an appraiser supposed to be making these judgments? Why is it supposed to be of any importance that anyone make these judgments? Goldman tells us nothing.

The problem is that, if it is characteristic of the nonregulative use of "justified" that it has no methodological import—that there is nothing in the set of rules to be consciously adopted by an inquirer that calls for her to determine whether any of her beliefs is justified in the nonregulative use of that term—then it is hard to see what point there could be to a system of evaluation dedicated to saying when it is that a person's belief is justified in the nonregulative sense. After all, in the sense of "justified" in question, it would seem that we might engage in inquiry as scrupulously and carefully as anyone can, yet never have occasion (and never suffer for our failure) even to *inquire* into whether our beliefs are justified!

Moreover (and here lies the second problem with the naturalist response), if it is characteristic of the nonregulative use of "justified" that it has no methodological import, it is hard to see on what basis one could judge (as the naturalists do in their critique of the arguments-on-paper thesis) that the expression, "justified," is being incorrectly applied.

To see why this is so, suppose that someone were to advance the following proposal: your belief that *p* is justified (in the nonregulative sense) iff you either find it psychologically impossible to doubt p's truth (p is indubitable for you) or you can produce on demand a derivation of p by truth-preserving rules from a set of propositions each member of which is indubitable for you. The proposal is a draconian one. Assuming that you are fairly normal psychologically, it is a proposal that would deem most of your beliefs—certainly those about the future, about everyday matters, about science—unjustified.

But is the proposal *mistaken*? Our immediate reaction may well be that it is. Surely any proposal that deems all these beliefs unjustified is, *eo ipso*, mistaken. But mistaken about *what*? The proposal is not, after all, suggesting that it is incumbent upon you to revise your doxastic attitudes toward the future, toward matters everyday and scientific. It is not suggesting that you should be uncomfortable about the fact that you harbor those doxastic attitudes. If it were suggesting *that*, then we would do well to regard it as mistaken. It would be issuing manifestly unacceptable methodological advice.

But, of course, the proposal cannot possibly be issuing unacceptable methodological advice. It is, after all, a proposal whose only pretension is to instruct us in *nonregulative* epistemic appraisal. Its only pretension is to tell us when, in the *nonregulative* sense of "justified," a person's belief counts as justified. That being the case, the draconian proposal cannot *have* any methodological consequences.

But, if this is so, then we are perfectly free to endorse the draconian proposal and continue (without fear of bad conscience) to persist in all the practices of belief-formation in which we are wont to engage. All our endorsement of the proposal would commit us to is a style of epistemic appraisal—a style of appraisal whose judgments are of absolutely no import to our conduct of inquiry—on which the practices in which we ordinarily engage in the course of inquiry do not yield justified belief.

And if that is all our endorsement of the draconian proposal would commit us to, then it is hard to see how we can possibly go wrong by making such an endorsement. Indeed it is hard to see how we could go wrong endorsing any other of the proposals with which the draconian proposal pretends to compete (such as the foundationalists', the coherentists', and the naturalists'). With no facts about what we are prepared (and not prepared) to believe capable of undermining any of these proposals, we can endorse any one we care to (or any pair or trio—why not commit ourselves to a variety of nonregulative styles?) without fear of having made a mistake. A mistake is only possible when there is some constraint on what counts as getting matters right. And here there is no such constraint. Cut loose from the obligation to answer to our practice of inquiry and criticism, proposals about how to make nonregulative judgments about what beliefs are justified answer to nothing.

But don't such proposals answer, at the very least, to facts about what we know? Goldman writes that "a prime motivation for a theory of justifiedness is the desire to complete the theory of knowledge"; that "justified belief is necessary for knowing"; that he is "interested in the conception of justification most closely associated with knowledge."[12] Can't we look to the facts about what we know for evidence as to whether a proposal that would proscribe the nonregulative use of "justified" is correct?

The answer is: "No." As Gettier has taught us, no matter how scrupulously a person weighs evidence and how carefully she adheres to the best methodological principles, it remains an open question whether even the true beliefs she forms as a result count as instances of propositional knowledge. And that means that no adequate principle for evaluating whether a person knows that *p*—no principle that would distinguish what she knows from what is merely one of her well-reasoned true beliefs—can be regulative. After all, since no person is in a position to make that distinction in the case of beliefs she currently holds, the principle cannot serve as part of a recipe she can use to guide her conduct. And, whatever might conceivably be at stake in how *we* distinguish between those propositions she knows and those in which she has but well-reasoned true belief, it can have nothing to do with how we would have her conduct inquiry. We have already granted that her conduct has been exemplary: she has scrupulously weighed the evidence, she has adhered to the best methodological principles. Thus, even when used by us to evaluate her, no principle that would distinguish knowledge from well-reasoned true belief can count as a regulative one.[13]

But that is just to say that there is nothing more to constrain our attributions of propositional knowledge than there is to constrain our nonregulative attributions of justified belief. We are free to answer the question of whether our agent's well-reasoned true belief counts as knowledge however we like—we are free to adopt any position concerning the nature and extent of propositional knowledge—without fear that there will be something in our (or anyone else's) conduct of inquiry that will have to be altered to conform to our verdict. We are free to take any position we like on the nature and extent of propositional knowledge without consequence.[14]

And that means that we cannot hope to support proposals concerning the nature and extent of justification (in the nonregulative sense of the term) by appeal to facts about the nature and extent of propositional knowledge. For it means that, bearing not at all on our conduct of inquiry and criticism, any substantive thesis as to the extent and nature of propositional knowledge will itself be every bit as immune to evidential constraint as are the proposals about the extent and nature of justified belief it is called upon to support.

But surely, it will be replied, such proposals are subject to a very substantial evidential constraint: they must answer to the rather sizable corpus of ordinary, commonsense intuitions we have about which beliefs count as justified. And what better proof can there be of this than that the arguments-on-paper thesis founders precisely because it runs afoul of one of those intuitions?

But does it *really* founder? Recall that the naturalist account of justification also seemed to founder on the reef of ordinary intuition—for example, the intuition that I am in a position to say that my belief that the earth orbits the sun is justified. Yet, with the aid of the distinction between regulative and nonregulative styles of epistemic appraisal, the naturalist account was saved.

That distinction in hand, we were able to explain both why the intuition appears to have such force and how the naturalist account can survive it unscathed. The apparent force of the intuition derives from the fact that, taking "justified" in the regulative sense, the intuition is quite correct. I am indeed in a position to say that my belief is justified, in the sense that my belief meets the standards of methodological hygiene. But (and this is why the intuition fails to do damage), the naturalist account of justification does not claim otherwise. The naturalist account is nonregulative in nature. Thus, it is only in the *nonregulative sense of "justified"* that (should I embrace the naturalist account) I will find myself in no position to say whether my belief is justified. The thing that I will find myself in no position to say has nothing to do with the methodological propriety of my belief.

But notice that we can float the arguments-on-paper thesis off the shoals of apparently recalcitrant intuition by exactly the same maneuver. The charge, recall, is that the arguments-on-paper thesis founders on the intuition that, regardless of whether a good argument is constructible for *p* from the propositions she believes, a person who believes *p* because she likes the sound of a sentence that expresses *p* is unjustified in that belief. But now, equipped with the regulative/nonregulative distinction, it is easy to say why the intuition appears to have such force and why the account it would seem to undermine nonetheless manages to emerge unharmed. The apparent force of the intuition, we can say, derives from the fact that, taking "justified" in its regulative sense, the intuition is quite correct: no sound methodology worthy of the name would sanction forming a belief in the manner described. But, we can say, the arguments-on-paper thesis does not claim otherwise. The arguments-on-paper thesis is nonregulative in nature: it is committed only to the claim that, *in the nonregulative sense of "justified,"* her belief is justified. And this claim implies nothing about what sound methodology sanctions.

Of course, what we have done to rescue the naturalist account and the arguments-on-paper thesis from apparent disconfirmation by intuition, we could do just as easily for the draconian proposal and any number of other proposals that would tell us under what conditions a belief is justified in the nonregulative sense of that term. Theses about justification in the regulative sense are fated to survive only at the pleasure of our methodological intuitions. But theses about justification in the nonregulative sense are answerable to none.

Thus, it seems to me, matters stand as follows. Maintaining that the naturalist account of justification is a nonregulative one does indeed provide refuge from the charge that the account has methodologically mad consequences. But it purchases that refuge only at the price of undermining the naturalist's claim to have shown that the arguments-on-paper thesis is mistaken. For that claim presupposes that it is possible to *be* mistaken in making a nonregulative judgment as to whether a person's belief is justified, that there is something to which such a judgment is called upon to answer. And neither of these presuppositions appears to be true. The conclusion seems unavoidable: maintaining that the naturalist account of justification is nonregulative saves it from the charge that is methodologically mad only at the cost of rendering the account empty.

III

Not that I think that the foundationalists and coherentists—the advocates of the arguments-on-paper thesis—are any better off. Consider why it is that they *are* advocates of the arguments-on-paper thesis. The reason is that they are committed to the view that no ordinary perceptual belief, such as my belief that I am seeing a table before me, is self-justifying. Any such belief stands in need of justification, a justification that requires a substantial bit of argument. Foundationalists and coherentists recognize, however, that they cannot expect a person to be able to produce on demand that substantial bit of argument. Apart from serious students of epistemology, few people can be expected to have much idea of what sort of argument is called for.[15] And even those who do have some idea of what sort of argument is called for are guaranteed to find the task of filling in the details of such an argument difficult, if not impossible.[16] So, rather than have to claim that we have few, if any, justified perceptual beliefs (a claim that they find unpalatable), foundationalists and coherentists opt for the arguments-on-paper thesis—they hold that it is sufficient for a belief to be justified that the right sort of argument for the belief merely exist.[17]

Now it seems to me quite clear that foundationalists and coherentists are right to shrink from requiring, as a condition of our being justified in harboring perceptual beliefs, that we be able to produce on demand the sort of arguments these philosophers think are required to justify the beliefs. The consequence of such a requirement would indeed be intolerable. Patently unable to do what is required to render our perceptual beliefs justified, we would be forced (insofar as we embraced foundationalism or coherentism) to draw the methodologically mad conclusion that we have no business harboring these beliefs—that we would be well advised to do what we could to effect their abandonment.

But how does the arguments-on-paper thesis avoid this mad methodological consequence? Only by telling us that we may with good conscience persist in a belief we know stands in need of substantive justification even as we recognize that we cannot now, and may not ever be able to, produce the justification it requires. But, while this is certainly a convenient and innocuous doctrine when applied to ordinary cases of perceptual belief—cases in which no reasonable person would ever challenge us to produce some justification for our beliefs—the doctrine is pernicious if universally applied. For it licenses a methodology on which one is free to persist in believing anything at all, about any matter at all, with no regard for whether one can produce even the most meager argument in the belief's favor. In opting for the arguments-on-paper thesis, foundationalists and coherentists simply exchange one mad methodological commitment for another.[18]

To be sure, the foundationalist and coherentist can seek to block this unhappy verdict by claiming their doctrines are being misread—that, properly understood, they do not have any methodological import. But in this the foundationalist and coherentist will fare no better than the naturalist did. Like their naturalist relative, the foundationalist and coherentist theories of justification can be stripped of methodological consequence only at the cost of rendering them immune to any and all evidential constraint. The conclusion we drew in the case of the naturalist account of justification applies just as well to the foundationalist and coherentist ones: if they are not methodologically mad, then they are empty.[19]

What has gone wrong with the naturalist critique of the arguments-on-paper thesis is, thus, *not* that the critique places the naturalist on the wrong side of the issue. On the contrary, as I have just finished arguing, the arguments-on-paper thesis is, as the naturalists maintain, mistaken. Where the naturalists go wrong is in their account of why the arguments-on-paper thesis is mistaken. Far from criticizing the thesis for its mad methodological consequences, the naturalists take for granted that the theory of justification to which the thesis means to contribute is not *supposed* to be of methodological consequence. The naturalists simply think that the foundationalist contribution is in error.

What we have seen is that this cannot be right. What we have seen is that, insofar as a theory of justification is not of methodological consequence, then it is simply empty. And insofar as it *is* of methodological consequence then it is adequate only to the extent that its methodological consequences are acceptable. What that would seem to mean is that the only way a theory of justification can make an honest living is by providing methodological insight and/or good methodological advice. Properly conceived, the job of a theory of justification is just to provide rules for (and insights into) the proper conduct of inquiry. The mistake the naturalists make (a mistake they share with the advocates of the arguments-on-paper thesis) is to suppose that a theory of justification can do anything else.

IV

But if the naturalist approach to the theory of justification is inspired by the mistake of thinking that whether a belief is justified is determined (at least in part) by the processes by which it is caused and/or sustained, it is not defined by that mistake. Naturalists are, after all, also advancing an independent, and substantive, conception of just how to go about improving the conduct of inquiry. It is a conception that means to make quite a departure from the traditional view of how methodological innovation is to be arrived at.

The traditional view is that at the heart of any good methodology must lie a conception of good argument, of evidential support. What we are looking for, after all, is beliefs for which we can muster good arguments, for which we have adequate evidential support. Coming up with an adequate conception of good argument and evidential support is largely a reflective exercise: a rehearsal of possible cases, possible scenarios, possible objections all by the light of our epistemic intuitions. Thus it is that, on the traditional view, a significant portion of the theory of justification as I have claimed it is properly conceived (as a theory that means to provide us with methodological insight and advice) can profitably be pursued in the comfort of an armchair.

But not on the naturalists' view. According to the naturalists, the methodological ambition of the theory of justification is to be pursued (in the words of Philip Kitcher) "by describing processes that are reliable, in the sense that they would have a high frequency of generating epistemically virtuous states in human beings in our world,"[20] where prominent among those epistemically virtuous states is true belief. It is an empirical, scientific task, the naturalists maintain—a task for which the armchair approach to methodology is entirely useless, hamstrung by its apriorism, i.e., by its nonempirical approach.[21]

The apriorism involved in the traditional sort of armchair methodological research, maintain the exponents of naturalism, founders on three fundamental difficulties. First, armchair apriorism must necessarily proceed in ignorance of the actual cognitive capacities of the human agents whose cognitive activities it seeks to govern. This renders it singularly ill suited to determine what cognitive processes are apt to be reliable in actual human agents. Second, having no ingress to what is apt to work in the actual world, armchair apriorism has no choice but to restrict itself to prescribing cognitive strategies that are optimal no matter how the world may be. This is a quixotic endeavor that leaves aside and (because it sets so high a standard of success) may even frustrate our attempts to find what we really want: strategies that will serve us well in the world we happen actually to inhabit. Third, armchair apriorism assumes that the fact that a methodology is in accord with our epistemic intuitions shows that it is worthy of our allegiance. But there is no reason why a methodology that satisfies some other set of epistemic intuitions, a set of intuitions harbored (say) by members of some other distant culture, might not serve our cognitive aims better. The fact that a methodology accords with our intuitions concerning rationality and evidential support is entirely compatible with its being quite unreliable at delivering us cognitively virtuous states in our world—much less reliable than some feasible alternative.[22]

Now, I confess that I am in considerable sympathy with the foregoing line of thought. The project which the naturalists favor—to devise strategies that are apt to lead beings such as we to achieve our goals in inquiry in the world we happen to inhabit—is surely a worthy one. And it is just as surely one that cannot plausibly be executed from an armchair. There are things we need to know about our environment, about our cognitive capacities, and the relationship between the two. (Perhaps a strategy that is apt to lead to disaster in most circumstances is pretty effective in the environments in which we are apt to use it.) This knowledge is not available apriori.

But I am at the same time struck by the fact, to show us all this, that what the proponents of epistemological naturalism have offered us is a series of arguments. And I am struck by the fact that they have not offered us any scientific evidence that, were we to believe what they would have us believe as a causal consequence of their having exposed us to these arguments, our belief would be the result of our having instantiated a process that is apt to have a high frequency of generating epistemically virtuous states in human beings in our world. (No surprise here: there is not—and probably never will be—any evidence of this sort available.) I am struck by the fact that they apparently think that their arguments are sufficiently cogent to show us that they are right.

But *are* their arguments cogent? So long as the naturalists mean to be showing their audience in spoken word and in print that their doctrines are correct,[23] this question will be an urgent one. But how are we supposed to go about trying to answer it? What are we to do—what *can* we do—to decide whether the naturalists' arguments are cogent?

It is hard to see what we can do except evaluate these arguments by the light of the very sorts of epistemic intuitions which the naturalists are so eager to disparage. Granted, we might well have had other intuitions.[24] Granted, had we those intuitions, we might well have very different views about what counts as a cogent argument. Granted, we do not know that heeding those other intuitions would not yield a higher frequency of epistemically virtuous states in human beings in our world than we achieve by heeding the intuitions we actually have.[25]

But none of this poses any worry that either we or the naturalist can afford to indulge. Were we unwilling to take the guidance of our epistemic intuitions until it had been shown scientifically that there is no other set of intuitions we might be capable of harboring that, if heeded, is apt to generate a higher frequency of epistemically virtuous states in human beings in our world, we would be forced to deny ourselves—now and for the foreseeable future— the only resources we have available with which to judge the cogency of *any* argument, the naturalists' arguments included.[26] Like it or not, the naturalists' attempt to show us the errors of aprioristic methodology depends for its success on our consulting, and finding naturalist arguments in accord with, the very sorts of armchair intuitions whose advice the naturalists would have us ignore.

Some naturalists will doubtless fail to be impressed by this line of argument. The day is coming, they will respond, when argument will not have the importance it now has, when our current preoccupation with the propriety of our propositional attitudes will seem quaint. It will be other attitudes towards other (perhaps hitherto unimagined) sorts of information-bearers that will occupy our attention.[27] But suppose they are right. Suppose there *will* come a day when we will give up all our dialectical chat for some yet-to-be discovered way of tweaking our cognitive mechanisms. It is still true that, until that day comes (if it ever does), the marshaling of arguments for and against the propriety of harboring various propositional attitudes towards hypotheses will continue to be central to the conduct of inquiry—for all of us, naturalists included. And, if so, there is still a place for a theory of justification that seeks to clarify and improve the standards by which we judge whether these arguments are cogent. It is precisely this place that the traditional apriori armchair approach to methodology occupies.

V

This last point, that the traditional approach to methodology is to be understood as offering a contribution to the understanding and improvement of the standards of cogent argument, deserves emphasis. It is a point that many naturalists apparently have failed to appreciate, as some of their criticisms of the traditional approach reveal.

For example, naturalists have often complained that the advice issued by the traditional approach—for example, that a person's beliefs should be consistent, that they should reflect her total evidence, that her states of confidence should be probabilistically constrained—is entirely unfollowable by any human being. We simply do not have the cognitive capacity. That the traditional approach issues such patently unfollowable advice only serves, they argue, to illustrate the fruitlessness of armchair apriorism.[28]

Now this much can surely be granted. The three pieces of advice just described *are* humanly unfollowable. And thus, if we think of these three pieces of advice as describing conditions for the violation of which a person is to be called on the carpet as a bad inquirer, then it is advice that is obviously mistaken. We cannot reasonably call someone on the carpet for failing to follow advice it was not in her capacity to follow. But if we think of the advice as contributing to a theory of cogent argument—if we think of the three pieces of advice as describing conditions the violation of which opens a person's state of opinion to legitimate criticism—matters look rather different. Then, what the advice comes to is this: we should consider an inconsistency in a person's set of beliefs, a failure of her beliefs to reflect her total evidence, a failure on her part to invest confidence in propositions in accord with axioms of probability calculus, grounds for criticizing the cogency of her beliefs (or, in the last case, of the way in which she has invested confidence in propositions). And, to judge from naturalist writings (thick as these writings are with arguments to the effect that, on pain of inconsistency, we must conclude so-and-so; with arguments to the effect that, given some unduly neglected bit of evidence, we must conclude such-and-such), this is advice to whose general propriety naturalists are (rightly) very much committed.

Is the advice correct in its every detail? Some may want to dispute that it is. They may, for example, think that the inconsistency involved in believing that at least some of your beliefs are false does *not* open your beliefs to legitimate criticism. Or, they may think that, the last piece of advice to the contrary, there is nothing wrong with investing more confidence in an explanatory theory than we do in a proposition that merely describes one of its observational consequences.[29] In my view, it is a mistake to think either of these things. But this is not the place in which to adjudicate this dispute.[30] It suffices to observe that the dispute is an intramural one, that how we adjudicate seems to depend entirely on how we deploy the resources of the traditional approach to methodology. Once we understand the traditional approach to methodology to be offering a contribution to a theory of cogent argument, we can see that considerations having to do with the cognitive capacities of human inquirers have absolutely no bearing on questions concerning the propriety of the advice the traditional approach issues.

The same thing goes for considerations having to do with the extent to which our cognitive tendencies are well adapted to our world. Consider one of the more conspicuous and powerful products of the traditional armchair approach to methodology: the canons of statistical inference. A large number of experiments conducted in the last twenty-five years or so have convincingly shown that inquirers (even trained inquirers) tend systematically to violate universally accepted canons of good statistical inference.[31] Many of those responsible for the experiments have found their results disheartening. But some naturalists beg to differ. Writing about two prominent purveyors of gloom, Hilary Kornblith writes that they

> compare the logical form of our inferences with the logic of statistical inferences, and on that basis, declare us sinners. Given the standards of proper statistical inference, our inferences receive a failing grade. But is the logic of statistical inference a reasonable standard against which to measure our own inferences?[32]

He thinks it is not. He argues, in the case of one sort of systematic violation, that we are cognitively adapted toward our environment in just such a way that the offending inferences we actually make (given the circumstances in which we tend to make them) are quite reliable. Kornblith concludes that the principles of statistical inference do not set appropriate standards by which to appraise human inference.[33]

Now, if he means by this that it is inappropriate to condemn people for their violations of the principles of statistical inference,[34] then Kornblith is surely right. Understood as a set of principles for the violation of which a person should be called on the carpet, the principles of statistical inference do seem quite unwarranted. But this, of course, is not how these principles are to be understood. They are, rather, to be understood as a set of principles the violation of which opens a person's inferences to cogent criticism. And, unless we are prepared to treat it as a matter of indifference whether the arguments we produce in word and print on behalf of our views are statistically fallacious (and I would wager that there is not a naturalist writing today who is prepared to do this), then we have little choice but to conclude that, so understood, the principles of statistical inference provide a perfectly reasonable standard against which to measure our own inferences.

VI

By way of closing, let me emphasize that I do not mean to be suggesting that a scientific study of human cognitive mechanisms offers no hope of method-ological advance. On the contrary. The better we know the biases, tendencies, strengths, and weaknesses of a tool, the more effectively we can deploy it to our ends. What I *am* arguing is that (many naturalists to the contrary) this scientific study of cognition is no substitute for the traditional approach to methodology. The methods and results of the traditional approach are indispensable to the scientific study of cognition, as they are to all inquiry. An epistemology that would pretend otherwise would be an epistemology denatured.[35]

NOTES

1. See, for example, "What is Justified Belief?" *Justification and Knowledge*, edited by George S. Pappas (Dordrecht, 1979), 1–13; "The Internalist Conception of Justification," *Midwest Studies in Philosophy V: Studies in Epistemology* (Minneapolis, 1980), 27–51; *Epistemology and Cognition* (Cambridge, Mass., 1986).

2. Hilary Kornblith, *Naturalizing Epistemology* (Cambridge, Mass., 1985 and 1992).

3. "The Naturalists Return," *Philosophical Review* 101 (1992): 53–114.

4. See, for example, Goldman, *Epistemology and Cognition*, 38–39. Goldman expresses some misgivings about the enterprise in "Psychology and Philosophical Analysis," *Proceedings of the Aristotelian Society* 89 (1988): 195–209. So does Hilary Kornblith, in his *Inductive Inference and its Natural Ground* (Cambridge, Mass., 1993), 4–5.

5. More properly, they hold that a person's belief that *p* is justified just in case, *if* p *is the sort of proposition that requires justification by argument* (and for foundationalists, not all propositions are of this sort), then there is a good argument for *p* that can be constructed from propositions she already believes. But in what follows, I will continue for the sake of convenience to omit the italicized qualification.

6. "Beyond Foundationalism and the Coherence Theory," *Journal of Philosophy* 77 (1980): 597–612, 509.

7. For evidence of the prominence this sort of argument has in the naturalist canon, see Gilbert Harman, *Thought* (Princeton, N.J., 1973), 30–31; Goldman, "What is Justified Belief?" 9, and *Epistemology and Cognition*, 81–93; Kornblith, "Beyond Foundationalism and the Coherence Theory," 599–602; Kitcher, "The Naturalists Return," 60.

8. These morals are spelled out with particular vividness in Kitcher, "The Naturalists Return," 56–74.

9. See, for example, Kornblith, *Inductive Inference and Its Natural Ground*.

10. I do not mean here to be denying that I find myself in a position to say things like "This belief is sustained by memory" or "This belief was produced by reasoning from some sort of evidence." But I do not for a minute suppose that this constitutes anything like a scientifically adequate way of identifying cognitive processes. And it seems to me that, in ignorance of how properly to identify cognitive processes and in the (consequent) absence of any investigation (serious or otherwise) into which cognitive processes thus identified have the appropriate justification-conferring property, it would be folly of me to suppose, nonetheless, that the three beliefs to which I have confessed are caused and/or sustained by cognitive processes that have that justification-conferring property. Alvin Plantinga makes much the same point in his *Warrant: The Current Debate* (Oxford, 1993), 202.

11. *Epistemology and Cognition*, 25–26. See too his "The Internalist Conception of Justification," 28–29.

12. *Epistemology and Cognition*, 76.

13. For a fuller elaboration and defense of the points made in this paragraph, see my "It's Not What You Know that Counts," *Journal of Philosophy* 82: 350–63.

14. This consequence of the nonregulative nature of knowledge attributions has, indeed, been embraced by some contemporary philosophers of skeptical bent, who rightly see in it a way to wax skeptical about the extent of our propositional knowledge without thereby opening themselves up to the claim that they are urging us to act as if we (say) don't know that the phlogiston theory is false or as if we don't know that we have teeth. See, for example, Barry Stroud, *The Significance of Philosophical Scepticism* (Oxford, 1984), ch. 2

and Bredo Johnsen, "Relevant Alternatives and Demon Skepticism," *Journal of Philosophy* 84 (1987): 643–53, esp. 652–53.

15. Indeed, even the most eminent of epistemologists have had difficulty saying to their own satisfaction (let alone to the satisfaction of others) what form of argument is called for. Roderick Chisholm, to take the most eminent among them, has been revising his account of how the argument should go for over four decades.

16. Laurence BonJour concedes that this is true of the argument from the coherence of a person's belief system he favors, allowing that no person has a sufficient explicit grasp of her system of beliefs to furnish such an argument (*The Structure of Empirical Knowledge* [Cambridge, Mass., 1985] 151–52). Given that there is no foundationalist alternative that does not itself involve some strong coherence constraint (see, for example, the coherence constraint that Chisholm imposes in chapter 6 of his *Theory of Knowledge*, 3rd ed. [Englewood Cliffs, N.J., 1989]), it would seem that a comparable concession is warranted from the foundationalist quarter as well.

17. For an expression of this line of thought, see (for example) William Alston, "Level-Confusions in Epistemology," *Midwest Studies in Philosophy* V, 144–45.

18. The commitment is not, however, so mad that it has failed to find philosophical voice. See, for example, Isaac Levi, *The Enterprise of Knowledge* (Cambridge, Mass., 1983), 1–2; Gilbert Harman, *Change in View* (Cambridge, Mass., 1986), ch. 4. But see David Christensen, "Conservatism in Epistemology," *Noûs* 28 (1994): 69–89.

19. The last four paragraphs constitute a compressed version of the argument that dominates my "Epistemology on Holiday," *Journal of Philosophy* 88 (1991): 132–54.

20. Kitcher, "The Naturalists Return," 75–76.

21. I am using the term *apriorism* here (and *apriori* below) only because it has been used as an epithet by such naturalists as Kitcher and because, understood in its colloquial sense, the use of the term makes vivid the contrast between a methodology that is itself an empirical, scientific enterprise and one which is a reflective one that can be pursued in an armchair. Nothing here will turn, or bear, on any views about what, if anything, counts as *apriori* knowledge.

22. For a lucid bill of indictment in this vein, see Kitcher, "The Naturalists Return."

23. As opposed to merely trying to sway their audience.

24. Our personal histories teach us that our epistemic intuitions tend to change over time. And the history of human inquiry teaches us that what epistemic intuitions are widely held in the scientific, and other investigative, communities has changed over time.

25. And we do know that some people have had intuitions that are—and that support methodological rules that are—quite mad. See chapter 4 of Stephen Stich, *The Fragmentation of Reason* (Cambridge, Mass., 1990) where Stich takes observations such as these to undermine the integrity of armchair methodology.

26. Indeed, we would be forced to deny ourselves these resources even if we demanded only that it be scientifically shown that our intuitions, when heeded, are apt to generate a reasonably high frequency of epistemically virtuous states in human beings in our world.

27. See, for example, Stephen Stich, *From Folk Psychology to Cognitive Science* (Cambridge, Mass., 1983); Patricia Churchland, "Epistemology in the Age of Neuroscience," *Journal of Philosophy* 84 (1987): 544–52; Paul Chruchland, *A Neurocomputational Perspective* (Cambridge, Mass., 1989).

28. See, for example, Christopher Cherniak, *Minimal Rationality* (Cambridge, Mass., 1986); Kornblith, *Inductive Inference and Its Natural Ground*, 5; Kitcher, "The Naturalists Return," 84–87.

29. Kitcher, together with a great many others of both naturalist and nonnaturalist persuasion, thinks the first of these two things (Kitcher, "The Naturalists Return," 85). Clark Glymour (*Theory and Evidence* [Princeton, 1980], 83–84) thinks the second. The latter is by far the more serious misgiving, striking at the heart of the last piece of advice.

30. I address that task in "Believing the Improbable," *Philosophical Studies*, (forthcoming) and "Confessions of a Modest Bayesian," in *Reconstructing Philosophy? New Essays in Metaphilosophy*, edited by J. Couture and K. Nielsen, *Canadian Journal of Philosophy Supplementary Volume* 19 (1993): 315–37.

31. See, for example, Daniel Kahnemann, Paul Slovic, and Amos Tversky, eds., *Judgment under Uncertainty* (Cambridge, 1982).

32. Kornblith, *Inductive Inference and Its Natural Ground*, 90–91.

33. Ibid., ch. 5.

34. I follow Kornblith in writing as if there is agreement on what those principles are. There is not. See Vic Barnett, *Comparative Statistical Inference*, 2nd ed. (New York, 1982).

35. I would like to thank Ken Gemes, Hilary Kornblith, Jamie Tappenden, and Joan Weiner for helpful and timely comments on this essay and Peter Haddawy for useful discussion in the early stages of its writing.

Kripke on Wittgenstein and Normativity

GEORGE M. WILSON

In Saul Kripke's *Wittgenstein: On Rules and Private Language*,[1] there are two main characters: a semantical skeptic and Ludwig Wittgenstein. Kripke himself, we can suppose, is the narrator. In the course of his narrative, the narrator often speaks for one or the other of the characters, and, when the characters are in agreement, he sometimes speaks for both. However, unlike Dr. Watson and Holmes, Kripke's Wittgenstein does not assent to all the skeptic's chief conclusions. Rather, Kripke's characters are related more in the manner of the governess and Mrs. Gross in *The Turn of the Screw*. The skeptic sees 'the super-natural' where Kripke's Wittgenstein sees only the skeptic's own delusion. Many commentators on Kripke's text have not done a good job of negotiating the question, "Whose voice is speaking in this passage? And now, who speaks in that one?" The upshot has been serious misunderstandings of the structure and content of the implicit dialogue that Kripke depicts in his book. Of course, the misunderstandings do not arise solely out of a deficient sense of 'point of view'; other factors encourage and support the confusions. These factors also need to be diagnosed. In any case, I will argue that the commentators have often been wrong about what the skeptic assumes, wrong about what Kripke's Wittgenstein concludes, and wrong, correlatively, to read some of the central arguments in a topsy-turvy fashion. My aim is to set these matters straight, commenting, where it seems especially illuminating to do so, upon the mistakes of several of Kripke's major critics.

I have noted that Kripke represents his characters as agreeing upon certain major issues. Upon what do they agree? Most notably, we are informed that they agree upon 'the skeptical conclusion'. And, what is that? Kripke varies his formulation of the thesis throughout the book, but here are two reasonably characteristic statements of the point. "Now Wittgenstein's skeptic argues that he knows of no fact about an individual that could constitute his state of meaning plus rather than quus" (p. 39). Or again, "But then it appears to follow [from the skeptic's argument] that there was no *fact* about me that constituted my having meant plus rather than quus" (p. 21). And yet, even these explicit formulations can leave one troubled, for, in their larger context, they seem dangerously ambiguous. One might be tempted to suppose, for example, that, suitably generalized, they say:

It is never a fact that a speaker means something by a term,

or

There are no facts that ascriptions of meaning could correctly describe,

or, considering other aspects of the discussion,

There are no (possible) facts that could constitute truth conditions for meaning ascriptions.

It is not merely that these statements might bear the sense of these crude paraphrases. In addition, each paraphrase roughly formulates a significant doctrine that figures in the developing argumentation. Hence, we will want to sort out at least three issues. How are the various 'skeptical' claims to be construed? Where do they stand within the different arguments that the protagonists deploy? And, returning to our first concern, which character voices any particular argument, and who is it that speaks for any given conclusion?

Since it will be important, as we proceed, to be as clear as possible about what Kripke's skeptic does and does not affirm, I will begin by attempting to state, in some detail, the perspective from which, as I see it, his skeptical arguments are developed. Here, for example, is an early statement by Kripke of one of the skeptic's basic presuppositions. "I, like almost all English speakers, use the word 'plus' and the symbol '+' to denote a well-known mathematical function, addition. . . . By means of my external symbolic representation and my internal mental representation, I 'grasp' the rule for addition. One point is crucial to my 'grasp' of this rule. Although I myself have computed only finitely many sums in the past, the rule determines my answer for indefinitely many new sums that I have never previously considered. This is the whole point of the notion that in learning to add I grasp a rule: my past intentions regarding addition determine a unique answer for indefinitely many new cases in the future" (pp. 7–8). Shortly afterwards, Kripke continues, "The basic point is this. Ordinarily, I suppose that, in computing '68 + 57' as I do, I do not simply make an unjustified leap in the dark. I follow directions I previously gave myself that uniquely determine that in this new instance I should say '125'. What are these directions?" (p. 10). These and related remarks lead into the summary statement of the skeptic's challenge that is offered on page 11. I quote that summary almost in full.

> [T]he challenge posed by the sceptic takes two forms. First, he questions whether there is any *fact* that I meant plus, not quus, that will answer his sceptical challenge. Second, he questions whether I have any reason to be so confident that now I should answer '125' rather than '5'. The two

forms of the challenge are related. I am confident that this answer also accords with what I *meant*. Neither the accuracy of my computation nor of my memory is under dispute. So it ought to be agreed that *if* I meant plus, then unless I wish to change my usage, I am justified in answering (indeed compelled to answer) '125', not '5'. An answer to the sceptic must satisfy two conditions. First, it must give an account of what fact it is (about my mental state) that constitutes my meaning plus, not quus. But further, there is a condition that any putative candidate for such a fact must satisfy. It must, in some sense, show how I am justified in giving the answer '125' to '68 + 57'. The 'directions' mentioned in the previous paragraph, that determine what I should do in each instance, must somehow be 'contained' in any candidate for the fact as to what I meant. Otherwise, the sceptic has not been answered when he holds that my present response is arbitrary.

It is these thoughts that we need to review with some care.

The skeptic, it seems, begins with a skeletal but plausible conception of what it is to mean something by a term. Restricting ourselves, first of all, to the exemplary case of addition, the conception runs as follows. If, during a certain period, I meant addition by "+", then, during that time, I must have adopted some *standard of correctness* for my actual and potential applications of the term. Meaning something by "+" essentially involves having a *policy* about what is to count as a correct and incorrect application of the expression. Moreover, the skeptic supposes, the wanted standard of correctness is, in this example, specified for me in terms of the arithmetic operation of addition itself. As a matter of mathematical fact, independently of my or anyone else's linguistic practices, the addition function yields a unique numerical value for any pair of natural numbers. This general arithmetic fact constitutes the basis for a suitable standard of correctness. What I must do to establish the standard for myself, the skeptic maintains, is to adopt a *rule* or a *commitment* to the effect that *correct answers* to queries of the form $\lceil j + k = ? \rceil$ are given by the values of the addition operation for the pairs of numbers that, query by query, are in question. Having adopted this linguistic rule for "+", correct applications of the term are *governed by* the infinite table of values that addition generates. Alternatively, we can say that, in meaning addition by "+", I must successfully 'single out' the addition function and, correlatively, form the *intention or purpose, concerning just that function*, that it is to determine correct applications of my use of the term. Hence, my acceptance of the linguistic commitment 'justifies' my answers to queries framed from "+" (when those answers are correct) in the sense that it supplies me with the standard of correctness that my applications of "+" are supposed to track.[2]

It is precisely at this juncture that the skeptic interposes his disturbing challenge. It is my contention that the skeptic does not doubt that the skeletal conception of what is involved in meaning addition by "+" is right. What he does doubt is that this conception can be intelligibly filled in with an account of *how* I (or any other speaker) achieve the adoption of the specified linguistic policy or commitment. What, he asks, does my adopting such a conception concretely consist in? In particular, what are the facts about me in virtue of which *it is addition* that governs correct applications of "+" for me and not some other initially similar but divergent arithmetic operation? What is it about me that makes it the case that I employ addition, and not (say) Kripke's quaddition, as my standard of correctness? In the discussion above, it was claimed that I must, in some manner, 'single out' addition and form an intention, about that function, that it is to settle correct applications of my use of "+". Well then, the skeptic asks, in what specific manner do I accomplish the task of 'singling out' addition so as to form the required intention concerning it?[3]

The ensuing skeptical argument purports to show that there are no acceptable answers to these questions. Some of the proposals that the skeptic considers cite facts about me that do not single out any particular arithmetic operation whatsoever. Other proposals cite facts which, if they do identify a specific function at all, wrongly identify an operation other than addition. All of them fail to explain how I have acquired a linguistic policy that is directed, as it should be, upon the addition function. The skeletal conception with which we started cannot be determinately grounded in facts about me that render it intelligible that it is addition that I have meant by "+".

As Kripke repeatedly emphasizes, the skeptic's problem is a general one: it concerns the meaningfulness of any speaker's use of a term. To lay hold of the broader point of view, it will be helpful to rehearse these last reflections in a more general fashion. Thus, let $\ulcorner \phi \urcorner$ be any term which a speaker X proposes to use as a general term or predicate. That is, $\ulcorner \phi \urcorner$, as X is to employ it, is to apply correctly or incorrectly, as the case may be, to the members of some open-ended domain of objects D. In particular, and without significant loss of generality, we can assume that $\ulcorner \phi \urcorner$ is to be a 'descriptive' term for X—a term that is applied correctly or incorrectly, in a given case, depending upon facts about the specific character of the candidate item. As before, the skeptic insists that X will not mean something by the term $\ulcorner \phi \urcorner$ unless she supplies for herself a standard of correctness for the envisaged use. But, from where is the appropriate standard to be derived? Well, let us take it for granted that each member of D (considered at a time when the pertinent item exists) exemplifies a range of determinant properties and does not exemplify a host of others. We can presume that the fact that a D-member has a certain property or the fact that it does not obtains independently of our beliefs about the matter and independently of whatever forms of language use we may have put in place. So, it seems, the standards of correctness for the descriptive predicates are to be established in terms of these properties of the D-members—in terms of these objective predicable conditions, realized or not as they may be, by the various objects in D. The skeptic repeats that what X must do if she is to mean something by $\ulcorner \phi \urcorner$ is to adopt the linguistic commitment that $\ulcorner \phi \urcorner$ is to be applied to a D-item o just in case o has just *these* properties, e.g., the properties P_1–P_n.

Varying the formulation, X is to have the intention, concerning P_1–P_n, that $\lceil \phi \rceil$ applies to o iff o exemplifies those conditions.

We should notice, since this will become important as we proceed, that X's meaning something by $\lceil \phi \rceil$, thus conceived, ensures that the meaning of $\lceil \phi \rceil$ for X enjoys a certain intuitive *normativity*. For an unbounded number of objects in D, X's semantic policy for $\lceil \phi \rceil$ determines, when relevant facts about the D-items are fixed, whether or not *it is correct* to apply $\lceil \phi \rceil$, on X's use, to the objects in question. Actually, as this formulation suggests, this determination of correctness is a two-stage affair. By adopting her semantic rule, X thereby determines *what has to be the case* if $\lceil \phi \rceil$, as she means it, is to apply. It is determined, as we have said, *which properties* a candidate for $\lceil \phi \rceil$ ascription is to have. But now, whether $\lceil \phi \rceil$ *does* apply to an object o (as it is at a time t) depends also upon the facts about o's character at t. It depends upon whether that character 'accords with' the defining properties, P_1–P_n. With this qualification understood, we can say that, on the present conception, meaning determines correctness and so is normative in relation to the speaker's prospective practice.

These considerations place us in a position to describe succinctly how the skeptic's negative argument proceeds. First, we have just observed that the skeptic endorses a natural and powerful conception of the normativity of meaning. He holds that

N_s) If X means something by a term $\lceil \phi \rceil$, then there is a set of properties, P_1–P_n, that govern the correct application of $\lceil \phi \rceil$ for X.

However, as we also observed in our discussion of "+", the skeptic insists that, if certain properties are to function as conditions of correct applicability for X's use of $\lceil \phi \rceil$, then there must be concrete facts about X which establish that it *is* just those properties which she has successfully singled out and about which she has formed a proper semantic commitment. The existence of conditions of applicability for a term must be intelligibly *grounded* in facts about the speaker's psychological and/or social history.[4] Therefore, the 'grounding constraint' says that

G) If there is a set of properties, P_1–P_n, that govern the correct application of $\lceil \phi \rceil$ for X, then there are facts about X that *constitute* P_1–P_n as the conditions that govern X's use of $\lceil \phi \rceil$.

Acceptance of this constraint moves us into the territory that the skeptic attacks. Naturally, the skeptic defends a number of skeptical-sounding conclusions, but what I take to be the basic skeptical argument attempts to show that the grounding constraint cannot be satisfied. That is, what I will call "the basic skeptical conclusion" states that

BSC) There are *no* facts about X that constitute any set of properties as conditions that govern X's use of $\lceil \phi \rceil$.

This is the conclusion for which the skeptic argues on a case-by-case basis. He investigates a range of suggestions, purporting to exhaust the possibilities, concerning the sorts of facts about X which might be thought to establish a set of properties as conditions of correct ascribability, and he tries to demonstrate that each of these suggestions is unacceptable. BSC), then, sums up the purported results of these investigations. In this essay, I will not attempt to assess the cogency of the case-by-case argument for BSC).

Nevertheless, simply setting up the structure of the skeptic's overall position in this form raises a number of significant questions. For example, I mentioned, at the beginning of this essay, that when Kripke frames what he calls "the skeptical conclusion," he tends to favor formulations such as

S) There are no facts that constitute X's meaning something by a term $\lceil \phi \rceil$.

It was this sort of formulation that seemed so provocatively elusive. But how, one may wonder, is my BSC) a plausible version of the troublesome form of words? Here, I believe, there are two related but distinguishable connections to be made. First, from the skeptic's viewpoint, BSC) simply says that there are no facts about X that constitute anything (i.e., any set of properties) as that which X means by $\lceil \phi \rceil$. After all, the skeptic thinks that what X means, if anything, by $\lceil \phi \rceil$ is a particular set of properties and that X's meaning some such set of properties by $\lceil \phi \rceil$ just is a matter of X's use of $\lceil \phi \rceil$ being governed by the properties in question.

However, there is another conclusion, potentially expressible by S), to which the skeptic is also directly committed. On the present reconstruction, the skeptic has held a view from the outset about the type of fact that X's meaning something by $\lceil \phi \rceil$ would have to consist in. In other words, the view says that statements of the form $\lceil X$ means ψ by $\lceil \phi \rceil \rceil$ uniformly purport to describe a fact of a certain kind, i.e., the fact that the relevant properties do govern X's use of $\lceil \phi \rceil$. But, the skeptic also contends that there can be no facts of that type unless they contain more specific facts about the speaker that fix for her the linguistic standards of correctness she is to pursue. And now, since BSC) is the thesis that no such standard-fixing facts exist, the skeptic concludes that there are and can be no facts that would be truly describable as $\lceil X$'s meaning something by $\lceil \phi \rceil \rceil$. There are no facts in the world to be correctly recorded by these ascriptions of meaning.

It will emerge, as we proceed, that it is important to keep these two connections to S)-style formulations sharply in mind. Although, as I have just indicated, the skeptic endorses both conclusions, the conceptual situation shifts dramatically when we turn to the framework of what Kripke calls "the sceptical solution." I will argue that this framework also incorporates BSC) (the skeptic and the skeptical solution agree on this), and, from a point of view different from the skeptic's, the skeptical solution agrees to the first of the reformulations offered above.[5] However, the thought expressed by my second formulation is quite a different matter. For reasons I will present later, the skeptical solution need not adopt the position that meaning ascriptions do not correctly describe or state facts about the speaker in question. But it will be easier to explain the import and the rationale for this remark only after the framework of the skeptical solution has been erected.

As I indicated above, since the skeptic draws several surprising conclusions, it is dangerous to speak of 'the' skeptical conclusion. It has probably not escaped notice that the three premises, N_s), G), and BSC), jointly entail the *radical* skeptical conclusion that

RSC) No one ever means anything by a term.

Kripke's skeptic plainly is committed to this. But what are we to say about Kripke's Wittgenstein in this connection? Kripke asserts that Wittgenstein accepts 'the' skeptical argument and agrees to its skeptical conclusion. Does this mean that Kripke thinks that Wittgenstein also holds or is committed to RSC)? The answer, I will urge, is "No," but to see *how*, on my reading of Kripke, this can be so will force us to explore some difficult terrain. In my judgment, the skeptical conclusion that Kripke's Wittgenstein accepts is just BSC), and it is the skeptical argument for *that* result that he endorses.

Consider, to begin with, an important remark that Kripke makes on pages 70 and 71; "Nevertheless I choose to be so bold as to say: Wittgenstein holds, with the sceptic, that there is no fact as to whether I mean plus or quus. But if this is to be conceded to the sceptic, is this not the end of the matter? What *can* be said on behalf of our ordinary attributions of meaningful language to ourselves and to others? Has not *the incredible and self-defeating conclusion* [emphasis added], that all language is meaningless, already been drawn?" The question that closes this passage refers to RSC), and the discussion that ensues unequivocally affirms that Wittgenstein does not draw this conclusion. In fact, it is natural to read Kripke as saying that it is a chief objective of the skeptical solution to explain why RSC) does not follow from BSC). Note that, in this quotation, RSC) is described as "incredible and self-defeating," and it seems obvious, in context, that this characterization is meant to reflect Wittgenstein's attitude also. So, Kripke does not suppose that Wittgenstein embraces RSC).

However, if Kripke's Wittgenstein accepts BSC) and rejects RSC), then the resulting conjunction has an immediate, important consequence. That is, according to Kripke's interpretation, Wittgenstein is committed to rejecting N_s) also, and that is the thesis that incorporates the skeptic's affirmation of the normativity of meaning. How plausible is this as part of a reading of Kripke's account of Wittgenstein? Many will wish to object that Kripke's Wittgenstein surely shares with the skeptic his emphasis upon the claim that meaning is normative. Any construal of Kripke's book that holds that its author represents Wittgenstein as repudiating 'normativity' must be mistaken.

In many ways, this objection goes to the heart of the reading of Kripke I propose, and it will take the remainder of the essay to develop fully my response. Here I can only adumbrate the strategy I will pursue. It will be my position that we need to be careful to distinguish a broad and somewhat schematic condition on meaning that articulates its normative character from the skeptic's more specific account of how normativity arises for a speaker's application of a term. I fully agree that Kripke's Wittgenstein, in rough harmony with the skeptic, accepts this normativity condition, and, guided by passages in Kripke's book, I will try to formulate the schematic condition as we proceed. Further, as I will try to show, not only does Kripke's Wittgenstein accept the condition, but from within the skeptical solution, he constructs a distinctive account of the *basis* of the normativity condition. On the other hand, N_s) encapsulates the skeptic's alternative conception of the basis of normativity, and this conception, I believe, *is* one that Kripke's Wittgenstein denies.

In any case, the following is my present hypothesis. The skeptic is committed to this argument:

N_s)
G)
$\underline{\text{BSC)}}$
∴ RSC;

Kripke's Wittgenstein is not; rather he is committed to the 'contrapositive' argument:

G)
BSC)
$\underline{\text{~RSC)}}$
∴ ~N_s).

Having just allowed that this hypothesis will require an elaborate defense, I hasten to add that, if it can be defended, there is a major interpretative benefit to be gained. Moreover, the benefit is accrued in relation to interpretative issues to which other commentators on Kripke have inadequately attended.

At the very beginning of his presentation of the skeptical solution, Kripke stresses that Wittgenstein rejects what he (Kripke) calls the "classical realist" theory or picture of meaning. Kripke provides a brief description of the sort of view he has in mind in this passage:

> The simplest, most basic idea of the *Tractatus* can hardly be dismissed: a declarative sentence gets its meaning by virtue of its *truth conditions*, by virtue of its correspondence to facts that must obtain if it is true. For example, "the cat is on the mat" is understood by those speakers who realize that it is true if and only if a certain cat is on a certain mat; it is false otherwise. The presence of the cat on the mat is a fact or condition-in-the-world that would make the sentence true (express a truth) if it obtained. (p. 72)

That Kripke believes that Wittgenstein rejects this classical realism has been widely noted, but he later makes a stronger claim whose import deserves deeper consideration. On page 85, Kripke writes,

In this way the relationship between the first and the second portions of the *Investigations* is reciprocal. In order for Wittgenstein's skeptical solution of his paradox to be intelligible, the 'realistic' or 'representational' picture of language must be undermined by another picture (in the first part). On the other hand, the paradox developed in the second part, antecedently to its solution, drives an important final nail (perhaps the crucial one) into the coffin of the representational picture.

Now, what does Kripke mean when he tells us that the skeptical paradox "drives a final nail into the coffin of classical realism"? It is my assumption that he means that Wittgenstein rejects classical realism because, perhaps along with other reasons, Wittgenstein supposes that the skeptical argument offers him the grounds for a definitive argument against the classical realist position. But, then, how is this argument supposed to run? If we see, as I think we should, that the skeptic develops his paradox from a conception of meaning that is itself classical realist, then, given my suggestion above, the argument is readily discerned. In effect, N_s) is a condensed statement of a central aspect of what the classical realist believes about meaning, and I have just outlined the way in which Kripke's Wittgenstein has a *reductio* of precisely that thesis.

When I first introduced and motivated N_s), I devoted some space to trying to convey what I take to be the skeptic's picture of what is involved when a speaker means something by a term. It was a part of my intention, in devoting as much space as I did to this conception, to bring out, at least implicitly, the way in which the skeptic himself is a (skeptical) classical realist. It is true that, when Kripke introduced classical realism (named as such) into his discussion, he focused on the idea that the meaning of a *sentence* arises from its supposed correlation with 'realist' truth conditions, i.e., with *a possible fact* whose realization in the world will render the sentence true. By contrast, I focused on *general terms* and on the thought that their meaningfulness depends upon their correct application being governed by *properties* or objective and exemplifiable conditions. However, these variant styles of formulation are easily intertranslatable. If, for example, in a sentence ⌈α is φ⌉, ⌈α⌉ names an object *o* and ⌈φ⌉ ascribes a property *P* to *o*, then ⌈α is φ⌉ is true just in case the possible fact of *o*'s being *P* obtains. So, to repeat. The skeptic has a classical realist background, and N_s) is his credo. Kripke's Wittgenstein endorses the skeptical argument to BSC), agrees also to the grounding constraint G), but, reasonably enough, denies the "insane and intolerable" RSC).[6] These components generate his *reductio* of N_s). Unlike the skeptic, Kripke's Wittgenstein sides with common opinion that people often mean something by the terms and sentences they use. But he claims to have shown that those sentences cannot have classical realist truth conditions (for sentences) nor classical realist satisfaction or truth-of-conditions (for terms). Hence, the meaningfulness of language for its users cannot consist in that.

I am reassured that my reading of Kripke's book is controversial by David Pears's discussion of the same material in his *The False Prison*, vol. 2. My last proposals simply contradict the interpretative impression he has formed. Pears states that the targets of Wittgenstein's attack are "Platonizing" accounts of meaning—theories that, as he puts it, hold that "the guidance given by a rule is complete, covering every possible case in advance and leaving nothing to be contributed to what counts as compliance by the mind of the person who is following it."[7] Now, although a lengthy process of sorting out and weighing would be required to support the claim, it strikes me that Pears's 'meaning Platonism' does not differ essentially from Kripke's 'classical realism' about meaning. Suppose that I am right about this, and consider a central objection that Pears makes to Kripke's views. "[I]t can be shown that the passages in the *Philosophical Investigations* which Kripke interprets as expressions of scepticism about rule-following are really nothing of the kind: they are part of a reductive argument directed against Platonizing theories of meaning."[8] I do not find Pears's exegesis of Kripke's argumentation easy to follow, but, details aside, I do not believe that this passage could have been written unless its author had failed to distinguish adequately the issues about which the skeptic and the skeptical solution agree from those about which they distinctly disagree. What I have been urging is that, if one does so distinguish, a major *reductio* of classical realism—what Pears calls "Platonism"—about meaning is present in the text and serves as a prolegomena to the skeptical solution. I conjecture that Pears does not believe that there can be a *reductio* in Kripke similar to the one that he outlines in his book because he supposes that Kripke holds that Wittgenstein shares the skeptic's conception of normativity. But then, N_s) represents a 'Platonizing' account of meaning, and so, Kripke's Wittgenstein cannot be arguing against that. As I acknowledged earlier, the appearances in support of Pears need to be explained.

Crispin Wright and Paul Boghossian also structure Kripke's reading of Wittgenstein quite differently than I do.[9] A few pages earlier, I signaled the fact that there is an issue about which of the skeptical conclusions Kripke's Wittgenstein is supposed to accept—an issue about the extent to which the skeptical solution is in agreement with the skeptic's position. It is precisely at this juncture, I believe, that Wright and Boghossian, in company with other commentators, commit a crucial error. But the issues are delicate and need to be developed with some care.

A symptom of my larger differences with Wright and Boghossian is to be found in their judgment that there exists a puzzling lacuna in Kripke's argumentative strategy. Both philosophers are well aware that Kripke's Wittgenstein rejects (classical realist) truth conditions in a global fashion, i.e., that he holds

S') *No* sentence has classical realist truth conditions.

But, Boghossian in particular charges that Kripke has neglected to specify how the skeptical solution arrives at S'). (He does think that the gap can be filled in and is prepared to suppose that Kripke sees the connection that he, Boghossian, supplies.)[10] Both authors also correctly record that the favored formulation of the skeptical conclusion is

S) There are no facts that constitute X's meaning something by a term $\lceil \phi \rceil$,

but they construe this to mean something like

S*) There are no facts about X that assertions of the form $\lceil X$ means ψ by $\lceil \phi \rceil \rceil$, even when they are correct by ordinary criteria, *describe truly*.

In response to this supposed result, they suggest that the skeptical solution incorporates a certain 'projectivism' about meaning at its core. Wright summarizes both the provocation and response in this way: " . . . Kripke's Wittgenstein may be seen as first, by the sceptical argument, confounding the ordinary idea that our talk of meaning and understanding and cognate concepts has a genuinely factual subject matter, and then, via the sceptical solution, recommending an alternative projective view of its content."[11] Thus, the skeptical solution is thought to feature the 'projectivist' thesis that sentences of the form $\lceil X$ means ψ by $\lceil \phi \rceil \rceil$ do not, as part of their semantic content, ever purport to describe facts. This, of course, is meant to take the sting out of S*). For if $\lceil X$ means ψ by $\lceil \phi \rceil \rceil$ does purport to describe facts about X, then the truth of S*) ensures that all such meaning ascriptions are either false or somehow incoherent. The projectivist thesis guarantees that S*) does not have this consequence and encourages us to search for an alternative account of the semantic function or functions of meaning ascriptions. Neither Wright nor Boghossian try to elaborate such an alternative, but, in the light of relevant parts of Kripke's presentation, one might be led to suggest, for example, that the semantic function of such ascriptions is to confer license upon or to acknowledge the license of a speaker to be a competent user of $\lceil \phi \rceil$ within the prevailing linguistic practices.[12] This at least hints at what 'projectivism' might amount to here, but, for present purposes, the details do not matter.

Therefore, on this construal of Kripke, the skeptical solution presents us with S*), and it seems plausible that a simple consequence of this is

S'') Sentences of the form $\lceil X$ means ψ by $\lceil \phi \rceil \rceil$ do not have classical realist truth conditions.

But now, Boghossian tells us that he cannot find in Kripke an explanation of what justifies the inference from S'') to the globally generalized S'), and, as I mentioned, he offers an explanation of his own. And yet, by my lights, there is no gap to be filled: Wright and Boghossian have got Kripke's argumentative structure back to front. It is my contention that the global S') is derived directly as part of the *reductio* of N_s)—it is an immediate result of that general argument. Naturally, S'') is also accepted, but it merely follows as an instance of S'). There is no reason to hunt for a route from S'') back to S').

My deeper disagreement with Wright and Boghossian, however, concerns a prior question. In my opinion it is highly doubtful that such a projectivist thesis figures in the skeptical solution. I find this thesis not only implausible on its own, but it seems irrelevant to the true concerns of Kripke's Wittgenstein.

Projectivism about meaning ascriptions is supposed to blunt the consequences of 'the skeptical conclusion', S*), but Kripke's Wittgenstein is not committed to S*). Kripke's skeptic *is* probably so committed, but, as we noted before and as we will see again shortly, that is another matter. It is easy to become tangled up in trying to formulate the issues properly. Contributing to the potential tangle is the fact that the version of skeptical conclusion Kripke spotlights (i.e., S): "There are no facts that constitute X's meaning [ψ] by ⌜φ⌝") can be read, with roughly equal naturalness, as expressing either S*) or S''). My claim is that only the S'') reading is correct. Moreover, Kripke's employment, in his book, of the phrase "states facts," where that applies to sentences, sometimes helps to encourage the confusion.[13]

The first point to be stressed is that S*) and S'') are not equivalent, at least, they are not when S*) bears a sense to which projectivism might be an appropriate response. I have already granted that it is plausible that S'') follows from S*), but the converse cannot be assumed to hold in the present dialectical context. More broadly, from

i) ⌜P⌝ does not have classical realist truth conditions

it does not follow that

ii) ⌜P⌝, even if 'correct', does not describe facts,

or, more guardedly and more to the present point, it would seem to be Wittgenstein's view that the inference is unsound. Consider what Wittgenstein says about 'family resemblance' terms such as his famous example "game."[14] Leaving aside everything else in his remarks on the topic, I take it that he contends that there is no single property and no single set of properties that govern the correct application of these terms. "Game" does not have classical realist truth (satisfaction) conditions. As an item of Wittgenstein interpretation this is not very controversial. However, I cannot see that the 'family resemblance' doctrine commits him, in any way, to the position that sentences like

a) This activity is a game,

b) John is playing a game,

and so on, do not, even when asserted correctly, describe facts. Such a commitment would surely be quite surprising. We have the conviction, I believe, that statements such as these *are, in some reasonable sense*, used to describe facts. There seems to be nothing projective about the content of such sentences. It is not, for instance, a part of their semantic function to express some attitude of the speaker's or to effect some sort of performative pronouncement. True utterances of a) and b), we want to grant, do function somehow to describe facts, and there is no reason why Wittgenstein could not agree with our conviction here.

One may well feel some hesitation over the questions just raised, because limited reflection makes it patent that the notion of a 'fact-describing' sentence is vague and problematic. One would like some minimal account of what the notion involves, and I feel certain that there are a number of non-equivalent but palatable accounts that could be developed. Nevertheless, through all the variations that might be played, a) and b) should come out on the 'descriptive' side. Further, nothing in the skeptical solution, as Kripke articulates it, precludes us from drawing a distinction (or, several alternative distinctions) between sentences that are used to describe facts and sentences that are not. That is, this distinction (or these distinctions) would be elaborated in terms of the framework that constitutes the skeptical solution.

As Kripke presents the skeptical solution, a meaningful sentence will have both assertability (justification) conditions and a "role and utility" within the language games in which it figures.[15] Kripke does not say much about the concept of the 'language game role and utility' of a sentence, but the road seems open to delineating the view that some sentences, given their overall use in the relevant language games, do have the role of describing (or stating or registering) facts. By contrast, other varieties of sentences, given their characteristic uses, will have other non-descriptive roles. Perhaps one will wish to grant, in a Wittgensteinian spirit, that the specific language game roles of sentences that count as 'describing facts' may bear only a family resemblance to one another. But, however the details might go, the envisioned distinction will be built as an added story upon the skeptical solution so that, presumably, the former will not contradict any component of the latter.

How will meaning ascriptions be classified by such a distinction? It is obvious that this will depend crucially on the particular character of the distinction that is drawn. My point here is that, at least in the absence of such a further distinction, the skeptical solution is or should be *agnostic* about the truth of S*). Hence, the skeptical solution need not and, in my opinion, does not incorporate projectivism about meaning ascriptions. Notice that if the inference from i) to ii) above were sound, then the global rejection of classical realist truth conditions in S') would enjoin a projectivist view of the content of all sentences. Whether for this reason or another, Wright thinks that Kripke's Wittgenstein is unwittingly stuck with this extreme position. Criticizing this supposed consequence, Wright says, "it is doubtful that it is coherent to suppose that projectivist views could be appropriate quite globally. For, however exactly the distinction be drawn between fact-stating and non-fact-stating discourse, the projectivist will presumably want it to come by way of a *discovery* that certain statements fail to qualify for the former class: a statement of the conclusion of the skeptical argument, for instance, is not *itself* to be projectivist."[16] I am urging that Kripke's Wittgenstein, properly construed, can endorse the second sentence of this passage wholeheartedly. Of course, if we mistakenly think that an argument for S'')—or, indeed, an argument for S')—is itself an argument for S*), then we will feel forced to inflate the skeptical solution with a projectivist remedy. But, I have also argued, on any reading of S*) that is plausible in the dialectical context, such a conflation just *is* a mistake.

I am not sure that Wright and Boghossian are actually guilty of conflating S*) with S''). It may well be that they understand S*) as a proposition, stronger than S''), which represents the central skeptical conclusion, the conclusion with which Wittgenstein is said by Kripke to agree. If this is the case, then, for reasons already sketched, they are mistaken about this different point. I explained earlier why Kripke's skeptic may well be committed to something like S*). The skeptic believes that, if a correct form of normativity is to be engendered, then X's meaning something by $\lceil \phi \rceil$ must be constituted by there being a set of properties to which X is committed as the conditions of correctness for her use of $\lceil \phi \rceil$. But, the skeptic also holds that, if there are or even could be facts of that type, there must be, constitutively, further facts about X that determine what that set of properties is. And now, the skeptic argues at length, there are and can be no such further facts. In other words, there cannot be any facts of the type that, on the skeptic's view, instances of $\lceil X$ means ψ by $\lceil \phi \rceil \rceil$ purport to describe. However, I also pointed out earlier that all of this rests on the skeptic's conception of normativity, encapsulated in N_s), or equivalently, on the classical realist picture of meaning that backs it up. In addition, it was a main thesis of that part of my discussion that Kripke's Wittgenstein decisively rejects N_s) and the 'classical realism' that goes with it. So, it *is* a mistake to imagine that Kripke's Wittgenstein buys into S*). He follows the skeptic only as far as BSC) and its consequences.

It is instructive to glance at Wright's general conception of how the skeptical argument proceeds. In broad terms at least, I suspect that many commentators share this conception.[17] In any case, Wright says,

> The initial target class of putative facts comprises those which you might try to express by claims of the form 'By E, I formerly meant so-and-so.' The relevant idealization will involve your total recall of all facts about your previous behavior and previous mental history, it being assumed that facts about your former meanings must be located in one of those two areas if they are located anywhere. The argument will then be that, even in terms of the idealization, no such claim is justifiable. It follows that your previous life in its entirety is empty of such facts, and hence that there are none.[18]

Now, as Wright and others have indicated, if this *is* the argument in outline, its basic strategy is deeply problematic. Kripke's Wittgenstein is deemed to start out from an assumption about the kinds of potentially relevant facts that exist and then to seek to 'locate' among these a suitable subject matter for ascriptions of meaning. But, given the types of facts that the skeptic appears willing to countenance (e.g., "facts about your previous behavior and previous mental history") locating a subject matter for such statements can involve nothing less than some form of reduction of meaning to the already accepted factual base. This has the consequence that it is open to the skeptic's opponent to reject the presupposition that a reduction is either possible or required. Why not say from the outset that, among the facts that exist for X to recall, is, e.g., the fact that X meant addition by "+", and that fact is just what it is and not another thing.

This conception of the argument misconstrues the kind of facts the skeptic wants specified and misunderstands the skeptic's reasons for his challenge. No wonder it winds up with a false idea of what the skeptical conclusion is. To reiterate once more, the classical realist and, hence, the skeptic believes that if X means something by a term, then there is a specific set of properties about which X has formed an intention (commitment, policy) that these properties are to be the standards for correct uses of her term. It is probably fair enough for the classical realist to resist an unmotivated demand for a reductive account of what it is to have the semantic intention or purpose in question, but it is much harder, without falling back on dogmatism or superstition, to turn aside the question, "*How* does X succeed in picking out the set of properties with which her intention is supposedly concerned?" There must be some way she does this and something to say about that way. *This* is where the 'facts about X' are needed—they are to be facts about how X's intention comes to be about just *this* set of properties and not any of *these* others. The skeptic argues that his question has no answer, and Kripke's Wittgenstein agrees.

We have reached the point at which it is imperative to say something positive about the question of the normativity of meaning. I have maintained that Kripke's Wittgenstein rejects N_s), and, so far, this is the only brand of 'normativity' we have. How, then, do I propose to explain the definite indications in Kripke's text that he thinks that Wittgenstein accepts, even insists upon, the normative character of meaning.

To make a beginning, consider what Kripke says in the passage that most directly formulates the idea that meaning is normative. He explains,

> Suppose I do mean addition by "+". What is the relation of this supposition to the question how I will respond to the problem '68 + 57'? The dispositionalist gives a *descriptive* account of this relation: if '+' meant addition, then I will answer '125'. But this is not the proper account of the relation, which is *normative*, not descriptive. The point is not that, if I meant addition by '+', I *will* answer '125', but that, *if I intend to accord with my past meaning of '+', I should answer '125'*. (p. 37, these last italics are my own)

Now, although there may be various questions to be raised about this passage and about the context in which they are set, one point seems fairly clear. The normativity of meaning is to be explained in terms of the correctness of a certain kind of 'normative' conditional concerning meaning: e.g., the kind of conditional of which the italicized sentence that concludes the quotation is an instance.

In some ways, Kripke's overview of the issue is presented more perspicuously in a segment of his summary account of the strategy of the skeptical solution.

> . . . [W]e must give up the attempt to find any fact about me in virtue of which I mean 'plus' rather than 'quus', and must then go on in a certain

way. Instead we must consider how we actually use: (i) the categorical assertion that an individual is following a given rule (that he means addition by 'plus'); (ii) the conditional assertion that "if an individual follows such-and-such a rule, he must do so-and-so on a given occasion (e.g., if he means addition by '+', his answer to '68 + 57' should be '125' "). (p. 108)

These remarks tell us explicitly that it is an essential task of the skeptical solution to provide, in the terms that it allows itself, an account of the acceptability of these normative conditionals about meaning. Thus, although the word "normativity" is never used in the later stages of Kripke's exposition, it is my belief that these and similar conditionals are to serve to define the concept that the word expresses.[19]

Let me, therefore, attempt to state more explicitly and more generally what it is for meaning to be normative. Kripke never offers such a general formulation, and, in the light of various qualifications he suggests, my formulation may be no more than a first approximation to a fully adequate explication of the concept. Nevertheless, I take it that the normativity of meaning rests upon the correctness of a generalized conditional of the form

N) For each of an unbounded range of (actual and possible) cases, if there is something that X means by $\lceil \phi \rceil$ during t, then, were the question to arise, X *must* [or: *should*] apply $\lceil \phi \rceil$, as she meant it at t, to the case in question.[20]

As I have already indicated, both the skeptic (or, more broadly, the classical realist) *and* the proponent of the skeptical solution are to be understood as assenting to N). Where they differ and differ radically is over the grounds there are for so assenting.

Why the classical realist accepts N) has been made all too familiar by our previous discussion. Since meaning something by $\lceil \phi \rceil$ is thought to involve there being properties that govern X's application of the term, X must or should ascribe $\lceil \phi \rceil$ to any item that has just those properties. That is, X must ascribe $\lceil \phi \rceil$ to an object from this class if, respecting the standards of correctness she herself has set, her ascription is to be, in fact, correct. Further, there will be an indefinitely large range of actual and possible cases that satisfy these standards.

The skeptical solution depicts this conception of how normativity arises as the product of a bizarre and ultimately incoherent mythologization of banal linguistic facts—of an interrelated complex of facts about familiar linguistic practice. The general character of the mistake with which the classical realist is charged can be illustrated with a simpler example whose moral is more transparent. Imagine that someone says this: "If Jones already knows *now* that Judy will divorce Jim in two weeks, then Judy *must* divorce Jim in two weeks."[21] It would be an outlandish misconception of what has been said if some Martian, learning English, were to interpret this 'normative' conditional to mean: knowledge that Judy will divorce Jim in two weeks is a psychological state, realized in Jones at the present moment, which, through its power to act upon the future, will somehow necessitate Judy's divorce from Jim in two weeks time. In the face of such a misunderstanding, we would want to explain that the speaker was simply asserting that, in this case as in others, its being the case that P is semantically required (along with other conditions) to sustain the judgment that Y knows that P. The conditional assertion is being used to remind us that Judy's divorcing Jim in two weeks is required to sustain the judgment that Jones knows now that such a divorce will take place.

Kripke's Wittgenstein contends, in a similar vein, that the classical realist supposes that, if X *now* means something by $\lceil \phi \rceil$, then this entails that there is something available *now* to X's language faculty that determines, *modulo* facts about the various candidate items, whether $\lceil \phi \rceil$ applies correctly or not. But, according to the skeptical solution, this picture reverses the true order of 'determination' and, in the process, grotesquely distorts the nature of the 'necessity' in play. The real basis of N) can be illustrated by suitable reflections on the following case.

We are wondering what Ralph means by the word "table" these days, and we notice that Ralph, his senses and intellect in normal working order, is situated so as to have a plain view of what we deem to be an exemplary table. But Ralph judges that this exemplary item is not a table. "That is not what I would call 'a table'," he insists. In virtue of his surprising claim, Ralph thereby supplies us with defeasible warrant for denying that he means table by "table," or, at least, for withholding judgment that this is what he means. Insofar as we regard ourselves as being thus warranted, we could naturally express the content of our warrant with the words, "If Ralph means table by 'table,' then he *must* apply 'table' to this object." The "must" in the statement simply registers a *requirement* that we are prepared to impose for judging that Ralph means table by "table." We require Ralph to agree with us that this paradigm is a table. Moreover, the requirement is a *primitive* requirement. It is established by our first and fundamental procedures in ascribing meaning, and it is not based upon a 'theory', e.g., about what speech behavior happens to be correlated with meaning 'table' by some term. In other words, what the normative conditional requires of Ralph constitutes an *assertability condition* for judgments about whether his use of the word means 'table'. Compare these reflections on Ralph with what Kripke says about similar conditionals. "By such a conditional we do not mean, on the Wittgensteinian view, that any state of Jones guarantees his correct behavior. Rather by asserting such a conditional we commit ourselves, if in the future Jones behaves bizarrely enough (and on enough occasions), no longer to persist in our assertion that he is following the conventional rule of addition" (p. 95). It is these and similar remarks in Kripke's book that I am trying to stress and elucidate.[22]

It will be useful to sketch, however crudely, the general pattern that the skeptical solution is invoking. By doing so, we can comprehend more precisely how Kripke's Wittgenstein agrees to N). Hence, where $\lceil \phi \rceil$ is an arbitrary term employed by X, let $\lceil\psi\rceil$ be a term or phrase that might specify a possible interpretation of X's use of $\lceil\phi\rceil$. I will say that an object o (as it is at a given time) is a *paradigmatic sample* for $\lceil\psi\rceil$ within a designated linguistic community just in case 'competent' members of the community generally agree in being prepared to ascribe $\lceil\psi\rceil$ to o when o has been presented to them under familiar, favorable 'test circumstances'. By "competent members of the community," I have in mind members who are competent in ascribing $\lceil\psi\rceil$, and they are to be the members who, having been subjected to a standard regimen of training in the use of $\lceil\psi\rceil$, regularly and systematically apply $\lceil\psi\rceil$ in overall agreement with one another. Given the role of the paradigmatic samples in relation to ascriptions of meaning to individual speakers, it follows that both positive and negative warrant for these ascriptions *presuppose* the existence of general agreement in the pertinent judgments of community members. This is a point much emphasized by Kripke in his development of the skeptical solution.[23] In addition, it should be noted that various remarks in Kripke's presentation suggest several refinements and modifications that may be in order here. For example, some passing phrases hint at the idea that we might stipulate that competent $\lceil\psi\rceil$-users should normally be disposed to ascribe $\lceil\psi\rceil$ to paradigmatic samples, optimally presented, "confidently and without hesitation."[24] In any case, I trust that the intuitive concept is clear enough. The paradigmatic samples for $\lceil\psi\rceil$ should more or less coincide with the objects that competent $\lceil\psi\rceil$-users would, as a matter of course, be inclined to treat as samples in the ostensive teaching of ψ.[25]

We can now arrive at N) by generalizing the earlier reflections on Ralph's prospective use of the word "table." Suppose that we are entertaining the possibility that X means something by $\lceil\phi\rceil$ during t, and let $\lceil X$ means ψ by $\lceil\phi\rceil$ during $t\rceil$ represent any hypothesis that we have occasion to consider. Finally, let o be one of the paradigmatic samples for $\lceil\psi\rceil$. As Ralph's case has illustrated, the skeptical solution maintains that we are entitled to affirm the normative conditional

n) If X means ψ by $\lceil\phi\rceil$ during t, then, were the question to arise, X must apply $\lceil\phi\rceil$ to o.[26]

As was also explained before, we are entitled to affirm instances of n), according to the skeptical solution, because n) is used to state a requirement that we impose upon the meaning ascriptions exhibited in the antecedents of these conditionals. The requirement is that X must ascribe $\lceil\phi\rceil$ to o if the judgment that X means ψ by $\lceil\phi\rceil$ is to sustain its warrant. Actually, two questions of warranted assertability are tied together here. A member of the community is warranted in asserting a given instance of n) just in case, failure to ascribe $\lceil\phi\rceil$ to o in favorable test circumstances warrants denying that X means ψ by $\lceil\phi\rceil$. The skeptical solution tells us that this is a requirement that we impose in our actual practice of assigning meanings to speakers' words and that we recognize, at least implicitly, that this is the case. So, on this basis, we are entitled to accept n).

However, we assumed nothing special about the object o. We are equally entitled to accept a generalization of n) which is prefixed by "For each paradigmatic sample, o, for $\lceil \psi \rceil$." This generalization of n) merely formulates the wider principle upon which each of the n)-style specialized requirements is based. The proponent of the skeptical solution believes that the same examination of what we do in ascribing meanings that convinces us of the propriety of instances of n) convinces us of the principle as well. Our realization that each instance is warranted provides us with warrant for the generalization. Finally, since we are concerned with both actual and possible paradigmatic samples for $\lceil \psi \rceil$, it is safe to assume that the range of these samples is unbounded—that it is indefinitely large in number. This point and the fact that $\lceil \psi \rceil$, the putative interpretation for X's use of $\lceil \phi \rceil$, has been an arbitrary term or phrase throughout guarantee that our generalization of n) entails N). And this is where we wanted to be. From the perspective of the skeptical solution, there are clearcut reasons to endorse the 'thin' normativity of meaning that N) is meant to capture.

To conclude this outline of the view I take Kripke to impute to Wittgenstein, let me briefly return a final time to the vexed issue of 'projectivism' in this domain. It has been a central tenet of my account of the skeptical solution that it does not include a projectivist explication of meaning ascriptions. However, in the light of the considerations just expounded, we possibly should allow that the skeptical solution does offer a projectivist conception of the 'hardness' of the semantical "must." That is, it may be that the reading of the modal terms embedded in instances of schema n) is projectivist in character. I hesitate over this point because of uncertainties I feel about what the doctrine of projectivism does and does not involve. In any case, the following is true. The skeptical solution denies that these normative conditionals are made true by some range of semantical facts generated by a set of standards that members of the linguistic community, individually or collectively, have pre-established as the basis of correct and incorrect application. This is the upshot of BSC). By contrast, the skeptical solution asks us to see the acceptability of the relevant n)-instances as the manifest expression of linguistic commitments or requirements imposed by the community in its actual practices of ascribing meanings. Perhaps this deserves to be called a 'projectivist theory' of the normative conditionals, and it may be of substantial philosophical interest if this is so. But, however this may be, projectivism of this sort does not seem to entail that meaning ascriptions (or, for that matter, the normative conditionals themselves) do not purport to state facts about a speaker's use of a term. For the reasons sketched earlier, that is a conclusion that Kripke's Wittgenstein has no obligation nor incentive to embrace.

The route to this result has been slow and laborious. But it has seemed to me important to be cautious here. In the first part of the essay, I argued that commentators have been seriously confused about the issue of the normativity of meaning. Noticing that Kripke says that both the skeptic and his Wittgenstein concur that meaning is normative, they fail to see that Kripke's Wittgenstein repudiates the skeptic's conception of normativity. Even this way of putting the matter verges on the paradoxical unless we distinguish sharply between two questions, "What condition or conditions define the normativity of meaning?" My answer to this has been, "The conditions laid down in N) or some improved version thereof." Here the two protagonists agree. The second question is, "What are the facts about meaning or about ascriptions of meaning in virtue of which the N-type conditions are satisfied?" Over the answer to this question, the skeptic and the skeptical solution diverge fundamentally. It is at the juncture of their divergence, I believe, that the heart of the whole topic is exposed.

A number of his critics have objected to Kripke's framing of Wittgenstein's investigation of 'following a rule' in terms of a debate about semantic *skepticism*. Some have denied that Wittgenstein's chief objective was to overcome a global skepticism about meaning; more have felt uncomfortable with the notion that Wittgenstein's views can be characterized as being even partially skeptical. To a considerable extent, it seems to me, these complaints tend to reflect the commentator's own attitudes toward classical realism about meaning. If one finds the classical realist account, whatever its local difficulties, to be natural, powerful, and intuitively persuasive, then Wittgenstein is likely to appear more plausibly in the role of a skeptic. On the other hand, if classical realism seems little more than a seductive and widely influential theory of truth and meaning, then Wittgenstein will probably arrive on stage as the subtle, commonsense therapist of a philosophical illusion. I doubt that there will turn out to be much substance to quarrels of this sort about the felicity of Kripke's drama of skepticism. Beyond this, these worries and complaints tend to miss one of the key factors that motivates Kripke's talk of skeptical problems and skeptical solutions. What is missed is the essence of Kripke's analogy to Hume.

Late in his book, Kripke gives a concise, instructive summary of the intended analogy. He says, "Wittgenstein's scepticism about the determination of future usage by the past contents of my mind is analogous to Hume's scepticism about the determination of the future by the past. . . . The paradox can be resolved only by a 'skeptical solution of these doubts', in Hume's classic sense" (pp. 107–108). We are presently well situated to grasp the comparison that this and similar remarks propose. Hume thinks that he can refute the idea that causation is an ontologically primitive relation between pairs of concrete events, a relation that implies that a cause necessitates its effect. Correlatively, his skeptical solution attempts to explain what we legitimately mean when we assert, e.g., "Event C caused E'" and "If the cause occurs, its effect must ensue." Of course, these analyses or explications purport to eschew the theses already repudiated in the previous skeptical stage. Similarly, Kripke's Wittgenstein denies that meaning something by a term or sentence involves the grasping of a something that semantically 'necessitates' the way the term or sentence is to be correctly used. The new skeptical solution tries to explain the content of meaning ascriptions in terms of their role and utility in the relevant language games, and the normative conditionals about meaning, which the classical realist misconstrues as describing a super-rigid semantical determination, are explained in terms of the requirements that our use of standard criteria for meaning ascriptions engender and enforce. I have wanted to emphasize the exact character of the analogy, because it is a significant virtue of my reading of Kripke that it enables us to make accurate sense of this. Many other readings do not.

Whether Kripke's interpretation is true to the thought of the actual Wittgenstein is another topic, one that I have not pursued. Nevertheless, I will close by making just one broad comment on this subject. In §185 the famous case of the wayward adder is introduced, and in §186 we find the following exchange.

> To carry it out correctly! How is it decided what is the right step to take at any particular stage?—"The right step is the one that accords with the order—as it was *meant*."—So when you gave the order +2 you mean that he was to write 1002 after 1000—and did you also mean that he should write 1868 after 1866, and 100036 after 100034, and so on—an infinite number of such propositions?—"No: what I meant was, that he should write the next but one number after *every* number that he wrote; and from this all those propositions follow in turn."—But that is just what is in question: what, at any stage, does follow from that sentence. Or, again, what, at any stage we are to call "being in accord" with that sentence (and with the *mean*-ing you then put into the sentence—whatever that may have consisted in).[27]

It is notable that, in this passage, Wittgenstein, who so often seems elusive, flatly asserts, "This is just what is in question." And we are told what that question is, i.e., "What, at any stage, follows from the cited sentence?" In §189 and §190, what I take to be a variant formulation of the question is employed: "What, at any stage, does a formula or the meaning of a formula determine as the next step?" From §190 through §243 many of the remarks are, indeed, focused on various facets of this question. Or, rather, the question under philosophical investigation in this section is, "*What is it* for a formula or the meaning of a formula to determine the next step?" (However, we need to be careful not to build in too much about the form an answer to this question has to take.) Now, I have argued that this is what Kripke claims Wittgenstein's central question to be, and it is the question that his dialectic is meant to address. But, this point will not be apparent if we misunderstand the issues he frames in terms of 'the normativity of meaning' or if we miss the fundamental position that they occupy in his exposition.

Further, it is clear that Wittgenstein believes that we are deeply and recurrently tempted to give an unsatisfactory answer to the problem about 'determination by meaning'—to form a wildly misleading picture of what meaning determination involves. In a more positive vein, many of the remarks in the 'following a rule' section are intended to help us set matters straight.

Again, if my exegesis of Kripke is right, it is the skeptic (*qua* classical realist) who gives expression to the misleading picture and to the unsatisfactory account it prompts. Correspondingly, the skeptical solution, by assembling a configuration of reminders about the nature and force of our practices in teaching and ascribing meanings, has the goal of shattering the bad picture by showing us the relevant plain facts that otherwise would be hidden. I realize, naturally, that these last observations of mine still leave it quite open whether the finer-grained execution of Kripke's interpretation mirrors the details of Wittgenstein's remarks accurately, but they do indicate that Kripke correctly portrays the basic structure of Wittgenstein's philosophical concerns. Even this modest assessment has been frequently denied. In any case, we will certainly be in no position to test Kripke's text against Wittgenstein's if we read the former through a pair of spectacles that invert the arguments he presents.[28]

NOTES

This essay is dedicated to the memory of David Sachs.

1. Saul Kripke, *Wittgenstein: On Rules and Private Language.* (Cambridge, Mass., 1982). Page citations in the main text are all to this book.

2. In this paragraph, I have deliberately used somewhat different formulations. That is, I speak of adopting a commitment, a policy, a rule, and also of forming a certain intention. I have done so in order to avoid whatever significant issues might be raised if one were to try to choose between them. On the other hand, I believe that none of the main questions discussed in this essay would be affected by such a choice. Also, in the second quotation from Kripke given above, he speaks of 'giving oneself directions' where I would use one of the locutions just mentioned. To my ear, this phrase of Kripke's too much conveys the idea of performing (outwardly or inwardly) a certain kind of speech act, and this distorts the general conception that the skeptic has in mind. In particular, the choice of words is particularly unfortunate when it is conjoined with Kripke's description of the first response to the skeptic's problem. The would-be response is stated in this way: "Rather I learned— and internalized instructions for—a *rule* which determines how addition is to be continued" (p. 15). This proposal is clearly rejected, but the similarity in formulation can suggest that the skeptic's basic conception of what must be involved in meaning addition by "+" is here being rejected. Rather, it seems to me, what is proposed and rejected is the idea that I *establish* which arithmetical operation is to constitute the standard of correctness for my use of "+" by giving myself a linguistic definition or set of instructions that specify the operation in question. But then, the obvious reply—given in Kripke's text—is that, because the puzzle about what it is I mean by a term is a completely general one, the puzzle will arise again and with equal force with respect to the relevant terms in the verbal definition or instructions I formulated for myself. Although this proposal is rejected, the skeptic's idea that, if I mean addition by '+', then something about me 'singles out' addition as that which governs my use of the term remains in place. In the first quotation, he speaks of 'grasping a rule', and I have similarly talked about 'adopting a rule'. But, standing by itself, these locutions can be understood as meaning something like 'accepting a linguistic or symbolic *formulation* of a rule'. So understood, the confusion just described can arise again. So I have been at some pains to counter this impression.

3. I realize that these formulations suggest that the facts about X that the skeptic will accept as relevant to his challenge are restricted, as it were, to 'individualistic' facts about X. Much of Kripke's discussion tends to carry the same suggestion—in some cases rather strongly. This suggestion leaves the skeptic open to the charge that he has illegitimately excluded, from the beginning, a kind of social version of a 'straight' solution to his puzzle.

Thus, very roughly, one might hold the following. First, it would be granted that there are facts about members of a linguistic community—in virtue of *their* complex, cooperative use of a term ⌜φ⌝—that establishes properties P_1-P_n as the standards that govern correct applications of ⌜φ⌝ among *them* or in *their* language. Second, it would be held that an individual member X of the community will mean P_1-P_n by ⌜φ⌝ only if his or her linguistic dispositions concerning ⌜φ⌝ situates him/her as a competent ⌜φ⌝-user in that community. Whatever the merits or demerits of this vaguely specified approach, I take it that Kripke holds that his skeptic rejects it and rejects it for reasons similar to the ones given in his main exposition of the skeptical problem. See, in particular, the brief remarks on p. 111. I assume that Kripke is here denying that Wittgenstein would accept the first plank in the approach adumbrated above, i.e., that there are facts about the linguistic community, even taken collectively, that constitute some set of properties as standards of correctness for their use of ⌜φ⌝. Again, I will make no attempt to assess the force of the considerations available to the skeptic against a position of this kind. However, I do mean to suppose in the text that the skeptic's arguments for his skeptical conclusion are to be understood as including non-individualistic solutions of this ilk. For many, I suspect, the skeptic's arguments will seem truly disturbing only if this supposition is made.

4. If one goes back to Kripke's summary statement of the skeptic's challenge, one finds the grounding condition indicated in the following statement: "The 'directions' ... that determine what I should do in each instance, must somehow be 'contained' in any candidate for the fact as to what I meant." Given the way in which I have formulated the issues, I would be inclined to put the point in this way. *The properties*, which constitute the standards for my use of ⌜φ⌝, and which thereby determine how I should apply ⌜φ⌝ in each instance, must somehow be 'contained' in any candidate for the fact as to what I meant. That is to say, the fact as to what I meant must itself partially consist in facts about me that establish which properties are to be my standards of correctness in using ⌜φ⌝.

5. When the skeptic affirms that there are no facts about X which establish some particular set of properties as that which X means by ⌜φ⌝, he presupposes that meaning ascriptions of the form ⌜X means ψ by ⌜φ⌝⌝ say that X's use of ⌜φ⌝ stands in the 'meaning-relation' (as he conceives of this) to a set of properties indicated by ⌜ψ⌝. Hence, his affirmation threatens to entail that X does not mean anything by ⌜φ⌝. However, the proponent of the skeptical solution rejects this crucial presupposition. As we will see later, it is central to the skeptical solution the skeptic has, in this manner, misconstrued the character of the meaning ascriptions from the very beginning. Thus, if we say, as I do, that the proponent of the skeptical solution endorses *this* affirmation of the skeptic, perhaps we should also say that he, unlike the skeptic, employs "means by" within scare quotes in this context and that the scare quotes are to signal the fact that he agrees to the claim only when "means by" is used as the skeptic (wrongly) understands it. See Kripke's remarks on what is essentially this same complication on pp. 76–77.

6. The characterization of a skeptical conclusion as being "insane and intolerable" occurs on page 60. I am taking this to refer to the radical skeptical conclusion, but, even in context, this is not so clear. Kripke simply says that *the* skeptical conclusion is insane and intolerable. But he cannot mean here 'the skeptical conclusion' with which Wittgenstein is supposed to agree. It has to be some conclusion drawn from the skeptic's argument which the skeptical solution is supposed to block. Admittedly, such remarks are confusing.

7. David Pears, *The False Prison*, vol. 2 (New York, 1988), 465.

8. Ibid., 457.

9. Crispin Wright, "Kripke's Account of the Argument against Private Language," *Journal of Philosophy* 81 (1984): 759–78. Paul A. Boghossian, "The Rule-Following Considerations," *Mind* 98 (1989): 507–49.

10. See Boghossian, "Rule-Following Considerations," 524. See also Wright, "Kripke's Account," 769.

11. Wright, "Kripke's Account," 761.

12. For remarks that could suggest such a view, see Kripke, p. 92. However, it should be clear that I do not take Kripke, in such passages, to be proposing a projectivist account of the semantic function of meaning ascriptions. He is merely attempting to bring out certain features of their assertability conditions and their 'role and utility' in relevant language games.

13. On the whole, when Kripke says that a sentence does not 'state facts', he seems to mean that the sentence does not have classical realist truth conditions. Or, so I interpret him. After all, talk of facts in relation to the question of sentence meaning is introduced when Kripke introduces the classical realist account of meaning. But, in some passages, his usage is not so clear. For example, on page 73, he says, "Since the indicative mood is not taken as in any sense primary or basic, it becomes more plausible that the linguistic role even of utterances in the indicative mood that superficially look like assertions need not be one of 'stating facts'." Especially when this is read along with fn. 62 at the bottom of the page, 'stating facts' here seems to mean "used to describe [or: report] facts" as I have been employing this phrase.

14. Ludwig Wittgenstein, *Philosophical Investigations* (New York, 1958), 31e–36e.

15. The concept in question is first introduced on pages 75–76. More on this notion, in relation to the "+" example, is found on pages 91–93.

16. Wright, "Kripke's Account," 770.

17. For example, Warren Goldfarb seems to have a similar notion of the strategy of the skeptical argument in "Kripke on Wittgenstein on Rules," *Journal of Philosophy* 82 (1985): 471–88. See his discussion on pages 473–80. For example, consider, "It [the skeptical argument] questions whether, if everything there is were laid out before us, we could read off the correct ascriptions of meaning to people. . . . Thus, it is the notion of fact, of 'everything there is', that is to provide the ground of the challenge" (p. 474).

18. Wright, "Kripke's Account," 762. Boghossian sees the argument in very similar terms.

19. For example, in Kripke's summary statement of the skeptic's challenge (which I quoted earlier), he says, "So it ought to be agreed that *if I meant plus, then unless I wish to change my usage, I am justified in answering (indeed compelled to answer) '125', not '5'.*" The conditional I have italicized is another variant formulation of the sort of condition that is meant to define the normativity of meaning. Indeed, that is its role in this passage, although, of course, the term 'normativity' has not yet been introduced.

20. The too brief qualification, "as she meant it $[\![\phi]\!]$ at t" is intended to do the following work. Suppose that a question about whether or not $\ulcorner\phi\urcorner$ applies to some object o arises at some time t^* that falls outside the period t mentioned in the relevant meaning ascription. Suppose also that X then incorrectly denies that $\ulcorner\phi\urcorner$ applies to o. At best, X's denial is grounds for denying that, *at t^*, X means such-and-such (for whatever interpretation of X's use of $\ulcorner\phi\urcorner$ is in question). X's denial, by itself, does not provide grounds for deciding anything about what X did or did not mean *during t*. To connect the denial at t^* with the question of what X meant by $\ulcorner\phi\urcorner$ during t, we need the assumption that what X means by $\ulcorner\phi\urcorner$ at t^* is the same as what X meant [or: will mean] at t. In fact, a formulation that explicitly conveys this condition would make N) clearer, but it also would make N) rather complicated and hard to read. As a compromise, I have settled for the briefer but possibly misleading phrase mentioned above. Since the condition that I have just explained will play no real role in the discussion below, I thought that the danger of misunderstanding could be accepted. On the other hand, I wanted N) to acknowledge the condition both because it is obviously needed and because Kripke several times mentions the condition briefly in formulations he gives.

21. For comparison, consider Wittgenstein's remarks in §187. I am not at all clear, however, that the use I have given in my example indicates the idea that Wittgenstein had in mind in this passage.

22. In his famous discussion of linguistic stereotypes, Hilary Putnam says, "The theoretical account of what it is to be a stereotype proceeds in terms of the notion of a *linguistic obligation*; a notion we believe to be fundamental to linguistics and which we shall not attempt to explicate here. What it means to say that being striped is part of the (linguistic) stereotype of 'tiger' is that it is *obligatory* to acquire the information that stereotypical tigers are striped if one acquires the word 'tiger'. . . ." "The Meaning of 'Meaning' " in *Minnesota Studies in the Philosophy of Science*, vol. VII, edited by Keith Gunderson (Minneapolis, 1975), 171. But see all of pp. 169–73. It is interesting to compare Putnam's notion of 'linguistic obligation' to the treatment of the modals in the normative conditionals proposed by the skeptical solution. I do not mean to suggest that Putnam expects his concept of 'linguistic obligation' to do the same overall theoretical work that Kripke's Wittgenstein expects from his treatment of the relevant modal terms.

23. For a discussion of agreement under that label see page 96. But much material on pages 88–100 is relevant.

24. For invocation of the concept of ascriptions made "confidently" and "unhesitatingly" see pages 86, 87, and 96.

25. Pears, in *The False Prison*, holds that he differs from Kripke, not only over the existence of a certain kind of *reductio* in the *Investigations*, but over Kripke's supposed failure to see the importance in Wittgenstein's thought, of "calibration on standard objects" (as he puts it). See, e.g., page 464 for the charge and chapter 14 for an account of what it amounts to. Re-reading Kripke in the light of the discussion of the role of what I am calling "paradigmatic samples," one might investigate the amount of difference between Pears and Kripke over even this topic. Notice that, since Kripke tends to develop his discussion quite extensively in terms of his "addition" example, the importance of "standard objects" or "paradigmatic samples" does not have great salience in his text.

26. Here and in the discussion that follows I drop the condition "as she meant ⟦φ⟧ at *t*" and the modest complications that would ensue in the discussion below if it were to be included. Nothing of significance, except simplicity turns on this. See my n. 18.

27. Wittgenstein, *Investigations*.

28. Earlier versions of this essay were read to colloquia at the University of Michigan, the University of Maryland, the University of Western Ontario, and the University of Connecticut at Storrs. I am grateful in each instance for helpful discussion that substantially improved the evolving work. I also want to thank the following individuals for help and encouragement: Margaret Gilbert, Jerry Levinson, Ed Minar, Bill Taschek, and especially Mark Wilson.

MIDWEST STUDIES IN PHILOSOPHY, XIX (1994)

Are Our Logical and Mathematical Concepts Highly Indeterminate?

HARTRY FIELD

I am going to begin with a rather familiar worry, about whether we have a determinate understanding of second-order quantification. Then I will consider an analogous worry about whether we have a determinate understanding of the notion of finiteness. At first blush the case for the second worry seems quite analogous to the case for the first; but for various reasons doubts about the determinacy of the notion of finiteness may seem harder to take seriously than doubts about the determinacy of second-order quantification. I will be considering a number of different reactions to this situation.

1. INTRODUCTION

1A. First Order Set Theory

I will start off the discussion not with second-order quantification, but with the notion of set; for the moment I will tacitly take our logic to be first order. How determinate is our understanding of the notion of set?

I think that familiar considerations against the determinacy of our notion of 'set' are fairly strong. I will remind you of two of them. The first concerns very central set theoretic questions such as the size of the continuum that are unsettled not only by the standard axioms of set theory but by any axioms that anyone has been able to think of that are intuitively compelling. The continuum example seems to me an especially striking one because it is not simply that there is an undecidable 'yes'/'no' question of whether the continuum hypothesis is true; it is rather that virtually every answer to the question of the size of the continuum is known to be consistent with the standard axioms of set theory, and with all known intuitively compelling extensions. (More exactly, it is known that one can consistently take the size of the continuum to be any infinite cardinal not cofinal with ω.) And even after arbitrarily choosing an answer to the size of the continuum, the size of its power set is still almost totally undetermined; and so on.

One sometimes hears it said that the continuum hypothesis should be regarded as false on the ground that it makes the set theoretic hierarchy too small. Certainly plenitude has its attractions: if you are going to have sets at all, you might as well have lots and lots of them. But of course increasing the number of sets does not obviously increase the size of the continuum; it can decrease it, by increasing the number of 1–1 correspondences. And even granting the assumption that a higher answer to the size of the continuum means a more plenitudinous set theory, one can hardly argue against the continuum hypothesis on the grounds that there is a more plenitudinous answer that is consistent, since this argument would tell equally against any other conceivable answer.

I guess I think that if one had to plump for a single answer, the Generalized Continuum Hypothesis might be best simply because it seems the least arbitrary. But I think it is more natural to say that we should not regard there as being a unique answer: for each infinite cardinal κ not cofinal with ω, we could refine our conceptions of set and membership into conceptions set_κ and ϵ_κ for which the size of the continuum is κ; and none of these conceptions of set and membership is privileged over any other. This point of view is of course a natural one for someone with fictionalist sympathies: each of these answers to the size of the continuum is an equally good fiction. But it seems to me that it is also natural from a platonist point of view, if platonism means simply that there are lots of abstract entities: indeed, the principle of plenitude seems to lead to precisely this viewpoint. What could be more plenitudinous than regarding all the consistent concepts of set and membership as instantiated side by side?[1] (By "instantiated side by side," I mean that we refuse to single out one instantiation as privileged and to regard all others as merely "unintended models" generated by the completeness theorem. For a clearer elaboration and a discussion, see the Appendix.) Of course, refining the concepts of set and membership to settle the size of the continuum would leave many other questions radically unsettled, including the size of its power set; there is no way to refine our concepts so that all questions will be settled. The picture then is that there are multiple mathematical universes, in which the answers to many set theoretical questions differ; and that nothing about our current concepts of set and membership serve to pick out a unique one, or even to narrow down the field enough so that questions like the size of the continuum get unique answers.[2]

The second consideration against the determinacy of 'set' is the one pressed by Putnam in the first half of [16]. It is based (in part) on the fact that even if one took the truths of set theory to be settled, there are alternative interpretations of 'set' and 'ϵ' that would generate these truths, by Skolem-Lowenheim and compactness arguments. That of course is not in itself a problem: it is natural to say that these interpretations are unintended. But Putnam's question is, *in virtue of what is "the intended one" uniquely intended?* Unless an answer to this question can be given, it would seem that the whole idea of a unique intended interpretation must be given up; if we put aside the fictionalist view that there is simply nothing in reality answering to these notions, the conclusion should be that 'set' and '∈' are referentially indeterminate. And I think Putnam argued pretty convincingly in the first half of [16] that in the case of 'set' there is a very serious problem in giving any account of "intendedness" according to which one interpretation is intended and all the others are not. (I will need to review this argument eventually, to distinguish it from an argument that Putnam gives later in his essay that attempts to generalize the conclusion to all concepts; that other argument seems to me clearly fallacious, but has nothing to do with the much more persuasive argument in the first half that is confined to the concept of set and related concepts.[3] But for now let me simply say that Putnam has raised a challenge that seems *prima facie* very difficult in principle to meet: explain in virtue of what we "intend" a standard as opposed to a nonstandard interpretation of 'set'.) If the challenge is impossible to meet, the natural conclusion would seem to be that *even taking the truths of set theory to be settled*, 'set' and '∈' are referentially indeterminate. And of course once one grants the referential indeterminacy of these notions, it becomes all the more natural to question whether claims like the continuum hypothesis have a definite truth value on our current understanding of 'set' and '∈'.[4]

It is often assumed that if we regard concepts like 'set' and '∈' as indeterminate, we cannot go on using classical logic in connection with them, but must use intuitionistic logic instead. But if there is a good argument for this, I do not know it. Indeterminateness seems formally a lot like vagueness, and there seems to be nothing at all incoherent about the idea that vague and indeterminate concepts obey classical logic. Of course, 'definitely true' is not a bivalent concept—a sentence A and its negation can both fail to be definitely true—but one does not have to give up the law of excluded middle, one can say that the disjunction $A \vee -A$ is definitely true even though neither disjunct is. An account of definite truth along these lines—supervaluation semantics—is obvious, intuitive, and well known. (See for instance [8].)[5] It is thus not at all obvious that the practice of standard mathematics presupposes the determinacy of the concept of 'set'.

For later reference I would like to make a final obvious observation: the case for the indeterminacy of 'set' and '∈' is unaffected by whether the set theory in question is a set theory like Zermelo-Fraenkel (ZF) that does not allow proper classes, or a set theory like Morse-Kelley that does.[6] For present purposes I take 'Morse-Kelley' to be a first-order theory that takes sets and classes to be distinct (i.e., which holds that no set is a class), and which employs separate membership relations ϵ_s and ϵ_c for sets and for classes, and which provides an embedding F of the sets into the classes such that for any sets x and y, $x \epsilon_s y$ iff $F(x) \epsilon_c F(y)$. As usual, there is an impredicative comprehension schema for classes. It is true that in Morse-Kelley the interpretation of 'set' and 'ϵ_s' are uniquely fixed (up to isomorphism) if we assume that the interpretations of 'class' and 'ϵ_c' are fixed, but of course the arguments for indeterminacy are arguments for indeterminacy of 'class' and class membership as well as 'set' and set membership.

1B. Second-order Set Theory

I have not yet discussed the details of Putnam's argument against the possibility of giving an account of what makes "the intended interpretation" intended and "the unintended ones" unintended, and some readers may feel that it is not as compelling as I have claimed. Let us not discuss this yet. Instead, let us consider whether that whole discussion can be obviated, by appealing to *second-order* set theory.

By second-order set theory I mean the theory (in impredicative second-order logic) that results from Zermelo-Fraenkel set theory by using a second-order replacement axiom instead of the first-order schema. (The second-order variables are understood either as plural quantifiers in the sense of George Boolos's [3], or as ranging over "logical classes," where this includes proper classes as well as classes that correspond to sets.) The Putnam argument presupposes there being a wide range of interpretations of set theory (e.g., interpretations that differ over the size of the continuum); we might want to claim that some of these interpretations are "unintended," but the heart of the argument is then that we cannot give an account of our intentions that *make* them unintended. But it may seem that the argument does not get off the ground in second-order set theory, for the presupposition is basically false. More accurately, the Skolem-Lowenheim and compactness theorems used for producing the unintended interpretations are false for second-order logic. Moreover, given any two interpretations of (pure) second-order set theory, one is obtained from the other by chopping off all sets of some inaccessible rank or higher; so that the most the Putnam argument can show is that it is indeterminate whether we are quantifying over *all* ordinals (that is, over sets of *all* ranks) or only over all of them up to a certain inaccessible. But this level of indeterminacy is not all that worrisome; indeed, many people doubt that the notion of *all* ordinals make sense, they think of the ordinals as an "indefinitely extensible totality." Certainly this "indeterminacy in height" is not one that could support the idea that the continuum hypothesis has no determinate truth value, for adding on more inaccessibles cannot affect the truth value of the continuum hypothesis. So (the response concludes) Putnam's argument lacks punch in second-order set theory. Indeed, this line of reasoning might seem to show not only that Putnam's *argument* is wrong but that its *conclusion* is, in which case there would be a uniquely correct answer to the size of the continuum (though perhaps we would in principle be unable to discover it).

But the response I have just reviewed seems to be quite misguided. Recall that there are at least two conceptions of interpretation for impredicative second-order logic: full interpretations, where the range of the second-order variables consists of all subclasses of the first-order domain; and general interpretations, where the range of the second-order variables is a collection (closed under second-order definability) of not necessarily all the subclasses of the first-order domain. These are both perfectly legitimate definitions of interpretation, and of course the Lowenheim-Skolem and compactness theorems do hold under the general notion of interpretation, and the claim about different interpretations arising only by cutting off the universe at some inaccessible is false for general interpretations. So if the response just reviewed works, it depends on restricting to full interpretations instead of general interpretations. Is it legitimate to make this restriction in this context?

I grant that in many ways the notion of full interpretation is more natural than the notion of general interpretation, more in correspondence with what we intend when we use the second-order quantifier: we intend our second-order quantifier to range over *all* subcollections of the domain of sets. However, in the present context where it is being questioned whether our intentions are as determinate as we usually assume, we must be careful about attaching too much significance to this: after all, in first-order ZF we intend 'set' to stand for all sets and 'ϵ' to stand for membership, but one could hardly shortcut the Putnam argument by restricting the word 'interpretation' to interpretations that are intended in this sense! Admittedly, the proposal to restrict attention to full interpretations is not quite as trivial as this: it is not directly a proposal to restrict the interpretations of 'set' and 'ϵ'. A fairer comparison would be the proposal to shortcut the Putnam argument for first-order Morse-Kelley by restricting the word 'interpretation' to interpretations in which 'class' and 'ϵ_c' stand for classes and class membership, but in which no restriction is explicitly imposed on the interpretations of 'set' and 'ϵ_s'. As noted earlier, this is enough to indirectly induce the restriction of 'set' and 'ϵ_s' to (something isomorphic to) their intended interpretations, but as noted there, this seems obviously to miss the point of the Putnam argument: if there is a problem seeing how what we do could make 'set' and 'ϵ_s' stand for all sets (or even, all sets of rank less than some inaccessible) and set membership, there is equally a problem in seeing how what we do could make our words 'class' and 'ϵ_c' stand for all classes and for class membership.

The same point holds for second-order quantification: if there is a problem seeing how what we do could make 'set' and 'ϵ_s' stand for all sets (or even, all sets of rank less than some inaccessible) and for set membership, there is equally a problem in seeing how what we do could make our second-order quantifier contribute to truth conditions in the manner of the full second-order quantifier. What in our practice determines that our truth conditions are governed by the truth rule

(1) $(\forall X)A(X)$ is true in interpretation J if and only if every subcollection of J satisfies $A(X)$?

Why not

(1*) $(\forall X)A(X)$ is true in interpretation J if and only if every F subcollection of J satisfies $A(X)$,

where F is some property closed under second-order definability? Of course, if we were to state a truth rule for the second-order quantifier we would state (1) and not (1*); but in virtue of what would our phrase 'every subcollection' mean *every* subcollection, rather than every F subcollection? If the Putnam argument works in the first-order case, it works equally in this case; and its conclusion is of course not that we might mean (1*) rather than (1), but that our second-order quantifier is indeterminate in its truth conditions (so that 'set' and '∈' are also indeterminate, even in second-order set theory). Consequently, we do not really have a determinate conception of a full interpretation. (Weston made this point in [19].)

My conclusion is that you cannot undermine Putnam's argument by appealing to second-order logic. Maybe Putnam's argument is basically wrong: in that case, you can explain what makes our words 'set' and '∈' stand for all sets (or all sets of accessible rank, or whatever) and for membership, without introducing second-order logic. But if Putnam's argument is correct, it undermines the determinacy of second-order quantification just as well. Shortly I will begin the discussion of which of these two alternatives is the more believable.

First though I should make clear that even if Putnam's argument is right, the conclusion is not necessarily that the full second-order quantifier is illegitimate, but only that we do not have a determinate understanding of the full second-order quantifier. To say that we do not have a determinate understanding of something is not to say that we have no understanding of it at all; indeed, on the basically supervaluational conception of indeterminacy advocated earlier, to say that a concept is not fully determinate does not rule out classical reasoning involving that concept.

It might be thought that in granting only an indeterminate conception of second-order quantification I am really granting the intelligibility not of a full second-order quantifier but only of a general second-order quantifier; but I think that is incorrect. I am willing to grant the intelligibility (and, for present purposes anyway, the legitimacy)[7] of a conception of second-order quantification which clearly departs from the general conception, in that competent users of the second-order quantifiers would refuse in general to infer from the construction within second-order set theory of a general model of not-A to the claim that A is not logically true. Their refusal to make such inferences is part of their inferential practice (albeit a negative part), and this part of their inferential practice is as important as the positive parts (the inferences they accept) in determining the contribution to truth conditions of their second-order quantifiers. Also relevant to their inferential practice, I think, is a general disposition to accept new instances of the second-order (impredicative) comprehension schema as new vocabulary is added to their language.[8] These aspects of their practice are enough I think to determine that the truth conditions of their thoughts and utterances involving the second-order quantifier are not appropriately modeled either by the truth rules for general second-order quantifiers or by the truth rules for any of the other standard weaker second-order quantifiers. But it is a big step from granting this to granting that there is something in their practice that determines a unique contribution of their second-order quantifiers to truth conditions: different contributions to truth conditions are compatible with all of their inferential practices and beliefs, even on this generous conception of 'inferential practices'.

1C. Finiteness

The basic Putnamian argument for the indeterminacy of our notion of set and of second-order quantification is that nothing in our practice with these notions seems as if it could possibly determine their extensions (or more generally, their contributions to truth conditions) at all uniquely (even up to isomorphism). To the extent that this is a problem for these notions, it would seem to be equally a problem for our notion of finiteness (and our notion of natural number).[9] We can define the quantifier 'There are only finitely many' set theoretically: $\exists_{fin}xA(x)$ iff $\{x \mid A(x)\}$ is in 1–1 correspondence with the predecessors of some natural number n. Or we can take it as a primitive. In the second case, our understanding of 'finite' seems to be exhausted by the inferential rules we lay down for it, where we allow as before both positive rules as to what follows from what and formalizable negative rules about what does not follow from what. This is ultimately so in the first case as well, because the definition is in terms of notions like 'set' and 'natural number' the understanding of which is exhausted by inferential practice. Whether 'finite' is defined or primitive, there will be non-standard interpretations of our practice, according to which many formulas of form $\exists_{fin} xA(x,y)$ will be satisfied by objects c for which there are really infinitely many b such that $<b,c>$ satisfies $A(x,y)$. In particular, 'natural number', though defined by a condition entailing 'Each natural number has only finitely many predecessors', will be satisfied in some interpretations of our overall theory of numbers by nonstandard "natural numbers" with infinitely many predecessors; and 'finite sequence of expressions' ('sequence with only finitely many initial segments') will be satisfied in some interpretations of our overall theory of finite sequences by nonstandard "finite sequences" with infinitely many initial segments. And so if the basic Putnamian argument is correct, it looks like we cannot have a determinate conception of finiteness, or a conception of the natural numbers that is determinate even up to isomorphism.

This conclusion seems *prima facie* much harder to swallow than the analogous conclusion about the notion of set or second-order quantification. It seems harder to swallow both because the notion of finiteness (or natural number) seems much more elementary, and because it seems presupposed even by our notion of inferential procedure. After all, an inference, or proof from given assumptions, is a finite sequence of expressions in which each is either a premise or a logical axiom or follows from predecessors in the sequence by certain rules; if we have no determinate notion of finite, then there is going to be an indeterminacy even in our notion of proof from given assumptions. And thus it seems we cannot even talk coherently about what our inferential procedure that supposedly fixes our indeterminate truth conditions is. Surely, it would seem, we have talked ourselves into an unacceptable situation.

There are three possible reactions to this situation. The first is that despite Putnam's argument (and the argument from the continuum hypothesis),[10] we do have determinate conceptions of sets and/or second-order quantification. If so then presumably we have a determinate conception of finiteness too.[11] The second possible position is that the radical conclusion about finiteness is to be swallowed somehow. And the third, intermediate, position is that there is a relevant difference between the cases of 'set' and second-order quantification on the one hand and the finiteness case on the other. Of course, each of these three positions subdivides: e.g., the first subdivides over the issue of *just where* the Putnam argument (which I still have not stated very explicitly) goes wrong.

In the remainder of the essay I will discuss at least one version of each of these three positions, without, I am afraid, reaching any totally definite choice between the second and third.

2. REJECTING THE PUTNAMIAN ARGUMENT: DISQUOTATIONAL TRUTH CONDITIONS

One way to argue that the Putnam argument in the first half of [16] is mistaken even in the case of sets (as is the continuum hypothesis argument) would be to argue that it is *incoherent* to suppose that our notions of set and of second-order quantification are indeterminate. Putnam himself suggests a version of this strategy at the very end of [16], albeit cryptically; his version seems to rely on his "internal realism without metaphysical realism," in particular, on his doctrine that neither sets nor anything else exist independently of our descriptions of them. But I think that there is a clearer version of the strategy that appeals to the disquotational properties of truth, and that is the version I will discuss.

Of course, to say that the conclusion of the arguments for indeterminacy is incoherent is not in itself to tell us just where these arguments go wrong; so for the "incoherence" strategy to be ultimately satisfactory, it must be supplemented to include such a diagnosis. But I will concentrate only on whether it is incoherent to suppose that the notion of 'set' is indeterminate.

The first step in the argument for the incoherence of the indeterminacy claim is to assume either "strongly disquotational" notions of truth and satisfaction, on which the disquotation schemas

(T) 'p' is true if and only if p

and

(S) For all x, x satisfies 'F' if and only if $F(x)$

are analytic; or at least "weakly disquotational" notions of truth and satisfaction that give these schemas a pretty much indefeasible status.[12] (Perhaps any reasonable notions of truth and satisfaction give them the required indefeasibility, but there is no need to decide this here.) The next step is to infer from this that

(T*) 'p' has the truth conditions that p

and

(S*) '$F(x)$' has the satisfaction conditions that x is F

have the same analytic or indefeasible status. And the final step is to infer that 'x is a set' has perfectly determinate satisfaction conditions, namely the condition of being a set, and that 'There is a set of cardinality between that of the rationals and that of the reals' has perfectly determinate truth conditions, namely that there is a set of such cardinality. To suppose that sentences containing 'set' do not have definite truth conditions would be incoherent; and similarly for sentences containing second-order quantifiers.

I do not deny the appeal of this line of argument (though I suspect that only the strongly disquotational version of it could be used to make even an initially plausible diagnosis of exactly how the arguments for indeterminacy go wrong). Nonetheless, I shall question the third (final) step. In my view it is highly problematic even on the strongly disquotational notions of truth and satisfaction according to which (T*) and (S*) are analytic.

That there may be a problem in the third step becomes evident when one reflects on vagueness. Surely any position on truth must be compatible with certain words such as 'bald' having borderline cases; but for someone (say Jones) to be a borderline case of 'bald' is for there to be no definite fact of the matter as to whether Jones satisfies the predicate. My general claim is that indeterminacy in the notion of 'set', or in the second-order quantifier, is rather analogous: there are certain objects which neither definitely are in the extension of 'set' or the range of the second-order quantifier nor definitely outside it. But it is best to look at the vagueness case in slightly more detail.

There are two main approaches to vagueness. On one, the law of excluded middle fails when it comes to vague sentences: if Jones is a borderline case of vagueness we cannot accept the sentence

Jones is bald or Jones is not bald;

more generally, we cannot accept the sentence

For all x, x is bald or x is not bald.

This view, combined with the disquotation schemas, implies that we also cannot accept either

'Jones is bald' is true or 'Jones is not bald' is true

or

For all x, x satisfies 'bald' or x does not satisfy 'bald'.

And this gives fairly clear sense to the idea that 'bald' does not have determinate satisfaction conditions.

This approach to vagueness could easily be carried over to the kind of indeterminacy that has been argued to infect the notion of set or second-order quantification. If we adopted this approach, then the indeterminacy in the notion of set or of second-order quantification consists in the fact that the law of excluded middle does not apply to it. The failure of excluded middle is fully compatible with the disquotation schemas (T) and (S) and (T*) and (S*).

I have said though that my own preference is to adhere to classical logic despite the indeterminacy. To see how this works, it is necessary to see how to make sense of vagueness without abandoning classical logic and without modifying the disquotation schemas (as least for one's primary notion of truth). How, that is, is the advocate of these schemas and of classical logic to say what differentiates a vague predicate like 'bald' from a fairly definite predicate like '(absolutely) square', given that the instances of (S) involving each of them are analogous? The only way to do this, I think, is with an object-language notion of 'definitely' or 'determinately' that extends first-order logic. 'Definitely p' implies 'p', but not conversely; so although either Jones is bald or Jones is not bald, it does not follow that either Jones is definitely bald or Jones is definitely not bald. (In classical logic the disquotation schemas do imply that either 'Jones is bald' is true or 'Jones is not bald' is true; but this is compatible with neither 'Jones is definitely bald' nor 'Jones is definitely not bald' being true, or equivalently, with 'Jones is bald' being neither definitely true nor definitely not true.) Analogously, it does not follow from the disquotation schemas that for any x either x is definitely a set or x is definitely not a set; or that for any x and y, either x is definitely a member of y or x is definitely a non-member of y. And so even adhering to excluded middle, it is compatible with the disquotation schemas that 'set' and 'ϵ' do not have definite satisfaction conditions.

[There is an ambiguity that is a possible source of confusion. To say that 'ϵ' has definite satisfaction conditions could be interpreted to be true simply on the grounds that

(2) For any x and y, it is definitely the case that [$<x,y>$ satisfies 'ϵ' if and only if $x \epsilon y$].

That of course does follow from the disquotation schemas plus classical logic plus reasonable assumptions about the definitely operator. But (2) implies only that 'ϵ' *definitely has satisfaction conditions*; what is relevant to the claim that it *has definite satisfaction conditions* is not (2), but

(3) For any x and y, [$<x,y>$ definitely satisfies 'ϵ' if and only if $x \epsilon y$].

The claim of indefiniteness is that this fails (as does any other sentence of form

For any x and y, [$<x,y>$ definitely satisfies 'ϵ' if and only if . . .]

in which a formula not involving 'definitely' goes in for the dots.) If there is any confusion about this, consider the analog for 'bald' in place of membership.]

I have been pressing an analogy between an uncontroversial phenomenon, vagueness, and a highly controversial one, referential indeterminacy in such notions as set membership and second-order quantification. The analogy is subject to a weak interpretation and a strong interpretation. The weak interpretation is simply that the two formal treatments I have considered for vagueness can be used for the referential indeterminacy of set membership too, showing how the claim of referential indeterminacy is compatible with acceptance of the disquotation schemas. The stronger reading is that the analogy is not simply a formal one: that the reasons that make 'bald' vague are indeed rather similar to the reasons that make 'set' indeterminate. The weak reading of the analogy is enough to undermine the view that it is incoherent to suppose our concept of 'set' indeterminate, but I am inclined to accept even the stronger reading of the analogy. What makes 'bald' vague—what makes it the case that there can be people who are not definitely bald or definitely not bald—is that there is nothing in our training with the word 'bald' that could plausibly be thought to determine its extension, plausibly be thought to determine whether or not people like Jones are bald. What makes 'set' and 'membership' indeterminate is that there is nothing in our training in the use of these terms that could plausibly be thought to determine their extension—e.g., that could plausibly be thought to determine the size of the continuum. If this is right then the analogy to vagueness is not purely formal.

3. COULD OUR CONCEPTION OF FINITUDE BE INDETERMINATE?

I now turn to a view on the other extreme, one which says that even the notion of finitude is referentially indeterminate. Actually I will begin by considering an especially radical version of this position: I will call it radical indeterminism. It and certain positions closely related to it will be discussed in subsections 3A–3C; then in 3D–3F I will return to a more general consideration of the view that the notion of finiteness is referentially indeterminate.

3A. Radical Indeterminism and Godel's Theorem

Radical indeterminism has it that at any time, a person's concept of finitude is exhausted by the maximal mathematical theory of finitude that he or she implicitly accepts at that time: more specifically, any mathematical claim about finitude that has different truth values in different models of someone's maximal theory has no determinate truth value on that person's current conception of finitude.[13] (Since claims about natural numbers are in effect claims about linear orderings in which every object has only finitely many predecessors, the same holds for mathematical claims about natural numbers.) If there is indeterminacy as to what exactly is the maximal theory a person implicitly accepts, then there is indeterminacy as to what indeterminate concept the person employs; and so there will be no determinate answer as to which questions have determinate answers. For part of my discussion I will ignore such "second-level" indeterminacy in discussing the radical indeterminist view, but I will argue in the end that nothing of importance turns on my doing so. (Also, for stylistic ease I will sometimes ignore interpersonal variation, and speak of the maximal theory "we" implicitly accept—or if second-level indeterminacy is taken into account, the class of reasonable candidates for such a theory.)

In stating the radical indeterminist view I have employed the notion of "implicitly accepting" a theory, but of course, this is quite vague. Roughly, we could say that I *implicitly accept* a sentence if I could fairly easily be brought to explicitly accept it without feeling I was learning anything essentially new; though this would require qualifications to rule out things I was brought to accept by fallacious arguments that I could be brought to see were fallacious. The extent to which what I implicitly accept goes beyond what I explicitly accept depends on how broadly we interpret 'fairly easily' and 'essentially new', but it seems clear that on any reasonable interpretations, what we implicitly accept is not closed under consequence.[14] We could roughly explain what it is to implicitly accept a mechanical inference rule in a similar (and similarly vague) manner. On any way of making precise the notion of implicitly accepting, take a person's *maximal theory* to be the closure of the set of sentences that he or she implicitly accepts under the set of mechanical rules that he or she implicitly accepts. So the class of reasonable candidates for a person's maximal theory is the class of theories that we get on different ways of making 'implicitly accepts' precise. This makes it clear that for any person at any time, there is indeed a non-empty class of reasonable candidates for the person's maximal theory at that time.[15] And a consequence of the radical indeterminist view is that any sentence not decided by any such theory has no definite truth value on that person's current conception of finitude.

It seems to me that on any reasonable way of making 'implicitly accepts' precise, the set of sentences and inference rules that a person implicitly accepts at a given time is almost certainly recursive (and might well be finite). Also, for most of us, what we implicitly accept (on any reasonable way of making this precise) entails the axioms of arithmetic. Consequently, each reasonable candidate for our maximal theory that is consistent has a Godel sentence that is undecidable in it. Let us now make the simplifying pretense that there is a uniquely best candidate for the maximal theory we accept at a given time. (I do not believe anything of substance turns on this simplifying pretense, though this will eventually require a bit of discussion.) And let us suppose this maximal theory M to be consistent. Then the radical indeterminist view has it that if G is the (any standard) Godel sentence of M, G has no determinate truth value (on our current understanding of the terms in M). This seems *prima facie* much more surprising than the claim that the continuum hypothesis has no determinate truth value. Among other things, few claim to have much certainty as to what the alleged determinate truth value of the continuum hypothesis is; but (especially if we know what our maximal mathematical theory is—and I do not see any principled reason why we cannot know this), don't we have available a good informal argument for believing the (any standard) Godel sentence of this theory to be true? And if there is such a good argument for its truth, there is certainly a good argument for thinking that it has a truth value, hence a good argument against radical indeterminism.

Against this, I will argue that the informal arguments for the truth of the Godel sentence of our maximal mathematical theory are unsound; but I need to explain away the illusion to the contrary. (The discussion will assume a platonist perspective; I will say something about the fictionalist perspective in Section 3C.)

The illusion to the contrary arises because we do have a very compelling argument for the truth of the Godel sentence of Peano arithmetic, and even for the truth of the Godel sentence of Zermelo-Fraenkel set theory. This argument depends on an informal inductive argument that since the logical and nonlogical premises of the theory in question are true and the rule of inference (*modus ponens*) preserves truth then the theorems are true.[16] (Given this, we can argue that if the Godel sentence is provable it is true; but by construction of the Godel sentence together with a Tarski biconditional, we also have that if it is unprovable it is true; so it is true.) That argument that the theorems of the theory are true is what is not formalizable in the theory in question. The most fundamental reason why it is not formalizable within the theory in question is Tarski's Theorem: there is no adequate definition of truth formalizable in the theory. But we do, I think, have a concept of arithmetic truth (definable in set theory), and of truth in ZF (definable only in more powerful set theories); and the informal inductive argument involving truth seems quite compelling, so I think that we do have grounds for regarding the Godel sentences of these theories as true.

One way to block this informal argument for the Godel sentence of our maximal theory would be to argue that Tarski's Theorem shows that we have no truth predicate for the language of this theory (since if we had one, it would be part of that theory, given that that theory is maximal). But this has two problems. First, the claim that we employ a language for which we have no truth concept is hard to swallow. (Doesn't the word 'true' express such a concept?) And second, this claim is *not* entailed by Tarski's Theorem; rather, Tarski's Theorem entails only that any such predicate must be nonclassical in that it cannot obey the Tarski biconditionals without restriction. That applications of 'true' *to sentences not containing 'true' and related terms* should obey the Tarski biconditionals is hard to deny; to avoid denying this while allowing the predicate to have unrestricted application, we must suppose that the predicate 'true' is not definable in substantially more basic terms in our maximal theory, but instead is primitive and governed by axioms that are part of the maximal theory.[17]

But if we do have a truth predicate for the language of our maximal theory M in that theory, and if as I shall assume we can use that truth predicate in inductions, then can't we inductively argue that all theorems of M are true? And can't we use this to argue for the Godel sentence of M in the way just reviewed?

I think it is clear that such an argument cannot be correct: for if it were correct, there would now be nothing to stop its being given in M itself, which is of course impossible if M is consistent. But to make this more convincing, we need to look at the details of why the argument cannot be carried out (either informally or in M).

To see why the reasoning for the truth of the Godel sentence is unsound, you do not need to preclude use of the truth predicate in inductions: indeed, we should not preclude it, for its use in inductively arguing that the theorems of Peano arithmetic and ZF are true seems perfectly fine. The problem rather is that to prove inductively that the theorems of M are true, you need to establish

(a) that all axioms of M are true

and

(b) that all rules of inference of M are true preserving.

Now, even if M did not contain a truth predicate, there might be difficulty in arguing for (a), if M is not finitely axiomatized. Certainly there could be a problem with a formal argument for (a): the assumption that a given axiom is true seems to amount to little more than the assumption of the axiom itself, but the generalization that all of them are true is a more powerful claim, one that might well go beyond the power of the theory M. A case could be made that we would still have an informal argument for (a), at least if we assume that the person whose maximal theory is M knows that he believes each axiom of M and does so for good reason; this is a rather delicate matter to decide. Fortunately, there is no need to decide this (or to decide on the finite axiomatizability of M either); for *the problem with adhering to (a) and (b) becomes very much more serious when one remembers that* M *contains a (non-classical) truth predicate.* For now the axioms of M must be taken to include axioms governing this truth predicate, and the rules of inference must include special rules governing the truth predicate; and it turns out that on all reasonable axiomatizations of the non-classical truth predicate, either the assertion of the truth of these truth axioms or the assertion of the truth-preservingness of these special rules of inference (or both) is inconsistent with the axioms governing 'true'. In other words, even if we assume that there is no special problem with knowing that all of the axioms of M *not involving 'true'* are true, and no special problem in knowing that rules like *modus ponens that do not specially involve 'true'* are truth preserving, this is not enough for the inductive argument: the inductive argument requires that we know that even the axioms of M that employ 'true' are true and that even the rules that employ 'true' are truth preserving. And the fact is that *on all the reasonable axiomatizations of the non-classical truth predicate, the assertion of the truth of THESE axioms of* M *and/or the truth-preservingness of THESE rules of inference of* M *would actually be inconsistent with* M. I leave the demonstration of this claim to a technical footnote.[18]

This shows why we cannot prove G, or True $<G>$, in M.[19] Does it also show that we cannot informally argue for it? I think it does. The informal argument would still have to be based on an inductive argument that the theorems of M are true; and the induction would have to employ the very same concept of truth employed in M, since it is the most general truth concept we have. (If we had a richer truth concept on which we could make inductions, then we would have a more powerful mathematical theory than M, contrary to the assumption that M is maximal.) But the considerations just mentioned (and elaborated in note 18) show that *the principles that would be required in the induction are not merely unavailable to us, they are incorrect in that they are inconsistent with* M. So the problem is not just that the informal argument employing those principles goes beyond M; rather, the problem is that the informal argument is unsound.[20]

I have been arguing that we have no good informal argument for the Godel sentence of our maximal mathematical theory;[21] if this is right, it removes one reason for thinking that there are mathematical claims unsettled by this theory that have determinate truth value on our current mathematical concepts. But it may be thought that my argument crucially presupposes the assumption that there is a uniquely best candidate for a person's maximal theory at a given time.

I do not think it does crucially presuppose this. Suppose that there is a class of candidates for my maximal theory; to be slightly crude about it, let's give each a numerical degree from 0 to 1 measuring how good a candidate it is for being my maximal theory, where the numerical degrees add to 1. Then for each theory M_i that gets a non-zero measure d_i for being my maximal theory, its Godel sentence G_i gets a non-zero measure of at least d_i (and typically much more)[22] for being epistemically unwarranted. And so we can consistently suppose that each such G_i gets no fully definite truth value.

I suppose that somebody might think that if G_i also has a non-zero degree of *warrantedness* then it must have a truth value, for anything having no truth value would be absolutely unwarranted. But this seems to me a mistake: the right conclusion is that if it has a non-zero degree of warrantedness then *to that degree* it has a truth value. If we think that if there were a best candidate for a maximal theory then anything unsettled by that theory would have no truth value, then the proper conclusion of there being no best candidate for the maximal theory is that there is also no best candidate for the set of sentences that have truth values. There is no reason to assume that any sentence that is a possible candidate for having a truth value definitely has one.

There is also another way to see that the indeterminacy as to what my maximal theory is should not affect the conclusion I have drawn. For surely (if my mathematical beliefs are consistent) there is a recursively axiomatized consistent theory M so powerful that it includes any reasonable candidate for my maximal theory (as I have defined that—see note 15). But then I have no good informal argument for its Godel sentence, if what I have said is correct; so again, considerations about informal arguments for Godel sentences cannot undermine the view that sentences not formally decidable in M do not have definite truth values on my current mathematical concepts.

3B. A Slightly Less Radical Indeterminism: Indefinite Extensibility

The view that our concepts of finitude and natural number are referentially indeterminate does not require the radical indeterminism outlined in Section 3A: one could posit a more limited referential indeterminacy that allowed the truth of the Godel sentences to be settled while not allowing the truth of all sentences to be settled. (One could even in principle posit a referential indeterminacy so limited that every sentence of arithmetic got a determinate truth value; but I doubt that indeterminacy not affecting truth values can be made plausible.)

But even if we regard the Godel sentence of our current maximal theory as not definitely true, one *may* not need to take quite as radical a line as I have suggested. An alternative view is suggested by Michael Dummett in his essay [4] on Godel's Theorem. In some ways, of course, Dummett's view is much more radical than the one I have outlined, for Dummett infers from the indeterminacy of the concept of natural number that we should give up the use of classical logic in number theory, and I have already remarked that I see no good argument for that inference. But if the intuitionism is thrown away,[23] and a certain additional doctrine to be discussed later that I think depends on the intuitionism is thrown away with it, then Dummett's essay suggests an interesting position not far from the one I have suggested, but perhaps slightly more palatable. The position is that our concept of number is *indefinitely extensible* (in a sense not quite the same as Dummett's):[24] it is indeterminate at any given time, but our usage dictates something about how it is to be refined. In particular, it dictates that we are to eventually accept the Godel sentence of even our current maximal theory, if the question should arise.[25] (The view does not, of course, involve the claim that our current usage dictates of each sentence or arithmetic whether it should be accepted if the question should arise; that view would not seem to me substantially different from the view that all answers to arithmetic questions have determinate answers.)

My worry about any view like Dummett's is a worry about its coherence: if our current usage dictates that we would accept the Godel sentence of M if the question should arise, then shouldn't we conclude that we now implicitly accept that Godel sentence, and hence that M cannot be our maximal theory? If we should so conclude, then the apparently more liberal line that Dummett's essay suggests really is not an option. I should however mention one consideration that may seem to support the indefinite extensibility view (and is basically what Dummett cites in support of the view). The consideration is that the mathematical theories we accept involve schemas: in particular, the schema of mathematical induction.[26] It is natural to interpret such schemas as not merely involving the assumption of each instance expressible in our language, but to involve a commitment to new instances as new terms are added to our language. But then, it seems, the commitment to the Godel sentence of our maximal theory follows: we get the Godel sentence from the induction schema, once we add a truth predicate for our language.

My doubts about this argument come at the last step: on my view, we already have a truth predicate for our language, so there is nothing to add. Of course, the truth predicate we have is nonclassical, i.e., does not obey the Tarski biconditionals; couldn't we add a classical truth predicate that does obey the Tarski biconditionals restricted to sentences that do not contain that classical predicate (but that may contain the non-classical one)? Yes, but then to deduce the Godel sentence of the old theory we need to use not just instances of the induction schema involving this truth predicate, but those Tarski biconditionals. Indeed, we need to add more: we need to add the generalization that a universal claim is true if and only if all of its instances are. These added principles are doing a large part of the work, not just the extension of the induction schema to the new predicate; so the argument that the eventual commitment to the Godel sentence of M was already built into our practice seems to me faulty.

One might try to defend the "indefinite extensibility" view by arguing that our initial practice dictates not only the extension of the induction schema to any predicates to be introduced, but also dictates those new principles governing a newly introduced classical truth predicate that are required for the deduction of the Godel sentence. To put it in a slogan, the proposal is that the concept of truth is indefinitely extensible, and that this together with the point about how accepting a schema commits you to accepting new instances of it is enough to imply the indefinite extensibility of the concept of number. This position deserves more discussion than I can give it here. I myself am skeptical of the view that the concept of truth is "indefinitely extensible" in the required sense. In the first place, this view seems to me to presuppose a Tarskian view of truth made obsolete (or anyway unnecessary) by the work of Kripke and others. In the second place, I have doubts about the coherence of the indefinite extensibility claim: we ought to be able to formulate a complete account of the rules governing our concept of truth; if a certain account C is proposed, but our usage dictates how our concept of truth is to be extended when applied to the sentences of C, then that simply shows that C did not give the required complete account of the rules governing our concept of truth. That is what I would be inclined to argue, but I will not discuss the issue further here.[27] My main goal so far in Section 3 has been to argue that we can coherently maintain at least one version of the view that our concepts of 'finite' and 'natural number' are so referentially indeterminate that the Godel sentences of our theories have no definite truth values; if the Dummett version (stripped of the intuitionism) can be maintained too, so much the better.

3C. A Still More Radical Variant, Involving Fictionalism

So far, in responding to the Godel sentence objection to radical indeterminism, I have assumed a platonist perspective, according to which we really believe our mathematical theories. There is also a more radical response, from a fictionalist perspective according to which we do not.

Though a fictionalist about mathematics does not believe mathematical theories, he does make a distinction between mathematical theories that are *mathematically acceptable* and those (such as inconsistent theories and perhaps ω-inconsistent ones) that are not; and presumably there are theories that he believes acceptable for which there is no strengthening that he believes acceptable (even if he believes that *there are* acceptable extensions of them). Let M be one such maximal theory. The fictionalist does not believe M, but he does presumably have certain beliefs about why it is acceptable. Let's start with a simple-minded fictionalism according to which a mathematical theory is acceptable if and only if it is consistent. (If the fictionalism in question involves fictionalism about number theory, then the notion of consistency cannot be formalized in the usual way of course; presumably it must be taken as a primitive notion, explained via axioms. There is no need here to go into details about how this might be accomplished: anyone skeptical that it can be

accomplished satisfactorily can imagine the fictionalism in question confined
to more powerful mathematical theories than number theory.)

The problem we were faced with in Section 3A can be put as follows: how
is one to plausibly avoid accepting all instances of the following "reflection
principle":

(P1)   For any T, go from accepting it to accepting the theory $T \cup \{G_T\}$,
        where G_T is the Godel sentence of T;

in particular, how can one avoid accepting the instance of P1 in which T is the
maximal theory we accept? P1 is equivalent to

(P1*)   For any T, go from accepting it to accepting the theory $T \cup \{CON_T\}$,
        where CON_T attributes the usual formalization of the property of
        consistency to the theory T (via some predicate that numeralwise
        expresses the property of being an axiom of T);

so how do we avoid accepting that? Section 3A gave what I think is the best
answer for the non-fictionalist; can our fictionalist do better?

At first glance it may seen hard to see how our fictionalist is better off:
after all, our fictionalist thinks that for M to be acceptable it must be consistent;
and putting aside worries about whether CON_M is the proper formalization of
consistency, this means that he is required to believe CON_M. So of course, he
must find $M \cup \{CON_M\}$ acceptable.

But this argument is fallacious: the last 'of course' is mistaken on at
least two grounds. Let's grant that if we believe CON_M and also believe
M, then we should believe $M \cup \{CON_M\}$. But our fictionalist is not concerned with believing theories, but only with believing their consistency. Let's
also grant that if theories imply their own consistency, then if you believe
$M \cup \{CON_M\}$ you should believe it consistent. But now the first, less important,
fallacy in the argument is evident: the assumption that theories imply their
own consistency is false, on the standard formalization of consistency; so on
that formalization of consistency you cannot get from believing $M \cup \{CON_M\}$ to
believing it consistent.

But there is a much more basic fallacy in the argument: there is no reason
why the fictionalist should believe $M \cup \{CON_M\}$; for even though he may
believe CON_M, he does not believe M! I believe the theory consisting solely of
'Snow is not white' to be consistent; I also believe 'Snow is white'; it does not
follow that I believe {'Snow is not white', 'Snow is white'} to be consistent.

An analogous point holds for a more sophisticated version of fictionalism, which requires more of a mathematical theory than consistency. Call a
mathematical theory T *sound* if for every formula A, if a sentence of the form
'There is a quantificational derivation of $<A>$' is derivable from T, then A is
quantificationally derivable. (Soundness is a limited version of 1-consistency,
and for standard impure set theory it is also virtually equivalent to what I
have elsewhere called conservativeness.)[28] It would seem at first blush that a
reasonable platonist would have to believe any theory he accepts to be sound;
however, the soundness of a theory entails its consistency (in any background

theory strong enough to prove the consistency of predicate logic);[29] so on the usual formalization of consistency it seems that no *platonist* can believe the soundness of his own maximal theory. Considerations like those in Section 3A are needed to make sense of how this could be.

It would also seem at first blush that a reasonable fictionalist should believe any theory he accepts to be sound. (Again, someone who is fictionalist even about number theory must show that 'derivable' in the definition of soundness can be made sense of on the fictionalist perspective, but I shall not discuss here how that might best be done.) But now we do not need to bring in considerations like those in Section 3A, because there is no reason why a fictionalist cannot believe the maximal theory he accepts to be sound. From *accepting* M and *believing* $SOUND_M$, there is no plausible way to conclude that one should *either accept or believe* $M \cup \{SOUND_M\}$; for the soundness of M and the truth of $SOUND_M$ does not imply the soundness of $M \cup \{SOUND_M\}$.

3D. More Basic Worries about the Indeterminacy of Finitude

So far I have tried to rebut objections to the indeterminateness of our conception of finitude and of natural number based on considerations involving Godel sentences or other reflection principles. But even if what I have said is correct, I think it leaves the deepest worries about the indeterminacy claim untouched. (These other worries are also broader in scope in that they affect versions of indeterminism that allow that the Godel sentences of our theories are true.)

Before trying to get clear what these deeper worries might be, I need to make clearer what the indeterminacy claim involves. One often hears it characterized—including by some of its advocates (Skolem [18]; Putnam [15] p. 22 and [16] p. 2)—as the view that the notion of finiteness makes sense only *relative to a model*. The motivation for this characterization is that set theory implies that there can be a model M of set theory in which a certain set A satisfies the condition "has only finitely many members," but where an expansion of the domain of the model to include new sets of natural numbers (but no new members of A) can lead to the same set satisfying the condition "has infinitely many members." (The set "looks finite" in M because M contains a function mapping it 1–1 onto an object b satisfying the predicate 'natural number' in M; but in the larger model, b does not satisfy the predicate 'natural number'.) One way of arguing for relativity would be to conclude from this that set theory implies that the set A is not really finite or infinite, but only finite or infinite relative to the model. But that conclusion is simply wrong: indeed, in the simplest examples of this situation, set theory implies that the set is infinite. The proper conclusion is just that set theory implies that there are models in which satisfying "has finitely many members" is compatible with infinitude. (That this is the proper conclusion has been frequently pointed out by those who take the finite-infinite distinction to be determinate. I am saying that we can and should recognize that this is the proper conclusion even if we regard the finite-infinite distinction as indeterminate.)

A slightly better variant of the above argument for relativity would be that the same set would be finite if M were the whole universe of sets and infinite if the larger set M' were; so the set is finite relative to M and infinite relative to M'. But among its other problems, this assumes that we can intelligibly talk of the same set occurring in a possible universe "given by M" and a possible universe "given by M'" (whatever exactly it might mean to say that a universe is "given by" a model); and the identification of sets across universes is dubious at best. (There is no difficulty in making cross-world identifications of sets that are uncontroversially hereditarily finite: such sets can be cross-world identified recursively, by a "cross-world extensionality principle," that is, by the principle that sets in different worlds that can be independently shown to have the same members should be identified. But that is no help in the case of a set A that is declared finite in M and a set B that is declared infinite in M', where M and M' are conceived as separate universes rather than embedded in a common universe of sets; for there A and B cannot be independently shown to have the same members by the cross-world extensionality criterion.)

To characterize the view that our notion of finiteness is indeterminate in terms of a relativity in the notion strikes me as thoroughly misleading. It suggests that the normal (unrelativized) notion of finiteness needs to be abandoned, and that in its place we put a new relativized notion of finite, not subject to the same difficulties. But I think this is doubly wrong. First, I do not think the normal notion does need to be abandoned, even if it is referentially indeterminate, any more than the referential indeterminacy of 'bald' forces us to give up the notion of baldness; indeed, the notion of finiteness is surely far too indispensable to be abandoned. Second, I do not think that there is any hope of introducing a relativized notion of finiteness that avoids the indeterminacy. The assertion "There are finitely many A's relative to model M" (where 'M' is a singular term for a model for some language L, and L contains a formula to which the model assigns the set of A's as its extension) does not seem to me any more referentially determinate than the unrelativized assertion that there are finitely many A's: models after all are sets of a certain type, so any indeterminacy in the notion of set is going to give rise to indeterminacy as to which model M we are referring to. And the problem does not arise only when we try to refer to a particular model: to say "There is a model (of such and such a sort perhaps) such that there are finitely many A's relative to that model" is equally indeterminate (if the basic Putnamian indeterminacy argument is correct), because of the indeterminacy as to what sets there are.

So let us dismiss the claim of the *relativity* of finitude as simply a mistake; the claim of interest is that the notion of finitude is referentially indeterminate, but not to be either relativized or abandoned.

I think that what is primarily worrying about the idea that our notion of finiteness is referentially indeterminate is that our notion of inferential procedure relies on this notion: any indeterminacy in our notion of finiteness will induce an indeterminacy in our notion of proving a claim from given assumptions according to a given proof procedure P, for it will induce an indeterminacy as to which discretely ordered strings of expressions (with first and last elements) that meet the other conditions for being a P-proof are genuinely finite and hence are genuine P-proofs. And the idea that it is indeterminate which strings of expressions are P-proofs (where P is a definite proof procedure) seems extremely hard to swallow.

I am not completely convinced, though, that the idea is one that it is impossible to live with. After all, any purported proof we come across will have less than (say) $10^{10^{10}}$ component formulas (each with less than say $10^{10^{10}}$ symbols). The indeterminacy we are contemplating, motivated as it is by Putnam's model-theoretic argument in [16], will not be so radical as to question that this is definitely finite, so it will not question that there is a definite matter of fact as to whether it is a proof. Slightly more generally, the model-theoretic argument does not question that there is a perfectly definite fact as to whether any given sentence (of less than $10^{10^{10}}$ symbols) is $10^{10^{10}}$-provable, that is, provable (in the given proof procedure) with a proof of less than $10^{10^{10}}$ component formulas each with less than $10^{10^{10}}$ symbols. And isn't this all the determinacy we have a right to be confident of?

Of course, we can set-theoretically describe infinite sequences of formulas in a discrete ordering with first and last elements; and when someone describes one, we all declare unequivocally that it is not a genuine proof. But that is also compatible with the indeterminacy of 'proof': in all cases where what we have described is clearly infinite, it clearly fails to meet the conditions we impose on proofs, since we impose finiteness as one of the conditions. That we reject discrete orderings that are clearly infinite as not genuine proofs is obviously not enough to show the determinacy of our concept of genuine proof.

Let us be clear on the consequences that we arrive at if we take the "Models and Reality" argument as showing that even the notion of finiteness is indeterminate. First, the argument only implies that there is indeterminacy about what is unprovable by any proof *however long*, not that there is indeterminacy about what is $10^{10^{10}}$-unprovable. (So though it may be indeterminate whether the Godel sentence of our maximal mathematical theory is true, as *radical* indeterminism claims, we should not expect any indeterminacy as to the truth of a sentence asserting its own $10^{10^{10}}$-unprovability.) Second, even the unbounded notion of unprovability is not illegitimate, and it will have perfectly determinate applications in certain cases, including those where we can *prove* unprovability in our maximal theory (at least, where we can $10^{10^{10}}$-prove it!). And even where it may have no determinate application, nothing prevents full classical reasoning using the notion.

3E. Dummett Again

Some advocates of the view that the notion of finiteness is indeterminate may think that it does not entail anything as strong as the view suggested in the last three paragraphs.

One invalid way to argue this would be as follows: the indeterminacy of finiteness shows that the extension of 'proof' is indeterminate: the candidates for its extension include not only the set of genuine proofs, but the set of *-proofs, where these are the things that satisfy all the condition on proofs other than being genuinely finite. But now we can introduce the idea of 'definitely provable', by saying that something is definitely provable if it is in all the candidates for the extension of 'provable'. And then if there are only *-proofs of a claim and no genuine proofs of it, it would not be definitely provable. That is the argument, but I hope the reply is obvious: the concept of 'definitely' employed here is itself indeterminate, for the quantification over "all the candidates for the extension" is indeterminate. ("Candidates for the extension" are abstract entities, which we may as well regard as sets; the Putnamian argument shows 'set' to be indeterminate, and it equally shows 'candidate for the extension' to be indeterminate.)

Dummett's article on Godel's theorem may suggest another line of argument for a less radical view. I have said that the concepts of number and proof are referentially indeterminate: they have indefinite extensions. What Dummett says is that despite the indeterminacy in our concept of number, it has a perfectly determinate extension: the indeterminacy in the concept resides not in any indeterminacy in its extension, but in an indeterminacy in the truth conditions of quantifications over all numbers. This at least appears different from what I have said: I have said that the extension of 'number' and 'proof' are indeterminate. Actually I am not at all sure that the difference with Dummett is genuine: it may be that when Dummett says that the extension of these notions is definite, what he means is simply that in any describable case it is a perfectly definite question whether or not that case falls under the concept, and that is the conclusion that I arrived at at the end of the last section. But let us see if we can interpret Dummett's claim literally, as saying that the full extension, not simply the extension restricted to humanly describable cases, is determinate.

If, as I have been doing, we assume classical logic and a classical or supervaluational view of truth, Dummett's claim can make sense only if we regard even the first-order quantifiers as indeterminate in their contribution to truth conditions; something I have not yet committed myself to. And Dummett does regard even first-order quantifiers as indeterminate: he holds that the concepts of set and ordinal are concepts of indefinitely extensible totalities, as is the concept of property; there is no "completed universe." It would be natural to argue that if the concept of property of natural numbers is the concept of an indefinitely extensible totality, then the concept of natural numbers is the concept of an indefinitely contractible totality (since an increase in the supply of properties can lead to a decrease in the things closed under these properties). But I do not think this would give Dummett his view that the extension of 'natural number' is determinate: presumably if the totality were indefinitely contractible, the extension of 'natural number' (which just is the totality) would be indefinite. In any case, Dummett denies that the concept of natural number is a concept of a contracting totality; and of course it is not a concept of an expanding totality either. Rather, the reason the concept is extendible, according to Dummett, does not have to do with changes in the domain, but *only* with changes in what we regard as properties of natural numbers and what we regard as grounds for asserting claims about all natural numbers.

And this makes clear that if we take Dummett at his word when he says that the truth conditions of universal generalizations about natural numbers are indeterminate even though the extension of 'natural number' is determinate, then his view makes no sense on a classical view of truth conditions (including a supervaluational view); *it makes sense only if we view truth as explained in terms of proof.* That of course *is* a view that Dummett elsewhere advocates, but it is a view that many of us find extremely unattractive (and a view that leads almost inevitably to giving up classical logic).

In summary, Dummett's view (that though 'natural number' and 'proof' are indeterminate, they have a perfectly determinate extension) turns out to have a higher cost than is initially obvious. I think we need not bear that cost: it seems to me that all that is clearly correct in the claim that the extension of 'proof' is determinate is that for each humanly describable case there is a definite fact of the matter as to whether it is in the extension of the concept; and that is a fact that the fully classical view described in the previous section captures.

3F. Still More Radical Indeterminacies?

Many will find the position reached in Section 3D radical enough; but actually it seems to lead naturally to a still more radical consequence so far suppressed. The consequence is that even the operators of first-order logic make no determinate contribution to truth conditions. The argument for this is straightforward in outline: our understanding of these operators is determined in part by the proof conditions of sentences containing them; to the extent that the notion of proof becomes indeterminate, the operators become indeterminate too.

Some may feel that this line of argument overestimates the role that proof theory plays in an understanding of logical operators. I disagree, and think that those who think so attribute to the theory of truth a role in understanding that it could not conceivably have. (Which is not to say that it has no role at all.) But I will not pursue this matter here. Let me simply say that the considerations at the end of Section 3D suggest that the extent of indeterminacy in the logical operators need not be great: it is not obvious that there need be any indeterminacy at all in their contributions to the truth conditions of sentences of humanly accessible length; indeed, maybe the only indeterminacy concerns strings of symbols for which it is indeterminate whether they are of finite length.

But there may be reasons for suspecting more indeterminacy in the contributions that our first-order logical notions make to truth conditions. One worry is this: to the extent that arguments for the indeterminacy of more powerful operators are based on model theoretic arguments like Skolem-Lowenheim and compactness theorems, they beg the question in favor of the determinacy of the first-order operators; for the notion of model builds in the contribution that the first-order operators make to truth conditions. This is certainly a fair worry, and I am inclined to think that taking it seriously would raise substantial questions about the determinacy of the first-order quantifiers (though not about the determinacy of the truth functional connectives, over and above the worries of the previous paragraph). But this is not a subject I will pursue here.

4. DOES PUTNAM'S ARGUMENT REALLY EXTEND TO THE NOTION OF FINITENESS?

Despite what you may believe, I am really a commonsensical guy, and would like to avoid the radical conclusions of Section 3 if I can. Here is my best attempt to do so.

I begin by noting that Putnam's argument in the first half of [16] is not based solely on the fact that there are non-standard models of set theory and nonstandard models of the second-order quantifier. If it were, it would surely extend to the notion of finiteness; but if you look at how the argument actually does work, the extension is very much more problematic. Putnam's argument is based rather on the fact that for set theory and second-order quantification there are nonstandard models *of a particular sort*; and in the case of finiteness, there are no nonstandard models *of that sort*. In the case of finiteness, you get the nonstandard models by the compactness theorem, rather than the downward Skolem-Lowenheim theorem that Putnam uses in his argument. And that, I claim, makes a very important difference.

To explain this, I need to review the details of Putnam's argument. Putnam begins by recognizing that there is no need for an advocate of the view that 'set' and '∈' have determinate extensions[30] to think that their extensions are made determinate solely by our uses of these terms in pure mathematics. For anyone who has learned the notions of set and membership can apply them to the world around us; indeed, these notions (and related notions like that of a function, that are usually defined in terms of set and membership) are used heavily in the usual formalization of physical theory. It is the entire range of uses of 'set' and '∈' that are available to determine their extensions.

But what is it about our usage of the words 'set' and '∈' that determines their extension, to the extent that their extension is determinate? Let us concede (as Putnam implicitly does) that the contribution that our first- and second-order logical operators make to truth conditions is determinate *up to the ranges of the quantifiers*.[31] (I think this concession is in fact pretty reasonable: it seems to me that our inferential practice does largely determine the contribution that our logical operators make to truth conditions [range aside, in the case of the quantifiers].) Let us concede further (as Putnam quite explicitly does in the first half of his essay, before taking it back in the second half) that the interpretation of our "observational vocabulary" is fairly fixed: it is fairly determinate what properties the observational predicates stand for. Or to put it in extensional terms, let us concede that it is determinate whether or not a given object (or *n*-tuple of objects) satisfies a given observational predicate, given that it is in the range of our first-order quantifiers. (Again I think this is quite plausible, ordinary vagueness aside: our practice of accepting and rejecting sentences containing observation predicates does largely determine whether any object or n-tuple of objects that we quantify over satisfies the predicates.) In fact, let's extend this a bit, from the "observational vocabulary" to the entire non-mathematical vocabulary of the language. And let us take that non-mathematical vocabulary to include the predicate 'non-mathematical', so that it is determinate of any object whether or not it satisfies 'non-mathematical' (or 'mathematical'). Even conceding all this determinacy in the non-mathematical and logical vocabulary, Putnam argues that nothing determines close to a unique answer to the question of which things satisfy the predicate 'set'.

The argument is that the only reasonable candidate for what determines the extension of the concepts of set and membership is our entire body of beliefs and deductive practice involving these concepts; and that the way this body of beliefs and deductive practice fixes their extension is that their extension is to be such that to the extent possible, the beliefs are to be true and the deductive practices are to preserve truth. Even allowing the beliefs in question to include our non-mathematical beliefs, and assuming the interpretation of the logical and non-mathematical concepts in that body of beliefs to be fixed in the way just described, there are three possible sources of indeterminacy. The first—which I do not want to emphasize, but must mention in order to formulate the others properly—is that not all of our beliefs can possibly come out true, *however* 'set' and 'ϵ' are interpreted: any person's beliefs are inconsistent, and even if you agree on a way to strip off the inconsistencies, any person's beliefs imply false observational claims; so only a proper subset of their beliefs can be made to come out true on some allowable interpretation, that is, on some interpretation that accords with the constraints imposed on the interpretations of the logical and non-mathematical vocabulary. And this means that there will be more than one choice of a maximal set of beliefs that can be made to come out true on some allowable interpretation or other. Presumably one such maximal set is more relevant (to the determination of the extension of 'set') than another to the extent that it is larger and contains more central beliefs, but it is highly unlikely that any one such maximal set of beliefs will uniquely come out most relevant (on any reasonable explication of 'most relevant'); that is one source of indeterminacy. But let us follow Putnam and put this source of indeterminacy completely aside: let's assume that a given such maximal set S of our beliefs has been identified.

A second source of indeterminacy, also not terribly interesting, is that for any allowable interpretation of the given maximal set S of beliefs and any permutation f of its universe *which leaves the non-mathematical objects fixed*, the new interpretation that results by replacing each object o by $f(o)$ in the extension of every predicate is also allowable (that is, it also satisfies the constraints on the physical vocabulary). But this is not terribly exciting, since in the case of mathematics few would expect more than uniqueness of interpretation up to isomorphism.

The most important source of indeterminacy, and the one that Putnam emphasizes early in the essay, is the downward Skolem-Lowenheim theorem:

any interpretation of the given maximal set of beliefs S will have a countable subinterpretation that also satisfies S. *The fact that it is a subinterpretation is important, for it guarantees that if the original interpretation satisfies the constraint on the interpretation of the non-mathematical vocabulary, the subinterpretation will too.*[32] Now, any natural interpretation of the given set of beliefs S will contain objects y that are "genuinely uncountable sets in the interpretation": that is, objects y such that there are uncountably many x such that $<x,y>$ satisfies 'Set(y) & $x\epsilon y$'. The alternative interpretations constructed by the downward Skolem-Lowenheim theorem violate this and so seem highly "unintended," and yet they satisfy all of the constraints, *including the constraints on the physical vocabulary.*[33]

From this presentation, it should be clear why the Putnam argument as it stands does not go over to show that there is any indeterminacy in the notion of finiteness. For if we use a compactness argument instead of a downward Skolem-Lowenheim theorem argument to get the nonstandard interpretation, there is not the slightest reason to think that the constraints on the physical vocabulary will be preserved. (And a downward Skolem-Lowenheim argument would not give you a nonstandard interpretation of 'finite': finite sets satisfy 'finite' in every interpretation in which the axioms of set theory come out true, since 1–1 correspondences between finite sets are themselves finite and hence exist in every such interpretation.)[34]

But even if Putnam's argument as it stands does not carry over to the finiteness case, it could still be that the standards he has imposed on an answer to the question of what determines the extension of 'set' and 'ϵ' and 'finite' are enough to prevent 'finite' from having a determinate extension. To argue that this is not so, one needs a positive account of how the extension of 'finite' (or, the contribution to truth conditions of '$\exists_{fin}$') might be determined. I will close with a modest suggestion about this; it is not entirely attractive, but I know none that is better.

The suggestion is that *if the physical world is as we typically think it is,* our physical beliefs are enough to determine the extension of 'finite'. Consider the one-place predicate $B(Z)$, defined as

> Z is a set of events which (i) has an earliest member and a latest member; and (ii) is such that any two of its members occur at least one second apart.

We typically think that any set Z of events that satisfies this will contain only finitely many members; moreover, that there is no finite bound on the size of the sets that satisfy it. Call these "our cosmological assumptions." (The first says in effect that time is Archimedean, the second that it is infinite.) From our cosmological assumptions (plus some set theory), we can infer the following:

> (*) $\forall Y \{Y$ is a set $\supset [Y$ is finite $\equiv \exists Z \exists f (B(Z)$ &f is a function that maps Y 1–1 into $Z)]\}$.

(Y is any set, not necessarily a set of events.) Now of course the theory S consisting of set theory plus our cosmological assumptions (which implies

(*)) has nonstandard models, in which certain infinite sets satisfy $B(Z)$ and hence in which certain infinite sets satisfy the predicate 'finite'. However, if our first cosmological assumption is true, any such model must assign a nonstandard extension to the formula $B(Z)$; and *in particular, it must either contain things that satisfy 'event' which are not events, or it must contain pairs of events which satisfy 'earlier than' or 'at least one second apart' even though the first is not earlier than the second or the two are not one second apart.* Either way, the model will violate the constraint on the interpretation of the physical vocabulary, viz. that the extension of such a predicate in the model can only contain things that actually have the corresponding property. In sum: if the first cosmological assumption holds then *no model of* S *in which 'event' and 'earlier than' and 'at least one second apart' satisfy the constraints on the interpretation of the physical vocabulary can be one where any infinite sets satisfy* B(Z). (Here 'infinite set' really means 'object y such that for infinitely many x, $<x,y>$ satisfies 'ϵ' in the interpretation'—see note 34.) But it is easy to see that no pair of an infinite set and a finite set can satisfy '$\exists f$ (f is a function that maps Y 1–1 into Z)' in any model; *so no allowable model of* S *can be one where any infinite sets satisfy 'finite'*. And of course there are no models of S where any finite sets fail to satisfy 'finite', since S includes set theory and genuinely finite sets satisfy 'finite' in every model of set theory; so (if the first cosmological assumption holds) *in every allowable model of* S, *a set satisfies 'finite' if and only if it is genuinely finite.*

This would be cold comfort if our second cosmological assumption were not also true: if it were false, no model meeting the constraints on the interpretation of our physical vocabulary could satisfy the theory S (since finite sets bigger than any sets that actually satisfy B would be constrained to be both finite and infinite); in that case, the interpretation of 'finite' could not be fixed by S. And dropping the second cosmological assumption from S would not restore the situation: for then (*) would have to be replaced by (*') $\forall Y \{Y$ is a set $\supset [\exists Z \exists f(B(Z)$ & f maps Y 1–1 into $Z) \supset Y$ is finite]$\}$; and while we could still argue that any allowable interpretation of (the weakened) S is such that only finite sets of physical events satisfy B in the interpretation, it would not follow that only finite sets satisfy 'finite' in the interpretation (since nothing would now prevent a set from satisfying 'finite' even if the interpretation contains no 1–1 mapping from it to a set of events satisfying B). In particular, there would be nothing to rule out nonstandard derivations in a given formal system, derivations that contain infinitely many formulas even though the set of formulas in them satisfies the predicate 'finite'. So if we want to argue that notions like 'provable in such and such a system' have a determinate extension on grounds like those here considered, we need the second cosmological assumption as well as the first.[35] But with the two assumptions together, the constraints on the physical vocabulary determine a privileged class of interpretations in which 'finite' determinately stands for what it should, thus providing a way around all the nasty consequences contemplated in Section 3.

I will close with four comments to help clarify this proposed solution. First, the proposal is *not* that (*) is an adequate definition of 'finite', in a sense that makes (*) anything close to analytic. Nothing prevents us from discovering that time is finite in extent; what is true is only that if it is finite in extent, then temporal considerations of the sort just reviewed do not determine a unique extension for 'finite'.[36] If time is finite but our cosmological assumptions about *space* are true, then conceivably an analog of (*) for space could determine a unique extension for 'finite'. But if both are finite in extent—as is surely a serious empirical possibility—the view being suggested here is that the notion of finiteness would have genuine indeterminacy of the sort discussed in Section 3. I am sure that some will feel that making the determinateness of the notion of finite depend on cosmology is unsatisfactory; perhaps,[37] but I do not see how anything *other* than cosmology has a *chance* of making it determinate.

The second clarificatory comment is that it is essential to the solution that the cosmological assumptions be *actually* true: you cannot solve the problem modally, using the mere *possibility* that they be true (even if the concern is simply to fix the extension of 'finite' as applied to pure sets, so that worries about sets changing their members in counterfactual situations do not arise). Why not? For instance, if the world were finite, couldn't we fix the extension of 'finite' for pure sets by the condition

(**) $\forall Y \{Y$ is a pure set $\supset [Y$ is finite $\equiv \Diamond \exists Z \exists f (B(Z) \ \& \ f$ is a function that maps Y 1–1 into $Z)]\}$?

No: this move to the mere possibility of a set Z of events satisfying the condition does indeed let all genuinely finite pure sets into the extension of 'finite', even if they have more members than the number of seconds in the history of the universe; but the same flexibility that allows them in also allows in many infinite pure sets, because of the possibility of an infinite set Z of events satisfying B.[38] The basic problem is that the move to possibility means giving up the use of the actual world as in some sense a standard of finiteness, so there is no longer a way to keep the nonstandard finite sets out.

My third clarificatory comment is that even if we had overwhelming evidence for our cosmological assumptions, it is not clear that skepticism about the determinacy of the notion of finiteness would be foreclosed: the skeptic could point out that since the physical theory that includes the cosmological assumptions has nonstandard models, all our evidence is compatible with the physical world itself constituting a nonstandard model of our theory, that is, a model in which time is non-Archimedean but satisfies all the sentences that we use to express the claim that it is Archimedean. If the physical world itself is such a nonstandard model of our theory, then the above argument for the determinacy of finiteness does not go through: that argument worked by using comparison to the physical world to rule out the nonstandard models. Actually there is some question in my mind as to whether it is even coherent to suppose that the physical universe might constitute a nonstandard model of our theory.[39] But even if this skeptical possibility is coherent, it is not particularly believable: so the skeptical possibility does not undermine the claim that if we have evidence for the cosmological assumptions we should believe the notion of finiteness to be determinate.

My final clarificatory comment is about how far the argument here can be pushed: if cosmological considerations can make 'finite' quite determinate in extension (thus somewhat constraining the determinations of 'set' and second-order quantification as well), can they make less elementary notions determinate (thus providing further constraints on 'set' and second-order quantification)? It might be thought that if the argument works for 'finite' it works equally for 'has cardinality $2^{\aleph_0}$'. For define $B^*(Z)$ as 'There are points of space a and b such that Z is the set of points on the line segment between them', where points are understood to be non-mathematical entities, and take as cosmological assumptions that there are sets Z such that $B^*(Z)$ and that any Z such that $B^*(Z)$ has cardinality $2^{\aleph_0}$. (The first of these cosmological assumptions would be false if lines in space were not made up of physical points (but points were only mathematical abstractions). The second assumption could err in either direction: there might be more than $2^{\aleph_0}$ points in any line segment in physical space if line segments contain points that are infinitessimally close; there might be fewer if line segments in physical space are ordered like intervals in some subfield of the real numbers.) Let S be set theory plus these cosmological assumptions. S implies that for any pure set Y, Y is of cardinality $2^{\aleph_0}$ iff there is a 1–1 mapping from a Z such that $B^*(Z)$ onto Y; can't we use this to argue as with 'finite' that in any allowable interpretation of S, a set satisfies 'has cardinality $2^{\aleph_0}$' if and only if it genuinely has cardinality $2^{\aleph_0}$?

No, for two reasons. First, even if we could assume that in any allowable interpretation the sets that satisfy $B^*(Z)$ have cardinality $2^{\aleph_0}$, we still would have no guarantee that the interpretation would not have sets of cardinality $2^{\aleph_0}$ that fail to satisfy 'has cardinality $2^{\aleph_0}$' in the interpretation; for the interpretation might not contain the 1–1 correspondence to a Z such that $B^*(Z)$. No such thing can happen in the finitude case, since any 1–1 correspondence between finite sets exists in every interpretation of set theory. Second, we have no right to assume that in any allowable interpretation the sets that satisfy $B^*(Z)$ have cardinality $2^{\aleph_0}$. Indeed a downward Lowenheim-Skolem argument shows that there are allowable interpretations where only countable sets satisfy B^* (and also allowable interpretations where only sets of any given uncountable size less than $2^{\aleph_0}$ do, if we assume the denial of the continuum hypothesis). Such sets will of course also satisfy 'has cardinality $2^{\aleph_0}$' in the interpretation; so being of cardinality $2^{\aleph_0}$ is neither necessary nor sufficient for satisfying 'has cardinality $2^{\aleph_0}$' in interpretations that satisfy the constraints on the physical vocabulary.

One might be tempted to strengthen the constraints on the physical vocabulary a bit: one might be tempted to assume that the domain of first-order quantification over the physical universe was determinate. (The constraints above guaranteed that in any allowable interpretation, quantifiers over the physical ranged *only* over physical things; the further constraint now being contemplated is that they include *every* physical thing.) In that case, 'has cardinality $2^{\aleph_0}$' would become slightly more determinate: it could no longer be satisfied in allowable interpretations by sets of cardinality less than $2^{\aleph_0}$. But it could still fail to be satisfied in allowable interpretations by sets of cardinality $2^{\aleph_0}$. The gain in determinacy would thus not be all that great, and would certainly fall far short of establishing the determinacy of 'set', or of second-order quantification generally. (Indeed, for cardinals greater than the cardinality of the physical universe we could not get even this much determinacy, as a modified downward Skolem-Lowenheim argument shows; and it is hard to see how to get this much determinacy for uncountable cardinals less than $2^{\aleph_0}$.) Moreover, it is not completely clear to me that the strengthening of the constraints on interpretation is reasonable: I do not think it is obviously determinate that our quantifiers range over all points of space rather than over some well-behaved subcollection of them (and it is worth stressing that I did not assume this to be determinate in arguing that suitable cosmological assumptions could make determinate the notion of finiteness). In short, the prospects of getting useful determinacy results for notions less elementary than 'finite' are minimal.[40]

APPENDIX: PLENITUDE

In Section 1A I say that if you are going to be an ontological platonist it seems natural to advocate extreme plenitude by holding that all the consistent concepts of (pure) set and membership are "instantiated side by side." What exactly does this mean? The idea is to regard all quantifiers over mathematical entities in a mathematical theory as implicitly restricted by a predicate to which all other predicates of mathematical entities in the theory are subordinate. In different mathematical theories the overarching predicate is different; so mathematical theories which appear to conflict with each other when written without their overarching predicates do not really conflict. It is not necessary to say that there is anything to preclude *meaningfully* quantifying over all mathematical entities at once, without an overarching predicate; one can say just that there is not anything interesting and true to say about so plenitudinous a realm.

The remark that the different universes of sets exist "side by side" suggests that nothing is included under more than one overarching predicate. Actually though it is better to say that there is no mathematical interest to the question of whether things falling under one overarching predicate also fall under another, and the matter can be conventionally decided either way. For instance, it is mathematically uninteresting whether the sets$_{\aleph_1}$ are included in the sets$_{\aleph_{817}}$, or the sets$_{\aleph_{817}}$ are included in the sets$_{\aleph_1}$, or neither inclusion holds. (If an inclusion does hold, the membership predicates $\epsilon_{\aleph_1}$ and $\epsilon_{\aleph_{817}}$ need not coincide on the common domain.) See [6], pp. 276–78. Perhaps the best decision is to say that neither inclusion holds, simply in order to emphasize that for mathematical purposes neither sets$_{\aleph_1}$ nor sets$_{\aleph_{817}}$ have privileged status.

Mark Balaguer persuasively argues in [1] that one of the advantages of such a "full blooded platonism" is that it undercuts much of the force of the epistemological challenge to platonism in Benacerraf [2].

But is such "full blooded platonism" really coherent? Usually when we speak of a theory (e.g., the theory of groups, or geometry without the parallel postulate or its denial) being satisfied in distinct universes with neither one having privileged status, we do so within the context of a broader set theory within which we can compare the universes. In conversation, both Stewart Shapiro and Shaughan Lavine have questioned the coherence of speaking of set theory itself in this way, since the view has it that there is no privileged set theory outside the universes within which to do the comparing. I do not think there is actually any incoherence here, but a certain amount of care is required.

It is true that on this view, if we try to compare the different universes from a universe-neutral standpoint, we cannot use set theory in the comparison: for instance, we cannot talk from a universal-neutral standpoint about isomorphisms between parts of one universe and parts of the other, since isomorphisms are set theoretic entities. (I will not explore here how much comparison we can do without set theory.) But we can in a certain sense compare the universes from the point of view of a given universe. More exactly, we can develop the usual theory of models and interpretations of set theory within each universe; in effect what this does is shows us how we can construct, within a "background" universe, representations of other universes, and compare these other universes to one another and to the background universe by comparing their representations.

But one must be careful in thinking about such comparisons of universes within background universes, or one *will* lapse into incoherence. Suppose you and I each advocate a standard set theory, but in my case containing the claim that the size of the continuum is $\aleph_{23}$ and in your case containing the claim that it is $\aleph_{817}$. [To avoid certain complications, we may suppose that these are "full" set theories, in that (i) each allows arbitrary sets of urelements (things it takes not to be sets) at the ground floor, from which other sets are built up, and (ii) each allows any vocabulary used in talking about such urelements to appear in its schemas (e.g., the replacement schema).] I then introduce the terms 'Set*' and 'ϵ*' within my universe of sets to represent your universe of sets and your membership relation, so I can use these in my replacement schema; similarly, you introduce the terms 'Set@' and 'ϵ@' to represent my universe and my membership relation, and use these in your replacement schema. But now when I interpret your theory in mine, I need to represent your symbols 'Set@' and 'ϵ@' as well as your symbols 'Set' and 'ϵ'. One might think that since these are supposed to be representations of my universe, the only adequate representations for me to use are 'Set' and 'ϵ'; but this would lead to contradictions. Rather, I must interpret your 'Set@' by a predicate 'Set@*' narrower in scope than the predicate 'Set*' which I use to represent your 'Set'. It is not mathematically interesting, either in my mathematics or yours, to ask which if either of my terms 'Set' and 'Set@*' is coextensive with your term 'Set@*': my terms 'Set' and 'Set@*' denote things in a universe where the continuum is of size $\aleph_{23}$, while your term 'Set@' denotes things in a universe where it is of size $\aleph_{817}$, and as noted in the second paragraph of this Appendix, questions of cross-universe identity have no mathematical interest. (Again the simplest convention is that these two "universes" are disjoint. In that case, my representation of your term can never be coextensive with your term.) All that can be asked of my representation of your term is that it play a roughly analogous role in the universe of sets$_{\aleph_{23}}$ to the role that your term plays in the universe of sets$_{\aleph_{817}}$. There is no contradiction in supposing that my term 'Set@*' bears this relation to your term 'Set@' while that latter term bears the dual relation to my term 'Set' and yet my terms 'Set' and 'Set@*' are not coextensive.

(I think these comments undermine recent attempts to get categoricity and quasi-categoricity results by "essentially first order" means: see [14], pp. 34–37, for the attempt to get such results in arithmetic; [17], p. 248, for the attempt to do so in analysis, and [11], sec. VII.4, for the attempt to do so in set theory.)

NOTES

1. I am talking about consistent conceptions of *pure* sets. For impure sets the situation is slightly more complicated, since theories postulating them can be internally consistent yet not consistent with the actual physical world: see [6], pp. 56–57, for a clearer statement of this and an example. This situation cannot arise however if the impure set theories are *conservative* in the sense of [6]; so the view in the text can be extended to impure concepts of set and membership by substituting 'conservative' for 'consistent'.

2. Note that I am not identifying the view that there are multiple "disjoint" universes of sets, different ones for different answers to the continuum question, with the view that our use of 'set' leaves the size of the continuum indeterminate. The first does not really entail the second: conceivably even if there are such multiple universes, there is something in our usage that determines which universe we are talking about, though it is hard to see what facts about our usage could do this. The second does not entail the first either: even if there is a privileged universe, there might be nothing in our practice to determine that 'set' applies to everything in the universe or that '∈' applies to the membership relation of the universe. But elaboration of this requires a different sort of argument than the one based on undecidable sentences; I turn to it next.

3. Putnam's attempt to extend his conclusions to non-mathematical concepts rests on confusing the view that reference is determined by e.g., causal considerations with the view that reference is determined by a description theory in which descriptions containing the word 'cause' play an especially prominent role. The fallacy has been often pointed out: see for instance [12]. The first half of [16] does not rely on this fallacy. It relies instead on the fact that in the case of 'set' nothing like a causal theory of reference seems as if it could play much role; so that our theory of sets has to be the main determinant of reference, and that theory has nonstandard models. A more careful statement of what it relies on will be given in Section 4.

4. The second consideration favoring indeterminacy is really a generalization of the first: if one could find a way to argue that we somehow manage to intend a unique interpretation of 'set' and '∈', then of course there would be a uniquely correct answer to the size of the continuum in this intended interpretation, whatever the difficulty in finding that answer. But the first consideration is worth separate statement to make clear the importance of worries about undecidable sentences.

5. Of course, the understanding of a notion like 'set' is prior to the understanding of a formal truth theory for sentences containing this notion. The claim is only that the super-valuational semantics gives as good a representation of the semantics of an indeterminate

notion of set as a standard model-theoretic semantics for set theory would give of the notion of set were that notion determinate.

6. The extra power of Morse-Kelley does of course constrain the interpretation of 'set' *somewhat.*

7. In the present essay I am not concerned with ontological issues; and my main doubts about the *legitimacy* of using second-order quantification in certain contexts (e.g., in basic physical theory) are ontological and hence not relevant here. (To some extent these doubts about legitimacy are overcome by Boolos's "plural quantification" interpretation of second-order quantification. Also, in some contexts we can get an ontologically cleaner interpretation of second-order quantifiers even without interpreting them as plural quantifiers: the quantifiers can be taken to range over parts of the mereological fusion of the objects in the first-order domain.)

8. The importance of such dispositions (even for schemas in first-order theories) is a recurrent theme of [11].

9. I talk mostly about the notion of finiteness rather than the notion of natural number to emphasize that the problem I am concerned with does not depend on the ontology of mathematics: it arises for mathematical fictionalists as well as for everyone else.

10. A reply to Putnam's argument would give rise to a reply to the continuum hypothesis argument as well: see note 4. The direct analog of the continuum hypothesis argument in the finiteness case concerns Godel's theorem, which I will discuss in Section 3A.

11. The latter is definable in set theory, and even without set theory, in second-order logic with relation variables or function variables. And though not definable in second-order logic with set variables only and no device for forming ordered pairs, it seems to me that there is no serious possibility of holding such second-order quantification determinate and finiteness not.

12. I am going to ignore considerations about the semantic paradoxes. (Perhaps it would suffice to replace (T) with the weaker claim that the inference from "'p' is true" to "p", and the converse inference, are always legitimate.)

13. There will be *non*mathematical claims about finitude that we *will* want to regard as factual even though they are not decided by any theory we accept: it may be that no theory we accept implies that there are only finitely many stars; but if in fact there are less than $10^{10^{10}}$ of them, and our mathematical theory implies that if there are less than $10^{10^{10}}$ Fs then there are only finitely many Fs, then of course we want to say that it is determinate that there are only finitely many stars. Here the failure of the mathematical theory to imply that there are only finitely many stars is due to its not having access to all the facts about stars, so we can grant that there is a definite fact here without granting that there are mathematical facts or facts specifically about finitude that transcend our theory.

14. The set of what we implicitly accept, as I have just defined it, might be inconsistent. It might be better to redefine 'implicitly accept' so that this could not happen, but it is simplest to stick to the definition given and to take the radical indeterminist as holding that if this set is inconsistent then none of our mathematical sentences have determinate truth value.

15. There is no obvious reason to think that this class of reasonable candidates has a largest member; for instance, it is not obviously closed under union. In other words, there may be no maximal reasonable candidate for being a person's maximal theory.

16. For simplicity I assume a formalization of logic with *modus ponens* as the only inference rule. On formalizations with a rule of generalization, the induction is not on truth but on having a true universal closure.

17. The idea that we should avoid postulating an increasing hierarchy of classical truth predicates by using instead a single non-classical truth predicate that avoids Tarski's Theorem has become pretty standard at least since Kripke [10]. Kripke proposed that we define the predicate set theoretically: however, to do so he had to take the predicate as applicable only to sentences whose quantifiers are confined to a specific set. (If we had a definition of 'true' in terms of other vocabulary, then certain applications of 'true' *to sentences containing only*

that vocabulary would have to violate the Tarski biconditionals (which is implausible if that vocabulary is substantially more basic): for the Tarski biconditionals fail for certain sentences containing 'true', and the definition would then give rise to failures for sentences in the defining vocabulary.) The idea of regarding a nonclassical truth predicate as undefined and unrestricted in its application and governed by explicit axioms has now become common: see [5], [13], and for an especially useful survey, [9].

18. In illustrating where the inconsistency will occur, let's confine our attention to theories that employ full classical logic. Then the assertion that all logical and nonlogical axioms of M are true and that all rules of M are truth preserving implies that $T(x)$ holds whenever x is a theorem of classical logic; indeed, whenever x is a theorem of Peano arithmetic (which I take to be part of M). So in what follows we can assume as a background theory this plus the truth-preservingness of *modus ponens*.

Most theories of truth employ both the rules of T-Introduction (A/T$<A>$) and T-Elimination (T$<A>$/A) (as well as perhaps the rules $-A$/$-$T$<A>$ and $-$T$<A>$/$-A$, which I will not consider here). The claim that T-Introduction is truth preserving implies the schema

    T-REP   T$<A> \supset$ T$<$T$<A>>$;

and the claim that T-Elimination is truth-preserving implies the schema

    T-DEL   T$<$T$<A>> \supset$ T$<A>$.

But the two rules of inference together with these two schemas is inconsistent in the background theory just mentioned. (T-REP, T-DEL and T-Introduction entail that every sentence is true; adding T-Elimination yields inconsistency. For a proof, see p. 16 of [9], whose notation I am following.) So you cannot accept both rules together with the claim that they are truth preserving.

To give up T-Elimination seems thoroughly unattractive. Besides, the situation with T-Introduction is unacceptable on its own: in combination with the further axiom that there is at least one sentence that is not true, T-Introduction and the claim that it is truth preserving (T-REP) are inconsistent. (Proof: Let L be the liar sentence, for which we can prove $L \equiv -$T$<L>$. So T$<L> \supset -L$; using T-introduction and the law T$<A \supset B> \supset$ (T$<A> \supset$ T$<B>$), we get T$<$T$<L>> \supset$ T$<-L>$; with T-REP, this gives T$<L> \supset$ T$<-L>$. But it is easy to see (using the background theory) that if at least one sentence is not true then not both T$<L>$ and T$<-L>$; so $-$T$<L>$. So by the unused half of the liar sentence biconditional, L. So by T-Introduction, T$<L>$; contradiction.)

Keeping T-Elimination while restricting T-Introduction is a possibility; but the restriction of T-Introduction means that it is not obvious that all axioms can be declared true. Indeed, I think that the only attractive view that restricts T-Introduction does so to keep the axiom T$<A> \supset A$; but this is inconsistent with its own truth, as Montague's theorem (or indeed, more elementary reasoning involving only a liar sentence) shows. I imagine there are sharper results about the inconsistency of adding assumptions (a) and (b) in the text to one's truth theory than I have given here; but these should give the general flavor.

The proof of the Godel sentence G requires not only the inductive proof I have been discussing: it also requires a restricted version of the conditional T$<A> \supset A$, or at least a restricted version of the principle $-A$/$-$T$<A>$. For the induction would give you

    If Provable$<G>$ then True$<G>$,

from which we can infer

    If $-G$ then True$<G>$;

but unless we have True$<G> \supset G$, we cannot get to $-G \supset G$ and thence to G. (And unless we have $G \supset$ True$<G>$, we cannot get to True$<G>$.) Alternatively, by formalizing the proof of the first incompleteness theorem we can get to G from CON, the formalization of the consistency of M; but then even if we had the claim that all theorems of M are true, we would need to infer $-$T$<0 = 1>$ from $-<0 = 1>$ in order to infer CON. I think though that reasonable axiomatizations of truth will allow at least restricted versions of these principles.

19. Some may think that in my account of why the Godel sentence of M is unprovable I am overestimating the importance of the fact that our maximal theory employs a truth predicate for which some of our usual assumptions about truth must break down, and underestimating the importance of the gap between asserting of each of a class of sentences that it is true and asserting that all of them are true. Vann McGee has suggested to me an interesting argument for this view: his argument is based on "Craig's trick" for obtaining bizarre recursive axiomatizations of recursively enumerable sets of sentences. Let $M*$ be the Craig reaxiomatization of the set of consequences of M not containing the truth predicate. $M*$ has a Godel sentence G that is undecidable in $M*$, and hence must be undecidable in M (since G does not contain the truth predicate). But for each axiom A of $M*$, T<A> its truth follows from M (since A does not contain the truth predicate); and M also implies the truth-preservingness of the rules of inference of $M*$. So here the obstacle to proving G can only be the gap between proving T(A) for each axiom A of $M*$ and proving the generalization that all the axioms of $M*$ are true; the role of the non-classical nature of truth predicates seems to have disappeared.

But I do not think that the role of the non-classical nature of the truth predicate really has disappeared. Suppose that N is a typical theory that does not employ a truth predicate, and that $N*$ is the Craig reaxiomatization of the class of theorems of N that meet a certain (decidable) condition C. If we believe N, and N is finitely axiomatized, then we have available a formal argument (in a metatheory employing a truth predicate for the language of N) for the truth of all the axioms of $N*$. (There is also a corresponding though somewhat more questionable informal argument when N is not finitely axiomatized but when we know that we believe each axiom of N and do so for good reason.) For in these circumstances we can argue that all theorems of N are true, hence that all the theorems of N meeting condition C are true, and the axioms of $N*$ are simply cleverly coded analogs of these theorems of N. In the case of the maximal theory M on the other hand, this argument for believing that all the axioms of $M*$ are true breaks down, since it depends on the lemma that all the theorems of M are true, which we do not get because M contains the non-classical truth predicate. So even though $M*$ does not contain the nonclassical truth predicate, the analysis of why we have no reason to think all its axioms are true does depend on the nonclassical truth predicate in the theory M from which it was obtained.

20. This is so even for the Craig theorem version of the argument discussed in the previous note: there, the argument is unsound because the premise that all the axioms of $M*$ are true is not determinately true. (It is not formally decidable in M. Equivalently, it can fail in nonstandard models of M, even though for each "genuinely finite" sentence A in $M*$ the claim that A is true is determinately true, because in nonstandard models the range of quantification includes nonstandard sentences.)

21. Actually there is a second strategy for trying to informally argue from M to its Godel sentence G. The argument would begin by noting that $M \cup \{-G\}$ is a highly unattractive theory: it is ω-inconsistent, and its ω-inconsistency is provable in M. (The ω-inconsistency might arise from an inconsistency in M, in which case $-G$ would be true.) The next step would be to argue from this unattractiveness in $M \cup \{-G\}$ to the claim

> (1) that if we found ourselves committed to $M \cup \{-G\}$ we would have strong moti-
> vation to revise our commitments: either by dropping $-G$ or by dropping part of
> M.

(Any reason to believe $-G$ would be a reason to take the second alternative in (1): this is not surprising, since $-G$ is equivalent (given a small fragment of M) to the standard formalization of the claim that M is inconsistent.) The third step would be to somehow get from (1) to

> (2) We have grounds based on the axioms and rules of M for disbelieving $-G$, and
> hence (by excluded middle) for believing G.

But the gap between (1) and (2) is a big one on any view: (1) may suggest that the axioms and rules of M give grounds for thinking that *if* –G *holds we should revise* M, but that is not the same as giving grounds for denying –G. (Maybe certain axioms and rules of *M* themselves give grounds for thinking we should revise *M*, even without the assumption that –G holds!) And the gap between (1) and (2) is especially big for the radical indeterminist, who denies that G has determinate truth value prior to a commitment to either G or –G.

22. Since G_i will typically fail to follow from many of the other M_js, as well as M_i.

23. Dummett actually intends the essay under discussion not to presuppose intuitionism: see pp. 199-200.

24. Dummett holds that the concepts of set, ordinal, and property are concepts of totalities such that any characterization of the totality brings forth new members of that totality. (I will not discuss just what this means or whether it is true.) He puts this doctrine by saying that these concepts are *indefinitely extensible*, but I will put it by saying that they are concepts *of indefinitely extensible totalities*. The concept of natural number certainly does not meet this condition—if anything, it is a concept of an indefinitely *contractible* totality—but because more gets built into the concept as the totality of properties expands, it seems natural to call the concept itself 'indefinitely extensible'. 'Indefinitely extendible' is thus on my usage a broader category.

25. It may be thought that note 21 entails that the radical indeterminist who is committed to avoiding ω-inconsistent theories is in the same position. Not so: there the position was that our current practice dictates that if we alter our practice so as to formally decide *G*, we must either accept *G* or give up part of our current theory; but the first of these alternatives has no privileged status.

26. If the induction principle is stated as a single sentence quantifying over sets or properties, then comprehension schemas about set or property existence are relevant instead.

27. Dummett's response is apparently contained in the following passage:

> The use of a mathematical expression could be characterized by means of a single formal system only if the sense of that expression were perfectly definite; when, as with 'natural number' [or, I assume, 'true'—H. F.], the expression has an inherently vague meaning, it will be essential to the characterization of its use to formulate the general principle according to which any precise formal characterization can always be extended. (p. 198)

But I do not see why the indefiniteness of an expression prevents it from being characterized in a single formal system. The disagreement here is presumably related to our different attitudes toward intuitionism, and also to a related difference in our conceptions of indefiniteness, to be discussed later.

28. See [7]; though the principle (MS*) discussed there uses a logical truth operator in place of the last 'is quantificationally derivable'.

29. If T is inconsistent it entails any claim of form 'There is a quantificational derivation of <A>'; but since quantificational logic is consistent, there are sentences A that have no quantificational derivations, so T cannot be sound.

30. I am speaking loosely: the naive interpretation of 'set' and 'ε' is such that they have no extension, since too many things satisfy them to be incorporated into a set. So a more accurate formulation of Putnam's conclusion would be that there is no determinate answer to the question of what satisfies the words 'set' and 'ε', or that it is indeterminate how they contribute to the truth conditions of sentences containing them.

31. I am assuming here that there is no non–first-order logical operator in the language except possibly a second-order quantifier. If other kinds of non–first-order operators are in the language, such as $\exists_{fin}$, the concession would have to be stated more carefully, so as not to rule them determinate by fiat.

32. In other words, if the original interpretation is such that for any two objects x and y in its domain, <x,y> satisfies 'heavier than' if and only if x is heavier than y, then this must be

so in the new interpretation as well; and analogously for each other physical predicate. (And for non-physical predicates too; though by combining the downward Lowenheim-Skolem argument with the trivial permutation argument of the previous paragraph, we would get models for which the extension to the non-physical predicates fails.)

33. It is worth noting that the transitive collapse of the alternative interpretation, which is isomorphic to the alternative interpretation, also satisfies the constraints on the physical vocabulary. For transitive ϵ-interpretations the "naturalness" condition is more snappily formulated as the condition that the interpretation contain uncountable sets, so the transitive collapse violates naturalness in this snappier formulation.

34. This formulation is really correct only for transitive ϵ-interpretations. (For interpretations generally, the actual finitude of a set is completely irrelevant to anything, since any mathematical object can play any role whatever in the interpretation.) The correct formulation is that in any interpretation in which the axioms of set theory come out true, *objects that are "genuinely finite sets in the interpretation"* satisfy 'finite'; where to say that an object y is a "genuinely finite set in the interpretation" means that it satisfies 'set' in the interpretation and is such that for only finitely many x does $<x,y>$ satisfy 'ϵ' in the interpretation.

Throughout the rest of the essay I will adopt the policy of talking about general interpretations in terms that are strictly appropriate only to transitive ϵ-interpretations. This saves considerable verbiage; the risk of misunderstanding is small; and it is routine to supply the correct reformulations.

35. To a large extent the argument of the last two paragraphs extends to the case where we do not have set theory but have a primitive quantifier $\exists_{fin}$. More fully, in that case, the truth of our cosmological assumptions would rule out at least the most noxious sort of indeterminacy in our concept of finitude, e.g., it would rule out indeterminacy in the notion of proof.

To discuss this, we first need a sufficiently comprehensive notion of model for a language containing $\exists_{fin}$ as primitive: one that allows nonstandard models. So: take a model for this language to be a model in the usual sense together with a distinguished collection of subsets of the domain (perhaps required to be closed under the subset relation), and regard a formula of form $\exists_{fin}xB$ as true in the model (relative to an assignment function) if the set of objects in the domain that satisfy B (relative to the rest of the assignment function) is in the distinguished collection. (A standard model will be one where the collection contains all and only the finite sets.)

Now suppose there is a 1-place predicate $W(x)$ such that the following are part of our overall theory:

    (i)   Any x such that $W(x)$ is an event;

    (ii) There is an earliest x such that $W(x)$, but no latest such x;

    (iii) For any distinct x and y, if $W(x)$ and $W(y)$ then x and y occur at least one second apart.

And make the cosmological assumption

    (iv) $\forall x[W(x) \supset \exists_{fin}y(W(y)$ & y is earlier than $x)]$.

(The other cosmological assumption, that time is infinite, is now built into (ii) and (iii).) Then (i)–(iv) will of course have nonstandard models; however, if our cosmological assumption is true, no model of (i)–(iv) in which 'event' and 'earlier than' and 'at least one second apart' have extensions in accord with the constraint on the non-mathematical vocabulary can be one in which anything satisfying $W(x)$ can have infinitely many "predecessors" satisfying $W(x)$. This imposes a strong constraint on the "distinguished collection of subsets" that serve as the "finite subsets" of the model.

In particular, consider any formula $Y(x,z)$ for which we believe $\forall z \exists_{fin} x Y(x,z)$. (Example: '$z$ is an expression of English and x is a subexpression of z.') Often—and in this example—

we will be able to define a formula $A(x,y)$ such that the following are part of our overall theory:

(v) $\forall x \forall x' \forall w \forall w'$[if $A(x,w)$ and $A(x',w')$ then $w = w'$ iff $x = x'$];

(vi) $\forall z \forall x [Y(x,z) \supset \exists w (W(w) \ \& \ A(x,w))]$

(In effect $A(x,y)$ defines a 1–1 mapping of $\cup_z \{x \mid Y(x,z)\}$ into $\{x \mid W(x)\}$; in this example, of the expressions of English into the W-events.) Then any reasonably comprehensive axioms for $\exists_{fin}$ will surely imply

(*) $\forall z \{\exists_{fin} x Y(x,z) \equiv \exists u \forall x \forall w [W(u) \ \& \ (W(w) \ \& \ Y(x,z) \ \& \ A(x,w) \supset w$ is earlier than $u)]\}$.

But in that case, the models that our cosmological hypothesis restricts us to are all ones in which for any object o satisfying $\exists_{fin} x Y(x,z)$, there are only finitely many o' such that $<o',o>$ satisfies $Y(x,z)$. Thus at least the most noxious nonstandardness has been eliminated.

36. Modified temporal considerations might. For we could reduce the strength of the second cosmological assumption, by weakening $B(Z)$ as follows:

Z is a set of events, no two of which are simultaneous, which (i) has an earliest member and a latest member, and (ii) is such that any two members with no member between them are the same distance apart.

The assumption that this weaker version of $B(Z)$ is satisfiable by arbitrary large finite sets is the assumption that time is infinite *in the large or small*, rather than in the large as before. But you do not get something for nothing: the assumption that only finite sets satisfy $B(Z)$ is correspondingly strengthened to the assumption of Archimedeanness *in the large and small* rather than just in the large: that is, events infinitessimally far apart as well as infinitely far apart must now be ruled out.

37. It may be worth noting though that the two cosmological assumptions are also presupposed by certain intuitive explanations of finiteness: for instance, that a finite set is one that a being who lived forever and could not count more than one object per second could finish counting. (The proposal in the text is a considerable improvement over that intuitive explanation. First, there may be obstacles to counting a set other than infinitude: consider for instance a finite set of real numbers that are not nameable in English. More important, the intuitive explanation gives incorrect results about finiteness when the cosmological assumptions fail, rather than making 'finite' indeterminate.)

38. It would of course do no good to strengthen the condition $B(Z)$ to require that Z be finite: the game is to look at interpretations of set theory plus (*) that satisfy the physical constraints, and if an extra occurrence of 'finite' is added into (*) it has to be subjected to the possibility of reinterpretation also.

39. In discussing such questions it may be important to distinguish two versions of the skeptical hypothesis: one in which our lives are of genuinely finite duration even though there are pairs of events whose temporal separation is merely pseudo-finite, the other (suggested to me by both Hilary Putnam and Shaughan Lavine) in which our lives are themselves merely pseudo-finite.

40. You get a bit more determinacy if you take arbitrary *regions* of physical space to count as non-mathematical, and construe arbitrary quantification over them to be determinate. Indeed, if you assume that every region contains a minimal region (a point) which is itself taken as non-mathematical, and make a completeness assumption about regions in addition to assuming that the regions form a Boolean algebra with zero element removed, then quantification over sets of physical points would be determinate on these assumptions, because the assumptions guarantee that it is closely associated with quantification over physical regions. Note though that because this view requires that regions are non-mathematical entities, we still would not have determinate quantification even over all sets of non-mathematical entities: that would require that quantification over sets of regions be determinate, which even our strong assumptions give us no reason to suppose.

For some very helpful comments on earlier drafts on this essay, I thank Shaughan Lavine, Vann McGee, and many of the participants in Matthias Schirn's 1993 conference on the philosophy of mathematics in Munich, especially Penelope Maddy, Stewart Shapiro, and Bill Tait.

REFERENCES

[1] Balaguer, Mark. "A Platonist Epistemology." *Synthese*, forthcoming.

[2] Benacerraf, Paul. "Mathematical Truth." *Journal of Philosophy* 70 (1973): 661–79.

[3] Boolos, George. "To Be Is To Be the Value of a Variable (Or Some Values of Some Variables)." *Journal of Philosophy* 81 (1984): 430–49.

[4] Dummett, Michael. "The Philosophical Significance of Godel's Theorem." In *Truth and Other Enigmas*. Cambridge, Mass. 1978.

[5] Feferman, Solomon. "Toward Useful Type-Free Theories, I." In *Recent Essays on Truth and the Liar Paradox*, edited by Robert L. Martin. Oxford, 1984.

[6] Field, Hartry. *Realism, Mathematics and Modality*. Oxford, 1989; revised edition 1991.

[7] Field, Hartry. "A Nominalistic Proof of the Conservativeness of Set Theory." *Journal of Philosophical Logic* 21 (1992): 111–23.

[8] Fine, Kit. "Vagueness, Truth and Logic." *Synthese* 30 (1975): 265–300.

[9] Friedman, Harvey, and Michael Sheard. "An Axiomatic Approach to Self-Referential Truth." *Annals of Pure and Applied Logic* 33 (1987): 1–21.

[10] Kripke, Saul. "Outline of a Theory of Truth." In *Recent Essays on Truth and the Liar Paradox*, edited by Robert L. Martin. Oxford, 1984.

[11] Lavine, Shaughan. *Understanding the Infinite*. Cambridge, Mass., forthcoming.

[12] Lewis, David. "Putnam's Paradox." *Australasian Journal of Philosophy* 62 (1984): 221–36.

[13] McGee, Vann. *Truth, Vagueness and Paradox*. Indianapolis, 1991.

[14] Parsons, Charles. "The Uniqueness of the Natural Numbers." *Iyyun, A Jerusalem Philosophical Quarterly* 39 (1990): 13–44.

[15] Putnam, Hilary. "The Thesis that Mathematics is Logic." In *Mathematics Matter and Method: Philosophical Papers, Vol. 1*. Cambridge, 1975.

[16] Putnam, Hilary. "Models and Reality." In *Realism and Reason: Philosophical Papers, Vol. 3*. Cambridge, 1983.

[17] Shapiro, Stewart. *Foundations Without Foundationalism*. Oxford, 1991.

[18] Skolem, Thoralf. "Some Remarks on Axiomatized Set Theory." In *Free Frege to Godel*, edited by van Heijenoort. Cambridge, Mass., 1967. Pp. 290–301.

[19] Weston, Thomas. "Kreisel, The Continuum Hypothesis and Second Order Set Theory." *Journal of Philosophical Logic* 5 (1976): 281–98.

Responsibility and History

JOHN MARTIN FISCHER AND MARK RAVIZZA

I. A DISTINCTION

We wish to begin with an intuitive distinction between "historical" and "non-historical" phenomena. The phenomena in question may be such things as states of affairs, facts, or properties. The simple basic idea is that certain phenomena are historical in the sense that they depend (in some interesting way) on features of their history. This idea will be elaborated and made more precise below, but it is sufficient at first simply to rely on the notion that whereas some phenomena do not depend in any significant way on the past, other phenomena depend in deep and interesting ways on features of the past. For example, a particular fact may depend on the past in the sense that its obtaining entails the obtaining of certain facts in the past; similarly, a property may depend on the past in the sense that an object's having it at a time entails the obtaining of certain facts in the past.[1]

A "current time-slice" phenomenon is a non-historical phenomenon. A current time-slice phenomenon is dependent solely upon its "snapshot" properties and not facts about its history. (The snapshot features of an object at a time are those that would be revealed by an optimally comprehensive snapshot of an object at a time. Less metaphorically but still somewhat roughly, we might say that the snapshot properties of an object at a time are the temporally nonrelational physical properties of the object at that time together with the properties that supervene on these properties.) A current time-slice phenomenon is resilient with respect to changes in its history; that is, holding fixed its snapshot properties, alterations in its history would not affect the phenomenon. In contrast, a historical phenomenon is responsive to changes in its history; if a phenomenon is historical, its dependence on the past implies that alterations in certain features of the past would imply alterations in the phenomenon, even given that its snapshot properties are held fixed.

II. SOME EXAMPLES

To see more clearly what we have in mind with the distinction between historical and current time-slice phenomena, consider certain aesthetic phenomena. Properties such as "smooth," "round," "bright," "colorful," "symmetric," and "shiny" are fairly clear examples of current time-slice phenomena. An object's having these properties is simply a function of its snapshot features and is not dependent in any interesting way upon facts about the past. In contrast, a painting's being a genuine Picasso (and not a fake) is intuitively not a current time-slice phenomenon—it is not solely dependent upon its snapshot properties. An object's being a genuine work of art and not a fake depends crucially upon its history. Thus, it is relatively clear that there is some interesting distinction between historical and current time-slice phenomena in the context of aesthetics.

Certain aesthetic features may be difficult to classify as historical or current time-slice. For example, it may seem obvious that being beautiful would be a current time-slice feature of an object. But some have argued that this is not so. In particular, it might be argued that if it is discovered that a particular lampshade is made of human skin of someone killed in a concentration camp, then the lampshade cannot be considered beautiful, irrespective of its snapshot properties. Others might argue that a distinction should be made between an object's beauty and *other* normative judgments about it and further that beauty is purely a current time-slice notion.[2]

Parallel to the issue of whether something is an original work of art or a fake is the issue of whether something is a particular natural artifact or a duplicate. Consider this example from Peter van Inwagen:

> Imagine a 'duplication machine'. This machine consists of two chambers connected by an impressive mass of science-fictional gadgetry. If you place any physical object inside one of the chambers and press the big red button, a perfect physical duplicate of the object appears in the other chamber. The notion of a perfect duplicate of the object may be explained as follows. A physical thing is composed entirely of quarks and electrons. A perfect physical duplicate of the physical thing x is a thing composed entirely of quarks and electrons arranged in the same way in relation to one another as are the quarks and electrons that compose x: and each of the quarks and electrons composing the perfect physical duplicate of x will be in the same physical state as the corresponding particle in x. If, for example, you place the Koh-i-Noor Diamond in one of the chambers and press the button, a thing *absolutely indistinguishable from* the Koh-i-Noor (since it is a perfect physical duplicate of the Koh-i-Noor) will appear in the other. If the two objects are placed side by side, and then moved in a rapid and confusing way, so that everyone loses track of which was the original and which the duplicate, no one, no jeweler, geologist, or physicist, will ever be able to tell, by any test whatever, which of the two

played an important role in the history of the British Raj in the nineteenth century, and which was created a moment ago in the duplicating machine.[3]

After the machine has created the duplicate, the two objects are identical with respect to their current time-slice properties. But clearly one is the Koh-i-Noor diamond, and the other is a mere duplicate. Which object is the original (and which is the duplicate) is a historical phenomenon.

Examples of allegedly historical phenomena can be found in various contexts. We shall here assemble some examples of putatively historical phenomena. (Below we shall ask whether these apparently historical phenomena are genuinely historical.) According to certain theories of linguistic reference, a word can refer to a certain object (and a person can refer to the object employing the word) only if a certain sort of causal process has taken place in the past. Although different causal accounts of reference posit different causal processes which are allegedly required in order to secure reference, they all evidently construe reference as a historical phenomenon. Similarly, certain philosophers argue that the content of beliefs is crucially dependent upon causal interactions with the world in the past. These philosophers typically invoke "Putnam-type" thought experiments (involving twin planets, doppelgangers, and so forth) to establish their claim that the content of our beliefs depends upon causal interactions with features of the world in which we live. If in the past I and my cohorts on earth had been in causal contact with XYZ rather than H_2O, then I would not now have beliefs about water.[4]

The medical context provides other examples of apparently historical phenomena. In the absence of the appropriate diagnostic technology, a physician can derive information important to a diagnosis from the patient's medical history. For instance, learning that a patient had previously taken a drug like Haldol would enable the physician to determine that the patient with partial paralysis and spasms of the neck and face suffers from a dystonic reaction to the drug rather than tetanus or botulism, other possible candidates with the same characteristic symptoms. Similarly, in the context of psychoanalysis facts about an analysand's past may be used to assist in the appropriate diagnosis of neurosis or psychosis brought about by repressed memories and thoughts. It might be claimed that precisely because the relevant present psychic states are repressed and unconscious, analyzing an agent's history is a necessary step to uncovering and understanding the agent's psychological state.

The examples just sketched are of allegedly historical non-normative phenomena. There are also various allegedly historical normative phenomena. ("Normative" is being used here broadly to encompass all ought-implying or value notions; thus, normative phenomena include but are not exhausted by moral phenomena.) We now turn to an area which is both normative (in this broad sense) and non-moral: justification and knowledge in epistemology.

Various philosophers have argued that justification of belief and knowledge requires some sort of causal condition. In the first instance, it is claimed that in order for a belief to be justified, there must be an appropriate causal relationship between the state of affairs which the belief is about and the agent's holding the belief. In his well-known paper, "A Causal Theory of Knowing," Alvin Goldman argues that knowledge requires that there be an appropriate causal connection between the state of affairs that makes an agent's belief true and the belief.[5] In his later paper, "What Is Justified Belief?" Goldman argues that justification requires that the agent's belief about a state of affairs be caused in a "reliable" way.[6] Other philosophers have also argued that knowledge of some state of affairs requires that the agent's belief about the state of affairs be caused by it (in some appropriate manner). Consider this Gettier-type example proposed by Marshall Swain:[7]

> Suppose that S is looking into a field, and in the distance he sees an object that has the shape of a sheep. In addition to seeing an object that looks like a sheep, he hears bleating noises, is aware of sheeplike odors in the air, and so forth. On the basis of this experience he comes to believe (truly) that he seems to see a sheep in the field. This evidence, in the context of the other relevant propositions that he believes, renders it evident for him that he does see a sheep in the field, and this latter evidence then renders it evident for him that there is a sheep in the field ($= p$). Suppose that, on the basis of his evidence, he comes to believe that there is a sheep in the field. . . . Now, suppose there is in fact a sheep in the field, but the sheep is in some far corner of the field where S cannot see. The object that S sees is a cement replica of a sheep placed in the field by the farmer for decorative purposes. Thus, S has a true belief that there is a sheep in the field, and his justification renders this evident for him. Yet S does not *know* that there is a sheep in the field. (p. 90)

Swain points out that one way to explain that S lacks knowledge in this case is to point out that his belief that there is a sheep in the field is not caused by the state of affairs in question—the sheep's being in the field. Thus, it seems that a causal condition suggested by this insight must be added to the analysis of knowledge.[8]

There are various moral notions which are arguably historical. For example, Robert Nozick has argued that distributive justice is essentially historical.[9] His point is that one cannot properly judge whether a given distribution of goods is just without knowing how it came about; an apparently very unequal distribution might have come about via voluntary interactions and transactions and thus not necessarily be unjust. (The "Wilt Chamberlain" example is invoked to support this sort of view.[10] In the Wilt Chamberlain example, thousands of individuals are willing to pay [and do pay] to watch Wilt Chamberlain play basketball; thus, this voluntary exchange of funds upsets whatever pattern had previously existed. But it is intuitively a permissible transition. Further, one could imagine quite a number of such voluntary interactions which at every point change the pattern of holdings. Also, this is the point of Nozick's claim that particular patterns and profiles can be upset by "capitalist acts between consenting adults.") It is reasonable to think that considerations of desert based on past effort, performance, and so forth are relevant to ascertaining whether a particular distribution is just. Notoriously, Nozick criticized Rawls for having an ahistorical or current time-slice model of justice, which was certainly at least in some respects an inaccurate characterization. But whether Nozick's criticism of Rawls was on target is not our concern here. What does seem undeniable is that distributive justice is in some important way a historical phenomenon.

In an intriguing passage, Nozick says:

> Incidentally, love is an interesting instance of another relationship that is historical, in that (like justice) it depends upon what actually occurred. An adult may come to love another because of the other's characteristics; but it is the other person, and not the characteristics, that is loved. The love is not transferrable to someone else with the same characteristics, even to one who 'scores' higher for these characteristics. And the love endures through changes of the characteristics that gave rise to it. One loves the particular person one actually encountered. Why love is historical, attaching to persons in this way and not to characteristics, is an interesting and puzzling question. (p. 167–168)

Another interesting example of a claim that a particular moral phenomenon is historical is the view that the virtues depend on certain processes of acquisition.[11] On this view, the virtues are not simply propensities or dispositions to behave in certain ways in relevant circumstances; they are these dispositions only provided that they have been acquired through certain appropriate processes of education and habituation. According to this approach, it is impossible in a strong sense that there be "virtue pills"—pills which one could take that would induce dispositions which would count as virtues. Whereas these pills might induce the pertinent propensities, these would not count as virtues insofar as they were not acquired in the prescribed fashion. This position implies that it is not simply a general empirical truth that certain methods of education and habituation are most conducive to the virtues; it is a conceptual and metaphysical impossibility that a person have the relevant virtue without having acquired it in the specified manner.

Similarly, notions of well-being and flourishing do not appear to be current time-slice notions. That is to say, simply attending to an agent's present condition without comparing it to past states (and perhaps alternative possibilities) will not adequately ground judgments of well-being or flourishing. As Thomas Nagel puts it:[12]

> Often we need to know [an individual's] history to tell whether something is a misfortune or not; this applies to ills like deterioration, deprivation, and damage. Sometimes his experiential *state* is relatively unimportant— as in the case of a man who wastes his life in the cheerful pursuit of a method of communicating with asparagus plants. . . . It therefore seems to me worth exploring the position that most good and ill fortune has as

its subject a person identified by his history and his possibilities, rather than merely by his categorical state of the moment. . . .

These ideas can be illustrated by an example of deprivation whose severity approaches that of death. Suppose an intelligent person receives a brain injury that reduces him to the mental condition of a contented infant, and that such desires as remain to him can be satisfied by a custodian, so that he is free from care. Such a development would be widely regarded as a severe misfortune, not only for his friends and relations, or for society, but also, and primarily, for the person himself. This does not mean that a contented infant is unfortunate. The intelligent adult who has been *reduced* to this condition is the subject of the misfortune. (p. 5)

It seems that Nagel is here suggesting that the notions of something's being a misfortune or someone's being in an unfortunate state are historical notions.

Finally, it has been suggested that the notion of moral responsibility is historical.[13] The motivation for this claim can be understood by thinking about the apparent inadequacies of various current time-slice models of moral responsibility. One particularly salient current time-slice approach to moral responsibility has been developed in a series of articles by Harry Frankfurt.[14] On one version of this theory, an agent is morally responsible for an action if there is conformity between his "second-order volition" (his preference as to which first-order desire should move him to action) and his "will" (the first-order desire that does in fact move the person to action). Roughly, the idea is that an agent is morally responsible for his action insofar as there is a mesh between what the person wills and what he wants to will.

In his later work, Frankfurt has proposed refinements (or perhaps further specifications) of his model of moral responsibility. Frankfurt stresses the way in which a person can identify with a particular desire. Such identification requires that an agent form an unopposed higher-order desire to make a particular first-order desire his will and that he judge that no further consultation with other even higher-order desires would lead to a reversal of this decision. Does it matter for Frankfurt how this mesh between higher-order volitions and the will (together with a judgment that future deliberation and reconsideration would not issue in a different decision) come about? Evidently not. Frankfurt's theory holds that an agent who identifies wholeheartedly with his will should be held responsible for his action, independent of his history (and in particular the history of the identification). Frankfurt says, "to the extent that a person identifies himself with the springs of his actions, he takes responsibility for those actions and acquires moral responsibility for them; moreover, the questions of how the actions and his identifications with their springs are caused is irrelevant to the questions of whether he performs the actions freely or is morally responsible for performing them."[15]

Another kind of "mesh" theory of moral responsibility is suggested by Gary Watson.[16] But Watson's theory is not a hierarchical mesh theory; rather, it is what might be called a "multiple-source" mesh theory.[17] Instead of positing a hierarchy of preferences, Watson posits different sources of preferences. According to Watson's theory, there are "valuational preferences" (which in some sense come from "reason" or reflect what reason recommends) and "motivational preferences" (which move one to act). A mere motivational preference would have its source somewhere other than reason, perhaps in "appetite." Roughly speaking, Watson suggests that the valuational preferences reflect what the agent takes to be defensible, considering his life as a whole. Employing the resources developed by Watson, one could say that an agent is morally responsible for an action insofar as there is a mesh between the valuational and motivational preference to perform the action.

An approach which combines elements from both sorts of mesh theories sketched above has been suggested by Charles Taylor.[18] He follows Frankfurt in employing a hierarchical apparatus, but follows Watson in requiring that a selected group of preferences reflect certain values. Taylor claims that these values must in some suitable way express deontological considerations such as rights rather than merely capture judgments about maximization or optimization. The details of this approach are not important here. What is relevant is that Taylor's approach is also a mesh theory; it claims that a certain mesh between a "strong-evaluation" (the pertinent higher-order preference based on appropriate moral considerations) and the preference that moves one to action is sufficient for moral responsibility.

The theories of Frankfurt, Watson, and Taylor are mesh theories of various sorts. They simply focus on the issue of whether there is a suitable connection or mesh between selected elements of one's mental economy. As such, these theories are purely structural—they look for a particular pattern in the relevant snapshot properties. Clearly, then, these theories are current time-slice approaches to moral responsibility.

Another influential mesh theory of moral responsibility posits a mesh between one's character (or particular traits of character) and choices (or actions) as sufficient for moral responsibility. On this view, one is morally responsible for one's behavior insofar as it expresses one's character (in some suitable way). The pertinent elements selected as the "mesh-elements" here are an agent's character (or perhaps particular traits of character) and the preferences and actions which result. (Here the mesh elements are not both particular *motivational states*, but a *disposition* or *propensity* and a motivational state or action.) David Hume suggested this sort of approach, and it has been defended by various contemporary philosophers.[19] A particularly salient articulation of this sort of theory is found in a recent *Yale Law Journal* article by George Vuoso, "Background, Responsibility, and Excuse":[20]

> The version of compatibilism I advocate claims that an agent can properly be held morally responsible for his actions to the extent and only to the extent that they reflect badly on his character. Thus, if an action is a moral wrong, and it was determined by the agent's character, in the sense that his character would be the predominant causal factor in an

accurate explanation of the action, then he generally would be morally responsible for it. . . . It clearly follows from this view that one's past is irrelevant to the assessment of his moral responsibility for a wrong he committed: all that is relevant is the extent to which his character was causally responsible for the wrong, or in other words, the extent to which the wrong was due to his bad character. . . . The sort of character a person has is relevant to assessing his moral responsibility for an action, but not how he came to have that character. (pp. 1680–81)

Similarly, Robert Cummins says:[21]

The fact that a bad habit or trait is not culpably acquired or maintained has no tendency to show that it is not a bad habit or trait. Vicious habits are like vicious dogs in that their viciousness does not depend on how they were acquired. . . . Most often, we want to know what someone is like now; whether they are good or bad now. Here it is plainly which traits are reflected in conduct that counts, not how those traits were acquired. (p. 224)

But we believe that the problem with *all* mesh theories, no matter how they are refined, is that the selected mesh can be produced via intuitively "responsibility-undermining" mechanisms. No matter what the mesh-elements are, they may be induced by such processes as (clandestine) electronic stimulation of the brain, hypnosis, brainwashing, and so on. More specifically, a connection between selected higher-order elements (even ones which reflect or embody certain values) and relevant lower-order elements, or between elements with different sources (such as reason and appetite, as specified by Watson), or between a preference and a character trait can be caused via (for example) direct electronic stimulation of the brain or any number of other clandestine responsibility-undermining processes. It seems that the problem with all such theories is precisely that they are purely structural and ahistorical. Moral responsibility however appears to be a historical phenomenon: whether an agent is morally responsible cannot be read off his snapshot properties, but is at least in part a matter of how the action came about. Given that the snapshot properties are held fixed, alterations in facts about the causal history of an action can elicit alterations in our views about the agent's responsibility.[22]

III. EVALUATION AND A FURTHER DISTINCTION

The examples assembled in the previous section were all instances of "apparently" or "allegedly" historical phenomena. But now we must inquire a bit more carefully into whether the phenomena are genuinely historical or merely apparently historical. Certainly, the claims about distributive justice and the authenticity of a work of art are very plausible: these phenomena seem to be genuinely historical. But other such claims may lose some of their appeal upon closer scrutiny. Ultimately, we will want to consider whether moral responsibility is genuinely or merely apparently historical.

Let us consider again the medical examples sketched above. It seems that the physician's understanding of the fact that the patient took a drug is helpful precisely because this past fact points the physician to the appropriate *present condition* of the patient's body. The past fact then is "epistemically" helpful—it helps to direct the physician to the pertinent snapshot properties. But the past fact is not important apart from referring the physician to a present condition which is assumed to be causing the symptoms in question. Thus, it is plausible to suppose that the importance of history in this sort of context is solely epistemic; the pertinent phenomena are thus not genuinely historical, but merely apparently so.

We shall say that certain merely apparently historical phenomena are "epistemically historical." The claim that a certain range of phenomena is epistemically historical is the claim that turning to the past is necessary, given the limitations of the relevant situation, in order properly to ascertain and evaluate the relevant snapshot properties. But it is evident that a claim of epistemic historicism does *not* imply a claim of genuine historicism. Epistemic historicism is an epistemological view; if something is epistemically historical, the past is a useful (although in principle dispensable) guide to us in describing and characterizing the present. In contrast, genuine historicism is a metaphysical position: if something is genuinely historical, its being the way it is entails something (of a certain sort) about the past.

To illustrate this point further, let us return to the example of psychoanalysis. In his early case studies on hysteria, Freud describes the case of Elisabeth von R., a young woman referred to him with severe leg pains.[23] The referring physician had "thought the case was one of hysteria, though there was no trace of the usual indications of that neurosis" (p. 135). Traditional examinations could not explain the pains which in two years had grown so severe that Elisabeth frequently had trouble walking. But while her present condition was of little help in diagnosing her illness, Freud discovered that her past did provide the needed information. According to Freud, Elisabeth's pains were the result of troubling ideas which were being repressed—in particular the memory of reaching her sister's deathbed and thinking that at last she could marry her dead sister's husband: "The girl felt towards her brother-in-law a tenderness whose acceptance into consciousness was resisted by her whole moral being. She succeeded in sparing herself the painful conviction that she loved her sister's husband by inducing physical pains in herself instead" (p. 157).

In this case, the pain in Elisabeth's leg is explained in terms of a conversion of the psychical pain from the repressed thought into physical pain. Thus the past influences Elisabeth's present state by causing some snapshot property (i.e., the repressed idea of loving her brother-in-law). In order to understand Elisabeth's present state, Freud needed to use her past to uncover the feeling she was presently repressing. But here the role of the past is purely epistemic: it is not the case that the past is alleged to affect certain features of the present without leaving a trace in the snapshot properties.

In the medical and psychological examples, then, the past is epistemically important. But it does not seem in these examples that the past can have an influence on certain features of the present without "casting a shadow" on the present or "leaving a trace" on the present.[24] Information about the past points us to pertinent snapshot features of the present. When a phenomenon is epistemically historical but not genuinely historical, there is something in the snapshot features of the present which fully grounds the judgments in question, and nothing is entailed about the past.[25]

Indeed, there are debates about whether various of the other phenomena (in addition to the medical and psychoanalytical phenomena) adduced in the previous section are genuinely historical. For example, "neo-Fregeans" of various sorts wish to argue that at least some of the phenomena of linguistic reference and psychological content mentioned above are not genuinely historical. Also, various epistemologists wish to deny that the notions of justification of belief and knowledge are genuinely historical. For example, such epistemologists as Ginet and Foley have argued that the notions of justification and knowledge are not appropriately analyzed causally.[26]

Let us briefly reconsider the Gettier-type examples which were used above to motivate the historical conception of these epistemic notions. S has based his view that there is a sheep in the field on his perceptual data. He is correct in believing this proposition quite by coincidence. The causal theorists hold that the only (or perhaps most effective) way of explaining why S does not know the proposition in question is by pointing out that some sort of causal condition is not met: the sheep itself must cause the belief (in some suitable way). But the anti-causalists argue that there are *other* ways of explaining why S does not know the proposition in question. For example, there is a fact which obtains at the time of S's belief—the fact that there is a cement replica of a sheep which is causing S's perceptual data—which is such that, if S were to be aware of it, his evidence would no longer render it evident or probable that the proposition that there is a sheep in the field is true. That is, there are snapshot features of the world at the time of the belief by reference to which the defective epistemic situation of the believer can be analyzed. Of course, this sort of fact has been dubbed a "defeater" in the literature in epistemology, and the approach sketched here is in the tradition that suggests that (say) knowledge is undefeated justified true belief. It is not uncontroversial or obvious that such an approach is ultimately tenable, and in any case any version of this sort of strategy would have to be developed with considerably more refinement and specificity in order to be deemed acceptable. Our point is only that such approaches exist and seem on the surface at least as plausible as the causal/historical theories.[27]

In thinking about whether certain of the apparently historical phenomena assembled above are genuinely historical, it is clear (in our view) that some of these phenomena—such as distributive justice and authenticity of works of art—are indeed genuinely historical. Other apparently historical phenomena are merely apparently historical. Among these, some—such as certain phenomena in the medical and psychoanalytical contexts—are epistemically historical. Other notions such as justification of belief and knowledge are quite controversial; we are not in a position to resolve the question of whether they are genuinely or merely apparently historical.[28]

IV. RESPONSIBILITY AND HISTORY

The question arises as to whether moral responsibility is genuinely historical. The considerations sketched above appear to indicate that it is. But there are also reasons to question this conclusion. The arguments just developed that certain notions are merely apparently historical suggest a parallel strategy in this context. That is, it might be argued that appeals to history are relevant to responsibility ascriptions only insofar as they point us to something about the present (or the time of the pertinent behavior); the claim would be that responsibility ascriptions are at best epistemically historical. On this approach, features of background and causal history are alleged to be relevant only to the extent that they point us to appropriate present conditions. Thus, the view is that scrutiny of an individual's childhood or past experiences can only be useful to responsibility ascriptions if the past is found to have left some trace or shadow on the present, just as in the psychoanalytic context discussed above.

The argument presented above for the conclusion that moral responsibility is a genuinely historical phenomenon relied on the point that the current time-slice view of responsibility tends to claim that a structural feature of the agent—a certain selected mesh—is a sufficient condition for moral responsibility. The claim was then that the selected mesh could be generated by an apparently "responsibility-undermining" process or mechanism, and thus the mere existence of the mesh is not indeed sufficient for moral responsibility; the history behind the mesh is also relevant. We wish here to focus, for ease of exposition, on the rather vivid context of significant direct electronic manipulation of the brain.

The anti-historicist might argue as follows. Suppose the direct stimulation of the brain is so significant that it induces a genuinely irresistible urge to perform a certain action. Here it is conceded that the agent is *not* morally responsible for his action, and thus the mesh theories are inadequate. But it does not follow that *no* nonhistorical theory will be adequate. And indeed (as with the medical and psychotherapeutic examples and perhaps also the epistemic notions of belief and justification discussed above) the resources for explaining the agent's lack of responsibility appear to reside in the current time-slice. That is, the past manipulation can be seen to rule out moral responsibility because it results in the presence of some snapshot feature which is sufficient to explain the lack of moral responsibility: the irresistible urge.

Suppose now that the direct stimulation of the brain is considerable but not so significant that it induces a genuinely irresistible urge to behave in a certain way. If the agent does behave in this way, then it will be pointed out that he *can* be held morally responsible for doing so. However, the nature of the causal process which issued in the behavior will have an impact on the degree of blameworthiness or praiseworthiness of the agent; these will presumably vary with the nature of the behavior and the degree of "pressure" placed on the agent. Thus, the phenomenon of manipulation may not indicate the necessity for a historical approach to moral responsibility, even if it calls into question purely structural or mesh theories. As we have just argued, if the manipulation issues in irresistible impulses, the agent is not responsible, and a nonhistorical account can accommodate this point. And if the manipulation does not issue in such impulses, the agent is indeed responsible (as the nonhistorical account would have it), but the appropriate reaction to the agent will depend on various factors including the intensity of the urge resulting from the manipulation. (Of course, a similar analysis would apply to other apparently responsibility-threatening factors, such as hypnosis, subliminal advertising, and so forth.) It might seem then that responsibility is, after all, a merely apparently historical phenomenon.

But this conclusion would be hasty. We believe that the dilemma posed above is misleading. The dilemma presupposes that an agent's basic values—the parameters of his practical reasoning—are immune to the envisaged manipulation (or other problematic influence), and it then offers the two alternatives of an irresistible and resistible urge as exhaustive of the field of possibilities. But it seems to be possible that an agent's values themselves be tampered with in significant ways.[29] And if so, then the agent may not be morally responsible for what he does, even if the urge is not irresistible.

To elaborate. Suppose that someone fundamentally alters an individual's relevant values by direct electronic stimulation of the brain. Imagine further that the agent has strong but not irresistible desires to act in accordance with these values (perhaps after deliberation). We believe that the agent is *not* morally responsible for his behavior, unless he has *taken responsibility* for the new values. It is possible for an agent to reflect upon and deliberate about his newly formed values and either alter them or accept them. If the agent undertakes this sort of activity, he can be said to *take responsibility* for his values and thus he can be morally responsible for the actions that flow from them (under certain circumstances). But an agent who has just been manipulated (or subjected to hypnosis, subliminal advertising, psychosurgery, potent drugs, and so forth) and who has *not yet* taken responsibility for the newly generated values cannot legitimately be held morally responsible for his actions. It is intuitively quite clear that if (some of) an individual's values have been suddenly and radically altered in the envisaged way—say a devoutly religious person has been rendered an atheist, or a feminist has been given chauvinistic values—and the agent has not yet had the opportunity to reflect on these values, he or she is not responsible for the resulting behavior. And this is so because of the nature of the individual's history—it lacks the crucial element of taking responsibility for important values and the parameters of practical reasoning.

Much more needs to be said about the notion of taking responsibility, and most of this will need to await another occasion. We hope that it will be enough here to rely upon some intuitive (and admittedly inchoate) conception of this notion.[30] In future work we intend to give a more explicit account of this notion, and to address the problem of whether this process itself can be induced by (say) manipulation. Our claim here is that taking responsibility is *necessary* for moral responsibility, and it is precisely this fact that renders moral responsibility a genuinely historical notion. (The sufficiency claim is quite another matter, but it is only the necessity claim which is required for our view that responsibility is essentially historical.) Taking responsibility for one's values and the basic mechanisms of one's practical reasoning can be explicit and deliberative, but it can also be implicit and nondeliberative. Our claim is that the plausibility of the view that an agent is morally responsible for his behavior in the case of a resistible urge in the original dilemma (in which the values have not been tampered with) issues from the presupposition that the agent has indeed taken responsibility for these values in some appropriate sense. The process of taking responsibility—although it need not be explicit or deliberative—is a prerequisite for moral responsibility.

Pursuing the other horn of the anti-historicist's dilemma, we wish to claim that even in the case of certain irresistible urges, it may be the case that the agent is morally responsible for his behavior, if (but only if) he has taken responsibility for the basic parameters of the practical reasoning which issues in the urges. For example, it may be that a mother has a literally irresistible urge to run into a burning house to save her children who are at risk.[31] It is highly controversial whether this is an accurate characterization of the situation, but it is at least possible that there are some such cases of "volitional necessity"—cases in which it would be literally unthinkable for the agent to behave otherwise.[32] In the case described above, the mother may be morally responsible for her behavior insofar as she has taken responsibility for the values that issue in her urge to save the children. In general, it may be the case that even action on literally irresistible impulses may be consistent with moral responsibility, given an appropriate process of taking responsibility in the past.

Thus, moral responsibility requires a certain sort of past process of taking responsibility. Both horns of the dilemma proposed by the anti-historicist can be denied: there may be cases of action on irresistible desires for which the agent is morally responsible, and there may be cases of action on resistible desires for which the agent is not morally responsible. In both cases the tenability of the responsibility ascription will depend on the agent's having taken responsibility; the relevant facts about moral responsibility cannot be read off the snapshot properties.[33]

As we stated earlier, Harry Frankfurt has frequently insisted that his approach to moral responsibility is purely structural and ahistorical[34] But consider now the following passage from Frankfurt:[35]

Let us distinguish two fundamentally different states of affairs. . . . In the first state of affairs the D/n [Devil/neurologist] manipulates his subject on a continuous basis, like a marionette, so that each of the subject's mental and physical states is the outcome of specific intervention on the part of the D/n. In that case the subject is not a person at all. His history is utterly episodic and without inherent connectedness.

. . . The other possibility is that the D/n provides his subject with a stable character or program, which he does not thereafter alter too frequently or at all, and that the subsequent mental and physical responses of the subject to his external and internal environments are determined by this program rather than by further intervention on the part of the D/n. . . . [There are no] compelling reasons either against allowing that the subject may act freely or against regarding him as capable of being morally responsible for what he does.

He may become morally responsible, assuming that he is suitably programmed, in the same way others do: by identifying himself with some of his own second-order desires, so that they are not merely desires that he happens to have or to find within himself, but desires that he adopts or puts himself behind. In virtue of a person's identification of himself with one of his own second-order desires, that desire becomes a second-order volition. And the person thereby *takes* responsibility for the pertinent first- and second-order desires and for the actions to which these desires lead him. (pp. 119–120)

But Frankfurt's remarks are puzzling, given that he repeatedly endorses a current time-slice model of moral responsibility. Notice first that he infers from the fact of continuous manipulation that the subject's "history is utterly episodic and without inherent connectedness." But surely this is a spurious transition, for continuous manipulation is compatible with continuity and intelligibility. Whether an agent's history is continuous or episodic in its content is quite a different matter from whether it is internally or externally generated. Further, the clear implication seems to be that a certain degree of historical continuity and connectedness is essential to moral responsibility, which would appear to be incompatible with a current time-slice model of moral responsibility.

But let these matters pass, and let us look carefully at what Frankfurt says about the second horn of his dilemma. This is the situation in which the D/n "provides his subject with a stable character or program, which he does not thereafter alter too frequently or at all." Frankfurt's claim is that the agent may become morally responsible by taking responsibility. We agree with Frankfurt about this, but we have an important disagreement about the nature of taking responsibility. We claim that some sort of *process* of taking responsibility is necessary for moral responsibility. And (of course) a process is essentially historical. In contrast, Frankfurt is committed to the view that taking responsibility is a current time-slice notion—it is a matter of attitudes and dispositions one has at a given moment. That is, Frankfurt's view (developed in "Identification and Wholeheartedness") is that one identifies oneself with (say) a first-order desire insofar as (a) one has an unopposed second-order volition to act in accordance with it, and (b) one judges that any further deliberation about the matter would issue in the same decision. This view reflects a slight refinement in the simple mesh theory of Frankfurt's early work; here, the mesh condition is supplemented by the "resonance" condition—in virtue of the judgment that further deliberation would simply issue in the same judgment, one's commitment is alleged to be "decisive" and to "resound" through the various levels of one's motivational states. But clearly this judgment can be induced in the same manner as the mesh, and even if the second condition addresses other apparent problems with Frankfurt's theory, it clearly does *not* address the problem of (say) manipulation.[36] At least part of the reason it is not successful here is that it posits an ingredient that may simply be another element in the mental economy of the agent at the time of the action which is induced in precisely the same manner as the mesh. What is needed, we have argued, is attention to the *history* of the action; what is needed here is some process of evaluation and scrutiny of the "program" or values which have been induced. And it is evident that this process requires that moral responsibility be a historical phenomenon. Frankfurt is correct in thinking that taking responsibility is crucial to moral responsibility, but he is wrong to think that taking responsibility can be analyzed simply by reference to snapshot properties.[37]

Finally, why exactly would one wish to insist that moral responsibility is a current time-slice notion? What is at stake? Frankfurt is a compatibilist about moral responsibility and causal determinism. If moral responsibility does not depend on history, then compatibilism would be easier to defend; perhaps this is part of the motivation for holding that moral responsibility is not historical. Indeed, an argument has been made that even if moral responsibility did not require alternative possibilities, it would not follow that moral responsibility is compatible with causal determinism insofar as causal determinism might constitute "actual-sequence compulsion."[38] According to this argument, even if responsibility does not require alternative possibilities, further work would have to be done in order to establish the compatibility of causal determinism and moral responsibility. But if moral responsibility were not a historical phenomenon, then this further task could be obviated.

Note however that the above strategy is not *required* in order to argue for the compatibility of causal determinism and moral responsibility. For example, it could be conceded that moral responsibility is essentially historical while insisting that causal determination need not in itself constitute the *kind* of past that rules out responsibility.[39]

V. TWO OBJECTIONS

Two related objections to our distinction between historical and non-historical phenomena (and our claim that moral responsibility is historical) issue from the worry that *too many* phenomena will be deemed historical. More specifically, if a historical phenomenon is one that *entails* something about the past, then the worry is that too many things will be counted as historical.

Va. The first objection points out that everything entails *something* about the past, in some sense of "about the past." So, for example, our writing this essay now entails that two plus two equalled four in 1900. Also, our writing this essay now entails that it was not the case in 1980 that we wrote our last essay. In general, the truth of *any* proposition about a time seems to entail the truth of at least *some* propositions about prior times. And if this is true, then all phenomena would turn out to be historical, and the distinction we have put forward would have been shown to be trivial.

No doubt, it is not an easy thing to give a precise account of the distinction between historical and non-historical phenomena. For our purposes, however, it is sufficient to say that a historical phenomenon entails the truth of a *certain sort* of proposition about the past. Alternatively, a historical phenomenon entails that a *certain sort* of fact obtained in the past. More specifically, the idea is that a historical phenomenon entails that an *immediate* fact obtained in the past, where an immediate fact is a contingent fact which specifies what is "really" going on in a basic sense at a given time. An immediate fact specifies what is happening in the "pure present" at any given time.[40] We do not purport (here) to give an *analysis* of immediacy, but must rely upon intuitively clear cases of immediate and non-immediate facts.[41]

At this point it is appropriate to note that historical facts are the "mirror image" of so-called "soft facts." (The following are soft facts: the fact that it was true on Monday that Mary would go to the movies on Tuesday, the fact that Jack went to sleep on Wednesday prior to eating breakfast on Thursday, and so forth.[42]) Both sorts of facts (historical and soft) are temporally relational. But whereas soft facts are implicitly about (or depend upon) immediate facts which obtain at *subsequent* times, historical facts are implicitly about (or depend upon) immediate facts which obtain at *prior* times. Indeed, Alvin Plantinga has suggested that the mark of a soft fact about a time is that it entails the obtaining of some intuitively immediate fact about the future.[43] Our suggestion is precisely the mirror image of Plantinga's: the mark of a historical fact is that it entails the obtaining of some intuitively immediate fact about the past. It is interesting to note that soft facts and historical facts are mirror image species of the genus, temporally relational facts.

Vb. A second objection issues from certain views about the essential features of individual objects (and perhaps also natural kinds). On a certain view of personal identity, it is a necessary condition of an individual's being (say) Max Smith that he have come from the particular sperm and egg cell from which Max Smith actually developed. Thus, it would appear (on the account of historical facts we have suggested) that such statements as "Max Smith is wearing a red shirt" express historical facts insofar as the truth of the statement entails that certain particular sperm and egg cells came together in the past to initiate the developmental sequence which issued in Max Smith. Also, on this sort of view, if this table is (and always has been) made of wood, it is an essential feature of it that it not have been originally made of ice. Thus, such statements as "This table is brown" would appear to express historical facts insofar as they entail that this table not have originally been made of ice, and so forth.[44]

We do not know whether these views about the identity of persons and particular objects are indeed true. They are controversial; if one denies them, one can of course block the objection. But even if they are true it does not follow that the distinction between historical and non-historical phenomena becomes trivial. For although (on this view) there will turn out to be more historical phenomena than one otherwise might have supposed, there is still a robust distinction insofar as such facts as "A person in such and such a location is wearing a red shirt," and "A table in such and such a location is brown" turn out to be non-historical. Indeed, for every (allegedly) historical phenomenon, there would seem to be various related intuitively non-historical facts. Thus, even on this "Kripkean" view about the essential features of objects, the distinction between historical and non-historical facts does not collapse.[45]

VI. SUMMARY

We began by sketching (in an admittedly somewhat vague way) a distinction between historical and current time-slice phenomena. A historical phenomenon is in some intuitive sense "dependent" on the past in a way in which a current time-slice phenomenon is not. Roughly speaking, a historical phenomenon entails that the past be a certain way, whereas a current slice phenomenon is solely a function of snapshot properties. We then assembled a number of examples of apparently historical phenomena from both normative and non-normative contexts.

But some apparently historical phenomena were found to be merely apparently historical. Even though some such phenomena were found to be epistemically historical, they were nevertheless deemed not to be genuinely historical. They were not thought to be genuinely historical because these phenomena could in principle be explained solely in terms of snapshot properties—the resources for explaining these phenomena all reside in the relevant current time-slice, even if they are difficult for us to identify without consulting the past.

Finally, we argued that moral responsibility is in the class of genuinely (and not merely apparently historical) phenomena. We argued that various possible cases impugn the idea that current time-slice resources can adequately ground and explain responsibility ascriptions. These cases point to a quite general truth that obtains even in relatively less unusual cases: moral responsibility requires a process of taking responsibility. This process *need not* always be explicit, conscious, or deliberate. But it has in fact almost always taken place, and it *must* have taken place, if the agent is to be held responsible: the arcane cases bring out and point us toward a quite general and important truth. And this truth—that moral responsibility requires the process of taking responsibility—helps us to see that moral responsibility is a genuinely historical phenomenon.

It just might be the case, finally, that there are two agents with precisely the same relevant snapshot properties and who perform precisely the same unfortunate action, but with very different pasts. It might be, for example, that one of the agents was subject to a long history of brutal and humiliating physical and psychological abuse. Specifically, it might be that one of the individuals was beaten and continuously abused in the past by her husband, while the other had no such history. Here it *may* be that—it is at least worth considering the proposition that—even though the relevant snapshot properties are precisely symmetric, the one agent is morally responsible, while the other agent is not.[46]

Stephen Daedelus complained, in Joyce's *Ulysses*, "History is a nightmare from which I am trying to awake." For some, history is a nightmare from which they cannot awake.[47]

NOTES

1. This is a rough first approximation to the idea of something's being historical. We further refine and discuss the characterization below.

2. We are grateful to Ruth Barcan Marcus for this example and conversations about it.

3. Peter van Inwagen, *Metaphysics* (Boulder, Colo., forthcoming). We have taken this passage from a pre-publication manuscript.

4. Hilary Putnam, "The Meaning of 'Meaning'," reprinted in Hilary Putnam, *Mind, Language, and Reality* (London, 1975), 215–71. Also, see Tyler Burge, "Individualism and the Mental," *Midwest Studies in Philosophy IV: Studies in Metaphysics* (1979): 73–121.

5. Alvin Goldman, "A Causal Theory of Knowing," *Journal of Philosophy* 64 (June 1967): 355–72.

6. Alvin I. Goldman, "What Is Justified Belief?" in *Justification and Knowledge*, edited by G. S. Pappas (Dordrecht, 1979), 1–23. Goldman in later work refers to his view as "historical reliabilism": Alvin Goldman, *Epistemology and Cognition* (Cambridge, Mass., 1986).

7. Marshall Swain, "Knowledge, Causality, and Justification," reprinted in *Essays on Knowledge and Justification,* edited by Papas and Swain (Ithaca, N.Y., 1978), 87–108.

8. And just as Goldman wishes to insist on a *certain sort* of causal sequence (a reliable or truth-conducive kind of causal chain), so Swain also must opt for an appropriate sort of causal sequence:

> Imagine the following variation [on the above example]. Suppose that S is looking into a field as before, and sees an object that he takes to be a sheep. And, as before, he hears bleating noises and is aware of sheeplike odors in the air. This time, however, he is seeing not a cement replica of a sheep, but rather a very cleverly engineered television image of a sheep, Someone, for reasons on which we need not speculate, has placed an invisible glass projection screen out in the field and with hidden projection equipment is projecting the image of a sheep on the screen. Moreover, the sheep whose image is being projected is off in some far corner of the field, where S cannot see. We may suppose that S's evidential beliefs, etc., are in this case just as they were in the previous example. Of course, in this case, as in the previous example, S does not know that there is a sheep in the field. (p. 95)

As a result of this sort of case, Swain concludes that the relevant condition on knowledge must specify a *certain sort* of causal connection (not just any causal connection), but the details are not important here. It suffices to note that various philosophers have argued that such notions as justification and knowledge are in the sense specified above historical notions: according to these philosophers, claims about justification and knowledge entail that the history of belief acquisition be of a certain sort.

9. Robert Nozick, *Anarchy, State, and Utopia* (New York, 1968).

10. Ibid., 161–63.

11. Robert C. Roberts, "Will Power and the Virtues," *Philosophical Review* 93 (April 1984): 227–47.

12. Thomas Nagel, "Death," in *Mortal Questions* (Cambridge, 1979), 1–10.

13. There is an argument that moral responsibility is essentially historical in John Martin Fischer, "Responsiveness and Moral Responsibility," in *Responsibility, Character, and the Emotions*, edited by Ferdinand Schoeman (Cambridge, 1987), esp. pp. 103–105. For a similar approach, see John Christman, "Autonomy and Personal History," *Canadian Journal of Philosophy* 21 (March 1991): 1–24.

14. Harry Frankfurt, "Freedom of the Will and the Concept of a Person," *Journal of Philosophy* 68 (January 1971): 65–80; "Three Concepts of Free Action: II," *Proceedings of the Aristotelian Society*, supp. vol. IL (1975): 113–25; and "Identification and Wholeheartedness," in *Responsibility, Character, and the Emotions*, 81–106.

15. Frankfurt, "Three Concepts of Free Action: II," 121–22.

16. Gary Watson, "Free Agency," *Journal of Philosophy* 72 (April 1975): 205–20.

17. Note that we mean "logical source," not "causal source" here.

18. Charles Taylor, "Responsibility for Self," in *The Identities of Persons*, edited by A. Rorty (Berkeley, 1976), 281–300.

19. See, for example, Richard Brandt, "Blameworthiness and Obligation," in *Essays in Moral Philosophy*, edited by A. Melden (Seattle, 1958), 3–39; and Robert Cummins, "Could Have Done Otherwise," *Personalist* 60 (October 1979): 411–14, and "Culpability and Mental Disorder," *Canadian Journal of Philosophy* 10 (June 1980): 207–32.

20. George Vuoso, "Background, Responsibility, and Excuse," *Yale Law Journal* 96 (February 1987): 1679–81.

21. Robert Cummins, "Culpability and Mental Disorder," *Canadian Journal of Philosophy* 10 (June 1980): 207–32.

22. Note that our criticism applies to "pure mesh theories"—those which claim that the mesh is itself sufficient for moral responsibility. If one wished to *add* some sort of historical condition to the mesh condition, then of course our criticism would not apply. In this case one would have abandoned the sort of mesh theory we are interested in, insofar as it is only the pure mesh theories which are current time-slice (and not historical) theories.

23. Josef Breuer and Sigmund Freud, *Studies on Hysteria* in *Standard Edition of the Complete Psychological Works of Sigmund Freud*, vol. 2 (London, 1955).

24. Compatibilists about causal determinism and freedom to do otherwise tend to argue that only features of the current time-slice are pertinent to ascriptions of freedom to do otherwise. They believe that the only way in which the past can matter to such ascriptions is by casting a shadow on the present: this is essentially the point of Keith Lehrer's "Shadow Principle" in *Profiles: Keith Lehrer*, edited by Radu J. Bogdan (Dordrecht, 1981), esp. pp. 30–39. In contrast, incompatibilists hold that the past can be *directly* relevant to current ascriptions of freedom to do otherwise (without casting any kind of shadow). They reject the shadow principle, replacing it with some sort of Dog's Tail Principle, according to which the past is like a dog's tail which must follow the dog wherever it goes. The shadow theorist may accuse the incompatibilist of allowing the tail to wag the dog, but we cannot go into this dispute here.

25. Not all philosophers have been careful to distinguish between phenomena which are genuinely historical and those which are merely epistemically historical. For example, in his book, *Philosophy of the Social Sciences* (Boulder, Colo., 1988), 107–108, Alexander Rosenberg says:

> As we saw in the case of Freud's theory, Marx's is also sometimes interpreted, defended, and attacked as 'historicist'. A theory or method is historicist, roughly if it holds that in order to understand and to predict subsequent states of a system . . . we must have detailed knowledge of the past states of the system. Even to predict the very next 'state' in the development of a neurosis or an economic system, we need to know about events long past in the life of the individual—usually the patient's infancy—or the society—sometimes even its prehistory. . . . When Marx's and Freud's theories are described as essentially or unavoidably historicist, what is meant is that past events really do continue to exercise control over future ones. . . . We need to study

the past . . . because over and above features of the present state, there are causes in the distant past.

Note that Rosenberg here *slides* from epistemic to genuine historicism.

26. Carl Ginet, *Knowledge, Perception, and Memory* (Dordrecht, 1975); "Contra Reliabilism," *The Monist* 68 (1985): 175–87; "Justification: It Need Not Cause But It Must Be Accessible," *Journal of Philosophical Research* 15 (1989–1990): 93–107; and Richard Foley, "What's Wrong With Reliabilism?" *The Monist* 68 (1985): 188–202; and *The Theory of Epistemic Rationality* (Cambridge, Mass., 1987).

27. The strategy just sketched pertains primarily to knowledge claims. But a similar approach can be employed in regard to justification. Consider this passage from "Justification" by Carl Ginet:

> For a fact to contribute to making me justified at a particular time in then adopting a certain belief, it is *not* necessary that it be part of what causes me to adopt the belief, but it *is* necessary that it be something in my field of awareness at that time so that it *could* induce me to adopt the belief should I be disposed to be influenced by it.
>
> Suppose, for example, that S knows that (a) certain medical tests she has undergone indicate, with 95% reliability, that she has a certain serious and incurable disease. She then has a reason, a strong reason, to believe that she does in fact have the disease. But she also has a reason not to believe that she does, a non-evidentiary reason, namely, the extreme disagreeableness of such a belief. A person in such circumstances need not be *compelled* by either of these reasons, need not either believe she has the disease without being able to help so believing or withhold believing she has it without being able to help doing *that*. A person in such circumstances may be in a position to choose whether or not to believe she has the disease (and I suspect that this is the position many of us would in fact be in).
>
> Now consider a person in such a position who knows that the test results are excellent evidence that she has the disease but who refuses to believe that she has it—she clings to the hope that she might be one of the 5% of false positives. She does this, that is, *until* she learns that the astrological signs indicate that she has acquired a serious disease, whereupon, having faith in astrology, she begins to believe that she has the disease. So the situation is that she *would not* believe that she has a serious disease if she had only the good reason for doing so (the evidence of the medical tests), but she *would* believe this if she had only the bad reason (the astrological signs) for doing so. Thus, it is not for the good reason but only for the bad reason that she believes it; it is because of her awareness of what the astrological signs say and not because of her awareness of the significance of the results of the medical tests that she believes it; it is solely the former that explains her believing it, the latter is not even part of the explanation. Nevertheless, the fact that she *is aware* that there is a good reason for believing it justifies her in believing it: she could turn aside any suggestion that she in her current circumstances ought not to believe such a thing by citing that good reason she then has for believing it. Her being aware of a good reason for believing it justifies her in believing it, even though it played no part in inducing her to believe it. (p. 100)

Again, the key insight here is that the fact which implies that the agent is justified in her belief resides in the snapshot features of the world at the time of belief: it is (allegedly) irrelevant how the belief is produced. The proponents of the epistemic strategies here described would argue that the crucial notions of justification of belief and knowledge are current time-slice notions; they would claim that these notions are merely apparently historical. Snapshot features of the world are available to explain the epistemic *defect* of S when he believes that there is a sheep in the field in the example discussed in the text, and snapshot features of the world are available to explain the epistemic *virtue* of the agent who believes that she will get the disease in Ginet's example.

28. The question of whether love and friendship are genuinely historical phenomena is an interesting and difficult one. Let us (somewhat morbidly) suppose that one's spouse and children suddenly die, but in an independent and incredible coincidence, exact duplicates come into being. These are molecule for molecule duplicates with exactly the same mental states, such as memories, as the "originals." Now it would seem almost impossible not to have the same attitudes of love toward these new persons as to one's old family, and yet one has never had any causal interaction with the new persons in the past (and the past is irrelevant to their coming into being). Of course, this is a fantastic scenario, and it is difficult to assess such possibilities sensibly. But we simply wish to raise some preliminary doubts about Nozick's suggestion that love and friendship are (like distributive justice) historical notions.

29. This claim can be challenged, but it is beyond the scope of this essay to evaluate these challenges carefully.

30. Ultimately, our preferred notion of "taking responsibility" will have core elements of the intuitive notion, but it will also depart from the ordinary intuitive concept in some ways. We believe that the ordinary intuitive concept of taking responsibility is too explicit and deliberative for our purposes. In cases in which it is tempting to say that an agent is morally responsible because he *should* have taken responsibility although he did not, we shall suggest that the temptation to suppose that the agent has not in fact taken responsibility may come from an excessively narrow conception of taking responsibility.

31. See, for example, Susan Wolf, "Asymmetrical Freedom," *Journal of Philosophy* 77 (March 1980): 151–66; and *Freedom Within Reason* (Oxford, 1991).

32. Harry Frankfurt, "Rationality and the Unthinkable," *The Importance of What We Care About* (Cambridge, 1988), 177–90.

33. We have focused on one particular anti-historicist argument. Of course, we do not deny that it is possible that there are other anti-historicist arguments, and thus we do not claim to have decisively established historicism.

34. In the recent essay, "Identification and Wholeheartedness," Frankfurt says:

> It is these acts of ordering and of rejection—integration and separation—that create a self out of the raw materials of inner life. They define the intrapsychic constraints and boundaries with respect to which a person's autonomy may be threatened even by his own desires. [The following is the footnote that attaches to this passage] The determining conditions that are pertinent here are exclusively *structural* arrangements. I mention this, although I do not pursue the point, since it bears on the familiar issue of whether *historical* considerations—especially causal stories—have any essential relevance to questions concerning whether a person's actions are autonomous. (p. 39)

35. Frankfurt, "Three Concepts of Free Action: II."

36. In his famous critique of Frankfurt's early formulation of his mesh theory, Gary Watson argued that simply adding higher levels in the hierarchy of preferences does not provide enough to ground the claim that an agent is acting freely (Watson, "Free Agency"). Roughly, the point is that if acting on a first-order desire is not itself sufficient for moral responsibility because of considerations pertinent to the second level, then surely acting in accordance with a second-order desire of a certain sort is not itself sufficient for moral responsibility because of considerations pertinent to the third level, and so forth. This might be called the "logical" problem with the simple mesh view, and Frankfurt's new view seems to address the logical problem (in virtue of positing the resonance condition). But the logical problem is clearly different from the "source" problem—the problem that the mesh can be induced in responsibility-undermining ways. (This problem for the simple mesh theory was nicely developed by Michael Slote: "Understanding Free Will," *Journal of Philosophy* 77 [March 1980]: 136–51.) Thus, it might be said that Frankfurt's new view addresses Watson's critique, but not Slote's—it addresses the logical problem, but not the source problem. Thus, the new view, even if it is successful in addressing the logical problem, does not in any way diminish the plausibility of the insight that responsibility is essentially historical.

37. In his fascinating and elegant Presidential Address to the Eastern Division of the American Philosophical Association, Frankfurt reiterates his attempt to analyze identification in terms of purely internal, snapshot resources:

> Hierarchical accounts of the identity of the self do not presume, however, that a person's identification with some desire consists simply in the fact that he *has* a higher-order desire by which the first desire is endorsed. The endorsing higher-order desire must be, in addition, a desire with which the person is *satisfied*. . . . Identification is constituted neatly by an endorsing higher-order desire with which the person is satisfied. (Harry Frankfurt, "The Faintest Passion," manuscript p. 23—delivered to the Eastern Division of the American Philosophical Association, December 1991)

But if identification is to do the work required of it in Frankfurt's theory of freedom and responsibility, matters cannot be as neat as he supposes: one must attend to the causal sources of the satisfaction in question. Frankfurt is here primarily concerned with analyzing such notions as ambivalence and wholeheartedness. Perhaps for *these* notions it is appropriate to employ a concept of identification that is analyzed by reference solely to snapshot resources; perhaps these notions are indeed simply a matter of patterns of internal attitudes quite independent of how the patterns are produced. But then this would simply reinforce the point that such notions as wholeheartedness and identification (thus construed) are not sufficient for moral responsibility.

38. John Martin Fischer, "Responsibility and Control," *Journal of Philosophy* 89 (January 1982), 24–40.

39. See Fischer, "Responsiveness and Moral Responsibility."

40. For a nice discussion of immediacy and the pure present, see Alfred J. Freddoso, "Accidental Necessity and Logical Determinism," *Journal of Philosophy* 80 (May 1983): 257–78.

41. For a selection of essays which explore various putative analyses of this problematic notion, see John Martin Fischer, ed., *God, Foreknowledge, and Freedom* (Stanford, 1989).

42. For discussion of the nature of soft facts and their role in debates about the relationship between God's omniscience and human freedom, see ibid.

43. Alvin Plantinga, "On Ockham's Way Out," *Faith and Philosophy* 3 (1986): 235–69.

44. For a defense of such views about identity, see Saul A. Kripke, *Naming and Necessity* (Cambridge, Mass., 1980).

45. Suppose a fact is composed of an individual and a property. Some facts are historical in virtue of their constituent properties, whereas others are historical in virtue of their constituent individuals (if the Kripkean view is correct). Thus, there are different "sources" of historicity of facts. Interestingly, there is a parallel here with soft facts. Some soft facts are soft in virtue of their constituent properties. But others are soft in virtue of their constituent individuals—or perhaps the *interaction* between the constituent individuals and properties (which themselves are not soft). Thus, there are different sources of the softness of facts. See John Martin Fischer, "Hard-Type Soft Facts," *Philosophical Review* 95 (October 1986): 591–601.

46. It might be argued that such a case is *impossible*, since there must be some differences at some levels of description between the two brains, if indeed the past history of the abused individual is to exculpate her. It is not however *obvious* to us that this is true, even if it is true. It is at least worth considering whether such a case is possible.

47. We thank Ruth Barcan Marcus for the example concerning the nature of beauty. We have benefited from very useful comments by Carl Ginet, Mark Lance, Nancy Sherman, Wayne Davis, Carl Hoefer, and Tom Senor. Also, we are grateful to Harry Frankfurt for a manuscript copy of his APA Eastern Division Presidential Address and to Peter van Inwagen for a manuscript copy of his book, *Metaphysics* (Boulder, Colo., 1993). Previous versions of this essay have been read at the University of California, Riverside, Georgetown University, and Occidental College.

Voluntary Motion, Biological Computation, and Free Will

PATRICK SUPPES

FREE WILL

What bearing does the general indistinguishability of determinism and indeterminism, as I argued for in a recent paper (Suppes, 1993), have on the classical philosophical problem of free will? Different answers, it seems to me, are possible. A conservative response might be that it has no bearing or relevance. According to this conservative response, free will is a manifestation of the causal efficacy of mental events. Such events are, in turn, manifestations of physical events, which unfortunately cannot be observed directly. But this language, suggesting, as it does, two kinds of objects, the mental and the physical, will be objected to by some. There are, so it would be said, just physical events, but under some descriptions we speak of them as mental events. In any case, I set this issue concerning the kinds of events to the side. This meant-to-be straightforward causal account of free will leaves no place for indeterminism or instability in the arena of human intention and action, even though it is entirely compatible with indeterminism in the behavior of elementary particles or black holes.

In contrast, the radical response is that the exercise of free will, as seen in the daily activity of humans and other animals high on the evolutionary scale, constitutes prima facie evidence of indeterminism in human affairs. This radical view, now not much defended by many philosophers, would obviously favor indeterminism over instability as the correct philosophical backdrop for the plain man's view of the world.

I do not intend these rough sketches of contrasting responses to be taken seriously. Rather, my purpose is to try to make clear a position that does not commit to either determinism or indeterminism in its account of free will. The attempt to be independent of either is just because of my earlier argument about the impossibility of providing data to choose between them. I argued in the essay referred to above that the choice between determinism and indeterminism is, at a fundamental level, transcendental.

There are, it seems to me, two central principles that should govern our account of free will. The first is that small causes can produce large effects.[1] The second is that random phenomena are maximally complex, and it is complexity that is phenomenologically evident in many human actions that are not constrained but satisfy ordinary ideas of being free actions. There is a third methodological principle I want to state before saying something more about these two principles. That principle is not to be intimidated by the kind of mechanistic argument derived from classical mechanics. Such arguments overwhelmed Kant in his metaphysical foundations of natural science and in his antinomy of freedom of the will. The case for determinism is not a strong one. The case for predictability of most phenomena is overwhelmingly a bad one. We need not be pushed by some metaphysical view of physics into being forced to create a dichotomy between deterministic physical processes and free human actions that seem to violate physical causality.

With these remarks as starters, I can sketch at this point the argument I want to make about free will. The central idea is that human intentions and actions exhibit in some cases the stability we anticipate of many parts of the physical world and in other cases the instability that is characteristic of many other kinds of physical phenomena. In human actions that appear unstable, either in their underlying intentions or in their triggering movements, we cannot in any direct way distinguish whether they are deterministically caused but unstable or, on the other hand, indeterministic. I said this before but in this context it is a litany that needs repeating. What we can say is that there are classes of human actions that are highly complex and essentially unpredictable. I give several examples in Suppes (1985).[2]

For the moment, I want to restrict myself to a single point, but an important one, that should illustrate my more general thesis about free will. In the case of movement of a limb, whether an arm or a leg, there are three kinds of actions or events that we can distinguish. One class consists of the movements themselves. Another consists of the forces exerted by the muscles, for example, a change in muscle tension to produce a movement, and the third consists of proprioceptive signals from the nervous system to the muscles to affect the forces exerted by the muscles. There is, of course, a great deal more to the system, at a gross level even, than I have indicated. For example, there is perceptual feedback generating the proprioceptive signals, but I shall ignore for the moment this additional critical perceptual part of the system. The important point is that there is no one-one correspondence between muscle force and movement. In fact, the evidence is very good that the differential equations are nonlinear in character, and have, as would be expected, extraordinarily complex solutions that are very dependent on initial conditions. The instability of the relation between forces and muscles requires constant revision of muscle tension by proprioceptive signals being sent to express the animal's intention in terms of what is desired as movement.

Now it might be thought that the aim of this kind of physiology and psychology is a mechanistic reduction of movement to an analysis of physical causes. But this is precisely what is not the case in any simple way. The extraordinary complexity of the system makes it impossible to pin down in any detail some simple mechanistic theory of the causal sequence. Whether the system is at heart deterministic but unstable or indeterministic cannot possibly be decided, and there is no hope with the framework of present science that the issue could be decided in decisive detail. The complexity is so great that there is little doubt that a strong argument could be made for irreducibly random elements in the phenomena, even though the central tendency of the mover's intention seems plain enough. One way of putting the indeterministic thesis in the present framework is that at heart the system is highly indeterministic but by continual proprioceptive correction the movement is kept on course.

It is this last point that I want to analyze with some care, for I think it contains the basis for one of the strongest arguments for the existence of free will regardless of whether "surrounding" phenomena are deterministic or not.

For much human and other animal behavior, continued perceptual feedback and proprioceptive correction of movement are obviously required. The first-level explanation of the ubiquitous perception-and-movement-correction data is in terms of goals and intentions. "Why is Mary turning the corner? Because she is going to the store." "Why is Henry moving backward so fast? He is trying to get to John's lob in time to hit the ball back across the net." This intentional feature of commonsense psychology is really denied by no one.

Such ordinary intentional actions bear the strongest possible witness to the existence of free will in the present framework. It is not the intentional aspect in its pure form that makes the case for free will. Rather, it is the ubiquitous necessity of correcting any complex movement continually in order to achieve the intended goal. Willful intervention, so to speak, is needed from moment to moment. The fact of such intervention is evident. Just as important, neither determinism nor indeterminism as a theoretical framework can shake the need for intentional intervention.

There is one fantasy about determinism that must be laid to rest. What is deterministic, so the fantasy goes, is not just the body that is moving, but the much larger system of the body plus environment plus perception plus feedback. This complicated total system is supposed to go its merry way without purposeful intervention. From what we know of complex systems, nothing could be less likely. Certainly we shall never, within the framework of present science, have the slightest chance of understanding in noninterventional or nonintentional terms even the simplest cases of human movement. But, given a goal, the phenomena become manageable even if still subtle and complex in physiological detail.

To believe in determinism simpliciter is on a par with believing in an omniscient God. In the real world of natural, as opposed to supernatural, phenomena, intention and will are evident and unproblematic. Intentional action is indispensable whether the world is indeterministic or deterministic. Which it is very likely we shall never know.

SOME QUESTIONS ABOUT VOLUNTARY MOTION

I now want to turn to a more systematic analysis of the general ideas just presented. Although the issue of free will or purposeful action can be analyzed from the standpoint of many different kinds of phenomena, ranging from the physiology of the heart to the evolution of the species, I want to use my earlier analysis of determinism and prediction (Suppes, 1993), and to concentrate just on the case of physical movement. There is, of course, already a large philosophical literature discussing human action involving physical movement, but it will not be my purpose to give a formal characterization of action but rather to concentrate on the more restricted notion of purposeful or voluntary movement.

The intuitive idea is quite simple. I shall define a physical movement of an object as *voluntary* if the movement of that object cannot be predicted by knowledge of initial and boundary conditions and laws of physics, but can be predicted by knowledge of a goal that is intrinsic to the object or that is set for this object by some other agent.

There are a number of distinctions that need to be dealt with, and unfortunately not all of these distinctions can be handled in an uncontroversial manner. I mean by this that serious arguments can be found on both sides as well as serious proponents supporting these arguments, and it is not clear that every issue can be resolved in an objective fashion. However, in order to make the case for the existence of free will, it will not be necessary to have a settled view on each of these matters. Let me mention some of the principal issues as I see them.

1. Is the motion of low-level organisms such as parameciums, which can be conditioned, to count as voluntary?
2. Is the motion intrinsic to a homeostatic device, such as a household thermostat, to count as an example of purposeful motion?
3. Is some at least rudimentary form of perception required to provide feedback and correction of the course of motion necessary in order for a motion to count as purposeful or voluntary?
4. Must an object exhibiting voluntary behavior be described as having intentions?
5. Does voluntary motion of an object imply consciousness of a goal by the object or an agent controlling the goal?
6. What level of accuracy of prediction is considered acceptable for purposeful or voluntary motion?

I shall consider these six issues in reverse order.

Accuracy of prediction. If my wife or I go to the nearest grocery store to purchase a bottle of milk and a loaf of bread, I can predict within a few feet or meters where the motion will stop, and then return to the house, again to a position known within a few meters or feet. I can, of course, even pick a few symbolic points, for example, the door of the grocery store or one of the doors into the house, to fix the accuracy of prediction well within a meter. Such predictions are pretty gross by the standards of good physics or engineering. If I ask for a more detailed prediction of the space-time trajectory—which would be the ordinary object of physical prediction—to the store and back, then quite gross errors can occur. First of all, the system is an open one, in the sense that there are disturbing causes easily entering the simple system defined. A typical example would be a traffic jam that had not been foreseen. Even the timing of approach to the automatic stop lights en route would lead to considerable variability in prediction. What is most important, however, is the intrinsic variability. There is no possibility, from physical knowledge of the initial conditions, as I or my wife leave the house, to calculate with any accuracy whatsoever the space-time trajectory to the store and back. The actual trajectory followed will require continual correction and modification based upon perceptual feedback of a variety of kinds en route. Thus we may conclude that prediction using just laws of physics is absolutely out of the question. There is no hope, using just the laws of physics and initial conditions, of being able to predict when someone would arrive at the entrance to the store, at a point whose location is known, within much less than a meter. On the other hand, the introduction of purpose and the concept of a goal do not make prediction come close to that ordinarily to be found in good physics or engineering, as already mentioned. What we get, with the introduction of purpose, in the sense of physical behavior oriented toward a goal, is that we can make very good predictions about one or two special aspects of the motion, namely, the aspects most central to achieving the goal. We can also, in terms of implicit aspects of the goal, make some quite reasonable predictions, but not highly accurate ones, about such features as the time the round trip will take. As already remarked, the pluralistic and decentralized character of the human motor-control system also argues against any possibility of highly accurate predictions of trajectories of purposeful motion. The important point, however, is the strong contrast between the essential unpredictability by physics of the critical points of the motion and the relatively accurate prediction of these critical points once a goal is introduced.

A second fundamental point is that in the framework of present science we are utterly unable to develop a detailed and accurate theory of voluntary motion. Moreover, it seems in principle impossible, and a mistaken idea to attempt to realize. The failure, it is important to note, can already be found in the analysis of complex open physical systems without any component of voluntary motion.

The voluntary aspect makes it all the more out of the question to develop a detailed trajectory prediction. From a physical standpoint, the course corrections characteristic of voluntary motion increase the openness of the system, and thereby increase the problems of physical prediction.

Consciousness. As I define the notion of voluntary motion, the requirement of consciousness is not part of the definiens. I have in mind examples that I want to include in which consciousness is certainly not an unequivocally definite aspect of behavior. When a bird dives from a hundred feet into the ocean to catch a fish it has seen, its complicated motion is certainly purposeful in both the weak and strong senses that I would want to use, but it is doubtful if we want to attribute consciousness to birds. It is not even clear that we want to attribute consciousness to dogs. A dog that is told to fetch the paper, certainly in the sense used here, engages in purposeful motion, but may not be conscious of the goal he is achieving because there is not the appropriate concept of consciousness to apply to the dog's mental life.

Intentions. Obviously I do not intend to make conscious intentions part of purposeful motion. On the other hand, a derivative sense of intention implicit in all goal-seeking behavior is innocent and unexceptionable, but the important point is that I do not intend to introduce a separate concept of intention that does any serious work in what is to follow.

Perception. Perception is another matter. Without perception and the consequent feedback mechanisms adjusting the motion of objects seeking a goal, I see no way to clearly distinguish purposeful from nonpurposeful motion, and therefore to distinguish physical predictability from what I shall term purposeful predictability. The way in which I or my wife depend upon perception to negotiate the physically complicated path from our house to the grocery store is obvious and certainly not a matter of essential controversy. On the other hand, as we move down the phylogenetic scale and on out to simple homeostatic mechanisms there can be differences about what is to be regarded as perception. In the case of lower animals, we can certainly go a long way down the phylogenetic scale and still be forced to accept that some sort of perception is taking place, because specific sensory input is demonstrably affecting the motion the animal is engaged in. The perception, and the perceptual system supporting these activities of the organism, can be extraordinarily simple in comparison with our own rich perceptual apparatus, but still I would claim it is perception when an ant follows a trail in pursuit of food or in returning to the nest. The acute visual perception of birds is well known.

Thermostat. But what about the thermostat as a simple example of an homeostatic system? It certainly is given a clear goal by the agent controlling it, namely, keep the ambient air temperature around the location of the thermostat itself in a certain small interval of values. Second, the thermostat has a rudimentary form of perception, for it is able to 'perceive' the temperature of the ambient air surrounding it much more accurately than a person can. It also can be claimed that it is not a simple matter whatsoever to predict from initial and boundary conditions at time t_0 when the thermostat will activate the furnace (or the air conditioner), or, if the furnace is on at t_0, when it will turn it off. In that sense the motion of the thermostat, that is, the mechanical motion of its parts, including the turning on of the furnace, would seem to qualify as voluntary motion—I leave aside the fact that much of the physical activity of the thermostat is electronic rather than mechanical, a point that does not bear directly on the issue at hand. Perhaps the disturbing point about the thermostat is that it is completely controlled in terms of its mode of operation by another agent who has the freedom to set the constant value the thermostat is striving to achieve, that is, its goal. We also find disturbing the fact that the design of the thermostat seems so transparent and understandable in purely physical terms. It is this absence of transparency, in fact, the absence of any serious detailed analysis at all, that is certainly responsible for much of what we consider important and significant about voluntary movement in higher organisms. It does not seem to me to be important to quarrel about exactly where to draw the line. I am prepared to say that in a weak sense a thermostat exhibits voluntary motion. On the other hand, I do want to stress that the thermostat is not an ideal example of a very simple object engaging in voluntary motion, because the thermostat itself is not moving but only its parts. I really want to restrict, for purposes of simplifying and making an analysis of one aspect of free will, the case of voluntary motion, where what one has in mind is the actual physical motion of the object as a whole. I have discussed the thermostat at some length just because it is a classical stalking horse for the sorts of philosophers who believe that intentions and free will are only embodied in complex structures of amino acids and their surrounding cellular materials.

MORE REMARKS ON VOLUNTARY MOTION

A methodological point. In offering an analysis of voluntary motion I am certainly operating in the philosophical rather than the scientific tradition. The systematic unsatisfactory character of my definition from a scientific or formal standpoint is evident. Unfortunately, the labor of converting it into something fully satisfactory is far from trivial, at least as far as I can see. On the other hand, the key notions used in the earlier informal definition are easy to describe, namely,

(i)   the concept of predicting by standard physical laws and initial physical conditions,

(ii) the concept of having a goal, and

(iii) the concept of adjusting motion on the basis of perceptual feedback.

I have made the conditions only sufficient and not necessary, just to commit myself to less. Concerning (i), in the present case what one has in mind is relatively quite simple. One neither knows nor can discover by physical means a goal that a moving object is attempting to achieve either through its own volition or through that of an agent controlling it. The problem is expressing that idea in some reasonable way. I have left it vague and general as stated.

The prediction requirement in (i) may seem relatively definite because of the reference to "standard physical laws," but in fact such a reference is clearly quite nebulous and indefinite and any satisfactorily detailed theory, about which we might prove some theorems, would require a specific narrowing down of the physical laws or theories available.

Clause (iii) uses the intuitively obvious but formally vague notion of perceptual feedback and the equally intuitive but equally formally vague notion of adjustment of the trajectory of the object. Again, it is clear to all what one has in mind, as in the case of an individual walking, running, or swimming to a given location that is a goal.

The analysis of voluntary motion was already a major topic in ancient philosophy, for it received systematic attention from Aristotle, and others as well. It is not in order here to look at the history of the concept, except to note that it is very old, and I do not mean to suggest for a moment that the idea of voluntary motion is a new one. The critical new ingredient I have introduced is the concept of unpredictability from the standpoint of standard physical theory, but even then there are clear harbingers of it in past analyses of voluntary motion. Of course, Aristotle does not discuss predictability of one kind or another, but rather the different kinds of causes that separate voluntary motion from involuntary motion. It is just part of my separation of determinism and predictability to put the emphasis here on predictability. In disentangling the issues concerning free will and determinism, in my own judgment the question of predictability is the most central.

Biology vs. ethics. Much of the philosophical literature on free will has been concerned with the relation between moral responsibility and freedom of the will. This is not merely a recent trend of modern moral philosophy but is already very much in the center of Kant's elaborate analysis of how freedom in the noumenal world can be seen as consistent with causal determinism in the phenomenal world.

In my view the emphasis on moral questions has been a disaster for the analysis of the problem of free will. Moral philosophy remains the soft underbelly of philosophy. The concepts and arguments of ethical thought are no match for the elaborate intellectual constructions of classical and modern physics, and their developed foundations. This intellectual mismatch may be seen already in Kant's placing on the side of experience all of physics, but essentially nothing of traditional philosophical concepts of moral behavior.

Aristotle had a more realistic approach. The expression of will—to use the modern term—is to be found first of all and most generally in the biological behavior of animals, not simply in the highly restricted domain of moral choices. Voluntary motion in animals is guided by reason, desire, or imagination. More generally, the analysis of biological structure and function is dominated by teleological principles.

As should be evident, I think that biological behavior of animals of all or nearly all species is the locus classicus of voluntary behavior. The analysis of voluntary motion alone shows the unfeasibility of reducing biology to physics. The next section will examine in more detail how this viewpoint recasts the philosophical problem of determinism and freedom of the will.

DETERMINISM AND FREE WILL

I now consider in more detail the relation between determinism, prediction, and free will, especially as exemplified in voluntary motion. There are several different ways to begin, but for both historical and conceptual reasons it will be useful to start with Kant's discussion in the Transcendental Dialectic of the *Critique of Pure Reason*, especially in the section on the explanation of the cosmological idea of freedom in connection with the general necessity of nature. As might be expected, I want to oppose Kant's conclusions, but not always his methods. First, let us consider in somewhat more detail what he has to say. I assume that we are all more or less familiar with the general idea that the empirical world of phenomena, covered by the laws of physics essentially, is quite distinct from the timeless world of noumena in which we find the proper setting for reason and freedom. Here is what Kant has to say in one important passage for our purposes:

> Every man therefore has an empirical character of his (arbitrary) will, which is nothing but a certain causality of his reason, exhibiting in its phenomenal actions and effects a rule, according to which one may infer the motives of reason and its actions, both in kind and in degree, and judge of the subjective principles of his will. As that empirical character itself must be derived from phenomena, as an effect, and from their rule which is supplied by experience, all the acts of a man, so far as they are phenomena, are determined from his empirical character and from the other concomitant causes, according to the order of nature; and if we could investigate all the manifestations of his will to the very bottom, there would be not a single human action which we could not *predict* with certainty and recognize from its preceding conditions as necessary. There is no freedom therefore with reference to this empirical character, and yet it is only with reference to it that we can consider man, when we are merely *observing*, and, as is the case in anthropology, trying to investigate the motive causes of his actions physiologically. (A549–550)

In this passage I have emphasized *predict* although Kant does not. This passage generally exemplifies what I just said in brief about Kant's ideas, namely, the separation of the phenomenal from the noumenal world and the fact that the empirical character of action must lie in the phenomenal world. The point I want to especially focus on here is Kant's assurance that we could predict with certainty any single human action if we investigated all the manifestations of the individual's will, as he says, "to the very bottom." What he means here, of course, is under the empirical character of the action, which would mean an investigation according to the laws of nature governed ultimately by physics. It is exactly my thesis that this conception of Kant rests on a mistake. We cannot, in fact, predict human action with certainty, even under the most idealized circumstances. Above all, we cannot analyze an action so that it becomes determined necessarily by preceding physical conditions.

At the end of the part on freedom from which I am quoting, Kant has this also to say:

> Our problem was, whether freedom is contradictory to natural necessity in one and the same action: and this we have sufficiently answered by showing that freedom may have relation to a very different kind of

conditions from those of nature, so that the law of the latter does not affect the former, and both may exist independent of, and undisturbed by, each other.

It should be clearly understood that, in what we have said, we had no intention of establishing the *reality* of freedom, as one of the faculties which contain the cause of the phenomenal appearances in our world of sense. For not only would this have been no transcendental consideration at all, which is concerned with concepts only, but it could never have succeeded, because from experience we can never infer anything but what must be represented in thought according to the laws of experience. (A557–558)

In this passage especially, Kant makes very clear his insistence that freedom lies outside the necessity of natural laws, and, more generally, outside of experience.

It has been a familiar thesis of a large number of philosophers that determinism is incompatible with free will, which is what Kant is saying at the level of phenomena, and that therefore so much the worse for free will, because it is well established from physics that the world is deterministic. As Jules Vuillemin has remarked to me on various occasions, the central argument that I want to make is to stand Kant's view on its head. It is free will that is given as the central, empirical data, and it is determinism that is fragile, insubstantial, and unsupported, in any direct way.

Remember also that I am making the argument here not upon the more nebulous ideas sometimes associated with free will but with the necessity of voluntary motion exhibiting motion that is continually corrected as a purposeful matter in order to achieve a goal. So my claim is that, above all, the central empirical phenomenon that is undeniable is that of continual correction of voluntary motion based on perceptual feedback and proprioceptive control of locomotion, in order to achieve a goal, that is, a new location of the organism as a whole, or some significant part of the organism, such as a hand, leg, or eye. Furthermore, it is easy to find a wide class of voluntary motions because of their demonstrable unpredictability from the standpoint of pure physics.

Following through on Kant's ideas, let us say in turn what is to be said, on the viewpoint I am defending, about determinism. Here, determinism assumes the metaphysical will-o'-the-wisp status that Kant assigns to freedom. Determinism is compatible with empirical data of every conceivable kind, but it is in no sense scientifically established as a correct, quite general theory about the nature of the universe. Separation of prediction and determinism in the decisive way illustrated by many examples discussed in Suppes (1993) makes it appropriate to say that the assumption of determinism as a completely general thesis about nature is a transcendental metaphysical assumption that goes beyond experience. It is only through the possibility of prediction for phenomena of every significant natural kind that we can hope to sustain in a detailed and serious way a scientific thesis about determinism. Given the impossibility of such prediction, determinism must have a transcendental status.

Indeterminism. It is a familiar form of philosophical argument to show that free will is incompatible with determinism, and also free will is incompatible with indeterminism. Therefore, there can be no free will. But the kind of argument I have given about determinism I also make about indeterminism, which as a universal thesis has a similar transcendental character.

There is, of course, the question of how to interpret quantum mechanics and whether there is at rock bottom an indeterminism in quantum mechanics as exemplified by the work of the last two decades surrounding Bell's inequalities and Bell's theorem. Even here the argument is not at all decisive. For a recent spirited defense of the de Broglie–Bohm deterministic interpretation of quantum mechanics, see Holland (1993).

So the Kantian thesis has been properly stood on its head. Free will, as exemplified in voluntary motion, is the hard empirical fact. Determinism (or, if you prefer, indeterminism) is the transcendental metaphysical assumption out of reach of detailed confirmation.

BIOLOGICAL COMPUTATION

The positive theory of voluntary motion cannot depend only on negative results about physical unpredictability. The best short description of the new biological concept that is needed is that of computation. I want to insist on computation taking place in the behavior of even very simple organisms or agent-designed devices like thermostats. Perception, simple or complex, is, from the viewpoint I am adopting, a special case of computation. On the other hand, as should be clear from what I said earlier, consciousness or intention in any rich human sense is not a necessary condition of computation. Because of my concentration on voluntary motion I put to one side whether genetic transmission in the form of DNA code is a form of computation, although it is my own view that it is.

The three basic kinds of computation that occur in voluntary motion are:

(i)   Setting a goal;
(ii) Perceiving something—object or phenomenon—in the environment;
(iii) Correcting the current trajectory.

Degenerate or special cases of this threefold analysis of computation in the context of voluntary motion are easy to give.

Stationary frog. A frog sitting on a rock "watching" for insects to eat is a good example. The frog does not compute a goal, and it does not correct its current stationary position or the motion of any of its parts. What it does do is respond more or less automatically to the perception of a small moving object by flicking out its tongue to catch the object. Perception is essential to the behavior of the frog.

Thermostat. It seems best to think of the thermostat as a simple man-machine system. Referring to the threefold analysis of computation just given, (i) the goal is set by a person, the desired approximate temperature, (ii) perceiving the actual temperature is done by the thermostat, and (iii) the correction of "trajectory" is made by the thermostat, when it turns the heat source off or on.

Automobile. A better man-machine system of voluntary motion is that of a person driving an automobile. (i) The short-term goal is set by the driver, who may be doing something for another person who sets the long-term goal; (ii) perception also is the driver's responsibility; and (iii) corrections of course are made by man-machine interaction. In a closely related kind of case, that of flying an airplane in bad weather, perception, under conditions of instrument navigation, is also a case of man-machine interaction.

Person walking to store. From the extended discussion of my going to the store in an earlier section, it is clear that this kind of activity is a paradigm of voluntary motion, and all three kinds of computation enter in a direct way. The same may be said of the behavior of an animal chasing a prey, or also of the behavior of an animal trying to escape a predator.

Question of more structure. It needs to be emphasized that the threefold division of computation introduced is not meant to be the end of the story. Each of the divisions introduced has its own complex and subtle structure. The setting of a goal, for example, naturally leads to the introduction of subgoals to provide a structured analysis of what must be accomplished to achieve the desired goal. The perceptual systems of all but the simplest animals are among the most complicated structures known, and much is yet to be discovered and understood about them. It seems to me obvious, and I shall therefore not pursue the point in detail, that the perceptual systems of all the higher animals perform computations of a complex kind, many aspects of which must be learned from experience.

Computation as a natural phenomenon. First of all, the computational power of higher animals evolved over many millions of years from simpler life forms, which in turn evolved even earlier from a soup of amino acids and other mixtures of carbon, oxygen, hydrogen, and the like. This naturalistic view is widely, even if not universally, accepted.

What is not as readily accepted is that computation is as natural a part of our world as the motion of planets or electrons. When I say *computation is a natural part of our world* I mean this in the strong sense that organisms and their computations are just as much an *irreducible* part of the world as is any simple mechanical system. This does not mean that biological organisms and their computational powers are ahistorically given or are in some strong sense universal. In fact their very evolution has surely depended on special environments of unstable energy configurations. The simple planetary systems magnificently studied by Ptolemy, Copernicus, Kepler, Newton, and Laplace could never, as conceived by any of these scientists, been a home for the evolution of life and biological computation. Turbulent environments with the right range of parameters of temperature and pressure, which may be analyzed within either a framework of unstable determinism or of indeterminism, were needed (Suppes, 1991). But any strong thesis of determinism or indeterminism is metaphysically irrelevant to gaining what understanding of these environments and their evolving organisms we are capable of. Almost all of the details are completely inaccessible, and not for historical reasons. The behavior of such complicated systems could be described only in the most gross fashion even if we were presented with a full panoply of instruments to make observations.

An obvious query at this point is how does what I have to say about the irrelevance of any general deterministic thesis square with the obvious deterministic behavior of a modern digital computer running a particular program. Are, so the query goes, biological computers fundamentally different; in principle, are not they too basically deterministic in character?

Let us deal with the case of the digital computer first. Given a proper stable physical environment with a proper source of energy and a syntactically correct program, the computational steps the computer will take are determined, even if not algorithmically predictable—as seen in the theorem on the halting problem for Turing machines. Of course, this computational determinism does not imply physical determinism of the computer, which is designed with certain physical tolerances in mind. But this issue is not really critical for the main point I want to make, modulo a remark about timesharing or multitasking.

Once timesharing or multitasking computers are considered, even the limited claim of computational determinism is suspect. For a fully loaded system, it is in general impossible to predict the next computational step that will be taken. Even modeling of timesharing as a real-time stochastic process is difficult if not impossible if quite detailed results are wanted.

What is critical is that what the computer will be computing tomorrow or the day after or next year is completely dependent on what program input it receives, and as our analysis of voluntary motion shows it is hopeless in principle to predict on physical grounds what program inputs will be received in the future. Moreover, there is no strong ground for believing a wider sense of predictability based on psychological and social concepts as well as physical ones has any possibility of being successful. Detailed predictability or determinism has no working place in such an extended study of computer use. Either concept is as out of place here as either would be in a year's data on the movements of a monkey, dolphin, or some other animal in the wild.

Given an appropriate physical environment, the computer remains ready to compute when it is given program input. It is a transcendental metaphysical fancy to think that its computational behavior over a period of a week or of a year can be analyzed without remainder in deterministic physical terms. The central reason is that the system is an *open* one. It is not possible to isolate the system because program inputs are continually arriving from a variety of sources for a variety of purposes. These inputs are like stochastic stimuli impinging on the peripheral nervous system of an animal and why, for the same central reason, animal behavior is that of an open system. Even purely physical systems that are open cannot be analyzed in detail either from the standpoint of determinism or of predictability.

What I have said about digital computers being open systems and therefore unpredictable applies in even stronger terms to biological organisms, which have evolved to survive in a much greater variety of environments and stimulus inputs. Biological organisms are necessarily open systems. As open systems they must make computations about their environments in order to survive. These computations, concerned in the case of voluntary motion with goal-setting, perception, and course correction, cannot be analyzed away either in terms of a sequence of deterministic causes or in terms of a sequence of probabilistic physical causes. Not only understanding but predictability requires use of the concepts intrinsic to voluntary motion.

Computation by biological organisms evolved along with other central features of life as essential to survival. The gist of the argument I am making is that free will as exhibited in voluntary motion is biological rather than merely moral in nature, and is essential to the survival of organisms.

The rational and moral tradition. In contrast to the biological view of computation and free will I have been arguing for, the greater part of the philosophical tradition has put the weight of the argument for free will elsewhere. One line of argument has been that the introspective evidence of deliberation is proof of the existence of free will in humans but not necessarily in other species. I see no reason for such a special focus. Deliberation is a form of computation, and what is biologically fundamental is the widespread role of computation in the continuing struggle to survive. Sometimes the argument about deliberation is given as one about rational belief, but this can only be taken as a further constraint on computation, not as a substitute for it.

The dominant philosophical tradition has been to make the existence of free will a necessary condition for the existence of moral responsibility. It is this tradition I want to examine again. The first point to note is that making free will a necessary condition of moral responsibility is a problem for the viewpoint I am advocating *only if* this relationship is made the primary focus of arguments for free will. But this is what is often done. The fact of the existence of moral responsibility in humans is used as the main—or sometimes, the only—argument for free will.

Although he certainly had predecessors, it was especially Kant who occupied the high ground of morality in his defense of free will, and I want to concentrate on what seems to be the central even if implicit assumption of Kantians and non-Kantians alike. This is that moral responsibility entails a kind of freedom that goes far beyond any biological account of the voluntary behavior of animals. The kind of freedom implied is one that derives from a theological rather than a scientific tradition. Again, it is to be seen in Kant, who presents as the great triad of problems for philosophy: the existence of God, the immortality of the soul, and the freedom of the will. Another but quite related way of expressing this view is that among the animals only humans have a moral conscience.

Admittedly the explicit theological source of this "high" ideal of freedom is often suppressed. In the tradition of much modern analytic philosophy, the argument that moral responsibility entails free will is made on as narrow a ground of common sense and moral psychology as possible. It is characteristic of these arguments to be very nonbiological. The behavior of other species is not seen as relevant to the argument. Indeed, it would not ordinarily be thought of as part of philosophical psychology to recognize the biological origins of the human species.

Putting the matter this way raises an important methodological issue that bears directly on the problem of the source of freedom. I have taken a biological line of argument that makes free will a natural concept exhibited in the behavior of other species. This is clearly a scientific line of attack. Those who center the argument for free will around the existence of moral responsibility implicitly or explicitly assume (or believe) that the grounds of the argument are philosophical rather than scientific.

It is also a feature of most of the purely philosophical arguments for free will in contemporary philosophy that the arguments are quite simple in structure. To a large extent they rest upon the premise that moral responsibility exists, and if an argument is wanted to back up this assertion it is that moral responsibility is a necessary concomitant of being a human being.

These facts or assertions I grant, and they are not the focus of dispute. What is in dispute is whether this kind of philosophical argument resolves the puzzle about free will and determinism. The proper philosophical focus, so I would claim, is to analyze away the apparent conflict between determinism and free will.

The resolution I have given should be evident, but I recapitulate the main strands of my argument, some of it given in Suppes (1993).

    I. Determinism does not imply predictability.
    II. Determinism and randomness are consistent.
    III. Universal determinism or universal indeterminism is a transcendental metaphysical assumption.
    IV. Voluntary motion has three characteristics:
        1. Physically unpredictable;
        2. Predictable given knowledge of goal;
        3. Perception and path correction required.
    V. Voluntary motion is characteristic of many animal species.
    VI. Voluntary motion requires several kinds of biological computation.
    VII. Biological computation has evolved as part of the struggle to survive and is a natural part of the universe.
    VIII. Biological computation exhibits free will.
    IX. The puzzle is resolved because there is no scientific theory of universal determinism (or indeterminism).
    X. There is no transcendental nonbiological origin of moral responsibility.
    XI. Moral responsibility is part, but only part, of the natural history of free will.

NOTES

1. This idea was already clearly expressed by Aristotle in *Movement of Animals*, 701b25.

2. One familiar line to take that is congenial to the framework I have been setting up, but does not go far enough for my taste, is this: actions are free, and therefore exhibit free

will, when they are not completely constrained by external causes. Here the problem is to clarify the idea of complete external causation. Constraints, of course, are the order of the day, even for actions that we think of as typical examples of being free. The movement of my hand, for example, is constrained by a great deal of obvious physics, such as the maximal rate of acceleration, the maximal rate of deceleration, the rate of final velocity, etc. But these constraints from physics are only partial constraints. There is much freedom left after they are satisfied—a point to be amplified later. On the other hand, if I grab your arm and force it to move without your consent, this is scarcely an example of free action. This ground has been tread before and I do not really want to retrace a path across it one more time.

REFERENCES

D. R. Holland. 1993. *The Quantum Theory of Motion: An Account of the de Broglie–Bohm Causal Interpretation of Quantum Mechanics.* Cambridge.

P. Suppes. 1985. "Explaining the Unpredictable." *Erkenntnis* 22: 187–95.

P. Suppes. 1991. "Indeterminism or Instability, Does It Matter?" In *Causality, Method, and Modality*, edited by G. G. Brittan, Jr. Dordrecht.

P. Suppes. 1993. "The Transcendental Character of Determinism." *Midwest Studies in Philosophy* 18: 242–57. Notre Dame, Ind.

If You Can't Make One,
You Don't Know How It Works

FRED DRETSKE

There are things I believe that I cannot say—at least not in such a way that they come out true. The title of this essay is a case in point. I really do believe that, in the relevant sense of all the relevant words, if you can't make one, you don't know how it works. The trouble is I do not know how to specify the relevant sense of all the relevant words.

I know, for instance, that you can understand how something works and, for a variety of reasons, still not be able to build one. The raw materials are not available. You cannot afford them. You are too clumsy or not strong enough. The police will not let you.

I also know that you may be able to make one and still not know how it works. You do not know how the parts work. I can solder a snaggle to a radzak, and this is all it takes to make a gizmo, but if I do not know what snaggles and radzaks are, or how they work, making one is not going to tell me much about what a gizmo is. My son once assembled a television set from a kit by carefully following the instruction manual. Understanding next to nothing about electricity, though, assembling one gave him no idea of how television worked.

I am not, however, suggesting that being able to build one is sufficient for knowing how it works. Only necessary. And I do not much care about whether you can *actually* put one together. It is enough if you *know how* one is put together. But, as I said, I do not know how to make all the right qualifications. So I will not try. All I mean to be suggesting by my provocative title is something about the spirit of philosophical naturalism. It is motivated by a constructivist's model of understanding. It embodies something like an engineer's ideal, a designer's vision, of what it takes to really know how something works. You need a blueprint, a recipe, an instruction manual, a program. This goes for the mind as well as any other contraption. If you want to know what intelligence is, or what it takes to have a thought, you need a recipe for creating intelligence or assembling a thought (or a thinker of thoughts) out of parts you already understand.

INFORMATION AND INTENTIONALITY

In speaking of parts one *already* understands, I mean, of course, parts that do not already possess the capacity or feature one follows the recipe to create. One cannot have a recipe for cake that lists a cake, not even a small cake, as an ingredient. One can, I suppose, make a big cake out of small cakes, but recipes of this sort will not help one understand what a cake is (though it might help one understand what a *big* cake is). As a boy, I once tried to make fudge by melting fudge in a frying pan. All I succeeded in doing was ruining the pan. Don't ask me what I was trying to do—change the *shape* of the candy, I suppose. There are perfectly respectable recipes for cookies that list candy (e.g., gumdrops) as an ingredient, but one cannot have a recipe for *candy* that lists candy as an ingredient. At least it will not be a recipe that tells you how to make candy or helps you understand what candy is. The same is true of minds. That is why a recipe for thought cannot have interpretive attitudes or explanatory stances among the eligible ingredients—not even the attitudes and stances of *others*. That is like making candy out of candy—in this case, one person's candy out of another person's candy. You can do it, but you still will not know how to make candy or what candy is.

In comparing a mind to candy and television sets I do not mean to suggest that minds are the sort of thing that can be assembled in your basement or in the kitchen. There are things, including things one fully understands, things one knows how to make, that cannot be assembled that way. Try making Rembrandts or $100 bills in your basement. What you produce may look genuine, it may pass as authentic, but it will not be the real thing. You have to be the right person, occupy the right office, or possess the appropriate legal authority in order to make certain things. There are recipes for making money and Rembrandts, and knowing these recipes is part of understanding what money and Rembrandts are, but these are not recipes you and I can use. Some recipes require a special cook.

This is one (but only one) of the reasons it is wrong to say, as I did in the title, that if you cannot make one, you do not know how it works. It would be better to say, as I did earlier, that if you do not know how to make one, or know how one is made, you do not really understand how it works.

Some objects are constituted, in part, by their relationships to other objects. Rembrandts and $100 bills are like that. So are cousins and mothers-in-law. That is why you could not have built my cousin in your basement while my aunt and uncle could. There is a recipe in this case, just not one you can use. The mind, I think, is also like that, and I will return to this important point in a moment.

It is customary to think of naturalistic recipes for the mind as starting with extensional ingredients and, through some magical blending process, producing an intentional product: a thought, an experience, or a purpose. The idea behind this proscription of intentional ingredients seems to be that since what we are trying to build—a thought—is an intentional product, our recipe cannot use intentional ingredients.

This, it seems to me, is a mistake, a mistake that has led some philosophers to despair of ever finding a naturalistic recipe for the mind. It has given naturalism an undeserved bad name. The mistake is the same as if we proscribed using, say, copper wire in our instruction manual for building amplifiers because copper wire conducts electricity—exactly what the amplifiers we are trying to build do. This, though, is silly. It is perfectly acceptable to use copper wire in one's recipe for building amplifiers. Amplifier recipes are supposed to help you understand how something amplifies electricity, not how something conducts electricity. So you get to use conductors of electricity, and in particular copper wire, as a part in one's amplifier kit. Conductors are eligible components in recipes for building amplifiers even if one does not know how they manage to conduct. An eligible part, once again, is an ingredient, a part, a component, that does not already have the capacity or power one uses the recipe to create. That is why one can know what gumdrop cookies are, know how to make them, without knowing how to make gumdrops or what, exactly, gumdrops are.

The same is true for mental recipes. As long as there is no mystery—not, at least, the *same* mystery—about how the parts work as how the whole is supposed to work, it is perfectly acceptable to use intentional ingredients in a recipe for thought, purpose, and intelligence. What we are trying to understand, after all, is not intentionality, *per se*, but the mind. Thought may be intentional, but that is not the property we are seeking a recipe to understand. As long as the intentionality we use is not itself mental, then we are as free to use intentionality in our recipe for making a mind as we are in using electrical conductors in building amplifiers and gumdrops in making cookies.

Consider a simple artifact—a compass. If it was manufactured properly (do not buy a cheap one), and if it is used in the correct circumstances (the good ones come with directions), it will tell you the direction of the arctic pole (I here ignore differences between magnetic and geographic poles). That is what the pointer indicates. But though the pointer indicates the direction of the arctic pole, it does not indicate the whereabouts of polar bears even though polar bears live in the arctic. If you happen to know this fact about polar bears, that they live in the arctic (not the antarctic), you could, of course, figure out where the polar bears are by using a compass. But this fact about what you could figure out *if you knew* does not mean that the compass pointer is sensitive to the location of polar bears—thus indicating *their* whereabouts—in the way it indicates the location of the arctic. The pointer on this instrument does not track the bears; it tracks the pole. If there is any doubt about this, try using Mill's Methods: move the bears around while keeping the pole fixed. The pointer on your compass will not so much as quiver.

Talking about what a compass indicates is a way of talking about what it tracks, what information it carries, what its pointer movements are dependent on, and a compass, just like any other measuring instrument, can track one condition without tracking another even though these conditions co-occur. Talk about what instruments and gauges indicate or measure creates the same kind of intensional (with an 's') context as does talk about what a person knows or believes. Knowing or believing that *that* is the north pole is not the same as knowing or believing that that is the habitat of polar bears even though the north pole is the habitat of polar bears. If we regard intensional (with an 's') discourse, referentially opaque contexts, as our guide to intentional (with a 't') phenomena, then we have, in a cheap compass, something we can buy at the local hardware store, intentionality. Describing what such an instrument indicates is describing it in intensional terms. What one is describing is, therefore, in this sense, an intentional state of the instrument.

It is worth emphasizing that this is not derived or in any way second-class intentionality. This is the genuine article—*original* intentionality as some philosophers (including this one) like to say. The intentional states a compass occupies do not depend on our explanatory purposes, attitudes, or stances. To say that the compass (in certain conditions C) indicates the direction of the arctic pole is to say that, in these conditions, the direction of the pointer depends in some lawlike way on the whereabouts of the pole. This dependency exists whether or not we know it exists, whether or not anyone ever exploits this fact to build and use compasses. The intentionality of the device is not, like the intentionality of words and maps, *borrowed* or *derived* from the intentionality (purposes, attitudes, knowledge) of its users. The power of this instrument to indicate north *to* or *for* us may depend on our taking it to be a reliable indicator (and, thus, on what we believe or know about it), but its *being* a reliable indicator does not itself depend on us.

Intentionality is a much abused word and it means a variety of different things. But one thing it has been used to pick out are states, conditions, and activities having a propositional content the verbal expression of which does not allow the substitution, *salva veritate*, of co-referring expressions. This is Chisholm's third mark of intentionality.[1] Anything exhibiting this mark is about something else under an aspect. It has, in this sense, an aspectual shape.[2] Compass needles are about geographical regions or directions under one aspect (as, say, the direction of the pole) and not others (as the habitat of polar bears). This is the same way our thoughts are about a place under one aspect (as where I was born) but not another (as where you were born). If having this kind of profile is, indeed, one thing that is meant by speaking of a state, condition, or activity as intentional, then it seems clear that there is no need to naturalize intentionality. It is already a familiar part of our physical world. It exists wherever you find clouds, smoke, tree rings, shadows, tracks, light, sound, pressure, and countless other natural phenomena that carry information about how other parts of the world are arranged and constituted.

Intentional systems, then, are not the problem. They can be picked up for a few dollars at your local hardware store. We can, therefore, include them on our list of ingredients in our recipe for building a mind without fear that we are merely changing the shape of the candy or the size of the cake. What we are trying to build when we speak of a recipe for building a mind is not merely a system that exhibits intentionality. We already have that in systems and their information-carrying states that are in no way mental. Rather, what we are trying to build is a system that exhibits that peculiar array of properties that characterizes thought. We are, among other things, trying to build something that exhibits what Chisholm describes as the first mark of intentionality, the power to say that something is so when it is not so, the power to misrepresent how things stand in the world. Unlike information-providing powers, the capacity to misrepresent is *not* to be found on the shelves of hardware stores. For that we need a recipe.

MISREPRESENTATION

Let us be clear about what we seek a recipe to create. If we are trying to build a thought, we are looking for something that cannot only say that x is F without saying x is G despite the co-extensionality of 'F' and 'G',[3] thus being about x under an aspect, we are looking for something that can say this, like a thought can say it, even x is not F. Unless we have a recipe for this, we have no naturalistic understanding of *what it is* that we think, no theory of meaning or content. Meaning or content, the what-it-is that we think, is, like intelligence and rationality, independent of truth. So a recipe for thought, where this is understood to include what one thinks, is, of necessity, a recipe for building systems that can misrepresent the world they are about. Without the capacity to misrepresent, we have no capacity for the kind of representation which is the stuff of intelligence and reason.

Jerry Fodor focused attention on what he calls the disjunction problem for naturalistic theories of representation.[4] The problem is one of explaining how, in broadly causal terms, a structure in the head, call it R, could represent, say, or mean that something was F even though (if misrepresentation is to be possible) non-F-ish things are capable of causing it. How, in roughly causal terms, can R mean that something is F (the way a thought can be the thought that something is F) when something's being F is (at best[5]) only one of the things capable of causing R? For someone trying to formulate an information-based recipe for thought, this is, indeed, a vexing problem. But I mention the problem here only to point out that this problem is merely another way of describing the problem (for naturalistic theories) of misrepresentation. For if one could concoct a recipe for building systems capable of misrepresentation—capable, that is, of saying of something that was not F that it was F—then one would have a recipe for meaning, for constructing structures having a content that was independent of causes in the desired sense. This is so because if R can misrepresent something as being F, then R is, of necessity, something whose meaning is independent of its causes, something that can mean COW even when it is caused by a distant buffalo or a horse on a dark night. It is, therefore, something whose meaning is less than the disjunction of situations capable of causing it. In the words of

Antony and Levine it is something whose meaning has been "detached" from its causes.[6] A naturalistic recipe for misrepresentation, therefore, is a recipe for solving the disjunction problem.[7] One way of solving problems is to show that two problems are really, at bottom, the same problem. We are making progress.

For this problem artifacts are of no help. Although clocks, compasses, thermometers, and fire alarms—all readily available at the corner hardware store—can misrepresent the conditions they are designed to deliver information about, they need our help to do it. Their representational successes and failures are underwritten by—and, therefore, depend on—our purposes and attitudes, the purposes and attitudes of their designers and users. *As* representational devices, *as* devices exhibiting a causally detached meaning, such instruments are not therefore eligible ingredients in a recipe for making thought.

The reason the representational powers of instruments are not, like their indicative (information-carrying) powers, an available ingredient in mental recipes is, I think, obvious enough. I will, however, take a moment to expand on the point in order to set the stage for what follows.

Consider the thermometer. Since the volume of a metal varies lawfully with the temperature, both the mercury in the glass tube and the paper clips in my desk drawer carry information about the local temperature. Both are intentional systems in that minimal, that first, sense already discussed. Their behavior depends on a certain aspect of their environment (on the temperature, not the color or size, of their neighbors) in the same way the orientation of a compass needle depends on one aspect of its environment, not another. The only difference between thermometers and paper clips is that we have given the one volume of metal, the mercury in the glass tube, the job, the function, of telling us about temperature. The paper clips have been given a different job. Since it is the thermometer's job to provide information about temperature, it (we say) misrepresents the temperature when it fails to do its assigned job just as (we say) a book or a map might misrepresent the matters of which they (purport to) inform us about. What such artifacts say or mean is what we have given them the job of indicating or informing us about, and since they do not lose their job—at least not immediately—merely by failing to satisfactorily perform their job, these instruments continue to mean that a certain condition exists even when that condition fails to exist, even when some other condition (a condition other than the one they have the job of informing about) is responsible for their behavior. For such measuring instruments, meanings are causally detached from causes for the same reason that functions are causally detached from (actual) performance. This is why thermometers can, while paper clips cannot, misrepresent the temperature. When things go wrong, when nothing is really 98°, a paper clip fails to say, while the broken thermometer goes right on saying, that it is 98°.

But, as I said, thermometers cannot do this by themselves. They need our help. We are the source of the job, the function, without which the thermometer could not say something that was false. Take us away and all you have is a tube full of mercury being caused to expand and contract by changes in the temperature—a column of metal doing exactly what paper clips, thumb tacks, and flag poles do. Once we change our attitude, once we (as it were) stop investing informational trust in the instrument, it loses its capacity to misrepresent. Its meaning ceases to be detached. It becomes, like every other piece of metal, a mere purveyor of information.

NATURAL FUNCTIONS

Though representational artifacts are thus not available as eligible ingredients in our recipe for the mind, their derived (from us) power to misrepresent is suggestive. If an information-carrying element in a system could somehow acquire the function of carrying information, and acquire this function in a way that did not depend on our intentions, purposes, and attitudes, then it would thereby acquire (just as a thermometer or a compass acquires) the power to misrepresent the conditions it had the function of informing about. Such functions would bring about a detachment of meaning from cause. Furthermore, since the functions would not be derived from us, the meanings (unlike the meaning of thermometers and compasses) would be original, underived, meanings. Instead of just being able to build an instrument that could, because of the job we give it, fool *us*, the thing we build with these functions could, quite literally, *itself* be fooled.

If, then, we could find naturalistically acceptable functions, we could combine these with natural indicators (the sort used in the manufacture of compasses, thermometers, pressure gauges, and electric eyes) in a naturalistic recipe for thought. If the word 'thought' sounds too exalted for the mechanical contraption I am assembling, we can describe the results in more modest terms. What we would have is a naturalistic recipe for representation, a way of building something that would have, quite apart from its creator's (or anyone else's) purposes or thoughts, a propositional content that could be either true or false. If that is not quite a recipe for mental bernaise sauce, it is at least a recipe for a passable gravy. I will come back to the bernaise sauce in a moment.

What we need in the way of another ingredient, then, is some natural process whereby elements can acquire, on their own, apart from us, an information-carrying function. Where are these natural processes, these candy-less functions, that will let us make our mental confections?[8]

As I see it, there are two retail suppliers for the required natural functions: one phylogenetic, the other ontogenetic.

If the heart and kidneys have a natural function, something they are *supposed* to be doing independently of our knowledge or understanding of what it is, then it presumably comes from their evolutionary, their selectional, history. If the heart has the function of pumping blood, if (following Larry Wright[9]) that is why the heart is there, then, by parity of reasoning, and depending on actual selectional history, the senses would have an information-providing function, the job of "telling" the animal in whom they occur what it needs to know about the world in which it lives. If this were so, the *natural* function of sensory systems would be to provide information about an organism's optical, acoustic, and chemical surroundings. There would thus exist, inside the animal, representations of its environment, elements capable of saying what is false. Though I have put it crudely, this, I take it, is the sort of thinking that inspires biologically oriented approaches to mental representation.[10]

There is, however, a second, an ontogenetic, source of natural functions. Think of a system with certain needs, certain things it must have in order to survive.[11] In order to satisfy those needs it has to do A in conditions C. Nature has not equipped it with an automatic A-response to conditions C. There is, in other words, no hard-wired, heritable, instinct to A in circumstances C. Think of C as a mushroom that has recently appeared in the animal's natural habitat. Though attractive (to this kind of animal), the mushroom is, in fact, poisonous. The animal can see the mushrooms. It has the perceptual resources for picking up information about (i.e., registering) the presence of C (it looks distinctive), but it does not yet have an appropriate A response (in this particular case, A = avoidance) to C.

We could wait for natural selection, and a little bit of luck, to solve this problem for the species, for the descendants of this animal, but if the problem— basically a coordination problem—is to be solved at the individual level, by *this* animal, learning must occur. If *this* animal is to survive, what must happen is that the internal sign or indicator of C—something inside this animal that constitutes its perception of C—must be made into a cause of A (avoidance). Control circuits must be reconfigured by inserting the internal indicators of C (the internal sensory effects of C) into the behavioral chain of command. Short of a miracle—the fortuitous occurrence of A whenever C is encountered—this is the only way the coordination problem essential for survival can be solved. Internal indicators must be harnessed to effector mechanisms so as to coordinate output A to the conditions, C, they carry information about. Learning of this kind achieves the same result as do longer-term evolutionary solutions: internal elements that supply needed information acquire the function of supplying it by being drafted (in this case, through a learning process) into the control loop because they supply it. A supplier of information acquires the function of supplying information by being recruited for control duties because it supplies it.[12]

Obviously this ingredient, this source of natural functions, whether it be phylogenetic or ontogenetic, cannot be ordered from a Sears catalog. There is nothing that comes in a bottle that we can squirt on thermally sensitive tissue that will give this tissue the natural function of indicating temperature, nothing we can rub on a photo-sensitive pigment that will give it the job of detecting light. If something is going to get the function, the job, the purpose, of carrying information in this natural way, it has to get it on its own. We cannot "assign" these functions although we can (by artificial selection or appropriate training) encourage their development. If the only natural functions are those provided by evolutionary history and individual learning, then, no one is going to build thinkers of thoughts, much less a mind, in the laboratory. This would be like building a heart, a real one, in your basement. If hearts are essentially organs of the body having the biological function of pumping blood, you cannot build them. You can wait for them to develop, maybe even hurry things along a bit by timely assists, but you cannot assemble them out of ready-made parts. These functions are the result of the right kind of history, and you cannot—not *now*—give a thing the right kind of history. It has to have it. Though there is a recipe for building internal representations, structures having natural indicator functions, it is not a recipe you or I, or anyone else, can use to build one.

THE DISJUNCTION PROBLEM

There are, I know, doubts about whether a recipe consisting of information and natural teleology (derived from natural functions—either phylogenetic or ontogenetic) is capable of yielding a mental product—something with an original power to misrepresent. The doubts exist even with those who share the naturalistic impulse. Jerry Fodor, for instance, does not think Darwin (or Skinner, for that matter) can rescue Brentano's chestnuts from the fire.[13] He does not think teleological theories of intentionality will solve the disjunction problem. Given the equivalence of the disjunction problem and the problem of misrepresentation, this is a denial, not just a doubt, that evolutionary or learning-theoretic accounts of functions are up to the task of detaching meaning from cause, of making something say COW when it can be caused by horses on a dark night.

I tend to agree with Fodor about the irrelevance of Darwin for understanding *mental* representation. I agree, however, not (like Fodor) out of the general skepticism about teleological accounts of meaning, but because I think Darwin is the wrong place to look for the teleology, for the functions, underlying *mental* representations (beliefs, thoughts, judgments, preferences, and their ilk). *Mental* representations have their place in explaining deliberate pieces of behavior, intentional acts for which the agent has reasons. This is exactly the sort of behavior which evolutionary histories are unequipped to explain. We might reasonably expect Darwin to tell us why people blink, reflexively, when someone pokes a finger at their eye, but not why they deliberately wink at a friend, the kind of behavior we invoke beliefs and desires (*mental* representations) to explain. I do not doubt that the processes responsible for blink (and a great many other) reflexes are controlled by elements having an information-providing function (derived from natural selection). After all, if the reflex is to achieve its (presumed) purpose, that of protecting the eye, there must be something in there with the job of telling (informing) the muscles controlling the eyelids that there is an object approaching. But the representations derived from these phylogenetic functions are not mental representations. We do not blink because we believe a finger is being jabbed at our eye. And even if we do believe it, we blink, reflexively, *before* we believe it and independent of believing it. So even if there are representations whose underlying functions are phylogenetic, these are not the representations we would expect to identify with *mental* representations, the representations that serve to explain intentional behavior. For that, I submit, one needs to look to the representations whose underlying functions are ontogenetic.

Nonetheless, wherever we get the teleology, Fodor thinks it is powerless to solve the disjunction problem and, hence, hopeless as an account of thought content. I disagree. There are, to be sure, some problems for which teleology is of no help. But there are, or so I believe, some aspects of the naturalization project for which functions are indispensable. Whether teleology helps specifically with the disjunction problem depends on what one identifies as the disjunction problem. Since I have heard various things singled out as *the* disjunction problem, I offer the following two problems. Both have some claim to be called the disjunction problem. I will indicate, briefly, the kind of solution I favor to each. Teleology only helps with one.[14]

1. If a token of type R indicates (carries the information that) A, it also indicates that A or B (for any B). If it carries the information that x is a jersey cow, for instance, it carries the information that x is either a jersey cow or a holstein cow (or a can opener, for that matter). It also carries the information that x is, simply, a cow—either a jersey cow, a holstein cow, etc. This being so, how does an information-based approach to meaning get a token of type R to mean that A rather than A or B? How can an event have the content JERSEY COW rather than, say, COW when any event that carries the first piece of information also carries the second? To this problem functions provide an elegant answer. A token of type R can carry information that it does not have the function of carrying—that it does not, therefore, mean (in the sense of "mean" in which a thing can mean that P when P is false). Altimeters, for instance, carry information about air pressure (that is *how* they tell the altitude), but it is not their function to indicate air pressure. Their function is to indicate altitude. That is why they represent (and can misrepresent) altitude and not air pressure.

2. If tokens of type R can be caused by both A and B, how can tokens of this type mean that A (and not A or B)? If R is a type of structure tokens of which can be caused by both cows and, say, horses on a dark night, how can any particular token of R mean COW rather than COW OR HORSE ON A DARK NIGHT? For this problem I think Fodor is right: teleology is of no help. What we need, instead, is a better understanding of information, how tokens of a type R can carry information (that x is a cow, for instance) even though, in different circumstances and on other occasions, tokens of this same type fail to carry this information (because x is not a cow; it is a horse on a dark night). The solution to this problem requires understanding the way information is relativized to circumstances, the way tokens of type R that occur in broad daylight at ten feet, say, can carry information that tokens of this same type, in *other* circumstances, in the dark or at two-hundred feet, fail to carry.[15]

The problem of detaching meaning from causes—and thus solving the problem of misrepresentation—occurs at two distinct levels, at the level of types and the level of tokens. At the token level the problem is: how can tokens of a type all have the same meaning or content, F, when they have different causes (hence, carry different information)? Answer: each token, whatever information it happens to carry, whatever its particular cause, has the same information-carrying function, a function it derives from the type of which it is a token. Since meaning is identified with information-carrying function, each token, whatever its cause, has the same meaning, the job of indicating F. Teleology plays a crucial role here—at the level of tokens. The problem at the type level is: how can a *type* of event have, or acquire, the function of carrying information F when tokens of this type occur, or *can* occur (if misrepresentation is to be possible), without F? Answer: certain tokens, those that occur in circumstances C, depend on F. *They* would not occur unless F existed. These tokens carry the information that F. It is from them that the type acquires its information-carrying function. At the type level, then, teleology is of no help. Information carries the load. Both are needed to detach meaning from causes.

There is a third problem, sometimes not clearly distinguished from the above two problems, that has still a different solution (why should different problems have the same solution?). How can R represent something as F without representing it as G when the properties F and G are equivalent in some strong way (nomically, metaphysically, or logically)? How, for instance, can R have the function (especially if this is understood as a *natural* function) of indicating that something is water without having the function of indicating that it is H_2O? If it cannot, then, since we can obviously believe that something is water and not believe that it is H_2O, a theory of representation that equates content with what a structure has the natural function of indicating is too feeble to qualify as a theory of belief. It does not cut the intentional pie into thin enough slices.

I mention this problem here (I also alluded to it in note 3), not for the purpose of suggesting an answer to it,[16] but merely to set it apart as requiring special treatment. The problem of distinguishing representational contents that are equivalent in some strong way is surely a problem for naturalistic theories of content, but it is not a problem that teleology (at least not a naturalistic teleology) can be expected to solve. To discredit a teleological approach to representation because it fails to solve this problem, then, is like criticizing it because it fails to solve Zeno's Paradoxes.

THE RECIPE

We have, then, the following recipe for making a thought-like entity. It does not give us a very fancy thought—certainly nothing like the thoughts we have every day: that tomorrow is my birthday, for example, or that I left my umbrella in the car. But one thing at a time. The recipe will do its job if it yields *something*—call it a proto-thought—that has belief-like features. I, personally, would be happy with a crude *de re* belief about a perceived object that it was, say, moving.

Recipe: Take a system that has a need for the information that F, a system whose survival or well-being depends on its doing A in conditions F. Add an element, or a detector system that produces elements, that carries information about condition F. Now, stir in a natural process, one capable of conferring on the F-indicator the *function* of carrying this piece of information. One does not quite "stir" these processes in (the metaphor is getting a bit strained at this point). Once you have got the right system, adding functions is more like *waiting* for the dough to rise. There is nothing more one can do. You sit back and hope that natural processes will take a favorable turn. Just as one cannot expect everything in which one puts yeast to rise (it does not work in sand), one cannot expect to get representational "bread" from everything in which needed indicators are placed. You need a reasonably sophisticated system, one with a capacity to reorganize control circuits so as to exploit information in coordinating its behavior to the conditions it gets information about. You need a system, in other words, capable of the right kind of learning. These are special systems, yes, but they are *not* systems that must already possess representational powers. We are not, in requiring such systems in our recipe, smuggling in tainted ingredients.

If all goes well, when the process is complete, the result will be a system with internal resources for representing—and, equally important from the point of view of modeling the mind, *mis*representing—its surroundings. Furthermore, that this system represents, as well as what it represents, will be independent of what we know or believe about it. For we, the cooks, are not essential parts of this process. The entire process can happen "spontaneously" and, when it does, the system will have its own cache of *original* intentionality.

RATIONALITY: THE FUNCTIONAL ROLE OF THOUGHT

Whether this is really *enough* to have supplied a recipe for thought depends, of course, on just what one demands of thought. What does it take to *be* a thought? If all it takes is possession of content, then, perhaps, we have supplied a recipe of sorts for making a thought. But the product is pretty disappointing, a mere shadow of what we know (in ourselves and others) to be the fullest and richest expression of the mind. What I have described might be realized in a snail. What we want (I expect to hear) is something more, something exhibiting the complex dynamics, both inferential and explanatory, that our thoughts have. To have a cow thought it is not enough to have an internal, isolated, cow representation. To be a cow thought, this representation must actually *do* what cow thoughts do. It must be involved in reasoning and inference about cows. It must, together with cow-directed desires, explain cow-directed behavior and rationalize cow-related attitudes and intentions.

There is validity to this complaint. If we are going to make a thought, we want the product to both look and behave like a thought. What we have so far devised may (to be generous) look a bit like a thought. At least it has representational content of the sort we associate with thought. Nonetheless, there is nothing to suggest that our product will behave like a thought. Why, then, advertise the recipe as a recipe for thought? I have, after all, already conceded that there may be representations of this sort, mechanisms in the body having an indicator function, which are not mental representations at all. When the underlying functions are phylogenetic (e.g., in the processes controlling various reflexes), the representations are not thoughts. They have a content, yes, but they do not *behave* like thoughts. They do not, for instance, interact with desires and other beliefs to produce intelligent and purposeful action. Why, then, suppose that when the functions are ontogenetic, when they develop in learning, the results are any better qualified to be classified as mental?

Since I have addressed this issue elsewhere[17] I will merely sketch an answer. A system that acquires, in accordance with the above recipe, and in its own lifetime, the power to represent the objects in its immediate environment will also, automatically, be an intelligent system, one capable of behaving (at least insofar as these representations are concerned) in a rational way. To see why this is so, consider a process by means of which an indicator of F might acquire the function of carrying information about the F-ness of things— becoming, thereby, a representation (possibly, on occasion, a misrepresentation) that something is F. In order to acquire this status, the element must acquire the job of supplying information about the F-ness of things. The only way an element can acquire this job description, I submit, is by being recruited to perform control-related services *because* it supplies this needed information. If R is drafted to shape output because it supplies needed information about when and where that output is appropriate, then, no matter what further services may be required of R, part of R's job, its function, is to supply this needed information. That is why it is there, directing traffic, in the way that it is.

In achieving its representational status, then, R becomes a determinant of need-related behavior, behavior that satisfies needs when R carries the information it is its function to carry. Since R represents the conditions (F) in which the behavior it is called upon to cause is need-satisfying, R must, when it is doing its job, produce intelligent (i.e., need-satisfying) output. Even when it is not doing its job, even when it misrepresents, the behavior it helps produce will be behavior that is rationalized by the F-facts that R (mis)represents as existing. According to this recipe for thought, then, something becomes the thought that F by assisting in the production of an intelligent response to F.

Something not only becomes the thought that F by assisting in the production of an intelligent response to F, it assists in the intelligent response *because* it signifies what it does. When the capacity for thought emerges in accordance with the above recipe, not only do thoughts (together with needs and desires) conspire to produce intelligent behavior, they produce this behavior because they are the thoughts they are, because they have *that* particular content. It is their content, the fact that they are thoughts that F, not thoughts that G, that explains why they were recruited to help in the production of those particular responses to F. This, it seems to me, vindicates, in one fell swoop, both the explanatory and rationalizing role of content. We do not need "rationality constraints" in our theory of content. Rationality emerges as a by-product from the process in which representational states are created.

Our recipe yields a product having the following properties:

1. The product has a propositional content that represents the world in an aspectual way (as, say, *F* rather than *G* even when *F*s are always *G*).

2. This content can be either true or false.

3. The product is a "player" in the determination of system output (thus helping to explain system behavior).

4. The propositional content of this product is the property that explains the product's role in determining system output. The system not only does what it does because it has this product, but what it is about this product that explains why the system does what it does is its propositional content.

5. Though the system *can* behave stupidly, the normal role of this product (the role it will play when it is doing the job for which it was created) will be in the production of intelligent (need and desire satisfaction) behavior.

This, it seems to me, is about all one could ask of a naturalistic recipe for thought.

NOTES

I read an early version of this essay at the annual meeting of the Society for Philosophy and Psychology, Montreal, 1992. I used an enlarged form of it at the NEH Summer Institute on the Nature of Meaning, co-directed by Jerry Fodor and Ernie LePore, at Rutgers University in the summer of 1993. There were many people at these meetings that gave me useful feedback and helpful suggestions. I am grateful to them.

1. Roderick M. Chisholm, *Perceiving: A Philosophical Study* (Ithaca, N.Y., 1957), chap. 11.

2. This is John Searle's way of putting it; see his *The Rediscovery of Mind* (Cambridge, Mass., 1992), 131, 156. I think Searle is wrong when he says (p. 161) that there are no aspectual shapes at the level of neurons. Indicators in the brain, those in the sensory pathways, are as much about the perceived world under an aspect as is the compass about the arctic under an aspect.

3. Despite even the *necessary* co-extensionality of "*F*" and "*G*". A thought that *x* is *F* is different than a thought that *x* is *G* even if *F*-ness and *G*-ness are related in such a way that nothing *can* be *F* without being *G*. This, too, is an aspect of intentionality. In *Knowledge and the Flow of Information* (Cambridge, Mass., 1981), 173, I called this the second (for nomic necessity) and third (for logical necessity) orders of intentionality. Although measuring instruments exhibit first-order intentionality (they can indicate that *x* is *F* without indicating that *x* is *G* even when "*F*" and "*G*" happen to be coextensional), they do not exhibit higher levels of intentionality. If (in virtue of a natural law between *F*-ness and *G*-ness) *F*s *must* be *G*, then anything carrying information that *x* is *F* will thereby carry the information that it is *G*. Unlike thoughts, compasses cannot distinguish between nomically equivalent properties.

My discussion has so far passed over this important dimension of intentionality. Though I will return to it, briefly, the point raises too many complications to be addressed here.

4. Jerry Fodor, *A Theory of Content and Other Essays* (Cambridge, Mass., 1990) and, earlier, *Psychosemantics* (Cambridge, Mass., 1987).

5. "At best" because, with certain "F"s ("unicorn," "miracle," "angel," etc.) something's being F will not even be *among* the things that cause R.

6. Louise Antony and Joseph Levine, "The Nomic and the Robust," in *Meaning in Mind: Fodor and His Critics* (Oxford, 1991), 1–16.

7. Fodor puts it a bit differently, but the point, I think, is the same: "Solving the disjunction problem and making clear how a symbol's meaning could be so insensitive to variability in the causes of its tokenings are really two ways of describing the same undertaking" (*A Theory of Content and Other Essays*, 91).

8. For the purpose of this essay, I ignore skeptics about functions—those who think, for example, that the heart only has the function of pumping blood because this is an effect in which we have (for whatever reason) a special interest. See, for example, John Searle, *The Rediscovery of Mind*, p. 238 and Dan Dennett's "Evolution, Error and Intentionality," in *The Intentional Stance* (Cambridge, Mass., 1987).

9. Larry Wright, "Functions," *Philosophical Review* 82 (1973): 139–68, and *Teleological Explanations* (Berkeley, 1976).

10. E.g., Ruth Millikan, *Language, Thought, and Other Biological Categories: New Foundations for Realism* (Cambridge, Mass., 1984) and "Biosemantics," *Journal of Philosophy*, 86, no. 6 (1989); David Papineau, *Reality and Representation* (New York, 1987) and "Representation and Explanation," *Philosophy of Science* 51, no. 4 (1984): 550–72; Mohan Matthen, "Biological Functions and Perceptual Content," *Journal of Philosophy* 85, no. 1 (1988): 5–27; and Peter Godfrey Smith, "Misinformation," *Canadian Journal of Philosophy* 19, no. 4 (December 1989): 533–50 and "Signal, Decision, Action," *Journal of Philosophy* 88, no. 12 (December 1991): 709–22.

11. This may sound as though we are smuggling in the back door what we are not allowing in the front: a tainted ingredient, the idea of a *needful* system, a system that, given its needs, has a use for information.

I think not. All that is here meant by a need (for system of type S) is some condition or result without which the system could (or would) not exist as a system of type S. Needs, in this minimal sense, are merely necessary conditions for existence. Even plants have needs in this sense. Plants cannot exist (*as* plants) without water and sunlight.

12. This is a short and fast version of the story I tell in *Explaining Behavior* (Cambridge, Mass., 1988).

13. Fodor, *A Theory of Content*, 70.

14. I was helped in my thinking about these problems by Peter Godfrey-Smith's "Misinformation."

15. In *Knowledge and the Flow of Information* I called these circumstances, the ones to which the informational content of a signal was relative, 'channel conditions'.

16. I tackled that in *Knowledge and the Flow of Information*, 215ff.

17. *Explaining Behavior*, chaps. 4 and 5.

Contributors

Laurence BonJour, Department of Philosophy, Illinois Wesleyan University
Sara Buss, Department of Philosophy, Princeton University
Panayot Butchvarov, Department of Philosophy, University of Iowa
Fred Dretske, Department of Philosophy, Stanford University
Richard Eldridge, Department of Philosophy, Swarthmore College
Hartry Field, Department of Philosophy, City University of New York
John Martin Fischer, Department of Philosophy, University of California, Riverside
Richard Foley, Department of Philosophy, Rutgers University
Richard Fumerton, Department of Philosophy, University of Iowa
Alvin I. Goldman, Department of Philosophy, University of Arizona
Richard E. Grandy, Department of Philosophy, Rice University
Peter Hylton, Department of Philosophy, University of Illinois, Chicago
Mark Kaplan, Department of Philosophy, University of Wisconsin, Milwaukee
Jeffrey C. King, Department of Philosophy, University of California, Davis
Hilary Kornblith, Department of Philosophy, University of Vermont
Stephen Laurence, Department of Philosophy, Rutgers University
Marina A. L. Oshana, Department of Philosophy, California State University, San Bernardino
Mark Ravizza, Department of Philosophy, University of California, Riverside
John R. Searle, Department of Philosophy, University of California, Berkeley
Frederic Sommers, Department of Philosophy, Brandeis University
Stephen P. Stich, Department of Philosophy, Rutgers University

Michael Stocker, Department of Philosophy, Syracuse University
Patrick Suppes, Department of Philosophy, Stanford University
Michael Tye, Department of Philosophy, Temple University
George M. Wilson, Department of Philosophy, Johns Hopkins University
Arnold Zuboff, Department of Philosophy, University College of London

Peter A. French is Lennox Distinguished Professor of Philosophy at Trinity University in San Antonio, Texas. He has taught at the University of Minnesota, Morris, and has served as Distinguished Research Professor in the Center for the Study of Values at the University of Delaware. His books include *The Scope of Morality* (1980), *Collective and Corporate Responsibility* (1980), and *Responsibility Matters* (1992). He has published numerous articles in the philosophical journals. **Theodore E. Uehling, Jr.**, is professor of philosophy at the University of Minnesota, Morris. He is the author of *The Notion of Form in Kant's Critique of Aesthetic Judgment* and articles on the philosophy of Kant. He is a founder and past vice-president of the North American Kant Society. **Howard K. Wettstein** is chair and professor of philosophy at the University of California, Riverside. He has taught at the University of Notre Dame and the University of Minnesota, Morris, and has served as a visiting associate professor of philosophy at the University of Iowa and Stanford University. He is the author of *Has Semantics Rested on a Mistake? and Other Essays* (1992).